Using Educational Research

A School Administrator's Guide

D0971385

Emil J. Haller
Cornell University

Paul F. Kleine
University of Oklahoma

Longman

New York San Francisco Boston
London Toronto Sydney Tokyo Singapore Madrid
Mexico City Munich Paris Cape Town Hong Kong Montreal

*To Evelyn and to our children, Barbara, Deborah, David,
and Gregory, who do us honor.*

E.J.H.

*To Eilene, whose love and support have been unending,
and to our children, Mark and Kathryn, who have
enriched our lives.*

P.F.K.

Series Editor: *Arnis E. Burvikovs*
Senior Marketing Manager: *Brad Parkins*
Production Manager: *Donna DeBenedictis*
Project Coordination, Text Design, and Electronic Page Makeup:
   Elm Street Publishing Services, Inc.
Cover Design Manager: *Wendy Ann Fredericks*
Cover Designer: *Diane Margolin*
Cover Illustration: © *PhotoDisc*
Manufacturing Buyer: *Al Dorsey*
Printer and Binder: *Courier – Westford*
Cover Printer: *Coral Graphic Services*

For permission to use copyrighted material, grateful acknowledgment is made to the copyright
holders on p. 399, which are hereby made part of this copyright page.

Library of Congress Cataloging-in-Publication Data

Haller, Emil J.
   Using educational research : a school administrator's guide / Emil J. Haller and Paul F. Kleine.
      p. cm.
   Includes bibliographical references and index.
   ISBN 0-8013-1635-9
      1. School management and organization—Research.   2. Education—Research—
Methodology.   3. School administrators.   I. Kleine, Paul F.   II. Title.

LB2806 .H29 2001
370'.7'2—dc21   00-028745

Please visit our website at http://www.abacon.com/edadmin

ISBN 0-8013-1635-9

1 2 3 4 5 6 7 8 9 10 — CRW — 03 02 01 00

Brief Contents

Detailed Contents

Preface

The Purpose of This Book

The purpose of this book is easily stated though not so easily accomplished. It is intended to contribute to the development of school administrators who are sophisticated, critical consumers of educational research. Two words, "administrators" and "consumers," are central to this statement of purpose.

First, the entire book is addressed to educational leaders and the problems they confront as they try to maintain and improve their schools. Thus, individual chapters are centered on the kinds of systemic problems practicing administrators often face: the dropout rate in a secondary school is too high; discipline in a middle school is bad and getting worse; under threat of state sanction, a district's achievement levels must be improved. Each chapter, then, draws together and examines research relevant to these sorts of problems. However, our purpose is not simply to examine studies pertinent to systemic administrative problems—this book is not a collection of literature reviews. Rather, we try to illustrate how research can inform administrators' thinking about the conundrums that lie at the heart of their work.

Second, we want to help practitioners become sophisticated, critical consumers of research. By this we mean administrators who possess certain identifiable skills. They are able to conceptualize their system's problems in fruitful ways. They can ask telling questions about those problems, questions that research has addressed. They know how to quickly locate pertinent studies that answer those questions. (Responsible administrators cannot spend months sitting in libraries doing the kind of literature searches that dissertations require.) They can sensibly read individual studies without becoming hopelessly mired in researchers' necessary but esoteric jargon. They are able to make judgments of quality—they know that some studies are more trustworthy than others. They are able to take the evidence gleaned from trustworthy studies and weave it together with local facts and important public and professional values to create defensible plans to resolve their schools' problems. That is, they can engage competently in practical reasoning. Finally, sophisticated and critical consumers of educational research are men and women who know that even if they become proficient in all of these skills, some problems will be recalcitrant; they will remain unresolved. They know that research, in itself, will not solve practical problems. But they also know that it can help them think more intelligently about those problems. And they know that thinking more intelligently about real problems is infinitely preferable to trial and error or—perhaps worse—mindlessly adopting every faddish "solution" currently making the rounds at administrators' conventions.

In this book we address all of the skills just noted. We hope to help school administrators develop a decent respect for credible evidence when they make important educational decisions. Good educational research is one source of such evidence (though certainly not the only one). Our purpose, then, is to help educational leaders learn how to avail themselves of it.

The Principles Behind This Book

This book is based on six principles we believe characterize the relationship between educational research and administrative practice. We would summarize these principles and their implications as follows:

1. The problems studied by researchers are not the problems faced by practitioners. This is obvious, of course, but the many practitioners who decry the uselessness of educational research betray that they do not understand this fundamental point. Sophisticated and critical consumers of research understand that the driving force behind the research institution most often stems from problems of understanding educational phenomena—of "knowing why." Such problems often derive from questions raised in other researchers' work, not from the questions raised by practitioners. In contrast, administrative problems arise in day-to-day practical affairs, when expectations are unmet or when interests clash. They concern "knowing what to do." Thus, in one sense educational research has limited bearing on educational practice. Yet, at a broader level, research problems are deeply rooted in problems of practice, and research is capable of usefully informing that practice.

2. Research cannot be "applied" to practical problems in any straightforward manner. When practitioners have such an expectation, they inevitably will be frustrated in their attempts to use research. Ideally, social research provides generalizable knowledge about the consequences of our actions. However, even if such information were absolutely trustworthy (which, of course, it never is), knowledge of consequences could not be a sufficient guide to practical decisions (Haller & Strike, 1997).

There are several reasons for this. First, administrative actions are necessarily shaped by their particular circumstances. They entail legal considerations that constrain actions, and they are further constrained by moral or ethical concerns. And there are always political considerations. Further, since practical problems are different from the problems studied by researchers, it is seldom clear what research problem(s) is relevant to a particular practical problem. Finally, research often involves explanatory concepts that have no obvious administrative referent. For example, even if research were conclusive in showing that anomie helps explain crime in general and school violence in particular, the concept of anomie has no inherent, administratively mutable analogue (Haller & Strike, 1997). For all of these reasons and others, sophisticated and critical consumers must be able to conceptualize a practical problem in a way that permits useful information to be derived from research literature, while recognizing that the information so derived is, at best, a less-than-perfect guide to practice.

3. Research problems have histories, and those histories are important for understanding and using research. Often the research on a problem spans decades, and it is punctuated by landmark studies that shape subsequent studies in fundamental ways. To understand what research has to say about some practical problem, sophisticated and critical consumers must be able to grasp the history of a research problem. They must be able to trace the development of a line of investigations that bears on the practical problem and arrive at a defensible synthesis with clear implications for action. (Sometimes the clear implication is that no action is warranted.) The sophisticated, critical practitioner knows better than to rely on "the latest research that shows. . ." Doing so is another reason for the faddishness that characterizes educational practice. Often we have "been there, done that."

4. The research that bears importantly on any practical problem is usually too vast, amorphous, and inconsistent to be sensibly "reviewed." Research relevant to a practical problem can only rarely be comprehended simply by reading it. For example, if the practitioner faces a problem of dropouts in his or her district, any attempt to review the research on dropouts will lead to frustration. That body of literature is very large, its boundaries are indistinct, its findings are often conflicting, and much of it bears no obvious relation to practice. Similar attributes will characterize the body of literature on nearly every important practical problem. The critical issue is to decide what counts as a relevant study before beginning a review. In order to do this, it is necessary to conceive of the problem in a useful way and to pose the right questions regarding it—questions that can be answered by the research literature and whose answers provide practically useful information. For practitioners then, reviewing research means attempting to answer useful questions posed by the administrator, not attempting to read all of the studies pertaining to a question posed by researchers.

5. Much of the published research that bears on a practitioner's problem isn't worth reading. Much research is of such poor quality as to be a dangerous guide to important practical decisions. Thus, knowledgeable administrators must be able to critically evaluate the research they turn up in a review of the literature. This means that they must be familiar with the technical criteria that researchers routinely use to judge the worth of a study, for example, logical coherence, fidelity in measurement, internal validity, and sampling adequacy. Equally important, they must be able to apply certain pragmatic considerations to the judgment of worth. As an example, they should understand the notion of practical significance (i.e., effect size), how that differs from statistical significance, and why the former is much more likely to be important to practitioners, though the latter is more important to researchers. Finally, they should recognize that many of the professional journals they rely on most heavily do not publish much in the way of research. Many of the articles that appear in the *Phi Delta Kappan* and the *NASSP Bulletin,* for example, are more akin to testimonials or editorials than they are to research reports.

6. When they are compiled and summarized, the results of trustworthy, relevant studies are an inadequate guide to practice. When research is simply compiled and summarized, the result is little more than a series of disconnected paragraphs: "Smith (1978) found . . ."; "Jones (1979) found . . ."; "Henry (1980) found . . ." ad nauseam. (One often sees such lists in the literature review chapters of dissertations.) Such compilations provide no useful guidance to practical decisions (or to theoretical ones, for that matter). In order to be useful, research results must be woven together and combined with appropriate and explicitly stated values in order to create an argument regarding a defensible course of action. Put another way, sophisticated and critical consumers are able to engage competently in practical reasoning. Practical reasoning differs from theoretical reasoning. Most notably it involves the ability to construct an argument that is based on both factual and value premises and one whose conclusion is a recommended action. Further, that argument must be accessible to laymen, not just other professionals, since school administrators must be able to explain and defend their recommendations to boards of education, parents, and taxpayers.

The Format of This Book

These six principles have guided the writing of this book. We develop these ideas in two stages. In the first part, consisting of chapters 1 through 4, we provide the necessary background concepts required for practitioners to understand and use research in educational administration. Chapter 1 addresses the following questions: What makes something a study in educational administration? Is there anything that distinguishes research in educational administration from, say, research in curriculum or teaching methods? If students are to use the research undergirding their profession, they must recognize it when they see it.

In chapter 2 we develop the idea of streams of research, often lasting decades, on particular administrative problems. The chapter stresses the importance of understanding these streams before attempting to apply research to practice. We use what is arguably the most influential study ever conducted in educational administration, the Coleman Report, (Coleman et al., 1966) to illustrate this idea. Published in 1966, this study and the questions it raised continue to shape the national research agenda. However, the chapter also stresses the difficulties that arise because of this need to see research in a historical perspective.

Chapter 3 illustrates the conduct of a research review regarding a practical and common educational and administrative problem (dropouts). It stresses the ideas developed in chapters 1 and 2, but it emphasizes the practical matters involved in reading research for the purpose of preparing a recommendation about a problem in schools. In particular, it emphasizes the fundamental difference between reading research for administrative decision making (i.e., to arrive at a defensible course of action) and reading research to prepare for doing more research (e.g., to prepare for writing a dissertation).

Up to this point, we have treated all studies as if they were equal—that deciding whether a body of research supports or does not support a course of action will be clear to anyone reviewing the literature. Obviously, that is rarely the case. Further, deciding whether a course of action is warranted is not simply a matter of taking a vote. Clearly, if students are to use research in a sophisticated and critical manner, they will need to be able to judge the worth of individual studies, which requires that they understand the criteria involved.

In chapter 4 we introduce the major criteria commonly used to assess research quality. We do not fully explicate and demonstrate the use of any single criterion in that chapter but instead provide students with enough of an understanding to begin to critically evaluate specific studies in the chapters that follow. The major criteria discussed include: the quality of the logic on which a study is based and of the argument supporting its conclusions; measurement and questions of validity and reliability; research design and threats to internal validity; sampling and threats to external validity; the logic of data analysis; and the question of practical significance.

In the second part of the book, we apply these ideas to actual problems faced by school administrators. The second part consists of chapters 5 through 10. Each of these follows a common format, opening with a brief case developing some practical problem in a school or district and the need to review the research regarding it. These cases focus on common problems—ones that most administrators will see as real issues and ones that many will actually be facing. For example, one chapter begins with a school principal facing a serious problem of student discipline. Another concerns a district's attempt to increase parent involvement. Each chapter then goes on to briefly review the research on the particular problem and concludes with a recommendation for practice based on that review, following the procedures described in chapter 3. These cases, then, are meant to put educational research in the context of practical problems and show how it can help practitioners think more intelligently about those problems.

Each of these chapters differs from the others in two important ways. First, one study turned up in the literature review is singled out for systematic, in-depth, evaluation. (For ease of reference, selected studies are reprinted in the book's end-of-chapter appendices.) Each of these is briefly evaluated using relevant concepts introduced in chapter 4. Second, in each chapter, one evaluation concept is the focus of attention. Thus, after completing these six chapters, students will have confronted the use of a major evaluation criterion six separate times on six distinctly different kinds of studies relevant to an important administrative issue, and each criterion will have been the subject of an in-depth treatment.

We recognize that the choice of studies to evaluate is important. We have chosen the focal study in each chapter with several criteria in mind. In addition to its significance as a study in educational administration, the aspect of each that we highlight for close examination is both visible and well-handled. Stated conversely, we do not set up bad studies to use as easy targets. Further, the study chosen is accessible. That is, it is not based on such esoteric theories or techniques that beginning administration students will be unable to grasp it. Each study is significant; it is influential in the research stream of which it is a part and influential in the world of practice. It should be substantively informative to students who are aspiring administrators. Finally, we have chosen studies that illustrate different research designs—experimental, causal-comparative, correlational, ethnographic, and so forth, which permit us to comment on particular strengths and weaknesses of each.

Chapter 11 closes the book by drawing together the major ideas that should govern sophisticated and critical administrators' use of empirical research to address practical problems in their schools.

Acknowledgments

We have had the benefit of the editorial competence and good advice of a number of people at Addison Wesley Longman. We are grateful to Art Pomponio and Arianne Weber for their guidance during the book's early stages, and to Amy Cronin and Matthew Ludvino who saw us through to its completion. Gina Linko at Elm Street Publishing Services gently, but firmly, kept the production process moving.

We also benefited from the comments of several people who read parts of this book and shared their reactions with us. These include Charles Achilles, James McNamara, and Janie Nusser. Maneesha Asundi and John Pijanowski ably assisted us at early stages of our work. And, of course, we are indebted to numerous colleagues at Cornell University and the University of Oklahoma for the stimulating discussions that make academic life so pleasurable. Perhaps most importantly, we are grateful to our students at Cornell and Oklahoma and to the practitioner-students at Nova Southeastern University who persisted in requiring that we make explicit the administrative relevance of educational research.

Emil J. Haller & Paul F. Kleine

References

Coleman, J. S., Campbell, E. Q., Hobson, C. J., McPartland, J., Mood, A. M., Weinfeld, F., & York, R. L. (1966). *Equality of educational opportunity*. Washington, DC: U.S. Government Printing Office. (ERIC Document Reproduction No. ED 012275)

Haller, E. J., & Strike, K. A. (1997). *Introduction to educational administration: Social, legal and ethical perspectives*. Troy, NY: Educator's Press International.

Introduction

We have a point of view. We believe that the competent practice of school administration requires practitioners to be sophisticated and critical consumers of educational research. Such practitioners are attentive to the importance of reasons and evidence when considering a solution to an educational problem in their schools. They formulate the right questions regarding their problem. They know how to efficiently locate and properly interpret the relevant research evidence. They are able to use that evidence to create a cogent argument in support of a practical course of action. And having done those things, they know that evidence—facts—can never be a sufficient guide to administrative practice.

Most of the texts dealing with educational research are less useful in creating these sophisticated, critical consumers than they might be. Typically, they are written for graduate students who are about to undertake research on their own—their masters theses or doctoral dissertations. Consequently, they have a distinct "how to" orientation, but the "how" concerns how to *do* research. There is very little discussion of how to *use* research to help address practical educational problems. Indeed, most texts are missing the practical problems that daily confront administrators. For the student preparing to undertake a dissertation, the traditional methods text is fine. For the student about to administer a school, it is substantially irrelevant. All of this is compounded by the dissertation itself, which teaches students to become experts on doing research that will fill a gap in our knowledge concerning a small, narrowly defined educational question, rather than teaching them to intelligently use research to help solve the complex, vastly amorphous, real-life problems that they will face in their schools.

In part, this situation is a consequence of the disjuncture between the historical purpose of university doctoral-level training and the composition of the graduate student body in most schools of education. In nearly every field, including the social sciences, the bulk of the graduate population is heading for a career in an academic or academic-like organization, where the conduct of research is a significant part of the role they will perform. It is sensible to train these people in the process of conducting research. In education, however, most graduate students are heading for careers in elementary and secondary schools or districts. A large proportion will go into administrative positions.[1] The vast majority of school administrators hold graduate degrees in some aspect of education, most commonly in administration itself (Haller, Brent, & McNamara, 1997). When these students earn their graduate degrees and return to their professional careers, most will never do another piece of academic research in their lives—that is, they will never write anything that resembles, even remotely, dissertations or the tightly focused articles that appear in scholarly journals. For these people the standard textbook and research methods course are largely hurdles that must be jumped on their way back to the world of practice.

This is not to say that research is irrelevant, however. Good research provides administrators with information and facts that can help them deal more sensibly with real problems in their schools: It can help them think more intelligently about those problems. Thus, it is important for practitioners to know how to become knowledgeable about what research has to say about educational problems. Becoming knowledgeable requires that they be able to locate, evaluate, and interpret the research that others have conducted. More importantly, they need to recognize when there is little or no research support for a program that they plan to implement. In either case, however, they do not need to know how to create that research themselves.

We are not so naive as to believe that the facts research can provide are all that are needed to resolve educational problems. Facts are never enough. For example, the vast bulk of the research on grade retention shows that this practice has few if any positive effects on children's achievement or social development. However, that fact is not sufficient, in itself, to justify a superintendent's decision not to implement a grade-retention policy in a school district. The superintendent would need to consider other factors as well, for example, the wishes of the community, the school board, and the faculty. Nevertheless, the fact that retention doesn't seem to work should certainly play a prominent role in the superintendent's thinking and discussion with anyone proposing that children be retained in grade in order to improve their achievement.

---

[1] Even when students major in something other than administration, many, in fact, enter administrative careers. The graduate student who earns an MA or Ph.D. in curriculum and instruction, for example, often ends up as a curriculum director in a district central office, that is, an administrator.

On Fads and Unwarranted Change, or Whatever Happened to All of Those Teaching Machines?

Many school administrators are quite unaware of what research has to tell them about a problem they are facing or if there is any research to support the efficacy of the particular solution they are advocating. For example, we are old enough to have taught in the public schools in the early 1960s and to remember the wave of enthusiasm that surrounded the introduction of "teaching machines" in the classroom. Long before computers were even a blip on the educational horizon, these machines were supposed to ensure student success in many subjects. Based on a straightforward extension of Harvard professor B. F. Skinner's theory and research on operant conditioning (Holland & Skinner, 1961; Skinner, 1953), these small, paper-fed devices were intended to guide students, in small easy steps, through a hierarchically arranged series of questions in a curriculum, from the very easy to the very complex. In theory, students were supposed to never miss a question, and correct responses presumably provided positive reinforcement, encouraging them to continue. When a response was correct, they were presented with slightly more difficult questions. If responses were incorrect, they were supposed to return to an earlier point in the series which, presumably, they didn't fully understand. When that point was mastered, they were permitted to progress to the next, slightly more complicated question. By proceeding in small easy steps, students were supposed to be able to master complex subjects. If you have the impression that many modern computer-based instructional programs are essentially multi-media versions of the same underlying theory of instruction, you are correct.

Despite their theoretical support and the evidence from psychologists' laboratories, the machines did not work in real classrooms. Students quickly lost interest in them; they were mechanized workbooks, and like workbooks, they soon became boring. Teachers objected when they found themselves relegated to the logistics and record-keeping involved with dispensing paper scripts to students. Good laboratory evidence showing that children could learn using these machines was no substitute for carefully evaluated, large scale implementations in real classrooms. The administrators who bought these machines and encouraged their use in schools did so without any satisfactory evidence that they would be effective. Thus, tens of thousands of hours of valuable instructional time and taxpayer dollars were wasted. We sometimes wonder what happened to all those machines. Undoubtedly most have long since disappeared into landfills. Perhaps a few molder in school attics. They did make useful, if expensive, door stops.

If teaching machines were an isolated episode in American education, little more could be said. However, the history of our field is replete with similar instances in which administrators have shown themselves unaware of research evidence that casts doubt on their favorite innovation, or have shown themselves willing to implement solutions to problems without any evidence that the solutions work. For example, Madeline Hunter's book *Teach More—Faster!* (Hunter, 1969, revised 1980) captured the attention of educators in the 1970s, promising, as the title implies, that student achievement could be significantly increased if the method were adopted. In the following decades uncounted numbers of teachers and administrators attended thousands of workshops to learn the Hunter method of instruction. It was not until 1988 that a large-scale, state-sponsored, evaluation of the method in North Carolina, involving almost half of that state's teachers, showed it to be ineffective (Mandeville, 1988 cited in Slavin, 1989). Before this bandwagon departed the educational scene, millions of dollars and hundreds of thousands of hours of educator's time were wasted. Had the method been implemented in several locations on a very small scale and then carefully evaluated—and had educators paid attention to the results of those evaluations—most of this waste might have been averted.

Other examples of educators' penchant to ignore research evidence bearing directly on an educational strategy, and their penchant to implement innovations on a large scale before evidence supporting their efficacy has accumulated, are easy to find. Consider the number of districts that have implemented programs to raise student self-esteem, absent any good evidence that high self-esteem improves student achievement. Now, when the evidence is clear that these effects are not regularly forthcoming (Kohn, 1994), numerous school districts are saddled with self-esteem programs that do not work. Consider also the current rush to implement "site-based management" programs across the country, when the evidence regarding their effectiveness in raising student achievement is only now beginning to trickle in, and that evidence is decidedly mixed (see, e.g., Townsend, 1996).

Perhaps the largest innovation ever implemented in U.S. schools was the consolidation of small, rural schools and school districts, an innovation that has taken place throughout this century. The number of school districts in the U.S. has declined from more than 150,000 in 1900 to fewer than 15,000 today, while one-room elementary schools and high school graduating classes of 20, which were once common, are now rare (Pipho, 1987). The consolidation movement was grounded in the firm conviction that larger schools and districts were both more effective and efficient. It was not until the 1960s and continuing until the present day that research has demonstrated that consolidation routinely achieves neither of these results (Barker & Gump, 1964; Monk & Haller, 1986; Monk & Haller, 1993; Sher, 1977). Indeed, we have many studies indicating the educational superiority of small schools (Cotton, 1996; Fowler & Walberg, 1991; Goodlad, 1984; Walberg & Walberg, 1994; Witcher & Kennedy, 1996). Now, at the turn of the millennium, we find ourselves struggling to make smaller schools from the larger ones we have created, for example, through schools-within-schools schemes. Undoubtedly you can think of other examples of educational fads and other instances of unwarranted educational changes.

School Administrators and the Problem of Fads

Certainly there are numerous reasons why educators tend to ignore the often painfully gathered evidence that bears on the practical problems that they face.

This tendency is partly rooted in what Lortie has termed an ethos of individualism, a belief that each classroom and school presents unique problems that must be addressed with unique solutions of the individual's own devising (Lortie, 1975). As long as this belief drives administrators' actions, research is largely irrelevant.

In part the problem is systemic. As Slavin has pointed out (Slavin, 1989), education has no equivalent to the Food and Drug Administration (FDA). The FDA requires that before any physician can administer a drug to a patient, that drug must pass sustained and rigorous tests that demonstrate that it is effective and that its side effects are known and within tolerable bounds. If a physician were to willfully ignore this requirement, he or she would be subject to severe penalties. In contrast, educational innovators peddle their wares to administrators undeterred by any requirement that they produce convincing evidence that their treatments work. And administrators are free to implement those innovations with no fear of penalty. This is another way we get teaching machines, the Hunter Method, self-esteem programs, and huge schools.

In addition to the ethos of individualism and the systemic problem, however, we believe that the tendency to ignore the need for evidence in administrative decision making is also simply a lack of knowledge. No school administrator is born with an understanding of the nature of administrative research, how that research can (and cannot) inform practice, how to decide when a study is relevant to a particular problem, how to know when that study is trustworthy, and how to use a series of studies to create an argument in support of a defensible course of action. This kind of knowledge is necessary if administrators are to recognize the uses and limitations of research and to use it intelligently when dealing with practical problems.

Knowledge, however, is insufficient. School administrators must also value the facts and evidence that research can provide and be willing to seek and use them effectively when dealing with others. When, for example, a school board seems bent on adopting an imprudent or unwarranted policy, the superintendent should be able to find and marshal the relevant evidence as part of a persuasive argument in opposition. Effective leadership should depend less on charisma, personality, and power than on reasoned persuasion, and this should be especially the case in educational institutions—institutions fundamentally committed to the development of individuals' capacity to reason.

We are not naive enough to think that a single textbook can negate the many forces that promote the faddishness that characterizes education. Nevertheless, knowledge is a necessary if not sufficient condition to improved administrative practice.

References

Barker, R. G., & Gump, P. V. (1964). *Big school, small school; high school size and student behavior.* Palo Alto, CA: Stanford University Press.

Cotton, K. (1996). *Affective and Social Benefits of Small-Scale Schooling. ERIC Digest.* Charleston, WV: ERIC Clearinghouse on Rural Education and Small Schools. (ERIC Document Reproduction No. ED401088)

Fowler, W. J., Jr., & Walberg, H. J. (1991). School size, characteristics, and outcomes. *Educational Evaluation and Policy Analysis, 13*(2), 189–202.

Goodlad, J. I. (1984). *A place called school: prospects for the future.* New York: McGraw-Hill.

Haller, E. J., Brent, B. O., & McNamara, J. F. (1997). Does graduate training in educational administration improve America's schools? *Phi Delta Kappan, 79*(3), 222–227.

Holland, J. G., & Skinner, B. F. (1961). *The analysis of behavior: a program for self- instruction.* New York: McGraw-Hill.

Hunter, M. (1969, revised 1980). *Teach more—faster!* El Segundo, CA: TIP Publications.

Kohn, A. (1994). The truth about self-esteem. *Phi Delta Kappan, 76*(4), 272-283.

Lortie, D. C. (1975). *Schoolteacher: A sociological study.* Chicago: University of Chicago Press.

Mandeville, G. K. (1988). *An evaluation of PET using extant achievement data.* New Orleans LA. (ERIC Document Reproduction No. ED295990.)

Monk, D. H., & Haller, E. J. (1986). *Organizational alternatives for small rural schools. Final report to the legislature of the State of New York.* Ithaca, NY: Department of Education, Cornell University. (ERIC Document Reproduction No. ED 281694)

Monk, D. H., & Haller, E. J. (1993). Predictors of high school academic course offerings: The role of school size. *American Educational Research Journal, 30*(1), 3–21.

Pipho, C. (1987). Rural education. *Phi Delta Kappan, 69,* 6–7.

Sher, J. P. (Ed.). (1977). *Education in rural America.* Boulder, CO: Westview Press.

Skinner, B. F. (1953). *Science and human behavior.* New York: Macmillan.

Slavin, R. J. (1989). PET and the pendulum: Faddism in education and how to stop it. *Phi Delta Kappan, 70*(10), 752–758.

Townsend, T. (1996). *School effectiveness and restructuring schools: What does the research tell us?* Paper presented at the Annual Meeting of the International Congress for School Effectiveness and Improvement, Minsk, Belarus.

Walberg, H. J., & Walberg, H. J., III. (1994). Losing Local Control. *Educational Researcher, 23*(5), 19–26.

Witcher, A. E., & Kennedy, R. I. (Eds.). (1996). *Big schools, small schools: What's best for students?* Bloomington, IN: Center for Evaluation, Development, Research, Phi Delta Kappa.

1

What Is Research in Educational Administration?

INTRODUCTION

Let us begin with a thought experiment. Imagine this. Suppose someone handed you copies of two empirical research reports. The first was an article from the *Journal of High Energy Physics,* and the second was from the *Educational Administration Quarterly.* Neither article, however, carried a title or identified the journal from which it was drawn. Could you tell the difference? That is, could you identify which research article reported the results of a study in high energy physics and which reported the results of a study in educational administration?

Undoubtedly you could. Even if you have not opened a physics book since high school, you're probably quite confident that you could tell research in physics from research in educational administration. You would expect to see numerous differences between the two studies—in the questions addressed, in research methods, and in style. For example, the study in physics might concern a question about some form of matter, say, one of the subatomic particles. The study would likely report the results of an experiment, and it would probably be short, heavily dependent on mathematical representation, and written in a highly specialized, arcane jargon that—for most of us—would be largely unintelligible. On the other hand, the study in educational administration would concern some question about schools or the people in them; its methods would probably involve some kind of statistical analysis of survey research data; its style would be relatively lengthy and discursive; and, while certainly not jargon-free, it would be reasonably intelligible to a professional educator like yourself, as well as to an educated layman.

Now let us repeat this imaginary experiment, but this time let us replace the article from the *Journal of High Energy Physics* with an empirical study taken from *Interchange,* a journal that publishes research primarily concerned with school curricula. Could you tell the difference now? That is, could you distinguish a research article about school administration from one about school curriculum? Both are likely to be about schools and the people in them, both are likely to involve survey methods, and both are likely to be lengthy, discursive, but reasonably intelligible reports. In short, is there anything distinctive about research in educational administration? What separates research in your field from research in other, related fields such as curriculum, educational psychology, and the economics of education?

In this chapter we want to address that question: What makes something a study in educational administration? We think the question is important. Throughout this book we will be arguing that research in your field can help you make better decisions about many of the practical problems that administrators face: How can we increase parents' involvement in the education of their children? What can we do to lower the dropout rate in our school? How can students' conduct be improved to give this school a better climate for teaching and learning? These are the kinds of questions that face administrative practitioners every day, and they are the kinds of questions about which research has something useful to offer. But if you are going to follow and use the research in your field, you must recognize it when you see it—that is, you must have a conception of the knowledge base that undergirds professional practice in educational administration.

What Is Research in Educational Administration? An Empirical Approach

How can we approach the question of what counts as research in our field? One strategy we might take would be empirical. By *empirical* we mean that our attempt to answer the question relies on experience, evidence, and observation —on data. At heart, an empiricist is someone who believes that all knowledge originates in sense impressions, that is, in sensations that impinge on our eyes, ears, and other senses. "Whatever is in the mind was first in the senses" is the empiricist's motto. Empirical research is concerned with creating facts through experiments, surveys, case studies, or other accepted methods, facts that can then be used to answer a question. The kind of educational research that concerns us in this book is empirical research.

Our task, then, is to generate evidence (data) that bears on the question of the nature of research in educational administration. How might we design such a study? What sort of data would help us answer the question: "What is research in educational administration?" One obvious empirical approach might be to ask. That is, we might simply ask people involved in doing studies in a field what it is that they do when they are engaged in research. For example, we can imagine posing the following query to a group of professors in university departments of educational administration: "What question are you trying to answer in your current research project?" Each response we receive could be considered data (or a datum, if you prefer) about what counts as research in our field. Indeed, we might ask that question of any field in which systematic research plays an important role, such as physics, sociology, or history.

Notice three things about this strategy. First, we have assumed away an important issue: We have assumed that everyone in departments of educational administration who does research does it in that field. Our empirical strategy becomes problematic if it turns out that many faculty members in those departments do research in some other field. While it is unlikely that any professors of educational administration do research in particle physics, it is not implausible that some might work on topics ordinarily found within the province of curriculum, educational psychology, and so forth. If a significant proportion of educational administration professors did that, any conclusion we reached about the distinguishing characteristics of research in our field would be misleading.

Second, notice the implicit definition of research: Research is about answering questions. Every study has at its heart a question that the researcher is trying to answer. Pick up any research journal in any field. There always is a question: "What is the mass of the top quark?" (physics); "What was the position of women authors in colonial America?" (history); "Have gun control laws affected crime rates?" (sociology). If we understand the question that is being asked, we understand the single most important aspect of a study. Generalizing that idea, if we understand the essential or prototypical questions asked by researchers in a field, we understand a critically important aspect of the field itself.

Finally, notice that we cannot ask a single professor and reach a conclusion about the nature of research in educational administration, since that single person is not likely to represent the entire field. At the least we should ask a representative sample of the professoriate in educational administration. However, if we ask a random sample of, say, 100 professors, what we would hear might, at first blush, sound like babble. That is, we are almost certain to get 100 different answers to the same question. Each of those researchers will be working on a different problem. This creates a methodological difficulty. How can we make sense of the babble—of 100 different responses?

Regarding the assumption that professors in educational administration do research in their own field, we will simply acknowledge that we are making that assumption. That is, if we were actually doing the hypothetical study discussed, we would explicitly state this as an assumption of our research. Every study rests on a set of assumptions, and this assumption would be an important one in ours. Regarding the methodological problem (how to make sense of the babble), we might listen, as the psychiatrists say, "with our third ear," meaning listening for the implicit message that lies beneath the explicit one. We might, for example, look for a common theme running through the answers of our

100 respondents: Is there some underlying quality that seems to characterize most of the studies that the professors are doing? If we define research as an attempt to answer a question, we might ask if there is a "central question" in the 100 different questions—a prototypical query that catches the essence of the 100 specific questions posed in professors' individual studies? We might argue, then, that this central question defines the essence of research in educational administration.

As we have noted, one might do this little study in any academic field: For example, we could ask what is the central question addressed by researchers in physics? Or sociology? We can imagine asking 100 physicists or sociologists what they do when they do research in their fields. If we did, we might find that those disciplines can be characterized by a central question. While the physicists or sociologists would certainly be studying a multitude of seemingly disparate questions, we might discover that the multitude is really only instances of a central question, a question that defines the discipline. For example, we might find that much of the research in physics, even since ancient times, has been an attempt to answer this central question: What is the nature of matter? In the case of sociology, we might phrase a central question as Thomas Hobbes, the 17th century English political philosopher, did. Hobbes noted that if we are all driven only by our own selfish motives, life would be a war of all against all. Or, in what he called "a state of nature," there would be "No arts; no letters; no society; and which is worst of all, continual fear and danger of violent death; and the life of man, solitary, poor, nasty, brutish, and short" (Hobbes, 1950, Ch. 13). But life is not like that—though it may seem like that some of the time. Sociology, then, might be thought of as a collective effort to answer the Hobbesian question: How is society possible?

If disciplines are characterized by a few fundamental questions, they are also characterized by a methodology, an accepted way to answer those questions. In physics, for example, legitimate answers are produced by experimentation and logic. Sociology, on the other hand, rarely uses experimental methods, largely because they are impossible (or unethical) to employ. When a sociologist asked the question, "Why did more Protestants than Catholics commit suicide in 19th century Europe?" (Durkheim, 1951), an experiment in which a randomly chosen group of people living a century ago are permitted to commit suicide isn't possible, even were it ethically acceptable. Sociologists, then, must often rely on "softer" methods than true experimental designs, for example, historical documents and surveys.

A Study of Dissertations in Educational Administration

Educational administration is not usually thought of as a discipline, at least in the sense of having both a few central questions and an accepted methodology. Nevertheless, it can be instructive to examine the kinds of questions researchers in the field address and to determine whether there is a question or two that captures much of the research that is done. Is there some analogue to "What is the nature of matter?" or "How is society possible?"

Some years ago Haller carried out a study along these lines (Haller & Knapp, 1985). The purpose of the research was to identify a central question that characterized research in educational administration. Instead of interviewing researchers, however, he selected a random sample of the abstracts of dissertations done in departments of educational administration at American universities.[1] From each abstract he identified the research question posed by the doctoral student conducting the study. Following is a representative sample of the questions those students asked. As you read the list, "listen with your third ear" and ask yourself: Is there a central question that runs through this sample of research studies in your field?

- What are the administrative opportunities available to 50 women religious school administrators?
- What causes stress for Illinois school administrators?
- What are the roles, satisfactions, and problems of assistant principals?
- What is the relationship between the Georgia Criterion Referenced Test and the Stanford Achievement Test?
- What congruence is there between the ideal and actual functions of academic deans?
- What are the best procedures to follow before and after a major school fire?
- How do former college presidents view changes in campus governance?
- What are the attitudes of male and female superintendents toward women administrators?
- Does experience as an assistant coach affect the *Leadership Behavior Description Questionnaire* scores of athletic directors?
- How do women school administrators feel about their work?
- What are the attitudes of Alabama superintendents toward collective bargaining? (Haller & Knapp, 1985)

There are at least two notable aspects to these questions. Perhaps the most obvious of these is what *is not* studied. With a couple of possible exceptions (e.g., the study of school fires), most of these studies had little to say about children. Indeed, it is possible to read entire dissertations in educational administration and never learn that schools have anything to do with students. Since shaping the minds and behavior of young people is the primary purpose of schools, and achieving organizational purposes is the central responsibility of administrators, it is disconcerting to find that much of the research in educational administration has little to say about the major responsibility of administrative practitioners.

---

[1] The decision to use dissertations instead of interviewing researchers or selecting articles from journals was deliberate. A dissertation is a piece of research, and since these dissertations were done in departments of educational administration, Haller assumed that they represented research in that field. More importantly, dissertations were selected because each was approved by one or more professors of educational administration. Hence, the studies presumably met the professors' criteria for research in the field. Thus, the sample reflected not only students' views but those of the professoriate as well.

What, then, did these researchers study when they did research in educational administration? With some exceptions, for example, the dissertation concerning test scores, the answer seems clear. They studied administrators. Haller concluded that the central question running through a substantial majority of the dissertations could be phrased as follows: "What are the attitudes, values or opinions of practicing school administrators about X" (where X can be virtually anything). The actual questions asked—"What are the attitudes of Alabama superintendents toward collective bargaining?"; "How do women superintendents feel about their work?"; "What causes stress for Illinois school administrators?"—illustrate this focus on the mental states of practitioners. In our view, the fundamental problem with these dissertations is that many confuse the study of educational administra*tors* with the study of educational administra*tion*. Clearly, one might spend a lifetime studying the former and learn little or nothing about the latter.[2]

Perhaps we can illustrate this distinction by considering another field of study. Suppose that a physics researcher becomes concerned about the federal government's cuts in its support of physics research. Suppose further that her concern leads her to send a questionnaire to a random sample of physicists around the country to determine their attitudes toward the cuts. After analyzing her results, she writes an article that is subsequently published in a physics journal. Is her study research in physics? Most of us would say no; it is a kind of public opinion polling, not research in physics (Gowin, 1972). Similarly, simply because a study has educational administrators as its objects of study (its *Ss* in the psychologists' jargon) that fact, in itself, does not make it research in educational administration.

Notice the value premise built into this judgment about the merit of these dissertations. We believe that research in educational administration should inform the *practice* of school administrators. Educational administration is an applied field, a field in which practitioners apply knowledge to solve real problems in schools. Research in an applied field should contribute to improving professional practice. If it does not, it is of less worth than it should be. Knowing the attitudes of Alabama superintendents toward collective bargaining seems likely to be of little help to a practitioner dealing with problems in his or her school—even if those problems grew out of a collective bargaining contract. Imagine if most of the medical school training of nascent surgeons was given over to studying articles and books about physicians' attitudes towards their jobs, their opinions

---

[2] There is a third aspect of this focus on attitudes and values that is worth mention. Academic research on individuals' attitudes and values is the traditional province of social psychology. That field has a rich history of theories and methods centered on just those topics. What is striking about most of the studies done by students of educational administration is the extent to which they show little if any acquaintance with those theories and methods. That is not surprising, of course, since they have spent most of their graduate time in classes concerned with school administration. However, this lack of knowledge is often painfully obvious, perhaps most so in the casual assumption that attitudes *cause* behavior, an assumption that has been treated as problematic by social psychologists for decades (e.g., McMahon, 1984).

of Medicare, or their beliefs regarding public control of medical practice. Few of us would be willing to put our bodies under the knife of a surgeon so trained.

What Should Research in Educational Administration Be? A Normative Approach

We have just taken an empirical approach to the question of what counts as research in our field. When we take an empirical approach, we are asking what *is*. What *is* the state of the field's research? If we do that, as we have seen, we may come to a disquieting conclusion: Much of the research in our field seems unlikely to be of much help to practitioners who must deal with the real and serious problems that burden their schools. In such situations we are prompted to take a normative approach to the same question.

What does it mean to take a normative approach to a question? The root of the word normative is *norm*, a rule for behavior. We see norms in operation everyday. If 15 people walk into a bank, and there is only one teller, they get in line. (Well, most do.) Why? Because they are obeying an internalized rule that specifies what people should do when many persons want simultaneous access to the same resource. Even small children can express the rule: "First come, first served."[3] Thus, when we take a normative approach to our question we are asking: "What should research in educational administration be?" When we approach a question normatively, we have entered explicitly into the realm of values.

Defining Terms: Research, Administration, and School

Before we address the question of what research in our field should be, we should clarify a few of its critical terms: *research, administration,* and *education.* If we are to develop an answer to our query, we should be clear about the central concepts that are embedded in it. We have been using these terms regularly for several pages, and we will continue to do so throughout this book, so it is important to explain what we mean by them.

We have already suggested a definition of research: it is an attempt to answer a question. That is a good start, but it doesn't go very far. The definition includes every activity that has as its purpose answering a question, for example, looking up a number in the phone book. That is a kind of research, we suppose,

---

[3] The example is interesting in part because it illustrates the importance of schools. It is likely that kindergartens are the first place that children regularly run into the problem of many people competing for a scarce resource, such as the teacher's attention, a pencil sharpener, food in the cafeteria, and so forth, and it is there that they learn this important norm. Today's typical family, in contrast, has so few children that there is no need to learn to get in line. Schools teach that skill. Incidentally, the learning of norms is one of sociology's answers to one of its central questions: "How is society possible?" See Robert Dreeben's classic discussion of the role of schools in teaching norms (Dreeben, 1967).

but it's not what researchers mean when they describe their work. Here, we will use *research* to mean *the sustained attempt to answer a question, using a legitimated methodology, when the answer to that question is not already known*. It is the final clause in this definition that separates what researchers actually do from looking up phone numbers in the phone book, or writing term papers in the library. In both cases the answer to the question is in the phone book or in the library's collection. The problem is simply finding that answer. On the other hand, researchers will go to great lengths to assure themselves that the question that they plan to answer in their next study hasn't already been answered. One's career is not furthered by answering a question that could have been answered by a quick trip to the library.[4]

In defining *administration* we will rely on a definition first offered by Gulick and Urwick in 1937. Gulick and Urwick were interested in administration qua administration: What does all administration have in common, regardless of where it is performed—in hospitals, the military, government, or industry? Their answer became a well-known acronym, POSDCoRB, standing for Planning, Organizing, Staffing, Developing, Coordinating, Reporting, and Budgeting. These are the activities that all administrators perform, regardless of what they are administering.

Applying the Gulick and Urwick definition to educational administration is useful, for it emphasizes that the primary orientation of an administrator is to a system, not to the components of that system. For example, suppose you were appointed superintendent of a brand new school district, one with a thousand children but no educational system at all. Your school board requires you to educate all of those children. You certainly wouldn't try to educate them yourself, so as an administrator you would design a system for doing that. You might proceed as follows: You might *plan* the tasks that need to be accomplished, for example, students would have to be taught, buses operated, lunches served, and so forth. Next you might *organize* those tasks by specifying how they relate to one another and who may initiate work for whom. An organization chart is a common way to do this. But since organization charts do not do actual work, you would need to *staff*—to put people in those empty boxes. Once everyone has been hired, they must be developed, that is trained. You would also have to concern yourself with *coordination*. Tasks need to be done at particular times and places, not when or where employees feel moved to do them. Part of your job would be to *report* (in other words, to evaluate), not just the performance of the people you had hired but, more importantly, the performance of the system you designed—are children getting educated? Finally, nothing would be accomplished until you had *budgeted*, or secured and allocated resources to the system.

---

[4] You might be wondering whether replications count as research, given our definition. Replication—basically, repeating a study—is highly valued in many fields. The answer is yes; replicating a study does count as research, in part because there is often doubt that the answer found by a previous researcher was correct and in part because of researchers' trained skepticism. It is also worth noting that replication seems to be much less valued in education than in many of the sciences, where important studies get replicated several times to ensure that their findings hold up. Recall the rush to replicate the "cold fusion" experiment a few years ago.

Notice that this is a process definition that proceeds roughly in the sequence named. Indeed, it is often referred to as "the administrative process." More importantly, the process is circular. Once complete, it begins again. After you designed and implemented the system for educating those thousand children, you would not be out of a job. You'd need to begin planning, organizing, staffing, and so on all over again. Further, each component is also a process, one that contains the entire sequence. For example, *budgeting* requires planning, organizing, staffing, and so forth. These circular processes give the conception its systemic character. In any given case, the process takes its significance from the purpose of the organization in which it is applied. With regard to schools, the processes of planning, organizing, staffing, and so forth attain their importance because of their contributions to educating children. This systemic view characterizes the practice of administration; we shall return to this point in a moment.

Finally, the last term we need to examine is *education*. We can make short work of it, because it is the wrong word. Administrators do not administer education, they administer organizations whose purpose it is to educate. Indeed, it is hard to imagine administration apart from organizations. In our field the basic organization is a school. Hence, we suggest that a better term is *school administration*, not *educational administration*. This is not simply a semantic quibble; it permits us to ask "What is a school?" rather than "What is education?" The former question is considerably more tractable than the latter.[5]

What is a school? We will rely on a conception of the sources of curriculum developed by Joseph Schwab (1978). Schwab proposed what he termed the four "commonplaces" of schooling: learners, teachers, subject matter, and milieu. Each of these could serve as the source of curriculum, for example, the needs of learners, the requirements of pedagogy, the character of the subject matter, the demands of society. We might also conceive of these four as the desiderata of a school—the things that must be present if we are to call something a school. One conception of a school, then, would be to think of learners as people who lack certain knowledge and teachers as people who possess that knowledge. The purpose of a school, then, is to take subject matter, a property of teachers, and make it the property of learners as well. (Subject matter was construed broadly by Schwab, not simply "the 3-Rs".) This transfer takes place in a locale, the milieu, which in Schwab's scheme is a compendium, including not simply the classroom and school itself but also the political and social communities in which they are embedded.

It is worth noting what is missing from this conception of a school: administrators. This tells us something about their necessity. They are not. We had schools for thousands of years before we had school administrators. In fact, only a century ago in this country, almost all schools consisted of a building with one classroom, a single teacher, and a local board of education that met irregularly to

---

[5] Despite our preference for *school administration* rather than *educational administration,* we will continue to use the terms more or less interchangeably for two reasons: In part we simply want to avoid ungainly repetition, and in part practitioners treat the two terms as synonymous.

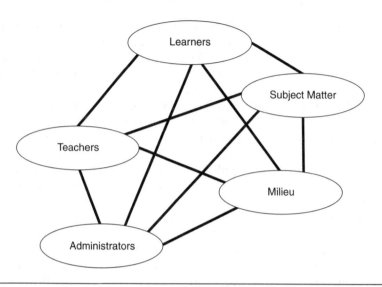

F I G U R E   *1.1*   **A Conception of Practice in Educational Administration**

Source: Based on Schwab, J. J. (1978). *Science, curriculum and liberal education: Selected essays of Joseph J. Schwab. Edited by Ian Westbury and Neil Wilkof.* Chicago: University of Chicago Press.

decide whatever needed deciding. If there was any administration to be done—any planning, organizing, or staffing—the teacher or the school board did it. It was only later in the century that, as a society, we decided that those one-room schools were inefficient and that they should be replaced by larger units. As schools became larger, however, administration became too complicated and difficult for a single teacher or school board to accomplish, and the profession of public school administration was born. We should remember, though, that as a society we could have decided otherwise—that despite their presumed inefficiencies, those one-room schools had advantages worth keeping. We could have opted to keep those little schools. If so, we would have no need for school administrators.

But we are not going back to the last century and rethinking a decision made then, nor are we going to build thousands of one-room schools to house today's students. For better or worse, administrators are an integral part of today's educational scene, and so we will add them to Schwab's conception. Finally, Schwab recognized that the commonplaces are not separate and discrete entities, existing in a vacuum; each is joined to all of the others. We represent this revision of Schwab's conception of a school in Figure 1.1.

What Is the Practice of School Administration?

With this conception of a school, and with the systemic view of administration captured in Gulick and Urwick's definition, we are in a position to define the *practice* of school administration. We begin by suggesting that the school administrator is not primarily concerned with any one of the five commonplaces, but with the relationships among them. That is, an administrator's responsibility is to plan, organize, staff, develop, coordinate, report, and budget that set of relationships that best accomplish the organization's purpose. In the case of schools, the fundamental purpose is to create prescribed changes in learners.

We need to discuss the relationships depicted in Figure 1.1. First note that each line represents a large number of possible relationships that exist between any two commonplaces. For example, consider the link connecting teachers and learners. In the primary grades, that line might represent a teacher's relation to learners as an instructor of reading, mathematics, or science, each of which is a distinct role. Further, our primary teacher also relates to his learners in the role of disciplinarian, a role that is captured in that single line as well. Finally, our teacher might stand as a father figure for his students, still another kind of relationship.

Here, however, we mean the relationships shown in the figure to stand for a much more circumscribed set of possibilities—the structured, deliberately chosen, and administratively mutable relationships that tie the commonplaces together. The key term is *administratively mutable*. Of the myriad relationships represented in Figure 1.1, only a few are under substantial administrative control. More are open to a degree of administrators' influence but not to their full control. Many relationships, moreover, are administratively immutable—they are outside of any administrative influence.[6] Consider the single line representing the relationships between teachers and administrators. One class of teacher-administrator relationship concerns school governance. One type of school governance relationship is the principal advisory committee. In most districts the composition and operation of these types of committees is left largely to principals' discretion. On the other hand, while principals may have some modest influence on aspects of their district's collective bargaining contract, these administrator-teacher governance relationships are primarily determined by others—namely unions and school boards. Finally, in states with tenure laws, due process rules stipulate in considerable detail principals' relationships to teachers judged to be incompetent. While those relationships are certainly administrative in nature, they are prescribed by legislatures and courts and are immutable from a school leader's perspective.

When administrators create or help to create a structured set of mutable relationships in their schools, they do so in order to attain some educational objective. For example, consider three elementary principals trying to deal with the same problem, unacceptably low mathematics achievement in the primary grades. The first principal is considering whether a program of cooperative

---

[6] An interesting way to think about leadership in educational organizations is to consider how administrators might extend their legitimate authority over relations among the commonplaces that are currently beyond that authority. How might relationships that are presently immutable be brought under administrative influence, and how might relationships that are presently open only to influence be brought under administrative control? For interesting empirical studies along these lines, see Kunz and Hoy (1976) and Hoy and Brown (1988).

learning would improve students' math scores. The second is thinking about ability grouping as a possible solution. The third is contemplating hiring a teacher specializing in mathematics to teach all of the primary classrooms. Referring to Figure 1.1, each of these schemes can be thought of as a specific variation on that set of relationships that tie together three of the common-places: learners, teachers and subject matter. Each has the same purpose: changing students' success in mathematics. Implementing each, moreover, is substantially (though not entirely) under the principal's control. In administrative parlance, these kinds of relationships are normally spoken of as *programs.* Cooperative learning, ability grouping, and a departmentalized curriculum are programs. Our idea of administrative practice is focused on the primary respon-sibility of school administrators for programs that create intended changes in learners. More formally, we offer the following definition: At its core, *the prac-tice of school administration consists of deliberately establishing, maintaining, and changing programs that have prescribed effects on learners.*

Notice the words *prescribed effects* in the definition. They are meant to remind us that as educators we are not free to decide what changes are to be worked on learners. In this country schools are institutions that are subject to democratic control, and it is the people, through their elected representatives, who decide how children are to be changed. This is simply another way of saying that the ends of education are primarily political matters (in the best sense of that term), while means to those ends are primarily professional matters. In the previous example, our principals are largely free to decide how mathe-matics should be taught. They are not free to decide whether it should be taught.

Research on Administrative Practice

Finally, then, we are ready to address the normative question that provoked this discussion: What *should* count as research in educational administration? We have already taken the position that educational administration is an applied field of research. By that we mean to emphasize that the fundamental purpose of its research should be to improve administrative practice. Of course, that should not be its only purpose, but to the extent that it neglects this fundamental goal, it comes to resemble research in other fields in the social sciences and is thereby increasingly hard to justify as an activity worth supporting within educational administration itself. If we accept this value, we can ask what kind of research would best support the conception of administrative practice that we devel-oped earlier.

We suggest that when administrative practitioners implement programs to achieve prescribed changes in learners, they are trying to predict the future. They take an action in the belief that it will cause some goal to be attained or some problem avoided. To follow our examples, the elementary principal who establishes cooperative learning, or ability grouping, or departmentalized math-ematics is predicting that his or her chosen program will improve mathematics achievement in the primary grades. But no one can predict the future. The prin-cipals are not, however, reduced to making blind guesses. Obviously, they will rely on their own past experience and best judgment. But everyone's experience is limited, and everyone's best judgment is sometimes misguided. They can improve on these methods by examining their profession's verified past experience. If these administrators know whether cooperative learning, ability grouping, and departmentalized mathematics have reliably increased student mathematics performance in previous times and in other places, they are in a better position to decide whether to try any of those programs in their own schools.

This is what research in school administration should provide, a verified past experience, if it is to be taken seriously in administrative practice. This is what we meant to imply earlier in using the phrases *sustained attempt* and *legitimated methodology* in our definition of research. We meant to suggest that in an applied field such as ours, a substantial part of our research effort should go to building up an extensive body of verified knowledge about the efficacy of specific, administratively mutable programs meant to affect learners. Thus, we offer this normative conception of research in our field: *Research in school administration should be primarily concerned with creating a methodologically sound literature of the effects on learners of specific, administratively mutable, educational programs.*

At this point we must offer a strong caveat. If our three administrators find that the research is unequivocal concerning their proposed programs, it does not follow that they should do anything in their schools. For example, if the research findings were unassailable that math scores are always improved under cooperative learning, ability grouping or departmentalizing primary grade mathematics, it does not follow that they must implement any of those programs in their schools. This is so for at least two reasons.

First and most obviously, each school is unique. A program that has worked in other places may not necessarily work in a particular school because that school differs in significant ways from those that were studied. Consider a few of the many factors that might militate against adopting a program that had an unblemished record of success in other times and locales. It might cost too much. Or the school staff might be so adamantly opposed to the innovation that its success would be unlikely. Or it might be antithetical to the school's culture, for example, a highly effective sex education program in a church-affiliated school. Finally, the students might differ in important ways from those that were involved in the research. Thus, even if a program has successfully solved the same problem in other schools, competent administrators might not adopt it in theirs.

Second, solving significant practical problems requires more than factual information. In part this is because many (most?) educational problems involve a consequential moral or ethical issue. In these cases, good solutions not only require that administrators get the facts right, they must also get the values right. For example, suppose research conclusively demonstrated that school integration made everyone's math achievement decline. Would it follow that we should not integrate our schools? Of course not, because integration serves an important moral (to say nothing of legal) value. The *fact* of score decline is relevant to a decision to integrate, but it would not *per se* determine the decision. Many people would argue that students must learn to live in a multicultural society, and integrated schools are important in achieving this goal. Hence, these people would seek ways to mitigate integration's effect on math achievement; they would not abandon integration.

We come back, then, to a point we made in the Preface to this book. Research cannot tell you what you should do when faced with some educational problem. Rather, all that research can do is to help you think more intelligently about your problem. Knowing with certainty that cooperative learning, ability grouping, and departmentalized primary instruction have had positive effects elsewhere isn't sufficient for our imaginary administrators to implement any of those programs in their own schools. But such knowledge is relevant to their decisions. It would help them to better understand their problems and better predict the effects of implementing those programs. In short, it would help them think more intelligently, and thinking more intelligently about real problems is not a trivial accomplishment.

Some Implications of the Normative View of Research in School Administration

Let us turn, then, to some of the implications of this view of what should count as research in educational administration by introducing a couple of basic research concepts. When you read a research article, you will often find the author talking about *independent* and *dependent* variables. What are they? A variable, of course, is simply something that varies. People's height varies. Among different school districts, expenditures per pupil vary. Commitment to school varies among students. Most simply, an *independent variable is something whose variation causes variation in something else.* For example, height affects the probability that people will play professional basketball. As expenditures per pupil vary, citizens' school taxes change. Students with a strong commitment to their schools are less likely to be truant.

When we apply this idea to our normative conception of research, we can say that the central independent variables in administrative research should be the relationships shown in Figure 1.1, that is, administratively mutable school programs. Studies of whether peer tutoring programs increase achievement, whether behavior modification programs reduce student disciplinary referrals, and whether employer-school cooperative apprenticeship programs increase post-high school student employment are studies in educational administration. All involve school programs that the effective exercise of administrative leadership might establish, maintain, or change.

Consider now dependent variables. When researchers use this term, they are referring to effects. *Dependent variables are variables that change as a result of variations in one or more independent variables.* What should be the dependent variables in educational administration research? We suggest that our primary focus should be on the foremost responsibility of practitioners: working prescribed changes in students. Our preferred dependent variable, then, should involve some form of student outcome. We would construe these outcomes broadly, not simply as the three Rs, and include numerous other forms of desired results such as critical thinking skills, valued traits of character, and selected physical abilities. In our examples here, higher achievement, reduced disciplinary referrals, and post-high school employment are desirable student outcomes dependent on peer tutoring, behavior modification, and apprenticeship programs, respectively.

Recall our earlier list of questions addressed in doctoral research, and notice what does not count as a study in school administration under the view we are advancing. Superintendents' attitudes toward collective bargaining is not a study in educational administration. Similarly, women school administrators' feelings about their work doesn't count. Nor does a study of former presidents' views of campus governance. All of these are studies of administrators' mental states, and mental states—including those of practicing administrators—are not school programs.

We are aware that this conception of appropriate research in educational administration is a highly restricted one. Certainly much that currently passes for administrative research falls outside its boundaries. We do not mean just the kinds of dissertations that we described earlier in this chapter—though dissertations represent, by far, the largest volume of research in our field. We also mean the many competently conducted studies that fill the major administrative journals, such as *Educational Administration Quarterly* and *Educational Evaluation and Policy Analysis*. For example, the study of leadership has been a staple of educational administration research for years. Many of those studies do not fit within the conception we have advanced here, especially those that treat leadership as a dependent variable, as in "How do principals' personalities, as measured by the Myers-Briggs Inventory, influence their leadership styles?" Such a study concerns neither an administratively mutable independent variable, nor a student outcome as a dependent variable. We are also aware that many, but by no means all, studies that meet our criteria are ordinarily thought of as *program evaluations* rather than *research*, though the boundary between the two, if there ever was one, has blurred to invisibility. (Is a metanalysis of a series of program evaluations of cooperative learning programs a kind of research or a kind of evaluation?)

We have tried to build a normative conception of what should count as the central core of research in the field of educational administration. We have argued that this core should consist of carefully executed studies assessing the effects of administratively mutable programs on student outcomes. We have not tried to fashion a Procrustean bed for researchers, for we do not believe that scholarly work in our field should consist only of such studies. Instead, we think that it is important for practitioners to have a conception of the sort of research that should be the center of their professional attention. There are at least three reasons for this.

First, without such a conception, virtually any study can be said to be important, at least potentially, to school administrators. If an economist carries out an investigation of trends in the international flow of capital, such a study is easily construed as significant, since local revenues for schools are surely affected by the movement of money and jobs overseas, and administrators are certainly concerned with school revenues. At the opposite end of the macro-micro continuum, when a psychoanalyst inquires into the nature of children's dreams and how those dreams manifest themselves in anxiety reactions, that inquiry, too, can be seen as significant, since children's anxieties surely affect their work in school, which is obviously a matter of administrative concern. Our point is that if our *only* criterion for deciding what counts as a study in our field is that the phenomenon investigated has the potential for affecting schools, there is little that can be excluded. However, the time administrators have to review the research literature of their profession is very limited. They cannot be expected to scan articles on economics, psychoanalysis, and everything in-between. They need some conception of the core of the research in their field to make managing it possible.

Second, we need a conception of the research center of our field because it permits us to make judgments of worth. Here we will use Scriven's (1990) distinction between merit and worth. A meritorious study is one that is of high quality—theoretically grounded, cogently reasoned, methodologically sound, and so forth. It does not follow, however, that a highly meritorious study has any worth, that it is of any use in improving professional practice. There are, quite literally, thousands of studies done each year by persons in educational administration. Even if all of those studies were of the highest quality, not all would be of equal worth to the profession. A study of the effects of variations in sick leave policies (a program) on student achievement (an outcome) is likely to be of more worth than a study of teachers' attitudes toward those policies.

Finally, and related to the previous point, a conception of the center of our field's research will help us set priorities in our research efforts. There is a large number of gaps in our knowledge about the practice of school administration. We cannot fill all of those gaps at once, and so we need to decide where work should be concentrated: What should come first? We have argued that the critical dependent variable in administrative research should be student outcomes because securing those is a fundamental responsibility of practitioners. Should we never consider other possible dependent variables, for example, teacher morale or parent involvement? Of course we should, but we think that it is desirable to show first that these are themselves linked to variations in student outcomes. Consider a research proposal to examine the effects of collective bargaining contracts on teacher participation in school decision making. Would such a study be worth supporting in our field? Well, perhaps. We would be more enthusiastic if we were certain that increasing teacher participation in decision making had some desirable effect on a valued student outcome. Since that is not certain (Conley, 1991; Conway, 1984; Taylor & Bogotch, 1994; Townsend, 1996), the proposed study would get a somewhat lower priority in our view. Put another way, a study to determine what effects (if any) participatory decision making of teachers has on student outcomes would have considerably more importance.

Some Concluding Remarks:
The Role of Research in Professional Practice

We want to close this chapter with a few remarks about the dissertation in educational administration, about the contribution of other educational specialties and other disciplines to administrative practice, and finally, about your responsibilities as a professional administrator.

If one listens to informal discussions among academics about the nature of the dissertation in their fields, it is possible to hear two quite different perspectives being expressed. One, the classic view, is a product of the turn-of-the-century German graduate universities. It holds that a dissertation should represent an original contribution to knowledge. To use Helmholtz's metaphor, each dissertation should add a brick to the edifice of knowledge.

Other academics take a quite different position. They hold a more recent belief, one that arose in American graduate schools during this century and that reflects a more pragmatic stance toward the dissertation. These academics view the dissertation as a training device. Its purpose is to permit neophytes to learn a field's research processes and traditions in an apprenticeship-like relationship with established researchers in that field. Professors who take this position will argue that it is unreasonable to expect original contributions to knowledge from novices. (These two viewpoints are often expressed most clearly when arguments erupt over whether a particular student's dissertation is "up to our standards.")[7]

In some academic disciplines the latter view has much to commend it. Many newly anointed Ph.D.s in history, for example, will take positions in universities, where the production of high-quality research is a major job expectation. Training them to meet that expectation makes sense. But the training view seems much less persuasive in school administration, where the vast majority of new doctorates take positions as practicing administrators. In those positions most will never be called upon to do any sort of research that looks remotely like a dissertation or the articles that appear in research journals. We suggest, then, that the most defensible rationale for dissertations in our field is the traditional one: dissertations should contribute to knowledge. In our case, however, we mean that it should contribute to the knowledge of practice.

Were dissertations to make such a contribution, they could make a substantial difference in administrative practice. Education is the largest doctoral producing field in American universities. Within it, Educational Administration is the largest specialization, producing more Ph.D.s and Ed.D.s than any other education specialty, such as curriculum or educational psychology. One estimate of the degrees granted each year in educational administration put their number at approximately 1,500 (Haller, 1979). Virtually all of those degrees represent a piece of research, the dissertation, since that is a requirement for a doctoral degree

---

[7] One sometimes hears another view expressed (usually by students), that the dissertation "trains a person to think." It is surprising to hear someone on the verge of a doctoral degree in Education take this position, since it expresses a largely discredited theory of learning.

at almost all universities. That is a great deal of research. Given this massive effort in numbers, time, and money, it is hard to see that professional practice has benefitted commensurately. However, with a sharper focus on the effects of administratively controlled programs and student outcomes, the massive research effort represented by doctoral students has the potential to contribute significantly to improving American schools.

Our emphasis on the problematic features of research in educational administration may have left you with the impression there are few worthwhile studies in the field, or that there is little research that can contribute to your professional practice. Such an impression would be completely wrong. In fact, the amount of high quality, useful research is enormous. Indeed, the point of this book is to show you how to access and sensibly use that research when you are dealing with practical problems in your school. The conception of research in educational administration that we have developed encompasses studies with particular characteristics, regardless of the field in which they originated. Excellent and useful studies in school administration are to be found in the research literatures of sociology, economics, psychology, political science, and medicine (to say nothing of other subfields in education, e.g., science education)—in short, in numerous fields and disciplines that may seem only remotely connected to administrative practice. The conception of research advanced here can help you identify a study in school administration regardless of the field in which it appears.

Finally, we would make a point about the conception of research that we have advanced. It is merely one possible way to answer the question with which we began: "What counts as research in educational administration?" Obviously, you are free to reject our answer. However, if you do, we think that you are obligated to create a defensible answer of your own. Our reason for saying this is rooted in the notion of professionalism.

Most educational administrators like to think of their work as a "profession." Now, whatever else that abused term means, it certainly means an occupation that is based on a verified, arcane, and theoretically codified body of knowledge. This body of knowledge has been deliberately and carefully constructed over a period of years (centuries in some cases); it continues to change and grow and is constantly being tested for its truth value; and it can be mastered only through intensive and lengthy study, usually at advanced educational levels. Indeed, it can never be fully mastered, because it is constantly growing and changing. Every occupation that deserves the honorific title "profession" is characterized by just such a body of knowledge that informs its practice. When you hear someone speak of a "professional ball player" or a "professional truck driver," they are abusing our language. Those are worthy lines of work, but they are not professions. Used in this loose way, "professional" only means that a person is paid for working, a definition that makes every job a profession.

When you claim that you are a professional administrator, you are implicitly claiming at least three things: that there is a verified, arcane, and codified body of knowledge that undergirds your work; that you have mastered and are mastering that body of knowledge; and that you practice the profession. This last idea, of a practice, is critical to understanding the nature of a profession. To practice means to apply a body of knowledge to particular cases. It is what separates a scholar from a professional; the former simply masters a body of arcane knowledge, while the latter masters that knowledge and tries to apply it to human problems. Consider a physician, for example. When you go to a physician's office because of a pain, what happens? She will begin to ask you questions about your distress, its location, severity, onset, and other, seemingly unrelated, symptoms. She might take urine and blood samples, thump your chest and poke your abdomen. She is practicing. That is, she is attempting to apply a body of knowledge to your particular case. When you claim the honorific title of "professional," you are claiming to practice.

Today, in most professions, the persons who are engaged in practice are not the same as those who do the research that forms its knowledge base (though that was not always the case[8]). This split of research from practice has had numerous benefits, but it has also created a great deal of mischief. As practitioners of the profession of educational administration, you need to use skillfully the knowledge that someone else has created—to become an intelligent, sophisticated consumer of research.

To be an intelligent consumer, it isn't necessary to become a researcher. But it is essential to know how to access, evaluate, and use research. That is what this book is about, and that is why we have spent this time trying to develop a conception of what counts as research in educational administration. In order to access, evaluate, and use the research that underlies the practice of educational administration, it is necessary to have a conception of what that research is. And that is why we suggest that if you object to the conception we have advanced, it is incumbent on you as a professional educational administrator to develop a defensible one of your own.

References

Conley, S. (1991). Review of research on teacher participation in school decision making. In G. Grant (Ed.), *Review of Research in Education* (Vol. 17, pp. 225-268). Washington, DC: American Educational Research Association.

Conway, J. A. (1984). The myth, mystery, and mastery of participative decision making in education. *Educational Administration Quarterly, 20*(3), 11–40.

Dreeben, R. (1967). The contribution of schooling to the learning of norms. *Harvard Educational Review, 37,* 211–237.

Durkheim, E. (1951). *Suicide* (J. A. Spaulding & G. Simpson, Trans.). Glencoe, IL: Free Press.

Gowin, D. B. (1972). Is educational research distinctive? In L. G. Thomas (Ed.), *Philosophical redirection of educational research: Part 1.* Chicago: National Society for the Study of Education.

---

[8] This is a relatively recent phenomenon. As late as the turn of this century, most medical knowledge was produced by practicing physicians who, in the course of their practices, made discoveries that they published in professional journals. We see vestiges of this in the many surnames that are attached to diseases, procedures, and anatomical structures, for example, "Addison's Disease," named for the 19th century British physician who first identified it.

Gulick, L., & Urwick, L. (Eds.). (1937). *Papers on the science of administration.* New York: Institute of Public Administration.

Haller, E. J. (1979). Questionnaires and the dissertation in educational administration. *Educational Administration Quarterly, 15*(1), 47–66.

Haller, E. J., & Knapp, T. R. (1985). Problems and methodology in educational administration: Introduction. *Educational Administration Quarterly, 21*(3), 157–68.

Hobbes, T. (1950). *Leviathan.* New York: Dutton.

Hoy, W. K., & Brown, B. L. (1988). Leadership behavior and the zone of acceptance of elementary teachers. *Journal of Educational Administration, 26*(1), 23–38.

Kunz, D., & Hoy, W. K. (1976). Leadership style of principals and the professional zone of acceptance of teachers. *Educational Administration Quarterly, 12*(3), 49–64.

McMahon, A. M. (1984). The two social psychologies: Postcrises directions. In R. H. Turner & J. F. J. Short (Eds.), *Annual review of sociology.* Palo Alto, CA: Annual Reviews Inc.

Schwab, J. J. (1978). *Science, curriculum and liberal education: Selected essays of Joseph J. Schwab. Edited by Ian Westbury and Neil Wilkof.* Chicago: University of Chicago Press.

Scriven, M. (1990). Teacher selection. In J. Millman & L. Darling-Hammond (Eds.), *The new handbook on teacher evaluation: Assessing elementary and secondary teachers* (pp. 76–103). Newbury Park, CA: Sage.

Taylor, D. L., & Bogotch, I. E. (1994). School-level effects of teachers' participation in decision making. *Educational Evaluation and Policy Analysis, 16*(3), 302–19.

Townsend, T. (1996). *School effectiveness and restructuring schools: What does the research tell us?* Paper presented at the Annual Meeting of the International Congress for School Effectiveness and Improvement, Minsk, Belarus.

CHAPTER 2

Research and Practice: The Case of *EEO*

INTRODUCTION

This chapter examines the institution of educational research and the complex—some would say convoluted—relationship between that institution and administrative practice. We'll do this by examining one study, *Equality of Educational Opportunity (EEO)* (Coleman et al., 1966) and its progeny, the multitude of studies it subsequently provoked. We will see how that study, rooted in an issue that was wracking the nation in 1964, and in a fundamental value conflict characteristic of modern democratic societies, raised important questions about our nation's schools. Those questions attracted the attention of numerous researchers in education and in other disciplines, most notably perhaps, in sociology and economics. These researchers began producing studies that, in turn, raised still more questions and attracted the attention of additional investigators. In this way several lines or "streams" of research grew out of *EEO*. These streams of work, often spanning decades, sometimes became detached from the issue that originally provoked *EEO* and in many ways detached from administrative practice. Nevertheless, those lines of work often had explicit implications for the practical problems that face practitioners daily.

In this chapter, then, we are going to try to better understand the research-practice relationship by studying a bit of history—the history and legacy of, arguably, the most important and influential study ever concerned with the administration of America's schools. Thus, we have two purposes in mind. First, we want you to see the ways in which research in your field relates to and does not relate to your professional responsibilities. Second, we want to do this by acquainting you with a study that has had a powerful influence on research in educational administration, and one with which every practitioner should be familiar.

Notice that we call *EEO* "important" and "influential." That is not the same as calling it "right." Studies can be important and wrong. In retrospect, *EEO* was probably wrong about several significant matters and right about several others. We will see that there are various criteria for judging the importance of a piece of research, only one of which has to do with the correctness of its findings. If you are to become sophisticated and critical consumers of administrative research, it is important that you understand these criteria and the dilemmas they provoke when you use research to address practical problems. It is important, too, we believe, for professionals to be familiar with the history of their own profession and the research that undergirds it. Again, we have chosen *EEO* not simply because it illustrates some of the complexities of the research-practice relationship but because it is such an important part of the history of U.S. school administration.

Further, as a sophisticated, critical consumer of research you will need to develop a conception of the ways in which research relates and doesn't relate to your work. Many administrators have a relatively naive view of this relationship. They expect that they can simply apply research to solve a practical problem. When they try to do that, however, the result is typically not a solution to the problem but frustration and disillusionment of the practitioner. We suspect that much of the common reaction of administrators to research—that it is "too theoretical," a "waste of time," and "not connected to the real world"—derives from just such experiences. *EEO* provides us with an opportunity to observe the *institution* of educational research and how its products, the thousands of reports that fill our professional books and journals, bear on and do not bear on practical administrative matters. We will see how the results of one study directly affected important administrative practices, national educational policy, and, ultimately, the lives of millions of students. But we will also see that the same study had no effect on important administrative practices or other national educational policies. And finally, we will see that this study affected practice, but those effects, while massive, were subtle, indirect, and not immediately apparent. We will find, then, that there is no simple answer to the question "Does research affect practice?" Indeed, it is not even a useful question. If you are to become a sophisticated, critical consumer of educational research, you must understand some of the complexities of the research-practice connection.

Putting *EEO* in Its Political and Legal Context

What was to become a landmark study in educational administration began in an obscure provision of the Civil Rights Act of 1964. Section 402 of the Act provided that a survey be conducted to ascertain the "lack of availability of equal educational opportunities for individuals by reason of race, color, religion, or national origin in public educational institutions at all levels in the United States . . ." and that the results of this survey be reported to the Congress and the President within two years (Coleman et al., 1966, p. iii). Notice the language. It presupposes the study's findings: The researchers would find that there was a lack of equal educational opportunities by reason of race, color, and so forth. Notice also that what was to count as equal educational opportunities was left entirely undefined. Both of these features of the statute were to play prominent roles in shaping subsequent developments. A sociologist, James Coleman,[1] then at Johns Hopkins University, was chosen to head the team of researchers that would conduct the study, and the finished document became familiarly known as the "Coleman Report."

In 1964 the nation was in the midst of the civil rights movement. *Brown* v. *Board of Education of Topeka* lay a decade in the past; ahead lay the King assassination, Watts, and our massive involvement in what was then an obscure country in southeast Asia. The Great Society and school desegregation were at the top of the national agenda. Although de jure separation of children by race was illegal, many Southern communities had, through one stratagem or another, managed to maintain racially segregated schools. By dividing the nation into regions (e.g., the Northeast, Plains, Southeast, etc.) and collecting data within each, it was thought that the Report would show the extent of the South's recalcitrance and how its delaying actions were denying black children equality of educational opportunity. As the report eventually showed, things were considerably more complicated.

The study was a massive undertaking. Well over one half million public school students, identified by race and ethnicity, filled out questionnaires and were tested on their academic ability and achievement. Approximately 60,000 teachers and 4,000 elementary and secondary schools were involved. Principals responded to questionnaires regarding their buildings. At the time it was the second-largest piece of social science research ever undertaken (Mosteller & Moynihan, 1972).[2] Segments of the report were given over to issues in colleges and universities, case studies of integration in local school districts, Project Head Start, guidance counselors, non-English speaking students, and vocational education. Perhaps because of the furor created by the major aspect of the study, (dealing with the achievement of children in public elementary and secondary schools), these special segments were largely ignored in subsequent discussions.

---

[1] It is worth pointing out that Coleman was not a public school educator, much less a school administrator, yet he and his colleagues produced a study that provided educational practitioners with important insights into their professional work. Experience as a practitioner, then, is not a necessary prerequisite for carrying out important, influential and high quality studies of administrative problems.

[2] All things considered, "Project Talent," a longitudinal study of educational achievement, was larger. That study, however, had little to say about race and equality of opportunity (Mosteller & Moynihan, 1972).

Putting *EEO* in Its Value Context: The Problem of Inequality

There is a deeper and more philosophical context to *EEO*, one that goes well beyond the problem of segregation in the United States. In most liberal western democracies many people carry around in their heads a rough conception of a just society. While there are innumerable variations, a basic idea is that all should have an equal opportunity to succeed—to secure for themselves a share of the good things in life. There are two things to note about this rough conception of a just society. First, justice consists in ensuring that everyone has an equal *opportunity* to secure the good things. It doesn't mean that everyone should get an equal *share* of the good things. If some people end up with more than others, that's fine, as long as everyone had an equal opportunity. Second, by "good things" we simply mean the things that all of us want no matter what else we want—the things that are primary instrumentalities in our pursuit of happiness. Money is a good thing. It helps us live the sort of lives we want to live. Not everyone wants to be rich, but everyone wants enough money to live the sort of life that they would like. Power is another good thing. We all want power, at least enough to have some control over our own lives. Prestige is still another; we would all like our neighbors to think well of us. The problem is that in every society there aren't enough of these good things to give everyone as much as they want. So every society faces the problem of how to allocate these primary instrumentalities. Who gets what, when, and how?[3]

On what grounds should some people get more than others? A common (but certainly not the only) answer to this question is that people who have abilities that benefit the rest of us should be rewarded for developing and using them. We are all better off, many would argue, if people who have the kinds of abilities needed to heal the sick, construct safe buildings, and teach our children are encouraged to develop and use those abilities. They should be rewarded for having done so, since we all benefit. If, as a result, they end up with more of the good things than others, that is all right. It is just.

Rewarding people for developing and using the abilities that benefit the rest of us isn't sufficient, however. Many people would go on to say that effort should be rewarded as well. Those who work hard should get more of the primary instrumentalities than those who laze about doing little for themselves or others. Both ability and effort should count. In fact, these people might say, individuals should be able to substitute one for the other. Someone with only modest abilities but who works especially hard should be rewarded as well, perhaps better, than a slothful person with a lot of ability. Finally, they might say that everyone should have an equal opportunity to develop their talents and demonstrate their effort. Usually what is meant by this is that certain things ought not to count in determining whether an individual has an opportunity to develop a talent or demonstrate effort. In particular, race ought not to affect a person's opportunities. Neither should modest circumstances at birth. A black

---

[3] This is Harold Lasswell's definition of politics (Lasswell, 1958).

child born into a poor family should have the same opportunity to attain the good things in life as a white child born into more affluent circumstances.

Notice what we are describing. We are portraying a rough normative conception of a just society, a conception that many persons might endorse. It is not an empirical description. We are not saying that our society—or any other for that matter—fits the description, only that many think that a just society ought to fit it.

There are some serious problems with this normative conception. We will mention two, but that hardly exhausts the list. Many of you will have already noticed an obvious one; it might be thought too harsh. What will happen to those who, through no fault of their own, have little or no ability, or who cannot demonstrate any appreciable effort? For example, what about children who are born with profound mental or physical handicaps? Are these children to be subjected to the modern equivalent of being put out on a mountain to die? Of course not, most of us would say. We would modify this normative conception so as to care for those who fate had denied equality of opportunity.[4]

Other problems remain with this normative conception of a just society. Perhaps the most serious arises because of a value that we hold about another fundamental institution, the family. Most people seem to believe that, within broad limits, parents should be free to raise children as they think best. In particular, we believe that parents should be free to sacrifice for their children, if they wish. Indeed, a conception of good parents is adults who put the needs of their child ahead of their own. The problem becomes obvious. Suppose that by some magic we could make real this normative conception of a just society, that is, suppose we could have true equality of opportunity: Individuals' rewards derived solely from their own abilities and efforts. Irrelevant factors such as race and gender did not count. What would happen? The just society would last only one generation, because parents will persist in helping their own children get a head start in life. Many parents, those who have been rewarded with a large share of the good things of life—wealth, power, education—will turn their justly earned rewards into their children's opportunities. And they will be praised for doing so, because that is what a good parent should do. But when this happens, wealth, power, and prestige are transferred across generations, and equality of opportunity becomes more shadow than substance.

There is a tension between these two deeply held values in this and other societies. On the one hand, we value equality of opportunity. On the other hand, we value liberty. Perhaps we especially value the liberty to help our children as much as we can. It is here, then, that two fundamental values come into conflict. We cannot fully satisfy both of these values, for to increase one usually requires

---

[4] This is a variation on what is often called the *distribution issue*. Is it permissible for a few people to reap huge rewards, based solely on their abilities and efforts, while everyone else receives little or nothing? Put another way, perhaps the good things in life should be distributed according to need, not according to ability and effort. As Marx (1992) expressed this alternative: "From each according to his abilities; to each according to his needs" (Marx, 1992).

that we decrease the other. We can, however, lessen the tension—or hope to. It is in part for this reason that public education is such a pivotal institution in America. In the Jeffersonian vision, and especially in that of Horace Mann, the public school becomes a mechanism for balancing these conflicting values. By sending all children to the "common school," where they would study the same subjects, working alongside the offspring of both rich and poor, and where ability and effort would be rewarded independently of home background, the children of those who had been less successful would be given an equal start to securing the good things in life. The public school would provide equality of opportunity.

In many respects that is a noble vision, a vision in which the public school acts as a great social leveler across generations, an institution that helps to prevent the rise of the kind of aristocracy of wealth, power, and prestige that characterized many European nations. Of course, most of us recognize that the public school is not so powerful an institution that, by itself, it could entirely overcome the advantages that accrue to the children of the affluent. But most people thought that the public school would help achieve this goal. At least they thought this until the publication of *EEO*. The study, then, is rooted not only in a political and legal conflict over school segregation, but in a fundamental value conflict concerning the role of schools in achieving a just society.

The Findings of *EEO*

Perhaps it was inevitable that the findings of a report dealing with such central issues as race and equality of opportunity should be controversial and frequently misunderstood. Even today, one often hears educators—who should know better—claim, for example, that "The Coleman Report showed that money has nothing to do with school quality," or that "Schools have no effect on student achievement." Of course, the report showed no such things. It is necessary, then, for school administrators to understand the findings of important studies, if for no other reason than they are likely to become the victims of other people's misinterpretations of them. Let's take the study's major findings one at time.

Racial Segregation

In 1964 the pace of desegregation was on many people's minds, including members of Congress. A major question for the study was to determine the extent of racial segregation in our nation's schools. After all, the Supreme Court had pronounced that segregated schools were inherently unequal. Hence, it was important to determine, ten years after *Brown*, whether black children were still being denied equality of educational opportunity as a consequence of having to attend schools primarily serving children of their own race.

The report's findings were unequivocal on this matter. In 1964 the vast majority of white children attended schools that served white children almost exclusively, and an analogous finding held for black children. For example, about 97% of all white first graders attended schools in which whites were in the majority, and the corresponding figure for black children was 87% (Coleman et al., 1966). If equality of educational opportunity was taken to mean the opportunity to go to school with children of all races, America had a long way to go to achieve it.

This first finding of the report was revealing. Everyone expected the study to show that most southern schools were still largely segregated. What was less expected was the extent to which northern schools, at least those in large cities, were also racially segregated. Obviously, much turned on what is meant by *segregated*. In the South, with its history of de jure segregation, slow progress was being made to integrate schools. While this was going on, however, the northward migration of blacks into the centers of large cities, and the movement of whites to the newly developing suburbs, was resulting in the de facto segregation of northern urban schools. Segregation, then, was not just a southern problem; it was a national problem.

The Achievement Gap

After analyzing segregation in U.S. schools, the report's authors turned to school outcomes, specifically to measures of educational achievement and motivation. As part of the survey, students in grades 3, 6, 9, and 12 were given tests of verbal and nonverbal ability, reading comprehension, and mathematics achievement. First graders were also tested, but only on their verbal and nonverbal ability. The first task of the report was to compare the achievement at each grade level of the five racial/ethnic groups that were studied: Indian Americans, Mexican Americans, Puerto Ricans, Oriental Americans, Negroes, and Whites.[5]

The results were both expected and surprising. It was expected that minority children would be achieving at lower levels than the white majority. For decades evidence pointing in this direction had been accumulating. However, the size of the achievement gap was larger than many expected, especially between black and white pupils. At every grade level the former scored approximately one standard deviation below the latter on the achievement tests used in the survey. It is important to understand what a gap of one standard deviation means. When one says that two groups differ by one standard deviation on some normally-distributed measure, one is asserting that there is a large difference between the two groups.

Figure 2.1, illustrating the group difference, represents two hypothetical distributions of achievement test scores for white and black students. The scores of both groups are distributed normally and have equal standard deviations of 10. If we arbitrarily say that the mean of the white students was 50 on this test, the mean score of the black students would be 40, that is, a gap of one standard

---

[5] Remember that the report was written in the mid-1960s, well before the terms *Indian, Negro,* and *Oriental* fell out of favor.

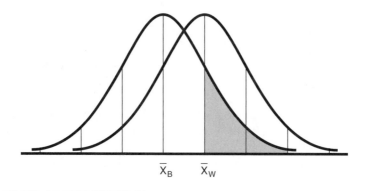

F I G U R E   *2.1*   **Hypothetical Distributions of Achievement Test Scores for a Group of White and Black Children Differing by One Standard Deviation**

deviation. Perhaps the best way to understand the magnitude of such a difference, however, is to focus on the shaded area of the figure. This represents the black children who have scored *above the mean* of the whites. When two normally-distributed groups differ by one standard deviation on any normally distributed measure, approximately 16% of the lowest scoring group are above the mean of the highest scoring group. Conversely, and in the present case, approximately 84% of the black students were achieving below the average white student. That is a very large difference. Further, *EEO* seemed to show that this one standard deviation gap between black and white children existed at every grade level. If school achievement is important to success in life, then a gap of this magnitude represents a serious threat to achieving equality of opportunity—one in which race was irrelevant to success in life.

Another finding concerned race or ethnicity and this achievement gap. There was considerable variation among racial/ethnic groups in mean achievement levels. In particular, Oriental-American students were doing as well or even slightly better in school than whites. This was puzzling, since in many cases Oriental-American families were relatively poor and the language spoken in the home was not English or even structurally similar to English. Thus, if poverty or speaking nonstandard English were the causes of low achievement, the success of children from Asian backgrounds seemed an anomaly that required explanation.

School Facilities and Expenditures

At this point the authors of *EEO* began to go beyond the requirements of Congress. What could account for the racial and ethnic variations in children's achievement? More generally, why do some children learn more than others? If the findings regarding segregation and the size of the black-white achievement gap were somewhat expected, those regarding school facilities and expenditures were startling. It was commonly understood that the schools attended by minority children were grossly inferior to those attended by whites. Indeed, Coleman himself predicted that *EEO* would show exactly that:

> . . . the study will show the difference in the quality of schools that the average Negro [sic] child and the average white child are exposed to. You know yourself that the difference is going to be striking. And even though everybody knows there is a lot of difference between suburban and inner city schools, once the statistics are there in black and white, they will have a lot of impact (Mosteller & Moynihan, 1972, p. 8).

It is important to understand the significance of this aspect of *EEO*. In 1966 there were certain matters that were virtually articles of faith: Some schools were of a higher quality than others; a school's facilities and services were important in determining its quality; and children learned more in high quality schools. Further, what counted as a high quality school seemed clear. For example, an excellent high school was one with a low pupil-teacher ratio, good chemistry, physics, and language laboratories, an extensive library, well equipped gymnasiums, athletic fields, plenty of free, recently published textbooks, and many ancillary services such as cafeterias, counselors, and nursing care. All students would learn more in such schools. Since all of these things cost money, it seemed to follow that expenditures per pupil would also be related to pupil learning: All else equal, the higher the per-pupil expenditure, the higher student achievement. Since black students were thought to be much less likely to attend schools with those characteristics than were whites, it should surprise no one that black achievement would be lower.

The report's findings were confounding on these matters. While on balance blacks attended schools that had less adequate facilities than their white counterparts, the differences were much smaller than were expected. For example, 94% of black students attended a high school with a chemistry laboratory, while 98% of white students did. The corresponding figures for a physics laboratory were 80% and 94%, a somewhat greater discrepancy. On some measures, however, for example, full-time librarians, black elementary students were better served than were whites (30% vs. 22%). Further, the greatest gap between the races in regard to school facilities was not in the South—where everyone expected it to be—but in the West.[6] These findings were startling not merely because they contradicted the conventional administrative wisdom of the time but because of what they portended for educational achievement. If children of different races were attending schools of approximately the same quality, any differences in "output" measures, say achievement test scores, could not be attributed to the quality of their schools—at least when "quality" was conceived in this way. It followed from all of this that expenditures per pupil should have little relation to student achievement, and that was precisely what the report's authors found.

---

[6] Keep in mind, though, that many more blacks lived in the South than in the West; thus, there was a much larger *number* of black pupils attending the less adequate schools in the South.

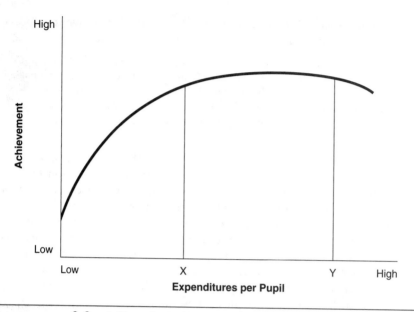

FIGURE   2.2   A Hypothetical Relationship Between Expenditures per Pupil
and Achievement

From an administrator's perspective this finding was anathema. For years
school administrators had claimed that if they were given more money, school
achievement would rise. EEO suggested otherwise. It is important to be clear on
this point, since it has often been misunderstood. Many people have claimed that
"EEO showed that money doesn't make a difference." EEO did not show that.
What it seemed to show was that *within the expenditure range then evidenced
by the majority of U.S. schools*, expenditures per pupil were unrelated to student
achievement.

Think of it this way. Clearly, if we spend no money on our schools, we
would have no schools, and most children would learn very little. A few children might learn to read and do simple arithmetic, but few would ever learn
anything about world history, Shakespeare, or calculus. Learning about those
things happens in classrooms, not on the street or at home. As school expenditures rise from zero dollars per pupil, children learn more. However, at some
point while expenditures continue to rise, achievement levels out and becomes
flat. This is no more than the economists' notion of "diminishing marginal
returns." Hypothetically at least, if expenditures continue to rise, achievement
might suddenly begin rising again, or conceivably it might actually decline as the
services and activities offered in an extraordinarily high-expenditure school
actually interfere with learning. Figure 2.2 illustrates this latter scenario.
Coleman's finding in EEO is most simply interpreted as showing that most
U.S. schools were currently (i.e., in 1964) operating in the expenditure range
marked by X and Y in the figure. Notice that between those two points the
curve is virtually flat, indicating that increasing expenditures were not associated

with changes in student achievement. The report seemed to show that within this range, increasing school district spending did not necessarily increase student achievement.

Teacher Qualifications

If money and improved school facilities have little effect on achievement, what could account for the fact of the racial and ethnic gap in achievement, or more broadly, the fact that some students learn more than others? At this point Coleman and his team turned their attention to teachers. Perhaps differences in teacher quality accounted for the achievement gap.

This notion seems commonsensical—students learn more if they are taught by good teachers. The issue turns on what one means by "good teachers." *EEO*'s authors took a seemingly straightforward approach to the matter. On average, good teachers were presumably well-educated and experienced teachers. Further, good teachers were probably ones who scored well on a test of verbal ability. Accordingly, the researchers analyzed the effects of each of these on student achievement.

Again the report produced surprising results. Neither teachers' degree levels nor their levels of teaching experience were related to most students' learning in anything but a trivial way. However, there was a modest positive relationship between these teacher characteristics and the achievement of black students, which suggested that having more highly educated and experienced teachers causes a small increase in their achievement. While students whose teachers had high scores on a test of verbal ability seemed to learn more than students whose teachers had low scores, this effect was a relatively small one.

We have called *EEO* an important study in educational administration. Here is another clear example of a straightforwardly important administrative finding. One only has to ask how we pay teachers to see its significance. The vast majority of public school teachers are paid according to a salary schedule in which degree level and teaching experience entirely determine an individual's salary. If Coleman and his colleagues were correct, we are paying teachers for qualities that are irrelevant to student learning: We might as well create pay schedules on the basis of hair color. Of course we recognize that we pay teachers for experience and level of education because it is administratively convenient. Nonetheless, *EEO* made it clear that more highly paid teachers were not, on average, better teachers.

Contextual Effects

Finding little evidence that traditional factors were important in affecting student achievement—facilities, expenditures, and teachers' attributes—the study's authors turned to other possible determinants. They cast the question in a purely sociological guise: Perhaps it makes a difference with whom students attend school. For example, perhaps poor children and minority children would do better if they attended schools serving predominately middle-class and white children. Phrased this way, the issue is one that in sociology is termed a *contextual effect*: In what way does the social composition of a setting influence individuals' behavior?[7] One can think of a school as a kind of functional community characterized by a set of modal aspirations and values that are not necessarily the attitudes and values on any particular member. These modal beliefs, in turn, affect the behavior, attitudes and values of individuals over and above their own family background and personal characteristics. For example, in a high school in which intellectual pursuits are prized, students who care little for such pursuits may come to value them.

Coleman's findings on this matter, especially in regard to minority students, were of major administrative (and political) significance. The report concluded that:

> Attributes of other students account for far more variation in the achievement of minority group children than do any attributes of school facilities and slightly more than do attributes of staff (Coleman et al., 1966, p. 302.)

If this finding was correct, *EEO* opened the door for administrators to have a direct effect on the achievement of students in their schools, regardless of facilities, expenditures, or teacher qualifications. All that was necessary was to ensure that poor and minority students went to the "right" school, that is, one whose student body was primarily middle class and white. Administrators could do this themselves; all it required of them was to draw the attendance boundaries properly or to run the buses in the right directions. As you might imagine, this finding of *EEO* created a great deal of interest among the nation's administrative cadre, policy makers, researchers, and the general public.

Social Psychological Attributes of Students

The report investigated three attitudinal aspects of students themselves: their interest in school, their self-concepts as learners, and their *fate control* or the degree to which people believe that they have some control over their own fate. In general, all racial and ethnic groups of children expressed, on average, relatively high levels of interest in school and good self-concepts. There were, however, particularly strong group differences between black and white students in the self-reported measure of fate control, with the latter scoring higher than the former. At the individual level, these three attitudes turned out to be the most important predictors of educational achievement of all the variables measured in *EEO*—more important than any aspect of the school facilities, teacher qualities, student body characteristics, and family background.

The report places considerable importance on these attitudes and their effects on school achievement. However, as many quickly noted (Mosteller & Moynihan, 1972), there is no obvious reason to believe that these social

---

[7] It is worth noting that this aspect of *EEO* was presaged by a very influential book written by Coleman in 1961, *The Adolescent Society,* a study of the composition and culture of schools and their effects on students.

psychological attributes of students actually *cause* student achievement. Indeed, it is at least as plausible to suppose that the reverse is true. For example, rather than believing that having favorable self-concepts of themselves as learners causes students to do well in school, it seemed equally credible to think that doing well in school leads students to develop favorable self-concepts of themselves as learners. Further, even if these attitudes did cause students to learn more effectively, it was not at all clear what schools could do to improve students' attitudes. Finally, regardless of the direction of causality, the relationship between attitudes and achievement, while among the strongest found in the study, was not large in an absolute sense.

Socioeconomic Status

Aside from the contextual effect described previously, the findings of *EEO* had been unremitting bad news for educators: there seemed little that was both under administrative control and that had a substantial effect on student achievement. If improving school facilities, increasing expenditures, or hiring more highly trained and experienced teachers had little effect on improving pupil learning, what could be done to close the achievement gap? The next finding seemed to promote an even more dismal view about the school's capacity to influence student achievement. Socioeconomic status (usually referred to as SES) was found to be a more powerful determinant of educational achievement than any attribute of schools that Coleman measured. Indeed, SES was so powerful a determinant of how much children learned in school that it swamped the effects of every other aspect included in the study.

It is also important to be clear about the magnitude of the SES effect, since it is one of the most misunderstood findings from *EEO*. Consider the following two assertions: (1) SES is a more powerful determinant of student achievement than any aspect of schooling measured in *EEO*. (2) SES is a weak determinant of student achievement. Both of these statement are true. They are not contradictory. Do you see why? It is not simply a consequence of the phrase "any aspect of schooling measured in *EEO*" in the first statement. That is, the two assertions aren't reconciled merely because other studies have sometimes shown schools to have stronger effects on achievement than SES. Rather, the two assertions make two quite different points. The point of the first is relative: Compared to school factors, SES is very powerful. The point of the second is absolute: SES has a small effect on children's achievement. The small effect of SES is simply much larger than the effect of any school attribute, such as teacher qualifications. For example, *EEO*'s findings suggested that if every student in America had a teacher with exactly the same number of years of experience, the variation in students' achievement would shrink by .009%—a virtually imperceptible amount. However, if every parent in the United States had exactly the same SES, the variation in their children's achievement would shrink by approximately 10%. Ten percent isn't very large in an absolute sense, but it is huge compared to .009%. (We shall have more to say about "variation" as a measure of effect in a moment.)

This is not a mere semantic quibble. The misunderstanding of this point has been pernicious. It has led many people—including many educators—to conclude that family background is so powerful that there is little that schools can do to help poor and minority children out of poverty. Worse, it has led some to shift responsibility for children's academic success to parents and to absolve the school of any obligation in the matter. In a sense *EEO* brought a hopeful message: If SES caused only 10% of the variation in children's school success, 90% must be caused by other factors. At least some of these might be open to alteration; hence, we might be able to work large positive changes in students' school success. Certainly it is incorrect to conclude on the basis of *EEO* that "SES is destiny."

The "80/20 Finding"

Finally, let us examine another important finding from *EEO*, one that is sometimes referred to as the *80/20 result*. In order to grasp the idea, you need to understand the notion of variation and its root term, *variable*. A variable, of course, can be anything that varies: people's weight, outdoor temperature, children's achievement. The goal of much research is to explain this variation. A physiologist might do research with the goal of explaining why some people are heavier than others. A meteorologist might study the causes of historical variations in climate: Is the earth really getting warmer? And, of course, trying to explain why some children learn more in school than others has been a preoccupation of many educational researchers. The goal of researchers in many fields is to "explain the variation" in some phenomenon of interest.

What does it mean to *explain variation*? Recall our discussion in the previous chapter of independent and dependent variables; changes in the former cause changes in the latter. Thus, our physiologist might conduct a study and reach the conclusion that people's genes (the independent variable) cause people's weight to vary (the dependent variable). Similarly, the meteorologist might conclude that variations in the thickness of the ozone layer (the independent variable) has caused historical changes in the earth's climate (the dependent variable). And educational researchers such as Coleman might decide on the basis of their studies that variations in per-pupil expenditures (the independent variable) have little effect on student achievement (the dependent variable).

Such conclusions are made more useful when we take the next step and ask *how much* change does an independent variable cause when compared with other independent variables? Returning again to our physiologist, suppose the researcher is interested in several factors besides genetic ones, say, nutrition and exercise. The question might be raised what is the relative influence of genetics, nutrition, and exercise on people's weight? If we think of all of the variation in people's weight as 100%, we can ask how much of this is due to genes, how much to diet, and how much to exercise. Thus, a researcher might carry out a study that leads to an estimate that 50% of the variation in peoples' weight is associated with genetic factors, 15% is associated with nutrition, and 5% is associated with exercise. (These figures are hypothetical.) The remaining 30% is due to unstudied (and perhaps unknown) causes.

We speak of this process as *explaining variation*—dividing it up into parts and associating each part with a factor that (presumably) causes it. One way to see what this means is to imagine that we could magically give everyone in a group exactly the same genes. If we did that, and if genes accounted for 50% of the variation in weight, the total variation in the group's weight would be reduced by 50%. People would become more alike in their weight because one of the causes of weight's variation, genetics, had been taken away. For instance, assume that the current weight of a group of people was distributed normally around a mean of 150 pounds. If every person were given the same genes, the mean weight of the group would remain the same, 150 pounds, but many more would be closer to that average.

This is analogous to the procedure used by Coleman. For example, in a subsequent analysis of the same data (Coleman, 1972), he divided the variation in student verbal achievement of a group of 12th grade students among the various factors that were believed to cause it. All family background factors (e.g., SES) explained 13.3% of students' achievement; all school facility and curriculum factors (e.g., the size of the library) explained 1.4%; all aspects of teacher quality (e.g., level of training) explained .9%; and all student body characteristics (e.g., the proportion students who were white) explained .8%. Thus, family background factors were estimated to be roughly 15 times more powerful than were teacher quality factors (13.3% vs. .9%). The remainder of the variance in student achievement, 83.6%, remained unexplained, that is, due to unstudied factors.

It is important to understand this notion of explaining the variance of a dependent variable not simply because it was the procedure used in *EEO*, but because it is a common goal in many kinds of statistical analyses used in the research that you will read, particularly correlational studies. If you understand the basic idea, you will be able to make sense of many research articles that are based on some highly esoteric statistical analyses. Essentially, the researcher is asking what causes something to vary and then tries to estimate how much of that variation is caused by the various independent variables included in the study.

You will often encounter a modification of this procedure when reading research reports, and this modification can be especially informative to school administrators. Consider a study in which the dependent variable is a measure of achievement gathered from students in a number of different schools. Taken together and without regard to which schools students attend, we can calculate the mean achievement of these students and how much their scores vary around that mean. We refer to the latter as the total variation in achievement. If we now take into account that these students attend different schools, this total variation can be divided into two separate components. The first is a measure of how different students are from the average student in their school. It recognizes the fact that all students within a school do not achieve at exactly the same level; they attain different scores that vary around their school mean. This is referred to as within school variation. For example, a school whose students score both very high and very low on a test would have a large within school variation, while a school whose students were quite homogeneous in their achievement would have a low within school variation.

The second component of the total variation recognizes the fact that not all schools are the same; the schools themselves have different mean achievement levels. For example, one school might have a very high average, while another's average achievement might be very low. This is referred to as between schools variation. Together the total variation in students' achievement scores is due to these two components, the part that lies within schools and the part that lies between schools.

We can then ask what proportion of this total variation results from each of these components. Investigators will often report the percent of the total variation in a dependent variable that lies within and between schools. Coleman gave this matter extensive discussion in *EEO*. Based on his analysis, a reasonable overall estimate would be that approximately 20% of the variation in student verbal achievement lies between schools and that 80% lies within schools. Of what significance is this?

The percentage of the total variation of a variable that lies between schools may be taken as an estimate of the upper bound of the effect of all school characteristics on that variable—expenditures, teacher quality, neighborhood, curricula, facilities, and so forth, regardless of what those characteristics are and regardless of whether they were actually measured in the particular study. The percentage of the variation that lies within schools, on the other hand, may be taken as an estimate of the effects of all personal characteristics of students on that variable—SES, ability, motivation, self-concept, and so on, again regardless of their nature and whether or not they were included in a study. Thus, when *EEO* seemed to show that no more than 20% of the variation in student achievement lay between schools, this was interpreted as saying that schools can have relatively little effect on student achievement. Eighty percent of the variation in student achievement was due to factors outside the school. In plain language, it means that most of the things that cause children to learn are largely beyond the control of school administrators.

When you read research that reports the within and between school variation in some dependent variable, pay particular attention to the between school percentage. If you are a principal, it is an estimate of the maximum influence that you might have on that variable relative to the influence of the personal characteristics of students. These kinds of analyses are not restricted to achievement as the dependent variable. For instance, Ho and Willms (1996) report that there are at least four kinds of parental involvement, and that the between schools variation of only one of these (attendance at PTO meetings) is greater than 20%. This can be interpreted to mean that the school principal may have little effect on other kinds of parental involvement.

The Conclusion of *EEO*

On the basis of the findings we have reviewed, Coleman and his colleagues reached a conclusion about the problem that provoked the study in the first place, equality of educational opportunity. If family background, neighborhood, peers, and individual psychological characteristics are vastly more powerful determinants of educational success than anything about schools themselves, and if educational success is important to success in life, then schools can do little to prevent the transmission of wealth, power, and status across generations. In perhaps the most damning paragraph ever written by an educational researcher about U.S. schools, the report's authors said:

> Taking all these results together, one implication stands out above all: That schools bring little influence to bear on a child's achievement that is independent of his background and general social context; and that this very lack of an independent effect means that the inequalities imposed on children by their home, neighborhood, and peer environment are carried along to become the social inequalities with which they confront adult life at the end of school. For equality of educational opportunity through the schools must imply a strong effect of schools that is independent of the child's immediate social environment, and that strong independent effect is not present in American schools (Coleman et al., 1966, p. 325).

Recall our earlier discussion of the deeper problem underlying the research: America had pinned its hopes on the public school as a means to offset at least some of the advantages that accrue to the children of the more fortunate. If the nation provided true equality of opportunity—a climate in which race and ethnicity had no lasting effects on individuals' success in life—it would also have to provide an institution that would offset the tendency for parents to pass on to their own children the advantages they had (justly) earned. The public school, *EEO* concluded, was failing to achieve one of its fundamental purposes.

Does Research Affect Practice?

With this basic understanding of the findings of the report, we can turn our attention to one of our reasons for revisiting a bit of the research history of educational administration: We can ask whether *EEO*, by all accounts the most significant piece of research in educational administration, had any influence on administrative practice. If we answer this question in the negative, it seems implausible to expect that the thousands of much less significant studies that fill our professional journals could affect practice.

Perhaps the first thing to note are the ambiguities in the phrase "affect administrative practice." One might consider the actions of particular school administrators and ask if the publication of *EEO* had an impact on a specific behavior they exhibit. That is, one way to think about how research might influence practice is to imagine that administrators read educational research journals while considering a problem they face and then apply the findings of relevant studies to that problem. There are numerous difficulties of such a view, not the least being that practitioners seldom read hard-line research journals (e.g., *The American Educational Research Journal*). They are much more likely to read journals that present popularized versions of research (e.g., *Phi Delta Kappa*, or

Educational Leadership), if they read research at all. Alternatively, since the report was prepared for Congress and was ostensibly commissioned to enlighten federal policymaking, it may be inappropriate to hold it to the standard of directly affecting individual administrators' actions. Instead, one might ask whether it influenced educational policies and whether those policies, in turn, influenced administrative behavior.

Viewed in this second way, it seems clear that *EEO* affected practice, primarily through its effects on federal, state, and local policy. Perhaps the clearest example of this can be seen in the impact of the report's apparent demonstration of a strong contextual effect on student achievement—the finding that if poor and minority children went to schools primarily serving middle-class and white children, their achievement would rise. This finding found its way into federal court decisions regarding desegregation and school finance (e.g., *Hobson* v. *Hansen,* 1967; *Keyes* v. *School Dist. No. 1 Denver,* 1973; *San Antonio Indep. Sch. Dist.* v. *Rodriguez,* 1973) and was a major part of the empirical support for the use of busing to bring about racial and socioeconomic balance in schools.

Similarly, the effect of *EEO* on compensatory education programs was immediate. While Head Start programs had been in operation for a few years before the study's results appeared, the study's impact on them was significant. If Coleman was correct that the achievement gap separating poor and minority children from middle-class whites was already apparent in the first grade, then it seemed obvious that the former groups would need to be reached prior to entering school. In the ensuing years compensatory education programs of various kinds were implemented around the nation, particularly in the inner cities. When early evaluations of these programs seemed to suggest that their long-term effects were negligible (e.g., Cain & Barnow [1973] and the Westinghouse-Ohio State study [1969]), other programs were designed to reach children at still earlier ages.[8] This trend to reach downward in the age distribution has now progressed to its logical endpoint: Pregnant and indigent women are provided prenatal care, in part because lack of adequate care before birth is recognized to cause handicaps that may deny a child equality of opportunity.

Despite examples of *EEO*'s substantial effects on practice, it is also easy to point to examples where the report seemed to have no effect. Perhaps the most obvious of these concern its finding that teachers' characteristics—their level of training and years of experience—had no effects on children's achievement. We have already noted the significance of this finding for teacher compensation plans. Its obvious implication is that other criteria, for example, measures of student outcomes or teachers' verbal abilities, should play a role in these plans. Yet while subsequent research has tended to support *EEO*'s findings on this matter (e.g., Hanushek, 1989), and after endless discussions of "merit pay," efforts to

---

[8] It is worth noting that there was considerable debate over the accuracy of these early evaluations of Head Start programs, and recent studies have generally concluded that the programs had modest but positive—if short-term—effects. (e.g., Wu & Campbell [1996]). Alternatively, the programs' failure has been attributed to causes outside the programs themselves (Lee & Loeb, 1995).

seriously modify compensation schemes have met with little success. (Monk & Jacobson, 1985; Stern, 1986).

It is a mistake, then, to think that research either has direct and obvious effects on practice or that it has none. Clearly it can have both, as *EEO* demonstrates. Perhaps more importantly, research can have important effects on the way we *think* about practice and, hence, indirectly, have important effects on practice itself. This is one of the enduring legacies of the study. Prior to 1966 most school administrators (and most of the public) had a straightforward understanding of what it meant to provide children with equality of educational opportunity; treat children the same. Indeed, the report itself was largely premised on this notion. If, for example, minority children were not doing as well in school as their white counterparts, it must be because we had not provided them with schools and teachers that were of equal quality to those provided most children. (As we have noted, Coleman himself believed this.) When the report's findings did not support this interpretation, our understanding of what was to count as equality of opportunity was turned on its head. If poor and minority children were coming to school at age six already behind middle-class whites, treating them the same as whites would only perpetuate the inequalities that they brought with them to the first grade. In order to give all children an equal chance of success in life, we could not treat them the same—we would have to treat them differently. Thus, we have redefined what is meant by equality of opportunity—from equality of inputs to equality of results—and this redefinition has had an enormous impact on the ways in which we administer schools. All of the categorical aid programs that specifically funnel additional resources to schools serving low-income families exemplify this reconceptualization. Coleman (1968) came to see this change in thinking as the most important outcome of the study.

Finally, we speculate that *EEO* has had a large effect on practice through its influence on the way that the public thinks of its schools. We have no direct evidence, but it seems clear that most Americans are much more cynical about the worth of public schools than they were in 1966. They seem, for example, much less likely to believe school administrators who claim that if taxpayers will simply provide more dollars, schools will be improved, or that if teachers' salaries are increased, children's achievement will rise. Today such pleas are likely to fall on deaf ears. There has been, we believe, a sea change in the public's support for its schools. Evidence for this is everywhere: the flight to private and religious schools and to home schooling, even among the working poor who had always been staunch supporters of public education; the support for vouchers and charter schools; the demand for national standards; and the distrust of "educational bureaucrats." Of course we would not claim that *EEO* caused all of this: The vast majority of Americans have never heard of James Coleman or his report. We do think, however, that the publicity that surrounded the release of the report in 1966, and the subsequent studies that followed up on various of its findings, have seeped into the public consciousness, fueling a pervasive disillusionment with public education. Thus, for example, while nowhere in *EEO* did its writers claim that money makes no difference, the popular media often interpreted it to have done so, and this (erroneous) idea has taken root in many people's understanding of the relationship between their tax dollars and the quality of their community's schools. You, as school administrators, must now deal with this pervasive cynicism. If we are correct in this speculation, *EEO*'s most powerful effect on practice has been its contribution to the creation of a cynical public.

A Developmental View of Research

Practitioners must understand the dynamic and changing nature of educational research if they are to better grasp its relationship to administrative practice. We will use the 80/20 stream of work that grew out of *EEO* to illustrate this dynamic quality.

Recall that the 80/20 finding refers to the estimate of within and between school variance in student achievement, that is, approximately 80% of that variance lies within and 20% between schools. This can be interpreted as saying that schools (and by extension, school principals) may have relatively little power to affect student outcomes. Many people took this to be bad news: If only one fifth of the variation in achievement could be affected by schooling, schools could have relatively little power to overcome the effects of home background. More broadly, the 80/20 finding suggested that we could not hope to achieve equality of opportunity using the public schools.[9] But was that finding correct?

Clearly this question was important, and it immediately attracted the attention of numerous researchers. In a short time a number of studies began to appear concerned with one version or another of *EEO*'s 80/20 finding. For some years these studies constituted a relatively coherent body of work, a stream of research, that you will certainly recognize. We will use this body of work and some of its subsequent transformations to illustrate the dynamic characteristics of these streams.

Research Streams Change, Sometimes Radically

Practitioners should first note that the research community is characterized by a trained skepticism toward its own products. This is especially so for the first study that poses and answers an important question. The findings of such a study are rarely accepted as definitive. Instead, other investigators attempt to replicate the study, and they attempt to evaluate it by testing the implications of its findings. Thus, from a researcher's perspective the most significant aspect of another investigator's study is not the answer it provided to the question it addressed but the questions it raises as a result of its findings. Put simply, the most significant products of a major study are some good questions. These questions trigger additional studies that refute, refine, or extend the initial work.

---

[9] The most famous and dramatic assertion of this point was made by Christopher Jencks et al. in their book, *Inequality* (1972).

This process began almost immediately after the appearance of *EEO*. Soon research began to appear that was commonly taken as showing that Coleman and his associates were in error regarding the relatively small between-school effects (Averch, Carroll, Donaldson, Kiesling, & Pincus, 1972; Brookover et al., 1973; Schneider & Brookover, 1974). A common tack taken by many of these studies was to identify a group of schools, all of which served low SES populations. The researcher would first show that some of these schools had higher average achievement than did others, and then argue that since all served low SES pupils, low SES could not, in itself, be an irremediable cause for the poor performance of some schools. Rutter's important study of a dozen London secondary schools is perhaps the best known of these (Rutter, Maughan, Mortimore, & Ouston, 1979).

Another common strategy was to use a statistical technique to predict the average scores of a group of schools and then to show that some of those schools serving low SES populations were achieving much higher than they were predicted to, while other schools serving high SES students were achieving considerably lower than predicted (Brookover & Schneider, 1975; Lezotte & Passalacqua, 1978). Both of these strategies led to an obvious question: If some low SES (and predominately minority) schools seemed to be doing well, what might account for their success? This question, in turn, led a number of researchers to do something that the authors of *EEO* hadn't done; they went into successful and unsuccessful schools and observed them closely in an attempt to identify what made them effective or ineffective.

The results of these studies have become common knowledge to educational administrators, even though most have never read the studies themselves: Successful schools seemed to be characterized by (1) principals who exercised strong leadership; (2) a staff that made deliberate attempts to involve parents in the education of their children; (3) a common set of goals toward which all members of the staff worked; (4) a high level of decorum in which pupils respected teachers and teachers respected pupils; and (5) a staff that was directly involved in school decision making. We refer, of course, to the so-called *effective schools research*. By the mid-1980s there were more than 100 such studies. For excellent critical reviews of this early work see Purkey and Smith (1983) and Rowan, Bossert, and Dwyer (1983). While the specific characteristics of effective schools varied somewhat from one study to another, the five listed are representative of the genre.

The research in the effective schools tradition continues to accumulate. For more recent critical reviews, see, for example, those by Levine and Lezotte (1990) and Sammons (1995). For our purposes, however, there are several things to note about this stream of research. First, it began in the ethos of skepticism of the research community and that community's unwillingness to accept an important finding at face value. Further, it began, at least for some, in a misunderstanding of *EEO*, that is, that "schools have no effects." Some researchers studying effective schools were at pains to demonstrate that this wasn't true but, as we have seen, *EEO* never made such a claim. This latter point is important for practitioners, because many seem to believe that the effective schools research refutes the findings of *EEO*. That is simply incorrect; the two are entirely complementary. Perhaps the best way to see this is to think of *EEO* as showing that schools might be able to control up to 20% of the variation in student achievement, while the effective schools research shows *how* that control might be achieved, that is, by principal leadership, parent involvement, and so forth.

Misunderstanding or not, the hundreds of studies that now make up the effective schools research tradition have their foundation in an intellectual issue, a question raised by *EEO*, not in the problems of practice. Yet this research has had numerous effects on practice. Site-based management and parent involvement policies are just two examples of direct outgrowths of the effective schools research. More generally, you should recognize that research streams can become self-perpetuating, driven by the questions raised by the individual studies that make them up. As this happens, a stream of work may transform itself. The effective schools research is in many respects quite different from *EEO* in both the questions it poses and the methods it uses, yet it has its intellectual roots deep in Coleman's study.

Research Findings May Become Increasingly Conditional

A second important lesson to be gained from the effective schools research program is that, with passage of time, studies may produce increasing ambiguity and tentativeness rather than increasing certainty. For example, as the research accumulated, obvious uncertainties in the original, relatively simple-minded conception of effective school characteristics became apparent. Why, precisely, should any of these characteristics produce better student learning? Exactly what does "effective leadership" mean? As researchers have pursued such questions, the seemingly straightforward application of the effective schools formula as a way of guaranteeing school improvement is no longer so obvious. Kratzer (1996), for example, in an ethnographic study suggests that as schools become caring communities they begin to evidence the traits that make them effective. It is, therefore, the former attribute that is important, not principal leadership, teacher decision making, or other factors. Shouse (1995), using a very different method and a subset of a national sample of schools, adds a further consideration to Kratzer's speculations by showing that a strong sense of community can result in a *decline* in achievement if that sense of community does not arise in a commitment to academic goals. Still further, Levine and Lezotte (1990) argue that the characteristics of effective schools are, at best, prerequisites rather than guarantees of success; that, for example, the context of a school is critical in determining whether the effective schools formula will work.

The consequence of such work is that the findings of a research stream that once appeared firm may become increasingly conditional. Initially it was claimed that greater parental involvement in their children's education would increase achievement. Now it appears that there are different types of involvement, and whether or not children's achievement is improved is conditional on the specific way that parents are involved (Ho & Willms, 1996).

Over Time Research May Become Increasingly Sophisticated

The effective schools research illustrates another way in which research streams change as time passes: They may become more sophisticated methodologically. For example, the statistical procedure used in *EEO*, multiple regression analysis, is seriously flawed for analyzing "nested" data, for instance, when the goal is to estimate the effect of a school-level factor, say expenditures per pupil, on an individual student-level outcome, say reading achievement. This is because students are nested within classrooms which are in turn nested within schools, a fact that may make the findings of regression analyses highly problematic. It was not that Coleman and his colleagues used the wrong analytical tool, it was that the right tool didn't exist in 1964—it hadn't been invented. It wasn't until the mid 1980s that statisticians claimed to have solved the nested data problem with the invention of a new analysis tool, hierarchical linear modeling (Bryk & Raudenbush, 1992).

As another example of this growing analytical sophistication, in the 1960s there was no appropriate statistical method for combining the results of many studies in order to quantitatively estimate the effect of some program on a student outcome. Instead, researchers had to "eyeball" a set of studies to assess whether or not some practice was having a measurable effect on achievement. It was in the late 1970s that the statistical procedure of meta-analysis was developed that permitted the aggregation of separate studies—even those using different metrics—into a single, numerical estimate of the size of the effect of a particular program (Glass, McGaw, & Smith, 1981; Hedges & Olkin, 1985). Further, it is not simply that better statistical analyses become available; perhaps more importantly, concepts are clarified and sharpened permitting a better understanding of educational phenomena. "Principal leadership," "school climate," and "parental involvement," to name three, are all constructs whose meanings have been sharpened over the last decade. As a consequence, we are able to speak more precisely about them than we were in the 1970s.

Studies in the effective schools tradition are now using these new procedures and ideas, and the outcome of this work is yet unclear. For example, the application of meta-analysis to studies of school finance has resulted in the re-opening of the question of expenditures and their effects on achievement. Some researchers now claim that, contrary to *EEO* and much of the subsequent research, spending more money has a direct and significantly positive effect on student achievement. Other researchers dispute this claim and marshal evidence in support of their view. Interested readers may find the exchange between Larry Hedges and Eric Hanushek of interest (Hanushek, 1989; Hanushek, 1994; Hedges et al., 1994; Hedges, Laine, & Greenwald, 1994). Similarly, hierarchical linear modeling is now used to identify effective and ineffective schools.[10] If it should turn out that those schools identified as effective under the new (and presumably better) procedure are not the same as those identified as effective under the old method, the characteristics of effective schools will be thrown in doubt.

---

[10] For examples of the application of hierarchical linear modeling to the identification of effective schools, see Harker (1995) and the work of Webster and his associates (1995; 1996).

Research Questions May Take an International Focus

A fourth developmental change in educational research concerns its spread to other nations. American school administrators should remember that the United States is not the only nation with a problem of inequality or with schools that are less effective than they might be. Effective schools research, having become broadly international in scope, is no longer simply an American enterprise. Numerous studies involving England, Sweden, Australia, Thailand, and Canada have appeared in the literature (Creemers, 1996; Harber, 1992; Hoyle & McMahon, 1986). In fact, there is an organization (the International School Effectiveness Research Program) devoted to the application of the effective schools techniques to other cultures to see what can be learned.

These studies are relevant to American school administrators on the same grounds that any cross-cultural study can be relevant: We learn about ourselves when we study others. More specifically, these studies clearly suggest that some aspects of the effective schools research may be context specific. For example, Townsend's study (1996) in Britain and New Zealand suggests that site-based management and involving teachers in school decision making may have little effect on student achievement. Kuroda's analysis of the Japanese educational system questions the importance of principal leadership (Kuroda, 1995). Scheerens and Creemers' studies in the Netherlands, and Grosin's work in Sweden reach similar conclusions about the cultural specificity of other effective schools characteristics (Grosin, 1985; Scheerens & Creemers, 1996). Lastly, van der Werf's careful, longitudinal study of Dutch children casts doubt on the ability of the effective schools model to raise the achievement of low SES students (van der Werf, 1993). Obviously, none of these cross-cultural studies invalidate U.S. research on effective schools. However, they do suggest the importance of the cultural context of school improvement efforts, and since the United States is a culturally diverse nation, the research from other nations implies that the efficacy of the effective school formula may vary substantially *within* this country, depending on the specific cultural context of a given school.

Questions Become More Discriminating and Research Streams Diverge

Finally, as the stream of research on effective schools developed, researchers began to ask more discriminating questions. Consider again the early studies that pointed to parent involvement as an important characteristic of schools. What, exactly, was meant by "parent involvement"? Clearly parents might be involved in their children's education in innumerable ways: They might attend PTA meetings, come out for school athletic events, discuss school events over the dinner table with their children, and supervise homework. Are all of these myriad ways equally effective in promoting achievement? If not, which might be more efficacious? Since research also suggested that family background was related to involvement, perhaps the link between SES and achievement might be partly a result of differences in particular kinds of parent involvement. The answers to such questions obviously have considerably more potential for improving administrative practice than simply knowing whether parent involvement is greater in effective schools. By the mid-1980s researchers were addressing such questions (Fehrmann et al., 1987; Lareau, 1987; Milne, 1986).

Further, as research streams differentiate, equity issues may arise. In the case at hand, if programs to increase parent involvement had their greater success with middle-class parents, would such programs effectively increase the gap in achievement between low and middle SES students (Lareau & Benson, 1984)? If involvement is important, shouldn't involvement include the right to choose which school one's child should attend (Chubb & Moe, 1990)? By the middle of the 1990s the research on parent involvement had become a substantial and distinct stream of research, separating from the effective schools research that had spawned it, and entirely disconnected from *EEO* in which it was rooted (Ho & Willms, 1996).

Lessons and Dilemmas for Sophisticated, Critical Consumers of Research

What can school administrators learn from this extended consideration of the most important study in their field? First and most obviously, it addressed a fundamental value issue in our society, the role of the family in creating inequality across generations and the power of the school to ameliorate the family's effects. It generated several lines of research that have stretched across decades involving many hundreds of studies. It shaped the way Americans think about their schools and the way they conceive of a critical value, equality of opportunity. It had a direct impact on the decisions of our federal courts. It directly impacted federal and state policies and thereby the actions of school administrators. In short, it helped us to think about schools in a new way.

The driving force behind research is seldom the problems that plague practitioners. While *EEO* was firmly attached to an eminently practical issue—school segregation—its authors quickly moved beyond the purely practical to consider much more theoretical and abstract questions. How does fate control affect achievement? How much of the variance in student achievement lies between and within schools? Is there a contextual effect on school achievement? In their attempts to answer these questions they raised other concerns and questions, which attracted the attention of researchers in education and other social science disciplines. Lines of research developed that became self-perpetuating and divorced from the original problem, segregation, that instigated *EEO*. In short, what drives research are interesting questions, where "interesting" means interesting to researchers, not necessarily to practitioners.

Good research has a history, a genealogy if you will, and that genealogy consists of the string of questions that link it to previous work. To paraphrase our definition in the last chapter, research is a disciplined attempt to answer a question. Those questions do not arise anew with each new investigation, nor are they idiosyncratic quirks of each investigator. If practitioners are to use research intelligently to help them address a practical problem, it is necessary to view that research as a stream of work, sometimes spanning decades, and not to rely on the results of the latest study that attracts the news media's attention. This view, however, raises certain dilemmas for the practitioner.

Dilemma 1: Questions vs. Answers

Consider the idea that what drives research (and researchers) are interesting questions. You might well respond that, as an administrator, you have little use for questions. You need answers to important and pressing problems in your school. The researcher might reply that he or she cares little for solving your problems but only for studying interesting questions. This is not a matter of arrogance or disdain for the practical. Solving your problem is, after all, your responsibility, not the researcher's. The latter's responsibility is to fill gaps in our knowledge. Put bluntly, that is how researchers earn their living. There is an inevitable disjuncture, then, between research and practice.

The disjuncture, however, is smaller than it might appear for at least three reasons. First, important and interesting questions often arise from problems of practice, though the link may not be immediately obvious. For example, the questions embedded in the contextual effect aspect of *EEO* (e.g., would minority children achieve more if they attended majority white schools?) arose directly from the problems of segregation and lower minority achievement, both important practical problems. Knowledge created by the stream of research on contextual effects speaks directly to these practical problems. Second, while streams of research often diverge sharply from the practical problem that provoked them, sometimes they return to it. Here, a good example is the effective schools work. It arose in *EEO* and for a while had a largely theoretical guise ("How much of the variance in achievement lies between and within schools?" Who but an academic would be interested in such a question?). When researchers stopped asking the question in this way, however, and began to ask what school factors control the between school variance, the answers they produced had immediate and practical application: School administrators who ensured that parents were involved, that teachers had some voice in school decisions, and so on, were likely to have more effective schools. Finally, there are numerous agencies that make it their business to bridge the research-practice gap by attempting to translate research findings into a more accessible form for administrators. Among these are the several ERIC Clearinghouses, including one devoted specifically to administrative issues, the numerous publications of such professional societies as Phi Delta Kappa, and the national associations of elementary and secondary principals.

Dilemma 2: The Problem of Time

There is another dilemma in the research-practice relationship revealed by the history of *EEO*. Recall that the magnitude of the contextual effect Coleman found was uncertain because of methodological problems in his study. In part because of this uncertainty, researchers turned their attention to trying to establish it more firmly. It wasn't until the 1980s that a reasonably clear picture began to emerge: Contextual effects, at least those resulting from racial and socioeconomic desegregation of schools, were smaller than originally thought (Crain & Mahard, 1981; Kroll, 1980; Levine & Havighurst, 1984). A practitioner might respond to this tale by saying "I can't wait 15 years to get the answers to important questions. I need the answers now." A researcher might reply, however, that good research takes time, that findings are never established as authoritative by a single study, or that science advances on the basis of replications. In short, practitioners must wait years to be able to treat a finding as reasonably established, and even then, after hundreds of supporting studies, it might be overturned. The more the supporting evidence, the more trust one can put in a finding, but to expect absolute certainty, especially from the social sciences at present, is mistaken.

The danger here is that if the practitioner acts on the basis of the latest research study he or she is in danger of jumping on a bandwagon from which it will be hard to exit. If, for example, on the basis of a recent and widely quoted study a principal implements a program to solve a problem, she may well find that in five or ten years that the study (and hence her program) has been discredited. More importantly, the school's problem will remain. Unfortunately, at that point it may be difficult to get rid of the program even though it is demonstrably ineffective. It may have administrators and tenured teachers connected with it, a traditional claim on a portion of the budget, and a supportive political constituency. Thus, the principal may find herself again consulting the latest research and implementing yet another program (probably on top of the existing one) that again might turn out to be a mistake.

Dilemma 3: What Are They Talking About?

Another lesson can be learned from *EEO* and its progeny. We have noted that as research streams develop, they are likely to become more sophisticated, both conceptually and methodologically. Distinctions are drawn that are unrecognized by practitioners. In practical terms, this means that the language education researchers use to discuss their work becomes increasingly arcane and less accessible to administrators. Practitioners need only pick up a recent issue of the *American Educational Research Journal*, for example, to see this. More generally, this progression from the conceptually simple to the more complex is a characteristic of all professions and fields of research as they mature. If one examines any well-developed profession or discipline, it is immediately obvious that its researchers speak a jargon that is simply not accessible to outsiders. This jargon is unique to their fields, and it is essential if the field is to make reliable contributions to human knowledge. The problem is that practitioners are always behind in this language progression, always finding it difficult to understand the researchers in their field. Physicians experience this when they read medical research reports, engineers when they read research in physics and chemistry, and school administrators when they read educational research. It is unreasonable for practitioners to demand that researchers speak in "plain

English." There is no plain English equivalent to such concepts as eigenvalue, positivism, and semiotics, which a researcher may require in order to convey, as precisely as possible, his or her meaning to colleagues.

Dilemma 4: How Can I Read All This Stuff?

Finally, another dilemma for the practitioner is evidenced by the history of *EEO*. If research generates its own momentum and develops streams of work that become increasingly complex, voluminous, and differentiated, how is the practitioner to stay current? In the last chapter we argued that school administrators must be conversant with the research in their field, if they are to consider themselves professionals. But how can busy practitioners stay conversant with rapidly developing, constantly elaborating, and increasingly arcane streams of research? It is difficult enough for researchers to keep up with the studies in their own narrow specialties. How can generalists, nonresearchers, and practitioners be expected to do so? Again we can use the effective schools research to illustrate this. When this stream of work began shortly after the publication of *EEO*, a consensus rapidly emerged about the characteristics of effective schools. These characteristics were few and relatively easy to understand—principals should be leaders, parents should be involved, and so on. There were perhaps a dozen or so studies that formed the core of this early work. Now, more than 20 years later, there are more than a thousand studies labeled as effective schools studies in the Educational Resources Information Center (ERIC) alone, and untold more to be found outside ERIC and in other social science disciplines. Further and worse, what it means to "be a leader" or to "involve" parents has been made problematic by this outpouring. Clearly it is not possible for a practicing school administrator to stay current with even this one line of work, much less all of the others in educational research that might be relevant to his or her school's problems.

We have raised four dilemmas facing the practitioner who wishes to become a knowledgeable research consumer. Each requires serious attention. A major purpose of this text is to help you develop responses to these dilemmas and to further your development as a sophisticated, critical consumer of research. The next chapter contains suggestions for addressing the last dilemma: How can a busy practitioner efficiently find and effectively use the research that is relevant to his or her particular problem, while avoiding becoming bogged down in the voluminous and complex research literature of educational administration?

References

Averch, H. A., Carroll, S. J., Donaldson, T. S., Kiesling, H. J., & Pincus, J. (1972). *How effective is schooling? A critical review and synthesis of research findings.* Santa Monica, CA: Rand Corporation. (ERIC Document Reproduction No. ED 058495)

Brookover, W. B., Gigliotti, R. J., Henderson, R. D., and Schneider, J. M. (1973). *Elementary school social environment and school achievement. Final report.* East Lansing, MI: Michigan State University. (ERIC Document Reproduction No. ED 086306).

Brookover, W. B., & Schneider, J. M. (1975). Academic environments and elementary school achievement. *Journal of Research and Development in Education, 9*(1), 82–91.

Bryk, A. S., & Raudenbush, S. W. (1992). *Hierarchical linear models: applications and data analysis.* Newbury Park, CA: Sage.

Cain, G. G., & Barnow, B. S. (1973). *The educational performance of children in head start and control groups. Final report.* (ERIC Document Reproduction No. ED 093452)

Chubb, J. E., & Moe, T. M. (1990). *Politics, markets, and America's schools.* Washington, DC: The Brookings Institute.

Coleman, J. S. (1961). *The adolescent society: the social life of the teenager and its impact on education.* New York: Free Press of Glencoe.

Coleman, J. S. (1968). The concept of equality of educational opportunity. *Harvard Educational Review, 38*(7), 7–22.

Coleman, J. S. (1972). The evaluation of equality of educational opportunity. In F. Mosteller & D. P. Moynihan (Eds.), *On equality of educational opportunity* (pp. 146–167). New York: Vintage Books.

Coleman, J. S., Campbell, E. Q., Hobson, C. J., McPartland, J., Mood, A. M., Weinfeld, F., & York, R. L. (1966). *Equality of educational opportunity.* Washington, DC: U.S. Government Printing Office. (ERIC Document Reproduction No. ED 012275)

Crain, R. L., & Mahard, R. E. (1981). Minority achievement: Policy implications of research. In W. D. Hawley (Ed.), *Effective school desegregation: Equity, quality and feasibility* (pp. 55–84). Beverly Hills, CA: Sage.

Creemers, B. P. M., Reynolds, D. M., and Swint, F. E. (1996). *The international school effectiveness research project quantitative and class study data, 1992–1994.* University of Groningen: Groningen Institute for Educational Research. (ERIC Document Reproduction No. ED 395380)

Fehrmann, P. G., et al. (1987). Home influence on school learning: Direct and indirect effects of parental involvement on high school grades. *Journal of Educational Research, 80*(6), 330–37.

Glass, G. V., McGaw, B., & Smith, M. L. (1981). *Meta-analysis in social research.* Beverly Hills, CA: Sage.

Grosin, L. (1985). *School ethos and pupil outcome: Research findings and some theoretical considerations.* Research Bulletins from the Institute of Education, University of Stockholm. (ERIC Document Reproduction No. ED 361875)

Hanushek, E. A. (1989). The impact of differential expenditures on school performance. *Educational Researcher, 18*(4), 45–51,62.

Hanushek, E. A. (1994). Money might matter somewhere: A response to Hedges, Laine, and Greenwald. *Educational Researcher, 23*(4), 5–8.

Harber, C. (1992). Effective and ineffective schools: An international perspective on the role of research. *Educational Management and Administration, 20*(3), 161–169.

Harker, R. (1995, April). *Analysis of school effects on school certificate results through the use of hierarchical linear models.* Paper presented at the Annual Meeting of the American Educational Research Association, San Francisco CA.

Hedges, L. V., Laine, R. D., & Greenwald, R. (1994). Money does matter somewhere: A reply to Hanushek. *Educational Researcher, 23*(4), 9–10.

Hedges, L. V., Laine, R. D., & Greenwald, R. (1994). Does money matter? A meta-analysis of studies of the effects of differential school inputs on student outcomes. *Educational Researcher, 23*(3), 5–14.

Hedges, L. V., & Olkin, I. (1985). *Statistical methods for meta-analysis.* Orlando, FL: Academic Press.

Ho, E. S.-C., & Willms, J. D. (1996). Effects of parental involvement on eighth-grade achievement. *Sociology of Education, 69*(2), 126–141.

Hobson v. Hansen. (1967). U.S. District Court for the District of Columbia, 269 F. Supp. 401.

Hoyle, E. E., & McMahon, A. E. (1986). *The management of schools.* East Brunswick, NJ: Nichols Publishing Co.

Jencks, C. S., Smith, M., Acland, H., Bane, M. J., Cohen, D., Gintis, H., Heyns, B., & Michelson, S. (1972). *Inequality: A reassessment of the effect of family and schooling in America.* New York: Harper & Roe.

Keyes v. School Dist. No. 1 Denver. (1973). Supreme Court of the United States, 413 U.S. 189; 93 S. Ct.

Kratzer, C. C. (1996, April). *Beyond "effective schools research": Cultivating a caring community in an urban school.* Paper presented at the Annual Meeting of the American Educational Research Association, New York, NY.

Kroll, R. A. (1980). A meta-analysis of the effects of desegregation on academic achievement. *Urban Review, 12,* 211–224.

Kuroda, K. (1995, October). *Effective schools research from a Japanese perspective.* Paper presented at the North-East/Mid-West Regional Conference of the Comparative and International Education Society, Buffalo, NY.

Lareau, A. (1987). Social class differences in family-school relationships: The importance of cultural capital. *Sociology of Education, 60*(2), 73–85.

Lareau, A., & Benson, C. (1984). The economics of home/school relationships: A cautionary note. *Phi Delta Kappan, 65*(6), 401–404.

Lasswell, H. D. (1958). *Politics: Who gets what, when, how?* New York: Meridian Books.

Lee, V. E., & Loeb, S. (1995). Where do head start attendees end up? One reason why preschool effects fade out. *Educational Evaluation and Policy Analysis, 17*(1), 62–82.

Levine, D. B., & Havighurst, R. J. (1984). *Society and education.* (6th ed.). Boston: Allyn & Bacon.

Levine, D. U., & Lezotte, L. W. (1990). *Unusually effective schools: A review and analysis of research and practice.* Madison, WI: National Center for Effective Schools Research and Development. (ERIC Document Reproduction No. ED 330032)

Lezotte, L. W., & Passalacqua, J. (1978). Individual school buildings: Accounting for differences in measured pupil performance. *Urban Education, 13*(3), 283–293.

Marx, K. (1992). Critique of the Gotha program. In M. Morgan (Ed.), *Classics of moral and political theory.* Indianapolis: Hackett.

Milne, A. M., Myers, D. E. Rosenthal, A. S., & Ginsburg, A. (1986). Single parents, working mothers, and the educational achievement of school children. *Sociology of Education, 59*(3), 125–139.

Monk, D. H., & Jacobson, S. L. (1985). Reforming teacher compensation. *Education and Urban Society, 17,* 223–236.

Mosteller, F., & Moynihan, D. P. (1972). A pathbreaking report. In F. Mosteller & D. P. Moynihan (Eds.), *On equality of educational opportunity* (pp. 3–66). New York: Vintage Books.

Purkey, S. C., & Smith, M. S. (1983). Effective schools: A review. *The Elementary School Journal, 83*(4), 427–452.

Rowan, B., Bossart, T. T., & Dwyer, D. C. (1983). Research on effective schools: A cautionary note. *Educational Researcher, 12*(4), 24–31.

Rutter, M., Maughan, B., Mortimore, P., & Ouston, J. (1979). *Fifteen thousand hours: secondary schools and their effects on children.* Cambridge, MA: Harvard University Press.

Sammons, P., Hillman, J. and Mortimore, P. (1995). *Key characteristics of effective schools: A review of school effectiveness research.* London, England: Institute of Education, University of London. (ERIC Document Reproduction No. ED 389826)

San Antonio Indep. Sch. Dist. v. Rodriguez. (1973). Supreme Court of the United States, 411 U.S. 1; 93 S. Ct.

Scheerens, J., & Creemers, B. P. M. (1996). School effectiveness in the Netherlands: The modest influence of a research programme. *School Effectiveness and School Improvement, 7*(2), 181–195.

Schneider, J. M., & Brookover, W. B. (1974, April). *Academic environments and elementary school achievement.* Paper presented at the American Educational Research Association, Chicago, IL.

Shouse, R. C. (1995, April). *Academic press and school sense of community: Sources of friction, prospects for synthesis.* Paper presented at the Annual Meeting of the American Educational Research Association, San Francisco, CA.

Stern, D. (1986). Compensation for teachers. In E. Z. Rothkopf (Ed.), *Review of research in education* (Vol. 13, pp. 285–316). Washington, DC: American Educational Research Association.

Townsend, T. (1996). School effectiveness and improvement initiatives and the restructuring of education in Australia. *School Effectiveness and School Improvement, 7*(2), 114–132.

van der Werf, G. (1993, April). *Differences in school and instruction characteristics between highly, average, and low effective schools.* Paper presented at the Annual Meeting of the International Congress for School Effectiveness and Improvement, Norrkoping, Sweden.

Webster, W. J., Mendro, R. L., Bembry, K.L., Orsak, T. H. (1995, April). *Alternative methodologies for identifying effective schools.* Paper presented at the Annual Meeting of the American Educational Research Association, San Francisco, CA.

Webster, W. J., Mendro, R. L., Orsak, T. H., Weerasinghe, D. (1996, April). *The applicability of selected regression and hierarchical linear models to the estimation of school and teacher effects.* Paper presented at the Annual Meeting of the National Council on Measurement in Education, New York, NY.

Westinghouse Learning Corp. & Ohio University. (1969). *The impact of Head Start: An evaluation of the effects of Head Start on children's cognitive and affective development. (Executive Summary).* Athens, OH; Ohio University. New York: Westinghouse Learning Corp. (ERIC Document Reproduction No. ED 036321)

Wu, P., & Campbell, D. T. (1996). Extending latent variable LISREL analyses of the 1969 Westinghouse Head Start evaluation to blacks and full year whites. *Evaluation and Program Planning, 19*(3), 183–191.

CHAPTER 3

Finding and Using Research to Address Educational Problems

INTRODUCTION

In Chapter 1 we developed a conception of research in educational administration by addressing what makes something a study in school administration. There we argued that, without such a conception, virtually any piece of social science research (and much physical and biological science, for that matter) is conceivably a study in school administration. As a consequence, every profession's requirement that its practitioners stay abreast of the research in their field becomes an impossibility. A full-time academic researcher could not begin to keep up with the avalanche of social science literature that fills hundreds of journals every year; certainly a practitioner, whose full-time responsibility is to administer a school, could not. Practitioners, especially, need to be able to put some kind of rough boundary around research that is likely to be relevant to their practice.

In the second chapter we developed a conception of the relationship between educational research and administrative practice. We saw that this relationship was not a straightforward one; that the same study could bear directly on practice and simultaneously have no relationship to practice, and that the relationship could affect practice powerfully but in indirect ways. We also suggested that research has its most obvious effects on other research; that important studies-such as *Equality of Educational Opportunity* (Coleman et al., 1966) generate streams of research that span decades. If administrators are to use research intelligently, they will need to be attentive to these streams and highly skeptical of the findings of the "latest study that shows . . . ," no matter how supportive it may be of their own favorite position on some educational issue.

In this chapter we want to apply these ideas to a practical matter, reviewing the research literature in order to *use* it to address real administrative problems. We will begin by contrasting literature reviews conducted for research purposes and those carried out for administrative purposes. While the two goals are alike in some respects, they differ in important ways. Next we will turn our attention to certain critical distinctions to keep in mind when trying to learn what research has to say about a problem in your school. Using these ideas, we will then consider some practical matters concerned with searching three types of research literature: secondary, preliminary, and primary sources. Finally, we will examine certain practical and ethical issues involved in using research and doing literature reviews.

Reviewing Research from the Perspective of Researchers and Practitioners

Some of you have had considerable experience perusing research literature. As an undergraduate and graduate student you probably did so when you wrote term papers. Some of you may have worked as a research assistant for a professor, where you were asked to prepare reviews for the professor's projects. Others may have completed Master's theses or have started on a doctoral dissertation, both of which require extensive literature reviews. As a consequence, many of you have knowledge and skills that will stand you in good stead. Your experience, however, may also create problems, for the purposes of a researcher and an administrator differ in important ways.

In one of the standard texts in educational research, Gall, Borg, and Gall (1996) identify six purposes for carrying out a literature review. Researchers, they suggest, need to carry out a thorough literature review in order to (1) delimit a research problem, that is, focus it narrowly; (2) find new lines of inquiry that others have ignored; (3) avoid approaches to an investigation that have proven fruitless in earlier studies; (4) provoke ideas about promising research methodologies; (5) learn what other investigators have recommended regarding further research; and (6) contribute to the process of building educational theory (Gall et al., 1996, p. 114–116). Underlying these objectives is the premise that the reason for doing research is to add to existing knowledge, and the point of a literature review is to contribute to that end.

Now consider a literature review from a practitioner's perspective. School administrators will almost never have in mind any of the six purposes described by Gall et al. when they consult published studies. They certainly are not attempting to make original contributions to human knowledge. Instead, they are attempting to find and use existing knowledge to help solve a problem. The need for literature reviews arises in the practical problems that make up the day-to-day stuff of administrators' lives: A program isn't working the way it's supposed to; the staff isn't as competent as it should be; parents are demanding immediate changes in a program; a sixth grade teacher is chronically late for work. In these situations, administrators are supposed to *do* something. For them, the end product of a literature review should be intelligent action. To repeat what we said in the first chapter, all that research can do is help you think more intelligently about practical problems. It cannot make the failing program work, improve the staff's competence, and so on, but it might help you devise more intelligent solutions to those problems.

There is a second difference in the approach of a researcher and practitioner to research reviews. With the six goals noted here and the ultimate purpose of making an original contribution to human knowledge, it is no wonder that Gall et al. stress the importance of thoroughness in doing a literature review. One cannot create new knowledge without being intimately familiar with existing knowledge. Thoroughness, however, takes time. It will take approximately three to six months to carry out a comprehensive literature review—more if you are unfamiliar with the topic (Gall et al., 1996, p. 114). Since few practicing administrators will be familiar with the research on their problem, the longer estimate is undoubtedly more accurate. For a practitioner this advice is certainly impractical and potentially disastrous. It doesn't take much imagination to predict what most school boards would do with an employee who, given an assignment to solve some problem, went off to spend six months in a library. For the practitioner, comprehensive knowledge about the research relevant to a practical problem, is not feasible. Nor is it necessary. Thus, while prior experience with reviewing research may be useful, it may also lead to misconceiving the nature of the work involved. We need to examine more closely the nature of the knowledge required for addressing practical problems and how the specialized knowledge derived from research fits into the problem-solving process.

The Nature of Practical Problems and the Knowledge They Require[1]

There is a fundamental difference in the notion of a *problem* as that term is used by researchers and administrators. Researchers often write of "the problem addressed in this study" in the reports of their investigations, by which they usually mean a gap in our knowledge that they hope their study will fill. Often such gaps undergird the research questions stated explicitly in the titles or opening paragraphs of their articles. For example, researchers have asked such questions as: How does the depth and diversity of a school's curriculum change as school size increases (Monk & Haller, 1993)? Do shared set of values and positive teacher-pupil relations really improve student achievement (Phillips, 1997)?

---

[1] This section closely follows the discussion in Haller and Strike (1997, pp. 1–9).

What is the role of a university's prestige in enhancing its graduates' careers in Japan and the United States (Ishida, Spilerman, & Kuo-Hsien, 1997)? While it is easy to see that studies such as these may have practical implications, their immediate purpose that motivated them was to fill a gap in our knowledge. No one knew whether schools' math, English, and foreign language curricula changed in the same way as school size increased, whether shared values actually caused achievement to increase, or whether going to a prestigious university had long-term effects on people's careers. The authors of these studies hoped their investigations would fill these gaps in our knowledge.

Administrators also seek to fill a gap when they address a problem. However, the gap is typically a discrepancy between a current condition in their schools and a desired state of affairs, not a gap in knowledge. While filling a gap in your knowledge might help you solve the problem in your school, it is rarely an end in itself. Using the language we adopted in Chapter 1, a practical problem exists when there is a gap between an empirical condition and a normative belief concerning that condition. A superintendent might claim: "Our students are achieving two grade levels below state norms in tested reading achievement" (an empirical claim). "We need to bring them up to grade level" (a normative claim). A high school principal might assert: "Morale among our staff is very low" (an empirical assertion). "We should raise it" (a normative assertion). A teachers' union official might say, "Our district's salary schedule is one of the lowest in the region" (an empirical statement). "It must be improved" (a normative statement). Practical problems such as these have certain characteristics.

Practical Problems Occur in Concrete Circumstances

First, practical problems are situated in a set of concrete circumstances (Haller & Strike, 1997, p. 1). They are not simply questions whose answers we do not know, that is, gaps in our knowledge. Most of us do not know the atomic weight of argon or the year of Shakespeare's birth, for example, but we do not find our ignorance of these matters problematic. More relevantly, none of us knows the exact chemical and electrical changes that occur in a child's brain when he or she learns something. This is a gap in our knowledge that lies at the very center of our profession, but we manage to operate reasonably effective schools despite this gap. These examples of our ignorance are simply not problems. Instead, problems exist when a specific set of circumstances does not meet our desires or expectations, or it conflicts with our values. Notice the consequence of this view: The same objective conditions may or may not be a problem to different people and, perhaps more importantly, the same objective conditions can be seen as quite different problems by different people. Students reading below grade level may be seen by one group as a problem of teacher inadequacy, by another as a problem of low parent socioeconomic status, and a third group as a lack of funds to support smaller classes. Indeed, there is almost an infinite variety of definitions of the problem of low reading scores. It follows that how we define a problem is critically important. The superintendent who defines low reading achievement as a financial problem and acts accordingly is unlikely to appease a group of parents who see it as a problem of teacher incompetence. In any case, for practicing administrators, problems are specific to a local circumstance. While a problem in district A may be similar to a problem in district B, it is never exactly the same problem.

Practical Problems Require Action

Obviously there are some problems about which nothing can be done, and still others which will go away by themselves (and savvy administrators are able to distinguish both of these from problems they must act upon). Nevertheless, problems are situations that need correction, school administrators are problem solvers, and solving problems requires action (Haller & Strike, 1997). It follows, then, that the kind of knowledge that administrators need is knowledge about what to do. We shall refer to this as *practical knowledge.* While theoretical knowledge, most generally knowledge about why things happen, is often essential for addressing practical problems, it is never sufficient. As we noted in Chapter 1, much educational research helps administrators little because it concerns matters over which they have little or no control. When researchers show, for example, that parent socioeconomic status has a significant effect on students' reading scores, they have provided no handle by which a principal might do something to raise the scores of students in his or her school. Such knowledge may be illuminating, but it is not necessarily helpful.

Practical Problems Can Be Thought About

Finally, problems can be thought about in productive ways, that is, ways that help us solve them (Haller & Strike, 1997). That is obvious, of course, but we have something more specific in mind. Previously we have said that research can help a practitioner think more intelligently about a problem. We need to say more about what that means. First, we think about something by using concepts. These concepts have various sources, notably for our purposes in education and the social sciences, but important and useful concepts are also derived from other fields, notably the law and from ethical systems. For example, it is helpful to understand the notion of diminishing marginal returns (a social science concept) when thinking about the financial aspects of a school system, due process (a legal concept) when disciplining students, and equality of opportunity (a moral concept) when planning curricula. These concepts permit us to think more productively about finances, discipline, and curricula—they illuminate these topics.

The second idea derives from the first: In order for concepts to be useful for thinking about problems, we need to see specific administrative actions as entailing those concepts. Consider a district's athletic director trying to improve the total sports program of his or her district. Even if allocating additional coaching staff to the successful football team will further improve its win-loss record, it does not follow that more staff effort should be allocated to football. Perhaps twice the improvement will be effected by allocating the additional staff to the losing track team; that is, the marginal return to the additional resources is greater for track. If the misbehavior of the baseball team when playing away from home has created public relations problems, understanding the concept of due process will help the director craft fair rules for athlete behavior. And if the director wants to establish a weight training program in the high school, seeing this as an occasion to apply the concept of equality of opportunity will help ensure that young women have equal access to the program. Thus, the athletic director of a school district is "thinking more intelligently about real problems" when he or she sees a decision about allocating staff effort among various sports in the light of diminishing marginal returns, setting rules for athletes as a means of ensuring due process, and implementing a new weight program as an opportunity to provide equality of educational opportunity.

Four Kinds of Knowledge Essential to Successful School Administration

We can now use these ideas to consider the knowledge that a practicing administrator needs in order to think more intelligently about a problem. There are at least four kinds of useful knowledge.

Local Knowledge. First, an essential kind of information concerns conditions in your school, the district, and the community. We will call it *local knowledge* (Haller & Strike, 1997). Much of this is informal and unwritten. It consists of knowing such things as local beliefs and customs, accepted practices in the school and district, who the powerful stakeholders are, and what individuals need to be consulted before actions can be taken. It includes being familiar with the characters and personalities of one's colleagues and clients. Extensive personal experience in an organization (or full access to those with that experience) is invaluable in helping you gain this knowledge and thereby helping you decide what to do about a problem. This kind of knowledge isn't gained from experience in other school districts, and it certainly cannot be gained in a library. Lack of local knowledge is what leads administrators new to a school and district to delay making consequential decisions until they get the lay of the land.

Legal Knowledge. A second kind of knowledge is essential when deciding what to do. You must know what is permissible and what is not (Haller & Strike, 1997). Every school system is enmeshed in a web of rules, regulations, policies, and laws that govern what administrators may and may not do. Rules often prescribe some actions and proscribe others when dealing with a particular problem. Some of these rules are made locally; school boards make written policies that have the force of law. Many rules and regulations derive from state and national legal requirements. It is customary to rail against all of these rules as bureaucratic red tape when they impede your actions to solve a problem. We often forget that they serve such necessary functions as ensuring predictable behavior, preventing the abuse of power, and making it possible to handle routine matters efficiently.[2] For example, school districts operate under strict accounting rules embodied in state laws. These rules are essential because the money administrators spend comes from other people's pockets. Principals who, without authorization, use money budgeted for salaries to buy library books, even when those books are badly needed, will quickly (and properly) find themselves in serious trouble. While practitioners cannot be lawyers, they must be generally knowledgeable of the policies, regulations, and laws that bear on the problem they seek to solve.

Ethical Knowledge. Knowing what is the right thing to do—what is morally or ethically demanded when dealing with a problem—is a third kind of essential knowledge (Haller & Strike, 1997). Perhaps it is the most important of the four. We suspect that relatively few administrators are fired because they are unfamiliar with the mores of their organizations, or they unknowingly violate policies, rules, and laws. Rather, we suspect that they are more often fired because they are perceived to behave unethically, deviously, or unfairly.

We need to say a bit more about ethical and moral knowledge because people sometimes claim that these are matters of personal values, and one's personal value judgments ought not to be foisted on others. Moral and ethical judgments are not the same things as value judgments. The former concern what is right, the latter concern what is good. If we say that canoeing is a good activity, and you reply that it is not, little more can be said. Each of us has made a value judgment: We value canoeing; you do not. Further discussion is largely pointless. However, if we say that law-abiding people shouldn't be permitted to own handguns, and you reply that they should, each of us has made a moral judgment. An extensive, substantive discussion is certainly possible, and a principled decision regarding guns can be made. Moral judgments are also not matters of personal opinion, meaning one person's opinion is as good as another's. If that were the case, we could not justify punishing those who break our laws. If, in your opinion, it is permissible to steal, that does not give you license to do so. Nor are moral rules simply collective judgments—even democratically chosen collective judgments. For example, during most of its history this country democratically decided to withhold the right to vote from women and blacks. A majority vote does not necessarily yield a moral decision. If it did, there could be no such thing as an unjust law.

It is also important to understand that facts alone cannot show that an action is a right one. Thus, true knowledge of the consequences of an action usually cannot, in itself, justify that action. Consider a school with a substantial number of incompetent teachers whose pupils suffer considerable harm as a result. Suppose you are appointed its principal with the explicit mandate to "clear out the deadwood," that is, fire the incompetent staff members. It may be

---

[2] The classic exposition of the functions of rules in bureaucracy is to be found in Weber (1947) and their dysfunctions in Gouldner (1964). For a discussion of the application of these functions and dysfunctions to schools, see Haller and Strike (1997).

factually correct that you can produce more reliable and valid information about individual faculty member's competence, and produce that information very quickly, by eavesdropping on classrooms via an intercom system. It may also be factually correct that with this information you could more accurately identify teachers that should be replaced and thereby more effectively end the harm they do to students. Despite all of these good consequences, most of us would demand that your eavesdropping be justified on ethical grounds, not simply on grounds of its good consequences. We would want you to show that eavesdropping was the right thing to do, not simply that it was an efficient thing to do.

Knowledge of Consequences. Fourth and finally, most problems require a knowledge of the consequences of a particular administrative action (Haller & Strike, 1997). Exact knowledge of this sort is, of course, impossible, unless one has a working crystal ball. Nevertheless, empirical knowledge about what has happened under similar conditions elsewhere surely will provide some useful guidance. Such knowledge may derive from the study of history, from educational and social science research, and from experience and common sense.

Most practitioners, of course, are wont to rely on the last pair of these, their experience and their common sense. They firmly believe that experience is the best teacher. In many cases it is. But experience and common sense can also be very misleading. What worked elsewhere or in the past, or what seems obvious, may not work now. Thus, your experience and common sense may easily lead you astray.[3] Evidence from research helps us decide what to do about some problem, if for no other reason than it can make us cautious about relying on our experience and what common sense tells us we should do. Suppose, for example, that you need to improve mathematics achievement in your school, and you are considering implementing a self-esteem program to accomplish that end. Perhaps such a program seemed to work in your former position and perhaps common sense tells you that self esteem is important to school success. However, evidence from numerous studies shows that self-esteem programs do not improve achievement (Kohn, 1994, provides an accessible review of this research). Of course these studies do not prove that a self-esteem program will not improve math achievement in your school, but they should make you very cautious about implementing one there, regardless of your personal experience and common sense. Thus, reviewing the research relevant to a problem in your school may help you predict the likely consequences of your actions. In the process, and if you are open-minded, the research can either confirm or cast doubt upon your own conjectures. It can help you think more intelligently.

We see now that knowledge of the research on a practical administrative problem is often a necessary condition of justified administrative practice, but it is never sufficient. It contributes to just one of four kinds of necessary knowledge, all of which are likely to play a role in the solution of practical problems:

---

[3] For a classic discussion of the limitations of common sense for solving practical problems, see Nagel (1961).

Administrators need to know the likely consequences of their actions, their local situation and its culture, which actions are permissible and which are not, and, perhaps most importantly, what is the right thing to do—what is just. Problems will vary in the extent to which they require each of these kinds of knowledge. The problem of improving pupils' math achievement is primarily one of identifying programs that are most likely to accomplish that improvement—the school's principal needs to predict the likely consequences of implementing a particular math program. The most useful knowledge in this situation may be knowing what programs have a demonstrated record of success in other places. Hence, reviewing the research on the effectiveness of various programs (including perhaps, programs to raise self-esteem) makes sense. On the other hand, the eavesdropping problem is primarily a moral issue and requires that the principal be able to construct moral arguments, though even here the other kinds of knowledge would likely play a role. For example, the principal would have to know the likely reaction of the staff and community to systematic listening in on classrooms, whether doing so was permitted by the teachers' contract, and so on. In any case, the point is that being able to skillfully access and use the research literature is a necessary but not sufficient condition to competent administrative practice.

An Administrator's Approach to Searching and Using Research Literature

Earlier we pointed out some of the differences that characterize a researcher's and a practitioner's purposes in doing a literature review. One of these concerned the requirement of comprehensiveness: Researchers trying to add to the knowledge base of a profession must necessarily gain a comprehensive grasp of existing knowledge. In contrast, practitioners do not need to know everything ever discovered about a problem, and they certainly do not have time to master the corpus of work on any significant problem. Instead, they must acquire just that subset of the knowledge base that is most likely to help them think more intelligently about their problem. They need to choose carefully the material they will read in the scarce time that is available to them. In this section we want to build on our earlier discussion by providing you with some concrete ideas about identifying and using studies that bear on a problem that you face.

Imagine yourself as a principal of East High School, a modestly large school in Pleasant View, a working-class suburb of a midwest city. Your district seems to be having problems. The proportion of its students classified as "at risk" is increasing, while its tax base is eroding. Recently it has experienced a large influx of non-English speaking immigrants from Asian and Latin American nations, putting a serious strain on its ESL programs. Further, it appears that 15% of its students quit school before graduation, a rate above the state average. Finally, the state has instituted a performance rating system of its districts, coupled with a program to reduce the funds of ineffective districts. This system puts a substantial weight on dropout rates. Now imagine that your superintendent, seeing the implications of the dropout percentages for the district's finances, asks that you recommend a strategy to lower that rate, and that you do so at next month's meeting of the Principal's Council.

You recognize that there is likely to be a substantial body of research on the problem of dropouts, research that may be helpful in preparing your recommendation. Out of curiosity, you run a quick search of the Educational Resources Information Center (ERIC) and find that there are over 1,000 documents that seem to concern dropouts. Now you have another problem: Clearly, you cannot read a thousand studies in the next month. How should you proceed?

We suggest that you begin by framing the problem carefully. You might state it as follows:

> The dropout rate from Pleasant View high schools was slightly over 15% last year and has been in that range for at least the last five years. We should attempt to reduce this rate to under 10% within the next three years.

Notice several aspects of this statement:

- The problem is not one of at risk students, inadequate ESL programs, the eroding tax base, or the state's performance system. Those are certainly related to the dropout problem, *but they are not the dropout problem*. Be clear about what your problem is and state it as precisely as possible.
- Don't confuse problems with solutions. Maybe if Pleasant View improved its ESL programs or its programs for at risk students, its dropout problem would disappear. But maybe not. Put another way, don't state the normative aspect of your problem as "We should improve our ESL programs for at risk students." If you do this, you have pre-judged the solution to the dropout problem. Perhaps a better program for ESL students would reduce the dropout rates in Pleasant View. But there may be something better, and you will not find it by researching ESL programs.
- It is a good idea to include an explicit and realistic goal in the normative aspect of your problem statement. For example, to say that you "should insure that all students graduate from high school" is to set yourself up for failure. Students drop out of high school for many reasons, most of which are probably not under your control. They are not administratively mutable. To strive to reduce the rate to 10% over a three-year period is more realistic.
- Notice the "for the last five years" phrase. Be sure that the problem you have identified is really a problem and not some random spike in the district's statistics. Thus, it is often useful to determine if the problem has existed for some time. If the dropout rate has stood at 15% for five years, it is probably not a blip in the data.

We will begin by suggesting what you should *not* do when carrying out a review of the research. Notice that the term *dropout* is a topic, not a problem. It is usually pointless to try to review the research on most educational topics. As the example illustrates, most significant topics in education have been the subject of hundreds, often thousands, of studies. (Imagine trying to read the research on the topic of reading. Your demise will occur before you finish.) If you try to review the research on dropouts, your literature review is likely to consist of a lengthy string of paragraphs, each devoted to the results of a particular study. The whole exercise will lack a point. The paragraphs will go on and on until you simply run out of time. Further, if you try to review the research on a topic, you will have no criteria for reading particular studies and ignoring others. Without criteria, if the topic of a study is dropouts, it presumably merits your attention.

Further, we recommend that you not think of your effort as an attempt to review the research on a *problem*. We have defined a problem as a gap between an empirical condition and a normative belief about that condition. Look again at the problem statement. Obviously, you cannot review the research on your problem because there will probably be none. That is, there is unlikely to be any extant research on the empirical aspect of your problem, unless someone has actually studied your school district. The empirical claim that your district's dropout rate is about 15% could only be verified by conducting your own research in your school system. Further, while there are likely to be numerous normative discussions of the problem of dropouts in the literature, their application to your district will be problematic and, again, you will have no criteria for selecting one study to read over another. Any discussion of why your district should lower the dropout rate must be based on the values of the Pleasant View community.

Asking Questions

How, then, should you proceed? Begin by asking yourself two questions: (1) "What do I really want to know about my problem, which the research literature can tell me and which will help me think more intelligently about the problem?" (2) "Why do I want to know that?" That is, sit down and think hard about the problem, concentrating on developing a list of questions whose answers would help you reason more carefully about the problem. Further, you should be able to give a good reason for wanting to know the answer to each question you pose. Answering even one question is likely to take hours. Therefore, think hard about why you want to know the answer to each one. "It would be nice to know" is not a good reason.

What kinds of questions might you generate? Figure 3.1 shows some of the questions that school administrators have suggested when we have presented them with the dropout problem in our classes. After each question we give a summary of the student's reasoning that led him or her to ask that particular question. Take a minute now to read these questions and their rationales carefully. The sample questions listed are hardly exhaustive—undoubtedly, you could add numerous others. (Why not try posing a few additional questions with their rationales? It will be useful practice.)

We need to say a few things about this process. Posing good questions is a critically important step in carrying out a useful research review. Taking the time to do it properly will ultimately save you time. You will also be much more likely to find helpful information efficiently. Consider the following suggestions:

- Pose questions that you expect researchers have addressed. Obviously, it may be difficult for you to know what those might be. However, recall our discussion in the previous chapter about the nature of research and the questions posed by investigators. If you find little or no research on the question you have posed, the chances are good that you have phrased it poorly.
- Do not confuse questions about the problem and questions about the problem as it exists in your school. For example, you will certainly have questions about the dropouts in your own school, but those questions will not have been answered by published research, except in the rare case when investigators have actually studied your school. If you need the answers to questions about your specific school, you will have to do the research yourself.
- List as many questions as possible, without excessively worrying at the outset about their wording or precision, but also without suspending your critical faculties. Call it "thoughtful brainstorming." You can clean up your questions later.
- Try to phrase your questions generally, rather than posing implicit hypotheses that you happen to favor. This is the difference between asking, for example, "Are there specific demographic characteristics that distinguish students who drop out of high school from those who do not?" (see Question 1, p. 64), and asking "Is student race related to dropping out?" "Is student age related to dropping out?" "Is student SES related to dropping out?" The latter questions presuppose that you know what the relevant demographic factors are, and you may not.
- Keep your own situation in mind when posing questions. Not all questions are equally relevant to all schools. For instance, if your school serves a demographically homogeneous population, a question about the demographic characteristics of dropouts may not be useful.
- Creating questions is best done as a small group activity. Suggestions from a few knowledgeable colleagues about important questions will be helpful. A small group of educators can generate a dozen or so useful questions about most educational problems in a short time.
- Do not be too concerned about overlap among the questions. For example, on page 64 Question 5 is arguably an instance of Question 4. Nevertheless, the local situation may provide good reasons for distinguishing the two. In any case, the next step of the process is meant to handle this issue.

After you have generated as comprehensive a set of pertinent questions as you can, you will need to throw most of them away. If you have posed two dozen questions, it is certain that you will not be able to answer all of them in the available time. For this reason, add a third question to the two we proposed earlier. Ask yourself: "Of all of the questions that I've generated, the answers to

1. Are there specific demographic characteristics that distinguish students who drop out of high school from those who do not?

Rationale: "If a majority of dropouts are characterized by specific demographic attributes, we might be able to better identify potential dropouts as targets for a prevention program. Further, since demographics change very slowly or not at all, we might be able to identify potential dropouts in the first grade, making early intervention possible."

2. What is a dropout?

Rationale: "Are there alternative definitions of the term *dropout*? The choice of a definition determines the resulting rate. For example, is someone who quits high school but later gets a GED still a dropout? Perhaps we should calculate our rates on the basis of more than one definition."

3. What happens to dropouts after they quit school?

Rationale: "We shouldn't rely on the media's depiction of dropouts. If most dropouts flounder around for a few years but eventually find jobs, raise families, and become contributing members of the community, what is the problem?"

4. Why do students drop out of high school?

Rationale: "When we know why something happens, we are in a much better position to prevent it from happening. We need to know why students drop out."

5. Are there identifiable characteristics of schools that promote high dropout rates?

Rationale: "We shouldn't focus only on students. We need to identify attributes of schools that cause dropping out. As administrators we can more easily change our schools than our students."

6. Are there existing programs that we might adopt that have been shown to be effective in preventing students from dropping out?

Rationale: "Let's not reinvent the wheel. If certain programs have proved successful, we should consider adopting one of them."

7. Why do students stay in school?

Rationale: "We should look at the problem from the opposite perspective. Most students do not drop out. If we knew why they decide to finish high school, we might be in a better position to help prevent those who intend to drop out from acting on those intentions."

Continued

F I G U R E   *3.1*   **Possible Questions About Dropouts to Guide a Review of the Research**

8. Are there any successful programs for attracting dropouts back to school?

Rationale: "Perhaps we cannot prevent most potential dropouts from doing so. We might, however, be able to attract them back to school after they've had a year or two to sample life outside school."

9. What educational characteristics distinguish dropouts from nondropouts?

Rationale: "If dropouts are frequently characterized by certain educational attributes (e.g., being discipline problems, getting low grades) that appear early in their educational careers, we could use these to help us identify students in need of early intervention programs."

which ones have the greatest potential for helping me think intelligently about my problem?" The number of questions you select must necessarily depend on the time you have. Select only those few that you think will have the greatest payoff in providing you with useful information. If it turns out that your review goes more quickly than you expect, you can always add another question from your list. Again, selecting the final questions is probably best done in consultation with your colleagues and staff. Finally, after you have selected the few questions that you will use, study them carefully and word them as precisely as you can.

All of this will take a few hours; however, it is time well spent because it provides a purpose for your library work. For most significant educational problems there are hundreds even thousands of studies that are potentially relevant. It will be impossible for you to read them all. If you begin with a question or two, you will be in a position to select that much smaller subset of work that is most likely to help you think intelligently about your problem. If a study addresses one of your selected questions, you should read it. If it does not, even though it is about the problem, you should not. Think of it this way: *Just because someone has carried out a study dealing with your problem, that is not a sufficient reason for you to read it.* You should read only those studies that directly respond to your question(s).[4]

Let's suppose that in discussion with your colleagues you conclude that you would most benefit from having the answer to three questions from the list in Figure 3.1: Question 2, "What is a dropout?" Question 4, "Why do students drop out of school?" and Question 6, "Are there existing programs that we might adopt that have been shown to be effective in preventing students from

---

[4] It is hard for a couple of academics like ourselves to write that you should read only the studies that address your question(s). We also believe that browsing in a good research library sometimes leads serendipitously to finding useful material. It is also intellectually rewarding even if you turn up nothing useful, and it is always fun. So, perhaps we should recommend that you browse if you can find the time, but focus first on the questions that you need to answer.

dropping out?" Your search of the literature, then, will be focused tightly on just these three questions.

Developing a Thesis

We have said frequently that research can help you "think more intelligently" about real problems. Now we can be more explicit about what this means in practical terms. The reason for selecting a few questions to guide your literature review is not simply to save time, to make your review manageable, or even to get the answers to some useful questions. Rather, the point is to help you craft a *thesis* regarding your problem. A thesis is a proposition in whose support you will argue. To argue in this sense is to state a set of premises that lead logically to a conclusion, the thesis. To argue is to reason. For school administrators who want to address a practical problem in their schools, a thesis is almost always a normative assertion about a course of action that should be taken, for example, "We should do X about this problem." Here, "X" is a proposed activity or program that will help close the gap between the current situation and our desires or expectations regarding it. Alternatively, a normative thesis might assert that we should stop doing X (if that program is already in place), or that we should do nothing about the problem (if ameliorating the problem isn't possible or worth the effort required). Each of these assertions is normative in form (notice the *should*); each is a prescriptive statement of actions to be taken or not taken. The point of doing a literature review, then, is primarily to provide the empirical evidence needed to support an argument for a normative thesis.[5] If you can advance a cogent argument in support of a course of action regarding a problem, you are thinking intelligently about that problem.

Now recall our earlier discussion concerning the four types of knowledge required for justified administrative actions: knowledge of likely consequences, knowledge of local conditions, knowledge of what is permissible, and knowledge of what is right. Reviewing the research literature should tell you the likely outcomes of your actions, that is, empirical knowledge. Recall also that empirical knowledge is never sufficient to justify a normative claim. Thus, when you prepare an argument advocating some course of action, that argument will be made up of a series of premises. Each premise will be drawn from one or more of the four kinds of knowledge, but at least one of those premises will be normative in form. Most likely it will be drawn from knowledge about what is permissible or what is right—from legal, moral and ethical sources.

The importance of a defensible thesis cannot be overstated. When you implement a program to address a problem in your school, you are intervening

---

[5] Remember to review other kinds of research. You might need to review the literature regarding the legal and ethical dimensions of your problem. For example, if your concern is to improve your district's teacher evaluation system, you might need to review the legal literature regarding the concept of due process in teacher dismissal cases and the concept of equal respect in the literature of ethics. In this book, however, we focus on ways to help you access and effectively use empirical research.

in the lives of other people's children. Even if the program does not directly impact students, you are spending money that your neighbors have labored to earn. You should be doing neither of these things without good reasons. Your thesis and its supporting argument provides those reasons. By stating your thesis plainly and arguing for it explicitly, you permit those who have a serious stake in your actions to critically evaluate the grounds for your proposal. This is important because it provides an error correcting mechanism. Others are often able to see flaws in our reasoning that we have overlooked. Further, in our view, creating defensible reasons for a course of action, and persuading others of the rightness and desirability of the proposed action, is at the heart of the idea of educational leadership. In a democratic society, educational institutions, of all places, should exemplify the role of reason and persuasion in governance.

It is highly unlikely that you will find a defensible thesis in something you read. After all, the authors of the books and articles that you study will not necessarily subscribe to the same normative beliefs that underlie your actions. They will not have the local knowledge that you possess; they will be unaware of many of the rules, regulations, and laws that prescribe and proscribe administrative actions in your district; they will be ignorant of the values that you and your community hold. Thus, your thesis will be the product of your own intelligence and imagination in interaction with the materials you read. *You create a thesis.* It emerges in your mind and is tested and modified as you continue to read. Your literature review may cause you to discard your pet thesis because it is unsupported by the evidence, and you will have to formulate an entirely new one. As soon as you begin to read the research on your problem the creation of a thesis regarding it should be foremost in your mind.

Reviewing Research: Secondary Sources

Now that we understand the purpose for reviewing research literature and how that literature contributes to practical decisions, we can examine some of the mechanics of actually carrying out a review. It is common to classify types of research literature into three rough categories: preliminary sources, secondary sources, and primary sources. We will use that classification because it is in common use, though it creates a problem: The terms themselves suggest that preliminary sources would be consulted first, but, with a minor exception, we suggest that you consult secondary sources first. In this section we will treat each of these types of literature and suggest some ideas about effectively using it. At places we will be following the work of Gall, Borg, and Gall (1996), who provide a discussion of the review process.

A secondary source is usually a published article or book written by a competent researcher who is an expert on the subject under discussion. It provides an evaluative overview and summary of the research on a particular topic. Succinctly, one might think of secondary sources as experts on a research topic critically discussing the stream of research on that topic. Often, a secondary source will explicitly address one or more of these questions: What do we know about this topic?

What do we need to know? What do we think we know, but really don't? The answer to the last question can be valuable. Often a kind of folklore or common sense grows up around educational problems that is either patently wrong or significantly in error. For example, many educators uncritically hold ideas that higher student achievement can be created by implementing site-based management, or by main streaming handicapped children. Both of these simple-minded and unnuanced ideas gloss over significant issues and contradictory research.

Our definition of secondary sources stresses that they are written by competent researchers. This is important because there are numerous secondary sources that are entirely unreliable for professional use. We are all familiar with the articles that appear in newspapers and national magazines such as *Time* and *Newsweek* that report the results of recently published research. These secondary sources purport to tell us what the current research says about some topic or problem. They do not. They are prepared by reporters who are largely ignorant of the bulk of the work on a topic and are meant for public, not professional, consumption. These articles focus on the latest, "most newsworthy" studies, even when those studies are seriously flawed. Often studies are termed "breakthroughs," or "path breaking," though experts in the field view the same studies as quite minor. In education, the popular press demonstrates a strong selection bias, tending to emphasize reports whose findings are critical of schools.[6] *The articles found in the popular press describing the findings of educational research are entirely unsuitable as bases for professional decision making.* Just as you would not knowingly put yourself under the knife of a surgeon who stayed abreast of medical research by reading *Time,* you should not expect parents to submit their children to school administrators who rely on *Newsweek* to stay up with the research in their field.

Useful Secondary Sources

What, then, are some secondary sources that you may trust? We will name and briefly describe the major, regularly published sources that cover the broad field of education, not simply educational administration. (Recall our discussion of research in school administration in Chapter 1, where we suggested that studies concerned with the effects of educational programs on student outcomes are to be found in a variety of sources.) The list is not meant to be exhaustive but to name specific sources as well as classes of sources. Note also that we do not touch on excellent books and journals that concern specialized fields, for instance, special education, mathematics education, and so forth. Finally, recall that a great deal of excellent research pertinent to educational administration is found in disciplines outside of education, such as sociology, economics, and others. These fields also publish reviews of research that may contain important secondary studies directly related to your problem.

---

[6] For example, consider the typical press coverage that accompanies the release of results from the international studies of educational achievement.

One source useful as a starting point when you are largely ignorant of the research on a topic is the *Encyclopedia of Educational Research* (Alkin & American Educational Research Association, 1992) Currently in its sixth edition, this four-volume work consists of short articles written by experts on hundreds of research topics. Each article gives an overview and bibliography of the research on a topic or issue. A somewhat similar work is the *International Encyclopedia of Education* (Husen & Postlethwaite, 1994), though it is somewhat less focused on educational research, per se. Both of these sources can provide you with a quick overview of many educational topics and problems, and they allow you to easily check topics related to your specific concern. Their major defect is that they are on a long publishing cycle. For example, the *Encyclopedia of Educational Research* is published every 10 years, so it may be substantially out of date when you consult it. However, because of its quality and breadth, we believe that it makes a sensible starting point, especially when you are entirely unfamiliar with the work on your problem.

Textbooks are another useful starting point. Recent texts by competent authorities often provide good reviews of the research on the topic of interest. Deciding whether a text is recent is easy, of course. Deciding whether the author is competent is considerably more difficult. Since you are presumably not an expert on the topic of your review, you are not in a position to judge the quality of the author's handling of it. We will have more to say about this problem in a moment.

Handbooks are other useful secondary sources. A handbook attempts to summarize current knowledge on a particular topic in a single volume. Its editor, a recognized authority on the topic, assembles a group of experts and commissions each to write a chapter on some aspect of the book's subject. Currently there are a number of high quality handbooks on educational topics. The "granddaddy" of them all is *The Handbook of Research on Teaching* (Wittrock, 1986) now in its third edition, a weighty tome that contains chapters summarizing the research on the teaching of various subjects and pedagogical practices. There are also research handbooks on a number of other educational topics including science teaching (Gabel, 1994), teacher evaluation (Millman & Darling-Hammond, 1990), curriculum (Jackson, 1992), and educational administration (Murphy & Louis, 1999), to name but a few. These provide competent summaries of the research on the entire area of the practitioner's responsibilities, justifying their purchase for personal use. For example, *The New Handbook of Research on Teacher Evaluation* is an excellent reference for any practitioner responsible for assessing teachers quality. In any case, be sure to check for the existence of a handbook relevant to your problem.

The *American Educational Research Association* (AERA), the primary professional organization of educational researchers, publishes two high quality secondary sources: The *Review of Educational Research* is a journal that is issued four times each year. Each issue consists of articles that review the research on a problem or research topic. The *Review of Research in Education* is issued once each year. Each chapter is a review of the research on a topic. Perusing the table of contents of each of these publications over the last several years will often turn up an article or chapter bearing on your problem. Both of these publications are likely to provide higher quality and more extensive research reviews than the encyclopedias mentioned previously; however, this is also their principal defect. Without some kind of introduction to the research on a topic, these sources can sometimes be overwhelming in the detail they provide. Further, the authors often write for an audience of researchers, so there tends to be a greater emphasis in their reviews of the literature on its implications for research than on its implications for practice. Nevertheless, the quality of these secondary sources commends them to your attention. Certainly they should be consulted in any competent literature review, but we recommend that you do this after a search of encyclopedias, handbooks, and textbooks.

The sources we have named above are arguably the major secondary sources in education. However, there are numerous other secondary sources that may be helpful, depending on the problem you are dealing with and the questions that you have posed about it. For example, the Educational Resources Information Center (ERIC) coordinates the activities of 20 ERIC Clearinghouses that monitor the research on particular topics in education. There are Clearinghouses devoted to educational management, handicapped and gifted children, elementary and early childhood education, and rural education to name but a few.[7] Many of these periodically issue summaries of the research on their areas of responsibility. The Clearinghouse on Rural Education and Small Schools, for instance, recently issued a summary of the research on the problems and benefits of small high schools (Cotton, 1996), which could be very useful to the principal of a small, rural school trying to deal with issues of school consolidation. Other useful secondary sources are the yearbooks published by the National Society for the Study of Education and the annuals issued by the JAI Press Incorporated and its companion firm, Ablex Publishing Corporation. At this writing JAI publishes yearly series dealing with advances in various educational fields including early education, educational administration, educational policy, educational productivity, and program evaluation, among others.

Why Review Secondary Sources First?

We have several reasons for recommending that you consult secondary sources as a first step in your literature review. First and most obviously, a few good secondary sources will efficiently provide you with the major research findings and conclusions about your problem. They will tell you what is known about a topic, what needs to be known, and what many mistakenly assume to be known. Related to this advantage, recall our stress on understanding the stream of research that typically develops around an important educational problem. Good secondary sources will provide you with a sense of this history.

Good secondary sources will also help you identify pivotal studies and authors. Identifying recognized experts on your problem is critically important. In practical terms, this means that you should pay attention to citations as you

---

[7] Gall, Gall, and Borg (1999, p. 510) provide the names and addresses of all ERIC Clearinghouses.

read secondary sources. If an individual's name turns up many times in your reading, and his or her work is discussed favorably by the authors of the reviews (who are themselves experts), this is useful knowledge. Later, when searching preliminary sources such as ERIC, you will be able to search for additional work by that person. Similarly, you can use this knowledge in making at least a rough assessment of the quality of textbooks. If the writer of a textbook is not among those cited as having done work on your topic, and he or she does not reference the studies cited as important by the authors of the research reviews you have read, you should be more skeptical of the information in that text.

We have said that a secondary source is usually a published book or article. However, when you have identified recognized authorities on your problem and have read some of their work, note their institutional affiliations (which are usually given in their articles and books) and call them to discuss the research on your problem. These authors become, in effect, another of your secondary sources. You should not be hesitant to call a recognized authority to discuss your problem after you have read some of his or her work. Most researchers will be pleased to discuss the practical implications of their work and the work of other investigators.

A third reason to consult secondary sources is to learn if there are characteristic weaknesses in a line of research. No study is perfect; each is flawed in some way. Indeed, a substantial portion of this book is devoted to examining the flaws that limit the trust we can put in any particular piece of research. However, it is also true that whole lines of work may have a characteristic weakness, and a good secondary source may identify it for you. This can be particularly helpful when you begin to read primary sources because you will be alerted to the flaw. For example, many studies of dropouts have addressed the question of why students drop out of school. Very often their methodology for doing this has been to interview students who have dropped out and ask them why they did so. Such a design is seriously flawed because it relies on students' memories and ignores both their tendency to put things in a favorable light and their capacity to recognize and articulate their own motives.[8]

Finally, another reason to first consult secondary sources is to assess the questions guiding your review. Recall that we suggested that you formulate a number of questions and then choose a few to try to answer by reviewing the research literature. It is possible that you have not chosen good questions or, more likely, that there is another question that would be more fruitful than one you have selected. Careful reading of good secondary sources can help you

---

[8] For example, a common reason given by former students for dropping out is low grades, and on this evidence researchers have concluded that low grades cause dropping out. However, it is equally conceivable that the reverse is true: dropping out causes low grades. Elementary students who dislike school may daydream and be otherwise inattentive (a kind of dropping out), learn less than is expected, and thereby earn low grades. The same students in junior high may begin to cut classes (another kind of dropping out) resulting in a further decline in achievement and grades. Finally, in high school, because they have not learned the necessary material in the earlier years, failure is more frequent, and they may be absent for whole weeks at a time (still another form of dropping out) with disastrous effects on their grades. In such cases it is not clear whether low grades caused the students to drop out or that dropping out caused their low grades.

recognize these mistakes and correct them before you expend a great deal of effort in your review.

Finding and reading several good secondary sources concerned with your problem may take a day or more, depending on such factors as the extensiveness of your search and the proximity of a good research library. When you have finished, you should have a set of notes about tentative answers to the questions you have posed, and the beginnings of a bibliography listing authors and studies that you want to read. Perhaps you have begun to form a thesis regarding your problem. At this point you should turn your attention to preliminary sources.

Reviewing Research: Preliminary Sources

A preliminary source is an index to a body of literature. That literature will be categorized into relevant subject headings, and full bibliographic data will be provided for each document in the index. Many preliminary sources also provide an abstract for each document contained in the index. In electronic indexes each document is usually referred to as a *record*. We will use that terminology here.

Electronic indexes are considerably more useful than their paper counterparts for several reasons, and we urge you to use them instead of their more cumbersome hard copy versions. The typical index, whether electronic or not, contains references to a much broader range of material than the books found in the typical library card catalog. It will usually index journal articles, government reports, critiques of published studies, reports by independent organizations (e.g., school districts), and unpublished materials such as papers given at conferences. Electronic indexes have additional advantages. Because each record is tagged by various descriptors, (terms used to describe the document's substantive contents), electronic searches can be much more sophisticated and narrowly focused than is possible using their paper-based versions. You are able to combine search terms using such logical operators as "and," "or" and "not." In our search of the literature for studies of dropouts, for example, entering the query "dropouts *and* high school *and* (race *or* ethnicity)" would yield studies of the race or ethnicity of high school (not college) dropouts.[9] Searching electronic databases is fast. Once search criteria are identified, locating documents that meet those criteria can be located in a matter of seconds. Finally, you may print out the results of a search including all of the necessary bibliographic information and abstracts.

Useful Preliminary Sources

There are a number of preliminary sources that index education-related documents. The best known, of course, is the Educational Resources Information

---

[9] The specific syntax of search queries varies somewhat among the different providers of these databases and also among the different databases.

Center, or more simply, ERIC. At this writing ERIC contains almost one million records. It is available at most university libraries in a print version, via networked computers as an electronic database, and on CD-ROM disks that can be read by personal computers. Thus, if you have access to the Internet, you should be able to search ERIC from your home or office. Electronic versions index education documents back to 1966 and some of these versions are updated monthly. In addition to full bibliographic information, ERIC provides a great deal of information about each document, for example, a source to write for hard or microfiche copies, the price per copy, the length in pages, the thesaurus terms (descriptors) used to classify the document, a unique accession number, and of course, an abstract, which (usually) will give you a reasonably good idea of the document's contents. This is not the place to go into the details of searching ERIC, but any good reference librarian can give you expert guidance. In addition, Gall et al. (1999) provide a useful guide to using both the hard copy and electronic versions of ERIC.

There are certain limitations to using ERIC, however. Perhaps most importantly, you cannot carry out a thorough literature review by relying on ERIC. The system has at least two serious limitations. First, its contents are largely confined to papers and articles; books and monographs presenting the results of research on educational topics are largely ignored. Second, recall our discussion in Chapter 1 in which we pointed out that much of the very useful research in educational administration is done in other social science fields. Coverage of these fields is largely missing from the system. Thus, even a thorough search of the database is likely to leave important studies undiscovered. In addition, you cannot trust the abstracts that accompany each document nor the descriptors used to classify it. Often the former are written by someone other than the author of the document and the latter assigned by someone with little expertise in the document's topic.

While ERIC is the major preliminary source of educational research, it is certainly not the only one that you should consult. There are several other electronic databases that may prove helpful to you. *Education Index* provides author and subject search capabilities (but not abstracts) for many of the same journals covered by ERIC, but it goes back to 1929 and covers books as well as journals. Recall our emphasis on searching in relevant social science fields. *PsychINFO* provides an easily accessible index to the research in psychology. Since some subfields of that discipline have a substantial focus on educational questions (e.g., developmental psychology, cognitive psychology) research in that field may bear directly on the questions you are trying to answer. *Sociological abstracts* indexes over 3,000 journals from the various branches of sociology, social work, and related fields. *EconLit,* provided by the American Economic Association, indexes books, journal articles, dissertations, and articles published since 1969. *Dissertation Abstracts On Line* is a definitive subject, title, and author guide to virtually every American dissertation accepted at an accredited institution since 1861. All of these are electronic databases and are likely to be available to you (possibly at a fee) if you have access to the Internet. Alternatively, they are available at most major libraries at no charge.

Increasingly, school districts make these useful databases available to their faculties. Even if you must pay for access, however, you are likely to find the time saved worth the cost, though it will pay for you to learn to use the system before accessing it, (from a librarian or by reading one of the texts cited earlier) so that your search will be as efficient as possible.

We should mention one final electronic preliminary source that may be unfamiliar to you, the *Social Science Citation Index (SSCI)*. This database does exactly what its name implies; it indexes citations in the social science literature. That is, it tells you who cited a particular author or article; it is an index of footnotes. The *SSCI* can be very helpful. Suppose in your search of secondary sources you have followed our suggestion and identified several seminal studies done some years ago on the questions you are trying to answer. By searching the *SSCI* on the authors or their works, you can identify other writers and their research who have cited these seminal studies in their own work. In this way you will be able to trace a stream of research forward in time to recently published material.

Earlier we suggested that, with a minor exception, a search of secondary sources should precede one of preliminary sources. The exception concerns ERIC. We suggest that you use ERIC to locate review articles dealing with your questions that have appeared in educational journals, that is, use a preliminary source to locate a secondary one. For example, in searching for articles that review the research on dropouts, it would be efficient to search ERIC for review articles that have appeared in the *RER*. That is, your search query might be "dropouts and Review of Educational Research"

After you have completed a search of preliminary sources you will have collected a bibliography of articles, reports, abstracts, and books that seem to address your question(s). You may be beginning to formulate a thesis about your problem. At this point you are ready to read primary sources.

Reviewing Research: Primary Sources

A primary source is an original report of research, prepared by the investigators who conducted the study. It describes the question the researcher was attempting to answer, the background of the study, its methodology, its findings, and a conclusion. Locating the primary sources that are most relevant to your question(s) is a major goal in conducting a literature review. You have not carried out a literature review when you have read only secondary sources and the abstracts found in preliminary sources.

Useful Primary Sources

There are several major primary sources in education that you should be familiar with. We will mention those sources that publish research concerning the general field of education, not its specialized subfields, such as special education. However, the general education journals often publish research that is concerned with a problem in one of the specialized areas. (Most of these specialized sub-fields also have journals given over to their concerns, and you should become familiar with those in your specialty and with their relative quality.)

Arguably the most important journal publishing educational research of general interest to the profession is the *American Educational Research Journal (AERJ)*. Like most research journals, it is published four times each year and may contain five to 10 original reports of studies. It is divided into two sections, the first dealing with social and institutional analysis and the second concerning teaching, learning, and human development. Studies in the first section tend to be sociological and historical, while those in the second tend to be more psychological.

A journal that is an exception to the four-times-a-year schedule is the *Educational Researcher (ER)*, which appears monthly. While this journal is primarily concerned with professional matters, such as employment opportunities, it also publishes original empirical and nonempirical research bearing on controversial issues, such as mainstreaming and tracking. *Educational Evaluation and Policy Analysis (EEPA)*, as the name suggests, is principally concerned with the results of major program evaluation efforts and research that bears directly on important policy matters. Of the three journals just mentioned, the last publishes a higher proportion of articles with direct and obvious administrative implications. All three of these are publications of the *American Educational Research Association*.

Other top quality journals devoted to general educational research include *The American Journal of Education (AJE)*, *Sociology of Education* (*SOE* is a publication of the *American Sociological Association*), and the *Harvard Educational Review (HER)*. Finally, while it is a specialized primary source, in a book aimed specifically at school administrators, we should mention the *Educational Administration Quarterly (EAQ)*, which is devoted entirely to research on school administration.

In several places we have referred to the high quality of these research journals. We mean by this that they are rigorously peer reviewed. That is, articles which appear in them have been critically evaluated by three or more experts before they are accepted for publication. These are blind evaluations whereby reviewers do not know the names of the articles' authors, nor do authors know the names of reviewers. This point is important for practitioners because it provides some assurance that the studies were competently conducted. It does not mean that they are flawless (a large portion of this book will be devoted to pointing out just those flaws), but it does mean that the reviewers did not find their flaws to be so debilitating as to invalidate the authors' findings. This is particularly helpful when considering methodological and statistical issues. It is unrealistic, in our view, to expect school administrators to become so knowledgeable in research methods and statistics that they are fully competent to judge a study's methodological quality. Suppose a study appearing in *AERJ* uses multiple analysis of covariance (MANCOVA) as a statistical tool for data analysis. While you may not have any idea what a MANCOVA is, since the study was published in a journal of the quality of *AERJ*, you can be reasonably confident that the technique was an appropriate one.

As you read the studies you have gathered, you will be formulating the answers to the questions you have posed and, most importantly, working through the process of creating a thesis regarding the problem you face. As we have said, that is a process that involves your own intellect and creativity in interaction with the research that you are reading. It is likely that you will make more than one false start on a thesis, and very probable that as you progress a point will occur to you that will lead you to check other studies. In any case, your goal is to create a set of normative and empirical premises, an argument, that supports a course of action addressing the problem in your school.

Creating an Argument to Support a Thesis: The Case of East High School's Dropouts

Now that we have an approach for conducting a literature review for administrative purposes, we can return to your hypothetical problem as principal of East High School and your superintendent's directive to prepare a recommendation for the Principals' Council regarding your district's dropout rate. In Figure 3.2 we illustrate a memorandum such as you might prepare for your colleagues' consideration.

We would draw your attention to several points about the memorandum and the literature review it embodies. First, note its brevity. As we tried to make clear in the beginning of this chapter, a review prepared for administrative purposes is not intended to be exhaustive of all of the studies on a problem. Instead, its purpose is to provide the empirical support needed for the thesis you create. That means that when you advance an empirical premise that is not obvious (e.g., your claim that there is considerable confusion regarding the definition of a dropout), you need to cite a study in support of your claim. Normally, if a premise is important to your argument (as this one is), you will want to cite more than one study to show that your premise does not rest on one study's unreplicated findings.

This view of carrying out a review has direct and obvious implications for the number of references that you cite. Too often administrators have the idea that the more references they throw into a paper, the better the paper. Not only is this view wrong, it acts as a deterrent to even undertaking a review of the research on problems. (The view is probably a holdover of their undergraduate term paper days.) The number of citations you need depends on the number of premises in your argument. In this case you have a relatively simply argument based on three empirical premises: First, there is no consensus on the definition of a dropout, hence, we cannot count them unambiguously. Second, we do not well understand the reasons students drop out. Third, there are no programs that have a well-established track record for successfully reducing dropout rates at documented costs. With three simple empirical premises, therefore, you might have 10 to 15 citations in your memorandum—not 50 or 100.

Notice also the way references are handled. The cited documents are not discussed; instead, they are simply used to support empirical premises. This is

MEMORANDUM

TO: Principals' Council, Pleasant View School District
FR: You, Principal East High School
RE: What Should We Do About Our Dropout Problem?

At last month's meeting of the Principals' Council I was asked to prepare a recommendation about ways to reduce the high school dropout rate in our district. In preparing this recommendation I have consulted with the staff and carefully reviewed the relevant district records. In addition, I have collected and reviewed pertinent educational research regarding dropouts. In deciding what was pertinent, I sought to answer three questions: (1) What is a dropout? (2) Why do students drop out? (3) Are there existing programs that have been shown to be effective in preventing students from dropping out? After expressing a set of principles that I believe should govern our responses to problems such as this, I briefly summarize the results of my efforts organized around these questions. I will be happy to amplify any of these points at our meeting next Wednesday.

My recommendation is predicated on the belief that any program we adopt must meet certain standards: It must address an existing problem or a problem that we know to be imminent. It should be based on a convincing rationale. It must have documented its effectiveness elsewhere, that is, we should implement programs that have a track record of success in other districts. Finally, any program that we adopt must be capable of being modified to suit local conditions in Pleasant View.

What is a dropout?

Definitions are critical. Dropout rates are computed in various ways, yielding widely different rates, ranging (at the national level) from 5% to 14%. Historically, rates have sharply declined. Differences among race/ethnic groups are disappearing. Blacks and whites are now dropping out at about the same rate (Coley, 1995; Hartzell et al., 1992; Hoffman, 1990; Williams, 1987).

We compute our school's rate using a variation on what is termed an "event rate" (Coley, 1995). However, because we compute our rate early in the school year, and because we do not have an adequate follow-up system to check on students who are presumed to have dropped out, our measured rate of 15% is certainly inflated by some unknown amount. In brief, we do not know our true rate. Hence, we do not know if we have a problem.

Why do students drop out?

The literature suggests numerous causes and correlates of dropping out (Deschamps, 1992; Ehrenberg & Brewer, 1994; Hendrick et al., 1989; Mirochnik & McCaul, 1990). These are often divided into categories: family factors (low SES, broken homes); school factors (school culture, urbanicity); and student factors (low grades, misbehavior). There are several problems with these factors. Many are not administratively mutable (family SES), or they are mutable only with great difficulty (school culture). Further, it is unclear which are causes of dropping out and which are effects. (Are low

Continued

F I G U R E   *3.2*   Memorandum

Figure 3.2 continued

grades a cause or an effect of dropping out?) Still further, factors commonly believed to be important in causing dropout may not be as important as we believe, for example, pregnancy in young women (Upchurch & McCarthy, 1990) and single-parent homes (Astone & McLanahan, 1991). In sum, the causes of dropping out are numerous, unclear (Kelly, 1993), and provide no clear approach to understanding and addressing the dropout problem (but see Hahn & Danzberger [1987] for an opposing view on this point).

Are there existing programs that have been shown to be effective in preventing students from dropping out that we might adopt?

There are a variety of extant programs intended to prevent dropping out. However, no one program or practice seems able to substantially reduce the rate by itself, and the evidence supporting many is very weak. Some of these programs have been expensive and have produced almost no reduction in rate. ("Project Yes" in Virginia cost 10 million dollars and, perhaps, reduced the statewide rate from 4.8% to 3.3% [Virginia Department of Education, 1993].) Moreover, most programs described in the literature have no price tag attached. Most have only short-term evaluations; I could not tell from the evidence whether their effects are long lasting. The general approach advocated by Wehlage does seem promising: (1) identify potential dropouts very early; (2) differentiate among the many and varied problems these students face; (3) develop programs to meet these individual problems (Wehlage et al., 1989). However, this is more of a way to think about dropouts than a program to prevent them. I am unsure, then, if there are any extant programs that will work here (assuming that we need a program).

My Recommendation

Based on the principles noted and my reading of the research pertaining to the three questions I posed, I recommend the following actions:

We should not implement a dropout prevention program at this time. Instead, we should adopt three intermediate objectives. After reaching each of these we will be in a much better position to take effective action, if that proves to be necessary. First, we need to agree on a definition of *dropout* and measure the dropout rate in our district. Second, we need to monitor the research for the appearance of more useful studies than those that now exist regarding the causes of dropping out. Third, we should monitor the evaluations of dropout prevention programs with a view of identifying those with demonstrated efficacy, based on a definition of dropout that we can adopt in Pleasant View.

MEMORANDUM REFERENCES

Astone, N. M., & McLanahan, S. S. (1991). Family structure, parental practices and high school completion. *American Sociological Review, 56*(3), 309–320.

Coley, R. J. (1995). *Dreams deferred: High school dropouts in the United States.* Princeton, NJ: Policy Information Center, Educational Testing Service. (ERIC Document Reproduction No. ED 392818)

Deschamps, A. B. (1992). *An integrative review of research on characteristics of dropouts.* Unpublished Doctoral Dissertation, George Washington University.

Ehrenberg, R. G., & Brewer, D. J. (1994). Do school and teacher characteristics matter? Evidence from "High school and beyond." *Economics of Education Review, 13*(1), 1–17.

Hahn, A., & Danzberger, J. (1987). *Dropouts in America: Enough is known for action.* Washington, DC: Institute for Educational Leadership. (ERIC Document Reproduction No. ED 282948)

Continued

Hartzell, G., McKay, J., and Frymier, J. (1992). *Calculating dropout rates locally and nationally with the Holding Power Index*. Omaha, NB: University of Nebraska (ERIC Document Reproduction No. ED 343953)

Hendrick, I. G., MacMillan, D. L., Balow, I. H. (1989). *Early school leaving in America: A review of the literature*. Riverside, CA: University of California, Riverside; California Educational Research Cooperative (ERIC Document Reproduction No. ED 320039)

Hoffman, L. M. (1990, April 16–20). *Issues in developing comparable national dropout statistics through the Common Core of Data Survey*. Paper presented at the Annual Meeting of the American Educational Research Association, Boston, MA.

Kelly, D. (1993). *Last chance high*. Ann Arbor, MI: Edwards Brothers.

Mirochnik, D., & McCaul, E. J. (1990). *Public school dropouts: A contextual approach. Occasional Paper Series: No. 5*. Orono, ME: College of Education, Maine University. (ERIC Document Reproduction No. ED 324152)

Upchurch, D. M., & McCarthy, J. (1990). The timing of a first birth and high school completion. *American Sociological Review, 55*(2), 224–234.

Virginia Department of Education. (1993). *Hypothesis for effective dropout prevention*. Richmond, VA: Virginia Department of Education. (ERIC Document Reproduction No. Ed 367748)

Wehlage, G. G., Rutter, R. A., Smith, G. A., Lesko, N., & Fernandez, R. (1989). *Reducing the risk: Schools as communities of support*. London: The Falmer Press.

Williams, P. A. (1987). *Standardizing school dropout measures. CPRE Research Report Series* (BBB07945). Washington, DC: Rand Corp., Center for Policy Research in Education. (ERIC Document Reproduction No. ED 298184)

another way in which doing a research review for administrative purposes can, in our view, legitimately differ from doing one for research purposes. In the latter case it is expected that individual studies will be critically discussed, sometimes extensively. Further, when reviews are carried out for research purposes, it is expected that the findings and methods of different studies will be compared and contrasted and judgments made about the quality of individual works. These expectations are not reasonably demanded of practitioners who need to use research for administrative decisions.

Next, notice the argument itself. It provides explicit evidence regarding your capacity to think intelligently about dropouts. In the second paragraph it states a set of beliefs—the normative principles that you think should guide the district's actions: The district should be sure that it has a problem before it moves to solve it; any program it adopts should be based on convincing reasons—a rationale; and any program it adopts should have strong empirical evidence that it has actually worked elsewhere and that it can be successfully modified for use in Pleasant View.

Stating these beliefs is important. Previously we pointed out that when administrators propose some action regarding a practical problem, they are, explicitly or implicitly, making a normative argument: They are claiming that some action *should* be taken. We also pointed out that it is a logical fallacy to reach a normative conclusion solely on the basis of empirical evidence. No amount of empirical evidence, by itself, is capable of supporting a normative conclusion. One often hears this expressed as "Is cannot lead to ought." Thus, for example, if it is absolutely certain that retaining children in grade is harmful to them, <u>it does not follow from that fact alone</u> that schools should not retain children. At least one normative premise is required in an argument that reaches a normative conclusion. For example, if the parents of your district strongly favor retention, does the fact that it is harmful entitle you to ignore their wishes? Similarly, if your school board has a policy that children should be retained under certain conditions, are you entitled to ignore those policies? Obviously you need a normative argument making the case that avoiding harm to children is a value that should take precedence over parents' wishes for their own children and over school board policies. And you must convince parents and board members that your position is right. Paragraph two explicitly states the beliefs that inform your argument. Stating them explicitly permits others to examine and question them.

The paragraph concerning beliefs is followed by three sections, each dealing with one of the questions you posed: What is a dropout? Why do students drop out? Are there existing programs that have been shown to be effective in preventing students from dropping out that we might adopt? Each section provides a succinct summary of your findings regarding the question, and each leads to a conclusion that serves as a premise in the argument you have created: Pleasant View is not sure that it has a dropout problem. Even assuming that it has, the research literature provides no clear understanding of the problem's causes. Finally, there are no programs with sufficient creditable evidence to warrant their adoption by the district. All of this leads to your recommendation: Pleasant View should not implement a dropout prevention program until it has achieved three intermediate objectives. It should choose a defensible definition of dropping out and improve its counting methods; It should monitor the research on dropouts for the appearance of more definitive studies on the causes of dropping out; It should monitor the research to check for programs with well-documented success.

By making your argument explicitly and in writing, you permit others to critically evaluate it. They may advance alternative premises and different conclusions. They may cite studies that contradict those you rely on or point out flaws in those you have cited. They may call attention to local conditions that you did not consider. They may question your normative premises and advance others in their place. All of this is to the good. You are not trying to win a debate but to reach better educational decisions. By making your thesis explicit, you raise the quality of the discussion that will occur when the Council meets. Thus, not only have you "thought more intelligently," you will have assisted your colleagues to do the same.

Notice the citations to Ehrenberg and Brewer, Astone and McLanahan, and Upchurch and McCarthy. The first is from the *Economics of Education Review,* a journal that is primarily aimed at economists interested in the field of education (both authors are labor economists). The latter two are both from the *American Sociological Review,* and all of their authors are practitioners of that discipline. These studies illustrate the point we made that useful research on educational problems can be found in literature outside of education. Indeed, they also suggest that the beliefs that educators hold about some educational phenomenon may not be shared by experts from other disciplines.

In closing, there are two ethical issues that arise when doing literature reviews for administrative purposes that bear discussion. Adopting the perspective we have advocated—that is, sharply restricting the scope of your literature review so as to address only a few questions—relieves you of the responsibility of having to read large numbers of studies. It does not, however, relieve you of the responsibility of reading the studies you have claimed to read, that is, the studies you cite. Recall our point regarding a thesis and your obligation to provide reasons for your proposed actions: Other people's children are involved, or at the least, other people's money. When your reasons rest on others' research, you must ensure that those studies have actually said what you claim they said. You cannot do that by cribbing citations from secondary sources or relying on abstracts of studies. You must read the studies themselves.

Finally, notice the citations to Hahn and Danzberger's study and to the book by Wehlage. Both suggest that one or more of your premises are wrong. If you find a competent study that seems to contradict your analysis, you may not ignore it in your review. Instead, your obligation is to point the study out to your audience and be prepared to fairly present its findings. In this way your colleagues are made aware that a competent authority disagrees with you, and they are in a position to question you on the matter. In educational research there are very few findings that are so ironclad that no one can reasonably disagree. Again, the point of providing the best argument that you can in support of your proposed action is not to win a debate but to raise the quality of the discussion and, eventually, to arrive at better solutions to educational problems. The students in your school and the citizens of your community will be the ultimate beneficiaries.

References

Alkin, M. C., & American Educational Research Association. (1992). *Encyclopedia of educational research.* (6th ed.). New York: Macmillan.

Coleman, J. S., Campbell, E. Q., Hobson, C. J., McPartland, J., Mood, A. M., Weinfeld, F., & York, R. L. (1966). *Equality of educational opportunity.* Washington, DC: U.S. Government Printing Office. (ERIC Document Reproduction No. ED 012275)

Cotton, K. (1996). *Affective and social benefits of small-scale schooling. ERIC Digest.* Charleston, SC: ERIC Clearinghouse on Small Schools. (ERIC Document Reproduction No. ED401088)

Gabel, D. L. (Ed.). (1994). *Handbook of research on science teaching and learning.* New York: Macmillan.

Gall, J. P., Gall, M. D., & Borg, W. R. (1999). *Applying educational research: A practical guide.* (4th ed.). New York: Addison Wesley Longman, Inc.

Gall, M. D., Borg, W. R., & Gall, J. P. (1996). *Educational research: An introduction.* (6th ed.). White Plains, NY: Longman.

Gouldner, A. W. (1964). *Patterns of industrial bureaucracy.* New York: Free Press.

Haller, E. J., & Strike, K. A. (1997). *Introduction to educational administration: Social, legal and ethical perspectives.* Troy, NY: Educator's Press International.

Husen, T., & Postlethwaite, T. N. (Eds.). (1994). *International encyclopedia of education* (2nd ed.). New York: Pergamon.

Ishida, H., Spilerman, S., & Kuo-Hsien, S. (1997). Educational credentials and promotion chances in Japanese and American organizations. *American Sociological Review, 62*(6), 866–882.

Jackson, P. W. (Ed.). (1992). *Handbook of research on curriculum.* New York: Macmillan.

Kohn, A. (1994). The truth about self-esteem. *Phi Delta Kappan, 76*(4), 272–283.

Millman, J., & Darling-Hammond, L. (Eds.). (1990). *The new handbook of teacher evaluation: assessing elementary and secondary school teachers.* Newbury Park, CA: Sage Publications.

Monk, D. H., & Haller, E. J. (1993). Predictors of high school academic course offerings: The role of school size. *American Educational Research Journal, 30*(1), 3–21.

Murphy, J., & Louis, K. S. (Eds.). (1999). *Handbook of research on educational administration* (2nd ed.). San Francisco: Jossey-Bass Publishers.

Nagel, E. (1961). *The structure of science: Problems in the logic of scientific explanation.* New York: Harcourt Brace & World.

Phillips, M. (1997). What makes schools effective? A comparison of the relationships of communitarian climate and academic climate to mathematics achievement and attendance during middle school. *American Educational Research Journal, 34*(4), 633–662.

Weber, M. (1947). *The theory of social and economic organization* (A. M. Henderson & T. Parsons, Trans.). New York: Free Press.

Wittrock, M. C. (Ed.). (1986). *Handbook of research on teaching.* New York: Macmillan.

CHAPTER **4**

Evaluating Research

INTRODUCTION

Each of the authors lays claim to a life outside of academia and pursues hobbies rather seriously. In the one case (Haller), fly fishing with all of its intricacies and frustrations serves as needed respite from faculty meetings and bureaucratic jousts. In the other case (Kleine), woodworking and stained glass hobbies provide needed diversion from the steady pressures of students, data, and bureaucratic bouts.

Years of pursuing these hobbies have provided a modest corpus of knowledge and skills that often remain unarticulated but nonetheless shape how we view examples of our crafts. Knowing where problems are likely to occur guides the eye to trouble spots and focuses the energy and effort in the area of greatest difficulty. Instead of randomly scanning a completed piece of stained glass or a prodigious fly cast, several subcomponents of the finished product or process are examined in detail and the routine segments ignored or given scant notice. Knowing where to look and, conversely, knowing what one can safely ignore, is the mark of the experienced practitioner of any craft or profession.

In the world of work, the notion of expertise providing practitioners with a set of criteria to guide them in making quality judgments should be relatively familiar. Picture the scene in northern California the morning after an earthquake.

Engineers examine the collapsed bridges and compare notes on what they have observed. It is safe to say that they will see things differently from what you and I might notice. With their eyes trained by years of attention to bridge designs, they may see fewer things than we do but what they do attend to will be examined in detail. Their eyes will be focused on the relatively few parts of the structure that their experience and training have told them to be points of vulnerability. While they and their colleagues might not agree on all the specific points, there will be reasonable agreement on which components of the bridge failed and why the structure collapsed. In contrast, our untrained eyes might scan the entire bridge, be impressed with the amount of the destruction, and miss the focal points that occupy the engineers. Ironically, we may see much more and understand much less.

What gives the engineers the edge in the ability to critique bridge designs? Put simply, the experts know where to look. They have studied bridge construction and have observed numerous examples of designs and their relative ability to withstand the stress of time and the impact of disasters. They know that each bridge design provides excellent solutions to some stress problems but leaves the structure vulnerable to others. The design chosen may have represented the best overall solution to the greatest number of threats to its stability, but given the constraints of cost, time, and the state of the science, however, weaknesses remain and good engineers know it.

The bridge engineer example is a useful metaphor for our development of this chapter. Like bridges, research designs represent compromises with reality: The reality of cost, time, ethical constraints, limited ingenuity, and the limitations of our knowledge. Each design solves some problems very well but leaves other threats relatively untouched.

As an educational administrator, you are required to make policy decisions that are based upon, among other things, a sound research base. A well-informed practitioner develops the expertise to differentiate among research studies so as to allow reasoned inferences regarding the trustworthiness of their findings. This chapter lays out the basic tools required to develop this expertise.

Several points undergird this chapter and can be stated quite straightforwardly. First, the quality of research varies widely, and the appearance in print of promising findings is no assurance of their validity. Second, it is essential that the educational administrator be able to make judgments regarding the quality and applicability of research. You are responsible for helping develop educational policy based in part upon research, and this responsibility cannot be avoided. Third, there is a set of concepts, skills, and criteria available by which research quality can be assessed, and these are within the reach of educational practitioners. This chapter introduces this set of concepts, skills, and criteria.

This chapter will briefly illuminate five important concepts for you to use when examining a piece of research. The remainder of the text will be required to explicate and apply the five concepts. The major concepts discussed in this chapter are: (1) the rationale on which a study is based and the argument supporting its conclusions; (2) questions of validity and reliability of measurement;

(3) research design and threats to internal validity; (4) sampling and threats to external validity; and (5) the issues of statistical and practical significance.

Study Rationale

Various terms have been used to describe the rationale of a study, and they are considered interchangeable by most researchers. Such terms include theoretical rationale, conceptual framework, and theory base, among others, but the underlying meaning remains relatively unchanged. At heart is the quality of logic on which a study is based and the quality of the argument supporting its conclusions. Contrary to an oft-heard expression, facts do not speak for themselves; good researchers do not mindlessly collect data, nor do they frame questions based on whimsy. A well-crafted study begins with a clearly stated research problem, which may be derived from gaps in the existing literature or may be a nagging, unsolved problem derived from practice.

The study rationale provides a linkage among the variables in a study and provides an explanation for their expected relationships. The explanation may draw on established theorists in the field, or it may be provided by the researcher, but in either case the reader should understand not only what is expected in the study but why it is expected.

Consider the following hypothesis: "There is a direct relationship between the amount of time spent on homework and school achievement." While the statement appears relatively straightforward regarding what is to be expected, a good study rationale would go further and provide a theoretical reasoning system that would explain why this increased achievement might occur. One rather obvious explanation might be that the increased practice in mathematics provided by the homework would increase the skill level of students, which in turn would be manifested in higher achievement test scores.

There are alternative explanations, and a good study rationale explores them. In addition to increased practice, systematic homework requirements might increase student-parent interactions centered on school work, thereby increasing student motivation. Still further, student-parent interactions might have their primary effect because parents serve as surrogate teachers during homework sessions. Each of these factors might contribute to increased school achievement as well as the simple practice effect of the first explanation.

By examining various possible rationales, a clearer and better defined study can result. For example, if the rationale for the "homework causes achievement" study is that parental teaching is the major cause for homework's positive influence, then provisions for controlling the possible confounding effects of increased practice and higher motivation can be included in the study's design. Finally, a cogent rationale is critically important in correlational studies, for it is the only basis on which we can make defensible causal inferences. We will have more to say about this topic in a moment.

A good rationale provides an explanation of the findings of the study. In this way, the research consumer is able to examine the logical steps embedded within the argument and to make an informed judgment regarding the tests of those steps. A clear study rationale also provides the reader with important information regarding why the results occurred or, equally importantly, why they did not occur. Understanding the logic of a study also provides useful information to the consumer of research regarding the limitations of applying research findings.

Measurement

It has been stated that research is fueled by theory but moves on the wheels of measurement. If this is correct, then it is appropriate to carefully examine the role that measurement plays in the conduct of research. In quantitative inquiry, the identification of variables must be followed by a careful definition and precise measurement. Two measurement concepts that require elaboration are validity and reliability.

Validity

Traditionally, most research textbooks have described validity as representing distinctly different types. A common list would include content, concurrent, predictive, and construct validities. More recently, researchers (e.g., Wiersma, 1991) have discussed validity as a unitary concept and referred to different sources of evidence for validity. This conceptual shift represents a different way of thinking about validity, but it does not affect the way in which the different sources or different types of validity are defined or calculated.

The unitary view of validity appears more straightforward and, following Wiersma's lead, we will refer to content-related evidence, concurrent-related evidence, predictive-related evidence, and construct-related evidence. We will discuss these four types of validity evidence as they apply to a measure of math anxiety, but remember that you should consider validity as an issue whenever any measurement is made, no matter how simple it may appear.

Content-Related Evidence. In our example of measuring math anxiety an obvious question could be raised: How do you know that your test is measuring math anxiety rather than, say, problem solving or computational math skills? Our first type evidence is the result of a logical analysis of test items to determine how well they represent a particular domain. A panel of three math anxiety researchers could be asked to indicate how well each item measures the domain of math anxiety. Those items that all three researchers agree are good indicators of math anxiety are retained while those that are judged to be deficient are deleted. This is a simple but useful test of providing content-related evidence of test validity.

Concurrent-Related Evidence. A different approach could be taken to answer the question of validity. Perhaps other researchers have spent time developing a test of math anxiety and have reported its use in the literature. It would be reasonable to ask if your measure of anxiety correlates with another measure of math anxiety concurrently being used. If it does correlate highly, at least you could claim to be measuring whatever it is the other test is measuring. The Wechsler Intelligence Scale for Children (WISC) was developed decades ago, and one of the first questions asked of its developer was to determine the extent to which it correlated with the existing Stanford-Binet test of intelligence.

Notice the dilemma facing the test developer in assessing concurrent validity. If the measure does not correlate with an existing measure, then the validity of the new test is brought into question. If it correlates too highly with an existing measure, then a question arises as to the need for the second measure. Also, the pursuit of concurrent validity makes it difficult to develop a measure that is markedly better than the existing ones.

Predictive-Related Evidence. In addition to the previous efforts, one could also reason that the validity of a measure could be assessed by its ability to predict future performance in related areas, such as whether the math anxiety score predicts future performance in university course work in math and in areas heavily dependent on math such as engineering. If students who are math anxious also fare poorly in future math and engineering courses this would be consistent with our predictions. The extent to which the math anxiety scale correlates with future performance would be considered predictive-related evidence.

Construct-Related Evidence. Construct validity represents a more complex approach to evidence of validity and is not represented by a single step or by a correlation as with concurrent or predictive evidence. Construct-related evidence is an approach that first teases out the theoretical underpinnings of the concept being measured and then explores how they might be related to other concepts. Construct validity approaches begin with a careful conceptual definition of the variable being measured and then a determination of how this definition differs from other similar concepts. Once we better understand the conceptual components of math anxiety, we can predict how it will correlate with certain variables and/or how it might be independent from others.

Illustratively, math anxiety will likely be higher among individuals who have previously failed math courses and/or have scored low on math achievement tests. On the other hand, there is no theoretical reason why math anxiety scores should correlate positively with writing skills or with general intelligence test scores. By examining the correlations with these variables and with a host of others that you might suggest, we can piece together a picture of the construct validity of our measure. If our measure consistently correlates with those variables that are conceptually linked to anxiety and if our measure consistently is not related to other variables that are not linked theoretically with anxiety, then our confidence in the measure increases accordingly. We cannot state with any degree of precision what the construct validity of a measure might be. The best

TABLE *4.1*

Types of Evidence and Their Characteristics Used in Establishing Validity

Type	How Analyzed	Example of Use
Content	Logical analysis of item content	A test of computational skills in fifth-grade arithmetic
Concurrent	Empirical analysis establishing the relationship between scores on the test and those on another measure obtained at the same time	Validation of a short history test against a long, standardized history exam known to be a valid measure of history achievement
Predictive	Empirical analysis establishing the relationship between scores on the test and those on another measure obtained at a later time	A comparison of high school seniors' SAT scores with their college GPA
Construct	Logical and empirical analysis	Analysis of a measure of anxiety to determine whether it relates to the underlying theoretical components of anxiety

we can do is summarize the state of our knowledge with regard to a measure's construct validity that emerges from the literature.

Each type of evidence, the analysis used, and an example of its use is provided in Table 4.1, which has been modified slightly from Wiersma (1991, p. 179).

In summary, each of the approaches to validity provides us with an estimate of the degree to which we can have confidence in our measures. Regardless of the care and concern with which we design our studies, no matter how carefully we select and describe our samples, in spite of how appropriately we select and implement appropriate statistical procedures, our efforts will be for naught if our concepts are measured with faulty instruments. We truly do move on the wheels of measurement.

Reliability

Reliability represents a relatively straightforward concept and does not stray far from its everyday meaning. A reliable measure is one that can be trusted to yield similar results when used a second time in similar circumstances. A reliable weight scale is one that gives consistent results as we step on, step off, and step on again. A reliable measure of math achievement should yield results that do not vary widely when administered at reasonable time intervals. Reliability coefficients are expressed in values from 0 to 1.0 with 1.0 representing a measure that is perfectly reliable.

Test-Retest Reliabilities. Just as different techniques have arisen to assess validity of a measure, there are also various ways to assess reliability. The simplest and most direct way is to administer the same test to the same group at a later date and to correlate the results. This technique is called, reasonably enough, test-retest, and a reliability may be expressed as a correlation coefficient (r). Thus, achievement test batteries will often display their reliabilities as $r =$. 91 or $r = .88$, indicating substantial agreement between the two administrations of the test. A question frequently arises regarding the optimum time that should elapse between the administration of the two tests. Conventional wisdom suggests a two-week interval, since this time period does not allow for subjects to be unduly influenced by the first administration of the test and also the subjects' knowledge may not have changed greatly in this rather short span of time.

Split-Half and Parallel Forms Reliability. Variations in technique have arisen to assess reliability in the event that a second administration of the test is not feasible. One such method examines the internal consistency of the test based on the argument that if the test does not yield consistency within itself, then it cannot be consistent across time. One technique used to estimate split-half reliability calls for the correlation of all the odd-numbered items with all the even-numbered items. This result is expressed in a correlation coefficient and is interpreted in the same way as the test-retest reliability coefficient. One often sees internal consistency reliabilities reported as "Kuder-Richardson" (or simply "K-R") coefficients or as "Cronbach's Alpha" (or simply "alpha").

It is a simple extension of split-half reliability logic to create parallel forms of a test by building matched sets of items and packaging them in permanent forms of the same test. Companies that produce norm referenced tests used to measure school achievement will provide alternate forms of their tests and will publish coefficients indicating the parallel forms' reliabilities as well as reliabilities derived from test-retest and split-half procedures.

Research Designs

Blue prints and architectural drawings for a home or business may be quite complex and confusing to the lay person although the purpose behind them is readily understood. Without a plan, building any project is an open invitation to disaster, even for a skilled builder. A plan allows one to think through the processes involved in advance and to make changes before the process becomes irreversible, impractical, or dangerous. Anticipating a second floor of a home may be information that the builder would like to have *before* the roof is constructed.

Similarly, while research designs may become quite complex and mastery of these intricacies does require a fair amount of sophistication, the underlying purpose of research designs is quite simple. A research design enables the collection of data in a manner that allows research questions to be answered, while minimizing the possibility of making erroneous interpretations of those data— and hence arriving at mistaken answers to those questions.

In addition, a research design gives the research consumer a clear description or set of specifics that were followed, enabling the reader to judge the quality of the research. By understanding the strengths and limitations of various designs, a research consumer may recognize problems with a design and not be swept away with the rhetoric of the researcher in drawing conclusions and recommendations. To return to the building analogy, a working knowledge of housing blueprints helps protect the buyer against the realtor's glowing descriptions of model homes. A design that calls for 2 × 4 rafters set 24 inches apart does not match the description of "solid construction throughout" offered in the Sunday newspaper supplement. Caveat emptor is a time-honored caution that carries over when one is "buying" research also.

Consider the following example to illustrate the need for an adequate research design. In your school a rather expensive program will be implemented. The program will allow eighth-grade students to access the Internet as a supplement to their science curriculum. Two science teachers have trained for the past three years by attending conferences, visiting university lab facilities, reading extensively, and working together on ideas for integrating the power of the computer into their classroom teaching. While the board of education was reluctant to pursue this on a broad scale, they did provide enough funds for the required technology and additional training for the two teachers involved. Additionally, they reduced the teaching loads of the two teachers by one class each and limited the size of their remaining classes to a maximum of 24 students, because each computer classroom was limited to 24 computer stations with access to the Internet.

The board requested a complete report at the end of the academic year regarding the relative effectiveness of the program. The two teachers are excited about the possibilities and the three of you are discussing ways to design a study that will assess the program's effectiveness. With a whole month before school is scheduled to begin, it should be relatively easy to plan for ways to collect data before and after the project. Perhaps a pretest given to the students in the pilot program as well as to all the remaining eighth-grade students could be compared with a posttest also given to both groups after the program has been completed. This might determine what differences, if any, could be attributed to the treatment. Also, one of the science teachers suggested that a pre and posttest of attitudes toward science should be given, because attitudes might be just as important a variable as student achievement. One teacher accepted the task of finding or developing a measure of student achievement and the other went in search of a valid and reliable measure of attitudes toward science that might be used or adapted for use with eighth-grade students. Your task was to pursue the support and approval of the other science teachers to help collect data from their classrooms. Data from students in the experimental program will be compared to equivalent data collected in these control classes.

Without benefit of all the concepts that are yet to be introduced, let us take a brief look at the design of this study and identify some of its inherent problems. Let us assume that after a full year there are large differences both in achievement and increased positive attitudes between the treatment and control groups. These differences strike you as very important and, on the face of it, appear to provide convincing evidence regarding the effectiveness of the program.

Before you present your results to the board and request additional funds to extend the program districtwide, you may wish to check on a few matters. Might these results have been due to one or more factors that you had not considered in your design? Are there other possible explanations for the differences you found that may have nothing to do with computer access to the Internet?

Let's look at your design. First, you had two teachers who have devoted three years to acquiring computer skills and applications to teaching science; this suggests they are highly motivated, competent, and current in their thinking. Attitude and achievement data from students in these two teachers' classrooms were then contrasted with students taught by the rest of the faculty who, though quite able, were unwilling to pursue this option with the vigor and excitement of the two project teachers. Quite possibly students in these two energetic and enthusiastic teachers' classrooms might have fared well without the Internet access.

Second, the board gave released time to each of the pilot teachers and reduced their class size to a maximum of 24 students. While hard to assess, it is reasonable to infer that this reduction in teaching time and student load might be a contributing factor to those healthy between-group differences.

Third, the two project teachers selected and modified the measures of achievement and student attitudes used in the study. To what extent were these tests slanted in favor of the treatment group? Whether intentional or not, it would be easy to imagine that items would be selected that would be particularly appropriate for measuring concepts likely to be acquired while surfing the Net.

A fourth possible problem could be cited. The excitement generated in the school by the selection of some classes but not others to be involved in a highly publicized venture involving computers might set motivational variables in play favoring the treatment group. From the opposite perspective, it is possible that not being included in an interesting venture could work to decrease the attitudes and achievement of control group students.

While the brief litany of problems listed is by no means exhaustive, it should underscore the importance of a good research design. An excellent design will reduce the number of competing interpretations to an absolute minimum. Ideally, in the example discussed, a study would have been designed that would leave very little doubt as to the reasons why the students in the treatment group achieved at a much higher level than the control group. We trust that you would share our conclusion that the study described fell far short of achieving that degree of confidence in the explanation. With mastery of the material in the following section, you will be able to recognize the design in use and be able to use this knowledge as you examine the strength and deficiencies of a research study.

Before we launch into the designs themselves, there are several assumptions about research designs that we should share at the onset.

Assumption 1. All Research Designs Are Flawed

Each design used represents a compromise between and among a host of factors including time, cost, effort, ethical constraints, access to data, and creativity of the researcher. With every building ever built or every product ever produced, numerous decisions were made that affected quality, and these decisions were hard choices forced upon the designers by the conflicting demands of these same forces. The implication of this assumption is to learn to recognize the inevitable flaws, determine their likely impact on the results, and determine if, in your setting, these flaws are fatal or merely cautionary.

Assumption 2. All Research Designs Are Useful

As the counterbalance to the first assumption, it is important to recognize that, for some problems, for some circumstances, *every* design has the capability of providing some useful information. Rather than asking, "Is this a good design?" a more fruitful framing might be to ask, "Is this the best design to enable the researcher to get data that will answer her or his question?" It should be clear that the match of design and research problem is of paramount importance.

Assumption 3. Research on Educational Problems Is Difficult

Educational research is frequently lampooned for its poor designs, flawed procedures and inadequate statistical techniques; frequently, the attacks are completely deserved. For a long list of both good and poor reasons, there are far more extant examples of shoddy workmanship than either of us would like to defend.

In spite of a fair amount of deserved criticism, it has frequently struck us that research in the so-called "hard" sciences has been given a "soft" ride. Research in the social sciences and in education faces problems that go well beyond those facing researchers in other disciplines. In addition to all the human frailties mentioned previously, the difficulties inherent in understanding the complexities of problems in education are frequently understated. As a simple example, consider the following comparison. If a doctor diagnoses a medical problem, a simple prescription of antibiotics might be given and the case is on the way toward resolution. The doctor assumes the patient will buy the prescription and take the medicine. In other words, the motivation of the patient is rarely a factor for the physician. It should be pretty obvious that the parallel problem is far more difficult for the educator. After diagnosing the problem of math deficiencies, it may be clear that students would benefit from a prescription of two weeks of specific drill and exercises to overcome this deficiency. May we safely assume all students will follow the prescription?

One implication follows from this assumption. Given the difficulties inherent in the task, even well-designed single studies should be viewed cautiously, and greater attention must be given to the accumulated research over an extended period.

A Quest for Causality

One might construe the researcher's efforts as a "quest for causality" in that an attempt is made to link factors in such a way that we better understand cause-effect relationships. Knowing that certain teaching methods appear to be associated with increased learning may be interesting, but knowing that a particular teaching strategy will *cause* an increment in achievement gives us a basis for action. While some study designs do not enable the researcher to draw causal inferences for reasons to be made clear later, one important outcome for research is to identify potential causal factors that contribute to improved administrative procedures that in turn may lead to improved student learning. Let us examine two broad categories of research designs that researchers use to pursue this quest for causality—qualitative and quantitative research.

Qualitative Research

The first step on the causal inference journey might begin with qualitative designs that enable the researcher to describe phenomena as carefully as possible. These careful descriptions may be useful in their own right or they may lead to other designs that further the researchers' purposes. While not limited to description alone, qualitative inquiry may include a wide range of approaches drawn from various disciplines within the social sciences. These approaches include case studies, participant observation, field studies, naturalistic inquiry, and ethnographic studies.

We offer the following definition derived from Denzin and Lincoln (1994) of the very dynamic entity known as qualitative inquiry: Qualitative research involves the studied use and collection of a variety of empirical materials—case studies, personal experiences, introspective accounts, life stories, interviews, observations, histories, and visual texts.

The underlying rationales and the wide variety of methods of qualitative research will be examined more fully in Chapter 7. This chapter will address only its strengths and weaknesses and offer several criteria for assessing its quality.

Strengths. Qualitative research studies can make an excellent contribution to our understanding of complex educational phenomena in several ways. First, a rich description of the context and setting in which the study occurs can be provided. Second, qualitative research provides a window to examine phenomena from the perspective of the individual who is living the experience. Third, the problem can be studied holistically rather than fragmented into its various components. Finally, the variables of most interest to researchers may not lend themselves well to quantitative measurement. Quantitative measures may have captured some of the meaning but much of the richness and complexity may have been lost.

Consider the example of studying teacher morale. Two teachers in neighboring schools may each feel that teacher morale is very high in her school.

Each enjoys coming to work, each values her colleagues, and each finds a high degree of professionalism in the building.

In spite of the apparent agreement we do not know how each defines "teacher morale." In the first case, the teacher may value the warmth, personal support, and concern for her and her family as the major ingredients of the concept and apparently finds those qualities in abundance in her school. In the second case, the teacher might resent the highly personalized involvement of her peers into what she considers her private sphere and may prefer the more formal, task-oriented, and work-related environment in which she is employed.

Qualitative researchers would argue that understanding the concept of teacher morale holistically, from the participant's perspective, and in its natural context, is of utmost importance before we proceed to aggregate responses across a variety of subjects. This example is not intended to negate the contribution that quantitative research can make to the study of teacher morale but, rather, to highlight what qualitative research can add to the process.

Limitations. The inverse of each research design's strengths is a convenient way to spot the weaknesses. For example, consider the three strengths mentioned previously. The full and rich description of individual cases makes it impossible to study phenomena across a wide range of settings. The personal perspective of the individual being studied adds dimension, but it does not offer the measured and perhaps less biased point of view of the outsider. Finally, examining cases holistically does not offer an opportunity to analyze the component parts in great detail.

Evaluation Criteria. While researchers continue to grapple with providing better ways to evaluate qualitative studies (Altheide & Johnson, 1994), there are several clues that can help you as you read and evaluate them. First, are the assumptions and biases of the researcher made explicit? Given the very sensitive interaction of the researcher and the researched, the study must provide you with a clear statement of the perspective from which the research was undertaken. Peshkin in his study of a Baptist school (Peshkin, 1986) and also in his study of a quad-racial high school (Peshkin, 1991) carefully outlined his views and values, which influenced his choice of sites studied and, even more importantly, his research findings and conclusions.

A second evaluative criterion is the degree to which the researcher provides a full and complete account of how the study was undertaken. At a minimum you should expect to see a good description of the subjects, the setting, the amount and type of data collected, and enough information on how the data were analyzed to allow you to have confidence in the results. Sometimes referred to as an "audit trail," the careful qualitative researcher should provide examples of interview questions, observation schedules, evidence regarding the amount of time spent on data collection, any uses of multiple sources of data, and examples of how data were processed and analyzed to determine the findings of the study.

A third criterion is the degree to which the researcher provides clear conceptual descriptions of the inferences drawn. If the researcher indicated that three themes emerged from the data, are those themes described in such a way that you clearly understand them? Are you able to see how each theme differs from the other two, and are you able to see applications of those themes to other settings?

A fourth criterion concerns whether the research study has provided sufficient data to underpin the inferences, categories, or themes described in the study. A well-executed qualitative study will not only give a clear understanding of what those categories mean but also will provide clear descriptions and examples of the data on which they were based.

One way in which qualitative researchers anchor their concepts in data is to provide excerpts from interviews or observations to buttress inferences they have drawn. As the following example shows, they can often do so with little need of further elaboration. Peshkin (1986) was examining the various ways in which teachers and administrators provided an environment for children in the Baptist school that would be safe from what they perceived to be unwholesome influences of the secular community. As he was exploring the nature of censorship of curriculum materials, one teacher provided him with the following examples of what she did with materials that she found to be offensive.

> I look for evolution. That's one of the things. I look for swear words. We take those out. I found a double page of monkeys developing into man and, of course, we don't approve of that at all, so I just sealed the pages together and it didn't bother the reading on either side. Then, in the beginning, there was a section on evolution. I bracketed that in black letters and wrote EVOLUTION across it so that anybody reading knows that it is evolution, rather than destroying the whole book, because a lot of it was good. If I find a naked person, I draw a little bathing suit on them or I put a little dress on, but just in a regular book that doesn't have anything to do with art. But in art, art is art, and if you find a person without any clothes on, that's what they drew. We had one storybook where the kids were all bathing in the nude. It was not anything, so I just put bathing suits on them. (Peshkin, 1986, pp. 262–263)

A fifth and final criterion for evaluating qualitative research is, consistent with the process itself, rather global in nature. Stated most simply, did the research provide you with a fresh, provocative perspective with which to think about the issues under investigation? Since one of the stated purposes of qualitative research is to illuminate hidden and complex processes, did the research provide a better understanding than you brought to the study, and does this understanding lead to further research questions and/or to better informed practice?

Quantitative Designs

Quantitative designs make up the second broad category of research designs. These designs can be categorized into three groups: (1) descriptive, (2) relational, and (3) experimental.

Descriptive research is used to provide clear and complete descriptions of individuals, events, or processes. An example of descriptive research would be an assessment of the characteristics of beginning teachers who leave teaching after one year. *Relational* research designs explore relationships between and among variables and include both causal-comparative and correlational designs. An example of the former would be a study of possible differences between males and females in math achievement scores. An example of a correlational study would be an examination of the relationship between the amount of time spent in school athletics and grade point averages of middle school students. The final category, *experimental* research, involves the manipulation of one or more variables and determining the effect of this manipulation on another set of variables. An experimental study might examine the effects of one hour of homework, 30 minutes of homework, or no homework on math and reading achievement scores.

We will examine each of these groups in order and will suggest clues to help you critique examples of these designs in future chapters. Consistent with the engineering metaphor offered earlier in this chapter, we would encourage you to look first at each design and be reminded of the points of vulnerability that are inherent in it. Just as certain bridge designs fall prey to particular stress points and weak welds, so it is with research. We will be explicit about where those points of vulnerability are in each design.

Survey Research. Survey research is a specific kind of descriptive research that ". . . involves collecting information about research participants' beliefs, attitudes, interests, or behavior through questionnaires, interviews, or paper-and-pencil tests" (Gall, Gall, & Borg, 1999). Numerous examples of survey research, both good and bad, surround us in everyday life. Opinion polls, voter preference polls, and marketing surveys are but a few of the thousands of surveys that are done each year.

Each research design may be examined as to points of vulnerability, and survey research has two places at which a particular study might be at risk. The first point is pretty obvious; good surveys contain good questions. A careful examination of each item in a questionnaire frequently reveals evidence of bias and/or a lack of clarity in the question. Even with the best of intentions, it is extremely difficult to write clear, unambiguous and unbiased items, particularly when measuring attitudes regarding a controversial topic. Consider the difficulties inherent in writing one clear item that measures peoples' attitudes regarding abortion. Each person in the country from the strongest pro-life advocate to the strongest supporter of abortion rights should be able to express his or her opinion on the item. The choice of the term "fetus" or "unborn child" in the stem could have a profound influence on responses to that item.

A second rather obvious point about surveys is that questions are frequently asked of a sample of people. Which people are sampled, how representative they are, and the influence of nonresponses, are questions of obvious importance. The 1–900 numbers that are posted on the nighttime news broadcast soliciting peoples' opinions on newsworthy issues of the moment are examples of the flaw that results from nonrepresentational samples. Persons who will spend 90 cents per minute to call the station regarding their opinions on the outcomes of the controversial issues of the day are probably not representative of a cross section of Americans.

In examining the quality of a survey study, the two points of *question quality* and *sample representativeness* are issues of great importance. We will discuss the latter in more detail when we discuss external validity later in this chapter.

Correlational Designs. Correlational research designs are used to investigate the relationship between two or more variables by examining the extent to which they co-vary. On the basis of a finding that two variables co-vary, researchers and others may argue that variation in one causes variation in the second. Here are a few examples of correlations to provide you with a clearer understanding of the concept.

1. Students with good attendance tend to score well on achievement tests. Stated as a correlation, we say that there is a positive relationship between student attendance and school achievement. We could check whether this proposed relationship holds by looking at a group of 100 students drawn from the fifth grade rosters in your district to see if, in fact, students who have high attendance rates also tend to have high achievement test scores. Conversely, do those students who have poor attendance tend to score lower on the achievement test?
2. Older teachers tend to miss more days of school due to illness than younger teachers, or, stated as a correlation, we say that there is a relationship between teachers' age and teachers' absenteeism. This proposed relationship could be tested by considering the age of each teacher and comparing it with the number of days each was absent over the course of a year. If older teachers were, in fact, absent more than younger teachers, it would indicate that teacher age and teacher absenteeism were correlated.

There exists a relatively simple technique that not only indicates that two variables are correlated but also indicates the strength of their relationship. The strength of a correlation is expressed on a scale which runs from 0 (indicating the two variables are completely independent) to 1.0 (indicating a perfect relationship between the two). In this way we can compare the strength of a relationship such as IQ and achievement ($r = .5$) with the strength of the relationship between SES and achievement ($r = .25$). These hypothetical correlations would tell us that the IQ-achievement relationship is much stronger than the SES-achievement relationship.

In addition to the magnitude of the correlation there is one more bit of information we need to understand before we can proceed with a discussion of design. Correlations can be either positive or negative in direction. In each of the two examples given in the preceding paragraphs the correlations were assumed to be positive in that high scores on one variable were associated with high scores on the other. For example, higher SES scores were related to higher achievement test scores. However, we could list numerous examples in which negative correlations would occur, that is, high scores on one variable would go with low scores on the other. For example, The University of Oklahoma faculty evaluation form asks students to rate their professors from 1–5 on a set of items assessing knowledge, attitudes, and classroom behavior. One is considered the high end of the scale while 5 represents the lowest score possible. It should be easy to see that if you correlated teacher evaluation scores with merit salary increases the correlations would be negative in direction. Those professors with the lower scores (i.e., better evaluations) would tend to get the higher merit allocations at salary time. Similarly, exercise and cardiovascular disease are negatively related: Those who exercise regularly tend to have fewer heart attacks. With the two dimensions of *magnitude* and *direction* clearly in mind we can proceed to think about problems and potential in the correlational designs.

Numerous opportunities exist to use correlational designs because of the ready availability of data sources that lend themselves to this purpose. Any time we have scores on at least two variables for a single group of people we can correlate those two variables and determine the strength and direction of their relationship. Further, while the examples we have chosen involve people, correlations can be computed using other entities. One might correlate school district wealth with a measure of curricular diversity: Do high schools in wealthy districts tend to offer more courses than those in poor districts? If so, how strong is that relationship? The ease and availability of correlational data are obvious advantages of the design, and we can learn a great deal from such studies.

Some examples of uses of correlational data include predictive studies of college success and vocational aptitude measures that predict both success and satisfaction with various jobs and careers. Additionally, correlational data help researchers identify variables that might be examined using other research designs to help further the quest for causal relationships.

There is a tendency even among the most cautious of us to infer causal relationships when correlations are found to exist, but these inferences are often incorrect. A strong correlation is just that: An indication that two variables were found to co-vary. The research consumer should carry a mental bumper-sticker that reads "Correlation does not prove causality."

Why is a strong correlation not proof of a cause-effect relationship? One explanation is that there may be (and often is) a third variable that may actually cause both of the variables in the study. Think back to the earlier example that posited a correlation between school attendance and school achievement. While it is tempting to think that students who attend school regularly might actually learn more than students who do not attend as regularly, there are several other reasons that might account for the correlation between attendance and achievement. It is possible that the kind of parents who take the time and effort to be sure that their children get to school regularly might also be the kind of parents who set high standards, help children with homework, and, in general, foster high achievement in the home. In other words, the causal inference based on the existence of even a very high correlation might be completely unfounded. Good attendance may not cause high achievement; parental behavior may cause both.

Our point about correlation and causation is not obscure academic carping—it has very significant practical import. When administrators fail to understand it (and they often do), they can waste large amounts of peoples' time and money and contribute to education's reputation for faddishness. For example, suppose an administrator is convinced that attendance has a powerful effect on achievement, despite the ambiguity of the correlational evidence. He or she might implement a costly program to increase the attendance of low-achieving youngsters in the hopes of improving their achievement, only to find that their achievement goes unchanged.

Another possibility is that the cause-effect relationship might be opposite of what is implied. Consider the following example drawn from educational research of several decades ago. Flanders (1970) developed a coding scheme that could be used to rate teachers from 1–7 on the basis of their degree of Indirect to Direct behaviors used in the classroom. Teacher silence and student initiated questions were considered evidence of an Indirect teaching style, while lecturing, coercive, and reprimanding behaviors were evidence of a Direct style. Over a period of several days teachers could be reliably coded on this scale and the ratio of their Indirect to Direct teaching behavior (the I-D Ratio) could be calculated.

With these numbers in hand it was a short step to determine the correlation between the I-D ratio and average student achievement in a sample of classrooms. A modest but consistent correlation was found, indicating that teachers with more Indirect styles were found in classrooms of higher achieving students. Few educators could resist the urge to draw a causal inference; teachers were taught to lower their I-D ratios and to develop a more indirect teaching style, so as to increase achievement when, in fact, no good evidence existed for this causal inference. Why not? Think about it for a moment. In high-achieving classrooms, children are motivated, ask questions, initiate activities, and work cooperatively; in this setting teachers may respond in a more indirect fashion. In low-achieving classrooms, the behaviors of children may lead to an increase in the amount of controlling or coercive behaviors found at the Direct end of the Flanders' continuum. Thus, one might make a good case that the behavior of children causes teachers' behavior rather than the reverse. In any event, a quick move to action based on correlational studies alone is usually a serious mistake.

This weakness in correlational designs creates a dilemma for researchers and practitioners alike. Ultimately, our best hope of preventing problems in education is to know what causes them. Indeed, a fundamental purpose for research in all scientific disciplines is to discover causes. Just as discovering the cause of smallpox and diphtheria led to the invention of vaccines that eradicated those scourges, so discovering the cause (or causes) of an educational problem gives the best hope for eradicating it. However, the only research design that permits us to be reasonably sure that we have found the cause of some phenomenon is an experiment. And for many educational problems experiments are impossible to perform, or they are ethically unacceptable. (In a moment we will discuss the nature of an experiment, and you will see why this is the case.) Thus, correlational studies (or the next design we discuss, causal-comparative) are the best we can do. But we can never prove causality with those kinds of studies. Thus, the research design we must rely on most often is incapable of unambiguously telling us what we most want to know. What, then, are practitioners to do?

Earlier in our discussion of a rationale, we alluded to this issue. When reading correlational research practitioners must pay close attention to the rationale that researchers offer. Recall that a study's rationale is the reason researchers advance for claiming that their independent variables are the causes of their dependent variables. In correlational and causal comparative studies the soundness of those reasons are ultimately our *only* basis for correctly inferring a causal relationship. When we have a good number of correlational studies, all with the same results, and all with logically sound rationales that variable A causes variable B, then we may make a reasonable inference that A does, in fact, cause B. At that point we may defensibly implement programs that embody A in the hope that we will be able to affect B. And at that point we will have made a leap of faith.

Causal-Comparative Designs

In the correlational design described previously, variables were examined to determine the extent to which they co-vary. A causal-comparative design is used to compare groups that differ on some characteristic to determine if this difference might be related to important variables of interest. As the name suggests, groups are *compared* to see if *causal* inferences might be drawn.

Examples abound both in the empirical literature and in the everyday assessment of our surroundings. Gender studies that examine differences in math achievement, studies that compare smokers and nonsmokers on incidences of lung cancer, and studies that compare achievement in public, private, and parochial schools are all examples of causal-comparative studies.

Intuitively this design appears very attractive, but caution is required. We see differences in our surroundings and we ask, "Why?" The reason for caution is that causal inference may be as problematic with causal-comparative designs as with correlational ones, though that is often less obvious. For example, if a researcher compared the math achievement of brothers and sisters and found the former performed better, it might be very tempting to attribute those differences to genetic differences based on sex. What else could it be? Students were raised in the same home environment, attended the same schools, and had the same teachers, textbooks, and classes. But sorting out the complex environmental influences from parental expectations, media portrayals, textbook illustrations, and teacher and peer expectations is difficult enough to occupy researchers in this area for a lifetime. Serious problems are caused in policy arenas because of our collective inability to prevent drawing simplistic inferences from the thousands of sex, race, and social class causal-comparative studies that are shared daily in the research journals as well as in the popular press.

Data from correlational and causal-comparative designs provide us with useful pointers for other research that might enable us to legitimately draw causal inferences. They represent rudimentary clues as to possible causes of complex behavior, and one should not fault the design for doing what it was intended to do. The fault lies, Pogo-like, with us as we overreach and overextend findings beyond what they were designed to tell us.

Experimental Research Designs

Moving up the ladder on the quest for causality, there are two designs that bear the term "experimental" although, strictly speaking, only one is deserving of the name. A true experimental design has two components that give it a great deal of power in laying claim to establishing cause-effect relationships. One component is the requirement that an experiment must have a treatment that is imposed on one set of subjects (the *experimental* or *treatment group*), while it is withheld from a second set of subjects (the *control group*). The second requirement is that subjects must be randomly assigned to the treatment and control conditions. When these two criteria are in place, the researcher's ability to lay claim to cause-effect relationships is vastly increased. This claim will be better understood in our discussion of threats to internal validity that follows this section.

In addition to the true experimental design described here, there is a variation on this theme that occurs frequently in the literature. Termed quasi-experimental, this design calls for giving a treatment to one group and not another and comparing the results, but it lacks the random assignment of subjects to the treatment and control conditions. Stated simply, the lack of random assignment in the quasi-experimental design reduces our confidence that the experimental and control groups are really equivalent before the experiment begins. Thus, it reduces our power to attribute causal effects to the treatment.

For reasons that should be clear to practitioners, it is unlikely that students can be randomly assigned to schools or even to classes for research purposes. Suppose, for example, a district is interested in learning whether a new science program for middle schools is more effective than its existing program. One middle school may be chosen to implement the new curriculum, while a second school serves as a control in a quasi-experimental study. It is a virtual certainty that the district will be unwilling to randomly assign students to each school for one year in order to carry out its study. But in this (common) situation, we have little assurance that the students in the experimental and control groups were actually equivalent when the study began. Perhaps, on average, those in the experimental school came from higher SES homes, had more ability, or had better preparation in elementary school. Any of these factors (and a host of others that are entirely unknown) might account for any science achievement differences that appear between the two schools at the end of the study.

Having little assurance of equivalence is not the same as having no assurance at all. Often researchers will match students or schools in the treatment and control groups of quasi-experimental designs, and this matching does provide a modicum of confidence that the two groups were equivalent at a study's start. In the hypothetical science study we are describing, the researcher could provide data showing that students in the treatment and control schools were of approximately equal SES, had similar ability test scores, and had elementary teachers of equal experience and training. That is, in quasi-experimental designs the researcher may try to equate treatment and control groups on variables believed to have an effect on a study's dependent variable, or at the least show that the two groups did not differ significantly on those variables when the study began. Such matching is better than nothing, but it falls far short of the power provided by the random assignment found in true experiments. As a practitioner, you should expect at least this much from researchers reporting a quasi-experimental study. It is understandable why quasi-experimental designs are frequently necessary, but it should be equally understandable that such a design severely limits the faith we can place in their conclusions.

Threats to Internal Validity

The ability to link a causal variable with outcome variables is one of the primary reasons we conduct research in education. For example, if a researcher examines the effect of a reading program on student achievement, it is important to know whether any changes in scores were due to the program or whether these changes were due to unknown factors within the environment of the study. Internal validity refers to the extent to which the treatment variable can be claimed to be causing the changes in the outcome variables of the study. In the previous section we provided you with a brief description of the major research designs used in education, and we alerted you to some of the flaws inherent in those designs. As we moved from descriptive to relational and then to experimental designs we noted an increase in our ability to draw causal inferences from the data. In this way we were able to examine the important role that research designs play in protecting us from drawing inappropriate inferences from a study.

If a study is well designed, and no other variables other than the treatment can be reasonably argued to have had an effect on the outcome variables, then the researcher considers it to be an internally valid study. Internal validity of a research study is one of the most important issues to be addressed by researchers and readers of research. In this section, we explore a set of concepts drawn from Campbell and Stanley (1963) that provide you additional help in interpreting research appropriately.

1. History. History refers to events occurring outside of a study that might impinge on its outcomes. Students not only attend classes and participate in an experimental science curriculum in a school district, they also read books, watch television, attend movies, and visit with their friends and relatives over the course of a year. Perhaps a national event focuses attention on science, and reading about this event and seeing it on television affects student knowledge of science and their tested achievement, quite apart from any effects of the science curriculum.

2. Maturation. Just as changes occur outside the individual, there may be biological or physiological changes that occur within the individual during the life of a particular study, and these could influence its results. Maturation is particularly a threat to internal validity when studies last a long time or when they involve students who are changing rapidly. For example, a study of the effects of a year long physical education program on the strength and agility of adolescents could be particularly vulnerable to maturational effects.

3. Statistical Regression to the Mean. This concept refers to the tendency of test scores that are extremely high or extremely low on one measure to become less extreme on a second administration of the same or a similar measure. Due to the importance of this concept for educators, we will spell it out more carefully and see what problems it can pose for us if it goes unrecognized.

Picture 1,000 fifth grade students in a particular district who have been given form A of a standardized test in reading comprehension. Now imagine that you administer parallel form B of the same reading test to the same 1,000 students two weeks later. Statistical regression toward the mean will occur in the second test: Students scoring at the very top of the distribution on test A will tend to drop slightly on test B. Conversely, students who score very low on test A will tend to increase their scores on test B. Why?

Consider a reading comprehension test made up of a single multiple-choice item with five alternatives, A, B, C, D, and E. A student selects B as the correct answer. If B is correct, there are two reasons why he or she got it right: The student either knew it or guessed correctly. If the student missed the item, we could surmise that he or she not only didn't know the correct answer, but we also can infer that he or she wasn't lucky enough to guess correctly.

Now picture a reading comprehension test made up of 60 items similar to the one described here. Again, we can surmise that students at the very top of the distribution are there for two reasons: They knew a great deal *and* they were lucky. If they take an alternate form of the test in two weeks, we would expect that they still know a great deal, but their luck will even out. Their scores will drop.

At the bottom of the distribution, we can infer that students scored low for two reasons: They didn't know very much and they were unlucky. Upon a second administration of the test, chances are they still won't know very much, but their luck will even out. Their scores will go up. And, so, statistical regression toward the mean works its magic at both ends of the distribution.

What are the implications of this phenomenon for research consumers? Suppose a researcher reports the results of a two-week intensive remediation program during the summer for students who scored in the bottom 5% on a standardized math test given in May. Following the program the researcher administers form B of the achievement test to ascertain the effect of the remediation efforts. What will happen? You guessed it. The scores are improved following the summer program, but was that due to the intensive remediation? Perhaps. Was it also due to statistical regression toward the mean? Almost certainly. And, therefore, the study has not controlled for this threat to internal validity.

4. Selection. When comparing the treatment outcomes of an experimental and control group, it is important that the two groups did not differ on those outcomes before the study began. As obvious as this might be, it frequently occurs that individuals volunteer to participate in a treatment group while controls do not. Think of the number of studies you have read that involve the training of teachers who have volunteered to participate in a summer workshop. These volunteer subjects, whom we assume had considerable interest and motivation in learning a new technique, are then compared the following fall to teachers who did not volunteer. Presumably, the latter group had less interest and motivation than the volunteers. It should hardly surprise us if the experimental teachers show greater evidence of using the new technique.

5. Experimental Mortality. The mortality referred to in this threat to internal validity is not the permanent variety but the kind that results from subjects withdrawing from the study before it is completed. While attrition of this type is inevitable and may not mean a serious flaw has occurred, it is a caution that should not be ignored. If the experimental treatment is time-consuming, difficult, or unpleasant, subjects are likely to withdraw from the study. It is possible those subjects who drop out are less motivated, and perhaps these very qualities may be important in the success of the treatment group. If just three of the less motivated subjects drop out of the experimental group of 15 subjects and none of the control subjects withdraw, it is easy to see the edge this gives to the experimental group.

While this abbreviated list of threats to internal validity is not exhaustive, attention to these five will go a long way in alerting you to possible flaws in quantitative research. In later chapters of the book we will address these threats again as we examine the ability of various research designs to address them.

External Validity

Following careful attention to the internal validity of the study, we now move to the next question that faces consumers of research. To what extent are the results of a particular study applicable to other subjects or settings? If the results of any research study were only applicable to that particular sample or that particular setting, their usefulness would be severely curtailed. If, on the other hand, we are able to extend those findings to a broad range of subjects and settings beyond the sample itself, then we would have results of much greater value. These questions address the important issue of the *external validity* of a study. Stated simply, studies are externally valid to the extent that the results can be generalized to other people, places, or times.

In this section we will begin by describing three aspects of external validity and their use in critiquing a research study. Bracht and Glass (1968) described these three components of external validity as *population validity, personalogical validity,* and *ecological validity,* and we will draw heavily upon their work in this section. Each of the concepts will be defined and then applied within a practitioner's context to help you think about external validity as you evaluate a piece of research.

Following our discussion of population, personalogical, and ecological validity as tools for critiquing research, we will turn our attention to the following question facing practitioners. Are the results of this study applicable to my setting? We will argue that this question is both important and not easily handled by the previous three concepts of external validity. We will make the case that the usual discussion of external validity, while helpful in examining the quality of a study found in the literature, does not speak directly to this question. To address the practitioner's concerns we will offer a term, *application validity*, and explain its meaning and use.

Population Validity

Let us begin with population validity, the first of the three terms used by Bracht and Glass (1968) to explain external validity. *Population validity* refers to the degree to which the results of a study done with a particular sample may be generalized back to the population from which the sample was drawn. Consider the following example. A researcher wishes to determine the vocational interests of high school seniors in Idaho; this is the study's *target population,* the group about which the researcher wishes to draw conclusions. With limited budget and time, the researcher cannot survey all of the target population but can randomly sample 10% of all high school seniors in Boise. The seniors of Boise are the *accessible population* and the 10% of the seniors in Boise who completed the survey represent the *sample.*

To determine population validity the researcher would need to establish a link between the sample and the accessible population and between the accessible population and the target population. In this case, demonstrating that a 10% random sample was drawn would be reasonably good evidence of the first link, but it might be much more difficult to demonstrate that the seniors of Boise were representative of the seniors from the rest of Idaho. The researcher would need to compare the two groups as carefully as possible on demographic variables such as SES, ethnicity, and so forth, and make the case for their similarity. As a consumer of research it is your task to examine how well the researcher has made the case for linking the target population, the accessible population, and the sample of the study.

Personological Validity

A second aspect of external validity is termed *personological validity* and is defined as an interaction between possible treatment effects and specific characteristics of subjects. This is not as complicated as it may sound. In some studies there may be positive treatment effects found, but the treatment may be more effective for some subjects than others. For example, in a teaching strategy study a researcher may report that the treatment was more effective for younger students than older ones, more effective for boys than for girls, and may have had no effect on students of above average reading ability.

Attention to personological validity may help you determine if strategies were found to be effective for students with particular characteristics. For example, a study of reading strategies that reports a sizable effect of the treatment on below average readers, but no effect on average readers, provides much greater precision and clarity than when this information is lacking. Even with a study that has established an acceptable level of population validity it would be wise to carefully attend to possible interactions between treatments and subject characteristics.

Ecological Validity

A third aspect of external validity is called *ecological validity* and, as the name implies, it refers to the setting, process, and procedures of the study being reported in the literature. An analogy might be instructive in understanding ecological validity. One of the authors struggles with gardening in Oklahoma. Plant varieties that thrive in the temperate, humid environment of the greenhouse frequently expire after a few days of unrelenting heat and drought in the real world of an Oklahoma summer. Our gardener should pay careful attention to the settings, processes, and procedures under which promising plant varieties were tested prior to their large-scale introduction in the family garden plot.

It often appears there is an inverse relationship between internal and external validity in that experimental studies with high marks for internal validity are often weak in external validity. An examination of ecological validity issues shows that the inverse relationship is not really so surprising. Studies high on internal validity often gain their strength through random selection of subjects and through removing those subjects from the messiness of classrooms into the more easily controlled laboratory setting. Conversely, studies done in the classroom with all procedures intact may be high on external validity but lack the controls to keep internal validity threats at bay.

The three concepts of *population, personalogical,* and *ecological* validity have great value in helping the practitioner make judgments about the external validity of a piece of research. Each concept provides you with a tool for determining the degree to which the researcher's claims for generalizing the results of the study are warranted. We will now return to the question facing practitioners: Are the results of this study applicable to my setting? It should be clear that a researcher may have provided excellent evidence of the population, personalogical, and ecological validity of a study and yet it may not be relevant for *you* in *your* district facing *your* problem. This question may be the most important for the person attempting to think his or her way through a particularly knotty problem. After determining the adequacy of the researcher's claims regarding external validity, the practitioner must answer a question that the researcher cannot; will the results of this study apply to my school?

Application Validity

We offer the term *application validity* as the fourth and final concept required to help the practitioner with this final link in the research to practice chain. We use the term to refer to those processes engaged in by the practitioner to determine the relevance of research results for his or her particular setting.

The argument for the three previous concepts of external validity is the responsibility of the researcher; however, it is up to the practitioner to make the case for the application validity of the study. How is this done? The information needed to determine application validity is drawn from the data provided for each of the three concepts we have been discussing. Let us begin with population validity. In the researcher's description of population validity there will be information that enables you to make explicit comparisons with your own setting. In the earlier example of the study of a 10% sample of Boise, Idaho, high school seniors, it should be relatively easy for you to compare the characteristics of the high school population of Boise with those of your own high school. Usually, the study will provide demographic data that include, age, sex, race, SES, or similar characteristics that allow you to judge comparability. Only you can determine the fit between that population and the population of concern to you. Of course, no sample used in a study will exactly match the population that concerns you. Small variations from the study to the local setting can be tolerated, but be alert to large differences that might invalidate promising results for consideration in your setting.

To further explore application validity you can examine the information provided in the study regarding personalogical variables. This information can be vital for helping you make the case for or against the study's applicability for your problem. In the study the researcher may provide information regarding subsets of the sample as the data were analyzed. Were there statements made about differential effects of the treatment for different categories of subjects? Did the treatment work better or worse for younger children? For boys rather than girls? For some ethnic groups and not others? For lower rather than higher ability students? If differences of these types were found it should easy to link those findings with your setting more directly.

A final approach to application validity can be made by examining the information provided regarding the study's ecological validity. Were the class sizes comparable to yours? Did the study have teacher aids for every class with 20 or more students? Was the treatment delivered in a manner that will be comparable to the one that you will be using? In short, was the treatment tested in an ecological environment reasonably similar to the one in which you work? These and other questions should provide you with clues as to whether a study's results might apply to your school.

In summary, population, personalogical, and ecological validity allow you to draw inferences about the generalizability of results beyond the sample studied. Drawing upon the information provided in the study about these three concepts of external validity, we have offered a fourth concept, application validity, to help you judge the relevance of a particular study's findings for your problem. A final thought—a study may get excellent marks for population, personalogical, and ecological validity and yet it could be completely inappropriate for your concerns. Only you can decide whether a study applies to your setting.

Statistical and Practical Significance

We now turn to issues beyond the design characteristics of research and address questions related to the analysis of data derived from the study. Researchers and practitioners are interested in attaching meaning and importance to the outcomes of a study, and two important issues of statistical and practical significance of results will be discussed. *Statistical significance* addresses the question "Are the differences found in this study real, or is it likely that they might disappear if the study were repeated?" Or, alternatively, "Are the apparent effects of the treatment in this research simply due to chance?" Practical significance addresses a quite different question: "Just how big is the effect of this treatment?" Or, alternatively, "Are the effects of treatment A larger than the effects of treatment B?" These are not trivial questions, and statisticians have devoted their careers to developing techniques to answer them.

First, a disclaimer needs to be made about the word "significance" as it is used in this context. In our opinion, it is very unfortunate that *the word* significance became associated with this concept because its meaning to statisticians is quite at odds with our everyday understanding of the term. We understand significant to mean "important," "useful," or "meaningful" as we talk about a significant relationship, a significant drop in tax revenue, or a significant pay increase. The statistician has no such meanings in mind as he or she discusses the term. To the statistician, the term might mean "rare" or "unusual," and while a statistically rare event might be useful or worthwhile, there is clearly no guarantee that this is so.

Statistical Significance

Undoubtedly you have seen the symbol "$p < .05$" or "$p > .1$" at the bottom of tables in research reports. This section will explain those symbols and help you understand the concept of statistical significance.

Consider this simple study. A computer interactive reading program was compared with a traditional reading program using 50 fifth graders who were randomly assigned to treatment and control groups. Let us ignore the many nuances of research design for the moment and focus on the results. The researchers reported a difference of 4 points on the reading achievement test favoring the computer interactive program. Could the researchers claim success for their computer program?

Before you raise money for more computers there are some simple issues to address. The first one is the trustworthiness of the 4 point difference. How can the researchers have confidence that this difference didn't occur as a simple chance fluctuation? How can they know that if they repeated the study on the next day they wouldn't find the traditional program group scoring 4 points higher?

Statisticians have ways to help with these questions. They have developed techniques to test for the possibility that a difference in observed scores (in our case, 4 points) might have been due to chance. They do this by starting with the assumption that, in two randomly assigned groups, the differences between the two group scores should be zero. There might be some random fluctuations from zero, but if measured an infinite number of times the true difference between the two groups would average to zero. The techniques they have developed allow them to draw inferences about the probability of finding any particular difference other than zero. It would seem reasonable that a very small difference of .1 of a point might occur from time to time but that a difference of 4 points might be much more rare.

When our helpful statisticians calculated the probability of finding a difference of 4 points they found that a difference of this magnitude would occur less than 1% of the time by chance alone or, as they phrased it, the difference was statistically significant with a $p < .01$. Note what this tells us and what it does not tell us. Its meaning is fairly straightforward; differences as great as these would occur by chance fewer than 1 time in 100. Does this tell us that our 4 point difference was not due to chance? No, this tells us that if it were due to chance it was a rather rare event. Note also that it tells us nothing about the importance of 4 points in any practical way. Four points may be a huge gain and worthy of great celebration or it may be a trivial gain that is not worth further pursuit. Those are questions for the following section on practical significance. It is sufficient to take what the statisticians have given us and to understand its contribution. A difference that is statistically significant is one that is unlikely to be attributed to chance; therefore, we may look further for what may have caused this 4 point gain. This may not seem like much, but without the notion of statistical significance we would be unable to reach meaningful conclusions about the trustworthiness of research results. Now the researchers may proceed to make the case for the factor or factors that brought about this difference. If there were no stable difference there would be no reason to proceed.

After you have the basic concept, the variations are easy to understand. Probability values can be infinite, but their interpretations remain the same. A $p < .001$ assigned to a result would indicate one that is statistically significant. To find a difference that would occur by chance less than 1 in 1,000 times should give you much confidence that the difference is real and trustworthy. To find a difference in which a value of $p > .5$ is assigned would tell us that half of the time you would find a difference of this magnitude if only chance were operating. Hardly something to enhance your confidence in the results.

There are conventional milestones that are commonly used in the literature such as $p < .05$, $p < .01$, or $p < .001$. While they are handy markers to indicate different levels of statistical significance, you should recognize there is nothing sacred about those levels. A study that reports a finding with a $p < .05$ is only marginally different from one that reports a finding with a $p < .06$.

Practical Significance and Effect Size

For the research consumer, the importance of the concept of effect size is hard to overstate. For the professional administrator attempting to make practical decisions, few questions are more important than "How much difference did it make?" Throughout this book we have argued that researchers and practitioners bring different agendas to the research table and the concept of effect size highlights these differences.

Researchers need to have data that are trustworthy and reliable before they proceed, if in fact they ever do proceed, to examining the usefulness of their findings. A story, perhaps apocryphal, has been attributed to Michael Faraday as he proudly displayed his small copper-wired armature spinning while attached to a dry cell battery. When asked what it was good for he responded to the question with a question, "What good is a baby?" Inherent in that response may well be some important differences between the researcher and the practitioner. Faraday may have meant a couple of things with his offhand comment. First, like a baby, research has an intrinsic value that does not depend upon the contribution it can make today. Or, he may have meant that, like a baby, research is valued for what it might become. In either event, Faraday was relatively unfazed by the pragmatic questioner and, fortunately for all of us who own electrical appliances, he continued to tinker with his "useless" toy.

While the preceding story is often used to keep the impatient practitioner at bay, we do not share it with you for that purpose. The question of practical significance is extremely important and the concept of effect size is a powerful tool, allowing research consumers to ask important questions about the issues that matter most to them. We will explain the concept of effect size, tell you how to calculate it, and illustrate its usefulness in areas of interest to practitioners.

When practitioners ask how much difference a treatment made in a study, the most simple and straightforward answer would be to compare the means of the two groups being studied. If an experimental program results in an average score difference of 5 points, that is the simplest and easiest bit of information to absorb from the study. If they were never going to read another study they could stop right there and have an answer to the question of practical significance.

For example, consider three different math studies that report differences of 5 points, 10 points, and 50 points between the experimental and control groups of each study. At first glance the studies appear to have had dramatically different results, but we must be cautious in our interpretation. Each of these studies used a different measure of math achievement, and it is not possible to make a simple comparison of the mean differences reported. We need to translate those values into a common standard to allow valid comparisons to be made. Just as measurements that are reported variously in inches, feet, and yards must be converted into a standard metric to allow comparisons, so we must also translate mean scores derived from different measures into a common denominator. When we convert each of those mean differences into a fraction of the standard deviation of that measure, we can then make comparisons from one study to the next that are meaningful.

Continuing with our math example above, let us convert each mean difference into a fraction of the standard deviation of that measure and see if we can make a judgment about the practical significance of the three studies. In our example above we had mean differences of 5, 10, and 50 points between the experimental and control groups in the three studies. Suppose the standard deviations of each study were 10, 50, and 500 points, respectively. When we divide the mean difference of the first study (5 pts.) by its standard deviation (10 pts.) we get a value of 1/2 or .5 SD. Stated simply, the treatment group of our first study averaged 1/2 of a SD higher than the control group, and this is usually expressed as an effect size (ES) of .5. When we do the simple calculations to determine the effect sizes of the other two studies, we get an effect size of .2 (10/50) for the second study and an effect size of .1 (50/500) for the third study.

Now we have effect sizes for each study that can be meaningfully compared. It is a simple matter to see that the first study yielded an effect size of .5, indicating that the treatment effect was of much greater practical significance than either of the other two studies that weighed in with effect sizes of .2 and .1, respectively. In this way, you can read a series of studies and compare effect size across all of them to assess the practical significance of each study.

A natural question may arise at this point. How large does an effect size have to be to be considered practically significant? There is an easy answer and a complicated one. The easy answer is similar to the one given to the question, "How much money do you want to earn?" Like salaries, an effect size should be as large as possible. If you have five different programs designed to improve reading and their effect sizes are .7, .2, .3, .2, and .1, respectively, which one would you choose, all other things being equal? Of course, .7 would be the winner. As we said, that is the easy answer.

The more complicated answer is that there are crude indicators that have been offered but, like their counterparts in statistical significance, they are quite arbitrary. Just as p values of .05 and .01 are simply bench marks for statistical significance, researchers have designated effect sizes of .3, .5 and .8 to be Small, Medium, and Large as indicators of practical significance. It should be obvious that these designations are only labels arbitrarily attached to numeric values. Even with these limitations the tool of effect size is an important one in the hands of the research consumer. With it you are able to answer the question "How much difference did it make?"

It should be clear that the two concepts of statistical significance and practical significance are important to you as a research consumer and that they should become an automatic part of your checklist as you evaluate a research study. First, statistical significance asks the question "Are the differences reported in this study likely to be due to chance?" Second, practical significance, or effect size, asks the question "How large in standard deviation units are the differences found in this study?" As you examine empirical research throughout your professional career, the use of these twin concepts should be a constant part of your critique format.

This chapter provided you with tools to help you assess the quality of empirical research that you encounter. The rationale of a study should be sought to give you an idea of the central question or questions being examined in a study. Which variables are being studied and how are they expected to relate to one another? Rather than a mindless search for relationships, how do these variables fit together in some coherent, meaningful framework?

After identifying and understanding a study's central question(s) and ratio-nale, your attention can be focused upon the measurement of variables in a quantitative study. To what extent are they *valid* and *reliable?*

After the essential ingredients of a study are laid bare, the next set of ques-tions arise as to the nature of the research design used. The particular design structure highlights the inherent strengths and weaknesses within each design.

Regardless of the design used, there are certain threats to internal validity that can be examined to help assess the researcher's claim for legitimacy of results. A study that accounts reasonably well for each of these threats is a well-crafted piece of research, and you can attend to questions of external validity and the likelihood that the results are generalizable to your setting.

Finally, the value of the researcher's findings need to be assessed relative to their statistical and practical significance. While it is important that the findings be statistically significant, the practitioner is further aided by the concept of effect size to ascertain the magnitude of the differences reported.

The remaining chapters will highlight these concepts within a framework of reviewing research on a particular topic. It is difficult to imagine any examina-tion of empirical research that would not contain these elements as keys to unlocking research findings.

References

Altheide, D. L., & Johnson, J. M. (1994). Criteria for assessing interpretive validity in qualitative research. In N. K. Denzin & Y. S. Lincoln (Eds.), *Handbook of qualitative research* (pp. 485–499). Thousand Oaks, CA: Sage.

Ary, D., Jacobs, L. C., & Razavieh, A. (1990). *Introduction to research in education* (4th ed.). Fort Worth: Holt, Rinehart & Winston.

Bracht, G. H., and Glass, G. V. (1968). The external validity of experiments. *American Educational Research Journal, 5,* 437–474.

Campbell, D. T., & Stanley, J. C. (1963). *Experimental and quasi-experimental designs for research*. Chicago: Rand McNally.

Denzin, N. K., & Lincoln, Y. S.(1994). Introduction: Entering the field of qualitative research. In N. K. Denzin & Y. S. Lincoln (Eds.), *Handbook of qualitative research* (pp. 1–17). Thousand Oaks, CA: Sage.

Flanders, N. A.(1970). *Analyzing teacher behavior*. Reading, MA: Addison-Wesley.

Gall, J. P., Gall, M. D., & Borg, W. R. (1999). *Applying educational research: A practical guide* (4th ed.). New York: Longman.

Peshkin, A. (1986). *God's choice*. Chicago: University of Chicago Press.

Peshkin, A. (1991). *The color of strangers: The color of friends*. Chicago: The University of Chicago Press.

Wiersma, W. (1991). *Research methods in education* (5th ed.). Boston: Allyn & Bacon.

Class Size in Irontown

Large-Scale Experiments in Education

INTRODUCTION

In this and subsequent chapters we begin the process of applying the concepts and ideas developed in chapters 1–4 to practical administrative problems. We want to demonstrate how practitioners like yourselves might use research to help address some of the common issues that they confront in their schools. In order to do this we have organized these chapters in a common format.

First, each chapter begins with a case study in which a school administrator contends with a practical problem: an urban district faces state sanctions because of its students' low achievement; the frequency of disciplinary problems in a school is unacceptably high; the climate of a high school seems to inhibit academic accomplishment. Each of these cases should be immediately recognizable to practitioners.

Next, the administrator involved in the case poses one or more questions about the problem and seeks the answers to those questions in the research literature. That is, he or she follows the procedure we recommend in chapter 3. We provide a brief description of the research on each problem, the kind of understanding that administrators can develop with a modest foray into the literature. Then we examine in detail one of the studies uncovered in the administrator's search. For your convenience, in all cases except chapter 6, that study is reproduced in full at the end of the chapter. We offer an extended critical discussion of that study using the criteria that we developed in chapter 4: For instance, we examine the quality of its rationale, its sampling procedures, and its research design. While we touch each of these topics in every chapter, one of them is the chapter's central focus. In every instance we approach that topic as we believe a practitioner should. That is, we illustrate how a practitioner can make defensible judgments of a study's quality. Each chapter closes with the administrator's recommendation regarding his or her school's problem, a recommendation that incorporates the results of the literature search. The object, then, of each chapter is for you to learn how to find and competently use research when you confront a practical problem in your school.

Without further discussion then, let us turn to Irontown's difficulties and the possibility of addressing them using the research on class size.

The Case: What Should We Do with All This Money?

Irontown, a city of 400,000 people, is located in the rustbelt of the northeast. At one time it was a thriving city of steel mills and heavy industry, but it fell on hard times during the late 1960s and never recovered. Unemployment is high, the welfare roles are swollen, the population is aging, and the schools are in disrepair. The city's infrastructure has deteriorated, many of the buildings in the downtown area are vacant, and crime rates are among the highest in the state. Irontown, in short, has more than its share of urban problems.

In one sense, however, the Irontown City School District is in an enviable position. The state has just bestowed on it a very substantial sum of money—$1,500,000—that is over and above its normal allocation of state funds. The money, to be disbursed in equal installments over a three-year period, is to be used to "make demonstrated and substantial improvements in reading and mathematics achievement in the district's pupils," according to the legislation authorizing the grant. Less enviable is the reason for the state's beneficence: The Irontown City School District is in danger of being declared "educationally bankrupt" and placed in state receivership. It ranks as the lowest performing urban district in the state.

Irontown's unenviable status is a result of the state's Education Accountability Act. Passed six years ago by the legislature, the Act requires that school districts identified as having consistently low student achievement improve their performance as measured by both nationally standardized and state-developed, curriculum-specific tests. Although the Act set no deadlines for demonstrating the required improvement, in each successive year offending districts came under increasingly strict state scrutiny coupled with additional resources to help make improvement possible. Ultimately, however, if a district failed to boost pupil achievement to satisfactory levels, the extra resources would come to an end and the State Education Department (SED) would take over control of the school system.

Given the district's problems, no one was surprised when Irontown was identified as a low-performing district during the first year following the implementation of the Education Accountability Act. What alarmed the district's school board and administrative staff was the realization that in the subsequent years not only did Irontown fail to improve, scores on both kinds of tests had actually fallen. Now, the district is at the last step in the process specified in the Act: There is to be one more carrot of extra money before the stick of takeover falls on the city's schools.

If nothing else, the threat of imminent state takeover galvanized the school board and central administration into action. A task force was appointed to recommend actions that would ensure the required improvement. The SED stood ready to assist in any way possible—state education bureaucrats were none too anxious to start running local school districts. The task force quickly identified possible strategies to improve student achievement, including establishing charter schools, radical decentralization of the district, computer-assisted instruction, and reduced class size, among others. Next, it appointed committees to examine each of these alternatives in detail, with the explicit instructions that each committee was to examine the evidence regarding a strategy's power to improve achievement and prepare a written report of its findings. These reports were to be a primary source of information in the task force's deliberations.

The Assistant Superintendent for Curriculum was appointed chair of the committee to examine the likely efficacy of reducing class size. The committee, consisting primarily of administrators and teachers, prepared a set of 10 questions about class size to be answered. These are listed in Figure 5.1.

You are Susan Resnick, the principal of the John Jay Middle School and a member of the committee on class size. George Castener, an elementary curriculum coordinator in the central office, Judith Cohn, a math teacher at Westside High School, and you are assigned the responsibility of determining what can be learned from the research literature regarding these questions and to provide the written results of your efforts to the committee at its next meeting. As the three of you examine the questions your committee has formulated, you recognize that only some of them can be answered by reviewing the research on class size. Others, while critically important to the committee's deliberations, must be answered by collecting data in the Irontown district. For example, knowing whether or not the district will be able to afford the required number of new teachers and whether constructing new classrooms will be necessary are essential to deciding if class size reduction is a feasible strategy in Irontown. These are not, however, questions that you, George, and Judy will address; other committee members will examine those questions. The three of you put your heads together and decide to find out what the research implies for questions 1, 2, 3, 4, 7, 8 and 9. You divide the questions among yourselves, with you taking primary responsibility for questions 1 and 2. Since each of you will undoubtedly find research bearing on others' questions, you agree to work closely together and share the results of your efforts.

You begin your work by checking secondary sources in an evening trip to the library of the branch campus of the state university located in Irontown.

1. What achievement benefits can we expect from making a substantial reduction in our district's average class size?
2. Just what does "substantial" mean in this case? That is, how far would we have to reduce our current class size to get a significant improvement in test scores?
3. If there are achievement benefits to be obtained, are there particular grade levels/subjects where those benefits are most likely?
4. Will any benefits show up on the tests that the state is using to measure the district's performance?
5. How many new teachers will the district be required to hire if it reduces pupil-teacher ratios to specific levels? Can the district's financial resources support such a reduction after the $1,500,000 is gone?
6. What are the implications of class size reductions in selected grade levels or subjects for the district's contract with its teachers' union? Will current provisions permit selective reductions or, if not, can they be negotiated as a caveat to the existing contract?
7. Do achievement benefits, if any, persist if students must later attend classes of normal size? That is, will reducing class size likely offer a permanent solution to the problem, or will Irontown be required to deal with another takeover threat a few years down the road?
8. Will benefits accrue to all students, or do particular types of students benefit more than others? Specifically, do poor and minority children benefit, since those groups make up a substantial part of the district's student body and are also the ones scoring lowest on the tests?
9. Are there any benefits of a non-cognitive nature likely to be forthcoming if we reduce our pupil-teacher ratio significantly? For example, will social interaction among students, teacher morale, or student discipline improve?
10. How much of a reduction in class size can we accommodate in our existing facilities? At what point and in which schools will new construction or temporary classrooms be required?

F I G U R E   *5.1*   **Questions to Address Concerning the Possible Effectiveness of Reducing Class Size as a Mechanism for Improving Student Achievement in Irontown**

Working to the closing hour, you review the relevant entries in the *Encyclopedia of Educational Research* (Alkin & American Educational Research Association, 1992) and the massive *International Encyclopedia of Education* (Husen & Postlethwaite, 1994), both of which provide relatively recent reviews of the class size research. You copy these to share with your colleagues. You also scan the table of contents of the last five years of the *Review of Research in Education*. Next, you run a quick ERIC search to look for the possibility of recent reviews of class size research in the *Review of Educational Research* and in the year-books of the *National Society for the Study of Education*. (The former turns up only one partially relevant article from 1979, which you decide to ignore, and the latter turns up nothing.) You search the library's online catalogue and find one edited book that appears relevant (Slavin, 1989). Finally, you run another ERIC search looking for research reviews on the topic of class size regardless of their source. You locate several likely candidates, which you also photocopy.

Your initial foray into the literature has produced more than enough to provide you with reading material over the next week.

On your second trip to the library you are armed with the information you have gained from reading the review articles. You have the titles and authors of what seem to be major studies that you want to read. You have the names of several researchers who have been particularly active in the field of class size, judging from the frequent citations to their work in secondary sources. Using the information you have gained, you make a more sophisticated search of the electronic version of the ERIC database using conjunctive terms. (You are not surprised to find that simply searching on "class size" alone turns up more than 2,000 references.) However, because you have learned that a technique called meta-analysis has played an important role in the research on this problem, a search on "class size and meta-analysis" produces several of these studies that weren't included in your original search of secondary sources. By searching on individual's names in the author field of databases, you locate additional writings on the subject by these researchers. Similarly, since you are particularly interested in reading and math achievement, the phrase "class size and achievement and (reading or mathematics)" considerably sharpens the results of your search.[1] You also search "PsychInfo" and "Sociological Abstracts," electronic indexes of the psychology and sociology literature. The former provides several promising citations, but the latter yields nothing. Finally, having identified two major studies that have apparently had a substantial impact on the class size literature, judging from the references to them, you run a check of the *Social Science Citation Index*, which provides several citations to recent, potentially useful publications that refer to these two major studies. Again making photocopies of selected items to share with your colleagues, and checking out an edited book with a chapter on the subject of class size, you call it quits for the evening.

Over the next week you meet with George and Judy, select the materials you feel you need to read in full text, and circulate selected materials among your subcommittee. At the end of that time you write your recommendations regarding questions 1 and 2.

The Class Size Research: An Introduction

Not very long ago a practicing administrator setting out to review the empirical research on the effects of class size on student achievement would face a daunting task. This was not simply because there were a large number of these studies, and they went back many years,[2] but because they spanned all levels of education, the construct "class size" was ambiguous, and, perhaps most alarming, the

---

[1] The specific syntax varies among the various ERIC electronic database providers.

[2] The earliest study uncovered by Glass and Smith (1978) in their review was carried out in 1902. Angrist and Lavy, cited in Achilles (1998), assert that the earliest claim that class size affected student achievement was made by the Talmudic scholar Maimonides in the 12th century! That must make the class-size issue the longest running issue in educational history.

results of these studies were seemingly contradictory. For every study showing that reduced size improved student achievement, there was another showing the reduced size had no effect whatsoever.

It was even possible to argue on the basis of empirical evidence that pupils learned more in large classes. For example, Tomlinson (cited in Finn & Voelkl, 1994) showed that over the period 1960 to 1984, the average pupil-teacher ratio in the U.S. declined substantially, from 30 to 24 pupils in elementary schools and from 27 to 22 at the secondary level. At the same time there was a decline "on virtually all standardized tests of academic aptitude and achievement, in all grades, among many different strata of students, in many subjects, and in every region" (Tomlinson, quoted in Finn & Voelkl, 1994). Similarly, cross-national comparisons of educational achievement seemed to support the same conclusion. For example, international studies of achievement in mathematics and science showed that the United States lagged countries with substantially larger pupil-teacher ratios in those two subjects (Finn & Voelkl, 1994). Of course, a multitude of factors could account for these results besides class size, but you see the point: The evidence regarding the effects of class size on student achievement was equivocal.

The last assertion—that the research was equivocal—is the kind of claim that leads practitioners to dismiss research and researchers. It may be difficult to find a teacher who believes that class size makes no difference in students' learning. And it is not just teachers who believe that small classes are better—many parents are clearly believers as well: They spend substantial sums paying tuition to private schools, in part because those schools often provide much smaller classes. Most programs for special education students and many for at-risk students are deliberately designed so that classrooms contain fewer pupils than is ordinarily the case—further evidence of educators' strong belief in the efficacy of small numbers. If research shows that reducing class size makes no difference in student learning, educators are likely to conclude that something is wrong with the research. Certainly nobody thinks that, all else equal, a first-grade child in a class of 100 will learn as much as he or she would in a class of 1, that is, with a private tutor.

When numerous studies seem to contradict common sense, or when a body of literature is rife with conflicting results, it is unwise to simply disregard the research. In the case at hand, rather than dismissing the many studies that suggested class size had no effect on achievement, an intelligent consumer of research can learn a great deal by asking what might account for the seemingly contradictory or anomalous findings. In part the equivocal findings are illuminated by the simple comparison made in the last paragraph. Just as a child with a tutor will learn more than a child in a class of 100, all else equal, we would be surprised if the research showed that there were substantial differences in achievement between classes of 30 students and classes of 29. Some of the ambiguity in the early research resulted from various definitions of what was to count as a small (or large) class. It seems better to ask where along the possible size continuum do achievement effects begin to show up. In classes of fewer than 25 pupils? Twenty?

This point is particularly critical to school administrators. Simply put, reducing the size of classes could be a very expensive endeavor. Personnel costs are the largest item in every school district's budget; typically over 70%of expenditures go to salaries and fringe benefits. Conceivably, cutting average class size in half might double the number of teachers required by a district and therefore nearly double its payroll. In fact, costs could be driven considerably higher, since additional classrooms might be required.[3] Setting class size, then, is a powerful administrative control over budgets and the reason it is such a vexatious issue in collective negotiations. Guthrie and Kirst (1988) estimated that it would cost California over $200 million to reduce the state's average class size by just one student. Given the huge costs involved, less-than-definitive research identifying the point at which size reductions begin to show improved achievement is a poor basis for forming public policy. If your committee concludes that Irontown should substantially reduce its class size in order to meet the state's demands for higher achievement, it will have to come up with some very convincing evidence.

Another cause of the conflicting interpretations regarding class size effects concerned what was to count as "higher" achievement. If a study shows conclusively that we can expect an average gain of 5 points on a standardized reading achievement test, is that a large gain? That is, it is not enough to demonstrate convincingly that achievement will increase. It is necessary to show that the increase is somehow worth the additional costs. Further, since investigators used different measures of student achievement, it was difficult to make comparisons across studies. Was a 5-point gain on a standardized reading achievement test more or less than a 12-point gain on a curriculum-specific test in plane geometry? In your case, since the task force will need to compare the potential gains from the various alternatives it is considering (computer-assisted instruction, decentralization, and so forth), your committee will need to provide evidence of the likely achievement effects of class size reductions in a metric that permits direct comparison among these alternatives. In other words, the task force needs to identify how it can get the biggest bang for it's one and one-half million bucks.[4]

Another issue that helped to make the early studies confusing was the ambiguity in the construct class size. Perhaps the best illustration of this is the frequent confusion of the constructs class size and pupil-teacher ratio (PTR), which were often treated as if they were synonymous. The former is typically constructed by computing the average number of pupils assigned to a set of classrooms. The latter is usually constructed by dividing the number of full-time equivalent students by the number of full time equivalent teachers in a school or larger unit (a

---

[3] It should be noted that whether reducing class size will result in large increases in expenditures is disputed. For an opposing point of view see Finn and Achilles (1998b).

[4] Recall our brief discussion of effect sizes in the previous chapter. These provide one tool to help answer the "biggest bang" question, that is, which program will most effectively achieve an organization's goal? (Note that this question is central to many administrative decisions.) We shall have considerably more to say about effect sizes in chapter 6.

district or even a nation). Both of these are open to various interpretations, and when they are conflated, confusion occurs. In the case of the first computation, the number of pupils assigned to any class is rarely the number of pupils in attendance on any given day. This is particularly the case in center-city schools, where absenteeism may be high. Further, it may not be the actual number of pupils assigned to a class that is important but the number actually involved in a lesson (Finn & Voelkl, 1994). In the case of the pupil-teacher ratio, account is rarely taken of noncontact time. Thus, in a school that provides preparation periods for teachers, the PTR is certain to be considerably lower than the average class size. A school's PTR may not indicate the number of pupils in any of its classrooms and is likely to mask very large variations among its classrooms.

Finally, much of the ambiguity in the research was (and still is) due to its a theoretical nature. That is, seldom were attempts made to specify exactly what it is about smaller classes that would lead to higher achievement. Because the mechanism explaining why class size affects student achievement was unspecified, it was (and still is) difficult to interpret studies. For example, if a study showed that there were statistically significant gains to be had from reducing average class size by 5 pupils, were those gains due to better individualization of instruction, teachers' ability to maintain better discipline, higher quality interaction among pupils, or reduced paperwork? If one study showed an achievement gain and another did not, perhaps it was simply because the teachers in the former adapted their techniques to take advantage of their smaller classes, while those in the latter did not. Perhaps certain teaching strategies are the real cause of any achievement gains that seem to result from reducing class sizes.

For all of these reasons, and others that we have not mentioned, by the 1970s the class size literature had become a quagmire for the unwary practitioner who approached it trying to get an answer to the simple question, Do students learn more in small classes? Indeed, as Glass and Smith (1979) suggested, many researchers had abandoned the topic as hopeless; they were convinced that there was no general, demonstrable relation between the number of students in a classroom and those students' achievement.

The Glass and Smith study is important for several reasons. It reawakened interest in the matter of class size. They claimed to show that researchers were wrong—there were achievement differences that could be attributed to class size. Further, Glass and Smith introduced a new methodology, *meta-analysis*, that seemed to demonstrate what every teacher already believed: small was better. As you might expect, there was a substantial amount of criticism of the Glass and Smith work. Nevertheless, we urge practitioners to acquaint themselves with the technique of meta-analysis, which has become commonplace in educational research and may be especially useful to administrators. In a sense it is analogous to a secondary source for research literature that we discussed in chapter 3. That is, it provides a way to combine the results of many different studies of an educational practice, and it allows us to estimate, numerically, that practice's effects. Hence, it permits us to directly compare the effectiveness of alternative programs intended to achieve the same goal and to compare the effectiveness of programs intended to achieve quite different goals. For example, is a program meant to improve math achievement in the primary grades as effective at achieving its goal as another program with the purpose of improving achievement in high school social studies?

If interest in the issue of class size was sparked by Glass and Smith, the matter was hardly settled. In the end, their analyses did not provide definitive answers to class size questions. It would take true experiments to do that. Beginning in 1985, the State of Tennessee sponsored project STAR (for Student-Teacher Achievement Ratio). As we shall see, however, while Project STAR gave us definitive answers about some of the questions concerning class size and achievement, it left many questions unanswered, and it raised some additional questions that were not previously considered. This project has produced a large number of studies, and more are on the way. One of these, by Jeremy Finn and Charles Achilles, is the centerpiece of this chapter.

The Background of the Tennessee Studies[5]

If meta-analyses did not provide a definitive answer to the question of whether reducing class size has an effect on student achievement, a series of studies conducted in Tennessee during the late 1980s and continuing to the present go a considerable distance toward doing so. Project STAR, (Word et al., 1990b), The Lasting Benefits Study (Nye et al., 1995a), and Project Challenge (Nye et al., 1995b) are arguably the most carefully designed, large-scale, policy-relevant experiments ever done in educational research. While they leave many questions unanswered, it is now very difficult to dismiss class size effects as nonexistent, or to argue that these effects are not important for raising the achievement of at-risk students. We will examine closely one article that emerged from Project STAR.

In the early 1980s a confluence of several events created the conditions necessary for establishing the STAR project. The Glass and Smith study and the controversy surrounding it had become common knowledge in educational circles. For the first time there was some reasonably clear evidence of the efficacy of small classes, at least at the primary level. The research evidence, however, was hardly unequivocal. For example, a well done experimental study in Toronto (Shapson, Wright, Eason, & Fitzgerald, 1980) essentially failed to find class size effects on achievement or other outcome measures, such as student satisfaction or teacher instructional strategies. (Interestingly, teachers involved in the project claimed that they were able to individualize instruction in small classes better, but trained classroom observers failed to detect that this actually happened.)

At about the same time, the State of Indiana had underwritten a large-scale project (Prime Time) to assess the effectiveness of reduced class size in the primary grades. Beginning in 24 classes, Project Prime Time examined the effects of reducing pupil-teacher ratios to 14:1. Bain and Achilles (1986) described Prime

---

[5] In this section we rely on discussions by Mosteller (1995) and Mosteller et al. (1996) and personal communications with Charles Achilles.

Time as yielding three important results. First of all, students in the smaller classes achieved at higher levels on standardized tests than did their contemporaries in larger classes. (However, recall Shapson et al., 1980.) Second, students in smaller classrooms created fewer behavior problems. Finally, teachers in smaller classes claimed that they were more productive and able to teach more efficiently in smaller classes. The Indiana General Assembly was sufficiently impressed with these results to reduce class sizes in the primary grades across the state, though they did not fund the project sufficiently to bring average class size below 18 (Bain & Achilles, 1986, p. 663).

Meanwhile, Lamar Alexander (later to become Secretary of Education under President George Bush) became governor of Tennessee. Alexander and the Tennessee legislature made the improvement of education a top priority. The legislature was aware that reducing class size, especially at the primary level, and especially to 15 or so pupils, might produce substantial gains in student achievement. They also knew that the evidence supporting their belief was not universally accepted. Finally, they were concerned that reducing average class sizes to 15 pupils in the primary grades of every school in Tennessee might be a very expensive initiative. A large number of new teachers would be required as well as additional space in many of the schools. Accordingly, in 1985 the Legislature appropriated 3 million dollars each year for four years to conduct a study that would provide firm evidence of the effectiveness of this strategy for improving Tennessee's schools. This study was Project STAR. The project has resulted in a number of publications, one of these, appearing in *The American Educational Research Journal* (Finn & Achilles, 1990) is found in the appendix of this chapter beginning on page 146. That article forms the basis of the following discussion.[6]

The Structure of Quantitative Research Reports: Evaluating Answers and Questions About Class Size

It is appropriate that the Finn and Achilles article, "Answers and Questions About Class Size," provide the example study in this, the first of several chapters in the book in which we closely examine actual research publications. We believe that it is possible for practitioners, largely untrained in research, to read and critically evaluate highly complicated research reports. Finn and Achilles' article is certainly that. For example, it involves both cross-sectional analyses (comparisons of the performance of two or more groups at the same point in time) and

---

[6] Remember that the Finn and Achilles article reports the results of Project STAR at about the halfway point of the project's duration, that is, after children had finished kindergarten and first grade. Additional studies followed these students as they progressed into the second and third grades, when the project came to a close. A summary of the results of the full four-year study can be found in the final report by Word and her associates (Word et al., 1990a). However, the final report is not as easily accessible as the Finn and Achilles article, nor does it serve our pedagogical purposes as well. If you are interested in the effectiveness of four years spent in a small class, we recommend that you read the project's final report.

longitudinal analyses (comparisons of changes in the performance of one or more groups across time). The statistics involved (e.g., multivariate analysis of variance) are highly esoteric and unlikely to be familiar to practicing administrators. The study's design, a large-scale true experiment, is quite rare in educational research. In short, it is not an easy read, yet it is the sort of study that fills the pages of our best research journals. What can school administrators gain from reading Finn and Achilles? We think a great deal. However, if you are to learn anything useful, obviously you must read it with a reasonable level of understanding and in a critical frame of mind. More generally, if we are correct that school administrators can make better decisions if they are familiar with the research bearing on a problem they face, those administrators must be able to critically read the articles that fill research journals. And they must be able to do so without spending three to five years earning a Ph.D. in educational research methods and statistics. We have some suggestions about how they can do this, which we will introduce and then apply to the Finn and Achilles article.

With some variation, most reports of quantitative research have a standard tripartite structure. We will refer to these as a study's *conceptual, methodological,* and *empirical* levels. Approach a study with these three levels in mind—they provide a kind of skeleton to which the flesh of most empirical, quantitative work is attached. Within each of these there are a few key elements that deserve your evaluative attention. If you have not already done so, read the study now and refer to it frequently as you read the following discussion.

The Conceptual Level: The Question, the Problem, and Evaluating the Study's Rationale

At the conceptual level, the author of a report explains the ideas that drive the study. The first several pages of most reports (after the abstract, acknowledgments, and so forth) are normally devoted to these ideas. The following topics are often discussed: the question (or questions) the research is to answer, why that question is conceived as it is, why it is important to ask, what the problem behind the question is, and how the study is related to previous work. All of this is usually explicit or implicit in the early pages. Authors will use various headings to label this section, for example, "The Problem," "The Research Question," " Purpose," "Hypotheses," "Literature Review," "Background," and so on. (Notice that Finn and Achilles use none of these terms; they simply launch into a discussion of the ideas behind their study. Nonetheless, each of the topics is embedded in their brief introductory remarks.)

Of the various elements making up the conceptual level of a report, two are critically important to your understanding of the research and your capacity to use it in making professional decisions. The most important to grasp is the question that the researcher has posed. Recall that in chapter 1 we defined research as a "sustained attempt to answer a question, using a legitimated methodology, when the answer to that question is not already known." For the moment, the significant aspect of that definition is the idea of answering a question: All research is an attempt to answer a question. The most powerful handle that you can get on a piece of research is simply to be clear about the question that it proposes to answer.

Fortunately, identifying the question posed in a study is usually straightforward. Often it is explicitly articulated in the title to the work itself. If you scan the tables of contents of many journals, you will be struck by the frequency with which questions appear. This should not be surprising, as a study's title can be thought of as its shortest abstract. If the question posed is the most important aspect of a study, putting that question in its title is sensible. By way of illustration, we happen to have at hand a recent issue of *Educational Evaluation and Policy Analysis* (volume 20, number 2). Two of the four articles pose questions in their titles: "Do new teaching standards undermine performance on old tests?" and "Does work inhibit cognitive development in college?" The point of these studies is immediately clear, and you could make a reasonably informed judgment just from reading these titles whether the articles might be relevant to your interests.

Even when the question driving a study isn't explicitly stated in its title, it is often articulated within the first few paragraphs. Sometimes, however, you will have to make a minor transformation, as when the author phrases the study's question as its purpose or its hypothesis. Each of these is an alternative way to phrase a question. For example, the author may say, "The purpose of this study is to determine the effect on teacher morale of assigning aides to classrooms." This can be read as a way of posing the research question: "What is the effect on teacher morale of assigning aides to classrooms?"[7] Again, Finn and Achilles are somewhat atypical. They do not explicitly pose a question, state a purpose, or propose a hypothesis. Nevertheless, within the first page of the article they make the major question they are posing quite clear. One way to phrase it might be the following: What is the effect of making a substantial reduction in class size on student achievement in grades K–1?[8]

Our stress on being clear about a study's question may seem to belabor the obvious. However, many educational practitioners simply begin to read a research report with no immediate objective in mind—they simply start to read. As a consequence many miss the point of the study—its question—and find themselves wandering about in a thicket of citations, methodological issues, and statistical procedures, until they throw up their hands in disgust. After a few such experiences they conclude that research has no practical worth. Most practitioners will know the topic of the study before they begin reading it (e.g., teacher morale in our example here or class size in the case of Finn and Achilles), but that is not a substitute for knowing its question. *A study's topic is not its*

---

[7] The choice of phrasing seems to be, in part, a matter of disciplinary tradition; psychologists conducting quantitative research tend to test hypotheses; sociologists and economists tend to address questions.

[8] This is the question that guided this particular study, and we will phrase it this way throughout this chapter. However, keep in mind that Project STAR covered 4 years, and the question that guided the entire project is more accurately phrased as follows: What is the effect of making a substantial reduction in class size on student achievement in grades K–3?

question. We strongly recommend that you scan the first few pages of every study to determine the question that the author has proposed to answer. Then, if the question and its answer are likely to help you deal with your practical problem, it might we worth your time and effort to read the study.

Further, to use research effectively in your administrative practice, you cannot simply read the stuff; you need to make judgments of its quality. As we have said, all research is not created equal. (Indeed, the remainder of this book is intended to help you make better judgments of research quality.) However, a judgment of quality must be rooted in the question that a study poses. One research method is not inherently better than another. Whether a methodological choice is good or bad depends on the question that is being posed. If a researcher asks: "What is the average salary of private school teachers in the United States?" a well-designed survey makes more sense than a tightly controlled experiment.

Once you have a study's question clearly in mind, you need to identify the problem that the research concerns. Recall that we defined a problem as a gap between what is and what ought to be, between an empirical situation and someone's desires or expectations for that situation. Since education is an applied field of study, educational research problems are typically (but not always) derived from a practical problem of schooling that you, as a professional educator, will immediately recognize. Problems are usually explicitly stated within the first few pages of a report. Even when they are not, you can often recognize them by first identifying the question the study addresses and then asking yourself: "Why would anyone care about answering this question?" That is, research questions in education are important because their answers may help to solve a real problem. Again, Finn and Achilles provide an illustration. They do not explicitly state the problem that they intend to study. However, if we ask why anyone would care whether a substantial reduction in class size affects achievement, the problem becomes clear: The achievement of children, particularly poor and minority children, is low. It should be raised. (Notice the empirical and normative statements.) Their study of the effects of reducing class size might reveal a mechanism for remediating low achievement of children generally, and of poor and minority children particularly. That is, the study also addresses the problem of equality of opportunity.

Identifying a study's problem can provide a test of its relevance to your work. Conceived simply as a study on the *topic* of class size, the relevance of the Finn and Achilles article to the problem of low achievement in Irontown may not be obvious. However, its relevance is clear when a reduction of class size is seen as a way of solving the problem of low student achievement.

Confusing a problem with a topic in this way is the cause of a common difficulty students have when they attempt to use research. They will search the literature and then report that they could find nothing on their problem. That is almost always an error, since virtually every significant educational problem will have dozens, perhaps hundreds, of studies relevant to it. Typically, these students have misconceived their problem. For example, a student recently said that she could find very little research on her problem, which she described as "salary banking," that is, giving teachers the power to take a voluntary 20% cut in salary for five years in return for a paid sabbatical leave in the last of those years.[9] That, of course, is not a problem in the sense that we have defined it. It is a topic. When pressed as to why she was interested in such a scheme, she replied that she believed that teacher stress and burnout were excessive, and she thought the plan might help reduce them. The problem, then, was not salary banking, which the student correctly perceived as having been seldom researched, but alleviating excessive burnout and stress among teachers, matters about which there has been a great deal of research. Salary banking was simply one technique among many that might alleviate the problem. If a review of this (extensive) research shows stress and burnout are not problems for teachers,[10] the need for a study on salary banking becomes much less compelling.

One last point about the notion of a problem. As we noted earlier, researchers sometimes speak of "the problem" in their study in a different sense than the way we use the term. They speak of a problem as a *gap in knowledge*. We do not understand some phenomenon, and that is a problem. For example, a researcher might say that the problem of his or her study is to identify the conditions required for a child to move from Stage 2 to Stage 3 of Kohlberg's theory of moral development. Without saying more, this is a purely theoretical problem—a gap in our knowledge. It might be rooted in a practical problem, such as unacceptably high levels of school violence, but no such connection is required on the part of the researcher. The practitioner, however, will probably want to forge such a link before reading the study. Why spend the little time he or she has available for reading research on a purely theoretical question, one without any bearing on educational practice?[11] Asking "Why should practitioners care about the conditions required to move from Stage 2 to Stage 3?" helps to create that link. The research question and the problem of a study are both critical aspects of its conceptual level and are worthy of careful evaluation.

With these understandings we can now evaluate the conceptual level of the Finn and Achilles article. In chapter 4 one of the criteria we proposed for assessing the quality of a study was its *rationale*—the logic on which a study is based. In research involving presumed causes and effects, a rationale should express a logical argument linking independent and dependent variables. If the study simply seeks to establish that certain variables are related, an explanation for why those relationships are expected is required. In the case at hand, the authors should tell us precisely as possible why decreasing class size should increase student achievement. What is the underlying causal relationship? In this sense, a rationale is often referred to as a study's *theoretical framework*.

---

[9] For a description of such plans, see Jacobson and Kennedy (1997).

[10] For an excellent review of the literature on teacher stress and burnout, one that casts significant doubt on the quality of the reasoning and the evidence on these topics, see Guglielmi (1998).

[11] The obvious answer to our question is "idle curiosity," which is always an excellent reason to read something. However, practically speaking, few school administrators have either the time or the inclination to indulge themselves in this way. Perhaps they should, but that is another matter.

You can see the importance of these theoretical frameworks. Without them it is often difficult or impossible to make sense of a study. Consider an absurd example. Suppose someone carried out a study in which they measured the length of people's big toes and their IQs and then correlated the two measures. Suppose further that they found the correlation to be .2. (Such a correlation is quite possible, since many attributes measured on the same persons tend to be slightly correlated.) Other than its artifactual nature, however, what sense can be made of the correlation? The point is that researchers shouldn't examine the relationship among variables without good reasons for expecting there to be one. Again, they should offer an argument. You should identify and critically evaluate the logic of that argument. In the example we just gave, unless the researcher offered an argument linking toe length and IQ, you would (and should) dismiss the study as mindless.

Now, consider a more realistic example. Many people have carried out studies in which they measured teacher morale and student achievement and then correlated the two. When they found a positive correlation (as most did), they interpreted it as meaning that high teacher morale *causes* high student achievement. They argued, for example, that teachers with high morale work harder and when teachers work harder students learn more. But this argument, this rationale, is highly suspect. It is just as likely—perhaps more likely—that when students have high achievement, teachers find their own work easier and more pleasant; hence, they have higher morale. The causal relationship is exactly opposite of the one the researchers have postulated. By critically evaluating the researchers' rationale for correlating morale and achievement, you would recognize the very serious weakness of the interpretation often made of these studies. Without a clear rationale linking the two variables, the existence of a correlation between teacher morale and student achievement provides little support for the idea that raising teacher morale will improve student learning.

Now let's apply these ideas to "Questions and Answers." Do Finn and Achilles offer a theoretical framework, a rationale, for expecting reduced class size to increase student achievement? Not only do they offer a rationale, they offer a number of them, albeit in a very sketchy manner. For example, they suggest that small classes facilitate student-teacher interactions, allow better pupil evaluation, and so on, and these in turn improve student achievement (p. 146). The first paragraph of the article mentions at least five possible rationales or theories, and the "Discussion" section at the end of their paper adds still more.

This is a problem. When a research area has many alternative theories to explain its findings, it is in serious trouble. It suggests that the area is poorly conceptualized. This is not only a problem with the Finn and Achilles' study, it is a problem with the research literature on class size. As a result of this study and others that have emerged from the Tennessee project, we are quite sure that reducing the number of pupils in primary grades has a positive effect on achievement. But we have virtually no good, theoretically sound idea as to why this happens. To their credit, Finn and Achilles recognize the seriousness of this issue and call for research on how classroom processes change as a result of fewer students being present. However, calling for more research on a problem is standard practice among researchers. It is not a substitute for a rationale. When you examine the conceptual level of a study, you should look carefully at its research question and evaluate it on the cogency of its rationale.

What might a practitioner say, then, about the conceptual level of "Questions and Answers"? Finn and Achilles' near failure to distinguish among the possible rationales for expecting class size to affect student achievement is disappointing, given the massive nature of Project STAR. That they were aware of the importance of theoretically linking size and achievement is evident from their discussion in this article, from the study's title, and in STAR itself.

The Operational Level: Methodological Considerations

At the operational level the researcher takes the question posed at the conceptual level of a study and transforms (or *operationalizes*) it in a way that permits it to be answered empirically, that is, on the basis of evidence. The quality of the finished study, and the level of trust we are willing to put in its findings, depends to a substantial degree on the quality of the methodological decisions that the researcher makes. Hence, it is important to be able to evaluate those decisions. The problem, of course, is that it is precisely on these methodological issues that research becomes most arcane and least accessible to the practitioner. Nevertheless, we think that competent practitioners can make important and accurate judgments about a study's methodological quality. In this section we consider how those judgments can be made. In subsequent chapters we will consider issues of sampling, measurement, design and data analysis in more detail.

Consider again the question posed by Finn and Achilles: What is the effect of making a substantial reduction in class size on student achievement in grades K–1? Note that it is not possible to answer this question empirically. Just what students are they talking about? What is "class size"? What do they mean by a "substantial reduction"? What kind of "achievement" is affected? How will they be sure that class size reductions really caused any increase in achievement? Every researcher faces equivalent questions after the conceptual question is formulated. Such questions are addressed in the methodological portion of a report. That section might be named "Methods," "Procedures" (the term used by Finn & Achilles), or something equivalent. In quantitative empirical studies the researcher will normally address the following topics: sampling, measurement, design, and data analysis. Let's look at each of these and the criteria that you can use to assess their quality as we apply these criteria to "Answers and Questions about Class Size."

External Validity. In chapter 4 we suggested that it is necessary to evaluate the external validity of a study: To what extent are its results applicable to other students and schools and to your students and school? There we suggested that there are four common approaches to doing this.

Population Validity. The first approach to external validity is termed population validity—the extent to which a study's results generalize to a larger population.

Investigators are rarely able to include the entire population of relevant research subjects in a study. Presumably Finn and Achilles are interested in the effects of small classes on all primary grade children in the United States—their *target population*. Clearly, it would be impossible to study all of the nation's K–3 classrooms. Further, it would be extraordinarily difficult even to draw a small random sample for all U.S. schools. Instead, they had access to the elementary schools in Tennessee, their *accessible population*. From this accessible population they selected a set of elementary schools that met their criteria (e.g., those containing at least three kindergarten classes). Are these schools reasonably representative of U.S. elementary schools, and will their findings generalize to their target population of all U.S. elementary schools? While their sample was drawn only from Tennessee, and contained only relatively large schools (since every school had to have at least three kindergartens), we see no a priori reason why their findings will not generalize nationally. That is, we can think of no convincing reason for believing that the class size effects they observe would not apply in other states or in smaller schools. In short, we think the study deserves good marks regarding population validity.

Personalogical Validity. A second type of validity concerns the interaction of a treatment and characteristics of a study's subjects. Is there any indication in "Questions and Answers" that the small class treatment was differentially effective for different types of students? Finn and Achilles analyze the effects of small classes on white and minority students separately. Similarly, they examine the possibility that class size might have different effects in rural, suburban, urban, and inner city locations. Particularly important, they uncover significantly different results for majority and minority students, results that suggest that the latter benefit particularly from small classes. Given the importance of improving the achievement levels of minority students (the problem behind this study), this is an important finding, and the researchers are to be commended for investigating the possibility that it exists.

Ecological Validity. A third aspect external validity should be a focus of your evaluation, ecological validity. Ecological validity refers to the degree to which the findings derived from a study are dependent on the setting of the study. Can its findings, for example, be generalized to real life. This is a serious problem when the research involves setting up a special situation in order to control outside factors that might make its findings problematic. Suppose an investigator tests a particular pedagogical technique in a laboratory, where children are instructed individually by trained researchers while wired to a computer that monitors their physiological reactions to the instruction as well as their learning. Suppose also that such an experiment is the best possible way to test the effectiveness of the pedagogical technique, best in the sense that we can be sure that the instructional treatment caused the experimental results. Finally, suppose that the technique turns out to be highly effective in increasing children's achievement. You might well question whether the findings of such a study meant that the pedagogy would work in the same way when employed in an ordinary classroom by typical teachers in Irontown. Ordinary classrooms aren't labora-tories, teachers aren't researchers, and students aren't taught individually in iso-lated surroundings while connected to computers. The experiment has poor ecological validity.

Now consider the ecological validity of the Finn and Achilles study. Ordinary children, the children that would have shown up for kindergarten in Tennessee regardless of the experiment, were used in the study. The classrooms they entered were the ordinary kindergartens in their local school. For the most part the teachers were the same teachers who were already employed in the local districts. (Finn and Achilles do not tell us in this report how many new teachers had to be hired to fill Project STAR's staffing requirements.) Further, at least in the first years, the teachers of the experimental classes (both the small classes and those with aides) were given no special training, so presumably they taught their pupils in whatever way seemed appropriate, and used their aides in whatever ways they wished.[12] This is to say that these teachers probably behaved as would other teachers not involved in the experiment. Further, there were no changes made to the normal curriculum used in Tennessee schools. Finally, pupil achievement was measured with some of the same tests that are widely used throughout the country and in the state. Therefore, the criterion of ecological validity in the Finn and Achilles study deserves high marks, especially contrasted with the hypothetical computer-laboratory achievement study described earlier. Many experimental studies in education are much closer to that end of the eco-logical validity continuum than to the end occupied by Project STAR.

Application Validity. From your perspective as an administrator, however, the issues of population, personalogical, and ecological validity are likely to be less pressing than knowing whether you can apply Finn and Achilles' findings to Irontown's schools. We have referred to this matter as *application validity*. Will the results of their study hold in your schools? In the end, of course, you cannot definitively know this, and you cannot expect researchers to answer this question for you. However, by judiciously considering the other forms of external validity, and by carefully examining a study's data in the light of those other forms, you may be able to reach an informed judgment about the matter. For example, the descriptive data Finn and Achilles report permit you to assess the study's popu-lation validity—do students, teachers, and schools reasonably represent Tennessee and U.S. schools? However, the same data permit you to compare the classrooms in Irontown and those used in the study on some important demo-graphic characteristics, notably the racial and socioeconomic composition of the classes. You would also note that their sample contained a relatively large number of "inner-city" and "urban" classrooms likely to be similar to those in your district. A consideration of the personalogical validity of the Finn and Achilles study should suggest that small classes might be an especially useful

---

[12] A sample of teachers with aides did receive three days of training in their use in grade 2. This is a trivial amount and, in fact, seemed to have no effect on student achievement (Finn, 1998).

treatment in Irontown, since there was a significant race by treatment interaction,[13] and Irontown's inner city and urban schools contain heavy concentrations of minority children. Finally, the strong ecological validity of the STAR research suggests that it might transfer readily to your district—reducing class size seems to be a robust treatment, that is, not dependent on special classroom conditions, extensive training of teachers, and so forth. For all of these reasons, you might conclude the Finn and Achilles study possesses considerable application validity for Irontown.

A word of caution is in order here. It is very easy to discern ways in which your students differ from those involved in a piece of research and then to conclude that the study's findings cannot apply to your situation. Does the fact that the schools in the STAR project were all larger than average and in Tennessee make the findings inapplicable to Irontown? In both cases our answer is "probably not." The point is not whether the characteristics of your school differ from those of the schools in a study (they always will), but whether your school differs in ways that are likely to invalidate the study's findings. Will the differences make a difference? We can think of no compelling reason for believing that Irontown's urban and inner-city minority children will respond differently to class size reductions than their peers in Tennessee. But note that deciding on a study's application validity is very much a subjective judgment that you, as a school administrator, will have to make based on your understanding of a study's external validity and of your own schools.

In summary then, we judge that Finn and Achilles did a good job in helping their practitioner-readers evaluate their study's application validity. By presenting their results separately by location and race, administrators in Irontown can at least focus on those children who most resemble those in their district. Practitioners should remember that very few published articles do a particularly good job of this, if for no other reason than journal editors have limited space available, and they may not allow their authors to give extensive descriptions of the samples or populations used. Despite this difficulty, a practitioner will need to make some assessment of a study's application validity. Earlier we recommended that you contact the authors of studies especially important to your problem and discuss their work with them. Questions about the demographics of a sample, interactions of treatments and subjects' characteristics, and the ecology of the study's setting are among the appropriate topics for such conversations.

Measurement: Validity and Reliability. In quantitative research, measurement is critically important. If the constructs embedded in the researcher's question are not properly operationalized, the study's results may be misleading.

---

[13] The idea of an interaction is straightforward. It means that the effects of a treatment on a dependent variable depends on the level of a third variable. In this case, the effects of a class size reduction on student achievement depend on the race of the student: Black students benefit more from a given size reduction than do their white counterparts.

We have referred to the idea of a *construct* several times. A construct is a particular kind of concept, one that is inferred from observation of sometimes diverse phenomena and used to name a commonality among those phenomena. The research question posed by an investigator will contain the key constructs of the study. It is important that you identify these constructs. Recall the research question posed by Finn and Achilles: What is the effect of making a substantial reduction in class size on student achievement in grades K–1? Student achievement in this question is a key construct, as is class size. Achievement and class size don't really exist except as constructs. They are not real things that can be seen or touched, and hence, measured. Rather, they are abstractions derived from our experience in many kinds of situations. For instance, in education we speak of students getting high grades, scoring well on tests, graduating from high school, earning scholarships, winning spelling bees and making the football team (among a host of other things), as all evidencing "achievement." But we cannot measure achievement in the abstract; the construct must be defined as one or more of such real-life indicators. When it is defined (or operationalized), say as a test score, it may vary from one person or case to another, and researchers will speak of the construct as a *variable*. Most researchers tend to use that terminology.

Every empirical study must operationalize its key constructs, and it makes a very big difference how that is done. For example, there are thousands of studies of student achievement, but none has actually studied that. Instead, they studied scores on nationally standardized tests, teacher-assigned grades in math, performance on researcher-created science tests, or high school graduation rates. The danger is that because most of these studies discuss their results as "student achievement," it is easy for the practitioner-reader to forget just exactly what was studied. An investigation that reports that Treatment A had a powerful effect on student achievement may be less impressive to an Irontown administrator who keeps in mind that achievement really meant scores on a specially constructed instructor-made test of unknown validity. After all, Irontown needs to increase its students' performance on specific, state-prescribed tests. It does not need to improve achievement in some abstract sense.

The Finn and Achilles research question contains two important constructs or variables—class size and student achievement. In addition, other ancillary variables played a role in their work, for example, socioeconomic status, academic self-concept, and academic motivation. Each of these needed to be operationalized. Class size was defined by the number of pupils assigned by the researchers to each room. Achievement was defined as reading and math scores on the Stanford Achievement Tests (SATs) and the Basic Skills First (BSF) tests, the latter designed as curriculum-specific tests for measuring Tennessee children's learning of the state's curriculum objectives. The average socioeconomic status of pupils in a classroom was measured as the percent receiving free or reduced lunch, and pupil self-concept and motivation was measured using the Self-Concept and Motivation Inventory (the SCAMIN) developed by other researchers.

Beyond attending to the nature of the operationalizations involved, when you evaluate a study's measures you should attend carefully to their technical quality. The criteria for making these judgments, as we discussed in chapter 4, are validity and reliability. In the Finn and Achilles research question, the central constructs or variables are class size and achievement. The authors' measure of the former has obvious content validity: The size of a class was measured by counting the number of pupils assigned to it. Recall however, our earlier discussion of the ambiguities that surround this construct. There are arguably more valid measures, for example, the number of pupils in average daily attendance (this is especially appropriate if absenteeism is high) or the number of pupils actually involved in reading and math lessons. If, for instance, a teacher divides a class of 15 students into three groups of 5, 7, and 3 pupils for reading lessons, these could be reasonably termed reading class sizes in that classroom. From an elementary principal's perspective, however, defining class size as the number of pupils assigned to a classroom would be evidence of good content validity. Likewise, this simple measure has high reliability—two observers of the same class should come up with the same student count.

The dependent variables of reading and math achievement also possess good validity and reliability. The Stanford Achievement Test, the SAT, of course, is an established and well-known test battery. Its reliability and validity are readily available from the publisher or from other standard sources such as *The Mental Measurements Yearbook* (1998). The Basic Skills First Test, BSF, is largely unknown outside of Tennessee, but Achilles and Finn provide a reference for their readers to check if they wish more information regarding its psychometric properties. Because it is a state-wide, professionally created measure developed to assess the performance of children on the curriculum actually taught in Tennessee schools, it is likely to have good validity and reliability. In fact, because it is specifically tied to the school curriculum, it probably possesses greater content validity than the SAT.

If the major independent and dependent variables used in this article have good validity and reliability, the ancillary variables are more problematic. While it is commonly used in educational research, the percentage of children on free or reduced lunch is at best a rough index of the socioeconomic status of a school's clientele, and the SCAMIN has only marginal reliability, which the authors report. However, neither of these ancillary constructs is critical to the question addressed in this study. Overall, then, we find the measurement aspects of this study quite acceptable.

Design: The Criterion of Internal Validity. As we noted in chapter 4, a study's design is its plan for collecting data that will answer the research question posed by the investigator. In the case of causal studies, for example, one seeking to show that a change in variable A caused a change in variable B, the purpose of a design is to rule out, as nearly as is possible, the likelihood that some extraneous variable other than A actually caused the change in B. In the Finn and Achilles research, then, the authors and their colleagues tried to design their study so as to effectively rule out the possibility that something other than reduced class size might actually cause the improved achievement of small classes. Researchers speak of this quality as a study's *internal validity*. A study with good internal validity has been designed so that extraneous variables have been largely eliminated as causes of any observed change in the dependent variable.

What might such factors be? In a classic exposition Campbell and Stanley (1963) listed eight such causes, which Cook and Campbell subsequently expanded to 12 (Cook & Campbell, 1979). For example, they discuss *testing*, and *maturation*. Testing as a source of invalidity occurs when a researcher gives a pretest to a "single group of students, administers a treatment of some kind, and then gives a posttest to the same group. If students improve on the second testing, that improvement might be the result of the treatment, but it also might be the result of students becoming "testwise" from taking the pretest. Maturation as a possible cause of invalidity is the result of the passage of time between initial and subsequent testing. For example, student scores may improve on a posttest not because the treatment worked, but simply because time has passed, they have become more mature, and they are therefore better able to answer the questions posed to them.

It may be less important for practitioners to be familiar with all of the various sources of internal invalidity than to recognize that true experiments provide the best protection against almost all of them. Recall our discussion in chapter 4. True experiments have two characteristics: First, the researcher must have administered a treatment to at least one group and withheld it from another—there must have been one or more experimental groups and a control group. Second, the subjects of the experiment must have been assigned to each group randomly. Random assignment requires that each subject in the study be assigned to treatment or control group using a method that guarantees that only chance determined their assignment. Usually this means that a table of random numbers was used in the assignment process. There are other kinds of research designs, including quasi-experimental, correlational, and causal-comparative studies that we will discuss more fully in subsequent chapters. These other designs are very common in causal educational research. However, none of them offers the level of assurance offered by a true experiment that an independent variable actually caused an observed change in a dependent variable.

The Finn and Achilles study is a true experiment. Two experimental treatments (a small kindergarten class of approximately 15 and a regular kindergarten class of approximately 25 with a teacher's aide) were established in each school. A control group consisting of a regular kindergarten class of 25 without an aide was also established in each school. Then, incoming children were randomly assigned to all three types of classrooms. In addition, teachers were randomly assigned to each type of class.

One of the striking aspects of the design was the investigators' requirement that participating schools had to have enough incoming kindergartners to permit all three types of classes to be established in every school. This effectively eliminated the possibility that school-level extraneous variables might have caused any observed changes in achievement. For example, every small classroom made up of children from a wealthy suburban neighborhood was matched by a regular classroom from the same neighborhood; every small classroom in a school with a highly effective principal was matched by a regular classroom with the same principal. Thus, wealth, suburban life, and principal leadership cannot explain the increase in achievement that Finn and Achilles report.

Even more striking, children in the small kindergartens were kept together for four years, through grade 3, each year with a randomly assigned teacher. Thus, the researchers were able to examine the cumulative effects of four years in a small class.

The Finn and Achilles study that you have read reports only the results of the experiment after its first two years. For a final report of the effects of all four years see Achilles, Nye, Zaharias, and Fulton (1993) and Finn and Achilles (1998a). Project STAR stands as a model of a carefully designed, long-term, experimental study in education. Its design effectively eliminates any serious doubt that the achievement gains of small classes are due to anything other than reduced class sizes in the primary grades. Just how substantial that is we will see in a moment.

The Empirical Level

The empirical level of a study is the third and final level of the tripartite division we described earlier. In quantitative studies, after researchers have described what question they are trying to answer and why (the conceptual level of a study), and what data they will collect and how they will analyze those data to answer that question (the operational level), they will report the results of their work in its empirical level: What is the answer to the research question, and what are the implications of that answer? Typical terms that mark this section of a report are "Findings," and "Results." Additional subheadings of the empirical level often describe other aspects: "Discussion," "Conclusion," and "Implications for Practice" are typical. Because Finn and Achilles compared the achievement effects of the three types of classes at the same grade level (a cross-sectional analysis) and then made a second comparison across time, comparing student growth in small classes to student growth in the other two types of classes (a longitudinal analysis), they report their findings in two sections corresponding to these two kinds of analyses.

The empirical phase commands a substantial proportion of the space in journal articles, and reporting this phase creates the most headaches for practitioners. Many of the terms used in describing data analyses are necessarily arcane: "multiple regression," "chi-square," "cannonical correlation" and, in the case of Finn and Achilles, "multivariate analysis of variance." Such terms are essential; they convey precisely the nature of the researcher's data analysis. It is pointless for practitioners to inveigh against this use and to demand that researchers speak ordinary English. Every profession develops a specialized vocabulary to convey exact meanings when conversing with colleagues. This is especially the case in regard to the methods by which researchers in the profession build its knowledge base. As a consequence, the more sophisticated a profession becomes, the more laymen and ordinary practitioners of the profession are excluded from conversations among researchers. Articles that appear in a profession's major research journals are simply not written for practitioners.

The *American Educational Research Journal* (in which the Finn and Achilles study appears) is one major outlet for quality research in education. The authors of its articles, however, seldom have practitioners in mind when they are writing their research reports. They write for other researchers.

This situation creates obvious problems for most practitioners, who have little training in research, but who want to read and understand the serious scholarly work pertaining to a problem in their schools. We can make some helpful suggestions. A practitioner should approach the empirical level of a study as follows: First, read this section of a research report with a very narrow purpose in mind. Keep the research question at the center of your thoughts and ask what answer did the investigator claim to find for that question? Once you have identified the investigator's answer, next ask if the researcher provides any assurance that the answer was not the result of chance. Could the findings of the study be nothing more than an accident? Finally, if the researcher's results are not likely to have been due to chance, and if the study seeks to identify the effects of an independent variable on a dependent variable, ask how big was the effect of the former on the latter.

Findings: Answers to the Study's Question. Let us apply these three steps to the Finn and Achilles study. Their research question concerned the effect of making a substantial reduction in class size on student achievement in grades K–1. Now scan the first section of the empirical level of their report, "Cross-sectional Findings." What is their answer to this question? Does class size affect achievement? In the case of quantitative research that reports its results in both tables and text, you should consult both to learn the researcher's findings regarding his or her question. By checking both tables and text, you are essentially cross-checking your understanding of a study's results. Many practitioners simply skip all tables, which is a mistake. Most tables are quite intelligible if you attend carefully to their titles and the headings of their columns and rows. You seldom need to understand *how* the numbers in the table were generated, that is, what statistical procedures were used to create them. Rather, it is usually sufficient to have a grasp of their nature: Are they percentages? Means? Measures of the effect of one variable on another? When it is not obvious from a table's title or headings, this kind of understanding can usually be gleaned by finding that portion of the text in which the table is discussed. With this rudimentary understanding many tables become intelligible.

For example, one table that should catch your eye immediately is on page 152 of "Answers and Questions," which we have reproduced here as Table 5.1. In it Finn and Achilles report the mean scores on their cognitive outcome measures by school location and class type. The column headings are the various types of achievement outcomes that they discussed earlier in their article (Word study skills, SAT reading, and so on). The rows give the four different kinds of school locations (Inner-City, Urban, Suburban, and Rural) and within each of these, the mean or average score of each kind of class (Small, Regular, and Regular with Aide).

TABLE *5.1*

Mean Scores on Cognitive Outcomes by Location and Class Type From Finn and Achilles (1990, p. 564)

	Measure				
Group	Word study skills	SAT reading	BSF reading	SAT math	BSF math
Inner-City	497.9	486.7	51.7	510.7	71.1
Small	506.0	493.9	61.2	517.4	77.0
Regular	491.9	482.4	46.3	505.9	66.8
Aide	495.2	483.2	46.6	508.5	69.1
Urban	534.5	518.8	65.4	530.8	81.9
Small	544.9	531.1	74.9	540.5	84.7
Regular	527.0	508.3	61.0	526.5	82.9
Aide	532.4	518.0	60.6	525.6	77.6
Suburban	528.0	513.1	62.6	528.7	83.4
Small	540.9	523.9	68.9	540.8	89.0
Regular	518.7	507.4	58.6	521.1	80.4
Aide	523.5	506.5	59.8	522.8	79.9
Rural	537.0	521.6	63.3	536.7	83.4
Small	541.8	528.9	68.3	541.6	85.1
Regular	531.9	512.9	57.0	531.8	80.1
Aide	537.0	522.5	64.2	536.2	84.7
Standard deviation	51.55	55.48	48.56	41.60	38.91

Notice how this simple grasp of the table's structure opens the study's findings to you. For example, as an administrator from Irontown, you would be particularly interested in the "Inner-City" and "Urban" comparisons, since schools in those locations are most like the schools in your district. Do small classes improve the achievement of these particular kinds of children? Looking across the "Inner-City" and "Urban" rows, it becomes clear that the average performance of first graders in small classes is higher than that of their peers in either classes with aides or regular classes, and that is true for all outcome measures. For example, on the SAT reading test, inner-city students in small classes averaged 493.9, while inner city children in regular classes averaged 482.4, and those in classes with aides 483.2. Similarly, on the BSF reading test, urban children in small classes outperformed their peers in regular classes without and with aides, scoring 74.9, 61.0 and 60.6, respectively.

Next find the place in the text where that table is discussed. Check your understanding of your reading of Table 5.1 (Finn and Achilles Table 3) by checking the discussion of that table in the text. Simply ignore all discussion of statistical techniques, computational methods, and so on, unless you are terribly

TABLE *5.2*

Small Class Advantage by Race. From Finn and Achilles (1990, p. 567)

Measure	White		Minority	
	Mean difference	Effect size	Mean difference	Effect size
Word study skills	7.9	.16	14.1	.32
SAT reading	8.6	.15	16.7	.35
BSF reading	4.8%	.10	17.3%	.35
SAT math	9.0	.22	11.6	.31
BSF math	3.1%	.09	7.0%	.16

interested in such matters.[14] On page 152 the authors summarize their findings to this point: "On the average, small classes positively affect student performance in first grade." By cross-checking between tables and text you are more likely to get a good grasp of the study's findings. By reading tables, you may also discover other useful findings that the author might not discuss.

Again, because you are from Irontown, Table 6 in the article (Table 5.2 above) should be of considerable interest. Because Irontown has a substantial number of minority students, you are especially interested in knowing whether reducing class size is of any special benefit to those students. In their Table 6 Finn and Achilles compare the mean differences in scores for white and minority students separately in small classes with their performance in both types of regular classes combined. This permits you to directly compare the gains made by each group. The improvement of minority students is, on all measures, greater than that of whites. For example, you can see on the BSF reading test that being in small classes increased the average number of white students who passed that test by 4.8%. In contrast, being in small classes increased the percentage of minorities passing by 17.3%. Checking the text's description of this table (on p. 154) corroborates this interpretation: "For all five measures, the advantage of being in a small class is greater for minority students than for whites."

Statistical Significance. After identifying the researchers' answers to the questions they posed, the next step is to be sure that those answers were not simply the result of chance. A major purpose of inferential statistics is to assess the possibility that the findings of a study are not simply the result of random factors. Suppose, for

---

[14] We recognize that many of our colleagues will take umbrage at our recommendation that you ignore the statistics involved in manipulating and analyzing data. We certainly agree that understanding the statistics would improve your understanding of research. However, only a tiny minority of school administrators will have the time to become sufficiently versed in statistics that they will understand the analyses undergirding most educational research that is published in today's journals. We think their time would be better spent on their primary responsibilities.

example, that small classes really have no effect on student achievement—that the real difference in mean SAT reading scores between small and regular classes is 0. After all, this is only one study. If Finn and Achilles drew another sample of schools and repeated their experiment, they certainly would not get exactly the same numbers that they report in this article. Perhaps, in this second study, there might be no difference at all between student achievement in different size classes. Or, perhaps they might find that regular classes are better. Given certain assumptions, for example, random sampling, inferential statistics allow us to estimate the likelihood that the real difference between small and regular classes is 0—that the results Finn and Achilles obtained were the result of a chance drawing from a population of schools in which class size has no effect on achievement.

Providing an estimate of this chance is the message conveyed by the ubiquitous p-values that one often finds in quantitative studies. Attached to a table of results, these symbols indicate the probability (p) that those results could be the consequence of a chance drawing of a sample from a population in which the true difference is 0. The example of $p < .05$ means that whatever finding is being presented is large enough that it had only 5 chances in 100 of occurring by chance, if the true difference in the population is 0. Conventionally, $p < .05$ is the standard for saying that the results probably did not occur by chance but are due to a study's treatment. This standard, however, is purely arbitrary; it could be set higher or lower and often is. When you are using the evidence from a quantitative study based on samples to arrive at a practical decision in your school, you want to be sure that whatever results it reports are not simply the product of chance. Thus, before you would rely on the Finn and Achilles study to make a recommendation to the Irontown school district, you would want to check the p-levels. These can be found in their Table 2 (on p. 152) for their cross-sectional results. You are primarily interested in the effect of class type on achievement. Reading across the row for type, you can see that all class-size differences were large enough to occur less than 1 time in 1,000 by chance, with the single exception of those for BSF math, which might occur 5 times in 100 by chance. It seems, then, that you can be confident (but not certain) that Finn and Achilles' findings are not the result of chance.

Practical Significance: The Effect Size. Finally, and only after deciding that chance is an unlikely explanation for a study's findings, you need to ask whether the effects it reports have any practical significance. After all, just because an event is rare does not mean that it is important. Imagine a new program to raise scores on the SAT reading test. Suppose a careful study shows that it almost certainly does this, that is, $p < .001$. It does not follow that you would want to adopt the program. If the program raised SAT scores, on average, one tenth of a point, that would not be considered an impressive amount. And if you also knew that the program was very costly, you would certainly not recommend its adoption by your district. The most important thing that you must remember about p-values is that they are very heavily dependent on the sample size used by the researcher: *The larger the sample size, the smaller the treatment's effect can be and still be statistically significant.* Thus, you want to be sure that a treatment's effect is not only statistically significant but also practically significant. That is the purpose of an effect size statistic.

In chapter 4 we discussed effect sizes (ES), and we will elaborate on that discussion in the next chapter. Suffice it to say that an effect size provides a standardized measure of the size of a treatment's effect in standard deviation units, where an ES of 1.0 means that the treatment raised a group's mean score by one standard deviation. Whether an effect size is large is ultimately a subjective matter, but in education an ES of .3 is usually considered practically important. A good study designed to assess the effects of a treatment on some educational outcome should report the effect size that the treatment produces. Certainly it should provide all of the information that you need to calculate the treatment's effect size yourself. (In chapter 6, we provide several opportunities to calculate effect sizes.)

Finn and Achilles provide the effect sizes of their treatment—classes of 15 students—and also for placing an aide in regular classes. These are shown in their Table 5 (on p. 155). There we can see that, on average, students in small classes gain about one fourth of a standard deviation on the various tests used, with the exception of the BSF math test where the ES was .13. While .25 is not large in the sense described previously, it is certainly not trivial. It is equivalent to raising the average child's SAT score from the 50th to roughly the 60th percentile. Perhaps even more importantly, in their Table 6 (on p. 156) we see that the effect size of small classes is substantially different for white and minority students. While the former gain roughly .15 of a standard deviation, the latter gain about .33. When you glean such information from tables you want to confirm your interpretation of those tables in the report's text. Confirmation can be found on pages 154 and 155 of the article.

Now try your hand at reading the empirical level of the study concerning the effects of small class size over time. How much did small classes affect children who were exposed to them for two consecutive years? Keeping this question in mind, use the tables and text to find the study's results and check those results for statistical and practical significance. The relevant findings are reported in the section labeled "Longitudinal Results" beginning on page 156.

Finally, check your interpretation of any study by carefully reading its concluding section. In "Questions and Answers" this begins on page 160 and is labeled "Discussion." (You can usually find a summary of a study's findings in the first few paragraphs of its concluding section.) Finn and Achilles interpret their research as showing conclusively that small class sizes markedly improve the reading and math achievement of pupils in the primary grades. With much less certainty, they believe that they have uncovered evidence that aides also improve performance. Since (as they acknowledge) this finding was not statistically significant, we suggest that practitioners treat an "aide effect" as an open question. On the basis of this study, you would not want to recommend to Irontown that it employ aides to improve achievement, knowing that the effect observed by its authors may be simply a result of chance. They find mixed support for special benefits for minority students. As they note, this is a critically important issue, one to which they return in subsequent studies.

Some Final Remarks

We would be remiss if we left the topic of class size without at least a brief mention of the Lasting Benefits Study and Project Challenge (Nye et al., 1995a; Nye et al., 1992). In your role as a committee member in Irontown, you would have discovered the final report of Project STAR (Word et al., 1990a) and these extensions of the project in your search of the literature. These reports would play a substantially larger role in your committee's recommendation than the single study that we have focused on in this chapter. You should note particularly Finn's summary for the Department of Education (Finn, 1998) and a recent addition of the journal *Educational Evaluation and Policy Analysis* (volume 21, no. 2, 1999) that was devoted entirely to issue of class size research and its implications.

STAR lasted four years, from 1985 to 1989. Children who had begun kindergarten in small classes continued to be assigned to small classes through grade three, and their performance was compared to their peers in regular classes with and without aides.[15] At the end of four years, the reading scores of children in small classes were, on average, about 8 percentile points above their peers in regular classes. In math the difference was about 7 percentiles. There was only a negligible difference favoring classes with aides over those without. The initially larger gain of minority students noted previously disappeared; after the second year both whites and minorities gained at the same rate.

When Project STAR ended all students entered regular size classes in the fourth grade and continued in them in subsequent years. Naturally questions were raised as to whether the benefits students experience from small classes would last. These questions provoked the Lasting Benefits Study (LBS), in which STAR children have been followed as they progress through school. When the children finished eighth grade, STAR students continued to show higher achievement levels than their peers, though their advantage declined with the passage of time (Nye et al., 1995a). It is worth noting that as the children moved up the grades, testing expanded to include subjects beyond reading and math (e.g., science and social studies). "The statistically significant advantages for LBS eighth-grade students, who had been in Project STAR small classes, form a strong pattern of consistency. Small-class students outperformed regular and regular-with-aid class students on every achievement measure" (Nye et al., 1995a, p. 19). Effect sizes for these differences averaged slightly over .06. An ES of .06

---

[15] It is worth noting that while students in small classes stayed in small classes, those in regular classes were randomly reassigned in the second year of the study to aide or non-aide regular classes. However, none were reassigned to small classes. This happened as a result of parent objections to having their children denied the benefits of small classes or aides. If you are a principal, you can imagine the difficulties principals in STAR schools undoubtedly experienced. To the administrators' and researchers' credit, they were able to maintain the small class groups intact, ensuring that they would be able to arrive at definitive conclusions about the effects of small classes. On the other hand, notice the ethical dilemma: After two years the beneficial effects of small classes was becoming evident, while the benefits of being in a classroom with an aid were far from obvious. Yet the researchers and school administrators continued to deny children access to the benefits of small classes.

may seem distinctly underwhelming. However, remember this is five years after the treatment ended. Minority students who had been in small classes in grades K–3 continued to outperform minority students who had not. This is an encouraging finding; it seems that the benefits of small classes linger for some years. It will be interesting to see whether students benefit when in high school, perhaps especially on noncognitive outcomes such as dropping out.

As another follow up to STAR, in 1989 Tennessee implemented small classes in the K–3 grades of the 16 school districts with the lowest average income of all districts in the state, that is, the districts with the highest proportion of children at risk. Thus, this project (Project Challenge) was a direct attempt to apply the lessons learned from STAR and LBS. In 1989, if one ranked all of the school districts in Tennessee in terms of student achievement (as measured by state-developed, curriculum-specific tests), Project Challenge districts were well below the state average. After five years of small primary classes, they were above the state average in mathematics and within 10 ranks of the average in reading. This suggests, according to Nye and her colleagues, that a small-class intervention begun in the earliest grades is capable of moving school districts serving populations that typically do least well on standardized tests to positions well within the average range. This is, of course, precisely the kind of movement Irontown needs to demonstrate. Note, however, that Project Challenge was not an experimental study and it was exposed to most of the threats to internal validity that plague such research.

The class size studies in Tennessee stand as a model of the kind of educational research that should drive educational practice. Project STAR was a true experiment, meaning students and teachers were randomly assigned to treatment and control groups. Its design effectively ruled out school and community-level factors that might have invalidated its results. It was implemented for a full four years, enough time for its effects to appear and be properly assessed. It was installed in a large number of ordinary classrooms taught by ordinary teachers, so that its findings were not the result of special conditions. Its sampling, measurement, and data analysis were well executed. It is fair to say that the study's finding are conclusive: Small classes in the primary grades can make substantial improvements in student achievement. There have been no studies of other educational innovations that provide as compelling evidence for the innovation's efficacy. Indeed, Frederick Mosteller, a Harvard professor of mathematical statistics and member of the American Academy of Arts and Science, described STAR as "one of the most important educational investigations ever carried out and illustrates the kind and magnitude of research needed in the field of education to strengthen schools" (Mosteller, 1995, p. 113).

This is not to say that all of the questions, or even the most important questions, about class size have been answered. We do not know whether reducing class size is the most cost-effective way of improving student achievement. We do not know how long the benefits of small primary grade classes last. We remain unsure of their lasting effects on poor and minority children, a question of huge national importance. We do not even know why reducing class size works. This last question is the one that Finn and Achilles use to open their paper and the one on which they close it. It provides the paper's title: "Answers and *Questions* about Class Size" [italics added]. Good research raises more questions that it answers.

In this regard we would make one final point about Project STAR. We have faulted Finn and Achilles for the lack of a rationale connecting class size and student outcomes. More precisely, we have faulted them for providing a plethora of rationales. In administrative perspective this may be an unimportant defect. In a sense, the important finding from Project STAR is that reducing class size works, and setting class size is an administrative prerogative. Class size is administratively mutable. The Finn and Achilles study and its follow-ups show that administrators, *by their own actions in setting reduced class sizes in K–3*, can have substantial effects on student achievement, regardless of teacher training, pupil background, and classroom equipment.

There may be other strategies for improving achievement, especially of poor and minority children, that have larger effect sizes. Cooperative learning, the subject of the next chapter, comes to mind. However, nearly all of those strategies depend on the compliance of teachers. If a strategy is to work in a district with Irontown's problems, all or nearly all teachers must be trained in it, they must be motivated and committed to its use, they must practice it daily, and the support systems the strategy requires must be in place in all or nearly all schools. When teachers leave the district their replacements must be trained, they must be motivated, and so forth. Even relatively simple school improvement schemes require constant maintenance. Complex procedures such as cooperative learning are very demanding in this regard. There are few school improvement schemes that will produce effect sizes in the .25 range that depend on little more than the will to commit the necessary resources and an administrative decision. It is also worth pointing out that most other kinds of improvement strategies can be coupled with a reduction in class size. Indeed, we suspect that many will be more easily implemented and maintained and be more effective in smaller than in regular classes (Finn, 1998). Thus, perhaps joining class-size reductions with other school improvement strategies offers the best hope of making major improvements in children's learning.

Having completed your review of the research on the implications of the class size research for questions 1 and 2, you prepare a memo to your fellow committee members stating your conclusions. We reproduce that memo in Figure 5.2. Notice that, unlike the literature reviews one finds in doctoral dissertations, master's theses, and research reports, your review is brief and to the point. Notice in particular that the review *uses* the studies to build an argument for a course of administrative action in Irontown. It does not discuss the studies themselves. It specifically addresses the questions to be answered and cites only research that bears directly on those questions. Remember, you are searching for pertinent research to help your district make practical decisions; you are not writing a literature review.

Memorandum

TO: Judith Cohn, Westside High School
       George Castener, Central Office, ICSD
FR: Susan Resnick, John Jay Middle School
RE: Class size questions and Irontown's problem

I have completed my review of the literature that speaks to the first two questions on our list. Below are my conclusions about each with a few of the most important references that directly concern those conclusions.

We'll meet to discuss these and the results of your work on the other questions next Wednesday at 4 p.m. in my office.

1. *What achievement benefits can we expect from making a substantial reduction in our district's average class size?*

If we reduce primary grade (K–3) class sizes, the achievement effect will not be huge but it will be substantial. The best estimate available (Word, et al., 1990) suggests that we may get effect sizes in the range of .25. This translates into an improvement of approximately 10 percentile points on the average child's scores on national, norm-referenced tests and curriculum specific tests. Of course we can't be sure the same result will apply to our state's tests, but I see no reason why it should not. While not all studies report effect sizes in this range, for example, Slavin (1989), or even conclude that reducing class size has a positive effect (Hanushek, 1989), the STAR studies in Tennessee seem definitive. (For a recent summary see Finn & Achilles, 1999.) Blatchford and Mortimor (1994) and Mosteller (1995, 1996) in careful reviews reach the same conclusion. A special issue of *Educational Evaluation and Policy Analysis* (volume 21, no. 2, 1999) is devoted to the topic and provides additional supporting (and some conflicting) evidence.

2. *Just what does "substantial" mean in this case? That is, how far would we have to reduce our current class size to get a significant improvement in test scores?*

On this point the research is rather clear. We would need to get down to 15 children in K–3. The Word et al. study cited above contrasted classes that averaged 15 with those that averaged 22, some of the latter having full-time teacher aides. Aides, incidentally, had little positive effect on achievement. When class sizes begin to range above 15, achievement effects appear to fall off sharply (Finn, 1998; Glass & Smith, 1979). It is not clear that reducing class size in upper grades has as large an effect (Blatchford & Mortimore, 1994)

I look forward to discussing the results of our work next Wednesday.

Continued

F I G U R E   *5.2*   Memorandum

Memorandum Reference List

Blatchford, P., & Mortimore, P. (1994). The issue of class size for young children in schools: What can we learn from research? *Oxford Review of Education, 20*(4), 411–428.

Finn, J. D. (1998). *Class size and students at risk: What is known? What is next?* Washington, DC: Office of Educational Research and Improvement, U.S. Department of Education.

Finn, J. D., & Achilles, C. M. (1999). Tennessee's class size study: Findings, Implications, Misconceptions. *Educational Evaluation and Policy Analysis, 21*(2), 97–109.

Glass, G. V., & Smith, M. L. (1979). Meta-analysis of research on class size and achievement. *Educational Evaluation and Policy Analysis, 1*(1), 2–16.

Hanushek, E. A. (1989). The impact of differential expenditures on school performance. *Educational Researcher, 18*(4), 45–51,62.

Mosteller, F. (1995). The Tennessee study of class size in the early school grades. *Future of Children, 5*(2), 113–127.

Mosteller, F., Light, R. J., & Sachs, J. A. (1996). Sustained Inquiry in Education: Lessons from Skill Grouping and Class Size. *Harvard Educational Review, 66*(4), 797–842.

Slavin, R. E. (1989). Achievement effects of substantial reductions in class size. In R. E. Slavin (Ed.), *School and classroom organization* (pp. 247–257). Hillsdale, NJ: Erlbaum.

Word, E. R., Johnson, J., Bain, H., Fulton, D. B., Boyd-Zaharias, J., Lintz, M. N., Achilles, C. M., Folger, J., & Breda, C. (1990). *Student/Teacher Achievement Ratio (STAR) Tennessee's K–3 Class Size Study.* Nashville, TN: Tennessee State Department of Education.

References

Achilles, C. M. (1998, April). *If not before, at least now.* Paper presented at the American Educational Research Association, Los Angeles, CA.

Achilles, C. M., Nye, B. A., Zaharias, J. B., & Fulton, B. D. (1993). Creating successful schools for all children: A proven step. *Journal of School Leadership, 3*(3), 606–621.

Alkin, M. C., & American Educational Research Association. (1992). *Encyclopedia of educational research* (6th ed.). New York: Macmillan.

Bain, H. P., & Achilles, C. M. (1986). Interesting developments on class size. *Phi Delta Kappan, 67*(9), 662–665.

Campbell, D. T., & Stanley, J. C. (1963). *Experimental and quasi-experimental designs for research.* Chicago: Rand McNally.

Cook, T. D., & Campbell, D. T. (1979). *Quasi-experimentation: Design and analysis issues for field settings.* Chicago: Rand McNally.

Finn, J. D. (1998). *Class size and students at risk: What is known? What is next?* Washington, DC: Office of Educational Research and Improvement, U.S. Department of Education.

Finn, J. D., & Achilles, C. M. (1998, April). *Tennessee's class-size study: Questions answered, questions posed.* Paper presented at the American Educational Research Association, San Francisco, CA.

Finn, J. D., & Achilles, C. M. (1990). Answers and Questions about Class Size: A Statewide Experiment. *American Educational Research Journal, 27*(3), 557–577.

Finn, J. D., & Voelkl, K. E. (1994). Class size. In T. Husen & T. N. Postlethwaite (Eds.), *International encyclopedia of education* (2nd ed.). New York: Pergamon.

Glass, G. V., & Smith, M. L. (1978). *Meta-analysis of research on the relationship of class-size and achievement.* (OB-NIE-G-78-0103). San Francisco, CA: Far West Laboratory for Educational Research and Development. (ERIC Document Reproduction No. ED168129)

Glass, G. V., & Smith, M. L. (1979). Meta-analysis of research on class size and achievement. *Educational Evaluation and Policy Analysis, 1*(1), 2–16.

Guglielmi, R. S., & Tatrow, K. (1998). Occupational stress, burnout, and health in teachers: A methodological and theoretical analysis. *Review of Educational Research, 68*(1), 61–99.

Guthrie, J. W., & Kirst, M. W. (1988). *Conditions of education in California: 1988*. Berkeley, CA: University of California, Policy Analysis for Education (PACE).

Husen, T., & Postlethwaite, T. N. (Eds.). (1994). *International encyclopedia of education* (2nd ed.). New York: Pergamon.

Jacobson, S. L., & Kennedy, S. (1997). Time, money, and the control of one's own work life: An examination of the deferred salary leave plan. *Educational Policy, 11*(3), 267–285.

Mosteller, F. (1995). The Tennessee study of class size in the early school grades. *Future of Children, 5*(2), 113–127.

Mosteller, F., Light, R. J., & Sachs, J. A. (1996). Sustained inquiry in education: Lessons from skill grouping and class size. *Harvard Educational Review, 66*(4), 797–842.

Nye, B., Boyd-Zaharias, J., Fulton, B. D., Achilles, C. M., Cain, V. A., & Tollett, D. A. (1995a). *The lasting benefits study: A continuing analysis of the effect of small class size in kindergarten through third grade on student achievement test scores in subsequent grade levels: Eighth Grade (1993–1994)*. Nashville, TN: Center of Excellence for Research and Policy on Basic Skills, Tennessee State University.

Nye, B. A., Boyd-Zaharias, J., Cain, V. A., Fulton, B. D., Achilles, C. M., & Tollett, D. A. (1995). *Project challenge fifth year summary report: An initial evaluation of the Tennessee Department of Education "at-risk" student/teacher ratio reduction project in sixteen counties, 1989–90 through 1993–94*. Nashville, TN: Center of Excellence for Research and Policy on Basic Skills, Tennessee State University.

Nye, B. A., Achilles, C. M. Boyd-Zaharias, J., Fulton, B. D., & Wallenhorst, M. (1994). Small is far better. *Research in the Schools, 1*(1), 9–20.

Plake, B. S., & Impara, J. C. (1998). *The thirteenth mental measurements yearbook*. (Vol. 13). Lincoln, NE: The Buros Institute for Mental Measurements, University of Nebraska Press.

Shapson, S. M., Wright, E. N., Eason, G., & Fitzgerald, J. (1980). An experimental study of the effects of class size. *American Educational Research Journal, 17*(2), 141–152.

Slavin, R. E. (Ed.). (1989). *School and classroom organization*. Hillsdale, NJ: Erlbaum.

Word, E., Johnston, J., Bain, H., Fulton, D. B., Boyd-Zaharias, J., Lintz, M. N., Achilles, C. M., Folger, J., & Breda, C. (1990a). *Student/Teacher Achievement Ratio (STAR) Tennessee's K–3 Class Size Study*. Nashville, TN: Tennessee Department of Education.

Word, E. R., Johnston, J., Pate-Bain, H., Fulton, D. B., Zaharias, J. B., Lintz, M. N., Achilles, C. M., Folger, J., & Breda, C. (1990b). *The State of Tennessee's student/teacher achievement ratio (STAR) project: Technical report*. Nashville, TN: Tennessee State Department of Ed.

APPENDIX

Answers and Questions About Class Size: A Statewide Experiment

Jeremy D. Finn and
Charles M. Achilles

A large-scale experiment is described in which kindergarten students and teachers were randomly assigned to small and large classes within each participating school. Students remained in these classes for 2 years. At the end of each grade they were measured in reading and mathematics by standardized and curriculum-based tests. The results are definitive: (a) a significant benefit accrues to students in reduced-size classes in both subject areas and (b) there is evidence that minority students in particular benefit from the smaller class environment, especially when curriculum-based tests are used as the learning criteria. A longitudinal analysis of a portion of the sample indicated that students in small classes outperform their peers in kindergarten classes of regular size and also gain more in reading outcomes during the second year. The question of why these effects are realized remains largely unanswered, but in light of these findings, is particularly important to pursue.

The question of class size continues to attract the attention of educational policymakers and researchers alike. To school personnel, small classes promise to facilitate increased student–teacher interaction, allow for thorough and continuous student evaluation, and provide greater flexibility in teaching strategies. Not only are these processes generally desirable, but they are exactly the processes that are likely to benefit students at risk for school failure (Slavin & Madden, 1987). Administratively, smaller classes reduce teachers' responsibilities for paperwork and record keeping, allowing them to allocate more time to instructionally relevant activities. Under ideal circumstances, a small class may also minimize discipline problems because the teacher can more easily keep all students under a watchful eye. At the same time, the cost of smaller classes is high, requiring investment in both additional teacher salaries and additional classroom space. This investment is unlikely to be forthcoming unless the evidence that positive outcomes will be realized is substantial and consistent.

This is not the case. In 1978, Glass and Smith undertook an extensive meta-analysis of class-size research aimed at settling the issue unambiguously. The authors concluded without qualification "that reduced class-size can be expected to produce increased academic achievement" (p. iv). Instead of settling the issue, the report was met with criticism (some of it compelling) and extensive debate about the very existence, not to mention magnitude, of the "class-size effect." Robinson and Wittebols (1986) also integrated a large number of empirical studies and arrived at a different set of conclusions:

> Existing research findings do not support the contention that smaller classes will of themselves result in greater academic achievement of pupils. . . . There is research evidence that small classes are important to increased pupil achievement in reading and mathematics in the early primary grades. . . . There is evidence that pupils with lower academic ability tend to benefit more from smaller classes than do pupils with average ability. (pp. 18–19)

Slavin (1989) reviewed eight well-designed studies, concluding that substantial reductions in class size do indeed have modest benefits among young children. However, the author noted that long-term studies indicate that the effects are not cumulative across grades and may even disappear in later years. The controversy over the existence of an effect continues, as well as its magnitude and whether it is more likely to accrue to student groups identified by age, gender, race or ethnic origin, or ability.

This article was originally published in *American Educational Research Journal,* Fall 1990, Vol. 27, No. 3, pp. 557–577.

Jeremy D. Finn is a Professor of Education at the State University of New York at Buffalo, 408 Christopher Baldy Hall, Buffalo, NY 14260. He specializes in multivariate analysis and school and classroom processes.

Charles M. Achilles is a Professor of Education at the University of North Carolina at Greensboro, NC 27412-5001. He specializes in educational administration.

Only randomized experiments can provide a definitive answer to these questions. Correlational studies, and studies that match children after they have been assigned to small or large classes, are confounded, at the very least, by the effects of differential selectivity of students or teachers, or both. The entire Glass and Smith meta-analysis included only five randomized experiments of nontrivial duration in which large and small class sizes were within the range found in most elementary and secondary schools.[1] The ten effect sizes for small class–large class comparisons that are derived from these studies range from –.29 to +.17. Robinson and Wittebols (1986) make no distinction among studies by methodology. Slavin (1989) included only one randomized experiment in his review, a large-scale study in grades 4 and 5 in Toronto, Ontario (Shapson, Wright, Eason, & Fitzgerald, 1980). The overall effect size for the study was +.17, but the small class–large class differences were negligible for reading (–.05 to +.01) and large for mathematics (+.22 to +.51). The smallest class size, 16, showed the most distinct advantage over classes of 23, 30, or 37 students.

The present study builds on the findings of this earlier research. It begins in the earliest years of school and continues for several years; it includes children identified by race and socioeconomic levels; and it is a controlled, randomized experiment. The reduction in class size is substantial, from an average of about 22 students present and providing data in the regular classes, to about 15 in small classes, a decrease of 32%.

However, an important qualification must be recognized. In this study, as in the others, a class with 25 students registered does not mean that 25 students actually attend class, and certainly does not imply that 25 students are present on any given day. For a plethora of reasons, the actual number may be somewhat smaller, much smaller or, on occasion, larger than 25. The problem of definition is complicated further when class size is used as an independent variable in an empirical study. The number of students actually *involved* in instructional activities may be more important to many outcomes than the number present, and class enrollment is only an approximation of this difficult-to-measure construct. In spite of these considerations, most studies do not indicate how enrollment figures were obtained, or their stability over time. Caution must be exercised in interpreting the effects of different degrees of class-size reduction. Attempts to study fine graduations in enrollment figures in particular—for example, by calculating ordinary correlations of class size with other measures—should be viewed with skepticism.

Procedures

All school systems in the State of Tennessee were invited to participate, with the state funding the cost of extra teachers and aides that would be needed.[2] About one third of the districts, representing 180 schools, expressed an interest in participating. After negotiation, the final sample consisted of 76 elementary schools that were large enough to have at least three kindergarten classes. Comparison of the participating school districts in 1986 showed that they were larger than the state average, had slightly higher per-pupil expenditures and teacher salaries, but were very similar in teacher-pupil ratios and percentages of teachers with higher degrees. Project schools scored slightly below the state average in second-grade reading and mathematics standardized test scores. Schools were classified as inner city, urban, suburban, or rural.

Within each school, children entering kindergarten were assigned at random, by the project staff, to one of three class types: small, with an enrollment range of

13–17 pupils; regular, with an enrollment of 22–25 pupils; or regular with aide, with 22–25 but with a teacher aide formally assigned to work with the class. Teachers were assigned at random to classes as a separate step. Except for this intervention, the school was to continue to operate as usual within district policies; that is, the study did not dictate any operational changes. No special training was provided for the teachers to help them take better advantage of the experimental settings.[3] The within-school design is particularly effective in controlling for contaminating sources of variability attributable to differences among school settings; these may include characteristics of the student population (e.g., socioeconomic status, community resources), of the school (e.g., availability of instructional materials, school administration), or of the district (e.g., policies, per-pupil expenditures). Larger schools allowed for more than one class of each type. The resulting sample consisted of 328 kindergarten classes and about 6,500 pupils.

Every class was to remain the same type—small, regular, or regular with aide—for 4 years beginning in the fall of 1985. The project staff randomly assigned a new teacher to the student group in each subsequent grade. The results reported here are for the end of Grade 1, the second year of the study.

Several operational complexities affected the composition of the sample between kindergarten and first grade. For one, kindergarten is not mandatory in the State of Tennessee. As a result, some youngsters did not attend kindergarten at all, and others were enrolled in nonproject kindergartens.[4] Participants entering the study in first grade were also assigned to classes at random; the process was monitored carefully by the project staff. The resulting sample from first grade, even with the loss of students who moved away from project schools, was larger than in kindergarten. The total number of classes was 347, with about 7,100 students; 34% had not participated in the project the previous year. After the data were screened for coding errors, 6,570 students in 331 classes remained for analysis (122 small, 111 regular, and 98 regular with aide) with the number of students varying slightly from one measure to another.

Two, to alleviate some parental concerns, about half of the regular-class students in kindergarten were randomly reassigned to teacher-aide classes in first grade, and half of the teacher-aide pupils were reassigned to regular classes. Youngsters in small classes were not reassigned. Thus, the comparison of teacher-aide classes with regular classes is confounded by the mixed composition of those groups in Grade 1. The comparison of classes by enrollment remains unconfounded.[5]

Information on race and a rough index of socioeconomic status (whether or not the individual participated in the subsidized lunch program) were obtained for each youngster.[6] These data are summarized in Table 1. At the extreme, 65 of 70 inner-city classes have only minority students, whereas there are no all-minority classes in the urban or rural samples, and minorities are a small proportion in the suburbs. There is a strong association between minority status and participation in the free lunch program. About 70% of the student sample are either minorities receiving free lunches, or whites not receiving free lunches; Yule's Q association measure is .78. An attendance index, the proportion of school days that the individual was present in class, was also calculated for each student. The mean proportion, .95, did not differ systematically by class type, school location, or race.

Outcome Measures

The Stanford Achievement Tests (SATs) in reading and mathematics were administered in the spring of each school year. In addition, beginning in first grade, a set of

TABLE *1*

Description of First Grade Cross-Sectional Sample

Quantity	Location			
	Inner-city	Urban	Suburban	Rural
Schools	15	8	15	38
Classes				
All white students	0	18	28	119
All minority students	65	0	13	0
Mixed	5	23	21	39
Total	70	41	62	158
Students	1495	804	1214	3059
Percentage receiving free lunch	91.2	46.6	33.2	42.8
Percentage of minorities	96.2	21.1	39.4	7.2

Note. Numbers of students vary slightly from measure to measure.

curriculum-referenced tests developed by the State of Tennessee, the Basic Skills First (BSF) tests, was administered to each student (Tennessee Department of Education, 1987). These were constructed from well-specified lists of objectives in reading and mathematics at each grade level, and could be scored either as the total number of items answered correctly, or as pass–fail. A student passes if he or she masters 80% of the objectives covered by the test items. The pass–fail system was used in the analysis reported here.

The Self-Concept and Motivation Inventory (SCAMIN) was given to the classes at the end of each school year (Milchus, Farrah, & Reitz, 1968). This group-administered instrument yields a measure of academic self-concept and academic motivation for each student. Its questions and answers, keyed to pictures of common objects and faces that appear happy or sad, is appropriate for children in the primary grades. Its reliability for early grades is only moderate, with alpha coefficients between .56 and .69 for subscales (Davis & Johnston, 1987; Davis, Sellers, and Johnston, 1988). Nevertheless, it provides convenient and useful measures for group comparisons such as required by this project.

Analyses

Means on each of the outcome measures were calculated for each class, and then separately for white and minority students in each classroom.[7] Two analyses were performed, a cross-sectional analysis of the entire first-grade sample, and a longitudinal analysis of the subset of pupils who were in the study for both kindergarten and first grade. Both analyses employed multivariate analysis of variance using the MULTI-VARIANCE program (Finn & Bock, 1985).

The outcome measures for the cross-sectional analysis were considered in three sets; reading, comprising the SAT word study skills and reading subscales and the BSF reading test; mathematics, comprising the SAT total mathematics scale and the BSF mathematics test; and motivation/self concept, comprising the two SCAMIN subscales. The reading subscale of the SAT is a composite of both word reading and reading comprehension measures (The Psychological Corporation, 1985). Each BSF measure was scored as the percentage of students in the class who passed. The percentage was transformed into a log-odds index, $1n(\%/100 - \%)$ for each class, to improve normality. Tests of significance for the class-type effect were accompanied by two contrasts, a comparison of small classes with the average of the other two class types, and a comparison of teacher-aide classes with regular classes.

The statistical design treated schools as a random dimension, nested within the four locations (inner city, urban, suburban, and rural). These were crossed with class type (small, regular, and aide) and race (white or minority). The mean scores for whites and minorities in each class were used as the basic units of analysis. The design has unequal Ns and many empty cells, and required multiple error terms to test all of the fixed effects.

Of the three instruments used in the study, only the SATs permitted a comparison of scale scores across grade levels. The Stanford Early School Achievement Test 2 form was administered in kindergarten and Primary 1 in first grade. The longitudinal analysis was performed on scores from pupils who participated in the same experimental condition in the same school location for 2 consecutive years—about 35% of the Grade-1 sample. Means were obtained on all three SAT scales—word study skills, reading, and total mathematics—for white and minority pupils in each class for both years. These became the data for a repeated-measures analysis of variance with grade as the within factor. The sample design was the same as the cross-sectional analysis previously described. The addition of the grade dimension permitted an examination of growth from kindergarten to first grade, and the interaction of growth with location, race, and class type. Multivariate tests of significance were obtained for the two reading scales jointly, and univariate tests were obtained for mathematics.

Cross-sectional Results

The analysis of variance results are summarized in Table 2 for the two sets of cognitive measures. This table, compiled from many computer runs, presents the multivariate test of each main effect and interaction, and separate univariate tests for each measure. Mean scores on the cognitive measures for the three class types, separated by location and race, are given in Tables 3 and 4, respectively.

The effects of location, race, and their interaction help to describe the context in which the experiment was conducted. Minorities score significantly below whites on all of the cognitive measures. There are significant differences among school locations, but the distinctions are not exhibited consistently across reading and mathematics subscales. However, when location differences are tested without eliminating the race main effect,[8] both multivariate tests are significant at $p < .001$, and all of the univariate F ratios are significant with the exception of the BSF reading measure. That is, there are substantial differences among locations in average cognitive performance, but they are attributable in part to the racial compositions of the communities.

The interaction of location and race reflects very distinct minority–white differences in rates of passing the BSF reading test. The rural difference, on the average, is 20 percentage points—67.3% of whites pass compared with 47.1% of minorities. The suburban and urban differences are 3.6 and 8.3%, respectively. Likewise, although not statistically significant, the minority–white difference is the largest in

TABLE *2*

Analysis of Variance for Cognitive Outcomes

	Reading				Mathematics		
Effect[a]	Multi-variate[b]	Word study skills	SAT reading	BSF reading	Multi-variate[b]	SAT math	BSF math
Location	$p < .01$	$p < .01$	$p < .06$	—	$p < .05$	—	—
Race	$p < .001$	$p < .001$	$p < .001$	$p < .001$	$p < .001$	$p < .001$	$p < .001$
Type	$p < .001$	$p < .001$	$p < .001$	$p < .001$	$p < .001$	$p < .001$	$p < .05$
Location × Race	$p < .05$	—	—	$p < .05$	—	—	—
Location × Type	—	—	—	—	—	—	—
Race × Type	$p < .05$	—	$p < .05$	$p < .01$	—	—	—
Location × Race × Type	—	—	—	$p < .05$	—	—	$p < .01$

Note. Only statistically significant results presented; dash indicates statistically insignificant results.

[a]The nonorthogonal design necessitated tests of significance in several orders (Finn & Bock, 1985). The results presented here were obtained as follows: each main effect was tested eliminating both other main effects; Location × Race tested eliminating main effects and Location × Type; Location × Type tested eliminating main effects and Location × Race; Race × Type tested eliminating main effects and other two-way interactions; Location × Race × Type tested eliminating all else. [b]Obtained from F approximation from Wilks' likelihood ratio.

rural schools on three of the four other cognitive measures. The pattern is reversed in inner-city schools, in which the average pass rate on the BSF reading test for whites is 46.9%, and 52.1% for minorities. Although the sample contains very few inner-city classes with white students, their performance is substantially below that of whites in other locations on every measure.

Do small classes provide an advantage to primary-grade children? The question is answered most directly by the class-type main effect. Comparing all three class types, there is a statistically significant effect for both multivariate sets and separately for each reading and mathematics measure. Further, Hotelling's T^2 for the comparison of small classes with the others is significant for both the reading and mathematics variable sets at $p < .001$; neither contrast of teacher-aide classes with regular classes is significant. The nonsignificant interaction with location confirms that the differences among class types occur to about the same extent regardless of the school setting. On the average, small classes positively affect student performance in first grade.

The mean scores for the three class types are given in Table 5 and are compared by effect sizes. The contrasts, small–others and aide–regular, are expressed in two different metrics. The first is the standard deviation of the particular subscale across all youngsters in the study who attended regular classes; the second is the standard deviation computed among the means of all regular classes. Although the former are more traditional effect-size measures, decreasing class enrollment is a classroom-level intervention. It is important to ask, What is the impact on the class' average performance, relative to the usual distribution of classroom outcomes? In general, it can

TABLE *3*

Mean Scores on Cognitive Outcomes by Location and Class Type

	Measure				
Group	Word study skills	SAT reading	BSF reading[a]	SAT math	BSF math[a]
Inner-City	497.9	486.7	51.7	510.7	71.1
Small	506.0	493.9	61.2	517.4	77.0
Regular	491.9	482.4	46.3	505.9	66.8
Aide	495.2	483.2	46.6	508.5	69.1
Urban	534.5	518.8	65.4	530.8	81.9
Small	544.9	531.1	74.9	540.5	84.7
Regular	527.0	508.3	61.0	526.5	82.9
Aide	532.4	518.0	60.6	525.6	77.6
Suburban	528.0	513.1	62.6	528.7	83.4
Small	540.9	523.9	68.9	540.8	89.0
Regular	518.7	507.4	58.6	521.1	80.4
Aide	523.5	506.5	59.8	522.8	79.9
Rural	537.0	521.6	63.3	536.7	83.4
Small	541.8	528.9	68.3	541.6	85.1
Regular	531.9	512.9	57.0	531.8	80.1
Aide	537.0	522.5	64.2	536.2	84.7
Standard deviation[b]	51.55	55.48	48.56	41.60	38.91

[a]BSF results tabled are average percentage passing. Statistical analyses were performed using the log-odds transformation. Standard deviations obtained by scoring each pupil 0 (fail) or 1 (pass). [b]Standard deviations for all pupils in regular classes only.

be observed that an increment of, say, x units is larger on the distribution of means than on the distribution of individual scores. This is correct. It reflects the fact that the effort required to raise a class average by that amount is generally much greater than that needed to augment one student's performance. For all effect sizes, standard deviations were obtained from regular classes only, as these were not impacted by the experimental interventions.

The benefit of the reduced class size is seen clearly for every measure. The effect sizes are about one fourth of a standard deviation among students, and range from about one third to two thirds of a standard deviation among class means. The difference in classroom pass rates on the BSF curriculum-based tests is 5.2% in mathematics and over 10% in reading. In fact, the univariate contrast values for comparing small classes with the others is significant at $p < .001$ for four of the five measures, and $p < .01$ for the BSF mathematics scale. If the SAT means are referred to the publisher's table of norms, the small-class advantage is at least $1\frac{1}{2}$ months for reading and $2\frac{1}{2}$ months for mathematics on the grade equivalent scale.

The effects of augmenting a regular class with a full-time teacher aide are not as large as the small-class advantage, and are not statistically significant in the multi-

TABLE 4

Mean Scores on Cognitive Outcomes by Race and Class Type

Group	Measure				
	Word study skills	SAT reading	BSF reading[a]	SAT math	BSF math[a]
White	540.2	524.8	66.5	540.1	86.2
Small	545.2	530.3	69.5	545.8	88.1
Regular	534.4	518.1	62.3	535.4	85.1
Aide	540.2	525.3	67.1	538.2	85.0
Minority	509.0	495.7	53.7	513.4	72.9
Small	518.6	507.1	65.4	521.3	77.8
Regular	503.5	489.0	48.0	509.2	69.4
Aide	505.6	491.7	48.3	510.3	72.2
	Standard deviations[b]				
White	50.42	56.04	47.26	40.37	34.34
Minority	44.58	47.71	49.90	37.97	45.16

[a]BSF results tabled are average percentage passing. Statistical analyses were performed using the log-odds transformation. Standard deviations obtained by scoring each pupil 0 (fail) or 1 (pass). [b]Standard deviations for all pupils in regular classes only.

variate model. However, the average performance in teacher-aide classes is higher than regular classes on each measure. Tests of the comparison of aide classes with regular classes on each measure separately are significant for the three reading measures at $p < .05$, if one-tail tests are made. Although these tests are not statistically independent, they indicate that using teacher aides in the primary years may be helpful in augmenting reading performance. Further data are needed before this speculation can be confirmed. The experiment will continue through third grade with no further reassignments. By that time, data will be available on youngsters who have been in teacher-aide classes for 3 years, providing clearer answers to this aspect of the investigation.

Differential Effects on Whites and Minorities

The significant interactions of type with race indicate that, for some outcomes, reduced class size does not have the same impact on white and minority students. This can be seen clearly by examining the small-class advantage—the difference between the average performance of small classes and the average of all other classes (large and regular)—for white and minority students separately (see Table 6). For all five measures, the advantage of being in a small class is greater for minority students than for whites. For example, the small-class advantage for white students is 8.6 points (.15 σ) on the SAT reading scale. In contrast, minorities in small classes outperformed their peers by an average of 16.7 points (.35 σ), more than twice the effect size for whites.

T A B L E *5*

Means and Effect Sizes on Cognitive Outcomes for Three Class Types

Class Size	Measure				
	Word study skills	SAT reading	BSF reading[a]	SAT math	BSF math[a]
	Means				
Small	535.5	521.8	68.0	536.9	84.4
Regular	520.6	505.1	55.9	523.7	78.1
Aide	527.2	512.7	60.0	527.7	80.2
	Effect Sizes[b]				
Small-Others					
Student SD^c	.22	.23	.21 (10.1%)	.27	.13 (5.2%)
Class SD^d	.62	.64	.51	.66	.32
Aide-Regular					
Student SD^c	.13	.14	.08 (4.1%)	.10	.05 (2.1%)
Class SD^d	.35	.37	.26	.23	.15

[a]BSF results tabled are average percent passing. Statistical analyses were performed using the log-odds transformation. Standard deviations obtained by scoring each pupil 0 (fail) or 1 (pass). [b]These are differences in standard deviations. [c]Standard deviations for all pupils in regular classes only. [d]Standard deviations across all regular class means. BSF class-level effect sizes based on log-odds transformation.

The Race × Class size interaction effect on the curriculum-based BSF reading test is so powerful that the difference in pass rates between whites and minorities is reduced from 14.3% in regular classes to 4.1% in small classes (see Table 4). Minority students in small classes pass the BSF reading test at a rate generally comparable to their nonminority peers. The same pattern, although not statistically significant, is seen for word study skills and for both mathematics scales. The effect on mathematics may have been more dramatic if the teachers had devoted more instructional time to this subject. Each teacher completed a 1-day log indicating the number of 15-minute time intervals spent on reading and mathematics instruction. On the average, teachers reported that 9.2 time intervals (2.3 hours) were spent on reading, and 3.5 (.9 hours) on mathematics. Although these data may not be highly reliable, differences in time spent on the two school subjects are substantial and consistent across locations and class types.

Both scales of the BSF test give indications of a three-way Location × Race × Type interaction. To investigate, separate Race × Type analyses were conducted within each of the four locations, with these two measures as criterion variables. The interaction of race with class type was not statistically significant in urban or rural schools, although the small-class advantage in reading was greater for minorities than for whites in both locations. The interaction was statistically significant ($p <$ .01) for BSF reading in both the inner-city and suburban schools.

There are very few classes with white students in the inner-city sample, so that a comparison between races may not be generalizable. However, for minorities the small-class pass rate is 64%, compared with 45.4% for the average of regular and

T A B L E 6

Small-Class Advantage by Race[a]

	White		Minority	
Measure	Mean difference	Effect size[b]	Mean difference	Effect size[b]
Word study skills	7.9	.16	14.1	.32
SAT reading	8.6	.15	16.7	.35
BSF reading[c]	4.8%	.10	17.3%	.35
SAT math	9.0	.22	11.6	.31
BSF math[c]	3.1%	.09	7.0%	.16

[a]Each value is Small − (Regular + Aide)/2; means from Table 4. [b]Mean differences divided by the standard deviation for all white students or all minority students in regular classes. [c]BSF results tabled are average percentage passing. Statistical analyses were performed using the log-odds transformation.

teacher-aide classes. In the suburban schools, fully 74.7% of minorities in small classes passed the reading test, compared with 53.1% in other class types. The small-class advantage is small or nonexistent for suburban white students, whose average pass rate is 65.5% in small classes and 63.4% in the others.

The Race × Type interaction was also significant in the suburban sample for BSF mathematics at $p < .05$, and approached significance in the inner city ($p < .08$). The same pattern occurs once again. In both locations, the difference in pass rates between small classes and the other class types is more substantial for minorities than for whites. In fact, in the suburbs, the average percentage of minority students in small classes who pass the BSF mathematics test is 90.3. This is well above the pass rate for suburban minority students in other class types (70.7%), and slightly above the average percentage of whites passing in *any* type of class in any location.

Motivation and Self-Concept

An analysis parallel to that performed for the cognitive measures was also applied to the motivation and self-concept scales. Only the location and race main effects reached statistical significance at $p < .05$, applying the multivariate test criterion. Univariate results reveal that differences among locations are significant for motivation but not self-concept, with urban and rural schools having slightly higher average levels than inner-city or suburban schools (see Table 7). The difference between white and minority students is statistically significant for self-concept alone, at $p < .01$; minority students have higher average levels of self-concept as revealed on the SCAMIN instrument. Although similar race differences have been found in previous research (Wylie, 1979), they have not been documented among children as young as these.

Longitudinal Results

An analysis of 2-year longitudinal data was conducted for that subset of youngsters who participated in the same classroom arrangement in the same geographic region

TABLE 7

Mean Scores on Noncognitive Outcomes by Location, Race, and Class Type

| Group | Measure | |
	Motivation	Self-concept
Location		
Inner-City	49.7	48.4
Urban	50.5	48.6
Suburban	49.7	47.9
Rural	50.2	47.7
White	50.2	47.7
Small	50.1	48.0
Regular	50.2	47.4
Aide	50.2	47.7
Minority	49.9	48.5
Small	49.9	48.6
Regular	49.9	48.5
Aide	49.9	48.3
Standard deviation	3.85	5.37

Note. Standard deviation is computed from all students in regular classes.

for both kindergarten and first grade, and who had complete data on the SAT achievement tests for both years.[9] Again, classroom means were computed for white and minority students separately, and these were used as the base data for analysis of variance. As with the cross-sectional analysis, if a mean was based on two observations or fewer, it was excluded from the analysis. Due to the number of students who did not attend kindergarten, those who were exchanged between regular and teacher-aide classes, and these additional data requirements, the resulting longitudinal sample consisted of 2291 youngsters—about 35% of the cross-sectional sample.

The composition of the longitudinal sample is described in Table 8. Altogether, 301 classes provided data (113 small, 99 regular, and 78 teacher-aide) compared with 331 classes in the cross-sectional analysis. The longitudinal sample comprises a smaller percentage of minority students and, with the exception of the inner-city schools, a smaller percentage of pupils in the subsidized lunch program. This may reflect a greater tendency for poor, minority children to begin school in first grade, and thus not appear in the 2-year data set.

The longitudinal sample is superior to the total group in terms of standardized achievement scores. Comparison of the first-grade means (Table 9) with those of Table 5 shows that the longitudinal sample outperforms the larger group on all three SAT scales in all class types. It is likely that youngsters who attend kindergarten come from homes in which early schooling is given a high priority. In addition, they enjoy the advantage of an extra year's school work. However, the rank order of means among small, regular, and teacher-aide classes is the same in both samples on every measure.

TABLE 8

Description of Longitudinal Sample

Quantity	Location			
	Inner-city	Urban	Suburban	Rural
Schools	15	8	15	36
Classes	60	38	51	152
Students	448	257	336	1250
Percentage receiving free lunch	92.8	37.0	28.1	36.5
Percentage of minorities	91.1	8.3	36.0	3.0

TABLE 9

Mean Scores and 1-year Growth for Longitudinal Sample

Measure	Class	All Students			White			Minority		
		K	1	Growth	K	1	Growth	K	1	Growth
Word study skills	Small	451.5	542.4	90.9	454.9	551.4	96.5	443.9	522.6	78.7
	Regular	444.1	525.0	80.9	447.6	538.3	90.7	436.8	497.3	60.4
	Aide	442.8	533.5	90.7	445.0	546.0	101.0	436.4	496.6	60.2
Reading	Small	442.4	529.5	87.1	446.1	536.6	90.5	434.3	514.2	79.8
	Regular	435.4	509.4	74.0	438.0	520.9	82.9	430.0	485.2	55.2
	Aide	534.1	520.3	85.2	436.9	530.9	94.0	429.8	489.0	59.2
Mathematics	Small	497.4	540.7	43.4	502.8	548.2	45.3	485.2	524.2	39.0
	Regular	486.8	528.1	41.3	489.4	538.5	49.1	481.5	507.0	25.5
	Aide	488.6	534.5	45.9	492.7	541.0	48.3	475.9	514.4	38.4

The repeated-measures analysis of variance yields results for location differences, race differences, and differences among class types that are consistent with the cross-sectional findings (see Table 10). Differences among the four geographic locations and between minorities and whites are statistically significant for the pair of reading outcomes and for all three SAT scales individually. Differences among classes types are also statistically significant: Small classes have a clear advantage over the other class types on all scales in both grades. Neither the Location × Race nor the Location × Type interaction is significant, indicating that the race and class size effects are found in all four geographic areas.[10]

There was significant overall growth from kindergarten to the end of first grade on all three SAT scales. The mean differences between grades are large (see Table 9) and are also distinguished by location, race and class type. That is, all three interactions are significant for the reading scales and Grade × Location interaction is significant for mathematics. Differential growth by location (means not tabled) is

TABLE *10*

Repeated Measures Analysis of Variance for SAT Scales

Effect[a]	Reading scales			Mathematics
	Word study skills	Reading	Multivariate	
Location	$p < .001$	$p < .001$	$p < .001$	$p < .01$
Race	$p < .01$	$p < .01$	$p < .05$	$p < .05$
Type	$p < .001$	$p < .001$	$p < .001$	$p < .001$
Location × Race	—	—	—	—
Location × Type	—	—	—	—
Grade	$p < .001$	$p < .001$	$p < .001$	$p < .001$
Grade × Location	$p < .001$	$p < .001$	$p < .001$	$p < .05$
Grade × Race	$p < .01$	—	$p < .05$	—
Grade × Type	$p < .01$	$p < .001$	$p < .01$	—
Grade × Location × Race	—	$p < .05$	—	—
Grade × Location × Type	$p < .05$	—	—	—

Note. Only statistically significant results presented; dash indicates statistically nonsignificant results.

[a]Tests of between-group effects were obtained as follows: Location differences were tested unconditionally; race and type differences tested eliminating both other main effects. Both two-way interactions were tested eliminating main effects and the other two-way interaction. Insufficient error degrees of freedom precluded testing the Race × Type or Location × Race × Type interaction, or interaction of either of these with grade.

largely attributable to smaller growth in the inner-city schools. For example, the kindergarten–Grade 1 mean difference in urban, suburban, and rural schools ranges from 84.5 to 89.9 points, but for inner-city schools it is 56.9 points. The significant Grade × Race interaction (means not tabled) is due to a greater gain, on the average, among white students—for example, 96.1 points on word study skills, compared with 67.9 points gain for minorities. Although not statistically significant, whites also gained more than minorities on both the reading and mathematics scales. The lack of significance may be explained in part by the small number of degrees of freedom for error[10] and also by the significant Grade × Location × Race interaction for reading. On this scale, minorities gained more than white students only in urban schools.

Class Size and 1-Year Gains

The Grade × Type interaction for reading is indicative of significantly superior growth among students in small and teacher-aide classes. The means (Table 9) further illuminate this finding. At the end of kindergarten, regular and teacher-aide classes had very similar performance—well below that of small classes. Students in small classes already had a decided advantage in reading and mathematics. Small classes maintained and even increased their superiority over regular classes by the end of the first grade. At the same time, teacher aides had more of a distinct impact in first grade than in kindergarten. Teacher-aide classes gained as much as small

---

TABLE *11*

One-Year Growth on Word Study Skills by Location and Class Type

	Class type		
Location	Small	Regular	Aide
Inner city	69.6	53.2	57.8
Urban	94.9	93.9	81.2
Suburban	95.4	74.7	91.4
Rural	95.7	91.3	105.0

classes during the year, narrowing but not closing the gap between them in final performance.

The univariate F ratio for the Grade × Location × Type interaction is significant for word study skills, although the multivariate test for the pair of reading scales is not. The average 1-year growth on word study skills is largest for small classes in three of the four locations (Table 11) but in rural schools it is exceeded by growth in teacher-aide classes. Also, classes with teacher aides improved more than regular classes in all but urban schools. In spite of this variability from one location to another, growth from kindergarten to first grade is greater in small than in regular size classes, and overall performance is higher in small classes than in either regular or teacher-aide classes in all locations on all three measures.

Although the longitudinal sample does not permit tests of significance for the interaction of class type with race, the mean 1-year growth is informative neverthe-less (see Table 9). White students' gains in mathematics were about the same regard-less of class type, whereas gains in reading were slightly greater in small and teacher-aide classes. In contrast, minority students were more differentiated by class type. The 1-year gains on word study skills and reading were substantially greater in small classes, and the 1-year gains in mathematics were notably larger in small and teacher-aide classrooms.

These outcomes may be viewed in terms of a white–minority achievement gap. In kindergarten, the race difference on word study skills is 11.0 points in small classes, 10.8 in regular classes, and 8.6 in teacher-aide classes—all about the same order of magnitude. By the end of first grade, the white–minority differential was 28.8 points for students in small classes and 41.0 and 49.4 points in regular and teacher-aide classes, respectively. The 41-point difference is closest to that which might have been expected if there were no intervention. However, with students attending small classes for 2 years, the difference was reduced to 28.8 points. This did not occur at the sacrifice of performance among whites, who also gained more in small than regular classes, but by giving an extraordinary boost to minority pupils. The same pattern is seen for reading and, to a lesser extent, for mathematics as well. It must be emphasized that these results are not confirmed by statistical tests. However, classes of 15 pupils appear to have benefited both white and minority stu-dents in terms of 1-year gains in reading and mathematics, with the greater relative benefit accruing to minorities.

Discussion

This research leaves no doubt that small classes have an advantage over larger classes in reading and mathematics in the early primary grades. In a large-scale experiment in which students were randomly assigned to treatment conditions within schools, first-grade students in smaller classes benefited in terms of improved performance on standardized reading and mathematics tests and pass rates on curriculum-based tests. Those pupils who had been in small classes for 2 years benefited in both kindergarten and Grade 1, and also showed significantly greater growth during first grade on standardized reading measures when compared with their regular class peers.

There is also some indication that regular-size classes benefit from the presence of a full-time teacher aide. In the first-grade cross-sectional analysis, teacher-aide classes outperformed regular classes on each achievement measure, but the results were not statistically significant. In the 2-year longitudinal subsample, teacher-aide classes gained as much as small classes, from the end of kindergarten to the end of first grade, on standardized reading measures. Continuing experimentation is needed to confirm this effect.

In addition to an overall class-size effect, there is strong indication that the performance of minority students is enhanced in the small-class setting. This important outcome is statistically confirmed only in inner-city and suburban areas, but the same trend is seen in urban and rural schools as well. Also, minority students in the longitudinal subsample experienced greater relative growth than white students in the second year of small-class participation.

In the cross-sectional analysis, the differential impact of small classes on minority students is revealed especially in the curriculum-based reading and mathematics tests. These tests are tied more closely to the instructional objectives and procedures of these classrooms than are the standardized Stanford measures. If classroom interventions for low-SES, minority, or at-risk students are attempted, they must be assessed in terms of the actual content that was presented and the actual extent to which students participated in learning that material.

The outcomes of this investigation differ from those of the Shapson et al. (1980) experiment that found "no significant differences attributable to class size for art, composition, vocabulary, reading, and mathematics-problem solving" (p. 149). However, the earlier study differs from the current one in important ways. For one, students in the smallest classes (16 pupils) and the largest classes (37 pupils) were not kept in the same size class for both years of the study. Perhaps of greater importance, students in the Shapson et al. study were enrolled in third and fourth grade. It is possible, as suggested by Slavin (1989), that reducing class size can have a greater effect in earlier years, especially if those are the years during which a particular subject area is emphasized. If reading as a separate subject is emphasized in first grade, then that is where we might expect the strongest effect. Shapson et al. did find a significant impact of class size on the understanding of mathematical concepts; perhaps mathematics received greater emphasis in Grades 4 and 5. The small-class advantage occurred only in classes of 16 students, close to the size of small classes in the present study.

Although this experiment yields an unambiguous answer to the question, Is there class-size effect?, other related questions remain unanswered. The issue of whether the benefits offset the costs involved is beyond the scope of this paper. However, it should be noted that few well-defined interventions have shown as consistent an impact as this one on the performance of minority students in inner-city settings, not to mention both their minority and nonminority peers in other settings.

The question of why, or under what instructional conditions, small classes work best is a complex but particularly important issue. Three dimensions of school process should be examined. First, teachers' enthusiasm and satisfaction may be enhanced when there are fewer students to teach; this may be perceived by the students and influence their own motivation for learning. The Glass, Cahen, Smith, and Filby (1982) meta-analysis concluded that "class size affects teachers. In smaller classes, their morale is better; they like their pupils better, have time to plan, and are more satisfied with their performance" (p. 65). Teachers in the Shapson et al. (1980) experiment indicated that they were especially pleased with their smaller classes, and informal comments from teachers in the present investigation confirm this view.

Second, reduced class size may directly impact on teacher–student interactions, allowing for more individual attention in particular; third, smaller classes may increase the extent to which individual pupils attend to and become involved in learning activities.

The few studies that obtained data on pupil participation or teacher–pupil interactions found very few differences between smaller and larger classrooms. For example, of many teacher and pupil variables observed in the Shapson et al. (1980) study, only the proportion of pupils addressed by the teacher as individuals increased significantly and monotonically as classes were reduced from 37 to 30 to 23 to 16 pupils. The Tennessee project did collect teacher logs—reports of how teachers spent each 15-minute interval of a typical school day. Each time interval was coded by subject area (reading, mathematics, other subject, or non-instructional time) and by the type of instruction (large group, small group, or individualized). Although the logs may have reflected teachers' lesson plans more than their actual classroom behavior, extensive analysis failed to uncover any systematic differences among small, regular, and teacher-aide classes.[11]

These critical questions about classroom process are not only pertinent to reduced size classes. It is clear from recent scholarly writing that students' active involvement in schooling, in various forms, is an essential requisite to the successful completion of 12 years of schooling (Ekstrom, Goertz, Pollack, & Rock, 1986; Finn, 1989; Hawkins & Lam, 1987; Wehlage, 1986). Reduced class size may be one of many ways to promote a greater variety and extent of participatory behavior. Augmenting regular classes with specialized teacher aides may be another, although we must seek to understand their roles and functions in the classroom better than we do now. In either case, it is important that the process issues—What is taught? How is it taught? How are students responding?—be addressed as well as the issue of learning outcomes.

Notes

The authors are grateful to the Project STAR directors and staff for providing the data for this investigation. Appreciation is extended to Elizabeth Word, Project Director; Helen Bain, John Folger, John Johnston, and Nan Lintz, the STAR Consortium; and DeWayne Fulton and Jayne Zaharias, data managers.

This manuscript was completed while the first author was Visiting Professor in the School of Education at Stanford University. Request for reprints should be sent to Dr. Jeremy D. Finn, Department of Counseling and Educational Psychology, State University of New York at Buffalo, 408 Baldy Hall, Buffalo, NY 14260.

1. These are studies numbered 3, 6, 7, 8 and 14, in Table A.1 of Glass, Cahen, Smith and Filby (1982). Study number 1 has also been excluded, because of irrelevant course content (tennis).
2. In May, 1985, the Tennessee legislature passed House Bill 544 authorizing and funding a major longitudinal study to consider the effects of class size on pupils in grades K–3. A four-university consortium worked with the State Department of Education to plan and execute the study, and to select an advisory committee and an external research design consultant.
3. Training was instituted at the second-grade level, but does not affect the first-grade results reported here.
4. About 10% of youngsters in Tennessee do not attend kindergarten at all.
5. The kindergarten analysis revealed no statistically significant differences in outcome between regular and teacher-aide classes (Achilles, Bain, Bellott, Folger, Johnston, & Lintz, 1988), although teacher-aide classes scored slightly better than the regular classes on each SAT scale. Thus, the comparison of small classes with the average of the others in first grade may be somewhat conservative.
6. Once the first-grade reassignments had been made, the percentage of minority students in small, regular, and teacher-aide classes was 32.8, 36.4, and 29.4, respectively; the percentage of students receiving free lunches was 47.5, 51.3, and 51.1, respectively. Small classes had somewhat fewer minority students and students from lower-SES homes when compared with regular classes. The difference in percentages is small, amounting to less than 1 pupil in a typical class of 15 or 22.
7. If a class had two white students or fewer, or two minority students or fewer, it was considered to be all-minority or all-white, respectively. The one or two "other" students were eliminated from all analyses.
8. Results not tabled.
9. Neither the BSF nor the SCAMIN measures are scaled to permit comparisons between kindergarten and Grade 1.
10. Due to the reduced sample size, no correct estimate of error variation is available to test the Race × Type or the Location × Race × Type interaction. Also, the race main effect is tested with very few error degrees of freedom; the error term is Schools × Race variation for which there are only 7 degrees of freedom. These restrictions affect the interactions of each of these terms with grade differences as well.
11. The Tennessee study has been collecting data on problems encountered by the teachers during the school year, and interviews each teacher at the end of the year. To date, these data have not been thoroughly analyzed. Also, a Grade-4 follow-up is planned, at which point all students will have returned to regular class settings. Questionnaires will be filled in by the fourth-grade teachers regarding the pupils' participation and initiative taking in class, as well as end-of-year achievement scores.

References

Achilles, C. M., Bain, H. P., Bellott, F., Folger, J., Johnston, J., & Lintz, M. N. (March 1988). *Project STAR technical report. Year one (1985–86): Kindergarten results.* Nashville, TN: State Education Department.

Davis, T. M., & Johnston, J. M. (1987). On the stability and internal consistency of the Self-concept and Motivation Inventory: Preschool/Kindergarten form. *Psychological Reports, 61,* 875–874.

Davis, T. M., Sellers, P. A., & Johnston, J. M. (1989). The factor structure and internal consistency of the Self-concept and Motivation Inventory: What face would you wear? Preschool/Kindergarten form. *Educational and Psychological Measurement, 48,* 237–246.

Ekstrom, R. B., Goertz, M. E., Pollack, J. M., & Rock, D. A. (1986). Who drops out of high school and why? Findings from a national study. *Teachers College Record, 87,* 356–373.

Finn, J. D. (1989). Withdrawing from school. *Review of Educational Research, 59,* 117–142.

Finn, J. D., & Bock, R. D. (19885). *MULTIVARIANCE VII user's guide.* Mooresville, IN: Scientific Software.

Glass, G. V., Cahen, L. S., Smith, M. L., & Filby, N. N. (1982). *School class size: Research and policy.* Beverly Hills: Sage.

Glass, G. V., & Smith, M. L. (1978). *Meta-analysis of research on the relationship of class size and achievement.* San Francisco: Far West Laboratory for Educational Research and Development.

Hawkins, J. D., & Lam, T. (1987). Teacher practices, social development and delinquency. In J. D. Burchard & S. N. Burchard (Eds.), *Prevention of delinquent behavior* (pp. 241–274). Beverly Hills: Sage.

Milchus, N., Farrah, G., & Reitz, W. (1968). *The Self-concept and Motivation Inventory: What face would you wear?* Dearborne Heights, MI: Person-O-Metrics.

Robinson, G. E., & Wittebols, J. H. (1986). *Class size research: A related cluster analysis for decision making.* Arlington, VA: Educational Research Service.

Shapson, S. M., Wright, E. N., Eason, G., & Fitzgerald, J. (1980). An experimental study of the effects of class size. *American Educational Research Journal, 17,* 141–152.

Slavin, R. E. (1989). Achievement effects of substantial reductions in class size. In R. E. Slavin (Ed.), *School and classroom organization* (pp. 247–257), Hillsdale, NJ: Erlbaum.

Slavin, R. E., & Madden, N. A. (1987). *Effective classroom programs for students at risk* (Report No. 19). Baltimore, MD: Johns Hopkins University, Center for Research on Elementary and Middle Schools.

Tennessee Department of Education (1987). *STAR criterion referenced test. Manual for test administration. Grade 1.* Nashville, TN: State Education Department.

The Psychological Corporation (1985). *Stanford Achievement Test Series. Technical data report.* Orlando, FL: Harcourt, Brace, Jovanovich.

Wehlage, G. G. (1986). At-risk students and the need for high school reform. *Education, 107,* 18–28.

Wylie, R. C. (1979). *The self-concept* (rev. ed., Vol. 2). Lincoln: University of Nebraska Press.

CHAPTER 6

Cooperative Learning, Statistical Significance, and Effect Size

INTRODUCTION

The first year on any job can be difficult, and beginning a new principalship can be particularly frustrating. Expectations are high as the new person occupies the office while fellow administrators, teachers, and parents watch and wait to see how he or she will perform. Usually a steady stream of suggestions, recommendations, complaints, and advice are offered by those who wish to give the new person the benefit of their experience.

Problems that have lain dormant for a few years may be dusted off and shared with the beginner, and the bearers of these problems may bring competing priorities to the office for administrative attention. Additionally, new problems may arise that vie for the principal's time and energy. As the first year progresses and the initial stream of faculty comments and suggestions is reduced to a trickle, the salient problems emerge more distinctly, and a set of priorities can be more clearly established.

Imagine yourself in the role of a new administrator facing the problem of declining math scores. Suppose that some of your teachers are interested in the possibility of implementing cooperative teaching strategies as an approach to the problem. When considering the adoption of such a major change in classroom organization and instruction, several important factors need to be considered.

First, there must be strong evidence that the strategy is effective with students who are comparable to those in your school. Second, complex procedures require the support of a large majority of teachers and administrators if they are to be successful. Anything less will make it difficult for you to implement and sustain the change. Third, teachers and fellow administrators will require a substantial amount of training to initiate and continue the innovation if it is to have an opportunity to succeed. Given the high costs in time, money, and political capital that are required for the introduction and maintenance of a major educational program such as cooperative learning, you would want to be confident of the program's efficacy before seriously considering its adoption.

In this chapter, we will examine the problem of declining math achievement and the effectiveness of cooperative learning strategies in dealing with it. We will observe Principal Beth Miller of Pleasant Valley Elementary School as she undertakes an examination of the problem and a possible solution. We will listen in as she and her colleagues think through the issue and as they examine the research evidence that relates to it. We will critique four studies that bear on cooperative learning using standard criteria, and, as the feature of this chapter, we will particularly focus on the concepts of statistical and practical significance. Finally, we will examine Miller's report to the faculty and her recommendations for action.

The Case: Math Problems in Pleasant Valley

The school year is finally winding down, and it has been a good but a tough one for Beth Miller. Beth is about to finish her first year as principal of Pleasant Valley Elementary School, and she feels as if she has been on a roller coaster since Labor Day and the car she is riding might be coasting to a stop. Well, not really a stop, but at least it is slowing enough for her to recognize faces moving past and to read an occasional billboard in the distance. It is Friday afternoon, and the building is almost empty except for the custodial staff and the "dedicated dozen" who tend to extend the workday well past contractual arrangements.

Beth kept the commandment she wrote for herself before the year began: "Thou shalt not tinker with anything until the first year is finished." While sorely tempted, she did not initiate any large-scale changes in programs or curricula until she had a reasonably clear picture of her parents, teaching staff, and students. Even without adherence to her "Eleventh Commandment," Beth had been busy enough tending to maintenance activities and learning the nuances of her first major administrative position to feel as if she had earned her paycheck for the year.

With the year coming to a fairly smooth close, now was the time to tackle a problem or two that required her attention. In fact, she had been bending her commandment a bit during the past couple of months as she chatted with teachers who stopped by after school. From time to time the issue of "doing something about the math achievement problem" arose, and several teachers expressed an interest in cooperative learning as a possible strategy to consider.

One of the teachers had taken a course in cooperative learning, had visited a neighboring district that was using it on a small scale, and was quite enthusiastic about trying it in grades 3 through 5. These conversations were usually short and hurried exchanges among tired teachers and administrators, but their staying power indicated a rather sustained interest in the problem. Within the next week, grades will be recorded, final reports either written or rationalized out of existence, and there will be time to take on the problem of math achievement a bit more seriously.

As we rejoin Principal Miller, she is deep in thought. The thought that has been rolling around in her head for a few days is that recurring phrase from some professor or some textbook (they tend to blur after a while) that asked cynically, "What is the problem for which your idea is the proposed solution?" What, then *is* the problem? The problem of concern to several 4th and 5th grade teachers is the gradual decline in norm referenced math scores over the past several years. While reading scores have shown modest increases and social studies and science scores have held reasonably steady, math scores in general and problem solving skills in particular have dropped a few percentile points each year for the last three years. School board members have not expressed serious concern, but they have noticed the decline and indicated that this issue might be something worth attending to in the near future.

A brief examination of the problem's context reveals that the previous principal had worked hard to implement ability grouping in grades 3, 4, and 5 in both reading and math. Homogeneously grouped classes in these two areas had been well received initially by teachers, but parents were less receptive to the idea and from time to time there are still a few complaints heard from the community. The gradual rise in reading scores has been touted by a few of the more senior teachers as evidence for the effectiveness of ability grouping while the math scores usually are not brought up during these discussions. Conversely, the younger teachers with concerns about math do raise the question of whether ability grouping might be contributing to the problem of lowered achievement. It is clear to Beth that she will need to tread gently as she pursues this problem.

There are several issues to be considered as Beth begins her quest for answers. First, the focus of the problem needs to be limited to math computation and problem solving abilities to reduce the likelihood of teacher resistance. Second, Beth is encouraged that teachers appear to be open to data that will speak to the effectiveness of programs rather than relying upon emotional persuasion. Third, teachers who are concerned about the problem do not appear to be committed to a narrow definition of the solution. While there seems to be an interest in cooperative learning as a possible strategy, there are a variety of cooperative learning strategies and there does not appear to be premature closure on any particular one.

Beth asks a couple of interested teachers to work with her on addressing the problem, and they spend several productive hours discussing ways to narrow it before they begin a review of the research literature. They frame several questions that they feel need to be answered if they are going to be able to make an intelligent report to the school faculty next fall. Their intent is to become as informed as possible over the summer and then to report back to the faculty during September and October. These meetings will raise additional questions that they and others can then explore. This will allow them to make an informed decision during the second semester of next year. In this way they will have ample time to implement any possible changes for one year from this fall.

The questions they initially decide to pursue are as follows:

1. What kinds of cooperative learning strategies are available?
2. What cooperative learning strategies have been found to enhance achievement in mathematics generally and in problem solving skills specifically with fourth and fifth grade students with widely varying levels of ability?

Beth and her two colleagues reviewed their questions by asking the ultimate one: "If we knew the answers to these questions, would we be able to make an informed decision about our problem?" Satisfied that, at the very least, they would be well on their way toward such an informed decision, they began their search.

Research on Cooperative Learning

The first question that helps frame this literature search asks: "What kinds of cooperative learning strategies are available? The rationale for cooperative learning has been offered by Slavin (1990) as an effort to move away from teacher-centered instruction and to provide opportunities for children to collaborate and actively participate in their attempts to construct meaning in the classroom. Cooperative learning provides instruction that focuses on various strengths and styles of students, attempts to foster personal and social gains for students, and also works to improve attitudes and social relations among students from diverse backgrounds. It has made claims to prepare children for life skills (Hamm & Adams, 1992; Sharan, 1980) as it creates a climate that attempts to simulate more realistic learning conditions in the child's world. Slavin (1990) claims that the benefits for students resulting from cooperative learning groups include improved academic performance, better social relations, and positive effects on self-esteem. Cooperative learning has been classified under a variety of meanings and applications by different researchers. Some classifications are based on how certain rewards and task structures are used for motivating students to cooperate or compete (Bossert, 1989), while others have identified approaches to peer-based instruction (Phelps & Damon, 1989) to understand the different ways in which these approaches influence student interaction, group composition, and the curriculum. Abrami, Chambers, D'Appolonia, Farrell, and de Simone, (1992) studied the relationships among group learning, attributional style, and academic achievement. Furtwengler (1992) and Slavin (1990) have presented the characteristics of these cooperative learning approaches, and their work forms the basis for the following overview. We will review only those methods that are appropriate for mathematics instruction.

Student Team Learning: In these learning methods, there are three important components, namely, team rewards, individual accountability, and equal opportunity for success. These methods stress both team goals and team success. Working together to learn and to share responsibility for the group's success are important elements of Student Team Learning. The different kinds of cooperative learning methods under this umbrella include the following:

A. Student Teams-Achievement Divisions (STAD). In STAD (Slavin, 1986), students are assigned to different heterogeneous teams based on achievement, sex, and race. Each team has four members. The teacher first presents the lesson to the large group and then children work in their smaller groups to ensure that each member has learned the material. All students then take individual quizzes without helping each other. These quiz scores are then compared individually with each student's own past averages to see if that student has made progress. Points are granted depending on the extent to which students meet or surpass their earlier performance. These points are then aggregated to form team scores, and teams that meet certain criteria may earn certificates or other awards.

We see the three distinguishing elements in STAD to be the following: (1) *team rewards* motivate children to help each member master the learning material so that the team may earn points, (2) *individual accountability* is evident because each child has to know the material to do well on the quiz, and (3) *equal opportunity* for success is built into this design because each student's performance is compared with his or her own past record. Hence, each child has a chance of success if he or she meets this criterion. Absence of norm-referenced comparison ensures that each child has an opportunity for earning points and everyone who makes progress contributes to the team's points.

B. Teams-Games Tournament (TGT). TGT (DeVries & Slavin 1978) operates on similar principles as STAD. The concepts of teacher presentations and teamwork are the same, but STAD and TGT differ in that weekly quizzes are replaced by weekly four-person tournament tables. Students with similar past records compete with members of other teams at each table. The winner of each table secures six points for his or her team. A "bumping" procedure changes students' table assignments weekly based on their performance in each tournament.

C. Team-Assisted Individualization (TAI). While STAD and TGT can be used to teach mathematics, TAI is designed to teach mathematics to students from grades 3–6. It is similar to STAD and TGT's four-member heterogeneously grouped teams, but it differs from them in that it does not use the same pace of instruction for the entire class. TAI combines cooperative learning with individualized instruction. First, the teacher provides instruction for the entire classroom. Next students enter an individualized instructional sequence determined by placement tests. Finally, each child in the team works on different units. The children check each other's work against answer sheets and help each other with difficult problems. Unit tests are taken without any team help and are scored by student monitors. Each week, the number of units completed by all team members is totaled, and certificates (or other team rewards) are awarded to teams that exceed a criterion score based on the number of final tests passed, with extra points for perfect papers and completed homework.

D. Jigsaw. This method was designed by Elliot Aronson and his colleagues (1978) and is based on task interdependence and personal interdependence. The teacher organizes the class into heterogeneous groups of six children in such a way that they have to rely on each other. The academic material is broken down into smaller units, and each member of a group is assigned one unit in which they are to become an expert. Next, members of different teams who have studied the same unit meet in the expert groups for discussion. Then, the students return to their teams and teach their teammates what they have learned.

E. Group Investigation. Sharan (1980) developed a procedure in which students work in small groups using cooperative inquiry, group discussion, and cooperative planning and projects. Students form their own groups ranging from two to six members and choose topics from a unit being studied by the entire class. These topics are broken into individual tasks and pursue activities necessary to prepare group reports.

F. Learning Together. This method developed by Johnson and Johnson (1989) involves students working in four- or five- member heterogeneous groups on assignment sheets. A single sheet is completed by each group and students receive praise or reward based on the group product. Four elements critical to this technique are face-to-face interaction (as they work in groups), positive interdependence (as they achieve a common goal), individual accountability and interpersonal skills.

With this background information on the various forms of cooperative learning, Principal Miller and her committee are now ready to pursue the empirical literature to help frame a response to their second question: What cooperative learning strategies have been found to enhance achievement in mathematics generally and in problem solving skills specifically with 4th and 5th grade students with widely varying levels of ability?

Four Studies of Cooperative Learning

As we review research findings on effects of cooperative learning techniques, we will select four of the most recent studies that meet the following criteria:

1. Focus on mathematics education.
2. Sample included elementary or middle school children.
3. Experimental and control conditions imposed on subjects.

These criteria should provide us with studies to evaluate the impact of cooperative grouping techniques and also facilitate the discussion of practical and statistical significance. As these two concepts are applied you should review their introduction in chapter 4. This chapter is not intended to serve as a comprehensive review of research on cooperative learning but rather to help you develop good questions that will facilitate a review and to allow you to apply your knowledge of threats to internal validity to several articles. The first two studies focus on critical components of cooperative learning while the last two are evaluations of types of cooperative learning programs. This chapter differs from chapter 5 and succeeding chapters in that we have not reproduced an article in the appendix for you to read. Rather, four separate articles will be reviewed to provide replication of the concepts of statistical and practical significance. Information will be provided about the study's design, variables, and sample; then we will focus on the results of this research. The concepts of statistical and practical significance will be applied to data tables that have been reproduced from the study. Finally, we will draw research implications from each study that respond to Principal Miller and her committee's problem of math achievement in Pleasant Valley Elementary School.

Study One

Hooper S. (1992). Effects of peer interaction during computer-based mathematics instruction. *Journal of Educational Research 85*(3), 180–189.

This study examined the effects of two learning contexts (individual and dyads) and the effects of group composition (ability grouping) on math achievement. A sample of 115 predominantly white 5th and 6th grade students participated in the study. Percentile scores were used to classify these students as high ability (above the 85th percentile) or average ability (at or below 85th percentile) on the mathematics subscale of the California Achievement Test (CAT). The mean CAT score of the high ability students was at the 95th percentile, while that of the average ability students was at the 64th. Students were then randomly assigned within ability groups to work either in dyads or to work alone.

Students also received training to promote intragroup interaction that emphasized summarizing and paraphrasing. They then completed a three-segment computer tutorial wherein they learned a rule-based arithmetic symbol system, learned to apply the rules to a series of questions, and learned the role of a special modifier. Instructions, practice questions, and a quiz appeared on the computer screen for each segment. Students automatically moved on to the next segment if they mastered the quiz or completed three attempts of the mastery quiz. Initial ability was assessed using a pretest, and achievement was determined by administering a posttest at the conclusion of the study.

Significant achievement differences ($p < .027$) were found for grouping (individual versus dyads) in the posttest scores with students who completed the assignment in groups scoring higher on the posttest than those who worked alone.

Capsule Critique. Before we explore the featured concepts of statistical and practical significance let us make a few assessments of the study itself. The researcher employed an experimental design to test the effects of students studying alone (individual condition) and students studying with a partner (dyadic condition). Additionally, this study examined whether individual versus dyad conditions had a different effect on high achieving versus average achieving students. Since an experimental design was used, the effects of many threats to internal validity were minimized, and we can be fairly confident that any observed differences between groups could be attributed to the individual versus dyadic condition.

How can all this information be inferred from this brief review? First and foremost, the 115 students were *randomly assigned* to treatment conditions. Remember from chapter 4, random assignment to groups provides the best possible protection against such threats as history, maturation, testing, and differential selection of subjects. We have no valid reason to infer that the individual and dyad groups should differ initially on ability or achievement, nor is it reasonable to infer that the groups differed on any variable except the one being studied— individual versus dyadic group membership. Therefore, we can be reasonably confident that the results, if any, can be attributable to the treatment conditions rather than prior differences or variables that could contaminate the study.

Next, and most central to our discussion in this chapter, what can we say about the differences in math achievement that may have been found between individual and dyadic groups? First consider the likelihood that any differences found might have been attributed to chance. You will recognize this as a question of *statistical significance,* and it is expressed as a probability estimate. For example, a statement $p < .05$, indicates that the researcher tested the differences found in a study using a statistical technique and found that these differences would have occurred by chance fewer than five times in a hundred.

Now, what did Hooper report? The Results section reveals the following sentence: "A significant difference was also found for assignment, $F (1,111) = 5.05, p < .027$. Students who completed the instruction in groups scored significantly higher on the posttest than did students who completed instruction individually" (Hooper, 1992, p. 184). The statistical technique used by the researcher demonstrated that the differences found were likely to occur by chance less than 3 times in 100 chances ($p < .027$). In short, while the differences may or may not be later found to be practically important, the researcher has reasonable confidence that the differences are not simply due to chance.

Having satisfied many readers that Hooper is dealing with differences that are real, we now address an issue that is of even greater importance to Principal Miller and her study team. How large are the differences found between individual and dyad groups, and are those differences smaller or larger for high versus average math students? These practical significance questions can be answered by examining the concept of effect size.

Review chapter 4 and remember that practical significance or effect size (*ES*) can be calculated by comparing the means of the two groups and dividing that number by the average standard deviation (*Av. SD*).[1] The formula calls for

---

[1] Effect Size can also be calculated using the *SD* of the control group as the denominator rather than the average *SD* of both the experimental and control groups as we are using. Using the common *SD* of both groups represents a third approach.

$$ES = \frac{M1 - M2}{Av.SD}.$$

Table 6.1 provides the posttest means and SDs for both individual and dyad groups and for each of the four types of math achievement: Facts, Application, Generalization, and Problem Solving. A Total Achievement score is also given. In this way, a more refined analysis can be made of the possible effects of Individual and Dyadic membership on achievement for both high and average ability learners.

In particular, Principal Miller and her committee framed part of their question to focus on problem solving skills, which makes that subtest of special interest in our analysis. Also, they were concerned with strategies that were effective with a wide range of ability and that would require an examination of the effects of cooperative learning on high as well as average ability learners. Fortunately, Table 6.1 will permit us to make those comparisons.

Table 6.2 provides you with the results of our efforts in calculating effect sizes from the information provided in Table 6.1. Frequently, research studies provide effect sizes so that you can judge the practical significance of the results. However, there are other times when only the means and standard deviations are provided, and you will not be able to determine the practical significance without additional steps. To assist you in these circumstances we have worked out two examples for you. These simple steps should reassure you that you can always calculate the effect size of an experimental treatment if you are given the means and standard deviations of treatment and control groups. Following these

---

T A B L E *6.1*

**Percentage Means and Standard Deviations of Achievement Data
(From Hooper, 1992)**

		Facts	Application	Generalization	Problem Solving	Total
High (Individual)	M	97.86	81.15	47.50	62.50	72.25
(n = 20)	SD	6.99	13.55	37.40	35.52	17.81
Average (Individual)	M	83.04	60.58	26.88	31.88	50.59
(n = 16)	SD	27.22	29.58	33.81	33.51	26.23
Total	M	91.27	72.01	38.33	48.89	62.63
	SD	19.99	24.13	36.84	37.48	24.21
High (Dyad)	M	99.62	83.40	59.21	67.11	77.34
(n = 38)	SD	2.32	17.39	32.16	24.26	15.18
Average (Dyad)	M	95.47	69.23	45.61	38.05	62.09
(n = 41)	SD	11.71	22.56	32.18	31.08	17.45
Total	M	97.47	76.05	52.15	52.03	69.42
	SD	8.79	21.33	32.69	31.44	18.01
Grand Total	M	95.44	73.89	46.81	50.08	66.55
	SD	13.53	22.75	34.44	33.46	20.58

TABLE 6.2

**Effect Sizes for Dyads versus Individual Groups
Calculated from Hooper (1992)**

Dyad vs. Individual Comparisons	Facts	Application	Generalization	Problem Solving	Total Math
High Ability	0.38	0.15	0.34	0.15	0.31
Average Ability	0.64	0.33	0.57	0.19	0.53
Total Dyad vs. Individual Comparisons	0.43	0.18	0.4	0.09	0.32

calculations, we will discuss the importance of these findings to practitioners and to Principal Miller and her committee.

Let us select several cells from Table 6.1 for computation and make the comparisons that are relevant to the question posed by the committee. First, we will examine the effectiveness of the treatment to enhance overall math achievement for high and average ability students. Second, we will examine the effectiveness of the treatment to enhance the specific component of problem solving skills for high and average ability students. Data on these two issues should provide the information sought by the committee for their second question.

To examine the effectiveness of the treatment for high as opposed to average ability students on the Total math achievement test, we will need to contrast those two groups by comparing their effect sizes (*ES*). We calculate the *ES* for both groups and then compare them to determine the relative degree of effectiveness or ineffectiveness of the treatment for these two ability groups.

Let us begin with the high ability group. In the right-hand column of Table 6.1, we find the high/dyad group has a mean score of 77.34 on the total math achievement test and the high/individual treatment group has a mean of 72.25. Substituting these values into our effect size formula yields

$$ES = \frac{77.34 - 72.25}{Av.SD}.$$

Subtracting those scores yields the following numerator in our formula:

$$ES = \frac{5.09}{Av.SD}.$$

Returning to the right-hand column of Table 6.1 for the appropriate *SD* values for the denominator we find a *SD* of 15.18 for the high ability/dyad group and a *SD* of 17.81 for the high ability/individual treatment group. Substituting those values into the formula and calculating them yields the following results

$$Av.SD = \frac{15.18 + 17.81}{2} = \frac{32.99}{2} = 16.5.$$

Completing our formula we have

$$ES = \frac{5.09}{16.5},$$

which yields an effect size of .31.[2] Now, we will have a point of comparison when we calculate the effect size for the Average ability students. We know that the $ES = .31$ indicates the dyadic condition yielded an increase on the total achievement test of approximately 1/3 of a standard deviation for the high ability group. To put it another way, if you attempted an intervention in your school to raise math achievement and found that it had an effect size of .31 on a standardized achievement test, that would be the equivalent of moving the treatment group from the 50th percentile to the 62nd percentile. An effect size of this magnitude would be considered practically significant. Let us now repeat the same steps to determine the effect size for the average ability students.

Returning to the right-hand column of Table 6.1, we find the mean score on the total math achievement test for the average/dyad group to be 62.09. In that same column we find the mean score on the total math achievement test for the average/individual treatment group to be 50.59. Subtracting these two values yields 11.5 in the numerator of our formula

$$ES = \frac{(62.09 - 50.59)}{Av.SD},$$

which reduces to

$$ES = \frac{11.5}{Av.SD}.$$

Locating the standard deviations for the average/dyad group (17.45) and the average/individual treatment group (26.23), adding them together, and dividing that value by 2 yields 21.84, which provides us with the last bit of information needed to complete our equation:

$$ES = \frac{11.5}{21.84} = .53$$

Completing that last bit of division yields $ES = .53$.

Now, we have two values that can be meaningfully compared. We learned in earlier calculations that the cooperative learning strategy had increased total math achievement for the high ability group by approximately 1/3 of a standard deviation ($ES = .31$). In the last set of calculations we learned that the cooperative learning strategy had increased total math achievement for the average ability group by approximately 1/2 of a standard deviation ($ES = .53$). This is good news for Principal Miller and her committee in that the strategy was effective for high ability students; the better news is that the strategy was even more effective for average ability students. On the total math achievement test this strategy met the criterion of enhancing math achievement for students that varied from high

---

[2] A typical interpretation of effect size is provided by Gall, Gall, and Borg (1999). They state that an effect size of .33 or larger has practical significance. While this estimate provides a guide for decision making, remember that any such determination is arbitrary.

to average ability. While this is encouraging, we must recall that Principal Miller and her committee are concerned with students of widely varying ability levels, and this study did not include those of below average ability.

Another issue raised in the committee's second question concerned problem solving skills. Let us compare the relevant means and standard deviations from Table 6.1. In the second to the last column in Table 6.1 we find the mean of the high/dyad group was 67.11 with a SD of 24.26. We contrast that with a mean of 62.50 and a SD of 35.52 for the high/individual treatment group. Placing these values in our formula yields the following equation:

$$ES = \frac{67.11 - 62.5}{\dfrac{24.26 + 35.52}{2}} = \frac{4.61}{\dfrac{59.78}{2}} = \frac{4.61}{29.89} = .15 \, .$$

The value of .15 is far smaller than those recorded for the total math component. There, the effect sizes were .31 for the high ability group and .53 for the average ability group. An effect size of .15 is approximately 1/2 of the value suggested previously as the criterion for practical significance. While it is encouraging that cooperative learning had a positive effect on problem solving skills, remember that the impact is a modest one.

Let us turn now to the calculation of the effect size for problem solving skills with average ability students. Perhaps the practical significance for these effects will be more encouraging. By returning one more time to Table 6.1 we find the mean and standard deviation for problem solving skills for average/dyad groups to be 38.05 and 31.08, respectively. The mean and standard deviation for average/individual treatment groups are 31.88 and 33.51, respectively.

The astute reader may have noticed the size of the standard deviations (31.08 and 33.51) and may have concerns that these large values will make it difficult to achieve an effect size of any magnitude. With such large values in the denominator it will take a substantial difference between the means to overcome this large amount of variation. Let us see if those concerns are well founded.

Calculating the values yields the following equation:

$$ES = \frac{(38.05 - 31.88)}{\dfrac{(31.08 + 33.51)}{2}} = \frac{6.17}{\dfrac{(64.59)}{2}} = \frac{6.17}{32.30} = .19 \, .$$

Apparently, the concerns of our astute reader were valid; the value of .19 is well below the .33 that has been suggested as a criterion for practical significance. The problem solving scores of both high and average ability groups of students were positively impacted by the cooperative learning treatment but only to a modest degree as evidenced by their effect sizes of .15 and .19, respectively. These values contrast with the more robust sizes of .31 and .53 we reported for the total math scores of high and average ability students. Therefore, while the total math achievement score was enhanced in a practically significant manner, the hoped for impact of cooperative learning on problem solving skills remains a concern for Principal Miller and her committee. An additional issue is the effect of cooperative learning on below average students; Hooper did not include students of below average math ability.

As Principal Miller examines the results of this and other studies, she must be attentive to the application validity issues discussed in chapter 4. As noted earlier, the ability levels of students in the study are one concern. Additionally, she will need to examine ecological validity issues as she compares the context of the study's setting with her own. Practitioners cannot simply apply research findings; they use research to help them think more intelligently about their problem.

Study Two

Fantuzzo, J., King, J., & Heller, L (1992). Effects of reciprocal peer tutoring on mathematics and school adjustment: A component analysis. *Journal of Educational Psychology, 84*(3), 331–339.

The second study we are examining does not directly address cooperative learning; however, it adds an important dimension of interest to Principal Miller and her committee. The previous study examined the impact of students working in dyads on math achievement, which was found to have practical significance for overall math skills. However, it had much more limited impact on problem solving skills.

Question 2 posed by the committee asked about particular cooperative learning strategies and their degree of effectiveness in raising math achievement. After examining the study of the use of dyads as opposed to individual instruction, questions could arise as to the degree of structure that is optimal for learning. Other questions emerge regarding the need for specific training for students before they become involved in this learning process. The Fantuzzo et al. study pursues answers to both of those questions. It also focuses on students who achieved in the lower half of the distribution.

The study used a true experimental design that assessed a reciprocal peer tutoring intervention to enhance mathematics achievement for at-risk students. There were three experimental groups and a control group based on the presence or absence of structure and reward conditions. The structure only condition gave children specific guidelines, teaching them how to act as instructional partners. The reward only component was a set of procedures allowing students to choose their group rewards and team goals from a series of options. The reward plus structure condition provided both treatment components. Finally, a fourth group served as a control in that neither rewards nor a planned structure was included.

Sixty-four African-American students from 4th and 5th grades in an urban school who scored below the 50th percentile on standardized mathematics achievement tests participated in the study for five months. Children were paired randomly and then randomly assigned as pairs to one of the four conditions. Eight such dyads made up one classroom, and each intervention session lasted for 45 minutes and occurred two to three times weekly during mathematics instruction.

While six dependent measures were reported from this study, we will limit our focus to the math computation test because of its direct relevance to our problem.

TABLE 6.3

**Means, Standard Deviations and Effect Sizes
Calculated from Fantuzzo et al. (1992)**

Measure		Reward Plus Structure	Reward Only	Structure Only	Control Group
Math	M	7.7	5.4	4.5	5
computation	SD	1.5	2.3	1.7	1.9
test	ES	1.59	0.19	− 0.28	0.00

Examine the mean scores given in Table 6.3 and note the following mean scores for the four groups: reward plus structure (7.7), reward only (5.4), structure only (4.5), and control group (5.0). An analysis of variance (ANOVA)[3] procedure was conducted that revealed a significant ($p < .01$) main effect for both the reward plus structure and the reward only treatment groups on computation math scores.

Since differences were found to be statistically significant among the four groups that made up the study, it remains to be seen exactly which groups were found to be different from which other groups. To answer this question a post hoc analysis indicated that students in the reward only group ($M = 5.4$) showed a significant increase ($p < .05$) compared with the controls ($M = 5.0$), while the reward plus structure group ($M = 7.7$) scored significantly higher ($p < .01$) than any of the other three groups.

These analyses give us the information we need to know regarding the differences and their likelihood of having occurred by chance. While research evidence cannot give us the certainty we may desire, it should be reassuring that the likelihood of these differences occurring by chance would be less than 5 times out of 100. Stated another way, the comparisons listed here should give us reasonable confidence that we are seeing real differences that were not likely to be chance events; therefore, we are free to ask important questions about the size of those differences or, as we have come to know them, effect sizes.

While it would be relatively easy for you to compute the effect sizes for students' computational scores, they are presented in Table 6.3 for your convenience.

While the differences were found to be similar in terms of statistical significance, it is clear from examining Table 6.3 that there are sharp differences in terms of the size of the effects. The combined reward plus structure condition

---

[3] As we have noted throughout this text, the consumer of research may not have the background knowledge to determine if a particular statistical technique is the appropriate one to use or if the technique has been executed correctly. That fact should not prevent you from examining the results of the researcher's efforts and from focusing on the statistical significance reported as a result of the data analysis. Your focus should remain on the twin issues of statistical significance and practical significance. Those issues are of vital concern to the practitioner and are well within your ability to interpret meaningfully.

had a pronounced effect as indicated by the *ES* value reported. Table 6.3 reveals that the reward plus structure treatment group had an effect size of 1.59 on math computation scores. Practitioners should examine research results for treatments that appear to make a substantial difference and a difference of 1 1/2 standard deviations is an extremely large effect. While other factors need to be examined, an outcome this large should be promising to Principal Miller and her committee.

Contrast these differences with those brought about by the reward only condition. The effect size reported under this column indicates a very weak *ES* of .19 for math computation that is well below the .33 we indicated as the typical criterion used for assessing practical significance. If improved math computation scores are the major interest of the practitioner, this study would indicate that both reward and structure are required components to build into a cooperative learning procedure. The reward condition resulted in a statistically significant difference in math computation but yielded a very weak effect size.

Capsule Critique. Given the experimental nature of this study design, we can be reasonably confident that most threats to internal validity have been protected against. Due to the random assignment of subjects to treatment conditions, we have no reason to infer that the differences found would be attributable to prior conditions or to factors extraneous to the study. The differences found were statistically significant and in the reward plus structure condition were practically significant. The effect size gives us confidence that the difference found would be an important one for practitioners to consider. In particular, the study indicated the additional potency that was derived from using both reward and structure conditions when implementing cooperative procedures. Finally, the study sample was drawn from the 5th and 6th grades, and this increases the confidence of the committee that the results might generalize to the 4th and 5th grade students in Pleasant Valley Elementary.

One word of caution regarding the sample should be noted: Only those students who scored below the 50th percentile on a standardized mathematics test were used in the study. While the focus on lower ability students was welcomed by Principal Miller and her committee, this also represented a limitation of the study in terms of generalizabilty. Any attempts to generalize the results of this study to the full range of student ability levels would be risky. Additionally, the sample of African-American students was different from the student population in Pleasant Valley Elementary School. Principal Miller will need to look for other studies showing similar effects that included the top half of the achievement distribution before she can safely conclude that these results might apply to all children in her school.

Study Three

Chambers, B., & Abrami, P. (1991). The relationship between student team learning outcomes and achievement, causal attributions and affect. *Journal of Educational Psychology, 83*(1), 140–146.

After examining two studies that explored components of cooperative learning, let us turn our attention to a pair of studies that examine types of cooperative learning that are directly related to Principal Miller's area of interest. The first, by Chambers and Abrami (1991), examined one of the types described in the earlier portion of this chapter. The method is called Teams-Games-Tournaments, or TGT.

A major purpose of this study was to understand how the effects of team learning mediate student achievement. Earlier laboratory research had suggested that successful learning outcomes of a team would relate to subsequent academic achievement as individuals. This field study was designed to test these findings in more a extended, naturalistic school setting. Elementary students from grades three to seven ($n = 190$) learned mathematics for five weeks with the Teams-Games-Tournaments (TGT) cooperative learning method. The TGT strategy calls for student teams to compete in a tournament as a group activity with the highest scorer of each tournament event being "bumped" up to a more difficult and challenging table for the next round and the lowest scorer at each table being "bumped" down.

Teacher rankings based on students' mathematics scores were used for assigning students to the initial four-member heterogeneous teams. Equality of prior achievement for the team was verified by calculating the mean ability rank of each team.

Each team received two copies of worksheets containing 30 questions, and group members worked together to answer these questions. The TGT strategy was then followed and students with similar past achievement records competed with members of other teams at each table. The winner of each table gained six points for his or her team. A "bumping" procedure changed students' table assignments weekly based on their performance in each tournament. At the end of the five-week program, the teachers administered math tests, attribution, and satisfaction measures.

The three factors of interest in this study were: prior achievement (high, average, low), individual TGT outcome (success, failure) and team TGT outcome (success, failure). Since students in different grades and different classes completed different tests, the raw scores were transformed to z-scores in order to make achievement measures equivalent. Prior achievement was defined as the mathematics achievement of the students as determined by their mathematics grades for the first term. Individual and team outcomes were calculated as the average TGT scores over the five-week period. The data were analyzed using analysis of variance procedures.

Relying on the twin concepts of statistical significance and practical significance (effect size) will be useful in understanding the results of the Chambers and Abrami (1991) data. The researchers reported statistically significant effects for team outcomes ($p < .05$), prior achievement ($p < .05$), and individual outcomes ($p < .05$). They concluded, "The hypotheses relating to the relationship between team outcomes and achievement, causal attributes, and affect were largely supported." (Chambers & Abrami, 1991, p. 142.)

TABLE 6.4

**Cell Means, Sample Sizes, Standard Deviations for Achievement
(z-Scores) from Chambers and Abrami, (1991)**

Prior achievement	Team outcome	Individual outcome	M	SD
High	High	High	0.94	0.67
High	High	Low	0.21	0.93
High	Low	High	0.76	0.99
High	Low	Low	0.74	0.67
Average	High	High	0.52	0.63
Average	High	Low	−0.15	0.96
Average	Low	High	0.14	0.97
Average	Low	Low	−0.47	1.27
Low	High	High	−0.19	1.11
Low	High	Low	−0.7	1.32
Low	Low	High	−0.82	1.19
Low	Low	Low	−1.44	1.17

So far, so good. As practitioners, however, we would like to know more about the amount of the effect and whether students at all levels benefited equally. Our first step is to examine the means and standard deviations of the different groups and to convert them to effect sizes.

In Table 6.4, Chambers and Abrami (1991, p. 142) provide the means and standard deviations that have been converted to z-scores to standardize them across all the different measures of achievement used in the various classrooms. What this means is that the scores have been converted to a scale with a mean of 0 and a standard deviation of 1. Since this conversion results in both positive and negative values, a few statements may be required to ensure a clear understanding of their meaning. The average student in the study would be assigned a score of 0. That means that half of the students would fall above this line and would be given positive values and the other half of the students would fall below this line and would be given negative values. Therefore, low achieving students in a particular treatment condition may have a mean score of −.82 that may appear quite low, however, when compared with another group of low achieving students in another treatment condition who averaged −1.44, the −.82 looks quite respectable. Perhaps a simple analogy of comparing the winter temperature in International Falls, Minnesota, of − 48 degrees on Monday climbing all the way to − 15 degrees on Wednesday may help make the point clearer.

By inspecting Table 6.4 you can easily see that the students with higher prior achievement all had posttest achievement means that were positive, ranging from .21 to .94. Those students in the average prior achievement group had scores that ranged from a −.47 to a +.52. Finally, those in the low prior achievement category had posttest scores ranging from a high of −.19 down to −1.44. These results offer few surprises, and neither Principal Miller nor any of her staff were expecting to see cooperative learning techniques that would place their top students on the bottom of the distribution, nor were they naive enough to believe a method existed that would bring their lowest achieving students to the top of the class distribution. What is significant to anyone interested in examining the effects of cooperative learning still lies concealed in Table 6.5. We need to ferret out the effect sizes of team and individual success on math achievement.

By comparing the results of the high team outcome students with the low team outcome students in Table 6.4 we are able to determine the effect that being on a successful tournament team had on student learning. Similarly, by comparing the high individual student scores with low individual student scores we are able to determine the impact that individual success in the tournament may have had on student achievement. Table 6.5 allows you to quickly see the effects each variable had on student learning. We encourage you to check our math by applying the formula for effect size that we have been using throughout this chapter.

To calculate the effect size for high versus low team outcomes in Table 6.5, we averaged the means found in Table 6.4 for the two high groups

$$\frac{(.94 + .21)}{2} = \frac{1.15}{2} = .58 \;.$$

We then calculated the average of the two low group means to get

$$\frac{(.76 + .74)}{2} = \frac{1.50}{2} = .75$$

and compared the high and low groups. We used the same method to average the standard deviations for the high group and found

$$\frac{(.67 + .93)}{2} = \frac{1.60}{2} = .80 \;.$$

The low group averaged out at

$$\frac{(.99 + .67)}{2} = \frac{1.66}{2} = .84 \;.$$

Inserting these values into our formula yields

$$ES = \frac{(.58 - .75)}{\dfrac{(.80 + .84)}{2}} = \frac{-.17}{\dfrac{1.64}{2}} = \frac{-.17}{.82} = -.21 \;.$$

The same procedure was used for each of the comparisons found in Table 6.5.

A comparison of the effect sizes reveals several items of interest. First, the team success or failure had very little effect on the high prior achievement students; in fact, there was a −.21 *ES*, indicating that team success may have actually lowered achievement for those students. The implication of these findings

TABLE **6.5**

Means, Standard Deviations and Effect Sizes for High and Low Team and High and Low Individual Scores Calculated from Chambers and Abrami, (1991)

High prior achievement		Average prior achievement		Low prior achievement	
High vs. Low team		High vs. Low team		High vs. Low team	
$M = .58$	.75	$M = .19$	−.17	$M = −.45$	−1.13
$SD = .8$	.83	$SD = .80$	1.12	$SD = 1.22$	1.18
$ES = −.21$		$ES = .38$		$ES = .57$	
High vs. Low Individual		High vs. Low Individual		High vs. Low Individual	
$M = .58$	.48	$M = .33$	−.62	$M = −.51$	−1.07
$SD = .83$	.80	$SD = .80$	1.12	$SD = 1.15$	1.25
$ES = .45$		$ES = .99$		$ES = .47$	

for Principal Miller and her committee appears rather straightforward. Building a successful team outcome in cooperative learning activities appears to have its greatest impact on low and average achieving students, and this was very encouraging news.

The effects of high individual success in the groups were much more consistent as indicated by effect sizes of .45, .67, and .47 in the high, average, and low achieving groups, respectively. Not surprisingly, prior individual achievement success was strongly linked with subsequent achievement. The committee found the results helpful in better understanding the role of success and failure in cooperative learning activities. They felt the following conclusion drawn by the authors was a reasonable one based on the data: "The implications for student learning are that students low in prior achievement who work in successful teams can benefit accordingly" (Chambers & Abrami, 1991, p. 145). However, the committee needed to be aware that the effect size analysis indicated that high team outcomes had a negative impact for students with prior high achievement. Of more interest to the committee was the finding that team success had a much greater effect on students with average and low prior achievement as evidenced by effect sizes of .38 and .57, respectively. Effect sizes in the vicinity of a half standard deviation are considered moderately large and would have the effect of raising a group of students from the 50th percentile to the 67th percentile.

Capsule Critique. The experimental study provided excellent protection against most threats to internal validity, and the use of students in grades 3 through 7 provided some assurance that the results would be generalizable to the students in Principal Miller's school. While not a fault of the study, the use of the Teams-

Games-Tournaments (TGT) style of cooperative learning was somewhat limiting in that it did not use the type of cooperative instructional strategies most frequently used in public schools. The use of three levels of achievement answered questions regarding the usefulness of cooperative strategies for various ability levels of students. Finally, the study was limited to a relatively brief five-week interval that leaves lingering doubts about the staying power of the intervention over a longer time period.

Study Four

Stevens, R. J., & Slavin, R. E. (1995). The cooperative elementary school: Effects on students' achievement, attitudes, and social relations. *American Educational Research Journal, 32*(2), 321–351.

The review committee members could hardly contain themselves when the Stevens and Slavin (1995) study emerged from their search. They were hoping to find a longitudinal study that assessed the effects of cooperative learning on elementary school students. Imagine their excitement when they read the opening words of the article abstract:

> This article reports the results of a 2-year study of the cooperative elementary school model which used cooperation as an overarching philosophy to change school and classroom organization and instructional processes. The components of the model include: using cooperative learning across a variety of content areas, full-scale mainstreaming of academically handicapped students, teachers using peer coaching, teachers planning cooperatively, and parent involvement in the school. After the first year of implementation, students in cooperative elementary schools had significantly higher achievement in reading vocabulary. After the second year, students had significantly higher achievement in reading vocabulary, reading comprehension, language expression, and math computation than did their peers in traditional schools." (Stevens & Slavin, 1995, p. 338)

The authors of this study made their purpose clear when they indicated they " . . . attempted to reorganize the school and classrooms in the school by using cooperative learning across the curriculum and using it as a theme to better integrate instruction between special and regular education" (p. 324). The current study was broader in curriculum scope than just mathematics and included the full range of elementary subjects. On the positive side this could help allay fears of teachers who had expressed concerns about not losing the gains that had been achieved in reading comprehension. Another positive aspect of the study, besides the obvious benefits of a two year longitudinal time frame, was the inclusion of both learning disabled students and gifted students in the sample.

The authors clearly identified the six elements of the cooperative learning study and elaborated upon each one.

1. Widespread use of cooperative learning in academic classes.
2. Mainstreaming learning disabled students in regular education.
3. Teachers coaching one another.

4. Teachers collaborating in instructional planning.
5. Principal and teachers collaborating on school planning and decision making.
6. Principal and teachers encouraging active involvement of parents.

Stevens and Slavin concluded their review of the research by selecting Cooperative Integrated Reading and Composition (CIRC) and Team Assisted Individualization-Mathematics (TAI) as the two methods that had been found to be among the most effective of all cooperative learning programs in raising student achievement.

Students in grades 2 through 6 ($n = 1,012$) in 5 schools comprised the total sample from which 21 classes in 2 schools were chosen for the treatment condition and contrasted with a matched set of 24 classes in 3 comparison schools to serve as controls. Random assignment of students to classes and schools was not possible and, therefore, comparison classes were matched with treatment classes on the basis of California Achievement Test scores for Total Reading, Total Language, and Total Mathematics. Additional matching was done to control for ethnic and socioeconomic background of students. Because of the need for cooperation from participating principals and teachers, the treatment schools were selected from among those schools whose faculty voted at least 75% in favor of participating in the project. Comparison schools were selected from among the remaining schools in the district whose students matched up well with classes in the treatment schools. The difficulties posed by the necessity of using a quasi-experimental design will be revisited in the Capsule Critique of this study. Suffice it to say at this time that there are gains and losses from this quasi-experimental design.

During the first year of the program, components of the training and of the cooperative learning model were gradually introduced. Staff development with both the CIRC and TAI was undertaken, and the reading program was begun early in the first year with the introduction of the full program by the beginning of the second year. Teachers were trained in Jigsaw II, which is a technique involving different students in different parts of a learning task and then "fitting" together their knowledge. Additionally, the techniques of Teams-Games-Tournaments (TGT) and Student Teams Achievement Division (STAD) were shared with all teachers in the treatment schools.

The results of the study compared pre and post achievement tests as well as pre and post measures of attitudes and social relationships. Table 6.6 provides a clear and concise assessment of the treatment results both in terms of statistical significance and effects sizes. Examining the second column from the right shows which outcomes were statistically significant—look for the asterisks denoting level of significance. Equally clear are the effect sizes printed in the right-hand column.

The results of the first year were quite limited. Reading vocabulary was the only outcome measure to be statistically significant ($p < .05$), and the effect size was a modest +.17. Results after the second year indicated more of the outcome

TABLE 6.6

Students' Achievement: Means, Standard Deviations, Analyses, and Effect Sizes Collapsed Across Grades (Adapted from Stevens & Slavin, 1995)

| Measure | Cooperative Elementary Schools | | | Comparison Schools | | | | |
	M	(SD)	HLM = fitted M	M	(SD)	HLM = fitted M	t	Effect Size[†]
Year 1								
Posttests								
Reading vocabulary	.04	(.99)	.08	−.14	(1.01)	−.09	2.14*	+.17
Reading comprehension	.03	(1.01)	.08	−.03	(.99)	−.05	1.63	+.13
Language mechanics	−.01	(.99)	.00	−.02	(1.00)	.01	<1.0	−.01
Language expression	.04	(1.01)	.04	−.04	(.99)	−.04	<1.0	+.08
Math comprehension	.02	(.99)	.06	−.01	(1.00)	−.06	1.34	+.12
Math application	−.07	(.98)	−.02	.08	(1.01)	.03	<1.0	−.05
Year 2								
Posttests								
Reading vocabulary	.05	(.98)	.10	−.04	(1.01)	−.11	3.04**	+.21
Reading comprehension	.08	(.98)	.15	−.07	(1.01)	−.13	3.62**	+.28
Language mechanics	.03	(.97)	.05	−.02	(1.02)	−.05	1.16	+.10
Language expression	.10	(.96)	.15	−.09	(1.03)	−.06	2.93**	+.21
Math computation	.03	(1.00)	.15	−.04	(1.01)	−.14	3.77**	+.29
Math application	−.03	(1.01)	.04	.01	(1.01)	−.06	1.24	+.10
N (students)	411			462				
Number of classes	21			21				

[†] Effect size equals the difference of the HLM-fitted means divided by the control group standard deviation.
* $p < .05$; ** $p < .01$

measures were statistically significant and, of great interest to Principal Miller's committee, the effect sizes were larger and more consistent across various subject matter areas. More specifically, tests of Reading vocabulary, Reading comprehension, Language expression, and Math computation had all shown statistically significant increases at $p < .01$. Again, remember that these results indicate that such differences between pre and posttests would have occurred less than 1 time in 100 if chance alone were operating. Therefore, these differences are likely due to some factor other than chance, presumably the cooperative learning intervention. Whether we can safely attribute those differences to the treatment will need to wait for a careful examination of the research design in our Capsule

Critique, but we will proceed to examine the practical significance, if any, of these results.

Table 6.6 provides the information we seek regarding practical significance in the right-hand column. The effect sizes ranging from .10 to .29 tell us that the students in the treatment group increased more than the comparison group during the second year of the study, and the increases ranged from 1 tenth to almost 3 tenths of a standard deviation on the California Achievement Test. Our earlier discussion of practical significance indicated that an effect size of .33 has been suggested as a criterion when considering what constitutes a difference worth the practitioner's time and effort. While the effect sizes in this study are promising and consistently positive, they fall short of that desired level. An additional disappointing finding was the effect size that occurred on the test of math applications; it was a minuscule .10 and failed to reach statistical significance.

The committee discussed the results at some length and finally concluded that with four of the tests in reading, language, and math showing effect size increases in the .21 to .29 range, they were willing to accept those levels as demonstrating practical significance of sufficient value to allow them to proceed. Additionally, they reasoned that the students had shown rather sizable achievement gains from the first year to the second year and that a third year might show even greater gains.

Note, here, that it is tempting to speculate that the committee may have fallen prey to a bit of wishful thinking as they reasoned (or rationalized) the issues in reaching a decision. However, it is the legitimate right and even obligation of practitioners to make a judgment as to what constitutes a difference that is practically important. Researchers can provide practitioners with tools and concepts to enable them to make statements about statistical and practical significance but, ultimately, it is the practitioner who must weigh and decide that a difference of .2 or .3 or .4 is large enough to justify implementation.

An advantage of using effect sizes in considering program implementation is that it allows you to make cost-benefit comparisons with other programs that are vying for the same resources. If you are able to achieve the same effect size with two different programs and the first costs half as much as the second, you are in a strong position to argue for adopting the first. While the practical significance of a research study is obvious, other factors such as program cost, faculty interest, and parental support are just a few of the issues that the practitioner must consider as the implementation decision is reached.

Examining other tables in the study that reported changes for special education students and for gifted students yielded promising results. Special education students showed gains in reading vocabulary, reading comprehension, language expression, and math computation that were statistically significant ($p < .01$) and showed effect size gains ranging from +.59 to +.85, which were quite substantial. Math application, while less robust, showed statistically significant gains ($p < .05$) and an $ES = .35$.

Examining the table that reported results for the gifted students was equally encouraging. Reading vocabulary, reading comprehension, and math computation scores were significantly improved ($p < .01$) and showed effect size gains over the comparison schools of +.59 to +.68. Again, while the math application scores were slightly improved, they failed to reach statistical significance, Miller and her committee are forced to conclude that those improvements could be due to chance.

Stevens and Slavin (1995) concluded their study in the following words: "While further research is needed to understand the effects of this program, the results of this study do suggest that cooperative learning can serve as a basis for school restructuring and can produce important benefits for a wide range of students" (p. 347). Principal Miller could take some solace from the results that indicated a wide range of subjects were positively impacted by cooperative strategies. The lower effect sizes demonstrated in math application gains were somewhat discouraging but, as the authors pointed out, reading was implemented from the very beginning of the first year while math strategies did not become fully operational until the beginning of the second year. It may be that insufficient time had elapsed to allow the gains to be demonstrated in the math area.

Capsule Critique. As indicated in our introduction to this article, the implementation of a rather major innovative strategy across five public schools posed special problems for the researchers. You will recall that Stevens and Slavin chose schools whose faculties had indicated rather dramatic support for the program. In fact, they would not be chosen for the study unless at least 75% of the teachers voted to participate. Doesn't this overwhelming support for the program indicate the faculty was positively predisposed to cooperative learning and might work exceptionally hard to make it succeed? Yes, it does. Doesn't the selection of two schools to participate give those faculty members a feeling of being special, thus enhancing their motivation to outperform the three schools who were not selected? Yes, it might. Then why didn't the researchers use the more powerful true experimental design rather than the less powerful quasi-experimental design?

While you are well aware by now of the great power that a true experimental design provides the researcher, your years as an educator also make you well aware of why a true experimental study would have been impossible in this case. Imagine the difficulties of imposing a program of this magnitude upon five schools in your school district without their voluntary participation. First, there would be a series of legal and political hurdles that might have precluded the attempt. However, the problems are deeper than that. Even if you could magically surmount those difficulties you would still be faced with serious problems. If you randomly assigned teachers to cooperative treatment groups there would be some teachers who would be enthusiastic about the possibilities inherent in the program and others who would be mildly interested and still others who might be openly antagonistic. If teachers were not willing to give the method a chance to be implemented, this opposition would certainly spoil any study attempting to determine its effectiveness. Additionally, teachers will need to be trained carefully in the method to give it a chance to be implemented properly. By the time you have won over teachers to undertake training in a particular method, the same possibilities exist for bias that occurred in the current study.

Stevens and Slavin addressed those questions quite directly and honestly. The choice facing the researcher was to do either a small scale effort testing one or two components in a more rigorously controlled setting using a true experimental design or to put the entire package together and test its effects in a longitudinal study within an existing district using the less powerful quasi-experimental design. Because there had never been a study that tried to examine the package in its entirety in a school district with all the real-world problems posed by such settings, they opted, correctly in our opinion, for the quasi-experimental design.

Having granted the soundness of the reasoning that went into the choice of the design, it remains true that all the problems posed by the quasi-experimental design still exist and cannot be willed away by good intentions or by the lack of good alternatives. It is not inappropriate to conclude that this study was both extremely well designed and was seriously flawed. The selection bias inherent in choosing two faculties who are excited about the possibilities inherent in implementing something new and challenging cannot be willed away. As evidenced by the more intensive and extensive faculty development meetings held in the treatment schools as in contrast to the comparison schools, there may well have been something special that motivated the teachers in the treatment schools. The researchers readily acknowledged the problems but argued that such initial excitement is difficult to sustain over a two-year period and that, in fact, the results became stronger rather than weaker as the program continued into the second year.

Given the difficulties discussed, what implications do we draw from the study? First, the results were consistent both statistically and practically. Second, the study does demonstrate what a faculty committed to implementing a program of this type can do over a sustained two-year period when teachers, administrators, and parents are involved in the process. Third, it is possible and even probable that the differences found might be inflated because of the sample selection problems discussed previously. The world of educational research is real, important, and messy. Principal Miller will have to weigh all these factors and make an informed decision based on the best available data. It should be apparent that the phrase "Research clearly proves" is not one that can be used with any confidence in making educational decisions.

We have now come to the end of our examination of four pieces of empirical research and have laboriously taken each one apart to examine the statistical and practical significance of the differences found in each one. You should now be well equipped with an important skill as you examine other research articles relevant to problems in your school. Each study that compares two or more groups and describes differences between them can be analyzed as to the likelihood that the differences were attributable to chance and to express that likelihood in terms of statistical significance.

In addition to statistical significance, the differences between and among groups often can be expressed in terms of an effect size. The effect size represents a fraction of a standard deviation and gives the practitioner an excellent way of determining whether a difference is sufficiently large as to warrant serious consideration for application to a school or classroom setting. At times the researcher will include the effect sizes in a table for easy reference but, in case they are not included, you are capable of calculating the differences when the relevant data are provided. By applying these twin concepts you are able to make intelligent decisions about the potential usefulness of a program for addressing a problem in your school.

Principal Miller's Decision

After concluding their review of the literature and examining the relevant studies in careful detail, what did Principal Miller and her committee conclude? The reader may recall that the committee set out the following questions to guide their deliberations:

1. What kinds of cooperative learning strategies are available?
2. What cooperative learning strategies have been found to enhance achievement in mathematics generally and in problem solving skills specifically with 4th and 5th grade students with widely varying levels of ability?

The review of the conceptual literature provided the committee with some excellent background information about cooperative learning models and strategies. Of these models of cooperative learning, the committee decided that the Student Teams-Achievement Divisions (STAD) and the Team-Assisted-Individualization (TAI) models were most promising to pursue for the teaching of mathematics to children in grades 4 and 5 in their school. Based on the conceptual descriptions of each one they felt encouraged to pursue the empirical literature for evidence of their effectiveness in improving student learning in math computation and problem solving.

Based on studies they reviewed, including the four studies chosen for examination in this chapter, what did the committee learn? First, while research with useful information was available, there was no one study that gave them exactly what they sought. One investigation examined math computation and problem solving but studied 7th graders instead of 4th and 5th graders. Another examined grade levels 5 and 6 but used only some components of cooperative learning—not the ones of greatest interest to Miller and her faculty. It was their task to read critically, to carefully draw inferences, and to use their best professional judgment regarding what recommendations to make to their colleagues.

The committee discussed their findings and, after deliberating for some time, composed an action memo to share with the full faculty meeting early in the fall semester. Of course, each of these points would be developed through discussion with all the teachers, but the memo (see Figure 6.1) would serve as an agenda to guide their deliberations and to help them plan their next steps.

AUGUST 15, 2001

MEMO

TO: Faculty members of Pleasant Valley Elementary School

FR: Math/Cooperative Learning Task Force

RE: Results of our summer's labor

We have spent a summer reviewing research on cooperative learning and math computation and problem solving skills. While we would not consider the work we did to be as exciting as some of the adventures you may have enjoyed, we did find it stimulating and interesting. We look forward to sharing the results of our work with you during the second faculty meeting of the year on October 8 at 3:30 P.M. in the library conference room. We hope you will think about the points we have raised and we encourage your active participation in the next phase of our efforts.

1. We found two types of cooperative learning strategies particularly well suited for teaching math computation and math problem solving for our students at Pleasant Valley. The first type is referred to as Student Teams-Achievement Divisions (STAD). In STAD, students are assigned to four person heterogeneous teams based on achievement, sex, and race. The teacher first presents the material in a large group setting, and then children work in their teams to ensure that each member of the team has learned the material. The second type is a slight variant of STAD and is called Team-Assisted-Individualization or TAI. This strategy has been specifically designed for teaching mathematics to students in grades 3–6, so we think it will be particularly appropriate for our 4th and 5th graders. It is similar to STAD in group composition and has the advantage of combining cooperative learning with individualization of instruction. Students enter an individualized instructional sequence on the basis of placement tests and then each child works on different units. We think this feature should be particularly appealing to some of our teachers who have been working with heterogeneously grouped classrooms.
2. The review of research yielded some very interesting results that look promising for our situation. While we will have to spend a great deal of time in our meetings this fall discussing the actual results, we found studies that indicated that cooperative learning strategies greatly increased student learning in math computation and also showed moderate increases in math applications and problem solving. Of even greater interest to us was that these studies demonstrated the gains could be achieved while integrating special education students and gifted students within the same learning context.

Several articles that describe the various types of cooperative learning strategies as well as four of the most relevant studies that looked at the effectiveness of the strategies in classroom settings are available for your perusal in the office. We encourage you to take a look at them over the next few weeks and be prepared to raise questions and issues when we get together on October 8.

Welcome back.

F I G U R E *6.1* Memorandum

And, so, we take leave of Principal Miller and her task force. Of course, the existing research did not provide them with easy answers to their questions. That is an unrealistic expectation. A careful examination of the research literature, however, did offer them ideas, insights, and possible ways to address their problem. It helped them think more intelligently about their problem. And, that is no small contribution.

References

Abrami P., Chambers, B., D'Appolonia, S., Farrell, M., de Simone, C. (1992). Group outcome: The relationship between group learning outcome, attributional style, academic achievement and self-concept. *Contemporary Educational Psychology* 17(3), 201–210.

Aronson, E., Planney, N., Stephan, C., Sikes, J., & Smapp, M. (1978). *The Jigsaw classroom.* Beverly Hills, CA: Sage Publications, Inc.

Bossert, S. (1989). Cooperative activities in the classroom. In E. Rothkopf (Ed.), *Review of research in education* (Vol. 15, pp. 225–250). Washington, DC: American Educational Research Association.

Chambers, B., & Abrami, P. (1991). The relationship between student team learning outcomes and achievement, causal attributions and affect. *Journal of Educational Psychology,*83(1), 140–146.

DeVries, D. L., & Slavin, R. E. (1978). Teams-Games-Tournaments (TGT): Review of ten classroom experiments. *Journal of Research and Development in Education, 12,* 28–38.

Fantuzzo, J., King J., & Heller, L. (1992). Effects of reciprocal peer tutoring on mathematics and school adjustment: A component analysis. *Journal of Educational Psychology, 84*(3), 331–339.

Furtwengler, C. B. (1992). How to observe cooperative learning classrooms. *Educational Leadership, 49*(7), 59–62.

Gall, J. P., Gall, M. D., & Borg, W. R. (1999). *Applying educational research: A practical guide* (4th ed.). New York: Addison Wesley Longman, Inc.

Hamm, M., & Adams, D. (1992). *The collaborative dimensions of learning.* Norwood, NJ: Ablex Publishing Corporation.

Hooper S. (1992). Effects of peer interaction during computer-based mathematics instruction. *Journal of Educational Research 85*(3), 180–189.

Johnson, D., & Johnson, R. (1989). *Cooperation and competition: Theory and research.* Edina, MN: Interaction Book Co.

Phelps, E. & Damon, W. (1989). Problem solving with equals: Peer collaboration as a context for learning mathematics and spatial concepts. *Journal of Educational Psychology,*81(4), 639–646.

Sharan, S. (1980). Cooperative learning in small groups: Recent methods and effects on achievement, attitudes, and ethnic relations. *Review of Educational Research, 50,* 241–249.

Slavin, R. (1986). *Using student team learning.* Baltimore, MD: Johns Hopkins University, Center for Research on Elementary and Middle Schools.

Slavin, R. E. (1990). *Cooperative learning: Theory, research, and practice.* Englewood Cliffs, NJ: Prentice-Hall.

Stevens, R. J., & Slavin, R. E. (1995). The cooperative elementary school: Effects on students' achievement, attitudes, and social relations. *American Educational Research Journal, 32*(2), 321–351.

CHAPTER 7

Teacher Empowerment and Qualitative Research

INTRODUCTION

The production of qualitative studies by educational researchers has grown rapidly in recent decades. These studies now appear frequently in journals formerly devoted entirely to quantitative studies, and new journals have emerged that are devoted specifically to their publication. Further, problems in education are being explored by researchers from other disciplines where qualitative methods are common, and the results of their work appear in our field's journals. As a result, practicing administrators are increasingly exposed to studies that use qualitative methods. Given these trends, it is appropriate that we devote time and effort to the concepts and methods that are unique to this form of inquiry.

Our chapter begins with a middle school principal, Bill Evans, trying to deal with a demoralized, dispirited faculty, one that is merely "going through the motions." We will observe him as he turns to the research literature in order to seek ideas to help him empower his staff and restore its commitment and enthusiasm for teaching. We explicate five criteria for evaluating qualitative research and apply these to a qualitative study that Bill uncovers in his search. Finally, implications will be derived from this study that will form the basis for the course of action that he adopts.

The Case: Can Lincoln's Faculty Be Empowered?

After three months on the job, most first year principals probably feel a bit overwhelmed. Being new to the district didn't help either as the daily demands from downtown seemed to bring a new set of incomprehensible requests for information and reports that were not readily available. Fighting through the blizzard of paper seemed to distract Bill Evans from larger problems he knew were lurking within his building. At moments like these, he also admitted that part of the reason he was distracted was that he wanted to be distracted. Quite frankly, he didn't know how to get a handle on those big problems, and the daily office chores gave him a needed excuse to avoid them.

Evans took the job even though good friends had recommended against it. The district didn't pay all that well, very little stability existed either in the district office or in the principalship of this school and the superintendent was fairly new and looking for success markers. Slow, steady incremental change was needed in Lincoln Middle School and the superintendent wanted results . . . now.

During the job interview the superintendent had been quite candid about the recent history of Lincoln Middle School. As he saw it, years of administrative neglect, aging teachers, new teachers who left as soon as possible, and a transient student population were not issues that lent themselves to easy resolutions. Of course, test scores reflected the dismal situation and placed Lincoln in the bottom third of the district and even lower on national norms.

So why did Bill Evans take the job? As he considered this question on the way home tonight he smiled as he thought, "Does the word *stupid* come to mind?" Maybe he was stupid but he also believed strongly that an average faculty and administrators with decidedly above average effort can have an impact. He had seen it work before and it was that experience that motivated him to take the job.

The question was, could it work here? And, could it work now? Evans had deliberately forged a low profile role for himself as principal the first couple of months. Partly by design and partly by default, he had not pushed any new ventures with the faculty. The *default* portion was explained by a sign he kept out of view in his office that read, "When you're up to your butt in alligators, it's hard to remember that your mission is to drain the swamp." Stated less bluntly, the day-to-day exigencies prevented him from effecting a large scale strategy for dealing with serious problems.

The *design* portion of his low profile was prompted by his suspicions that the current faculty felt beaten down by conditions. It seemed as though they were waiting for the new principal to come in with a game plan that would either succeed and solve their problems or, more likely, fail, leading to another new principal who would repeat the cycle. As the veterans liked to remind each other, "Principals come and principals go."

And so, the first couple of months were spent looking, listening, and dealing with the administrivia of Lincoln Middle School. No great tragedies had occurred but, in all honesty, the school was in no better shape than when he got there. It struck him that a stand-off was occurring. He was waiting for leadership to emerge from the faculty, and the teachers were waiting for him to earn his salary and lead them from the edge of the abyss.

As Bill Evans pulled into his driveway on the day before Thanksgiving he knew that the impasse would need to be overcome. This weekend would give him some time to effect a strategy for energizing the faculty to address the difficult issues they all faced. Maybe the nap after tomorrow's turkey dinner would bring him the inspiration he needed.

During the Thanksgiving break, Bill decided on a game plan. He pulled some thoughts together and recalled some conversations he had previously with three or four faculty who seemed committed to the long haul of improving Lincoln Middle School. Two of these teachers had been there for from six to eight years and had some sense of history of the place. A couple more were dynamite young teachers who had not yet received their cynicism implants and were well regarded as "good, young hires."

What Evans liked about this group was that they really weren't a group . . . yet. He saw this as an advantage in that building upon any existing factions within the faculty was probably an invitation to failure. While he may have been overgeneralizing from earlier experience, he couldn't overcome the feeling that the social structure of the school was not a healthy one. The groups appeared poised to attack any and all who dared threaten their conclusion that nothing would really improve their lot, and that anything that might be tried was bound to make more work for teachers. In the end, everyone would feel worse for having tried and failed. "Wow," Bill thought, "Am I *really* that depressed?"

Rightly or wrongly, those were some of the perceptions driving Evans as he planned for moving on the school's problems. Other perceptions were less negative. The school and its surrounding community were not in a deteriorating condition. The faculty and pupil turnover were typical for this type of community, and parents seemed like good, decent people who were concerned about their kids' education. Sometimes. At other times, the parents he met seemed to be going through the same ritualistic dance perfected by many of his faculty. Occasional sparks of hope were struck by faculty and parents, but often they seemed resigned to accept the fate of the consistently denied.

The attitude of "you're here, I'm here, let's make the best of it" had to be changed. Some way, some how, teachers as individuals, teachers as groups, parents as individuals, and parents as a total community must help each other gain or regain a sense of efficacy about their lives and work. Somehow, the concept of empowerment needed to be developed, nourished, and used to effect changes in curriculum and teacher practice, and through these vehicles to make changes in the lives of students. It may sound a bit hokey, but that is why Bill Evans took this principalship. "Plus," he mused, "don't forget the part about being stupid."

We take leave momentarily from our beleaguered principal and begin our discussion of qualitative research issues. We will return to Mr. Evans when he has thought through his problem a bit more carefully and when he is ready to pose guiding questions to be addressed by the research literature.

Qualitative Research in Education

Remember that qualitative research comes in a wide variety of sizes and shapes. While this may be true of quantitative research as well, arguably the approaches and perspectives in qualitative research are more numerous and varied than their counterparts in the quantitative realm.

Numerous reasons for these differences could be listed, but the two major ones appear to be the recency and origins of qualitative research. Quantitative research methodologies have been the mainstay of doctoral level training for decades. Most practicing administrators received their entire research training completely within the quantitative tradition, often taking a quantitative research methods course and a semester or two of statistics. Few, if any, took even one course in qualitative data analysis. Few doctoral programs preparing administrators today give equal time to qualitative research skills, and the typical pattern may include two or three quantitative courses and one qualitative course. Clearly, qualitative research has more recently arrived and has not matured to the point where consolidation of the differences in approaches has occurred.

Perhaps more important than its recency, the origins of qualitative research in education are rooted in several disciplines, each of which has developed a long history and tradition. Psychology, sociology, and particularly anthropology have developed variations of qualitative inquiry, and each of these traditions has influenced researchers working on educational problems. The anthropologist studying artifacts and indigenous peoples, the sociologist observing and participating in street gang cultures, and the psychologist observing primates though video lenses all share a common interest in nonquantitative data to help them understand their phenomena. However, it should be clear that these settings can lead to vastly different methods, techniques, and philosophical assumptions. As educators borrowed, extended, and modified these approaches in seeking answers to educational questions, it should be clear that qualitative research was not a single entity. Perhaps the point could be best made by simply noting that the first *Handbook of Qualitative Research* (Denzin & Lincoln, 1994) has 36 chapters and 643 pages.[1] With these cautions behind us, we will try to simplify the comparisons and share several distinguishing characteristics of qualitative research.

Tenets of Qualitative Research

Wilson (1977) emphasized two differences between qualitative and quantitative orientations. While no distinction is iron clad, he argued that those researchers who draw on the qualitative tradition tend to differ from their quantitatively-oriented colleagues in the importance they attach to the *phenomenological*

---

[1] While the *Handbook* is the most extensive collection of work available on qualitative research methods and techniques, it is written at a level of complexity that might not be useful to practitioners. We would recommend one of the following texts: Glesne (1999), LeCompte and Preissle (1993), Miles and Huberman (1984), Yin (1989) or Wolcott (1994).

perspective of the individuals being studied and the role of *context* as it influences those individuals.

Wilson describes the phenomenological perspective in the following words: "Those who work within this tradition assert that the social scientist cannot understand human behavior without understanding the framework within which the subjects interpret their thoughts, feelings, and actions" (p. 246).

The role of context is defined by Wilson as follows: "Many social scientists believe that human behavior is significantly influenced by the settings in which it occurs. They, therefore, believe that it is essential to study psychological events in natural settings" (p. 244).

While few researchers would disagree with the presence of these two factors, you will find sharp differences in the importance attached to them. Consider the following example. If researchers from the quantitative tradition wish to study the concept of teacher morale, a rather typical approach might be to carefully define the concept by examining the research literature to determine its typical usage and then to refine it as clearly as possible. Next, an instrument might be developed to provide a valid and reliable indicator of morale. Teachers might be consulted during the validation process, but the researcher would be responsible for applying psychometric principles to develop a measure that was clearly related to the conceptual definition of teacher morale. Next, the researcher might move to the field to examine a variety of legitimate questions. Are there differences in teacher morale among middle schools? Are there correlates of teacher morale that might account for these differences? Is teacher morale related to administrator behaviors? Can teacher morale be modified by specific interventions?

Certainly these questions are worth pursuing and their answers could help a school administrator be more effective at her or his central role: providing an environment for enhancing pupil learning. Equally certain is that a qualitatively-oriented researcher would not approach these tasks in a similar fashion.

Based upon Wilson's two principles, the qualitative researcher may be puzzled by the previous approach and may reason as follows: "When I think about teacher morale, I remember a teacher at Irving Middle School who said that teacher morale was really high there. Other teachers demonstrated concern for you and your family. They got together socially and kept up with each other's children. They greeted you in the teacher lounge with questions such as, 'How are the kids doing? How are your azaleas growing?' Teacher morale at Irving couldn't be better.'"

"But," the hypothetical qualitative researcher continued, "I also know a teacher at Longfellow Middle School who thought teacher morale was also excellent in her setting. Teachers expressed concern for school achievement, school board policies, curriculum issues, and classroom management problems. They didn't greet you in the teacher's lounge with questions about your kids and your azaleas. Teacher morale at Longfellow couldn't be higher."

These two forays into hyperbole are intended to make the point that the qualitative researcher would have trouble comparing these two teachers' responses on a single scale of teacher morale no matter how carefully it was constructed. Wilson's tenet of phenomenological perspective would loom large for the researcher in that she or he would value highly the perspective and meaning that the participant would attach to the concept. Second, the role of *context* would also loom large in that the values and norms that have developed over time at Irving might shape the teachers' concept in very important ways that will be different from the norms and values of Longfellow. The qualitative researcher might approach the problem of teacher morale from precisely the opposite perspective of the quantitative researcher. Teacher morale might be explored, not for its similarities among the participants, but for the differences in point of view held. What one research tradition takes for granted, the other makes problematic. The two traditions offer interesting, but different, slants at understanding phenomena; both slants are necessary. Many years ago, Homans (1962) articulated a position we find relevant today:

> "We need both stricter ideas of what we are trying to get at—deductive explanations—and more toleration for the many different ways of getting there—our methods of investigation . . . No method can go far wrong that puts human behavior under close scrutiny." (p. 49)

Criteria for Assessing Qualitative Research

Before we examine research related to empowerment of teachers, we need to explore criteria for judging the quality of qualitative research. Some concerns are shared across both qualitative and quantitative research traditions but take slightly different forms in each, while other concerns are not at all comparable. We will discuss criteria that address five areas of concern to every qualitative research consumer: (1) the research problem, (2) the setting of the study, (3) data quality, (4) data analysis techniques, and (5) researcher perspective.

Research Problem. In qualitative research, it is not uncommon to begin the study with a broad, somewhat hazy outline of the problem, and a clear problem statement can be a product rather than a prerequisite of the study. Malinowski (1984) referred to a "foreshadowed" problem as the appropriate metaphor for anthropologists. For example, one may begin with a broad definition of teacher morale or with various conceptions of teacher morale, and the purpose of the study is to provide the clarity and details that are currently lacking. One could argue that if, in fact, a clear and precise definition of teacher morale were available, perhaps a qualitative study might not be the preferred approach.

Lack of precision should not be seen as a license for ambiguity, however. Casting the problem as clearly as the research literature will allow and describing the problem in as clear and precise a manner as possible are still the prerequisites for good research of either genre.

One way to think about problem specificity might be to consider exploring a cave in search of rock formations when you are the first known person to enter it. If you assume, based on exploration of previous caves, that you know exactly what you will find, you will not be open to the possibility that this cave holds unique mysteries. In contrast, ignoring the existing evidence that others have gathered and attempting to enter the cave without any preconception of what you will find is neither possible nor advisable. Malinowski's foreshadowed problem attempts to capture the essence of the appropriate degree of problem specificity required in a good qualitative study.

As you evaluate a research problem in a qualitative study you should focus on the questions that will be addressed. Those questions may be more in number and broader in scope than their counterparts in a quantitative study, but they should be explicit, clearly written, and related to the problem.

The Setting. The setting of the study includes the physical setting as well as the sample of participants who are being studied. A careful qualitative researcher concentrates on the physical characteristics of the setting and describes it in rich detail. Since context plays such a vital role, it is important to spend time observing and describing it. It is not enough to describe a setting as a school district in the Southwest United States. The district, its geographic location, the community, and its cultural and political history are all features that need to be described, if these characteristics play an important role in participants' behavior.

In addition to the physical aspects of the setting, the sample of participants need to be carefully described. Large, representative samples are highly valued in quantitative research because they enable the researcher to generalize the results of their findings to similar settings. Because qualitative researchers are usually limited to small, unrepresentative samples, they are properly cautious about generalizing the results of their studies. Sample selection in qualitative research is frequently undertaken for a very different purpose. Samples in qualitative studies may be chosen precisely because they are unrepresentative of the population at large and therefore enable the researcher to explore a particular phenomenon not widely found in the general population.

For example, if dissident parent groups rarely rise up and demand the termination of a building principal, this highly atypical event might serve as an ideal opportunity to examine the factors and conditions that galvanize parents to take action. Of course, by its very nature as a rare event, one must be cautious about generalizing these results to districts that have not witnessed such disruptive upheavals.

Selection of an appropriate number and variety of subjects serves a different purpose for the qualitative researcher. One selects sufficient *numbers* and *types* of people so that the phenomenon being investigated is adequately represented. To return to the study of teacher morale, a sample of one or two math teachers taken from a middle school does not allow for different conceptions of morale to surface if, in fact, they exist. However, a sample of 12 to 15 teachers of varying ages, experience, subject background and ideological perspectives might allow the researcher to tap a wider range of morale conceptions. Put another way, if differing conceptions of teacher morale exist in middle schools, then intensively interviewing 12 to 15 teachers from various segments of a school greatly increases the likelihood of discovering those conceptions.

The requirement of intensive data gathering usually sets the upper limits of how many participants can be properly studied. Note again the different focus brought to bear upon the sample in a qualitative study. Rather than seek a larger, more representative sample to increase generalizability of findings (a quantitative researcher's concern), the qualitative researcher seeks a large and diverse enough sample so that the phenomenon being studied manifests itself.

The setting and sample descriptions in a qualitative study can take on added importance for the practitioner. When done well, the rich description of the context and the clear identification of the study participants can sharpen the similarities and differences between the study and the practitioner's home setting.

Data Quality. Miles and Huberman (1990) remind us "Unless we can develop more of a tradition of making our methods explicit . . . it will keep on being hard to trust the results of qualitative inquiry . . ." (p. 349). Fortunately, there are ways to evaluate the quality of data in a study. Lincoln and Guba (1985) addressed the issue as one of establishing trustworthiness in the following words, "How can an inquirer persuade his or her audiences (including self) that the findings of an inquiry are worth paying attention to, worth taking account of? What arguments can be mounted, what criteria invoked, what questions asked, that would be persuasive on this issue?" (p. 290).

Lincoln and Guba suggest three specific researcher activities that can enhance the credibility of data collection. These three activities are: (1) prolonged engagement, (2) persistent observation, and (3) triangulation. *Prolonged engagement* allows the researcher sufficient time to establish trust with participants and overcome initial resistance to share perceptions and learn the culture in which the study takes place. A limited encounter will not allow the researcher to detect the distortions that could creep into the data. Group members will, intentionally or unintentionally, mask feelings and opinions from the researcher until such time as trust is established and the participants feel it is safe to share their perceptions. No amount of skill or technique can be used to gather data if the participants are unwilling or unable to share with the researcher

A second researcher activity is described by Lincoln and Guba as *persistent observation* (p. 304). Persistent observation can be manifested in a study through the number and length of observations and/or interviews conducted and the amount of time the researcher spends in the field during the data collection phase. While prolonged engagement refers to the duration of the study, persistent observation describes the frequency and intensity of data collections efforts in the study. Clues regarding this criterion are available in the Methods and Procedures section of most qualitative studies, and you should be able to draw inferences regarding data quality based on these clues. An oft-repeated maxim in anthropology refers to the quest as "making the familiar strange and the strange familiar." It takes time, effort, and persistent observation to achieve these goals.

Finally, Lincoln and Guba refer to *triangulation* as an activity that adds to data credibility. This concept has been around in a variety of disciplines for a rather long time. Surveyors and airline pilots use triangulation as a means of tracking multiple sources of information to pinpoint a location. Analogously, journalists and qualitative researchers seek corroboration from other sources to lend credibility to their observations. Concretely, evidence that the researcher has used more than one *source* of data (e.g., multiple participants), more than one *method* of collecting data (e.g., interviews, observations, and documents), or more than one *observer* (e.g., other researchers) should help us gain confidence in the quality of the data.

The research consumer should ask for careful documentation, either in the body of the report or in an appendix, of the collection, transcription, and processing of the data. If interviews were conducted, were the interview procedures and questions clearly described? If observations were undertaken, did the researcher share with the reader important information as to length, type and frequency of the observation? In short, how clearly did the researcher describe how the data were collected? With this information you should be able to form an opinion regarding the prolonged engagement, persistent observation and, triangulation criteria for judging data quality. Good data do not guarantee a good study, but bad data certainly go a long way toward ensuring a weak, shallow, and superficial investigation.

Data Analysis Techniques. The qualitative researcher lacks the convenience of pointing to specific techniques such as analysis of variance, correlational analysis, or *t*-tests to indicate how the data were examined. While lacking these time-honored techniques of the quantitative researcher, the quiver of the qualitative researcher is not completely empty. There are a variety of techniques available to show what the researcher did with the data that enabled him or her to arrive at the interpretations or conclusions that were drawn in the study.

Great caution needs to be exercised by the research consumer at this phase of the evaluation process. Too frequently, the qualitative researcher may offer a rather terse "The data were analyzed to determine patterns that existed" or some such phrasing. This type of response is not acceptable. How were the data analyzed? Were they read through once and the first impression garnered written down as evidence of a pattern? Was one highly articulate respondent used as the source for all or most of the patterns that were reported? "Three patterns emerged from the data," is a phrase that has continued to amuse us. The image of murky and amorphous data simmering in a hollow with three patterns slowly and distinctly rising from the swamp is a tempting vision, but it does not square with the reality known to most qualitative researchers. Patterns do not "emerge." They are pushed, pulled, manipulated, modified, and merged, but they do not emerge magically from the data.

What techniques are available to the researcher who seeks to analyze qualitative data? Glaser and Strauss (1967) and Glaser (1978) developed an approach that they called the *constant comparative method*. This procedure calls for coding data from interviews, observations, or documents under headings that appear to capture the theoretical properties of that category. Each coded category is then described as succinctly as possible to capture the meanings inherent in it. Then, using that category, all new and existing data are constantly compared to determine the descriptive adequacy of the category. Revisions and modifications of the category continue until the researcher is satisfied with it. Additional categories are identified, tested, and modified in a similar fashion. Finally, linkages between and among categories are forged as an important part of a *grounded theory* (Glaser & Strauss, 1967) approach.

The constant comparative approach, or modification of this procedure, should be evident in the data analysis section. Not all researchers will refer to the procedures by name and not all researchers will strictly adhere to its painstakingly thorough steps, but some data analytical procedures should be clearly identified if the research is of high quality. Absence of any description of how meaning was extracted from the data leaves the reader with an appropriate degree of skepticism.

Certain techniques add credibility to a qualitative data analysis. One is called *negative case analysis* (Lincoln & Guba, 1985) and represents a slight extension of the constant comparative method. In negative case analysis, the researcher combs the data looking for examples that contradict the category under active consideration. Kidder (1981) drew upon an earlier study by Cressey (1953) to explicate the concept of negative case analysis. He stated:

> Cressey formulated and revised his hypothesis five times before he arrived at his conclusion about the causes of embezzlement. Each time he formulated a new hypothesis, he checked it against not only new interviews but also all of his previously recorded interviews and observations. . . . Negative case analysis requires that the researcher look for disconfirming data in both past and future observations. A single negative case is enough to require the investigator to revise a hypothesis. When there are no more negative cases the researcher stops revising the hypothesis. . . ." (Kidder, 1981, p. 241)

Kidder drew an interesting parallel between negative case analyses and statistical techniques in quantitative studies. He wrote: "Both are means to handle error variance. Qualitative research uses 'errors' to revise the hypothesis; quantitative analysis uses error variance to test the hypothesis. . . ." (Kidder 1981, p. 244)

One final technique will be cited. Lincoln and Guba (1985) described the importance of *member checks* in establishing qualitative data credibility. This procedure may be as informal as returning to one participant to make sure the researcher "got it right" or as formal as returning all transcripts of interviews and observation notes to the participants to determine their accuracy. At times researchers will share copies of the report at various draft stages to determine the participants' perceptions of the researcher's analysis. While this raises potentially serious problems when participants see themselves portrayed in a bad light, it does serve as a check on distortions and inaccuracies that may have crept into the data. The researcher is not obligated to accept the participants' criticisms, but a careful researcher would certainly benefit from knowing what they were.

These techniques are not used by all qualitative researchers, and there are other strategies that could be argued to be equally important as the ones cited. The presence or absence of any particular technique is not the salient issue. What is important is that the qualitative researcher should document techniques used in her or his data analysis. An important yet simple question should guide the research consumer: How did the researcher get from the data collected to the inferences drawn?

Researcher Perspective. One of the exciting, but troubling, aspects of qualitative inquiry is the important role that the personal beliefs, values, and experiences of the researcher play in the research process. It is exciting because it enables the researcher to draw upon all his or her knowledge, skills, and life experiences to help extract meaning from the data. It is troubling because those very qualities can also influence the findings in unknown ways. Many have argued that, in qualitative inquiry, the researcher *is* the instrument.

While it is tempting to try and avoid problems of researcher perspective by striving for objectivity or neutrality, this is never completely an option. Certainly, biases and value-laden opinions should be consciously checked at every phase of the research process, but careful qualitative researchers argue that an additional step be taken. Researchers need to understand their subjectivity by carefully delineating their core values.

Peshkin (Glesne & Peshkin, 1992) traced his personal values history by being attentive to his feelings as he undertook several extensive research projects. He identified several stages in the process that began with reflecting upon an earlier work and recognizing that *what* he chose to describe was partly a function of *who* he was as a person. In *Growing Up American* (Peshkin, 1978), he realized that his strong sense of community was being tapped for insights as he wrote about a rural community and its struggles with school consolidation.

Peshkin's struggle with the researcher's perspective reached its apex in *God's Choice* (Peshkin, 1986), in which he came to grips with the influence his Jewishness had on his examination of a fundamental Baptist school. He recognized that the Baptist school represented a strong community not unlike the rural village he had previously admired, and yet he perceived this one very differently. Peshkin described his feelings as follows:

> In research terms, this setting provided entry to the world of true believers, a world that I had never known before. Never before had I felt so alien, so distant from where I lived, while being geographically so close to home. I was proselytized by persons who were certain I was condemned to eternity in hell unless I was born again by accepting Christ as my personal savior. I had to learn to perceive proselytizing as the acts of persons who sincerely wished me well, rather than as an act that offended my integrity as a Jew. (Glesne & Peshkin, 1992, p. 103)

While qualitative researchers struggle against the negative aspects of their subjectivity, they should also strive to capitalize on the positive aspects that bring a wealth of insights to a study. Again, we turn to Peshkin for his description of the next stage of the quest for understanding the researcher's perspective:

> In short, the subjectivity that originally I had taken as an affliction, something to bear because it could not be foregone, could, to the contrary, be taken as 'virtuous.' My subjectivity is *the* basis for the story that I am able to tell. It is a strength on which I build. It makes me who I am as a person *and* as a researcher, equipping me with the perspectives and insights that shape all that I do as a researcher, from

the selection of the topic clear through to the emphases I make in my writing. Seen as virtuous, subjectivity is something to capitalize on rather than to exorcise. (Glesne & Peshkin, 1992, p. 104)

With the importance attached to the role of researcher perspective, the researcher should share relevant aspects of his or her life experience that might influence the study. While no one expects an autobiographical treatise as a preface to each qualitative study, the researcher should provide sufficient information so that the reader can make informed judgments about the particular perspective being brought to bear upon the research. In a study of labor conflict and its impact upon a local community, it would be helpful to know the researcher's beliefs and values regarding the role of teacher unions. It is possible for a person to conduct an excellent study from either a pro-labor or a pro-management perspective, but it will certainly be helpful to know in advance which set of life experiences is driving the study.

To return to the example of Peshkin and the Baptist school study, it is instructive to contrast the different stories that might have emerged if the school had been studied by Alan Peshkin, a Jewish professor from a research university, or by Reverend X, a Baptist professor at a theological seminary. Could each of these people do a good qualitative study of this school? Of course. Would these studies focus on very different aspects of the Baptist school? Most likely. Would the reader be better informed by knowing the background of these two researchers? We think so.

Different perspectives bring different skills and values to the table, and qualitative research benefits from examining phenomena from as many different orientations as possible. No one perspective can lay claim to "truth," but each can offer an alternative and valuable version of truth as seen through the eyes of the researcher. In examining a qualitative study it is important to look for evidence that the researcher is attempting to come to grips with the role the researcher's perspective brings to the study. Limitations on article length may not allow the full disclosure that Peshkin could pursue in his book, but some information should be provided. Researchers can share assumptions that drove the study and include personal information that may be relevant. As an important aspect of research credibility, read carefully for any information that provides clues about these matters.

Unfortunately, many beginning qualitative researchers carry over the tradition of assumed neutrality and objectivity that has been the goal of quantitative researchers. While oversimplified, one could contrast the two traditions by how they deal with subjectivity. Quantitative researchers attempt to safeguard the quality of the study by developing valid and reliable instruments and statistical techniques that reduce the effects of researcher perspective. Qualitative researchers cannot rely on these efforts and hope to accomplish the same goal by clearly explicating and sharing their perspectives with the reader and thereby limiting the negative aspects and capitalizing on the positive ones. However, Glesne and Peshkin warn us: "Reading, reflecting, and talking about subjectivity are valuable, but they are no substitute for monitoring it in the process of research (Glesne & Peshkin, 1992, p. 106).

Review of Empowerment Literature

Keeping in mind the criteria that prepare us to address qualitative research, we are ready to return to Bill Evans and his challenging task of revitalizing his faculty. Specifically, Bill said, "Some way, somehow, teachers as individuals, teachers as groups must help each other gain or regain a sense of efficacy about their lives and work." Bill recognized the problem he wished to ultimately solve was the enhancement of the learning environment of students at Lincoln Middle School. He reasoned that there was a prior problem that needed to be addressed if any headway were to be made on that problem. He wanted to find a way to galvanize the faculty and staff into a cohesive force to be able to address the larger problems facing the school. As he saw it, the initial problem was to address the low sense of empowerment of faculty. He turned to the research literature to address his problem.

Rather than undertake a literature search on all aspects of teacher empowerment, Bill wisely began with a list of questions he felt were important. After poring over a list of 8 or 10 questions, he settled on these two:

1. What is known about the concept of teacher empowerment that would help me better understand my faculty?
2. What strategies or techniques impact faculty members' sense of empowerment?

Teacher Empowerment

Exploring definitions of empowerment proved to be a difficult task. At first glance, it appears easy. Teacher empowerment would appear to refer to increasing the ability of teachers to influence those decisions that are important to teaching. But, which decisions? In which areas? It is commonly reported that teachers work in very isolated settings with little or no close supervision. If this is so, then it would appear that teachers already have a great deal of control over their day-to-day activities in the classroom.

If, on the other hand, teacher empowerment refers to control over decisions related to type of content taught, length of the school day and the school year, and other aspects of the school program, then other questions are raised. Some of these decisions are clearly in the hands of the state legislatures as they have set minimum requirements for length of school year and length of school days. Similarly, school boards and their hired officials (e.g., superintendents and principals) are responsible for determining policies and procedures for meeting state and local mandates. If teachers are to be "empowered," who is to be "disempowered"?

Bill found the literature less than helpful in his search to pin down a definition. Frequently, the concept of empowerment was undefined or vaguely defined. Maerhoff (1988) devoted a monograph to the topic and stated, "Empowerment, as viewed in this book, is a term somewhat synonymous with professionalization. It does not necessarily mean being in charge, though that is possible; more than anything else it means working in an environment in which a teacher acts as a professional and is treated as a professional. The inevitable result is empowerment." (p. 6) Bill wished it were that easy.

Hart and Robottom (1990) referred to empowered teachers as researchers and participants in the decision-making process. Kreisberg (1992, p. 108) stated ". . . to be empowered means to be able to effect change. Empowerment is the process by which individuals and groups become able to 'make a difference.'" Kreisberg extracted that definition from six case studies of teachers who were involved in a multiyear study. One teacher stated that "Empowerment works two ways. . . you can empower somebody, you can be empowered. . . the end is the individual having both the skills and the confidence to make change. . ." (p. 107). Another teacher added "I guess you might describe or define [empowerment] as a state in which a person feels that he or she has some control over his or her life. . ." (p. 107). And, a third teacher in the study commented, "[For me, empowerment means] to feel like I make a difference, that I have something to say that matters to other people. . ." (p. 107–108).

With these general definitions of empowerment as background, Bill began focusing more specifically on his first question, "What is known about the concept of teacher empowerment that would help me better understand my faculty?" Sarason (1971) sought the commitment of teachers to the reform process in his early work. Other researchers such as Havelock (1971, 1973) and Huberman (1984) were described by Gitlin and Margonis (1995) as constituting the "first wave" within the school change research literature. They described the "first wave" as a focus on providing strong outside support and resources to overcome the initial resistance to change that was said to characterize teachers' responses to school reform.

Gitlin and Margonis characterized a second "wave" of research as representing a slight advance over the earlier researchers in that it recognized the importance of the culture of teaching in facilitating or impeding school change. Hargreaves (1993) argued that the "top-down" approach of the previous orientation to school reform should be altered to win over and persuade teachers to become actively involved in the change process. Rosenholtz (1989) presented evidence that collaborative schools supported continued change while noncollaborative faculties were less productive. Similarly, Fullan, (1993) suggested that collaborative work cultures raised morale and teacher enthusiasm.

Bill found the Gitlin and Margonis critique helpful in giving him a historical perspective with which to think about his own situation. The authors seemed to be saying that while the change literature had progressed from the stage of trying to overcome teacher resistance by eliciting outside forces, to the stage of trying to persuade and win over teacher support by eliciting teacher support from within, both views suffered from the same fatal flaw. Both waves viewed teacher resistance as ill-informed, negative, and wrong-headed. Gitlin and Margonis developed the thesis that teacher resistance often contains insights about the preconditions needed for reform and should be substantively examined rather than routinely ignored. Rather than overpowered from without or won over from within, they argued that the expressed resistance might be derived from a knowledge of local conditions that need to be recognized, understood, and dealt with rather than side stepped.

Gitlin and Margonis (1995) based their argument for recognizing and dealing with expressed resistance on a study they conducted in an elementary school. They had been invited by the principal of that school to conduct an evaluation of the change process and were given access to teachers, administrators, and classrooms for extended data collection. The researchers found the initial set of concerns raised by teachers were ignored by the principal and an alternative faculty structure was chosen to pursue the issues that mattered to her.

Specifically, the principal had requested the teachers to provide a list of "central issues we can do something about" and they offered the following concerns:

1. Everyone has a job that creates work for others.
2. Too many meetings are being held.
3. Machines don't work and the workroom doesn't function.

Rather than respond to the issues that were raised, the building principal chose to interpret these responses as resistance to change that needed to be overcome. She chose to take advantage of a career ladder structure that existed in the district and to use these teachers to plan a second meeting. The second meeting resulted in a new set of goals that included restructuring of math assessment, direct instruction on social skills, and the implementation of instructional strategies in cooperative learning and whole language learning.

This action by the principal yielded predictable results. While the faculty voted unanimously to implement the site-based management goals put forward by the second committee, teachers effectively undermined the process in a variety of ways. Gitlin and Margonis reported that some teachers graded papers and polished bowling shoes during faculty meeting discussions of the proposed changes. The researchers noted two specific examples of how they came to be viewed by the teachers. Some faculty referred to them as "cooperative learning police" and other teachers would not allow them to observe in their classrooms even though they had previously agreed to this arrangement.

Gitlin and Margonis examined the teachers' original list of concerns over the course of the study and found ample evidence to suggest they were legitimate issues that had previously limited their teaching effectiveness and should have been taken seriously. They concluded their analysis in these words: "Our interpretation of the insights of resistant teachers indicates that reformers might be better off focusing on the preconditions for reform: Giving teachers the authority and time they need to teach in ways they find educationally defensible" (p. 403).

Bill felt he had gained some perspective on his problem. He had clearly recognized all the signs of teacher resistance among his faculty but may have dismissed them too quickly. He certainly had entertained thoughts of ways to circumvent or overcome these "obstructionist" teachers before he had made any efforts to understand them. Bill was particularly struck by one of the researchers' suggestions to develop a climate ". . . where teachers work together to examine and articulate the implicit insights embodied in resistant acts" (Gitlin & Margonis, 1995, p. 403)

A second caution was suggested by his reading. While he had entertained thoughts of cultivating a small group of teachers to serve as "change agents," the results of Gitlin and Margonis study suggested this might need further thought. The last thing he wanted to do was drive a further wedge between and among factions on his faculty.

Strategies for Impacting Teacher Empowerment: Learning from a Qualitative Case Study

What strategies or techniques exist that have been found to impact faculty members' sense of empowerment?

A study turned up in Bill's literature search will serve both as our example of qualitative research as well as provide substantive results that respond to his second guiding question. We will first examine the quality of this study using the criteria discussed previously and then turn our attention to the substantive issues.

Case Study Critique. The featured study of this chapter (Hart, 1994), is entitled Creating Teacher Leadership Roles and is described as a comparative case study. We would suggest you turn to the appendix on pages 218–237 and carefully examine this study before you continue reading the chapter. Two junior high schools in one district implemented a strategy to redesign teacher work roles in an effort to achieve three outcomes: (1) improved peer supervision, (2) shared decision making, and (3) collegial assistance. The plan called for two categories of teachers: the teacher leader and the teacher specialist. Only current faculty within each school who had three or more years of experience were eligible to apply for these two positions. A school committee comprised of the principal and two teachers selected 10% of the teachers as teacher leaders, giving them 12 months salary in addition to an annual stipend of $1,000.

The general role description of the teacher leaders called for the supervision and assistance of new teachers and, upon invitation, of experienced teachers. They were also expected to design and deliver in-service training, serve as department or team heads, and to write and test curriculum as needed.

The selection committee chose 40% of the teachers to serve as teacher specialists from among those who applied. The teacher specialists were to function as subject matter specialists in elementary schools and to assist with curriculum enrichment activities at the secondary level. They were to receive the $1,000 stipend and a few additional contract days of work for their efforts.

The comparative case study method was chosen because it allowed the examination of two replications of the same intervention and an examination of both the similarities and the differences in the outcomes as well as the processes that led to these outcomes. Yin (1989) and Miles and Huberman (1984) would refer to this as a qualitative, multiple-case method and would cite its advantages in verifying common patterns through replications.

Earlier in this chapter we suggested five issues that need to be addressed in a good qualitative study. These were: (1) the research problem, (2) the setting of the study, (3) data quality, (4) data analysis techniques, and (5) researcher perspective. We will explore each of these issues in turn with regard to the Hart study.

Problem Statement. The research problem was stated in its most general terms as follows: "In this article, I take advantage of a naturally occurring field experiment in school reform to examine organizational change in the form of teacher work redesign (Hart, 1994, p. 218). Scattered throughout the first few pages of the article are hints regarding more specific aims of the study. On page 218, Hart stated: "The goal of this comparative analysis was to learn from the people involved in the reform, to explore their assessments of the important values and activities in their schools affected by a change in teaching and leadership roles."

While implicit in the article, the most specific problem addressed in the study might be phrased as follows: To improve student performance, a plan for restructuring teacher roles was implemented in two middle schools. These role changes focused on clinical peer supervision, shared decision making, and collegial assistance.

The clarity of the research problem left something to be desired in that hints were scattered throughout the introduction to the article but were not explicitly stated in one place. While qualitative research problems are often stated at a rather general level of abstraction, they can still be stated clearly and explicitly. After careful reading, the problem (as we have phrased it) appears to be an important one, and if our inferences are correct, it appears to be an appropriate level of abstraction for qualitative research.

The Setting. The physical setting of the study as well as the sample participants were carefully described in the Hart study, although the description was uncharacteristically located under the heading of Findings. The physical setting of the district, its size, and political and fiscal conservatism were clearly stated. Additionally, the similarities and differences in the two middle schools were carefully delineated regarding principal tenure and leadership styles, faculty tenure, and ideological proclivities.

Careful attention to context is of vital importance for two reasons. First, it enables the reader to draw inferences about the correspondence between the setting of the study and the reader's own setting. Second, it provides the context for making sense of the researcher's data analysis and interpretations. Since one of the strengths of qualitative analysis is its ability to be sensitive to a much wider range of contributing factors than is often possible in a quantitative study, it is vitally important to provide a rich description of those background factors. Hart's description gives the reader a reasonably clear picture of both middle schools' settings and cultural context.

Data Collection. Extreme care was taken by Hart in describing each aspect of the data collection process. The procedures for gaining permission to do the study were detailed and thorough. Specific types of data included both systematic field notes and structured and unstructured interviews that were described as to frequency, duration, and type. Classes observed, meetings attended, surveys, teacher journals, and audio tapes of meetings not attended were also described.

In our earlier discussion of data quality, we stressed documentation, prolonged engagement, persistent observation, and triangulation. The researcher documented field notes covering two days a month at each school for an entire school year; 164 structured interviews of 30–60 minutes each; surveys; meeting notes; 41 classroom observations; journal reflections of 6 teacher leaders, 23 probation teachers, and 3 teacher specialists; and other data sources.

Based on the careful documentation of data collection, the reader can draw inferences regarding data quality. We give the study high marks on each of the mentioned criteria. Adding to researcher credibility in this area was her candid discussion of the weaknesses inherent in the teacher journals. Hart discussed the episodic nature of the journals and their tendency to record crises or highly charged emotional responses rather than as a record of the more mundane but important nuances of day-to-day changes.

Data Analysis and Interpretation. Some specific information was provided regarding data analysis procedures. For example, the steps taken to code raw data were briefly listed as follows: "Transcripts . . . were coded using basic concepts of role theory. Data summary sheets were prepared by collecting quotations and field note notations directly from the data. . . . Comparison matrices then were developed to facilitate the analysis of interaction patterns. . ." (Hart, 1994, p. 220). While useful, these procedures were less well documented than they might have been.

A strength of the data analysis and interpretation section was the careful exploration of role theory that guided the analysis. One difference often cited between quantitative and qualitative research deals with the greater use of inductive analysis in qualitative research. Rather than using theory to drive the design and implementation of a study, as may occur in quantitative studies, qualitative researchers either develop "grounded theory" (Glaser & Strauss, 1967) from their data or draw upon an existing theoretical framework to interpret their findings. Hart's use of role theory to interpret her data was consistent with the approach described by Glesne and Peshkin (1992):

> Typically, qualitative research is neither invariably nor explicitly driven by theory, but researchers often use empirical generalizations or middle-range propositions to help form initial questions and working hypotheses during the beginning stages of data collection. As they begin to focus on data analysis, they may seek out yet other theories to help them examine their data from different perspectives." (p. 21)

Another strength of the data analysis and interpretation procedures was the attention paid to mitigate researcher effects and/or bias in interpreting data. A teacher at each school was asked to check for any changes noted during or after observations and interviews. Several pieces of data were shared that provided reassurance that researcher effects, after an initial "flurry of activity" (p. 220) appeared to be minimal.

Another researcher activity involved identifying one teacher in each school who was respected by her or his colleagues but who was not involved in the project and who was, in fact, an opponent of the new structure. Actively seeking opposing points of views strengthens the reader's confidence in the interpretations and conclusions that are provided by the researcher.

Finally, following the completion of the study, ". . . the strength and explanatory value of conclusions were checked with teachers and administrators of each school" (p. 220).

A careful reading of the data analysis and interpretation section highlights several researcher activities that we have listed as criteria for a quality study. The coding of data, while less explicit than desired, gives evidence of a modified "constant comparative" method. The selection of opponents of the project and attention to their positions is related to the technique of "negative case analysis" and could provide a healthy check on the researcher's conclusions. Finally, consulting faculty and administrators in both schools regarding conclusions drawn is clearly an example of "member checking."

Overall, the data analysis and interpretation procedures appear solid and indicative of the care that good qualitative researchers bring to their task. Note, also, that in most cases Hart did not make specific reference to the constant comparative method, negative case analysis, or member checking, and yet she attended to the concerns addressed by these concepts.

Researcher Perspective. Given the importance of researcher perspective in qualitative research, it was rather surprising that the reader was provided with little information regarding the author of the study. The journal provided a brief biographical paragraph on each author published in this issue and we learned that Hart is a Dean of the College of Education and professor of Educational Administration at the University of Utah. Was the researcher a former teacher or administrator in the district? Did she have a consulting relationship with the district? Did she have a personal involvement in the development of the plan being implemented in the two schools? We don't know the answers to the previous questions, but having this knowledge would provide us with a better context within which to interpret the results. We are told (p. 219) that this article is based upon data collected and reported earlier in Hart (1990), which together with a reference to a still earlier study (Hart, 1987) suggests that the author has had a sustained, seven-year interest in the research topic.

One reason for a lack of personal information about the author may be the journal's reluctance to provide it. Researchers from the quantitative tradition attempted to downplay personal qualities of the researcher in their attempt to pursue greater objectivity. While one might argue that researcher perspective can influence all research efforts, it is arguably less critical in a quantitative study due to the greater number of safeguards provided by instruments and statistical techniques for collecting and analyzing data. The norms of journal editors, which were based on quantitative traditions, may remain unchanged, despite the increased number of qualitative studies.

The lack of information about researcher perspective, while disappointing, need not be a fatal flaw in an otherwise strong study. Knowing more about the researcher's values, experience, and degree of involvement in the setting is simply one more way to validate the credibility of a qualitative study.

Case Study Results

We now use the Hart (1994) study to help Bill find information regarding his second guiding question: "What strategies or techniques exist which have been found to impact faculty members' sense of empowerment?"

We will see in our examination of this study that Bill's question, while helpful, is not the one that emerges from the research. What Bill was hoping for was an intact plan that had been found to work elsewhere. What Bill got were solid clues about how to address his current situation in Lincoln Middle School. Note that this is *not* an insignificant gain. Remember that we have continued to stress the outcome of a good literature review should be to help you think more intelligently about your problem.

Findings of the Study. One of the first things Bill noted about the qualitative study was that "Findings" were not so easy to find as in a quantitative study. No neat tables gave him yes or no answers to research questions or hypotheses. Instead, woven throughout the narrative was a series of insights, observations, and comments that were supported by the data, commented upon by the author, and offered for the reader's consideration.

Additionally, many of the findings were examined in light of the particular context of the schools studied. To accomplish this, the author provided additional information about each of the two schools' faculty and administrators to make the data meaningful. In presenting the findings in a qualitative study, several points are noteworthy: (1) it takes more space to adequately describe a context than to report statistical outcomes, (2) outcomes of a qualitative study lack meaning unless they can be embedded within the particular context from which they emerged, and (3) the practitioner has more information upon which to base an evaluation of the usefulness of the analysis for his or her particular setting than is found in most quantitative research reports.

Bill read with interest the following paragraph.

> Relationships among teachers and administrators were in flux at the time the case study was undertaken. At North, the principal, although an old-time insider in the district, was new to the school. At South, the principal of three years was an outsider (in a district where outsiders were uncommon and sometimes resented) who had well-known disagreements in philosophy with several prominent teachers in the school (most notably the past president of the union), and the majority of teachers chosen as teacher leaders at the two schools had a history of union activism. At North, one teacher leader had served as a national delegate to National Education Association (NEA) conventions and as a building NEA

representative. The faculties had reputations with administrators as two of the most "difficult" in the district and were not reticent to criticize and comment freely. . . . In both schools, interest in the teacher specialist positions was low. Committees chose some teacher specialists with less than three years' experience, because no one with more experience applied. This created a situation where relatively new teachers were instructing their more experienced colleagues. Neither school provided tranquil waters on which to launch organizational change." (p. 224)

Bill was particularly attentive and quietly pleased to note the less than ideal conditions that existed in both schools at the beginning of the study. Frequently, he read research studies describing idyllic conditions foreign to his experience. The closing comment about "tranquil waters" gave him reason for hope.

The findings of the study yielded sharp differences between South and North schools in the acceptance of the reorganization plan. In South School, the following conclusions were drawn: "Morale improved. Even teachers who did not like the idea of teaching careers that drove the reform concurred. Said one teacher, 'Although the career ladder idea is not for me, I'll have to admit that morale in the faculty is a lot higher this year.' By the end of the year, teachers wanted more visits and conferences than teacher leaders had time to give and more in-service training sessions and program assistance than teacher specialists' compensation justified offering" (p. 225).

The reactions of the North faculty were sharply different: At North, "Teachers often interpreted the assistance from peers that teachers at South praised profusely as torture. . ." One veteran said in an interview in early October, 'A mentor can also be a tormentor.' A beginning teacher complained, 'Sometimes you get the feeling you're going to be watched a lot under career ladder. It causes anxiety.' Others called for more emphasis on 'helping the school as a whole.' Career ladder teachers on many occasions said they were 'beating their heads against a stone wall'" (p. 225).

The real contribution of the study for Bill was the excellent examination of the reasons for the differences between the two schools. Here the extensive use of role theory that guided the study was put to the test. What could be learned about reasons for these sharp differences that might illuminate the problem Bill faced? Clearly, neither the North nor the South Schools mirrored Lincoln Middle School very precisely, but there were strong hints that could save Bill much anguish, and more importantly, help him and the faculty address the serious problems they were facing.

The first insight from the analysis pointed to something rather obvious but quite important. Any attention to changing the roles of teachers required a change in the principal's role. Further, it was no small task to undertake role changes in a social system that has a long history of rather clearly defined expectations for teachers and for administrators. Changing these roles did not happen easily, and any change had consequences, some that could not be clearly anticipated.

Additionally, some role changes proceeded more smoothly than others. Although all changes were designed to ". . . provide chances for teachers to grow professionally and contribute to school performance," (p. 226) some of these activities were perceived as being "administrators' work."

In the more successful setting, career teachers and the principal moved quickly to design and implement activities that teachers had defined as important to them. At the less successful North School the researcher reported that no one talked about the changes as a contribution to students' learning. The crucial step of involving teachers in an active redesign of their own job functions, while patently obvious, was just as blatantly missing. Hart stated, "The core group concept that so powerfully nurtured implementation activities at South was missing. . ." (p. 226).

Another important insight provided by the study dealt with the teachers' professional identities and how they were developed in the two settings. At South, teachers came to view the new roles as opportunities to enhance their status; in the words of one faculty member, it made teaching, ". . . more of a profession." At North, the exact opposite result occurred. Teachers interpreted the plan as an attack on their autonomy and moved successfully to define the teacher leaders' job descriptions as narrowly as possible. After a series of faculty meetings they developed job descriptions limiting the teacher leader roles to include substitute teaching, doing roll books, and making bulletin boards (p. 229). Perhaps more telling, the teacher leaders complained that these roles were demeaning, but they accepted them anyway.

Other important differences were cited. The teachers at South were actively engaged to discuss, debate, and argue about the nature and form the new roles should take. Teacher leaders set up a formal planning meeting one Saturday a month, requested and gained control over half the scheduled faculty meetings, and took initiative in designing large-scale improvement projects. The rest of the faculty at South responded actively by requesting and receiving frequent reports on what was being done by the teacher leaders and in assessing their effectiveness. Complaints and dissident faculty views existed, but they were processed and dealt with actively by the principal and the core of newly defined teacher leaders.

In sharp contrast, the prevailing norms of privacy and isolation at North were not overcome and the principal admitted, "I've dropped the ball." (p. 233) Debate and discussions were not productively focused, and the criticism became cynicism as teachers turned on teacher leaders and teacher leaders turned on each other. Teachers noticed the principal had little to say when these criticisms surfaced. On one occasion he indicated that he liked to hire good people and then let them alone. Another time he complained that he was too busy responding to crises to deal with the criticisms. In the words of the author:

> In the absence of positive articulation at North, *nonverbal cues, gestures, and innuendo*—'body language' as one teacher leader put it—filled the void. These cues had the desired chilling effect, and two of the three teacher leaders and most of the teacher specialists at North decided it was not *worth the cost;* they did not reapply for their positions. As one teacher leader put it, the year was devastating, like 'being blown out of the water'" (p. 233).

Study Conclusions. Bill Evans took stock of what he thought he had learned from the study and listed the following points:

1. The powerful effect of existing teacher roles should not be underestimated. The long history of the teaching profession and the number of years each teacher has spent in the profession must be carefully examined and understood, and any proposed changes need to be made in light of these roles.
2. The particular context of the school was a powerful determinant of the success or failure of an attempt at change. Hart summarized that point in the following words: "No matter how carefully planned or how thoughtfully integrated with good instructional practice, the new work design for teachers in the comparative case analysis ultimately was shaped within each school and, in terms of individual roles, nested in that school" (Hart, 1994, p. 235).
3. Any changes in teacher roles will require concomitant changes in principal roles. The two roles exist within a dynamic social system and cannot be viewed independent of one another.
4. The principal's attention and efforts are very important during any proposed changes to the social system of the school. The new roles for both teachers and principal require a period of transition during which those changes are negotiated. Any retreat from active involvement by the principal leaves a vacuum that could have deleterious effects. Hart phrased it as follows: "Principals should not underestimate the need for their diligent, supportive, visible, and frequent reinforcement of the real power of teacher leaders, nor should they ignore the social-emotional adjustments in professional self-concept leadership that opportunities bring with them" (p. 235).

A Plan for Action

With this backdrop of information from the literature review available, Bill was now ready to chart a plan of action to address the fundamental issues facing his school. The following figure represents Bill's first draft of an action plan. It will need much thought and work before it is finished, but here were his initial thoughts.

Memorandum
Lincoln Middle School
January, 2001

MEMO
Fr: Bill Evans
To: Bill Evans
Re: Action Plan Notes

I need to address these fundamental issues:

1. I'll have to garner the support of Supt. O'Brian to engage in a broad, comprehensive plan for incremental change. O'Brian is going to have to give me some relief from the pressures for instant improvement in standardized test scores and a commitment that he will be supportive for the long haul. Garnering this type of support from the superintendent will require setting a reasonable timetable with progress markers that can be measured and reported.
2. I will need to engage the faculty in a full scale discussion of the problems of Lincoln Middle School as *they* perceive them. Clearly, I will need to contribute heavily to that discussion, but I need to bring an open mind to the discussions.
3. Together, the faculty and I will need to develop a leadership structure that responds to the problems identified by the faculty rather than imposed upon them. I will need to pay particular attention to the following issues from the research literature: Hart (1994) presented solid evidence that when the teacher roles are not closely aligned with instructional functions they will be aggressively resisted. Also, Gitlin and Margonis (1995) provided evidence that teacher resistance carries a rational component that should not be ignored.
4. The faculty will need time and resources to address some of the same issues that I have encountered in my search for answers. To accomplish this, I will need to devote time at several faculty meetings for an examination of the Gitlin and Margonis (1995) and Hart (1994) studies. Copies of both studies will need to be shared with the faculty as background reading for faculty meetings.
5. With one half of the school year remaining the entire semester should be devoted to addressing problems that faculty identify as important. No specific action plans should be sought during this time: Attention will be focused on *problem identification* and not *problem solutions* in the short run.
6. If possible, teams of faculty members wishing to address particular problems can be formed as needed. Rather than require all faculty to address the same problems, it may increase commitment to encourage teachers to work on problems currently identified or to identify others they feel are more important. Over time, the most important problems may emerge from the process.
7. Modest funds can be provided from the district office to offer stipend support for up to eight teachers to work one month of the summer to define problems and suggest strategies to address them. Based on the reactions of teachers in the Hart study, it is very important to allow teachers to determine how these funds should be spent. It could undermine the efforts of empowering faculty by creating divisiveness resulting from the selection of teachers for additional stipends and responsibilities.
8. During next fall's orientation meeting, a full faculty discussion of problems, strategies and structures should take place. Priorities can be set and a few of the most important issues could form the professional agenda for the next academic year.

FIGURE *7.1* Memorandum

References

Cressey, D. R. (1953). *Other peoples' money: A study in the social psychology of embezzlement.* New York: Free Press.

Denzin, N. K., & Lincoln, Y. S. (Eds.). (1994). *Handbook of qualitative research.* Thousand Oaks, CA: Sage.

Fullan, M. (1993). *Change forces.* London: Falmer Press.

Gitlin, A., & Margonis, F. (1995). The political aspect of reform: Teacher resistance as good sense. *American Journal of Education, 103,* 377–405.

Glaser, B. G. (1978). *Theoretical sensitivity: Advances in the methodology of grounded theory.* Mill Valley, CA: Sociology Press.

Glaser, B. G. & Strauss, A. L. (1967). *The discovery of grounded theory: Strategies for qualitative research.* Chicago: Aldine.

Glesne, C. (1999). *Becoming qualitative researchers: An introduction.* New York: Addison Wesley Longman.

Glesne, C., & Peshkin, A. (1992). *Becoming qualitative researchers: An introduction.* Longman, NY: Longman Press.

Hargreaves, A. (1993). Individualism and individuality: Reinterpreting the teacher culture. In Little & McLaughlin (Eds.), *Teachers' work: Individuals, colleagues, and contexts* (pp. 51–76). New York: Teachers College Press.

Hart, A. W. (1987). A career ladder's effect on teacher career and work attitudes. *American Educational Research Journal, 24*(4), 479–503.

Hart, A. W. (1990). Impacts of the school social unit on teacher authority during work redesign. *American Educational Research Journal, 27*(3), 503–532.

Hart, A. W. (1994). Creating teacher leadership roles. *Educational Administration Quarterly, 30,* 472–497.

Hart, E. P., & Robottom, I. M. (1990). The science-technology-society movement in science education: A critique of the reform process. *Journal of Research of Science Teaching, 27*(6), 575–588.

Havelock, R. (1971). *Planning for innovation through dissemination and utilization of knowledge.* Ann Arbor: University of Michigan Press.

Havelock, R. (1973). *The change agent's guide to innovation in education.* Englewood, Cliffs, NJ: Educational Technology.

Homans, G. C. (1962). *Sentiments and activities.* New York: The Free Press of Glencoe.

Huberman, A. M. & Miles, M. F. (1984). *Innovation up close: How school improvement works.* New York: Plenum.

Kidder, L. H. (1981). Qualitative research and quasi-experimental frameworks. In M. B. Brewer & B. E. Collins (Eds.), *Scientific inquiry and the social sciences* (pp. 226–256). San Francisco: Jossey-Bass.

Kreisberg, S. (1992). *Teacher empowerment and school reform.* Albany, NY: Suny Press.

LeCompte, M. D., & Preissle, J., with Tesch, R. (1993). *Ethnography and qualitative design in educational research* (2nd ed.). New York: Academic Press.

Lincoln, Y. S., & Guba, E. G. (1985). *Naturalistic inquiry.* Beverly Hills, CA: Sage.

Maerhoff, G. I. (1988). *The empowerment of teachers: Overcoming the crisis of confidence.* New York: Teachers College Press.

Malinowski, B. (1984). *Argonauts of the western Pacific.* Prospect Heights, IL: Waveland. (Original work published in 1922)

Miles, M. B., & Huberman, A.M. (1990). *Animadversions and reflections on the uses of qualitative inquiry.* In E. W. Eisner & A. Peshkin (Eds.), *Qualitative inquiry in education* (pp. 339–357). New York: Teachers College Press.

Miles, M. B., & Huberman, A. M. (1984). *Qualitative data analysis: A sourcebook of new methods.* (2nd ed.). Newbury Park, CA: Sage.

Peshkin, A. (1978). *Growing up American: Schooling and the survival of community.* Chicago: University of Chicago Press.

Peshkin, A. (1986). *God's choice: The total world of a fundamentalist Christian school.* Chicago: University of Chicago Press.

Rosenholtz, S. (1989). *Teachers' workplace.* New York: Teachers College Press.

Sarason, S. (1971). *The culture of the school and the problem of change.* Boston: Allyn and Bacon.

Wilson, S. (1977). The use of ethnographic techniques in educational research. *Review of Educational Research, 47*(1), 245–265.

Wolcott, H. F. (1994). *Transforming qualitative data: Description, analysis, and interpretation.* Thousand Oaks, CA: Sage.

Yin, R. K. (1989). *Case study research: Design and methods.* (2nd ed.). Newbury Park, CA: Sage.

===

APPENDIX

Creating Teacher Leadership Roles

Ann Weaver Hart

A comparative case study revealed divergent emerging judgments of a teacher career ladder in two schools. Educators in the two sites strongly disagreed over the relative salutary impact of the new tasks and responsibilities on instruction and student learning. In an earlier analysis, the use of work structure and group-level frameworks fell short in providing a full explanation for site-specific differences in teachers' individual perceptions of the career ladder reform. Therefore, a deductive analysis of the cases was conducted applying role theory constructs. It revealed individual-group dynamics embedded in group conceptions of role. Conclusions support the assertions that interpretations drawn from the immediate environment have profound impacts on "objective" tasks associated with work characteristics and their outcomes and emphasize the ambiguity of innovation in established organizations.

The effects of change remain a central concern in school reform research. In search of improved student performance the "restructuring" of schools throughout the 1980s ranged in scope from the reform of governance and finance structures at state levels through site-based management and participative decision making to the redesign of teaching work (Bacharach, 1990).

School reforms provide an opportunity to examine organizational change. Many reforms change teachers' long-accepted and respected activities and challenge established authority patterns. Others violate teachers' core professional norms of equality, cordiality, and privacy (Hart, 1990; Johnson, 1990; Lortie, 1975; Malen & Hart, 1987). At the same time, some of these changes appeal to the career advancement and professional growth needs of teachers (Bacharach, Conley, & Shedd, 1986; Murphy, Hart, & Walters, 1989; Schlechty & Joslin, 1984). In this article, I take advantage of a naturally occurring field experiment in school reform to examine organizational change in the form of teacher work redesign. A comparative case study of two schools provided data about changes that differentiated previously

This article was originally published in *Educational Administration Quarterly,* Nov. 1994, Vol. 30, No. 4, pp. 472–497.

undifferentiated work, benefited some members of the organization and not others, and created new work tasks and authority relationships. The purpose of this particular analysis was to seek theoretical explanations for different observed patterns of teachers' attitudes and actions and the social processes associated with these patterns.

Method: A Comparative Case Study

The goal of this comparative analysis was to learn from the people involved in the reform, to explore their assessments of the important values and activities in their schools affected by a change in teaching and leadership roles (Spradley, 1980). A comparative case study had a number of advantages. The replication and sampling logic of the qualitative, multiple-case method strengthened the verification of common patterns (Yin, 1989) and provided opportunities to identify variance in the experiences of similar groups. It also made comparisons between the groups possible because patterned behavior existed at each school before the career ladder was implemented. In addition, the research required data tracing of organizational change over time, because discreet, one-time measurements of attitudes and performance failed to reveal emerging dynamics (Brousseau, 1978; Steers & Mowday, 1977).

This article presents the analysis of previously collected data (Hart, 1990). Earlier inductive analysis revealed the impacts of the two schools' social environments on teachers' career attitudes and morale. Data on perceptions of the reform's effect on instruction and student performance (rather than its incentive value) are used for this new analysis. Work structure (rather than its incentive value) are used for this new analysis. Work structure features and school-level attitudes left much of these data unsatisfactorily explained. Consequently, I searched for existing theories that could elaborate the individual teachers' perceptions about effects on students within their schools. Role theory provided this theoretical framework. After summarizing the original data collection process, I describe the data analysis procedures used for this deductive application of role theory to an existing case study data set. I then provide a summary of the analytical framework and report the results of this analysis. I close with a discussion of some implications for organizational change in schools and principals' roles in this process.

Data Collection

After the superintendent and school board granted permission to conduct the study, principals in the district were contacted. The study was explained to teachers and administrators in a regular faculty meeting. The educators in two junior high schools (North and South) agreed to participate. Three teachers (two at South and one at North) refused to join the study. Data came from a variety of sources, and conclusions were checked with participants. Consequently, it was possible to view multiple perspectives (Yin 1989) from multiple sources (McClintock, 1985). At least one day a week from September through May (1983–1984) was spent at each school.

Two types of data were gathered directly: (a) systematic field notes collected by nonparticipant observation for two days a month at each school (September through May); and (b) structured and unstructured interviews. Notes from the observations were expanded into systematic field notes and divided into three sections: (a) an objective narrative; (b) descriptions of affective aspects of the interview or observation such as emotions, rushed or relaxed atmosphere, and cooperative or reticent attitudes; and (c) reflections and preliminary themes. Structured interviews with teachers (career ladder participants, nonparticipants, and novice teachers), principals, and assistant principals were conducted in three cycles—fall, winter, and spring. These interviews (164 structured interviews lasting 30 to 60 minutes) were recorded and transcribed. Informal, unstructured interviews with teachers, students, and administrators were recorded throughout the year in field notes.

Other data included surveys, transcripts of audiotapes from meetings the researcher did not attend, teacher journals, and notes and transcripts of 17 post-observation conferences between teacher leaders and novice teachers. Journals and reflection of the 6 teachers leaders, 23 probationary teachers, and 3 teacher specialists; a midyear survey of teacher "leaders" and novice teachers assessing the frequency, content, and process of supervision under the new structure (with a return rate of 95%); and notes from 41 classroom observations by teacher leaders and 20 observations by principals prepared exclusively for the study. Participants failed to keep their journals consistently, tending instead to record thoughts and incidents that struck them as significant, so journal data reported crises, emotionally charged experiences (both negative and positive), and impressions emerging from moments of reflection. The greatest advantage of the journals was their spontaneity. They highlighted issues dominating teachers' perceptions. Because they were episodic, however, the journals sometimes left weeks at a time out of the record.

Documents relating to the career ladder but not generated for the study included the career ladder plan, job descriptions for each school, newsletters and in-service training materials prepared for and by career ladder teachers, official minutes and teachers' notes of task force and faculty meetings, and newspaper articles related to career ladder events. These data were used primarily as background and reference material and to check for the consistency of participants' accounts.

Several procedures were used to mitigate researcher effects and to check emerging conclusions with the participants. First, a teacher at each school was asked to watch for any changes in behavior that occurred during or immediately after observations or interviews. A North, the teacher reported that career ladder efforts took off with a "flurry of activity" after the researcher visited the school. In 6 to 8 weeks people ignored the researcher, and for weeks career ladder activity languished. The site monitor at South reported no impact of the research commenting, "They really don't care what you think." Second teachers and administrators were asked to name one teacher at each school who was experienced, respected by other teachers, an opponent of the new structure, and not a participant in the career ladder. Two teachers were quickly identified. These teachers were interviewed before December. Many informal conversations with them appear in the field notes. Several unsuccessful applicants for career ladder positions and members of the selection committees at each school also were interviewed. Finally, in the autumn following the study, the strength and explanatory value of conclusions were checked with teachers and administrators at each school. Cases were written from this pool of data.

Data Analysis

Data analysis for this article followed established procedures for case study and naturalistic research when applying an existing theoretical framework to qualitative case data (Miles & Huberman, 1984; Yin, 1989). Transcripts of interviews and meetings, teaching observation notes taken by participants, journals, and field notes of earlier inductive analyses (grouped under the general category of student performance effects) were coded using basic concepts of role theory. Data summary sheets were prepared by collecting quotations and field note notations directly from the data. These summary sheets were, therefore, long collections of specific examples illustrating the manifestation of a concept in the raw data. Summary sheets also contained notations of the specific role (teacher, teacher leader, principal, etc.) associated with each entry, the school, and the date of occurrence. Comparison matrices then were developed to facilitate the analysis of interaction patterns. These matrices compared occurrences of data points illustrating each concept (and frequency counts) across time, by school, and by position, seeking insight into role-specific clues to strong feeling centered around perceptions of performance effects.

This analysis draws primarily on unpublished data originally grouped as participants' explanations for the new jobs' effects or lack of effects on student performance. These data were inadequately explained by work structure and redesign theories. Although the teacher-to-student relationship clearly was important, previous analyses left it poorly elucidated. The present analysis is by no means exhaustive. The job characteristics model of work redesign, for example, suggests that the task, autonomy, and feedback features of the teacher leader and teacher specialist jobs might have affected their motivational potential (Hart, 1987). Preexisting features of each school's social unit shaped events in the two schools (Hart, 1990). Yet these initial differences were only part of the story. They framed the roles people played, but individual roles and the political jockeying among core groups also shaped this educational reform.

Analytical Framework

Role theory provided the conceptual framework for this analysis. Role theory had several advantages. It provided a model for individuals' behaviors within the social system. It also provided a conceptual structure for tracing natural social processes. Finally, its cross-disciplinary approach to the study of behavior in natural settings contributed an expanded perspective on organizational change.

Specifically, role theory provided three critical insights. First, characteristic patterns of interaction among people filling set roles provide the internal structure for social systems. Consequently, roles such as that of teacher are associated with established social positions. Patterns in the group associated with each role are independent of the people who fill them, and the sum of roles makes up the culture of the group. Characteristic behaviors identify members of each role. As group members share expectations, they induce stable roles, and established members teach and enforce appropriate behaviors (Biddle, 1979; Biddle & Thomas, 1966; Turner, 1988; Wentworth, 1980). New members and members in transition to new roles modify and mold them (Wentworth, 1980). Consequently, role taking and role making both occur. When people adopt or take on an existing role (role taking), they read, interpret, and model others' behavior. When they assert or make a new role, they shape new expectations in the group (role making) (Mead, 1934; Turner, 1962). During major role transitions, people may change substantially as they develop new skills and attitudes, or they may modify the role they fill and its functions in the group (Louis, 1980a, 1980b; Nicholson, 1984).

Second, although not static, established social patterns are resilient, and social pressure that reinforces existing roles often is heightened during change or transition. Enforcement pressures need not be conscious to be powerful. Research on which role theory is based reveals that pressure for change can cause stress. Role stress can result from disparities among central beliefs and actual behaviors. It can take the form of conflict, ambiguity, and overload and may affect performance and attitudes (Diamond & Allcorn, 1985; Dubinsky & Yammarino, 1984; Latack, 1984; McEnrue, 1984).

Finally, a school's social system is part of its members' shared world. Interaction creates the system (Mead, 1934), and members of the system read and interpret each other's meanings and intentions.[1] Thus people construct reality and fact as they interact with each other and interpret information (Garfinkel, 1967). Scholars often label this social information processing, a process through which shared beliefs are constructed and judgments are reached (Kulik, 1989; Salancik & Pfeffer, 1978). A number of factors affect social information processing, including the salience and potency of the information source (Salancik & Pfeffer, 1978).

These three components of role theory provided the general categories for the case study analysis reported here: (a) roles existing as identities within systems, (b) the enforcement and evolution of roles, and (c) the social processes that construct inter-pretations—a shared reality. The analysis revealed features of the career ladder jobs as a set of new positions within the social system. This perspective differs from the more common view of career ladder jobs as minor changes in the structure of an existing role—teacher. It raised issues omitted from the prevailing school reform lit-erature, which tends to view recent reforms as implementations of new curriculum or instructional methods, public choice, or new school governance structures that leave the work of teachers essentially untouched (participative decision making and public choice, for example) (Conley, 1990, 1991; Murphy, 1990; Shanker, 1990). The deduc-tive use of role theory in this analysis highlighted an often overlooked impact of reforms: The "role and function" of teachers became unclear during the process of change, muddied by conflict over whether the reform was a fundamental restructuring of teaching or the introduction of modified job categories for teachers (Fullan, 1991).

The present analysis also revealed the importance of a mutually supportive core group within the social system when teacher leadership roles are created that violate long-standing assumptions about teachers' work (Firestone & Bader, 1992).

The Findings section that follows include three components: the district, North Junior High, and South Junior High. Following a description of findings in these three settings, I discuss the findings in terms of the three ideas from role theory pre-sented earlier—individual roles within the social system, role enforcement and evo-lution, and constructed interpretations.

Findings

The District

The setting for the study was a school district in which a "career ladder"[2] for teach-ers was implemented. Located in a city in the northern United States, the district had a student enrollment of about 12,000 when the study began. The community was politically and fiscally conservative, and the level of financial support given to the career ladder subjected it to close scrutiny.

New work structures that are labeled career ladders are common in the move-ment to redesign teachers' work (Cornett, 1988; Smylie & Denny, 1990) but contain many different features. Clinical peer supervision, shared decision making, and collegial assistance—not permanent career advancement—were the basic components of this career ladder. Consequently, it redesigned work within an established organizational structure. The district plan included a variety of tasks expected of those filling the career ladder positions—curriculum assistance in subject specialties, in-service training, teacher observation, consultation on instructional techniques, leadership of school programs (e.g., positive reinforcement and reward systems, enrichment weeks exploring subjects outside the regular curriculum, science fairs, school climate projects), and communication (within each school and throughout the district). Whatever the tasks or labels, the plan's designers emphasized that teaching should remain the central activity of participants. This insistence on sustaining the teaching career while creating career growth opportunities generated a heated and ongoing debate about the nature of teaching work, the boundaries between administration and teaching, the nature of professional growth and opportunity, and the appropriateness of new tasks for teachers. The explicit outcomes expected by those who designed the career ladder (touted in newspaper articles and described in the literature that circulated among teachers, board members, parents, and community members) were the following: (a) improved earning potential for career teachers, (b) use of expert teachers for the overall improvement of curriculum and instruction, and (c) increased involvement by teachers in professional decisions affecting schools. Improved student outcomes, broadly conceived, were the expected result.

A task force designed the career ladder. The superintendent chaired the task force that included teachers representing every school in the district and three administrators. As work on the plan progressed, the assistant superintendent, counselors, special education teachers, and the president elect of the teachers' union joined the task force to speak for their constituencies. The president of the district Parent Teacher Association (PTA), although not a task force member, criticized and commented on the plan. After agreeing on the basic structure and selection procedures, the task force forwarded the plan to the schools, where job descriptions tailored to each school were written by teachers and administrators. People credited this participation in the process of designing the plan for early and widespread support in the initial months of implementation (Firestone & Bader, 1992; Rosenholtz, 1987).

The plan included two categories of positions for teachers: teacher leader and teacher specialist. In addition, all teachers received their salary schedule pay rate for work days in the school when students were not in attendance. Schools used most of these days before school opened in the fall. The number of teachers in each school determined the number of career ladder positions. Only current faculty within each school and teachers with more than 3 years' experience qualified to apply (unless no one else in the school was interested or qualified). A school committee including the principal and two teachers selected teachers' leaders (10% of teachers). Many teacher leaders worked nearly 12 months. In addition, they received a small stipend of about $1,000. Overall, this provided a substantial earning increase—more than 35% for some teachers. Teacher leaders supervised and assisted new teachers and, if invited, experienced teachers; designed and delivered in-service training (e.g., instructional methods, curriculum, classroom management); led grade-level or department groups; and wrote and tested curriculum. A few became district-level curriculum supervisors while retaining their teaching positions. Appointments were for 1 year (later extended to 2 years), and leaders could reapply and compete for their positions.[3]

The committee chose teacher specialists (40% of teachers) for more narrowly defined 1-year positions, often implementing district instructional or curriculum goals. In elementary schools, they functioned as subject matter specialists or as project directors focusing on special needs such as writing or computers. In the secondary schools, they supervised curriculum enrichment activities, positive reinforcement and discipline plans, academic extracurricular activities, or subject area departments. Specialists received the stipend and a few additional contract days of work.

Two junior high schools were chosen as sites for the study. The schools, called North and South here, were similar in demographic characteristics conventionally used to assess comparable contexts in schools. North Junior High drew its students primarily from upper-middle and upper-class neighborhoods. A faculty of 34 teachers taught its student body of more than 700. The professional staff included a principal, an assistant principal, a counselor, and a psychologist and a social worker (both part-time). South Junior High was larger, with 855 students and 43 teachers. Its administrative and support staffs were of the same size and ethnicity as North's. South's student body was almost exclusively middle-class, although boundary gerrymandering by the school board to create more comparable schools increased the proportion of students from upper-class neighborhoods. Both South and North had small numbers of minority students, primarily from Hispanic and Pacific Islands backgrounds. The district allocated three teacher leaders to each school. North had six teacher specialists, and South had eight.

Relationships among teachers and administrators were in flux at the time the case study was undertaken. At North, the principal, although an old-time insider in the district, was new to the school. At South, the principal of 3 years was an outsider (in a district where outsiders were uncommon and sometimes resented) who had well-known disagreements in philosophy with several prominent teachers in the school (most notably the past president of the union). Teachers at both schools were active in the union, and the majority of teachers chosen as teacher leaders at the two schools had a history of union activism. At North, one teacher leader had served as a national delegate to National Education Association (NEA) conventions and as a building NEA representative. The faculties had reputations with administrators as two of the most "difficult" in the district and were not reticent to criticize and comment freely. Teachers universally reported that "hard feelings" toward the career ladder, resulting from the selection process the previous spring, were prevalent during the summer and autumn in both schools. Whereas their peers described all the teachers chosen for the positions as among the best teachers, teachers and administrators only acknowledged one, a teacher leader at North, as "probably the best teacher in the school." In both schools, interest in the teacher specialist positions was low. Committees chose some teacher specialists with less than three years' experience, because no one with more experience applied. This created a situation where relatively new teachers were instructing their more experienced colleagues. Neither school provided tranquil waters on which to launch organizational change.

South

The prevailing assessment at South was that the career ladder positions had potential as a means for improving instruction, the curriculum, and teacher morale. Even though teachers recognized stumbling blocks and flaws, optimism about the future continued and, at year-end, teachers and administrators were planning to use their experience to improve the new roles' usefulness to the school. New teachers frequently praised the positions and said they intended to apply or positions as soon as they were eligible. Experienced teachers also applied, many of whom had held back the first year, and the number of skeptics decreased. Of the three teacher leaders eligible to reapply for their positions, all three did so and were reappointed.

Teachers willingly explained why most of them felt good about the new job. Most felt that people worked together to the benefit of the school more frequently and effectively. "Every school now can have a resource pool within its own faculty focused on improvement of the entire school." "Having someone else. . . is a variable that people have noticed that's different from other years." They also believed that this affected students. "I can see that the career ladder is helping my teaching, which, in turn, must be helping the students." They communicated more. Teachers experienced "a lot more discussion" and more substantive faculty meetings in which they vigorously debated critical school-level issues and made decisions. As one teacher put it, "We really talk about issues and don't just get announcements." Another teacher said she was now "more aware of [her] profession" and "a little bit prouder to be a teacher."

The consensus: Morale improved. Even teachers who did not like the idea of teaching careers that drove the reform concurred. Said one teacher, "Although the career ladder idea is not for me, I'll have to admit that morale in the faculty is a lot higher this year." By the end of the year, teachers wanted more visits and conferences than teacher leaders had time to give and more in-service training sessions and program assistance than teacher specialists' compensation justified offering.

North

The prevailing assessment at North was that the career ladder positions caused more problems than they solved and were yet another burden imposed by the legislature and school administrators on already overloaded and exhausted teachers. Teachers expressed frustration and confusion over their belief that the career ladder seemed to work in other schools but not in theirs. Any praise for individual career ladder teachers' contributions to the school failed to influence the overall negative assessment. Accusations flew that the reform movement was a thinly disguised move toward merit pay. New teachers remained almost universally confused about the "real" purpose and motives behind the reform and, wary of participation, several veteran teachers were openly hostile opponents, and only one of the three teacher leaders reapplied for the position the following year. Of the remaining two, one said he was "informed" that he should not reapply, because the faculty would "make sure he wouldn't be appointed"; the other said she had enjoyed the experience but did not want to do it again.

Career ladder advocates failed to overcome this interpretation. Even supporters described the prevailing point of view when asked how the career ladder was doing in their school. Teachers blamed the new positions for "dissension," "pain," and "anguish." Teachers who actively sought career ladder positions explained their participation: "It's the only game in town."

Teachers often interpreted the assistance from peers that teachers at South praised profusely as torture at North. One veteran said in an interview in early October, "A mentor can also be a tormentor." A beginning teacher complained, "Sometimes you get the feeling you're going to be watched a lot under career ladder. It causes anxiety." Others called for more emphasis on "helping the school as a whole." Career ladder teachers on many occasions said they were "beating their heads against a stone wall."

A Role Analysis of Findings

Individual Roles Within a Social System

The nature of legitimate teaching work and the adjustments in professional self-concept that the redesign required emerged as major issues surrounding teachers' roles in the schools. "What is teaching?" The new positions sparked vigorous debate about teachers' legitimate tasks. The critical behaviors that identify teachers as a general group were in flux. Teachers actively undertook new activities and activities that were previously the responsibility of administrators (e.g., observation and supervision of other teachers, in-service training, schoolwide planning of instruction, student reinforcement, and student discipline). Although the task force that developed the job guidelines and the school committees that designed the positions tried to plan activities that would provide chances for teachers to grow professionally and contribute to school performance, accusations that the career ladder was administrative work in disguise were common. Teachers said in interviews, in faculty room conversations, on surveys, and in official meetings that career ladder teachers were being assigned "administrative work."

Although they agreed that the line between administrator and teacher was blurred by the reform, career ladder teachers and the principal quickly moved to design and to define activities aimed at accomplishing goals that faculty members said were important. They talked about teaching and interacted with other teachers in formal and informal settings. They defined the new work structure as an outgrowth of a teacher's initiative:

> [Schoolwide] responsibility hasn't been pushed on us. We have done it because we
> have wanted to do it, because it is benefiting the school. There are great benefits
> for all of us in this school as a whole if we can get the [program] to work (TL,
> transcript, April meeting).[4]

By late fall, other teachers agreed that career ladder teachers were helping the school by doing valuable work central to teaching. They acknowledged that much of this work was new. Teachers praised a new "focus on schoolwide problems by teachers" not possible under traditional assignments (new teacher, interview, November). Career ladder teachers were energized. They seized the opportunity to shape thinking about the school. Teachers saw them functioning as a leadership unit, independent of the principal.

Although new relationships began to develop and all but two or three teachers said the career ladder was a success, some ambiguity over the distinctions between administrator and teacher remained. For example, in a spring meeting in which plans for the coming year were discussed, a teacher leader argued that the schoolwide discipline plan they had worked so hard to design and implement should be "taken over by the administration."

Unlike the teacher leaders and the principal at South, no one at North talked about schoolwide work as a contribution to students' learning or as an expanded opportunity for teachers. Each of the career ladder teachers pursued his or her tasks independently. The core group concept that so powerfully nurtured implementation activities at South was missing:

> [A] tenured teacher today . . . expressed resentment that they were teaching a class
> in an area they were unqualified and uncertified to teach in because a teacher
> leader who had been teaching that class in previous years was now free that period
> doing career ladder work (TS, journal entry, November, emphasis in the original).

In the fall, a major conflict erupted over one teacher leader's supervision of new teachers. Who was he, teachers asked indignantly, to define how teachers should behave, teach, and dress? No one—administrator, teacher, or staff—could describe tasks or behaviors that distinguished career ladder teachers from other teachers. New positions remained the responsibility (and burden) of individuals.

A second pattern related to teachers' roles in each school's social system involved their professional identities or self-concepts. Reflecting ambivalent feelings about the nature of their work, teachers became introspective about their identities as "professionals." At both schools, teachers bristled whenever stories denigrating the intelligence and performance of teachers were bandied about. Over time, however, teachers at South came to see the new positions as a way to enhance status, saying that the career ladder made teaching "more of a profession." Teachers at North interpreted the career ladder as an assault on their professional identities, an implicit attack on their career choices.

Successful applicants for the new roles and new teachers at South who were planning to apply for positions in the future said they hoped that the career ladder would help make teaching a more stable career choice. They said that it made "teachers feel more appreciated and professional" and made teaching feel "less like a dead-end job." They believed it could "keep things interesting so that you do not have to do the same thing year after year" (TS, interview, March). The career of one teacher leader, a young man who quickly rose to prominence in the union hierarchy, personified this hope.

Teachers at South described themselves as "more cohesive" and "professional," a "variable that people have noticed that is different from other years." The new jobs made cooperation to improve instruction "more likely to happen" (teacher interviews and field notes, October and November). Teachers contrasted the redesigned work with their past:

> My previous experience was very different. I received no supervisory help, zero help, and the idea that the evaluation process was supposed to help teachers was non-existent. I have experienced more help, trust, and involvement so far at [South] this year than in my previous six years combined. (teacher interview, March)

At North, conflict increased as career ladder teachers continued to work independently rather than as a leadership team. Each teacher stood alone. Actions that defined teachers' professional self-concepts became clouded:

> Teaching is so much a part of one's being. "I am a teacher." They really tie personal feelings into what they do as teachers. If you openly or blatantly attack what someone does as a teacher it can be very devastating for those individuals who have not learned to disassociate behaviors from personalities. (TL, interview, April)

Access to the new roles became increasingly entangled with judgments of individual worth. As time passed, no generally accepted norms of behavior for the new jobs developed. Career ladder teachers looked to others to delineate their roles for them, whereas the "others" coalesced into opposition groups determined to undermine them. "The issues are beginning to pressure us. We really need to get going. We need to know what we should do. [The principal] should tell us what we should do, and we should all be doing the same thing" (TL, interview, October). In successive interviews, from over-heard conversations, and in official meetings, the teachers and administrators at North reinforced a growing consensus that the career ladder sparked "animosity and jealousy," caused a "feeling that three people are now super-visory personnel," and built a "system in which teachers must compete with each other." All these effects were in direct conflict with their espoused beliefs about teachers professional identities.

Enforcement of Old Roles

The supportive environment and norm of teamwork at South induced the develop-ment of new roles (promoting role making), whereas fragmentation at North left teachers subject to strong conventional-role enforcement and little or no innovation (role taking). In both schools, proponents and opponents of the career ladder agreed on dominant norms and values. Role stress was apparent at both schools but clearly hampered teachers at North because it was virtually unrelieved.

The principal and lead teachers at South used expectations to induce behavior through constant emphasis on the professional resources to improve teaching pro-vided by career ladder teachers. Teachers echoed the principal's rhetoric: "Every school has some very good teachers. Career ladders allow me to tap their knowledge and experience. Every school now can have a resource pool within its own faculty focused on improvement of the entire school" (second year teacher, journal, October). People throughout the school joined the storytelling, recounting incidents in which teacher leaders had provided valuable assistance. Teachers noted training, supervision, and assistance with lesson plans and instruction; the principal gave speeches in faculty meetings, emphasizing that only teachers "have the power to change practice in a profound manner." Career ladder teachers pointed out that they had taken a number of responsibilities on themselves.

As teachers talked about the instructional assistance they received, other teachers began to ask the teacher leaders for help. The principal talked enthusiastically about the things career ladder teachers were doing. Teachers said they could "do more if they want to." Even cynics saw and described this pattern that induced action.

Career ladder teachers at South were highly visible, and the accountability system made career ladder teachers accountable not to the principal, but to the fac-ulty at large. Faculty meeting presentations about career ladder activities became rou-tine. One group of teachers asked for a written account at the end of the year from each teacher leader, so teachers "can see if [they] really helped." "People wonder what was done," one said (teacher interview, April).

The faculty and administrators at South accepted the assumptions that career ladder teachers must be very busy and visible, that they must serve other teachers, and that they are accountable to all teachers. These assumptions guided expectations for public activities, faculty meeting reports, written accounts of the work, and explanations to the faculty. The teacher leaders at South joined to exert influence over their developing positions. They set up a formal planning meeting for one Saturday each month, requested and received control over half of the regularly scheduled faculty meetings, and selected and redesigned the major career ladder pro-jects undertaken during the year. They became articulate advocates for the reform.

Whereas the career ladder teachers and the principal at South induced new roles that conformed to core instructional values and served the school, those at North retained their commitment to individual benefits and the protection of traditional con-cepts of teaching (adding privacy to the values they enforced). Visibility and busyness were rare. Teachers limited their praise to the few programs that were highly visible and that brought immediate benefits—an enrichment week and a positive school cli-mate reward program. However, the teachers who arranged these programs seldom received credit from anyone but the principal and other career ladder teachers (and then always as individuals, not as incumbents in new roles). In reference to an enrichment week program, for example, the principal pointed out that "teachers said, 'Oh, that is a nice thing,' but they didn't realize how we got it" (interview, May).

Paralyzed by doubt about their place in the faculty, teacher leaders gradually turned on each other, amplifying individualism. Although they had received training in supervision techniques in the summer and fall, two did nothing, waiting to be invited by teachers or ordered by the principal. They used the hour they were released from teaching for career ladder duties to prepare for their own teaching. In the face of intense criticism from experienced and new teachers alike, the teacher leaders met and decided to delay all classroom visits (a major part of their job descriptions) until mid-November, then until after the holidays in January. School-level instructional improvement and enhanced student outcomes never surfaced. Instead, teachers focused on enforcing individualism.

At North, teachers enforced conformity to long-established conventional practice in a number of ways. First, they ostracized the teacher leader who attempted to complete his assigned supervision visits. He described what it felt like to have a stony silence fall over the faculty room when he walked in the door as "being frozen out." A group of teachers told him directly that he should not apply for a teacher leader position the following year. The other two teacher leaders got the message more gently. One said, "They let you know you're not one of the gang anymore." Second, in a series of faculty meetings, the teachers moved to take control over the boundaries defining the new roles. They developed job descriptions that could most charitably be described as glorified attendance clerk and teachers' aide (substitute teaching, compiling roll books, making bulletin boards). Teacher leaders described these activities as demeaning, although they accepted them. The result was that teachers called the teacher leaders "expensive substitutes." People described all activity in traditional terms. Finally, the faculty demanded rigid explicit job descriptions for the next year and elaborate accountability procedures to assure them oversight over career ladder teachers, insinuating that "particularly with some of these teachers" everything should be "carefully written down" (teachers, field notes, May). In April, one teacher called the career ladder at North "role-playing."

One teacher felt "a little like I'm making up activities for myself." (South TL, field notes, May). Many identified strongly with the traditional teacher role.

One teacher leader at North said he "needed to find some way to help without looking holier than thou," but a new teacher he was assigned to help complained that "he seems to feel like he can't come in my class unless I invite him" and said his "mentor" had not visited his classes formally even late into the fall. This new teacher argued that the teacher leaders "need to be about their job contacting, helping, observing, and getting into the instruction of the school." Another new teacher shared her frustration but with a different teacher leader. She complained that she would "really like to interact with [my teacher leader] more. . and have more assistance from her," because she heard "so much about . . . how good she is" (interviews, November/December).

Resistance coupled with lack of initiative led teachers (late in March) to say, "Nobody seems to know what is expected of them." The principal attributed this to "having trouble with the job descriptions." A new teacher was less charitable: "They are sitting there using their two preparation periods for classroom preparation just because nobody told them what they should be doing. Well, let's take some initiative; let's go find out."

Dissidents could be found in both schools, but without exception the participants, including the administrators, accurately described the prevailing beliefs within their schools even if they personally disagreed. Although they might personally disagree with prevailing norms and values powering the enforcement of old roles or the inducement of new ones, people accurately described them as a driving force in each school. The unanimity was striking.

At South, the prevailing norms and values supported teamwork along with the career ladder teachers as new roles evolved. At North, they reinforced individualism and isolation. Dissidents to the prevailing point of view at South came from diverse quarters. One teacher, a 20-year veteran, described morale as "much improved" while explaining that the career ladder was "not for me."

North's dissidents were the career ladder's supporters. One teacher specialist filled his journal with the criticisms and complaints of teachers about the new positions, interspersed with reflections on the success of activities launched by career ladder teachers and his conviction that the school was a better place for both students and teachers than it had been in previous years. The teacher leaders pleaded in private interviews and conversations for understanding and patience from their peers, then joined in the criticisms of other career ladder teachers in public.

Just as it had been at South, ambivalence over the exclusivity and permanence of positions was felt by the career ladder teachers at North. A teacher specialist suggested in his journal that "all non-probationary teachers be evaluated comprehensively every year . . . and all teachers who meet a predetermined level of performance be given a rating of either professional or teacher leader, along with the appropriate responsibility and pay." Rumors asserted that he was bitter over failing to land a teacher leader role. He also described the faculty as "extremely competitive."

Growing role stress was the final factor that influenced role inducement and enforcement. Teachers and administrators at both schools talked about time pressure, ambiguous expectations, and teachers doing administrative work.

At South, overload was the most common source of role stress. In a spontaneous comment in the hall in late spring, one career ladder teacher summed up her feelings: "My gosh, it is an animal that is going to eat us." Another was more explicit about the need to define the limits of their positions: "I really think that we have got a responsibility . . . in defining what a teacher leader is, so that they aren't expected to be God on a peasant salary" (interview, FL, May). Some of this pressure was self-imposed, a result of the variety and scope of activities the career ladder teachers designed for themselves as they worked to promote acceptance of their efforts. The addition of the new positions to traditional expectations caused considerable overload: "If you are supposed to do this in addition to teaching a full load of courses . . . it's just too much" (TL, transcript, April).

The role conflict felt by career ladder teachers at South emerged in association with supervision, selection processes (a recurring focus of hurt feelings and conflict,) accountability demands, and task expectations. Teacher leaders altered their observation and conference techniques to distinguish themselves from the principal, and they worried that they were seen as rate busters who worked too hard (so they could get reappointed). Teachers felt they *had* to work hard to justify their existence in the new roles.

More prevalent at North, role stress emerged as overload, ambiguity, and conflict. The principal felt role overload most keenly, not the teachers in the new positions. "It is a matter of having the time . . . whatever is the hottest issue gets the time" (interview, April). He felt buffeted, constantly reacting instead of acting.

Ambiguity was ubiquitous at North. Faculty and administrators recognized and identified the confusion surrounding career ladder activities. One teacher specialist said, "They are not quite sure what to do" (interview, January). Her assessment matched a journal entry made in October by another specialist: "She [a TL] felt a little frustrated in her job in that she was a little unclear on exactly what she was supposed to be doing." In an attempt to alleviate the discomfort and paralysis resulting from this ambiguity, teachers and administrators turned to tighter codification and oversight. A teacher leader offered one look at this frustration:

> The teacher leaders have not really been given any feedback from administration or [anywhere] other than what we have been able to pick up in innuendoes, body language, or whatever . . . That makes it kind of frustrating because you don't know if you are going on the right track or if you are not. (interview, May)

Participants identified conflict between the new roles and established equality, cordiality, and privacy norms in teaching (Lortie, 1975; Waller, 1933): "We want to be objective, but nice . . . You try and mince your way around it . . . It is kind of scary," said one teacher (field notes, January). Another pointed out,

> It is just a new concept, that a colleague is going to come in and point out things or observe . . . If your best friend comes up and asks, "What do you think of my dress?" you aren't going to say, "It is the ugliest thing I have ever seen." (interview, April)

Career ladder teachers at North also described conflict between their responsibilities as teachers and as leaders:

> Even though I'm a teacher leader, I'm struggling with the concept of career ladders. I am concerned with the conflict between loyalty and honest criticism that I feel. Personally, I feel both obligated as a teacher leader to be loyal to the school administration as part of the team and the need as a professional teacher to offer honest and constructive feedback and criticism. (TL, interview, April)

Constructed Interpretations

By interpreting or processing information, the two groups created two different interpretations, statements of meaning and value, judgments of motive and worth, and actions. As interpretations developed, subgroups began to form coalitions to promote their points of view. At South, teachers openly acknowledged the coalition of teacher leaders, the principal, and some teachers. At North, few would admit that subgroups wanted to undermine or change the career ladder, although one teacher stopped the researcher in the hall one day in late fall and said, "If you're hearing good things about the career ladder, you're not talking to the right people."

Information processing—making sense as a group of the career ladder experience and coming to a shared understanding of what was happening—shaped interpretations. Information exchange and judgments eventually created the roles people filled at the two schools be defining the tasks, activities, and relationships that were accepted as legitimate. The data associated with the development of a shared reality at the two schools revolved around the frequency and directness of communication, the articulation and clarity of beliefs and expectations, feelings of isolation versus a sense of community, the frequency and form of criticism, the influence and status of the most powerful information source, the salience of the information in relation to central norms, perceptions of nonverbal cues, and interpretations of personal costs to those taking on positions. The selection process, again, became the focal point of these dynamics.

Many people at South accepted responsibility for information exchange and communication directed toward the interpretation and clarification of the career ladder. The principal saw it as a principal part of his role; he also expected the career ladder teachers, particularly the teacher leaders, to assume responsibility for giving and interpreting information. As we noted previously, the teacher leaders held a monthly planning and discussion session. They also wrote a monthly newsletter. Whenever they questioned whether their decisions might "step on the toes of the administration" or when they felt the need for the support of formal authority, career ladder teachers went directly to the principal and requested a planning meeting, time in faculty meetings, and clarification. Other teachers noticed a change in communication. One said, "We talk a lot about what is going on and what modifications we need to make in the ladder. Sometimes, [the talking] becomes very vigorous" (interview, December). A teacher specialist agreed, arguing that "discussions are open. We can discuss problems. I don't think it's a threat to people here."

The processes creating positive interpretations at South failed to have the same effect at North. Communication was infrequent and indirect, taking the form of mandated training sessions and written directives from the district. The principal was invisible. Mutual blaming accompanied this paucity of information in support of the new roles. The principal said that he chose "good people and [let] them run with it" (interview, November). Teacher leaders said that they "didn't know what to do" and needed direction from the principal (TLs, interviews, October and November).

Influential members of the faculty, administrators, and the career ladder teachers said that they believed it was their responsibility to "explain" their function and usefulness as well as perform new tasks. They occasionally felt frustrated and discouraged with having to defend the career ladder and the performance of career ladder teachers, but they believed that the outcome and longevity of the reform in part depended on their making sense of it for people. Consequently, the data from South portray a well-articulated communication effort characterized by clarity, shared belief, and positive interpretations and led by the formal leader of the school. This important leadership was not apparent at North.

Shared beliefs and expectations also were apparent in reference to a sense of community, social support, and the increased influence of all teachers in the school. Although no one went so far as to claim that all teachers had the power and influence of teacher leaders, they described themselves as "talking more about issues," having longer faculty meetings because people debated professional questions more freely, and having a high awareness of what the career ladder teachers were doing. The tasks performed as part of the career ladder were visible and understood by many of the faculty members. The career ladder teachers described the principal as supportive. "He has supported us tremendously," said one (TL, interview, October). Another pointed out that the interaction they had because of the career ladder had improved their relationships with teachers and between teachers and administrators. "It [the career ladder] seems to have strengthened our collegiality" (TL, interview, May).

The absence of deliberate exchange left the articulation of the career ladder to the rumor network at North. During the month of November, administrators, teachers, secretaries, and custodians spent much energy spreading and elaborating rumors about a teacher leader who used his career ladder time to work on a home remodeling project in the school's wood shop but no one, including the principal, took initiative to affect the storytelling.

Another important part of the shared reality developing in the schools centered in the frequency and intensity of criticism of the new positions and those filling them and the isolation this caused. Although debate and critique surrounding professional issues increased, people did not frequently call this talk criticism. Teacher leaders and the principal often "sat in his office and brainstormed and worked together" (TL, field notes, November). Teachers who criticized the level of effort and performance of individual career ladder teachers (most frequently the teacher specialists were the targets) did not associate their disappointment with potential or usefulness of the concept of a career ladder. "Lots of good discussion and arguing" took place (teacher, interview, November).

Where teachers at South described a new sense of community and interaction, those at North lamented over their isolation. The lack of communication and cooperation among teacher leaders grew into alienation by January, when their interviews, conversations in the faculty lounge, and the accounts of other teachers show they were joining in the chorus of criticism, turning on each other. Their work was at first a mystery—"the teacher leaders' work is very invisible"—and then a subject of scorn.

The status and influence of those praising and reinforcing the career ladder positions at South played an important part in the positive interpretation of activities. The relative reticence of the principal at North to speak out and lead out on the career ladder stood in stark contrast. The administrators at South actively engaged in the information exchange, teacher union leaders praised the tasks undertaken, and respected veterans either praised the new positions, stayed neutral, or admitted that they had improved morale. These were salient sources of validation for the career ladder. Teachers saw almost all the actual tasks and programs undertaken as teacher initiatives at South. Many felt the program had "brought a lot more control back to the school" (TL, meeting transcript, April).

The teacher leaders at South joined to exert influence over their developing positions. They set up a formal planning meeting for one Saturday each month, requested and received control over half of the regularly scheduled faculty meetings, and selected and designed the major career ladder projects undertaken during the year. They became articulate advocates for the reform.

A teacher who went directly to North's principal to complain said it made her feel "like a little narc" for violating the privacy of another teacher, an important norm. Confusion over the expectations and tasks associated with the new positions increased with time. In the fall, one teacher leader asked the researcher what she should be doing with her preparation period (field notes, October). "I feel that the staff development role and mentoring of probationary teachers that we should be doing is not very well articulated, and we are unclear in our direction and what is expected of us," said another teacher leader in March. The principal admitted, "I've dropped the ball."

Debate and discussion at North took the form of blanket criticism of the career ladder and of specific teachers. Even the principal acknowledged that "much of the criticism here has centered around one teacher leader. . . He does too much." The discussion was pervasive but not productive. "In our faculty meetings it seems like everybody is always griping about career ladders" (teacher, interview, April). Those filling the positions were subjected to vilification no matter what they did: First, they were chastised for observing and supervising, then they were ridiculed for not taking initiative and coming into classrooms to offer assistance. Teachers noticed that the principal had little or nothing to say. "It's not one of his priorities." He argued that he was "a busy person" and the "squeaky wheel gets the grease."

In the absence of positive articulation at North, *nonverbal cues, gestures, and innuendo*—"body language" as one teacher leader put it—filled the void. These cues had the desired chilling effect, and two of the three teacher leaders and most of the teacher specialists at North decided it was *not worth the cost*; they did not reapply for their positions. As one teacher leader put it, the year was devastating, like "being blown out of the water."

Summary and Implications

The role theory framework used for this analysis of case study data offers one inter-pretation of how social system dynamics affect interpretations and, consequently, outcomes of a work redesign for teachers. It frames interpretations as emerging through a progressive interaction of established role characteristics with new role behaviors associated with the career ladder in an environment of negotiation and ambiguity. The competition between the enforcement of old role behaviors, norms, and values and the inducement of new roles challenged teachers' and principals' professional self-concepts. Coalitions of administrators and teachers formed around change versus enforcement activities and vied for control over the interpretations that constituted and defined work in each school. This last factor illuminated the process through which the role constructs exerted influence (see Firestone & Herriott, 1981). Two schools looking very much alike in common demographic details were actually very different.

This analysis also supports the assertion of Salancik and Pfeffer (1978) that interpretations drawn from the immediate environment have profound impacts of "objective" tasks associated with work characteristics and their outcomes. For exam-ple, the occupational identity of teachers played a major part in responses of teach-ers and administrators to the new positions in both schools. At South, the career ladder teachers and the principal acted quickly when challenges to their identity as teachers were mounted. The teacher leaders formed their own ad hoc leadership committee, worked together to define and support their roles, publicized their activ-ities, and openly confronted questions about the legitimacy of their activities. The principal deliberately structured visible opportunities for them to exert leadership. At North, each career ladder teacher remained isolated to stand or fall alone (even though their job descriptions were far more alike than those at South). The new posi-tions never developed around an accepted set of behaviors, and no core-group of adherents emerged. Individual teachers thus were vulnerable to attack, because no systemwide concepts and beliefs developed on which their actions could be judged. Each teacher lasted on the basis of a "perceptual control variable" of sorts (Cziko, 1992). The principal remained silent.

Another explanation for the different outcomes in these two schools is related to the social processes that created judgments of benefits and costs associated with the new positions. At South, the principal and career ladder teachers moved quickly to emphasize instructional benefits to the school. Teachers filling career ladder positions (and creating the role in many cases) found they could manage the coping pressures coming from the role-making process. Assertive action by a number of different groups induced new roles at South. A paucity of conceptual development and an enforcement of conventional expectations of equality, cordiality, and privacy pre-vailed at North.

Building on the enforcement of roles through values and norms, the interpretation of words, gestures, and events functioned as the primary mechanism through which teachers and administrators at both schools defined their experiences. Interpretations developed through which the new roles exerted influence on outcomes. Teachers and administrators at South talked about curriculum development, improved instruction, support for professional growth, and enhanced communication. They acted on this talk. In some ways, they recreated the career ladder, changing it from a promotion and incentive scheme closely resembling merit pay (which violated long-established professional norms) to a staff development and school improvement intervention (which appealed to long-standing beliefs in intrinsic motivation and student learning).

Role theory predicts that the enforcement of roles and information processing will be powerful forces in stable organizations, and this analysis supports a view that, during periods of change, roles and social systems may exert an even more powerful influence. This impact emerged in part as coalitions of subgroups within the organization (teachers against the career ladder at North; career ladder teachers and the principal at South) jockeyed for influence over the dominant interpretation of reality emerging from the redesign process (see Bacharach & Mundell, 1993). Where teachers interpreted the new jobs as important contributions to the overall instructional system, thus improving students' performance throughout the school, they supported them.

These findings inform understanding of school change efforts and principals' leadership responsibilities. No matter how carefully planned or how thoughtfully integrated with good instructional practice, the new work design for teachers in the comparative case analysis ultimately was shaped within each school and, in terms of individual roles, nested in that school. This suggests that much thought to the particular function of teacher leadership in each unique context is warranted. Enhanced, visible relationships between leadership roles and the core instructional work teachers' valued improved actual outcomes described by participants. The relationship took on the dynamics of an amplified feedback loop system. One might argue that good work will stand on its own, but the present analysis belies this conclusion. Without the support of core leaders in context, one could predict little change.

This analysis revealed that leaders should attend to individual teacher's roles and the group assessment of, and support for, those roles. When the district implemented a major work role change in schools (to affect the incentive system or to improve instruction or both), time and resources for planning were valuable to promote the success of each teacher.

Finally, the principals' attention and contribution strongly affected the importance that teachers attached to the new leadership roles. The two principals in this study sent very different cues about the importance, real power, and professional authority of the teacher leaders to the faculties. The new roles lacked intrinsic authority and needed time to acquire legitimacy. Principals should not underestimate the need for their diligent, supportive, visible, and frequent reinforcement of the real power of teacher leaders, nor should they ignore the social-emotional adjustments in professional self-concept leadership that opportunities bring with them.

In conclusion, role theory offers insight into processes through which interpretations of the work influence objective job characteristics during school reform. In these two case studies, enforcement pressures competed with pressure for change. The power to interpret the meaning and to judge the utility and worth of the tasks enforced old patterns at one school and facilitated development and change at the other. Where a core support group including the principal functioned well, teacher leaders were able to act as leaders, create their new roles, and contribute to the school's instructional system.

Notes

1. This process sometimes is described as a blending of symbolic interactionism with concepts of role (Mead, 1934; Turner, 1962).
2. Although the work redesign differed substantially from conventional conceptions of a career ladder as a series of progressively higher steps for which people can prepare and on which they can count as they formulate career plans, its designers called it a career ladder. Teachers who participated recognized the ambiguity in the name, remarking, "A career ladder's not a ladder if you fall off it automatically every year," and calling it a "stepladder . . . you step on and you step off."
3. In the years since this career ladder was first implemented, teacher leader positions have turned over with decreasing frequency. Positions are now virtually assured unless teachers choose not to reapply. See Firestone and Bader (1992) for a more complete description of this kind of gradual entitlement process during teacher work redesign.
4. In all subsequent citations from the data, the abbreviated CL will be used to designate career ladder, TL will designate teacher ladder and TS will designate teacher specialist.

References

Bacharach, S. B. (Ed.). (1990). *Education reform: Making sense of it all.* Boston: Allyn & Bacon.

Bacharach, S. B., Conley, S. C. & Shedd, J. B. (1986). Beyond career ladders: Structuring teacher career development systems. *Teachers College Record, 87,* 563–574.

Bacharach, S. B., & Mundell, B. (1993). Organizational politics in schools; Micro, macro, and the logics of action. *Educational Administration Quarterly, 29,* 423–452

Biddle, B. J.: (1979). *Role theory: Expectations, identities, and behaviors.* New York: Academic.

Biddle, B. J., & Thomas, E. J. (1966). *Role theory: Concepts and research.* New York: Wiley.

Brousseau, K. R. (1978). Personality and job experience. *Organizational Behavior and Human Performance, 22,* 235–252

Conley, S. C. (1990). A metaphor for teaching: Beyond the bureaucratic-professional dichotomy. In S. B. Bacharach (Ed.), *Educational Reform: Making sense of it all* (pp. 313–324). Boston: Allyn & Bacon.

Conley, S. C. (1991). Participative decision making: A review of research. In G. Grant (Ed.), *Review of research in education 17* (pp. 225–265). Washington, DC: American Educational Research Association.

Cornett, L. (1988). *Is "paying for performance" changing schools?* (SREB career ladder clearing-house report 1988). Atlanta, GA: Southern Regional Educational Board.

Cziko, G. A. (1992). Perceptual control theory: One threat to face educational research not (yet?) faced by Amundsen, Serlin and Lehrer. *Education Researcher, 21*(9), 25–27.

Diamond, M. A., & Allcorn, S. (1985). Psychological dimensions of role use in bureaucratic organizations. *Organizational Dynamics, 14,* 35–59.

Dubinsky, A. J., & Yammarino, F. J. (1984). Differential impact of role conflict and ambiguity on selected correlates: A two-sample test. *Psychological Reports, 55,* 699–707.

Firestone, W. A., & Bader, B. D. (1992). *The redesign of teaching: Professionalism of bureaucracy?* New York: SUNY Press.

Firestone, W. A., & Herriott, R. F. (1981. Images of organization and the promotion of education change. In A. Kerchoff & R. Corwin (Eds.), *Research in the sociology of education and socialization* (Vol. 2, pp. 221–259). Greenwich, CT: JAI.

Fullan, M. G. (1991). *The new meaning of educational change* (2nd ed.). New York: Teachers College Press.

Garfinkel, H. (1967). *Research in ethnomethodology.* Englewood Cliffs, NJ: Prentice-Hall.

Hart, A. W. (1987). A career ladder's effect on teacher career and work attitudes. *American Educational Research Journal, 24*(4), 479–503.

Hart, A. W. (1990). Impacts of the school social unit on teacher authority during work redesign. *American Educational Research Journal, 27*(3), 503–532.

Johnson, S. M. (1990). *Teachers at work: Achieving success in your schools.* New York: Basic Books.

Kulik, C. T. (1989). The effects of job categorization on judgments of the motivating potential of jobs. *Administrative Science Quarterly, 34,* 68–90.

Latack, J. C. (1984). Career transitions within organizations. An exploratory study of work, nonwork, and coping strategies. *Organizational Behavior and Human Performance, 34,* 296–322.

Lortie, D. C. (1975). *Schoolteacher: A sociological study.* Chicago. University of Chicago Press.

Louis, M. R. (1980a). Career transitions: Varieties and commonalities. *Academy of Management Review, 5*(3), 329–340.

Louis, M. R. (1980b). Surprise and sense making. What newcomers experience in entering unfamiliar organizational settings. *Administrative Science Quarterly, 25*(2), 226–251.

McClintock, C. (1985). Process sampling: A method for case study research on administrative behavior. *Educational Administration Quarterly, 21,* 205–222.

McEnrue, M. R. (1984). Perceived competence as a moderator of the relationship between role clarity and job performance. A test of two hypotheses. *Organizational Behavior and Human Performance, 34,* 479–486.

Mead, G. H. (1934). *Mind, self, and society: From the standpoint of a social behaviorist.* Chicago: University of Chicago Press.

Miles, M. B., & Huberman, A. M. (1994). *Qualitative data analysis: A sourcebook of new methods* (2nd ed.). Newbury Park, CA, Sage.

Murphy J. (Ed.). (1990). *The educational reform movement of the 1980s: Perspectives and cases.* Berkeley, CA. McCutchan.

Murphy, J. Hart, A. W. & Walters, L. C. (1989, April). *Satisfaction and intent to leave responses of new teachers in target populations under redesigned teacher work.* Paper presented at the annual meeting of the American Educational Research Association, San Francisco.

Nicholson, N. (1984). A theory of work role in transitions. *Administrative Science Quarterly, 29,* 172–191.

Rosenholtz, S. J. (1987). Education reform strategies: Will they increase teacher commitment? *American Journal of Education, 95,* 534–562.

Salancik, G. R., & Pfeffer, J. (1978). A social information processing approach to job attitudes and task design. *Administrative Science Quarterly, 23,* 224–253.

Schlechty, P.C., & Joslin, A. W. (1984). Recruiting teachers—future prospects. *Journal of Children in Contemporary Society, 16,* 51–60.

Shanker, A. (1990). The *conditions* of teaching: Flexibility and authority in the classroom. In S. B. Bacharach (Ed.), *Educational reform: Making sense of it all* (pp. 354–361). Boston Allyn & Bacon.

Smylie, M. A., & Denny, J. W. (1990). Teacher leadership: Tensions and ambiguities in organizational perspective. *Educational Administration Quarterly, 26,* 235–259.

Spradley, J. (1980). *Participant observation,* New York: Holt, Rinehart & Winston.

Steers, R. M., & Mowday, R. T. (1977). The motivational properties of tasks. *Academy of Management Review, 2,* 645–658.

Turner, J. (1988). *A theory of social interaction.* Stanford, CA: Stanford University Press.

Turner, R. H. (1962). Role-taking process versus conformity. In A. M. Rose (Ed.), *Human behavior and social processes: An interactionist approach* (pp. 20–40). Boston: Houghton Mifflin.

Waller, W. (1933). *The sociology of teaching.* New York: Wiley

Wentworth, W. (1980). *Context and understanding: An inquiry into socialization theory.* New York: Elsevier.

Yin, R. K. (1989). *Case study research: Design and methods* (2nd ed.). Beverly Hills, CA: Sage.

CHAPTER 8

Quasi-Experimental Research Designs, External Validity, and the Matter of School Discipline

INTRODUCTION

There are a handful of problems capable of bringing about faculty dissatisfaction, parental concerns, and, ultimately, administrator termination in a public middle school. Of this handful, a deteriorating school-wide discipline problem may be the one most feared by building principals because of its clear visibility. Parents, visitors to the school, teachers, and former teachers all add to the rapid manner in which reputations spread about the degree of order or lack thereof that exists in a particular building.

Such fears often push administrators and teachers to move quickly to head off a problem in its earliest stages. "We've got to do something about it before it gets out of control" is a common plea for help from beleaguered teachers. This pressure for a quick and decisive solution can race ahead of a clear understanding of the problem. Frequently, any action is applauded as long as it appears to be quick, incisive, and consistent. And if word spreads that discipline at Adams Middle School just does not measure up to what it is reputed to be at Charley Good-Principal's school, then the principal at Adams may be headed for the chopping block.

These pressures for taking decisive action make principals a receptive audience for proposals that promise quick and effective solutions to discipline problems. Workshops, training materials, and consultants bring word of highly successful ventures in other schools. Given the pervasiveness and seriousness of many school discipline problems, these resource providers have a long and promising future.

The Case: Are These Kids Getting Out of Control?

Lynne Michaels cycled through a dozen or more options as she thought about the upcoming school year, the third of her tenure at Adams Middle School. The hypothetical discipline scenario sketched previously is an unfortunate reality for her. Adams Middle School has undergone some changes recently and they have probably all contributed to the discipline malaise that she admits is becoming a bit oppressive. Adams does have discipline problems and it does little good to tick off the possible causes (although she runs through the list every few hours when she thinks about the problem).

One contributing factor was the recent reorganization of the district, which resulted in four middle schools rather than three, and with redrawn school boundary lines. While the fourth school was absolutely necessary and the boundary lines made sense when they were first drawn, that was nearly five years ago. Today, a larger proportion of low-income students are coming to Adams from the growing number of apartment buildings and mobile home parks that seemed to sprout in the Southeast quadrant of the county. Each year the poverty indicators of her students seemed to grow, and with those indicators, the ability, motivation, and morale of her faculty seemed to wane proportionately.

A second decision was made by the central administration at the same time they added the fourth middle school. The board accepted the superintendent's recommendation to reshuffle the teachers and administrators among the four schools. This decision was prompted by a desire to break up existing faculties which, in the eyes of some, had become rather set in their ways and would benefit from a new work setting, new challenges, and different colleagues. The same argument was advanced in the hope that reassigned principals would bring new vigor to their jobs.

One more complication for Lynne Michaels was more personal in nature. While two of the building administrators had served as middle school principals in the district for 8 and 12 years, respectively, she and one other were new to the district. Adding to the problem is that the other new principal, Walter Murphy, had been hired very early in the process and had played a role in the reorganization of faculty. The original intent had been that Murphy would serve as the building administrator at the newly built Adams school, but during his six months in the central office, Murphy changed his mind when Charley Kraus, a principal of long standing, retired a year early.

Word had it that Kraus saw the potential problems inherent in a district-wide shakeup and decided his retirement options suddenly looked far more attractive. This retirement left open an existing middle school that had a reputation for being a good school with a stable population in a good residential neighborhood. Add to these positive qualities of the existing school the fact that the new building was about three months behind schedule, and rumor had it that the school would open with more construction workers than teachers in the building.

Not too surprisingly, Murphy examined his options and applied for the existing building, which meant the district was now looking for another principal for the nearly finished Adams Middle School. And so, Lynne Michaels applied for the exciting job of beginning a new school and developing a new faculty, but with very little knowledge of all the behind-the-scenes maneuvering that led up to the position being available. Michael's last year was not one she would consider a personal best, and on the last day of school, her patience, good humor, and her staff's professionalism seemed to end together. But, she has recovered some of her energy and enthusiasm over the summer and is ready to face the school world again. As she anticipates her third year at the helm of Adams Middle School she feels ready to move beyond the survival stage. She is pleased with the overall quality of the faculty; they are as concerned about the growing discipline problems as she is. Many of them would admit they are better prepared to teach their subject matter than they are to cope with the wide range of personal, emotional, and behavioral problems of their students. The new building and its problems and potential have been realized; a reasonable working relationship has been developed among faculty, staff, and administrators; and the beginning of a leadership infrastructure is emerging. Finally, parents are starting to feel comfortable with the new school in their midst and are a source of support to Adams and its programs.

Having said all this, it seemed clear to Lynne that a potentially serious discipline problem was emerging at Adams. She was tempted to bypass the problem identification phase because the problem itself seemed obvious. Also, teachers might resist lengthy discussions and debates about the issue; they may well crave answers, not questions, and solution finding, not problem finding. Lynne wisely resisted the pressures for finding solutions and maintained her focus on refining the problem before she proceeded. She addressed the following questions as they applied to her school. Are there discipline problems over and above what occur anytime 700 young adolescents are housed together for six hours a day? If so, what type of discipline problems are they, and what are their frequency and intensity? Are these problems spread across the entire school or concentrated in one grade level or within one content area? Are these problems increasing from year to year or from grade to grade or have they begun to level off?

Examining the data available from the past two years helped provide partial answers to these and other questions, and a sharper understanding of the problem began to emerge. After the first three months of the chaotic first year during which so many things were in flux that no consistencies seemed apparent, the remaining year and two thirds showed some interesting patterns. First, there has been a sharp increase in the number of serious offenses of fighting, insubordination, harassment, and truancy. Additionally, there has been an even steeper increase in the use of out-of-school suspensions as the administrative response. While serious incidents had increased by 25% from year 1 to year 2, the total number of student suspension days was up over 40%. The faculty pressure for tougher penalties was felt most strongly by Lynne's assistant principal, and he responded accordingly.

Teachers expressed concern over what they saw as a growing number of students who were being drawn into misbehavior. Granted, it was difficult to feel confident about these patterns given such a limited data base, but the teacher concerns were real and strongly expressed. While all expressed concerns over the increased number of referrals for serious offenses, they did not all share the same concerns about the sharp increase in suspension rates. Some faculty shared Lynne's doubts about the efficacy of longer and stiffer suspensions, but other faculty felt the suspensions were not long enough and were not being consistently administered.

A second set of discipline problems seemed distinguishable from the first by the seriousness of the offenses. There were hundreds of nuisance activities—constant talking in class, failure to have homework done or on time, dawdling in the halls, being late for class, pranks, and goofing off instead of working—that resulted in students' being sent to the office or written up. While of far less serious concern to teachers as a whole, there were many who argued that these activities should not be ignored because their sheer numbers might be interfering more with instruction than the more serious offenses. Serious or not, these offenses seemed to be increasing over time. In particular, when Lynne contrasted the final quarter of both years, she found a 30% increase from last year to this year. That got her attention.

As Lynne shaped the problem to be addressed, she recognized that it had a dual focus. One piece of the problem dealt with serious offenses. These offenses were dangerous to fellow students and teachers as well as the individuals committing the offenses. Tied to this issue were questions about the effectiveness of suspensions as a means of addressing this problem. The other aspect of the problem was the large number of irritation behaviors that interfered with effective instruction, not only for the offenders but for the rest of the class.

Lynne posed the problem as follows: A small but increasing number of students is behaving in ways that put them and others at physical and educational risk. Additionally, a large and increasing number of students is behaving in ways that interfere with the learning environment for themselves and their schoolmates. We need to reverse these trends at our school.

During a faculty meeting devoted to major issues to be faced in the upcoming year, teachers easily reached a consensus about assigning school discipline the highest priority. In that same meeting, three faculty members volunteered to serve as a committee to work with Lynne on examining the discipline problem at

Adams and to review the research literature on the topic. The committee was asked to make recommendations to the faculty for specific steps that might address their concerns when they had completed their work.

The committee developed a list of eight questions to help them think about their problem. From this list, one specific and one more general question survived the screening process:

1. How effective are out-of-school suspension programs for reducing serious discipline incidents in middle schools?
2. What programs for middle schools have been found to be effective in improving overall discipline?

The Research on School Discipline: An Introduction

One point we have tried to make is the importance of narrowing the guiding questions to those that will speak directly rather than indirectly to the problems faced by the practicing administrator. This point was underscored during the literature search that Lynne and her colleagues undertook on school discipline.

The search for studies that spoke to the effectiveness of comprehensive discipline programs in the middle schools yielded a small but helpful set of studies. Along the way, however, Lynne and her associates encountered two other groups of articles that were far more numerous but of considerably less help to her.

One of the larger bodies of literature that proved interesting but unhelpful came from national surveys and popular journals. This literature described the severity of the discipline problem in U.S. schools. For example, the annual surveys of public opinion that appear in the *Phi Delta Kappan*. Polls gave ample documentation that discipline was ranked by parents and teachers as the biggest issue facing local schools. If the categories of drug abuse, lack of discipline, and fighting/violence/gangs are combined, a whopping 45% of the parents indicated that behavior problems were the most important issues facing local schools in 1996 (Rose, Gallup, & Elam, 1997).

The reason these data are described here as ample but unhelpful is that, for Lynne, comments from parents and teachers and her own school data were persuasive enough for her to realize that she was facing an important problem. In fact, even if the national sample had not indicated serious concerns about school discipline problems, her parents were concerned, and that made the problem relevant for her.

A second set of plentiful but unhelpful articles was given to her by colleagues and friends who knew she was grappling with a discipline problem. These articles and newsletters crossed her desk on a daily basis and could be characterized as testimonials from concerned professionals. While these articles often described realistic-sounding programs in vivid terms with a great deal of compassion, they provided precious few data on their effectiveness.

The structure of these articles was highly predictable. First, the practitioner-author described in vivid terms how discipline had gotten out of hand in his or her school. Next, the author would go on to describe—with few details—a program that was implemented to correct this situation. Finally, the article would close by describing the current scene as "Things are not yet perfect at Run-A-Muck Middle School, but we are getting there quickly." Lynne softly vowed to herself that she would never again read another testimonial that did not offer clear descriptions of what had been done followed by hard data on the effectiveness of that treatment.

The discrepancy between the goal of responsible citizenship for students and the harsh realities depicted by the national poll data cited earlier is hardly a new phenomenon. Bear (1998) reflected on this discrepancy with a historical account of Thomas Jefferson and the creation of his model school at the University of Virginia. The goal of self-governing students with a clear understanding of the link between virtuous, caring behavior and the survival of the young democracy was countered by a strong dose of colonial reality.

Bear quoted Brodie (1974) in the following words:

"Jefferson at first was in favor of self-government for the students and a minimum of discipline, but a student riot, which he himself at 82 helped to quell, and which resulted in three expulsions (one of his own nephew) and eleven severe reprimands, convinced him that severer regulations were essential." (p. 604)

Lynne thought about Jefferson's struggle with school discipline and realized these problems preceded TV, drugs, rock and roll, and single parent families. Perhaps the tension between self-regulation of behavior and the appropriate level of external controls and sanctions was just a way of life for maturing adolescents of all times and places.

Bear's article also provided a conceptual scheme for thinking about school discipline issues and a framework for authoritative teaching that comprised three interrelated components: (1) classroom management strategies for preventing behavior problems, (2) strategies for short-term management of behavior problems, and (3) social problem-solving strategies for achieving long term goals of self-discipline. Additionally, he reviewed the literature that bore on these three components. He concluded that proactive classroom management strategies that parallel the authoritative parenting literature have had empirical support. In addition to delineating a set of 16 strategies adapted from the literature, he described the authoritative teaching style as " . . . characterized by a combination of warmth and acceptance, clear rules and expectations, and activities that promote autonomy and positive self-concept" (p. 19).

The second component of Bear's scheme involved the use of operant learning strategies for responding to short-term behavior problems. The research literature is reasonably clear on this component: The use of mild punishment techniques and the reinforcement of appropriate behaviors by means of privileges and social rewards have proven to be effective. Martens and Meller (1990) and Walker, Colvin, and Ramsey (1995) also support the efficacy of operant strategies for control of short-term behavior problems.

The third component, social problem-solving strategies, involves the use of such processes as empathy (Eisenberg & Harris, 1997), moral reasoning (Bear, Richards, & Gibbs, 1997), negotiating strategies (Selman & Schultz, 1990) and impulse control and anger management (Lochman, Dunn, & Klimes-Dougan, 1993). Bear (1998) indicated that empirical support for the effectiveness of these social problem-solving mechanisms was lacking at this time and argued that the popularity of such approaches lies more in their conceptual contribution to our understanding of school discipline problems than in their demonstrated effectiveness.

Research Question 1: Are Suspensions Effective?

How effective are out-of-school suspension programs for reducing serious discipline incidents in middle schools? The definition of serious discipline offenses traditionally included fighting, insubordination, harassment, and truancy. More recently, the use of drugs and alcohol has been added to the list. While uniformity does not exist in the use of the term, Baker's (1996) definition of Major Disciplinary Violations (MDVs) as describing students who are truant, involved in fighting, insubordinate, or in possession of drugs or alcohol appears adequate for Lynne and her colleagues. These acts threaten the safety of teachers and other students in the building and are clearly of concern to all educators as problems in their own right. In addition, these behaviors have been found to predict later encounters with the law for students who disproportionately drop out of school (Peng, Fetters, & Kolstad, 1981; Wehlage & Rutter, 1986).

Truancy differs conceptually from the more aggressive forms of disciplinary infractions listed here; however, totally removing oneself from the learning environment has serious short-term consequences as well as a decided impact on the rest of the student's academic career. Truancy is therefore of serious concern to educators.

Responses available to educators for dealing with serious offenses are strikingly few. Equally striking is the lack of examination as to their effectiveness. In general, parents and teachers agree that removing the troublemakers from the school is appropriate. An overwhelming proportion (92%) of a national survey of parents indicated support for such a response (Elam, Rose, & Gallup, 1996).

School suspensions (and ultimately expulsions) are often the final weapons in the arsenal of school personnel, and they are used more often as offenses increase. Gottfredson, Gottfredson and Hybl (1993) described the interactive nature of discipline offenses, increased failure rates, and spiraling suspensions. In their study of one district's middle schools, the percentage of students who were one year over age for their grade level rose from 34% to 48% in five years, while the suspension rates also rose sharply. They reported that suspensions rose from 41 per 100 students enrolled to the rate of 100 suspensions for every 100 students enrolled. (Of course, not all students in the district were suspended; rather, this statistic indicates that if there were 400 students enrolled in a particular school, there were 400 individual suspensions recorded for the year.)

For just one school year the combination of out-of-school and in-school suspensions amounted to 7,932 lost instructional days for the district's middle schools. Clearly, as a strategy, suspensions carry a high cost in time and lost instruction.

Studies have documented the rise in frequency of discipline incidents and the corresponding rise in detention and suspension as responses to those increases (Tobin, Sugai, & Colvin, 1996). Gottfredson et al. (1993) and Uchitelle, Bartz, and Hillman (1989) are examples of researchers who have discussed these increases and challenged the efficacy of increasing suspensions as a strategy to reduce MVDs.

Another problem cited in the use of suspensions relates to the issue of frequency and recidivism. Wu, Pink, Crain, and Moles (1982) examined national data samples and found 11% of all students were suspended at least once during their school careers, which suggests the widespread use of this method of discipline. More troubling, perhaps, was the finding by Costenbader and Markson (1994) that 42% of all suspensions were for students who had been previously suspended one or more times. Clearly, the high rate of recidivism suggests (but does not prove) that the suspensions were not effective in reducing the occurrence of major discipline incidents.

Other criticisms have been raised regarding suspensions and zero-tolerance approaches as a means of improving student behavior. In addition to efficacy, questions have been raised about consistency of application (Pisarra & Giblette, 1981) and the disproportionate number of low SES students and minority students who receive suspensions for MDVs (Brantlinger, 1991; Davis & Jordan, 1995).

In one carefully documented study, Skiba, Peterson, and Williams (1997) examined an entire district's middle school population of over 11,000 students in 19 schools. The study's recency, its large scope, and the similarity of student populations with those in Lynne's district led her to be particularly interested in it. The authors examined office referrals and suspensions, seeking patterns in the types of referrals, the responses chosen by the administrators to those referrals, and the relationship between the severity of the offenses and the severity of the responses. Finally, they examined the relationship between suspensions and race, gender, and SES of the students.

What Lynne and her committee learned from this study was disturbing. Over the course of one year, 4,521 students (41.1%) were referred to the school office with an average number of referrals per student of 3.77. Of this total of 17,044 referrals, 5,673 (33.3%) were given out-of-school suspensions. When added to the 1,721 in-school suspensions, this resulted in 43.4% of all office referrals ending in suspensions. While no total of lost instructional days was given, the suspensions ranged from 1 to 5 days. If we assume that the suspensions averaged 2 days each, the 5,673 out-of-school suspensions would result in over 11,000 lost pupil instruction days for suspended students during one year in one school district.

The researchers reported statistically significant differences in suspension rates based on race ($p < .001$), SES ($p < .001$), and gender ($p < .001$). Unfortunately, they did not report effect sizes, nor did they provide means and standard deviations of these variables, which prevented Lynne from calculating their effect sizes. This omission prevented her from estimating the actual size of the differences to determine their practical significance.

A second study reported in the same article by Skiba, Peterson, and Williams (1997), which pursued one middle school in depth, was a part of the district-wide study reported earlier. The follow up provided data about the nature of the incidents that prompted a referral, where it occurred, previous actions taken with the student prior to this incident, and the staff member's recommendation to the administrator. Finally, the action taken by the administrator was recorded.

The middle school examined had 610 students with a total minority population of 12% with 9.2% being African-American, 1.5% Asian-American, .8% Hispanic, and .5% Native-American. The school size, ethnic composition, and SES of the student body closely resembled Adams Middle School. Lynne and her committee were able to infer from the sample and population characteristics of the study that it would have good application validity for Adams. The results indicated a large percentage (52%) of all referrals fell into a category coded "lack of cooperation." The second category, "insubordinate/verbal abuse" yielded nearly 40%, and it was obvious that these two categories accounted for a large proportion of the total referrals. The major incidents of fighting (6%), threats and intimidation (4%), and sexual harassment/assaults (1%), while serious in nature, were relatively infrequent.

The conclusions drawn from this study reinforced the preliminary data that Lynne and her staff had collected at Adams: The most serious infractions were relatively infrequent and these infractions were done by a small number of repeat offenders. Typically, these students were suspended and returned to school only to offend again, thus perpetuating an offense-suspension-offense cycle.

The large bulk of offenses were minor in nature, but their frequency amounted to a great deal of lost time by students, faculty, and administrators who had to deal with these nagging incidents. Taking both studies together, over 40% of the district's students had been referred to the office for 1 or more disciplinary referrals.

Skiba et al. (1997) inferred from the high degree of stability in referrals across the three grade levels that the punitive actions taken by administrators had not been effective in reducing their occurrence from grade 6 to grade 8. They cautioned against suspensions as a treatment for disciplinary infractions with the following words: "One must be very concerned about a procedure that puts a student at-risk for school alienation on the street for days at a time where the most available peers will be those who have already chosen an antisocial course." (p. 312)

In summary of their findings on research question 1, Lynne and her colleagues concluded that there was no compelling research evidence to show that suspensions reduced the number of serious discipline offenses. In addition, there were side effects that argued for caution in the use of suspensions. Removing a student from instruction when academic problems may have played a role in contributing to the major violations did not appear to be conceptually sound. Additionally, there were suggestions that race, SES, and ability levels of students may have been contributing factors to selecting suspensions as the response to MVDs. Finally, the data suggested that a great deal of inconsistency existed in applying suspensions.

Based on these factors Lynne and her committee concluded that a judicious use of suspensions may be required for the immediate safety of students and staff in certain cases, but they found little evidence that, by itself, it served as a strong deterrent to either the person being suspended or to the other students in the school. Phrased another way, one committee member stated that it may be a necessary but not sufficient strategy for dealing with their problem.

Research Question 2:
What Discipline Programs Have Been Found to be Effective?

Having examined a portion of the literature exploring the effectiveness (or, ineffectiveness) of suspensions as an attempt to reduce Major Disciplinary Violations, it was time for Lynne's committee to move to the next phase of their task. The faculty had expressed concern about the impact of two types of discipline events: The more serious but infrequent MDVs as well as the less violent but more frequent problems that caused referrals to the office. The second question asked, "What programs for middle schools have been found to be effective in improving overall discipline?"

The high rate of referrals has caught the attention of researchers, resulting in attempts to examine the effect of gender, grade level, and SES on referral rates. Freiberg, Stein, and Parker (1995) examined the referrals for the month of October in one middle school of 1,285 students in grades 6, 7, and 8. These results closely mirror others (Wu et al., 1982; Kazdin,1987; Stattin & Magnusson,1989) in several ways. First, the rate of referrals is extremely high. Freiberg et al. (1995) reported 895 referrals in the month of October, which would yield over 8,000 referrals in one academic year. This staggering number obviously occupies a considerable amount of time for teachers, administrators, and staff.

Second, gender and grade level differences are found consistently, with 7th grade males tagged with the most number of referrals (Blyth, Simmons, & Carleton-Ford, 1983; Skiba, Peterson, & Williams, 1997). In addition to 7th graders being identified as the most frequent offenders, they were also the most likely to be referred for serious offenses of fighting or insubordination. Other than vague references to a lack of respect for authority, these studies provided few insights into the reasons for these differences.

Third, these same studies suggested that a relatively large percentage of students were referred one time and a smaller set of "hard core" offenders were responsible for a large proportion of the total number of referrals. Freiberg et al. (1995) reported that, of the 895 total referrals for the month of October, 203 students accounted for 709 of them. These 203 students averaged 3.5 referrals per month, and if those rates held constant over the course of a school year it would be possible that 203 students could make more than 6,300 trips to the principal's office. These data struck Lynne and her colleagues as troublesome and, unfortunately, similar to their own numbers at Adams Middle School.

Managing Adolescent Behaviors: A Multiyear, Multischool Study

An important study by Gottfredson, Gottfredson, and Hybl (1993) offered a comprehensive program designed to address discipline problems in the middle schools. This research article will be highlighted as the featured study of this chapter, and we urge you to turn to the appendix on page 259 and read it carefully before you proceed. We will refer frequently to the study and its findings. We will use the tripartite structure of *conceptual, operational,* and *empirical* levels introduced in chapter 5, focusing particularly on the elements of research design and external validity of the study.

The Conceptual Level. At the conceptual level, researchers describe the research question(s), the research problem, and the rationale that undergirds the study. Let us examine each of these. What research question drove the Gottfredson et al. (1993) work? The opening sentence in the abstract gives us a strong indication of the underlying question of the study: "A 3-year study in eight middle schools tested a program to improve adolescent conduct" (p. 259). Coupled with their discussion introducing their research, the question they address is clear. We would phrase it as follows: Will a comprehensive discipline program designed for middle school students reduce misbehavior? If this is the question, then we will be attentive throughout the study for data that will help answer it. The question will help us find our way through the array of data tables and should reduce the likelihood of our being distracted or overwhelmed by complex statistical procedures.

After determining the research question, it is useful to identify the research problem being addressed by the study. As indicated in an earlier chapter, you can often locate the problem by asking yourself: "Why would anyone want to know the answer to the researcher's question?" If the authors do not explicitly address this matter, and if you cannot develop a good reason for wanting to know the answer to the research question, then possibly there is no problem of worth being investigated. The abstract in the Gottfredson et al. study indicated in general terms that the purpose of the study was to test ". . . a program to improve adolescent conduct" (p. 259). However, Gottfredson et al. were more explicit on p. 262 as they described their research problem in terms of high rates of student suspensions in a particular school district and extremely high scores on a measure that compared students' misbehavior in this district with other students in urban secondary schools in the United States. The problem was clearly rooted in practice and was cast as a classic contrast between the empirical claim (students in this district had very high rates of student misbehavior) and the normative claim (these student misbehavior rates should be reduced). In the introduction to the article, the authors make their case for the importance of the problem of reducing disruptive behavior by citing data indicating that 29% of public school teachers reported they were seriously considering leaving the profession because of student behavior problems, and 33% reported that such behavior interfered with their teaching. It would appear the researchers are addressing an important problem that would be of high concern to many educators.

Another element in the conceptual level of a study is the *rationale* or theoretical framework that drives the research. A well-conceived study rests on a clear argument or rationale that helps explain the relationship between and among its variables. This rationale should be informed by the existing research literature and should be crafted by the researchers to provide a set of propositions that guide the study. After reviewing the literature and exploring the *nature* and the *causes* of disruptive behavior, Gottfredson et al. state their rationale in the following words:

> We were driven in the design of the program by a belief that a systematic, integrated approach to discipline management that provided a mix of activities that targeted the entire school, classrooms within the school, and individuals within the school would be most beneficial. We expected that the interventions would work in concert with one another, producing a larger effect on student behavior than would have been possible had we targeted only individual-level factors that place a student at elevated risk for misbehavior, only classroom-level factors, or only school-level factors. The components for this integrated approach were selected because they had withstood evaluation scrutiny and were linked directly to several of the determinants of misbehavior identified in prior research (summarized earlier). The study was designed to assess the total effect of the system. It is incapable of assessing the independent effect of any piece of the system, and it is incapable of assessing how one program component may have facilitated another. These questions must be left for future research. (pp. 265–266)

In general terms, the researchers listed three important elements in their rationale: (1) the components that were selected had been linked in the research literature to several determinants of misbehavior, (2) their belief that the components would be more effective in concert than when implemented individually, and, therefore, (3) an integrated system that targets student behavior at the school, classroom, and individual level should be effective in reducing misbehavior. While we would wish for an explicit theoretical explanation of how each component affected each outcome variable both individually and in combination, that information is beyond the knowledge available at this time. We believe the researchers provided as clear and explicit a rationale as the state of our knowledge will permit. If the results of the study indicate that the discipline program yielded reductions in student misbehavior, then that is an important contribution. Future research studies might examine the relative contribution of individual program components, which would add to our theoretical understanding of the problem.

We feel the researchers have identified a research question, developed and defended a problem of importance, and presented a rationale that, while lacking precision, does provide an argument in support of the researcher's plan. Additionally, the review of literature provided both a context for the study and support for the selection of program components and outcome variables.

The Operational Level. In this part of the study, the researcher attempts to transform or operationalize the variables in a way that allows the empirical examination of the research questions. We will examine the following topics: (1)

sampling, (2) measurement, (3) design and, (4) data analysis and apply each one to our featured study.

Sampling. The quality of a study's sampling procedures is important in assessing the external validity of a study. We have highlighted population, personalogical, ecological, and application validity in order to explore the issue of generalizability of the results of this study. Lynne and her colleagues are working in a specific setting within a particular context, and it matters a great deal to them if they can have confidence that the results of the study are relevant to their students and their setting.

While less than explicit in the article, it appears that all 8 of the middle schools in the district were involved in the study and, therefore, no sampling was involved. Data regarding the 6 treatment schools and the 2 comparison schools are provided in Table 1 (p. 267). The treatment schools varied from a 27% to a 97% minority population. An affluence index based on number of students receiving free lunch showed a wide range in SES family characteristics. Finally, the schools were located in urban, suburban, and mixed urban and suburban settings. Because sampling was not involved, there should be no problem extending the results to the district involved in the study (that is, there is no issue of population validity), but we will defer our judgment regarding the applicability of the results to Lynne Michael's school. However, the data provided in Table 1 (p. 267) will be helpful as she and the committee make a judgment about that.

Personological validity provides an opportunity to examine the differential effects, if any, of the treatment on different types of students. Because the data were analyzed by school, it was possible to examine the results of a particular school whose demographic characteristics matched up well with those of Adams Middle School. We will explore that possibility shortly as we examine the results of the study. It is also interesting to note that in the suggestions for further research the researchers call for future work to ". . . determine the relative effectiveness of approaches to behavior change that target individual students at elevated risk for behavior problems and those that alter the classroom and school environment to prevent misbehavior" (p. 287).

Ecological validity addresses the issue of the context in which the study was undertaken and the resources or other special arrangements made available for implementing a treatment. If, for example, a program was implemented with a reduced teacher-pupil ratio, then the reader should realize that the results might be difficult to replicate if these resources are lacking in the reader's home district. On the other hand, if the context of a particular study is carefully described and if those conditions are similar to those of the reader, concerns about ecological validity are eased. The authors of our study described the implementation of the treatment rather carefully (pp. 262–266) and provided detailed information about how each component was adopted (or, in some cases, adapted) by each school. The three-year, comprehensive intervention used available teaching and administrative staff and, other than providing specific training to implement the discipline program, there did not appear to be any special considerations provided that could not be replicated in the average school district.

Lynne and her committee were now ready to raise the important question of application validity as they thought about the relevance of the study for Adams Middle School. Lynne noted the careful description of the students involved. The range of student characteristics seemed to be somewhat greater than at Adams, but several of the treatment schools were similar to their own. In particular, because the data were analyzed separately for each school, they were able to examine the results from those schools most like Adams. Further, they were reassured by the adherence to typical staffing ratios and the attempt to implement this program across a wide range of schools and over a three year time period. The Gottfredson et al. study shared an ecology with Adams Middle School, which assured Lynne and her committee of increasing application validity. She and her colleagues felt reasonably confident that results could be applied to Adams. At a minimum, they felt comfortable considering its findings as they developed their own solutions.

Measures. In the Gottfredson et al. study, the researchers attempted to assess the impact of a program to reduce misbehavior and increase appropriate behavior of middle school students. It should be obvious that the entire study rests on a careful delineation of what constitutes the *program* and on how validly and reliably the researcher would be able to measure student behaviors.

The program components are described on pp. 262–263 of the article and the amount of article space devoted to that description is an indication of the importance of this matter. The reader needs to have sufficient details to understand what is being evaluated. A weakness of many program evaluation studies is that a vaguely defined program is tested and the results are reported. Even if the results are highly significant and practically important, they are of little help to the practitioner if the program that brought about these results cannot be replicated. For this reason Lynne appreciated the care Gottfredson and her colleagues had given to a description of the program and its components.

What about the dependent variables used in this study? Under the heading entitled *Measures* beginning on p. 267, the data sources and measures used for each dependent variable are described. In quantitative studies researchers need to provide measures of these variables and address their validity and reliability. The same care and concern that was given to the program description was also evidenced in the authors' discussion of outcome measures. The measure for each variable was described in sufficient detail to make an assessment of the content validity of the instrument. Additionally, the researchers provided information about the reliability and validity of several instruments in the footnotes and on one occasion referred the reader to a source that would provide additional information about the measures. While we cannot address each measure, we encourage you to reexamine the authors' discussion of them.

Design of the Study. All 8 public middle schools in one district served as the locus of the study; 6 schools were selected to implement the program while 2 schools were chosen as comparison or control schools. The authors described the study design as a ". . . nonequivalent control group design" (p. 266), which we would call a quasi-experimental design. This quasi-experimental design had an experimental treatment imposed on one or more intact groups (schools, in this case) and withheld from others. Students were not randomly assigned to treatment or control schools as they would be in a true experiment.

A great deal of power was lost when random assignment was not used to create experimental and control conditions. The possibility existed that, for a variety of reasons, the 6 treatment schools might have characteristics that would affect the study's outcomes. This is an inherent weakness of a quasi-experimental design.

Before we are unduly critical, however, we need to consider the realities faced by the researchers. Rather than ask, "Is this the perfect design?" we should ask, "Given the circumstances, is this the best available design to examine this problem?" While the researchers did not explicitly address the issue of alternatives, it appears clear that if the study was going to be done, it would have to be done within the real-world constraints of a public school district. These constraints include the existence of 8 middle schools, each having students assigned to it from the surrounding residential areas. The researchers were well aware of these student differences and made several attempts to compensate for the resulting threats to internal validity.

First, they selected 2 of the 8 schools to serve as comparison schools based on demographic information. Table 1 (p. 267) indicates the 2 comparison schools included the highest and lowest values on an affluence index, while the 6 treatment schools fell between those two on this measure. The selection of comparison schools that would be evenly matched to the treatment schools was an important and difficult task facing the researchers. By selecting the two schools representing the highest and lowest values on the affluence index to serve as comparisons with the 6 schools distributed in the middle of the index, the authors were attempting to even the playing field as much as possible. This does not solve the problem created by a lack of randomization, but it is an attempt to address the issue.

Second, and more importantly, the researchers collected pretest information on all 8 schools that could serve to statistically control for preexisting differences between treatment and comparison schools. Such statistical controls are frequently used in quasi-experimental, causal-comparative, and correlation studies. You should be familiar with their purpose. Basically, these controls adjust outcome measures (that is, dependent variables) to take into account preexisting differences on variables that might affect those outcomes. In the study at hand, for example, Gottfredson, et al. adjusted schools' scores on classroom order by using pretest scores to make it as if all schools began with the same level on that variable.

While this strategy is useful and very common, you should know that it also can introduce serious and unknown errors into the analysis. It is far less desirable than random assignment to treatments found in true experiments. Additionally, as the researchers indicate on p. 283, the possibility that schools in one condition may have been changing at different rates prior to the study is not compensated for completely by the use of statistical controls. As is often the case, the use of this method provides only a partial solution to a complex problem. However, if this step had not been taken, the reader would have less confidence that differences between treatment and comparison schools could be attributed to the discipline program being assessed. Given the choices available, we support their use of this approach to control for initial differences between and among schools.

A final difficulty added to the design problems faced by the researchers. They indicated the two comparison schools were exposed to some parts of the treatment. While not stated explicitly, the reason for collecting and sharing quarterly data with all 8 schools, and involving administrators of all 8 schools in feedback and planning sessions, may have been based on the political realities of the school district. Principals in comparison schools may have demanded access to discipline data and to planning sessions as a precondition for participating in the study. Clearly, this is speculation on our part, but it indicates the complexities faced by researchers who attempt to research problems within the constraints of a public school setting. The researchers are to be commended for sharing all aspects of the study that might have a bearing on the outcome.

In summary, the quasi-experimental design was an appropriate choice for conducting this study. Limitations due to the possibility of differences between experimental and comparison schools exist, but the researchers made appropriate efforts to acquaint the readers with the possible pitfalls. The researchers also tried to reduce the potential negative impact of these design flaws both through selection of comparison schools, which attempted to reduce differences, and through the use of pretest data to statistically control for them. Having said all that, the lack of randomization still hampers the clear attribution of outcomes to the treatment program.

The Empirical Level. We have termed the third and final section of a study its empirical level. It is here that authors present the results of their work and their conclusions based on those results. Clearly, the results of a study command our attention; they provide us with answers to the researcher's questions and represent the culmination of the entire project. In a similar way, conclusions are important because they may influence our decisions about practice and policy.

Study Results. The 6 treatment schools differed by level of implementation, which led the researchers to divide the schools into two groups of high and medium levels of implementation. These two treatment groups were then contrasted with the comparison schools to examine changes in program outcomes.

Statistically significant ($p < .01$) changes were reported from 1987 to 1989 on the program outcomes of classroom order, classroom organization, and rule clarity. (see Table 4, p. 278) We can have a reasonably high level of confidence that these differences are not likely to be due to chance, and we can now proceed to our next level of analysis. An examination of the right-hand column of Table 4 yields information about the practical significance of these differences. As practitioners, Lynne and her committee particularly noted the impressive effect sizes listed for these three variables for the high implementation schools. Those schools that came closest to a full implementation of the program showed an ES of .62 for classroom order, .53 for classroom organization, and .55 for role clarity. Changes in excess of one half of a standard deviation in the desired direction are certainly noteworthy. This assessment of practical significance will be of value later in our discussion of the cost-benefit analysis of the program.

Study Conclusions. The researchers drew cautious but clear conclusions as follows: "Results for the measures of disruptive behavior agree with the conclusion that the program had beneficial effects on student behavior when it was well implemented" (p. 283).

In their discussion of the results, the authors provided an excellent analysis of alternative hypotheses—one of the marks of a good piece of research. On page 283 they ask the crucial question that gets at the internal validity of the study: "Are beneficial outcomes related to actual implementation of program components?" In other words, granted that differences occurred that favored the treatment schools, are there other explanations for these differences than the hoped for treatment effects?

The researchers candidly addressed three separate alternative hypotheses that might have accounted for the differences found between the treatment and comparison schools. First, did the treatment program occur at the same time as some unknown event that occurred in the high-implementation schools that may have made the difference in the results? The reader may recognize this as the threat of history to internal validity, which needs to be considered when random assignment to treatment and control conditions has not been done. The researchers reject this alternative hypothesis on the grounds that no other major programs or changes coincided with the treatment program. While we have no reason to quarrel with the authors regarding their assertion, we would simply point out that it is an assertion. The best that researchers can do is what Gottfredson et al. have done; they have examined the available evidence for the alternative hypothesis and have rendered a judgment that it was not supported.

The authors conclude that they cannot definitely rule out two additional rival hypotheses. One of these suggests that the program may have interacted with preexisting conditions in such a way that the treatment effects were enhanced. For example, the readiness of the treatment school staffs for accepting the treatment conditions may have provided a context that enabled the treatment to be successful. The quasi-experimental design does not rule out this possibility. The second rival hypothesis suggests that the ". . . teachers and administrators in the high-implementation schools were on a steeper change trajectory to begin with, and their schools would have improved at a faster rate in the absence of a treatment" (p. 283). While attempts were made to statistically control for initial differences, these controls do not rule out this alternative hypothesis.

Perhaps an example would help. If you were concerned about controlling for initial differences in sprinters' speeds, you might handicap them according to their previous times in the event. For example, you might have the runners begin the race at different starting points. While this would certainly result in a closer race than if you had not controlled for initial differences, there still is a problem with this procedure. It is possible that the faster sprinters were improving more rapidly than the slower runners right up until race time, and that the former would still win despite the handicap you imposed. This is the point being made by the researchers regarding rival hypothesis three, and we commend the authors for their careful examination of it. While these considerations do not negate the primary research hypothesis that attributes reductions in student misbehavior to the discipline program, it should give us pause in asserting that the program caused those reductions. We must remain cautious that, in spite of our best efforts, there may be unknown factors contributing to the results of this study.

One puzzling outcome of their work was examined in depth by the researchers. Several outcome measures improved more in the comparison schools than in the medium implementation schools. On the face of it this appears to be very troubling: A no-treatment school was superior to the medium treatment schools. In many ways comparison school 8 had outcomes that matched those in the high implementation schools.

The researchers went to great pains to examine this issue by interviewing a total of 40 teachers, 10 high-performing teachers from each of the three High implementation schools and 10 high-performing teachers from comparison school 8. The results of the interviews indicated that the comparison school teachers had, in many ways, implemented components of the program very successfully with a minimum amount of training and support.

How did this happen? The comparison schools had been involved in the general planning and data sharing that went into the planning year. They also were involved in the quarterly meetings that continued throughout the three years of the program. Further, the comparison schools had been assured they would be high on the list to implement the program in the following year. Perhaps most importantly, the assistant principal of the comparison school had provided a two day discipline workshop during the first year of the program that incorporated some of the same components as the program being evaluated. The researchers summarized their post-hoc analysis as follows: "In summary, one of the low-implementation schools was clearly engaged in a major behavior management program, and the program resembled in many ways the program that was implemented in the high-implementation schools" (p. 286). It should be mentioned that the analysis conducted is somewhat suspect in that it was done after the fact to explore possible reasons for unexpected outcomes. Nevertheless, the effort expended by the researchers to explore those alternative interpretations of their results was appropriate.

This example also demonstrates the high degree of difficulty of undertaking a large comprehensive research study within the context of the public schools. One certainly cannot fault the principal and faculty of comparison school 8 for jumping the gun to implement the program, but this benign act did add to the complexities of interpreting the results of this applied research project.

You will recall that the effect sizes in the study were all at the .5 level or above and would be considered practically significant. The researchers examined the relative costs of implementing the discipline program by comparing it with other projects vying for district dollars and time. These comparisons appeared to justify their prudent and refreshingly candid conclusions, which were a welcome contrast to the unsubstantiated claims Lynne had encountered earlier in her search. Gottfredson et al. conclude: "The modest improvement in student behavior seems to have been obtained at a significant, but not unreasonable cost" (p. 287).

Note that, even in the best of studies, there are flaws inherent in all designs and practitioners should look for replications of studies wherever possible. It would be wise to contact the investigators involved in a study and get an update on their current efforts. Perhaps they have tested the program in another setting and have additional important insights. Perhaps they have modified the treatment program and these modifications have added to their understanding of the program's effectiveness. Further, it makes sense to contact the administrators in the schools involved to get their current views regarding a program's success. (Remember that by the time you read the report of a study in a research journal, two or more years may have elapsed since the study ended.) In any event, it is always wise to draw on as many data sources as possible when making an important implementation decision.

Action Steps

The authors' cautious conclusion could serve as the starting point for an action step for Lynne and her faculty. She knew better than to expect an explicit plan that could be transplanted into her school, watered once a week, and then ignored as discipline referrals dropped and serious offenses began to disappear.

What she had received was a reasonably clear answer to the first question regarding the efficacy of out-of-school suspensions as a deterrent to serious discipline infractions. At Adams Middle School they simply had to find a better solution to the increase in serious offenses, one that was more likely to address the root causes of student misbehavior.

Second, while not an easy task, the comprehensive program described and evaluated by Gottfredson et al. (1993) bore promise for Adams Middle School. The four components of the program included, (1) school discipline policy review and revision, (2) computerized behavior tracking, (3) improved classroom organization and management, and (4) positive reinforcement. These four steps provided a road map for an attack on the problem that Lynne was facing.

The committee met one last time to write up their suggestions for the fall faculty meeting. They knew that additional time would be required by the entire faculty to read and absorb summaries of the research they had read over the summer. Also, given the differences of opinion on the use of out-of-school suspensions, it would require time and active discussions to arrive at a decision that would unite rather than divide the faculty.

Another decision reached by the committee was to attempt a carefully sequenced attack on the overall discipline environment of the school much as they had seen in the Gottfredson et al. (1993) study. They wanted to take the

---

Memorandum

School Discipline Committee Recommendations for Action

1. **Review** and **revise** the school discipline policy. The focus of this review would be to increase clarity and consistency and to design rewards for positive behavior as well as enforceable punishments for misbehavior.
2. **Communicate** the discipline policy to every student and every parent through a series of instructional steps that include large and small group student discussions, large and small group parent discussions, and parent-teacher conferences. Additionally, an attractive brochure would be developed and its contents placed on a newly developed web page for Adams Middle School.
3. **Modify** and **improve** the database for tracking student behavior referrals. Careful attention should be given to the limitations in the current system that prevent teachers and administrators from using the available data to make better informed decisions.
4. **Test** the revised behavioral tracking system for one month during the current year to examine the frequency and intensity of referrals and to examine variables that relate to referral data. The Freiberg, Stein, and Parker (1995) study of one middle school could serve as a model for examining similar data at Adams. As part of the data-gathering process, the studies bearing on the efficacy of various form of suspensions will be examined by the faculty involved.
5. **Contact** Gottfredson and her colleagues to discuss details of the discipline program and its current implementation status. Perhaps a visit could be set up with a school currently using the program, and/or one of the researchers might become involved as a consultant to Adams Middle School.
6. **Select**, **modify**, and **implement** a comprehensive classroom organization and management program based upon the outcomes of steps 1–5.

F I G U R E *8.1* Memorandum

entire next year to plan and develop a discipline program that would involve teachers, administrators, and parents in a comprehensive approach.

To accomplish their goals, they established the action steps (see Figure 8.1) for discussion at the fall faculty meeting.

Clearly, Lynne and her committee had described a full year's worth of hard work in planning to be followed by a couple of more years of equally hard work in implementing the plan. The problem had been at least three years in developing and the solution to the problem could hardly be expected to take less than that. They were committed to take the steps necessary to make a difference in the learning environment of Adams Middle School.

References

Baker, A. (1996). Major disciplinary violations in a junior high school: An exploratory study. *Research in Middle Level Education Quarterly, 19*(3), 1–20.

Bear, G. G. (1998). School discipline in the United States: Prevention, correction, and long-term development. *School Psychology Review, 27*(1), 14–32.

Bear, G. G., Richards, H. D., & Gibbs, J. C. (1997). Sociomoral reasoning and behavior. In G. G. Bear, K. M. Minke, & A. Thomas (Eds.), *Children's needs II: Development, problems, and alternatives* (pp. 13–25). Bethesda, MD: National Association of School Psychologists.

Blyth, D. A., Simmons, R G., & Carleton-Ford, S. (1983). The adjustments of early adolescents to school transitions. *Journal of Early Adolescence, 3*(1, 2), 105–120.

Bracht, G. H., and Glass, G. V. (1968). The external validity of experiments. *American Educational Research Journal, 5*, 437–474.

Brantlinger, E. (1991). Social class distinctions in adolescents' reports of problems and punishment in school. *Behavioral Disorders, 17*, 2–10.

Brodie, F. M. (1974). *Thomas Jefferson: An intimate history.* New York: Bantam.

Costenbader, V. K. & Markson, S. (1994). School suspensions: A survey of current policies and practices. *NAASP Bulletin, 78*, 103–107.

Davis, J. E., & Jordan, W. J. (1995). The effects of school context, structure, and experiences on African American males in middle and high school. *Journal of Negro Education, 63*(4), 570–587.

Eisenberg, N., & Harris, J. D. (1997). Prosocial behavior. In G. G. Bear, K. M. Minke, & A. Thomas (Eds.). *Children's needs II: Development, problems, and alternatives* (pp. 1–11). Bethesda, MD: National Association of School Psychologists.

Elam, S. M., Rose, L. C., & Gallup, A. M. (1996). The 28th annual Phi Delta Kappa/Gallup poll of the public's attitude toward the public schools. *Phi Delta Kappan, 78*(1), 41–59.

Freiberg, H. J., Stein, T. A., & Parker, G. (1995). Discipline referrals in an urban middle school: Implications for discipline and instruction. *Education and Urban Society, 27*(4), 421–440.

Gottfredson, D. C., Gottfredson, G. D., & Hybl, L. G. (1993). Managing adolescent behavior: A multiyear, multischool study. *American Educational Research Journal, 30*(1), 179–215.

Lochman, J. E., Dunn, S. E., & Klimes-Dougan, B. (1993). An intervention and consultation model from a social cognitive perspective: A description of the anger coping program. *School Psychology Review, 22*, 458–496.

Kazdin, A. E. (1983). *Conduct disorders in childhood and adolescence.* Newbury Park, CA: Sage.

Martens, B. K., & Meller, P. J. (1990). The application of behavioral principles to educational settings. In T. G. Gutkin & C. R. Reynolds (Eds.), *Handbook of school psychology* (pp. 612–634). New York: Wiley.

Peng, S. S., Fetters, W. B., & Kolstad, A. J. (1981). *High school and beyond: A national longitudinal study for the 1980's.* Washington, DC: National Center for Educational Statistics.

Pisarra, J., & Giblette, J. F. (1981). Administrators' perceptions of aggressive behavior. *NAASP Bulletin,* 49–53.

Rose, L. C., Gallup, A. M., & Elam, S. M. (1997). The 29th annual Phi Delta/Gallup poll of the public's attitude toward the public schools. *Phi Delta Kappan, 79*(1), 41–56.

Selman, R. L., & Schultz, L. H. (1990). *Making a friend in youth: Developmental theory and pair therapy.* Chicago: The University of Chicago Press.

Skiba, R. J., Peterson, R. L., & Williams, T. (1997). Office referrals and suspensions: Disciplinary intervention in middle schools. *Education and Treatment of Children, 20*(3), 295–315.

Stattin, H., & Magnusson, D. (1989). The role of early aggressive behavior in the frequency, seriousness, and types of later crime. *Journal of Consulting and Clinical Psychology, 57*(6), 710–718.

Tobin, T., Sugai, G., & Colvin, G. (1996). Patterns in middle school discipline records. *Journal of Emotional and Behavioral Disorders, 4*(2), 82–94.

Uchitelle, S., Bartz, D., & Hillman, L. (1989). Strategies for reducing suspensions. *Urban Education, 24*, 163–176.

Walker, H. M., Colvin, G., & Ramsey, E. (1995). *Antisocial behavior in school: Strategies and best practices.* Pacific Grove, CA: Brooks/Cole.

Wehlage, G. G., & Rutter, R. A. (1986). Dropping out: How much do schools contribute to the problem? *Teachers College Record, 87*, 374–393.

Wu, S. C., Pink, W. T., Crain, R., & Moles, O. (1982). Student suspensions: A critical reappraisal. *The Urban Review, 14*(4), 245–303.

APPENDIX

Managing Adolescent Behavior
A Multiyear, Multischool Study

Denise C. Gottfredson
Gary D. Gottfredson and Lois G. Hybl

A 3-year study in eight middle schools tested a program to improve adolescent conduct. The program sought to increase clarity of school rules and consistency of rule enforcement, improve classroom organization and management, increase the frequency of communication with the home regarding student behavior, and increase reinforcement of appropriate behavior. An organization development approach provided a context to achieve strong implementation by increasing communication, collaboration, and planning at the school level. The strength and fidelity of implementation differed across schools. In schools in which the program was well-implemented student conduct improved significantly.

Disruptive behavior in school harms both the misbehaving individual and the school community. Students who misbehave also drop out of school, use drugs and alcohol, and engage in delinquent behavior at higher rates than do their more conforming peers. Later, they tend to make poorer occupational and marital adjustments (Bachman, Green, & Wirtanen, 1971; Jessor & Jessor, 1977; Robins, 1966; Wolfgang, Figlio, & Sellin, 1972). These predictable outcomes reflect a stable pattern of antisocial behavior for some individuals, but they also suggest that school misconduct may play a part in producing negative outcomes. Suspension, a common response to school misconduct, limits students' opportunities to learn. Teachers may lower their expectations for troublesome students and limit these students' opportunities for learning by asking fewer questions, for example. Conventional peers may avoid misbehaving students, pushing them toward more deviant peer groups.

Student misbehavior also has negative consequences for the school community. In a recent national survey of public school teachers, 11% of urban teachers mentioned fear of student reprisal as a major limitation on their ability to maintain order, 29% said they seriously considered leaving teaching because of student misbehavior

This article was originally published in *American Educational Research Journal,* Spring 1993, Vol. 30, No. 1, pp. 179–215.

Denise C. Gottfredson is an associate professor at the Institute of Criminal Justice and Criminology at the University of Maryland at College Park, College Park, MD 20742. Her specializations are delinquency, prevention, and evaluations.

Gary D. Gottfredson is a Principal Research Scientist at the Center for Social Organization of Schools at the Johns Hopkins University, 3505 N. Charles St., Baltimore, MD 21218. His specializations are measurement and education.

Lois G. Hybl is a research assistant at the Center for Social Organization of Schools at the Johns Hopkins University. 3505 N. Charles St., Baltimore, MD 21218. Her specialization is education.

problems, and more than 33% of teachers reported that student misbehavior interfered with their teaching (National Center for Education Statistics, 1986). The consequences of fear—teacher withdrawal, nonparticipation, alienation, and high turnover rates—coupled with erosion of the learning environment (reductions in engaged learning time, and frustration for teachers and students) are among the costs of student misconduct.

In this article we review what is known about the nature and causes of student misbehavior, describe a middle-school program designed to reduce misbehavior, and report the results of a 3-year study to assess the program's effect in six middle schools.

Nature of Disruptive Behavior

Behavior that results in disciplinary actions at school is best viewed as one facet of adolescent problem behavior (Jessor & Jessor, 1977). Students who lie and cheat in school also lie and cheat at home and in the community. Students who steal and fight in school are also often charged with criminal offenses by the police. These same students frequently become involved with drugs. Adolescent misconduct is usually not specialized.

Unsocialized behavior is common among adolescents (Williams & Gold, 1972). In a national sample of adolescents, 21% reported destroying others' property and 10% reported carrying a concealed weapon sometime in the last year (Elliott, Ageton, & Huizinga, 1979). In a survey of junior and senior high school students, 50% of the boys admitted hitting or threatening to hit another student (G. D. Gottfredson, 1987). But the conception of student misconduct as common must be tempered with the knowledge that there is substantial variation among individuals in the seriousness and frequency of problem behaviors. Several studies have demonstrated that more than half of the officially-recorded crimes are due to a relatively small percentage of individuals (six to seven percent; Shannon, 1982; Wolfgang, Figlio, & Sellin, 1972). The distribution of disciplinary referrals across individuals in secondary schools is also lopsided. In one of the middle schools included in this study, 10% of the students in the school were responsible for 45% of the office referrals during one school year.

Causes of Disruptive Behavior

Misbehavior in school has both individual and environmental determinants. Some environmental characteristics raise the probability of disorderly behavior in the environment and some personal characteristics make it more likely that a particular individual will misbehave.

Individual-level Correlates. Misbehaving students are more likely to be male than female (Kazdin, 1987). Misbehaving youths display less academic competence, have limited career and educational objectives, dislike school, have more delinquent friends, and have lower levels of belief in conventional social rules than do their more conforming peers (G. D. Gottfredson, 1987; Hirschi, 1969). They tend to display poor interpersonal relations and are often rejected by peers because of their aggression and poor social skills (Coie, 1990). They are less likely to defer to adult authority and be polite in their interactions with adults, and they are deficient in problem-solving skills such as identifying alternative solutions to problems and taking the perspective of others (Kazdin, 1987).

Studies that have followed individuals from preschool and first grade through adolescence show that teachers' ratings of classroom disturbance, impatience, disrespect, and defiance (Kellam & Brown, 1982) and "ego under-control" (inability to defer gratification, emotionality, being easily irritated and angered: Block, Block, & Keyes, 1988) predict misbehavior and psychological problems during adolescence. In short, much disorderly behavior in schools apparently reflects troubling but stable characteristics of certain individuals.

Classroom-level Correlates. Classroom organization and management practices also influence behavior. Disorderly behavior occurs more frequently in the absence of clearly defined classroom activities that constrain and structure student behavior (Doyle, 1986). The type of activity, physical characteristics of the setting, and level of familiarity of the student work also affect the level of disorder a classroom experiences. For example, behavior during teacher-led small group discussions is generally more orderly than behavior during independent seat work. Loosely structured lessons, open-space physical arrangements, and high levels of student choice and mobility provide greater opportunity for disorderly behavior to occur. Routine tasks such as spelling tests and worksheets are associated with less disorder than are more complex tasks such as word problems and essays. Perhaps in the typical classroom complex tasks decrease familiarity with work, leading to off-task behavior and greater opportunity for disorderly behavior.

Evertson and Emmer (1982) highlighted the importance of teachers' organizational practices in maintaining order. Their observations of effective and ineffective classroom teachers revealed differences in the clarity of communication, styles of monitoring and responding to student behavior, extent of student responsibility and accountability for work, and methods of organizing instruction.

School-level Correlates. Disorderly schools tend to be characterized by (a) teachers with punitive attitudes; (b) rules that are not perceived as fair and clear and are not firmly enforced; (c) ambiguous responses to student misbehavior; (d) disagreement among teachers and administrators about rules and appropriate response to misbehavior; (e) students with low levels of belief in conventional social rules; and (f) a lack of resources needed for teaching (G. D. Gottfredson & D. C. Gottfredson, 1985). School orderliness is related to the presence of a clear focus on appropriate student behavior; clear expectations for behavior; much communication about the rules, sanctions, and procedures to be used; formal discipline codes and classroom management plans; and expressed concern for students as individuals (Duke, 1989).

In summary, research implies that misbehavior in school has determinants at three levels: (a) Some individuals are more likely than others to misbehave; (b) Some teachers are more likely than others to produce higher levels of misconduct in their classrooms by their management and organization practices; and (c) Some schools more often than others fail to control student behavior. Behavior change programs that reduce risk for misbehavior at all three of these levels are most likely to be effective.

The Program

The program described in this article included school-, classroom-, and individual-level interventions aimed at reducing the misbehavior of middle school students.

Context

The program was implemented in the Charleston County School District (CCSD) between fall, 1986, and spring, 1989. The educational and political climate in 1986 reflected a "get tough" approach to education. Like many urban school districts during the 1980s, standards for promotion from grade to grade were increased as part of a state-wide educational reform. Increased standards immediately increased student grade retention rates and resulted in an accumulation of "overaged" students in Charleston's middle schools. The percentage of CCSD's eighth-grade students who were at least one year behind grade level increased from 34% in 1983 to 48% in 1988. As the age of the population increased apparently so also did levels of student disattachment and misconduct. The discipline program described in this paper was an attempt to cope with a crisis of student misconduct that was produced by the accumulation in the middle schools of large numbers of students with diminished investment in education.

The Problem

The suspension rate in the CCSD middle schools rose from 41 to 100 suspensions per hundred students between 1981 and 1986, the year this project began. This high overall rate masked large differences from school to school. For example, during the 1986–87 school year two middle schools with similar student populations had rates of 2 and 100 suspensions per hundred students.

High rates of out-of-school suspension translate into many lost instructional days. Data from the 1987–88 school year in the six intervention schools showed that 2,042 suspensions resulted in approximately 3,850 student-instructional days lost to out-of-school suspension. In-school suspensions increased the number of lost instructional days to 7,932 during the same school year. Evidence from the Effective School Battery (ESB; G. D. Gottfredson, 1984b) student survey, which was administered to all middle school students during the baseline year of the study, also indicated high levels of suspension and other forms of punishment for misbehavior. Each of the eight schools surveyed scored higher than the average score for schools included in the norming sample for this battery (mostly urban secondary schools in the U.S.) on a measure that asked students to report the frequency of punishment received in school. Only one of the eight Charleston schools scored within one standard deviation of the mean, four were more than two standard deviations above the mean, and two were at the 99th percentile.

Program Components

The program, designed in collaboration with educational administrators and teachers, is described in the following paragraphs.

School Discipline Policy Review and Revision. The first component of the program revised the discipline policy to increase rule clarity, specify the consequences for specific infractions, and achieve consistency in school-wide and individual classroom policies. Revised discipline policies provided for systematically *rewarding* desired student behavior as well as punishing misbehavior.

Behavior Tracking System. Programs that involve parents in providing consequences in the home for student behavior in school have proven effective for reducing undesirable behavior. Home-based reinforcement programs (Atkeson & Forehand, 1979; Barth, 1979; Bailey, Wolf, & Phillips, 1970), which encourage parents to provide rein-forcers in response to positive school behavior, are effective for increasing desirable behavior. One element of home-based reinforcement involves frequent communica-tion between the school and the home to inform the parents about the students' behavior, an activity that many schools find difficult to accomplish systematically and frequently. An objective of the program was therefore to increase the frequency of communication with parents about student behavior in school and to ensure that parents learn about positive as well as negative behavior.

A computerized Behavior Tracking System (BTS) stored information about every positive and negative referral to the office. It was used to record referral infor-mation, generate letters to the home regarding positive and negative referrals to the office and about disciplinary actions taken, and generate reports for managing school discipline (e.g., detention lists, lists of students and teachers with more than a specified number of referrals, summary reports of suspension). The system was developed to promote consistency in rule enforcement by reminding the administra-tor of the disciplinary responses allowable for each offense, according to the school's discipline code.

Classroom Organization and Management. This third program component was designed to replicate as closely as possible the intervention developed by Texas researchers Emmer, Everton, Sanford, Clements, and Worsham (1984), who demon-strated a reduction in classroom disorder using a teacher training intervention focus-ing on classroom organization and management. The Emmer et al. materials were used, and two of the Texas researchers provided the training. The Texas system of classroom observations for monitoring implementation of classroom practices was adapted for use in the present program.

Positive Reinforcement. Research (summarized by D. C. Gottfredson, Karweit, & G. D. Gottfredson, 1989) supports the efficacy of a variety of behavioral strategies for reducing misbehavior. The fourth component of the behavior management program was based on the assumption that misbehavior results in part because the environ-ment reinforces undesirable behaviors and fails to reinforce desirable behaviors. It was designed to help educators structure the school environment so that (a) expec-tations for student behavior were understood by students and staff, (b) consequences for misbehavior were understood by students and staff, (c) misbehavior was responded to consistently and in accordance with well-communicated rules and con-sequences, and (d) desirable behavior was reinforced. A teacher's manual was devel-oped and used in conjunction with a practical book on modifying classroom behavior (Buckley & Walker, 1978). Teachers were taught to incorporate these behavioral practices into their instruction. During the second year of the program, students who were identified as at especially high risk for behavior problems were targeted for special assistance using behavioral techniques.

Method and Implementation

Field research often fails because the intended interventions are not implemented as anticipated. A simplified form of the Program Development Evaluation (PDE) method (G. D. Gottfredson, 1984a; G. D. Gottfredson, Rickert, D. C. Gottfredson, & Advani, 1984) was used to increase the strength of implementation of the interventions.

Specifically, we sought to (a) ensure that the goals and objectives of the project, its theoretical rationale, and the performance standards for each component were clearly understood; (b) provide timely feedback about the extent to which goals, objectives, and performance standards were being met; (c) assess organizational obstacles to strong implementation and develop plans to overcome them; and (d) clearly delineate each person's responsibilities.

School Improvement Teams. During the planning year for the project, the principal in each school appointed a team of teachers and administrators to prepare the school for the program that would begin the next fall. Two team members from each program school became members of a multischool team with responsibility for specifying concrete performance standards for each program component, and working with their individual teams to modify the standards as appropriate for their schools. The school teams reviewed and revised their school discipline policies, oriented their faculties to the program, developed strategies for school-wide implementation of the new practices, and recruited 6 to 10 additional classroom teachers to join the school improvement teams and to become part of a staff development effort in the schools. Team members attended a training workshop to learn about the classroom organization and management and behavior change strategies. They then organized and carried out staff development workshops covering these strategies for teachers in their schools, monitored implementation of the new strategies in their colleagues' classrooms, and provided constructive feedback and ongoing technical support to their colleagues as they implemented the new practices. Two members of each school team attended quarterly meetings throughout the duration of the project to share their experiences with team members from other schools, receive formal feedback, and identify and solve problems. The team members were given the option of receiving a small stipend ($100) or graduate credit through a local college.

Some schools elected to rotate different faculty members onto the team in the second implementation year. The renewed teams received the same training at the beginning of the second program year that the original team members received.

Information Feedback. Frequent feedback was used as a mechanism to foster implementation. Feedback to individual teachers occurred informally when team members provided assistance and suggestions about ways to improve classroom practices. Teachers also received individualized feedback twice each year from student and teacher Classroom Environment Assessments (CEA; to be described later), and they received feedback about their disciplinary referrals at the discretion of the assistant principal or principal.

During the first implementation year, all teachers completed logs to record which behavior change strategies they used with their students and classes. These logs were used by team members to monitor teacher use of the new strategies.

School averages on measures of classroom environment were reported to the school teams four times per year, and results from a comprehensive school assessment battery (the ESB; G. D. Gottfredson, 1984b) were presented to the administrators of the participating schools annually.

Disciplinary incidents, punishments, and rewards were recorded in the computerized BTS. School teams received quarterly reports on the number and nature of disciplinary incidents and days lost to suspension for each quarter compared with the same quarter from previous years. The BTS also provided schools with the capability to generate on-the-spot summaries of referrals by teacher or student.

When the program was well implemented, the components were blended together by the school team to create an integrated discipline management system for the school. The program took on a different character in each school as the teams molded it to fit their local environments. Each team created a student handbook describing school rules and consequences for them, but in the best schools the handbooks also discussed a system of rewards for appropriate behavior (e.g., "student of the month" contest, or a system by which students who performed good deeds would receive a certificate that they could deposit in a box from which a weekly prize-winner would be drawn). The best schools used the computerized behavior management system not only to monitor misbehavior but also to generate reports for team use in its role as facilitator for other teachers (such as lists by teacher of all referrals made to the office during a certain time period) and to generate letters to inform parents of positive teacher referrals. Teachers in these schools participated voluntarily in the positive referral program by informing the office of instances of desirable or improved student behavior.

The classroom organization and management component was facilitated by the school team in the schools with the strongest implementation. The team organized refresher training sessions and divided the faculty into smaller teams for reinforcement and technical assistance. Team members also used the planning periods to observe the classrooms of other teachers and to provide feedback on organization and management skills. This arrangement worked particularly well in schools that folded the school team duties into the existing organizational structure by, for example, asking department chairs or master teachers to be team members.

The positive reinforcement component seemed particularly amenable to creative adaptation by the school team. Each team developed its own system of reinforcers. In one school, high-risk youths were assigned to volunteer teachers who monitored the students' behavior by having the student carry a "report card" from class to class, having each teacher rate the child on the target behavior. The designated teacher saw the student daily and provided some type of reinforcer (generally of a social nature) at the end of each successful day. A more substantial reward (e.g., pizza party) was provided at the end of each successful week. In a school in which the program was well implemented, one might observe bulletin boards with pictures of successful students, see students purchasing supplies at the school store with tokens they had earned for good behavior, listen to PA system announcements recognizing student achievements, hear much praise in the classroom, and encounter many special events such as Friday parties.

To summarize, the program had four components: (a) school discipline policy review and revision, (b) computerized behavior tracking, (c) improved classroom organization and management, and (d) positive reinforcement. All interventions were aimed ultimately at decreasing student misbehavior and increasing appropriate behavior in school by (a) decreasing punitive measures taken in response to misbehavior and increasing positive reinforcement of appropriate behavior; (b) increasing clarity of expectations for student behavior and student perceptions of the fairness of the rules governing their behavior; (c) increasing consistent following-through in response to student behavior both in school and at home; and (d) improving classroom organization and management. All four components were expected to affect each of these intermediate outcomes.

We were driven in the design of the program by a belief that a systematic, integrated approach to discipline management that provided a mix of activities that targeted the entire school, classrooms within the school, and individuals within the school would be most beneficial. We expected that the interventions would work in concert with one another, producing a larger effect on student behavior than would have been possible had we targeted only individual-level factors that place a student at elevated risk for misbehavior, only classroom-level factors, or only school-level factors. The components for this integrated approach were selected because they had withstood evaluation scrutiny and were linked directly to several of the determinants of misbehavior identified in prior research (summarized earlier). The study was designed to assess the total effect of the system. It is incapable of assessing the independent effect of any piece of the system, and it is incapable of assessing how one program component may have facilitated another. These questions must be left for future research.

The "technological" components were implemented in the context of limited organization development activity aimed at increasing school staff commitment to and ownership of the program and providing school staff with the information, planning, and management skills needed to implement the program.

Method

Design

This study used a nonequivalent control group design. This design provided for a comparison of before-and-after differences for groups receiving and not receiving the program. The before-and-after measurement allows the researcher to establish temporal precedence of the independent to the dependent variables, which is not possible with a posttest only comparison group design or a survey research design. The pretest and the use of a comparison group allow the researcher to measure and statistically control for preexisting differences between the treatment and comparison group, thus helping to rule out selection threats to internal validity.

The design had its drawbacks, the most important of which was the "selection by maturation" threat to internal validity. In the presence of this threat, the research cannot definitely attribute a greater amount of change in one experimental condition to the treatment because the units (in this case, schools) in one condition may have been changing at different rates to begin with, and hence the same result might have been obtained in the absence of any treatment.

Cook and Campbell (1979) point out that the often-used nonequivalent comparison group design is interpretable in most cases.

Subjects

The subjects were all staff and students in eight public middle schools in Charleston, South Carolina. Principals in the eight schools selected by central administrators agreed to participate, and then the researchers designated two of the eight schools as comparison schools. This assignment was made primarily on the basis of demographics in an attempt to ensure that the comparison group was as diverse as the treatment group.

The two comparison schools were exposed to some parts of the treatment. The same data (except for data on quarterly referrals generated by the BTS system) were collected and fed back to the administration. The assistant principals participated in quarterly feedback and planning sessions with the treatment schools. In these schools

TABLE *1*

Selected Characteristics of the Participating Schools

School Number	Total Enrollment	Percentage White	Affluence Index[a]	Location[b]
Treatment				
1	554	73	1.38	S
2	944	51	1.87	M
3	460	3	2.51	U
4	724	49	2.26	M
5	781	36	2.07	M
6	1050	50	1.65	S
Comparison				
7	490	70	1.35	S
8	716	0	2.69	U

[a]Affluence index is scored "1" if student does not receive free or reduced lunch cost, "2" for reduced lunch cost, and "3" for free lunch. Index is based on all students Grades 6 and 8 in Spring, 1987. [b]S = suburban; M = mixed (urban and suburban); U = urban.

teams were not formed, and teachers received no training in the behavior and classroom management strategies, although the administrators had access to all program materials.

Table 1 shows some characteristics of the eight schools as we found them in 1986. All schools served Grades 6 through 8. The schools range from majority white to majority black and from small to medium in size, and they served diverse communities.

Measures

Several different data sources and measures were used to assess the level of implementation of the program components, the intermediate outcomes of each intervention, and the ultimate program outcomes. Table 2 summarizes them. A complete description of the measures appears in D. C. Gottfredson, G. D. Gottfredson, and Hybl (1990). Each data source is briefly described below:

Classroom Environment Surveys. A brief Classroom Environment Assessment (CEA) instrument was administered to all teachers and students in all classes (except physical education classes and classes for visually and hearing-impaired students) at the end of each of the 12 academic quarters during which the program was being planned or in operation. The percentage of the eligible classes that turned in completed student and teacher surveys was high each quarter, ranging from 79% to 100% for any school in any given year. The average response rates for classrooms in the treatment schools for 1987, 1988, and 1989 were 93%, 84%, and 100%. For comparison schools the same percentages were 87%, 92%, and 100%. Nonresponse was mostly a result of administrator error.

Several items from the Classroom Environment Scale (Moos & Trickett, 1987) were combined with items we generated. Factor analysis guided the formation of one scale from the teacher questionnaire (Classroom Order) and four scales from the student questionnaire (Classroom Order, Order and Organization, Rule Clarity, and Teacher Support).

These scales are *classroom-level* scales intended to measure changes in classroom environment. The student survey scales are formed for each classroom by averaging the classroom means for each of the items. Factor analysis and reliability assessments used classroom averages for all classrooms included in one quarterly assessment.

The Classroom Order scales measure changes in classroom orderliness, a desired outcome of all program components. The Order and Organization and Rule Clarity scales measure primarily the effect of the classroom organization and management intervention. Although increasing teacher support was not an objective of the program, items to measure it were included because previous experience with programs that sought to increase rule clarity and consistency of rule enforcement suggested that an unintended side effect of such programs might be a decline in students' perceptions of teacher support.

Teacher Ratings. Teachers whose classrooms were included in each quarterly survey were asked to rate how often each student in the selected class "attends to academic work (i.e., pays attention, does homework, participates in class, completes classroom assignments, is cooperative, and is motivated to learn)" and "disrupts the classroom (i.e., leaves seat, makes disruptive noises, speaks without permission, talks back to the teacher, fights or argues with other students, and comes late to class)." The teacher ratings for each student were averaged for all four quarters so that each student's score is based on one (12%), or the average of two (16%), three (31%), or four (41%) different ratings in each year. Variation in the number of ratings averaged to form each student's score resulted from in- and out-migration and from excluding physical education and certain handicapped classrooms from the sample. These ratings are intended to measure student classroom conduct, a major outcome targeted by all components of the program.

Effective School Battery. The Effective School Battery (ESB; G. D. Gottfredson, 1984b) student questionnaire was administered each Spring during the 3-year project. All students in the eight schools were included in the administration. The response rates ranged from 87% to 100%. The average response rates for the treatment schools for the 3 years were 93%, 90%, and 87%. For the comparison schools these averages were 93%, 96%, and 91%.

Several ESB measures were used in this study.[1] The Rebellious Behavior scale asked students to report how often they engaged in a variety of misbehavior ranging in seriousness from coming late to class to trying to hurt other people. The School Rewards and Avoidance of Punishment[2] scales measured student perceptions of the level of positive reinforcement and asked them to report how often they were punished in school because of misbehavior. These scales were scored at the student level.

Student ESB reports of Clarity of Rules, Respect for Students, and Fairness of Rules were expected to capture the efforts of all program components. Schools that made a successful transition from a primarily punitive disciplinary system to one that emphasized fairness, consistency, and respectful treatment of students were expected to improve over time on these climate measures. These measures were scored only at the school level.

Teacher Survey. A teacher survey was administered to all teachers in the eight participating schools at the end of the program. The response rates for this survey were 95% for the treatment and 94% for the comparison schools. Teachers were asked to rate the effectiveness of the school team in five different areas, to provide a global rating of the program, to report how often they used the positive reinforcement strategies in their classes, sent positive and negative communications to the home, and used the preventive management techniques included in the organization and management component. They were also asked to report on their level of use of the program materials.

School Discipline Records. The BTS provided records of referrals to the office for positive and negative behaviors. These records were used to measure the level of implementation of the positive referral system. Examination of quarterly reports of suspensions and disciplinary referrals from the BTS revealed that these measures reflect primarily administrator discipline style. Five of the six program schools experienced at least one administrator change during the project period. The suspension and disciplinary referral rates changed dramatically with these shifts, rendering them useless as measures of student behavior.

Analysis Strategy

Outcome Measures. Changes in school means from the 1986–87 school year (the year during which plans were made and baseline data collected) to the 1988–89 school year were examined for all outcomes. Changes were reported separately and compared for comparison ("low implementation") and treatment schools and for treatment schools that implemented the program with high and medium levels of fidelity to the implementation standards. Multiple measures were collected at different levels of aggregation. Table 2 summarizes the levels of measurement and analysis for each measure, and shows which statistics were used to test the significance of the change.

In most cases, data were analyzed at the lowest level of aggregation at which they were collected. For classroom and school climate measures, student and teacher measures were averaged to form reliable measures of climate. Individual variation around the group mean is regarded as error in the measurement of classroom and school climate.

We used *t*-tests for comparing average student and teacher scores over time. For school climate score comparisons we used the standard errors of measurement for each climate scale provided in the ESB user's manual to form a confidence interval around the Time 1 to Time 2 climate score difference. Hence, for the school climate measures, statistical significance was calculated using the distribution from the norming sample for the ESB rather than the distribution of schools included in this study.

Effect sizes are reported for all outcome measures. For individual-level measures, these are the differences between the 1988–89 and 1986–87. Score divided by the standard deviations for the 1986–87 score. For school climate measures, the standard deviation reported in the user's manual is used in the denominator.

TABLE 2

Summary of Measures and Analysis Strategy

Name of Measure	Number of Items	Alpha Reliability	Source	Level of Measurement	Level of Analysis	Comparisons	Statistics
Measures of student misbehavior (ultimate outcome)							
Rebellious Behavior (1–5; 1 = never, 5 = always)	19	.94	Effective School Battery (ESB) Student Questionnaire	Student	Student	Change over time, by level of implementation	t-tests within each level of implementation
Attends to work (1–5; 1 = almost never, 5 = almost always)	1	–	Teacher rating	Student	Student	Change over time, by level of implementation	t-tests within each level of implementation
Disrupts classroom (1–5; 1 = almost never, 5 = almost always)	1	–	Teacher rating	Student	Student	Change over time, by level of implementation	t-tests within each level of implementation
Classroom Order, Student (1–5); 1 = never 5 = almost always)	14	.96	Classroom Environment Assessment (CEA) Student Questionnaire	Student	Teacher	Change over time in teacher averages, by level of implementation	t-tests within each level of implementation
Classroom Order, Teacher (1–5; 1 = never, 5 = almost always)	16	.94	CEA Teacher Questionnaire	Teacher	Teacher	Change over time in teacher averages, by level of implementation	t-tests within each level of implementation

Table 2 continued on page 271

Name of Measure	Number of Items	Alpha Reliability	Source	Level of		Comparisons	Statistics
				Measurement	Analysis		
Measures of intermediate outcomes							
School characteristics							
Clarity of Rules (0, 1)	4	.67	ESB	Student	School	Change over time, by level of implementation	Time 1 to Time 2 difference relative to standard error of measurement
Fairness of Rules (0, 1)	3	.76	ESB	Student	School	Change over time, by level of implementation	Time 1 to Time 2 difference relative to standard error of measurement
Respect for Students (0–2)	3	.85	ESB	Student	School	Change over time, by level of implementation	Time 1 to Time 2 difference relative to standard error of measurement

Table 2 continued on page 272

Table 2 continued

| Name of Measure | Number of Items | Alpha Reliability | Source | Level of | | Comparisons | Statistics |
				Measurement	Analysis		
Classroom characteristics							
Order and Organization (1, 2); 1 = False or mostly false, 2 = True or mostly true)	5	.89	Student CEA	Student	Teacher	Change over time in teacher averages, by level of implementation	t-tests within each level of implementation
Rule Clarity (1, 2; 1 = False or mostly false, 2 = True or mostly true)	3	.80	Student CEA	Student	Teacher	Change over time in teacher averages, by level of implementation	t-tests within each level of implementation
Teacher Support (1, 2; 1 = False or mostly false, 2 = True or mostly true)	3	.82	Student CEA	Student	Teacher	Change over time in teacher averages, by level of implementation	t-tests within each level of implementation
Student characteristics/experiences							
Rewards (0, 1)	4	.56	ESB	Student	Student	Change over time, by level of implementation	t-tests within each level of implementation
Avoidance of Punishment (0, 1)	4	.54	ESB	Student	Student	Change over time, by level of implementation	t-tests within each level of implementation

Table 2 continued on page 273

Name of Measure	Number of Items	Alpha Reliability	Source	Level of Measurement	Level of Analysis	Comparisons	Statistics
Measures of program implementation							
Global rating of program (0, 1; 0 = negative or no opinion, 1 = positive)	1	–	Teacher survey	Teacher	Teacher	High and medium level of implementation	t-tests separately for all teachers and for team members
Team effectiveness rating (1–3; 1 = not effective, 3 = effective)	5	.90	Teacher survey	Teacher	Teacher	High and medium level of implementation	t-tests separately for all teachers and for team members
Reports of level of implementation	7 single items	–	Teacher survey	Teacher	Teacher	High and medium level of implementation	t-tests separately for all teachers and for team members
Practices: (1–5; 1 = never use, 5 = always use)							
Read books: (1–4; 1 = never saw book, 4 = read book and used)							
Ratio of negative to positive referrals	1	–	Behavior Tracking System	Student	School	Comparison of ratios to implementation standard	None

273

Implementation Measures. Measures of implementation come primarily from teacher-survey addenda administered only at the end of the program. For these measures, posttreatment comparisons between high- and medium-level implementation schools (see paragraphs that follow) were made and *t*-statistics reported.

Results

Level of Implementation

The activities of and support for the school improvement teams varied from school to school, and the variation was predictable from informal assessments of building-level support for the program during the planning year. A report on project implementation discusses this variation in detail and speculates about the sources of the variation (Hess, Mack, & D. C. Gottfredson, 1989). A summary of these differences follows.

In one of the six schools (School 5 on Table 1), the program was poorly communicated to the teaching staff during the planning year. The BTS component was overemphasized, and the components that would require more intensive staff effort were underemphasized. Team members in this school were not fully briefed on the program or their responsibilities prior to the team training. The principal was replaced at the end of the planning year, and the assistant principal (who was primarily responsible for the program) left after the first implementation year. In this school, the program was initially met with hostility from the teaching staff and the team was unable to overcome these negative feelings. The administrative team that subsequently took over was strong and supportive, and conditions improved steadily over the 2-year implementation period, but the support came too late to transform an initially resisted program into a strongly supported one.

In a second school (School 6), the principal who had agreed to participate in the program was replaced just prior to the opening of the planning school year. The new principal never became extensively involved with the program because he saw it as a discipline program and delegated it to the assistant principal. The assistant principal who helped to design the program during the planning year was replaced at the end of the first implementation year by an assistant principal who was not a strong leader for the program. The team in this school was unable to make much headway without support from the administrators.

In a third school (School 4) both administrators provided only weak leadership for the program. The assistant principal was replaced at the end of the first implementation year by a stronger leader, but the new assistant principal and the team suffered under the weak leadership of the principal through the end of the program period, when he was replaced.

The other three program schools and the two comparison schools enjoyed medium-to-high levels of support and fewer administrative changes over the 3-year period. These five schools had a total of four administrator changes, whereas the three discussed above experienced five. The changes that did occur in the remaining five schools did not affect the administrative support for the program, which was initially high and remained high to medium.

The frequent meetings to provide feedback on the strength and fidelity of program implementation and the high level of communication among the school teams and between the teams and the researchers provided ample opportunity to observe differences in the levels of implementation and enthusiasm from school to school.

Information from these meetings showed that the schools differed on level of implementation of the program components. All six schools produced and published a revised school discipline handbook that described school rules, the consequences for breaking each rule, and provisions for positive rewards for appropriate behavior. All six schools used the BTS to enter their office referrals and administrative responses, but two schools (Schools 4 and 6) entered only partial information (the research staff completed the records). These same two schools never used the BTS to record positive referrals to the office and positive responses. The other four schools did.

These differences in the level of administrative support and the quality of program implementation were visible immediately, and the planning team composed of key leaders in each school, central office administrators, and the researcher developed an expectation that the success of the program would be different for three sets of schools: "Low-implementation" schools (the two comparison schools that participated only in some aspects of the program), "medium-implementation" schools (the three treatment schools that experienced visible implementation problems or low levels of administrative support), and "high-implementation" schools (the three treatment schools that enjoyed administrative support and had no visible signs of implementation breakdown). The BTS and school leadership indicators that led to the placement of schools into the medium and high implementation levels are shown in Appendix B.

Few systematic data were collected on the level of teacher use of the program strategies. Teacher observations were conducted by team members and many teachers kept logs of behavior management strategies used, but these data were not representative of the school populations. Systematic data about use of the positive reinforcement and organization and management strategies come primarily from a teacher survey administered only at the end of the project. The use of these data as measures of program implementation is limited because we are unable to assess the increase in use of these strategies from the beginning to the end of the project. However, if we are willing to assume that the medium- and high-implementation school teachers were similar prior to program in their use of the program strategies, the data support the planning team's observation that these schools differed in their level of implementation of the program. Table 3 shows the teacher reports of use by level of implementation. Appendix B shows school-by-school scores.[3]

The teacher reports of use of contingent reinforcement of student behavior (rows 1 through 4) were higher in the high-implementation than the medium-implementation schools. The differences were significant ($p < .01$) or close to significant ($p < .08$ and $p < .15$) for all items except negative communication to the home, which was emphasized less than were the positive responses. The differences between team members' reports in high- and medium-implementation schools are larger than differences for the general population of teachers, and this interaction of team membership with level of implementation is statistically significant for negative communications to the home ($p < .05$) and almost significant ($p < .10$) for positive communications and rewards for individual behavior.

The level of implementation was also higher for team members in the high-implementation schools than for the general teacher population in their schools. This was not the case in the medium-implementation schools where the level of implementation was equivalent for team and nonteam teachers. Although the program targeted all teachers and was not intended to produce a difference between team members and other teachers in their practices, the different patterns in the high- and medium-implementation schools converge with other information about differences in level of implementation found for the high- and medium-implementation schools.

Two items on the teacher addendum asked about the level of implementation of the classroom organization and management strategies. For both the general-teacher and the team-member populations the reports of intervention to prevent misbehavior were higher in the high-implementation schools. Teachers in the medium-implementation schools, however, reported that they had read the Emmer et al. (1984) book as carefully as teachers in the high-implementation schools probably because the principal in one of these schools mandated that every teacher read the book.

The number of team members at any given time ranged from 4 to 11 per school, with a mean of 8. The percentage of the faculty represented on the team ranged from

T A B L E *3*

Means and Standard Deviations on Measures of Program Implementation, by Level of Implementation and Team Membership

| | Level of Implementation | | | | | |
| | High | | | Medium | | |
Implementation measure	*M*	*SD*	*N*	*M*	*SD*	*N*
Teacher reports: all teachers						
Rewards for individual behavior	4.08	.80	105	3.89	.82	113
Rewards for group behavior	3.88[a]	.94	104	3.44	.92	113
Negative communication to home	3.82	.78	105	3.70	.76	115
Positive communication to home	3.80	.75	105	3.65	.81	114
Read contingency management book	2.14	1.14	86	2.06	1.02	102
Intervenes to prevent misbehavior	4.02[a]	.76	105	3.74	.62	115
Read organization/management book	2.16	1.12	86	2.18	1.08	104
Percentage "thumbs up"	.59[a]	.49	98	.33	.47	110
Team effectiveness	2.32[a]	.58	98	2.05	.62	107
Teacher reports: team members only						
Rewards for individual behavior	4.36[a]	.63	14	3.77	.59	26
Rewards for group behavior	4.28[a]	.73	14	3.46	.71	26
Negative communication to home	4.14[a, b]	.86	14	3.56	.75	27
Positive communication to home	4.07[c]	.83	14	3.48	.89	27
Read contingency management book	3.08	.95	13	2.68	1.11	25
Intervenes to prevent misbehavior	4.28[a]	.61	14	3.74	.66	27
Read organization/management book	3.15	.99	13	2.68	1.14	25
Percentage "thumbs up"	.86[a]	.36	14	.42	.50	26
Team effectiveness	1.38[a]	.45	14	1.78	.65	24

[a] Differences between high- and medium-implementation schools is significant at the $p < .01$ level. [b] Team membership by school level of implementation interaction is significant at the $p < .05$ level. [c] Difference between high- and medium-implementation schools is significant at the $p < .05$ level.

6% to 23%, with a mean of 16%. The percentage of team members who remained on the team for a second year ranged from 20% to 57%, with a mean of 36%. The ratio of teachers to nonteachers on the teams ranged from 0.7 to 8, with an average of 2.9. No differences between the medium- and high-implementation schools were found on any of these team characteristics.

Global teacher ratings of program effectiveness, shown in Table 3, provide additional evidence of differential implementation. Teachers in the three high-implementation schools were generally more favorable to the program and reported that the teams were more effective than teachers in the medium-implementation schools. Team members in the high-implementation schools were also more favorably impressed with the program than their counterparts in the medium-implementation schools. Team members in the medium-implementation schools, however, rated their own effectiveness higher than the team in the high-implementation schools.

Program Outcomes

Tables 4 through 6 report changes from baseline to the end of the program on the primary outcomes of the program—classroom order and student behavior. Tables 4, 6, and 7 report changes on intermediate program outcomes targeted by the program. All tables show change in measured outcomes for all treatment and comparison schools combined and for high- and medium-implementation schools. Means are further disaggregated in Appendix A, which reports all outcomes separately by school.

Table 4 shows that treatment schools improved significantly on student report of classroom order, classroom organization, and rule clarity. The low-implementation (comparison) schools did not improve. The breakdown by level of implementation shows that the treatment effects are found mostly for the high-implementation schools except for Rule Clarity, on which the medium-implementation schools also improved significantly.

Figure 1 shows the quarterly scores for student reports of classroom orderliness. The graph shows that the medium- and low-implementation schools' performances were similar: They are marked by the same pattern of seasonable variation in classroom orderliness, but there is gradual improvement, albeit slight, over the 12 quarters. The high implementation schools started off with significantly lower classroom order but ended up with the highest. Their scores are marked by the same ebb and flow pattern as the other schools, but their improvement is more dramatic over the project period.

Table 5 shows the average teacher ratings of student behavior for 1987 and 1989. Teacher ratings of student attentiveness increased and ratings of student disruptive behavior decreased significantly in the high-implementation schools. Teacher ratings of disruptive behavior increased significantly in the medium-implementation schools. Neither ratings changed significantly in the low-implementation schools. Effect sizes are generally small.

Table 6 shows means for students' reports of their own misbehavior and their schools' responses to appropriate and inappropriate behavior. Rebellious behavior significantly increased for all groups between 1987 and 1989. These increases were most marked in the medium-implementation schools. Students' reports of the level of punishment they received in school declined[4] significantly over the time period for treatment but not comparison schools. The positive effects were due only to the

TABLE **4**

**Means and Standard Deviations for CEA Measures, 3 Years,
by Level of Implementation**

Behavior and Group	1987			1989			Effect Size
	M	SD	N	M	SD	N	
Classroom order, students							
All treatment	3.28	.49	211	3.45[a]	.52	226	.35
High implementation	3.20	.52	103	3.52[a]	.50	117	.62
Medium implementation	3.36	.44	107	3.37	.53	109	.02
Low implementation	3.44	.39	59	3.43	.45	62	−.03
Classroom order, teachers							
All treatment	3.71	.61	211	3.75	.58	229	.07
High implementation	3.72	.66	103	3.79	.61	117	.11
Medium implementation	3.71	.55	107	3.69	.55	109	−.04
Low implementation	3.90	.50	59	3.85	.46	61	−.10
Classroom organization							
All treatment	1.67	.16	211	1.72[a]	.16	226	.31
High implementation	1.65	.17	103	1.74[a]	.16	117	.53
Medium implementation	1.69	.14	107	1.70	.17	109	.07
Low implementation	1.73	.14	59	1.70	.15	62	−.21
Rule clarity							
All treatment	1.83	.10	211	1.87[a]	.10	226	.40
High implementation	1.81	.11	103	1.87[b]	.11	117	.55
Medium implementation	1.84	.09	107	1.87[b]	.10	109	.33
Low implementation	1.85	.07	59	1.85	.09	62	.00
Teacher support							
All treatment	1.66	.16	211	1.68	.15	226	.13
High implementation	1.63	.17	103	1.69[b]	.14	117	.35
Medium implementation	1.68	.16	107	1.67	.16	109	−.06
Low implementation	1.68	.16	59	1.65	.15	62	−.19

[a] Difference between 1987 and 1989 score is significant at the $p < .01$ level. [b] Difference between 1987 and 1989 score is significant at the $p < .05$ level.

high-implementation schools. Increases in student reports of rewards received in school increased significantly in all groups.

Table 7 shows changes in three school climate indicators targeted by the program—Respect for Students, Clarity of Rules, and Fairness of Rules. The effect sizes for all these measures are moderately large for the high-implementation schools, but only the increase in Fairness of Rules exceeds the standard error of measurement reported in the ESB user's manual for this measure.

Change from 1987 to 1989 in Teacher Ratings of Students' On-Task Behavior, by Level of Implementation

Behavior and Group	1987			1989			Effect Size
	M	SD	N	M	SD	N	
Attends to academic work							
All treatment	3.87	.93	4011	3.88	.96	4066	.01
High implementation	3.91[a]	.89	1951	3.99	.91	1973	.09
Medium implementation	3.82	.96	2060	3.77	1.00	2093	−.05
Low implementation (comparison)	3.87	.88	1162	3.90	.83	1215	.03
Disrupts the classroom							
All treatment	2.00	.96	4006	2.01	.98	4064	.01
High implementation	2.02[b]	.94	1952	1.91	.92	1977	−.12
Medium implementation	1.98[b]	.97	2054	2.10	1.02	2087	.12
Low implementation (comparison)	1.95	.90	1160	1.95	.93	1214	.00

Note: Coded "5" = almost always; "1" = almost never. [a] Change from 1987 to 1989 is significant at the $p < .05$ level. [b] Difference from 1987 to 1989 is significant at the $p < .01$ level.

T A B L E 6

Change from 1987 to 1989 in Student Reports of Misbehavior, Rewards, and Punishment, by Level of Implementation

Behavior and Group	1987			1989			Effect Size
	M	SD	N	M	SD	N	
Rebellious behavior							
All treatment	.86[a]	.67	2991	1.04	.87	2865	.27
High implementation	.90[a]	.71	1476	.98	.85	1474	.11
Medium implementation	.81[a]	.63	1515	1.09	.88	1391	.44
Low implementation (comparison)	.85[a]	.64	936	.97	.80	979	.19
Rewards							
All treatment	.32[a]	.31	3392	.36	.32	3180	.13
High implementation	.33[b]	.31	1686	.35	.32	1617	.07
Medium implementation	.31[a]	.30	1706	.37	.32	1563	.19
Low implementation (comparison)	.32[a]	.30	1058	.36	.31	1065	.11
Avoidance of punishment							
All treatment	.72[a]	.28	3394	.74	.27	3179	.06
High implementation	.70[a]	.28	1688	.75	.27	1618	.19
Medium implementation	.75	.27	1706	.73	.28	1561	−.07
Low implementation (comparison)	.66	.27	1061	.68	.28	1065	.07

[a] Change from 1987 to 1989 is significant at the $p < .01$ level. [b] Change from 1987 to 1989 is significant at the $p < .05$ level.

TABLE 7

Change from 1987 to 1989 on Student Reports of School Climate, by Level of Implementation

Level of Implementation	Respect for Students			Clarity of Rules			Fairness of Rules		
	1987	1989	Effect Size	1987	1989	Effect Size	1987	1989	Effect Size
All treatment	1.027	1.053	.18	.772	.790	.28	.565	.587	.24
High implementation	1.023	1.083	.40	.773	.793	.33	.577[a]	.623	.52
Medium implementation	1.030	1.023	-.04	.770	.787	.22	.553	.550	-.04
Low implementation (comparison)	1.020	1.065	.25	.785	.775	-.25	.605	.620	.17

Note. "Effect size" is the difference between the climate scores for 1989 and 1987 divided by the standard deviation for schools reported in the ESB user's manual (G. Gottfredson, 1985, page 57).

[a] Difference between 1987 and 1989 score exceeds one standard error of the mean.

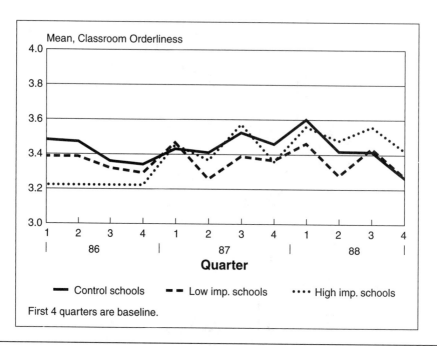

FIGURE *1*   **Student Reports of Classroom Order by Level of Implementation, 12 Quarters**

Summary

Measures of implementation of the "technological" program components suggested that the School Discipline Policy component, including provisions for school-wide positive reinforcement for appropriate behavior, was implemented in all six treatment schools. The computerized BTS was fully implemented in all high-implementation and one medium-implementation school. The classroom-level positive reinforcement and classroom organization and management components were implemented more faithfully in the high- than in the medium-implementation schools. Teacher ratings of program effectiveness were highest in the schools in which the program was most faithfully implemented.

Changes from pre- to posttreatment on measures of program outcomes generally indicated a positive change for the high-implementation schools only. Significant changes in the desirable direction were found for the high-, medium-, and low-implementation schools for 9, 2, and 1 of the 13 differences examined. Significant changes in the undesirable direction were found for 1, 2, and 1 of the differences examined for the three levels of implementation.

Examination of the direction of the effects, regardless of the magnitude, also indicated a positive change for the high-implementation schools only. Changes for 12 of the 13 outcome measures examined were in the positive direction for the high-implementation schools ($p < .01$, using the Sign Test described in Siegal, 1956). The before-and-after differences for the medium- and low-implementation schools were in the negative direction about as often as in the positive.

Results for the measures of disruptive behavior agree with the conclusion that the program had beneficial effects on student behavior when it was well implemented. Students' reports of their own rebellious behavior generally increased over the 3-year period, but the increase was smaller in the high-implementation schools than in other schools. Teachers' perceptions of their students' behaviors improved in the high-implementation schools, deteriorated in the medium-implementation schools, and were unchanged in the low-implementation schools. Students' reports of the orderliness of their classrooms increased in the high-implementation schools only.

The measures of intermediate objectives of the program also supported positive change in the high-implementation schools only, but the results were more mixed. Students reported less punishment in the high-implementation schools. Students at all three levels of implementation reported receiving more rewards. Effect sizes for Respect for Students, Fairness of Rules, and Clarity of Rules were moderate and in the desired direction for the high-implementation schools only.

Discussion and Supplementary Exploration of the Results

Are beneficial outcomes related to actual implementation of program components? Records of school-level disciplinary practices as well as teacher and team member reports of program strategy use were higher in high-implementation schools than in medium-implementation schools (Table 3) and beneficial program outcomes were more often observed in these schools. At least three alternative explanations rival the interpretation that the program improved practices in high-implementation schools and the improved practices resulted in positive outcomes—that is, that there was a treatment effect. The program could have coincided with some other unknown event in the high-implementation schools that actually produced the positive outcomes (a history threat). We reject this possibility. No other major programs or changes coincided with the program. Two more plausible rival hypotheses are that (a) the program interacted with some preexisting conditions in the schools in such a way that the positive effects were "facilitated" by preexisting conditions (a selection by treatment interaction effect), and (b) the teachers and administrators in the high-implementation schools were on a steeper change trajectory to begin with, and their schools would have improved at a faster rate in the absence of a treatment (a selection by maturation interaction effect).

The selection by treatment interaction hypothesis cannot be ruled out. Improvements from the year prior to the program to the end of the program may be attributable to unmeasured conditions that produced different contexts onto which the program elements were laid. Such differences may have affected teacher commitment to and participation in the program *and* produced differences in the outcomes of the study. The nonequivalent control group design and the absence of a priori knowledge of the conditions that may have interacted with the treatment to produce different results do not permit systematic examination of this issue. Technical reports (Hess, Mack, & D. C. Gottfredson, 1989; D. C. Gottfredson, G. D. Gottfredson, & Hybl, 1990) provide more detail about variation in the school contexts and provide some hints about contextual conditions that may have interacted with the treatments to produce the observed outcomes. The study design does not eliminate this ambiguity.

The selection by maturation interaction hypothesis suggests that the observed outcomes would have occurred in the absence of the project interventions. This alternative explanation cannot be completely ruled out, but evidence from disaggregated analyses that the level of utilization of the program strategies within the school was related to improvements in targeted outcomes would raise doubt about its plausibility. Generally, measures of implementation and outcome measures were collected and analyzed only at the school level because the program involved primarily school-level interventions. Individual teachers were asked to change their classroom management practices, but all other interventions were coordinated by the school improvement teams. These teams modified school discipline policies, established reward systems, and coordinated direct services to youths. Implementation data collection efforts were geared towards documenting the activities of the team rather than of individual teachers. This makes within-school analyses relating the level of implementation to outcomes a difficult task—one not anticipated in the design of the study. However, such an analysis is possible for the CEAs that were identified at the classroom level. It is reasonable to expect that team members used the program strategies in their classroom more than did other teachers, at least in the high-implementation schools where the teams seem to have been more effective. If the classrooms of team members improved from the pre- to postintervention period more than the classrooms of other teachers, the argument that the program was instrumental in improving outcomes would be strengthened.

Supplementary regression analyses in which each teacher's average CEA score from the four quarters of the final program year were regressed on a dummy variable measuring team membership and the same Classroom Environment Assessment average score from the teachers' class in the previous year were conducted. These analyses are based on the relatively small number of teachers for whom classroom assessments for both 1988 and 1987 were available. Only 67% of the 1988 teachers were also present in the schools in 1987, and the minimum pairwise number of cases was 58 in the high-implementation and 63 in the medium-implementation schools. For all schools combined—and with the prior year's measure controlled—team membership was hardly related to 1988–89 teacher reports of classroom orderliness (beta = .02, p = .66). A significant (p = .02) interaction was found for team membership with the level of implementation of the program, however. Team membership was nearly significantly related to increased classroom orderliness (beta = .30, p = .08) in the high implementation schools. These results, though admittedly exploratory, help to reject the alternative hypothesis that the higher level of implementation reported by teachers and team members in the high implementation schools—and the beneficial outcomes observed for these schools—can be explained by factors other than the level of implementation of the program.

Why did low-implementation schools perform better than medium-implementation schools? The two low-implementation schools were intended to be no-treatment comparison schools. Practical considerations prevented them from being left entirely alone, however. They were considered to be part of the district planning team that was charged with developing, implementing, and evaluating the program. They were promised top priority in the next phase of the program, which was to extend the effective elements from the experiment into other middle schools. The comparison schools, then, were very much a part of the program. Their assistant principals attended all planning and feedback sessions and were given all materials. Their principals participated in annual feedback workshops.

Several of the outcome measures in the study improved most in the high-implementation schools and least in the medium-implementation schools. The effect sizes for changes in the low-implementation schools were greater in the positive direction or smaller in the negative direction than those for the medium-implementation schools on teacher ratings of student behavior, Rebellious Behavior, Avoidance of Punishment, Respect for Students, and Fairness of Rules. A closer look at the low-implementation schools helps to explain why.

Appendix A shows that for the most direct measures of student behavior, large differences exist in the before-and-after changes observed for the two comparison schools. In one (School 8), significant increases in teacher ratings for attending to work and significant declines in teacher ratings of disruptive behavior were observed. In the other school (School 7), significant changes in the undesired direction on both ratings were observed. School 8's students reported more rebellious behavior over the 3-year period, but (as in the high-implementation schools) the increase was not statistically significant. School 7's students reported significantly more rebellious behavior (as did students in the medium-implementation schools). School 8's students reported significantly less school punishment and significantly more rewards over the period. Clearly, School 8 resembles the high-implementation schools on many of the measures that might be expected to be most responsive to changes in the consequences for misbehavior at the school, and School 7 resembles the medium-implementation schools. Note that differences between School 8 and School 7 were not apparent for outcomes expected to be more responsive to the organization development or classroom organization and management activities in the school.

In an attempt to discover what discipline practices at School 8 might have produced results similar to those in high-implementation schools, we performed informal, open-ended interviews with teachers in the three high-implementation schools and School 8. Ten teachers from each school were selected on the basis of positive changes in their classes' classroom environment assessment scores. A research assistant interviewed all forty teachers about their usual discipline practices. Through these interviews we learned that the assistant principal in School 8 provided a 2-day discipline workshop during the 1987–88 school year (after the planning year for our project). This workshop used the Assertive Discipline model (Canter & Canter, 1976) to focus on increasing clarity and consistency of rule enforcement at the classroom level. Sixty four percent of the teachers interviewed in School 8 (compared with 67%, 44%, and 11% in the other schools) mentioned Assertive Discipline as having helped them with discipline problems. Eighty-two percent (compared with 67%, 78%, and 44% in the other schools) specifically mentioned using a "checks on the board" system to introduce progressively harsher penalties for misbehavior. When asked to state the single most important factor in their success as disciplinarians, the School 8 teachers mentioned rule clarity and consistency of enforcement at much higher rates than the teachers in the high-implementation schools (73% versus 33%, 56%, and 56%).

We also learned that the teachers in School 8 used strategies for contingent reinforcement of behavior at a high rate. Eighty-two percent of the teachers in School 8 reported that they apply consequences for behavior according to a prearranged plan. In the high-implementation schools, 78%, 78%, and 67% of the teachers reported frequent use of these methods, which were part of the program training. Roughly the same percentage of teachers in School 8 mentioned using specific behavior change methods included in the program training as teachers in the high-implementation schools (91% versus 89%, 100%, and 100%). Many of the specific methods for positive reinforcement mentioned by School 8 teachers were identical to those used in the high-implementation schools.

Teachers in the high-implementation schools mentioned the specific program materials, help from the school team, and feedback produced as part of the program as having been helpful. None of the teachers in School 8 mentioned these specific materials and support structures. They also mentioned classroom organization and management issues as important in maintaining discipline more than did teachers in School 8, and they reported having special plans for improving behavior of at-risk youth more than the teachers in School 8. For example, 80%, 67%, and 83% of the teachers in the high-implementation schools said they used contracts with at-risk youths. Only 50% of the School 8 teachers used this program strategy. However, one teacher in School 8 reported that the assistant principal targeted specific high-risk individuals for special assistance and used the kind of monitoring and contracting strategies included in our program materials.

In summary, one of the low-implementation schools was clearly engaged in a major behavior management program, and the program resembled in many ways the program that was implemented in the high-implementation schools. It included a positive reinforcement component and those segments of the classroom organization and management component that overlapped with Assertive Discipline—those focusing on clarity and consistency of classroom rules. It did not include the other organization development components or the computerized behavior management system with frequent communications to the home. These differences help to explain the beneficial changes observed for School 8 and lend credibility to the conclusion that the program, when well-implemented, was effective for reducing behavior problems.

Conclusions

Emmer and Aussiker (1989) recently reviewed research on four popular discipline programs. They found some evidence of positive effects on teacher attitudes, beliefs, and perceptions, mixed evidence for efforts on teacher behaviors, and almost no evidence supporting a positive effect on student behavior. The work summarized here implies that schools can intervene to improve student behavior. The features that distinguish this moderately effective program from those reviewed by Emmer and Aussiker are that (a) researchers and practitioners collaborated in the development and implementation of the program, (b) the technological components of the program were supported by organization development activities and structures, and (c) the program targeted sources of misbehavior from multiple levels.

Enthusiasm for this approach to improving student conduct in the middle grades must be tempered. First, schools differ in their capacity to implement large-scale changes such as the one described in this report. Variation in the level of implementation appeared to be related—at least in part—to the level of administrative support for the program and the team. Additional research and development is needed to learn how to foster organizational competence to support change. We now assume that much effort is wasted when training programs are not augmented with school-level structures to facilitate change.

The classrooms of those teachers who participated as members of a school improvement team that was responsible for providing leadership for the program and for tailoring the program to fit their schools' unique needs had more positive outcomes (at least in the schools in which the team received strong administrator backing). These teachers received more training in the program components than the other teachers in the school, but the study results suggest that it was the team participation rather than the additional training that led to the improved outcomes. Teachers in the schools whose teams were ineffective also received more training, but their classes did not improve. This outcome underscores the importance of organizational support for professional development as opposed to mere training, a point that has been emphasized by others as well (Berman, 1981, Miles, 1981).

The modest improvements in student behavior attributed to the program must also be weighed against the effort expended to achieve the outcomes. We can not quantify the costs of the program, but we can comment on our perceptions of them. The local effort applied to the project was high, but clearly within the range of normal staff development activities for the school district. The efforts expended by school staff to learn about and maintain the new strategies were somewhat greater than those expended on, for example, the districts school-based management program. The efforts expended by school and district staff were far less, however, than those expended on the districts Program for Effective Teachers. The level of technical assistance provided by the researchers was unusual for the district, but not beyond the realm of possibility for a school district to obtain. The modest improvements in student behavior seems to have been obtained at a significant, but not unreasonable cost.

Some Speculations

The study provides some insights about the design of effective discipline programs. All of the schools in the study clarified their school discipline policies, implemented a computerized behavior management system, and developed a school-level system for providing rewards for appropriate behavior. These changes probably produced increases in students' reports of clarity of rules and rewards, but these changes were not sufficient to reduce student misconduct and rebellious behavior. Those schools that *in addition* significantly reduced the amount of punishment and changed the school climate in the direction of respectful, supportive, and fair treatment of students experienced beneficial student outcomes. This suggests that simply adding a cosmetic system of positive reinforcement onto a punitive system is not productive. The underlying approach to discipline must be examined to produce a coherent system.

Schools that implemented only the school-level components did not experience positive change. Most misbehavior can probably be traced to classroom- and individual-level sources that the school-level components did not alter. Although the school-level components probably helped to set the context for alterations in these more proximate domains, they were unable to stand on their own.

Classroom-level changes, on the other hand, appeared effective for modifying student behavior. We are unable to disentangle the effects of preventive classroom management changes from changes that targeted troublesome students (e.g., contracting), but it is clear that a combination of these approaches was effective for producing improvements both in the orderliness of the classroom environment and in teacher and student reports of student behavior.

Future work in this area should determine the relative effectiveness of approaches to behavior change that target individual students at elevated risk for behavior problems and those that alter the classroom and school environment to prevent misbehavior. Although recent statements on the future of discipline programs seem to favor classroom environmental approaches (Doyle, 1986), we lack strong tests of the relative efficacy of plausible targeted programs on the one hand and plausible environmental programs on the other. Targeted programs that use behavioral and cognitive approaches to teach students how to manage their own behavior appear highly effective for replacing inappropriate behavior with appropriate (Alexander & Parsons, 1973; Barth, 1979; Manning, 1988; Patterson, Chamberlain, & Reid, 1982; Schinke & Gilchrist, 1984; Spivack, Platt, & Shure, 1976). In all likelihood, a behavior-management program that combines these theoretically plausible targeted approaches with plausible environmental change approaches should prove most beneficial.

Notes

    This research was supported in part by the U.S. Department of Education, Office of Educational Research and Improvement by Grant No. OERI-G-90006 to the Johns Hopkins University for a Center for Research on Elementary and Middle Schools and by Grant No. R117 R90002 for a Center for Research on Effective Schooling for Disadvantaged Students. The opinions expressed do not necessarily reflect the position of the Office. We are grateful for the help of Nancy L. Karweit in designing and helping to implement the BTS and to Barbara Clements and Julie Sanford for providing classroom organization and management training. Renee Castaneda, Roger Jarjoura, Laurel Wiersma, and Mark Melia provided research assistance. Many people in the Charleston County School District of South Carolina were partners in this research. Jeff Erickson, Larry Bolchoz, and Barbara Hess provided leadership from the district level. Karen Coste, Karl Bunch, Walter Pusey, Deward Brame, Jeff Erikson, Bob Ephriam, Barbara Cohn, Figgins Frayer, Roberta Papineau, Walter Dodson, and Nancy Gorchik led school teams. Andrea Heyer and Darlene Venable coordinated the program in the comparison schools. The help of the team members and support staff who assisted with the project is gratefully acknowledged. We also thank the teachers and students who dutifully completed surveys each quarter for 3 years.

1. Descriptions of the scales and information about the reliability and validity of the scales are taken from G. D. Gottfredson (1984b).
2. Measures of internal consistency for the ESB Avoidance of Punishment and Rewards scales shown in Figure 1 are for measurement at the individual level. Modest reliability in individual measurement does not bias the results. Statistical efficiency in examining changes in means over time depends mainly on sample size (Stanley, 1971).
3. Tables 3 through 7 report results for multiple nonindependent *t*-tests, inflating the number of significant comparisons found. One way to adjust for this is to require a more conservative alpha level for significance. The basic results of this study would not change if we required an alpha level of .01 for significance. Also, the number of significant differences found in the study far exceeds the number expected by chance: One significant effect at the .01 level would be expected by chance; 24 were found. Three significant differences would be expected by chance at the .05 level; 9 were found.
4. Note that the scoring is in the positive direction such that high scores indicate fewer reports of punishment.

References

Alexander, J. F., & Parsons, B. V. (1973). Short-term behavioral intervention with delinquent families: Impacts on family process and recidivism. *Journal of Abnormal Psychology, 81,* 219–225.

Atkeson, B. M., & Forehand, R. (1979). Home-based reinforcement programs designed to modify classroom behavior: A review and methodological evaluation. *Psychological Bulletin, 86,* 1298–1308.

Bachman, J. G., Green, S., & Wirtanen, I. D. (1971). *Youth in transition: Vol. 3. Dropping out—problem or symptom?* Ann Arbor: University of Michigan Institute for Social Research.

Bailey, J. W., Wolf, M. M., & Phillips, E. L. (1970). Home-based reinforcement and the modification of predelinquent classroom behavior. *Journal of Applied Behavior Analysis, 3,* 223–233.

Barth, R. (1979). Home-based reinforcement of school behavior: A review and analysis. *Review of Educational Research, 49,* 436–458.

Berman, P. W. (1981). Educational change: An implementation paradigm. In R. Lehming & M. Kane (Eds.), *Improving schools: Using what we know.* Beverly Hills, CA: Sage.

Block, J., Block, J. H., & Keyes, S. (1988). Longitudinally foretelling drug usage in adolescence: Early childhood personality and environmental precursors. *Child Development, 59,* 336–355.

Buckley, N. K., & Walker, H. M. (1978). *Modifying classroom behavior.* Champaign, IL: Research Press.

Canter, L., & Canter, M. (1976) *Assertive discipline.* Los Angeles, CA: Lee Canter & Associates, Inc.

Coie, J. D. (1990). Towards a theory of peer rejection. In S. R. Asher and J. D. Coie (Eds.), *Peer rejection in childhood.* New York: Cambridge University Press.

Cook, T. D., & Campbell, D. T. (1979). *Quasi–experimentation: Design and analysis issues for field settings.* Chicago: Rand McNally.

Doyle, W. (1986). Classroom organization and management. In M. C. Wittrock (Ed.), *Handbook of research on teaching* (3rd ed.). New York: Macmillan.

Duke, D. L. (1989). School organization, leadership, and student behavior. In O. C. Moles, *Strategies to reduce student misbehavior.* Washington, DC: U.S. Department of Education.

Elliott, D. S., Ageton, S. S., & Huizinga, D. (1979). *1978 self-reported delinquency estimates by sex, race, class and age* (Report No. 9). Boulder, CO: Behavioral Research Institute.

Emmer, E. T., & Aussiker, A. (1989). School and classroom discipline programs: How well do they work? In O. C. Moles, *Strategies to reduce student misbehavior.* Washington, DC: U.S. Department of Education.

Emmer, E. T., C. M., Sanford, J. P., Clements, B. S. & Worhsam, M. E. (1984). *Classroom management for secondary teachers.* Englewood Cliffs, NJ: Prentice-Hall.

Evertson, C. M., & Emmer, E. T. (1982). Effective management at the beginning of the school year in junior high classes. *Journal of Educational Psychology, 74,* 485–498.

Gottfredson, D. C., Gottfredson, G. D., & Hybl, L. G. (1990). *Managing adolescent behavior: A multiyear, multischool experiment* (Report No. 50). Baltimore: Johns Hopkins University, Center for Research on Elementary and Middle Schools.

Gottfredson, D. C., Karweit, N. L., & Gottfredson, G. D. (1989). *Reducing disorderly behavior in middle schools* (Report No. 37) Baltimore: Johns Hopkins University, Center for Research on Elementary and Middle Schools. (ERIC Document Reproduction Service No. ED 320 654)

Gottfredson, G. D. (1984a). A theory-ridden approach to program evaluation: A method for stimulating researcher-implementer collaboration. *American Psychologist, 39,* 1101–1112.

Gottfredson, G. D. (1984b). *Effective School Battery: User's manual.* Odessa, FL: Psychological Assessment Resources.

Gottfredson, G. D. (1987). American education—American delinquency. *Today's Delinquent, 6,* 5–70.

Gottfredson, G. D. & Gottfredson, D.C. (1985). *Victimization in schools.* New York: Plenum.

Gottfredson, G. D., Rickert, D. E. Gottfredson, D. C. & Advani, N. (1984). Standards for program development evaluation plans. (Manuscript No. 2668) *Psychological Documents, 14,* 32.

Hess, B., Mack, D., & Gottfredson, D. C. (1989). *Interim report on Project BASIS* Unpublished manuscript, Johns Hopkins University, Center for Research on Elementary and Middle Schools, Baltimore.

Hirschi, T. (1969). *Causes of delinquency.* Berkeley: University of California Press.

Jessor, R., & Jessor, S. L. (1997). *Problem behavior and psychosocial development: A longitudinal study of youth* Boulder: University of Colorado Institute of Behavior Science.

Kazdin, A. E. (1987). *Conduct disorders in childhood and adolescence.* Newbury Park, CA: Sage.

Kellam, S. G., & Brown, C. H. (1982, December). *Social adaptational and psychological antecedents in first grade of adolescent psychopathology 10 years later.* Paper presented at the Research Workshop on Preventive Aspects of Suicide and Affective Disorders Among Adolescents and Young Adults, Harvard School of Public Health, Boston, MA

Manning, B. H. (1988). Application of cognitive behavior modification: First and third graders' self-management of classroom behaviors. *American Educational Research Journal, 25,* 193–212.

Miles, J. (1981). Mapping the common properties of schools. In R. Lehming & M. Kane (Eds.), *Improving schools: Using what we know.* Beverly Hills, CA: Sage.

Moos, R. H., Trickett, E. J. (1987). *Manual for the Classroom Environment Scale.* Palo Alto: Consulting Psychologists Press.

National Center for Education Statistics. (1986). *Discipline in public secondary schools.* Washington, DC: U.S. Department of Education.

Patterson, G. R., Chamberlain, P., & Reid, J. B. (1982). A comparative evaluation of parent training procedures. *Behavior Therapy, 13,* 638–649.

Robins, L. N. (1966). *Deviant children grown up.* Baltimore: Williams & Wilkins.

Schinke, S. P., & Gilchrist, L. D. (1984). *Life skills counseling with adolescents.* Austin, TX: Pro-Ed.

Shannon, L. W. (1982). *Assessing the relationship of adult criminal careers to juvenile careers.* Washington, DC: Office of Juvenile Justice and Delinquency Prevention.

Siegel, S. (1956). *Nonparametric statistics for the behavioral sciences.* New York: McGraw-Hill.

Spivack, G., Platt, J. J., & Shure, M. B. (1976). *The problem-solving approach to adjustment.* San Francisco: Jossey-Bass.

Stanley, J. C. (1971). Reliability. In R. L. Thorndike (Ed.), *Educational measurement* (2nd ed., pp. 356–442). Washington, DC: American Council on Education.

Williams, J. R., & Gold, M. (1972). From delinquent behavior to official delinquency. *Social Problems, 20*(3), 209–29.

Wolfgang, M. E., Figlio, R., & Sellin, T. (1972). *Delinquency in a birth cohort.* Chicago: University of Chicago Press.

APPENDIX A

School Means for All Outcome Measures, 1987 and 1989

| | High Implementation | | | | | | Medium Implementation | | | | | | Low Implementation (comparison) | | | |
| | School 1 | | School 2 | | School 3 | | School 4 | | School 5 | | School 6 | | School 7 | | School 8 | |
Outcome Measure	1987	1989	1987	1989	1987	1989	1987	1989	1987	1989	1987	1989	1987	1989	1987	1989
Classroom order, students	3.38	3.65[a]	3.17	3.50[b]	3.07	3.42[b]	3.27	3.26	3.43	3.52	3.42	3.32	3.40	3.31	3.47	3.52
Classroom order, teachers	3.79	3.90	3.59	3.81	3.85	3.68	3.60	3.57	3.79	3.89	3.76	3.61	3.90	3.72	3.90	3.95
Classroom organization	1.68	1.77[a]	1.63	1.73[b]	1.66	1.72	1.67	1.68	1.69	1.73	1.70	1.68	1.71	1.64	1.75	1.75
Rule clarity	1.78	1.87[b]	1.80	1.87[b]	1.87	1.85	1.85	1.87	1.83	1.89[b]	1.84	1.83	1.81	1.81	1.89	1.88
Teacher support	1.61	1.66	1.63	1.70[a]	1.67	1.69	1.71	1.69	1.69	1.70	1.64	1.62	1.62	1.58	1.72	1.71
Attends to academic work	4.02	4.10	3.81	3.95[b]	3.96	3.90	3.83	3.74	3.78	3.75	3.85	3.82	4.06	3.93[a]	3.73	3.87[b]
Disrupts the classroom	1.89	1.91	2.16	1.94[b]	1.93	1.86	2.07	2.24[b]	1.87	1.95	1.96	2.15[b]	1.88	2.16[b]	2.00	1.77[b]
Rebellious behavior	.87	.94	.96	1.08[b]	.96	.95	.81	1.16[b]	.87	1.10[b]	.86	1.11[b]	.91	1.09[b]	.83	.90
Rewards	.28	.35[b]	.34	.33	.36	.39	.32	.34	.33	.39[b]	.30	.38[b]	.34	.33	.31	.38[b]
Avoidance of punishment[a]	.76	.79[a]	.70	.75[b]	.63	.70[b]	.73	.69[a]	.78	.77	.74	.72	.71	.71	.62	.65
Respect for students	1.11	1.15	.88	1.07[c]	1.08	1.03	1.07	1.08	1.01	1.04	1.01	.95	.95	.98	1.09	1.15
Clarity of rules	.78	.75	.74	.85[c]	.80	.78	.83	.82	.70	.75	.78	.79	.75	.73	.82	.82
Fairness of rules	.57	.57	.50	.66[c]	.66	.64	.63	.59	.50	.50	.53	.56	.48	.49	.73	.75

[a] Difference between 1987 and 1989 score is significant at the p < .05 level.   [b] Difference between 1987 and 1989 score is significant at the p < .01 level.

[c] Difference between 1987 and 1989 score exceeds two standard errors of measurement.

APPENDIX *B*

School Means for All Implementation Measures

Implementation Measure	High Implementation			Medium Implementation		
	School 1	School 2	School 3	School 4	School 5	School 6
BTS (1988–89):						
Number pos. responses	1252	935	1321	0	943	0
Ratio of negative to positive responses	.38	2.97	1.32	–	3.06	–
Teacher reports (posttest):						
Rewards individuals	3.97	4.05	4.30	3.92	3.97	3.80
Rewards groups	3.77	3.78	4.18	3.47	3.50	3.36
Negative communication home	3.80	3.77	3.92	3.73	3.83	3.57
Positive communication home	3.83	3.70	3.92	3.64	3.86	3.48
Read contingency mgt. book	2.08	2.00	2.50	2.16	2.29	1.76
Intervenes to prevent	3.83	4.21	3.96	3.81	3.94	3.50
Read org. and mgt. book	2.12	2.03	2.47	2.31	2.26	2.00
Percentage "thumbs up"	.39	.60	.88	.63	.17	.20
Team effectiveness	1.13	1.33	1.61	1.33	.90	.94
Rating of leadership support for program	5	6	6	1	3	2

Note: Leadership support ratings were derived as follows: Each school was rated for each of the 3 program years on a 3-point scale (0–2) indicating low to high support. The three ratings were summed. Teacher reports of implementation are taken from a survey administered at the end of the project only.

CHAPTER 9

Correlational Designs, Parental Involvement, and the Question of Causality

INTRODUCTION

In this chapter we will examine a problem faced by many school administrators—a lack of active parental involvement. Principals and teachers are aware of the importance of involving parents in the life of the school, and they work at this problem on many fronts. Parent-teacher conferences, Parent Teacher Organizations, music, art, and athletic events are just a few of the efforts made to encourage parental involvement.

Additionally, teachers, parents, and administrators interact in countless other ways on an individual basis through telephone calls, notes sent home with students, and personal visits between parents and school staff. In spite of these efforts, the problem of parental involvement continues to be of concern to school administrators.

We will briefly describe a school facing a problem of parental involvement. In our case study, the principal appoints three faculty members to examine the problem, and we follow them as they develop a set of questions to guide their search. We then review selected research studies that address those questions and highlight one rather complex study for more intensive analysis. The particular methodological focus for this chapter will be on correlational research designs, and we will highlight the criteria used for making judgments about this type of research. Finally, we will draft an action step to be shared with the principal based upon the committee's findings and deliberations.

The Case: How Do We Get Our Parents More Involved?

J. D. Davis is midway through his fifth year as principal of Jefferson Middle School. Currently, he is mulling over a conversation he had with several teachers. Parental involvement is a topic that returns each time parent-teacher conferences are held, and the usual stories are shared of parents who should attend but don't as well as a few who do show up and teachers wish they hadn't. Usually the flurry of suggestions and finger pointing about parents who "just don't care" passes quickly, and the topic of parental involvement is shelved once more under the heading, "Things to Gripe About When Reviewing Our Most Recent Parent-Teacher Conferences."

Jefferson Middle School (JMS) has more than its share of problems with parental involvement. Situated in a deteriorating inner city location, students come to school from a variety of home situations that challenge the school's efforts at increasing their school-home interactions. Davis worked from time to time with the Parent Teacher Organization (PTO) officers as they planned for a meeting or helped parents schedule fundraisers for purchasing sports equipment, but he knew this was not getting the job done.

On occasion, J. D. expressed his frustration in working, on the one hand, with the most active members of the PTO who were likely to be leaving the district the following semester, and, on the other hand, with the "problem" parents who were permanently entrenched in the community. Or, so it seemed to J. D. Of course, this was an overstatement. There were dozens of parents who were willing to support the school and its programs in any way that they could.

In fact, these concerned parents were the source of the greatest frustrations for Davis and his faculty. How do you get these people more involved in their children's educational efforts? How can JMS initiate programs that work both to *inform* the parents of what teachers are doing with and for their children and to *involve* the parents in taking an active part in the process? What has worked with parents in settings similar to Jefferson Middle School? There must be some research out there to help with this problem.

Davis shared his musings with Jolene Watkins, his assistant principal. He expressed an interest in going beyond the gripes and groans about parental involvement and hoped they could do something positive. He wanted to go beyond the usual urgent plea to attend parent-teacher conferences or the colorful bulletin that went home with students to announce the PTO meeting.

Jolene smiled as she drove home thinking about J. D.'s carefully chosen words: "He hoped *they* could do something positive to improve parental involvement." Jolene had learned that the plural "they" usually meant the singular "she," and she understood she had just been assigned a task to perform. Different administrators delegate in different styles, and J. D.'s preferred method was the plural to singular transfer of responsibility. And, if truth were told, Jolene preferred that to the more direct, "I want you to undertake this assignment" bit of business. At least she could delude herself into thinking that she had chosen to undertake the assignment on her own initiative.

Jolene's plan of attack included a request for two teachers to assist her in a review of research and practice to uncover what the literature on parental involvement could tell them. Sharlene, an 8th grade science teacher, and Mark, a 7th grade social studies teacher, agreed to work with her under the stipulation that they had the support of the administration to implement something if they came up with a workable plan. As Sharlene put it, "I don't want to mess around for six months and wind up with a panel discussion at a PTO meeting on 'Improving Parent-Teacher Relations.'"

Given the assurance that they had the complete support of the principal and perhaps even some financial resources if a feasible plan were forthcoming, the committee set about its task. After the usual time spent in comparing proposed solutions, the committee gradually reached the point where they were ready to focus on the problem.

While knowing where to begin a committee assignment is never easy, Jolene, Mark, and Sharlene had a particularly difficult time defining their task. The initial attraction to find several programs that worked and to select one that seemed to fit their situation at JMS proved difficult to resist. Jolene pushed the group to spend some time determining what they thought to be the question or questions for which they should be seeking answers. Mark thought the question was self-evident: "What can we do to improve parental involvement at Jefferson Middle School?" Upon further discussion it became less clear what each meant by parental involvement. Sharlene seemed concerned that most parents paid little heed to the assigned homework she required in her 8th grade science classes and rarely responded to her written pleas to sign the work as evidence they had at least monitored if not helped with it. She argued that mechanisms were needed to impress upon parents that teachers cannot do it alone and that parental support was necessary to get kids to take school seriously.

Mark acknowledged the importance of Sharlene's concern but felt little could be done about that problem. He argued that parents in this neighborhood were not capable of providing the kind of homework help Sharlene was expecting and that the most they could hope for would be to develop greater interest on the part of parents in attending parent-teacher conferences and to participate in their children's activities such as sports or school functions. As Mark put it, "Is it too much to ask for parents to come to one PTO meeting a year to show they care whether their children succeed or fail?"

Jolene struggled with her response because she feared she would be misunderstood. As the only African-American on the committee and one of four African-Americans on the school faculty, she sensed the problem ran deeper than getting parents to sign off on homework or to attend a PTO meeting or two. And race wasn't the only issue, although she was convinced it contributed substantially to their task of creating a strong climate of cooperation between and among parents, students, faculty, and administration at JMS. She raised the question of "What does parent involvement mean to parents and to teachers in our school?" She reasoned that if it meant different things to each member of the committee there was a strong likelihood that parents and teachers would be viewing involvement from differing perspectives as well.

The discussion continued into the second meeting and, finally, questions started taking shape. The committee agreed that any research they would pursue should help them with several issues. First, they felt a need to examine what people had written on the topic of types of parental involvement. The conceptual confusion that lumps together PTO attendance, parental help with math assignments, and parental expectations for high achievement needed to be addressed. Second, they wanted to know if there was any evidence to show that any of the various types of parental involvement made any difference in student achievement. Finally, they wanted to focus their search on literature that addressed parents and schools quite similar to their own. Jolene agreed to draft the questions and the committee adjourned their second meeting with Mark's semi-serious comment, "This may be more than I wanted to know about parental involvement!" The next day the following memo was placed in Mark's and Sharlene's mail boxes, and the committee was off and running.

PARENTAL INVOLVEMENT COMMITTEE

DRAFT QUESTIONS

1. What types of parental involvement are there and what is known about each type?
2. What evidence exists regarding the effect of parental involvement on student achievement, particularly in lower income, African-American middle school settings?

FIGURE **9.1** Parental Involvement Committee

Overview of the Research

As research articles and book chapters emerged in the search, it quickly became apparent to the committee that parental involvement was neither a simple topic nor one that could be easily separated from broader social and legal issues. A journal issue devoted to the topic of parental involvement and public choice in education (Goldring, 1991) yielded several promising articles that were photocopied and read by each member of the committee. Lindle and Boyd (1991) pointed up the inherent conflict that can exist between parents and educators in the following words: "As professionals, teachers and school administrators need substantial autonomy to carry out their work. As clients of schools, parents and interested citizens have a major stake in how schools operate. Consequently, they need some voice and involvement in school. How to balance these competing needs is far more than an academic issue" (p. 323). A further tension between parents and teachers was noted in the balance theory of Litwak and Meyer (1974), which argued for a balance between intrusive parental involvement and completely autonomous professionals. The growing pressures for professionalization of teaching, while perhaps laudable in some aspects, was argued by some scholars (cf. Goldring, 1986; Lightfoot, 1978) to have widened the gap between experts and nonexperts. The increased bureaucratization of the school organization as a result of population growth and centralization was contrasted with the more informal organization of the family unit, which could deepen the chasm between parents and teachers.

Comer (1980, 1988) added a further complication, arguing that professionalism had promoted a more technocratic dimension to teaching and school administration, which had reduced the emphasis on affective and social dimensions of schooling and favored more cognitive outcomes. The committee was particularly interested in Comer's comment that the neglect of affective issues and personal and group relationships had hampered educators' efforts in working with children from poor families. Each of the issues raised seemed to underscore the difficulty faced by the faculty and staff of JMS.

From a different perspective, Mawdsley and Drake (1993) examined a century of court cases and found a change in parent-school relationships over that period of time. Their reading of the cases led them to conclude that the judicial opinions had created greater deference for the education decisions of schools that ". . . has made schools relatively impervious to the legal demands of parents to change school programs and curricula" (p. 1). These authors echoed Comer's concerns that the effect was most pronounced on parents of the poor, non-English speaking, and disadvantaged children. While the previous writers provided a framework within which the committee could think about their task, the committee now turned to the empirical research to seek more specific information regarding their guiding questions.

Lindle and Boyd (1991) reported a qualitative study based on interviewing 10 families from each of 4 elementary schools. While the sample of elementary school parents raised questions of application validity, the contrast of middle and lower SES populations made the study of interest. With 60% of the lower SES school parents being classified as single parents, the committee reasoned that an examination of the results might yield clues that would be useful for their setting. Additionally, as a qualitative study, the specific responses of parents might yield useful information about their views. The committee was also aware that the downside of this study was that one had to be very cautious about generalizing results from such a small, non representative sample. With these concerns in mind, the committee examined the study in some detail.

Parents expressed many of the same concerns raised by teachers at JMS. For example, one parent said, "This area has a high transient population: Little consistency exists." Another said, "I watch the kids in the neighborhood. They have no discipline. But how much can a school do"? A third commented, "Vandalism is a problem here . . . recently three boys broke into the junior high and all the principal did was suspend them. He said his hands were tied."

Another category of responses emerged that expressed parents' concerns about balancing work demands and the time needed for assisting their children. For example, one parent said, "I'd like to be more involved, but I'm afraid to leave my kids at night. I can't afford a babysitter." Another parent commented, "I help with homework everyday. . . . What am I going to do next year when he's in school a full day, and I'm gone to work by the time he gets home?"

The study reported two clusters of responses of special interest to the committee. One category was labeled "communications in general" and the second was "conferences." In the general category, parents expressed a preference for communications to be more informal and did not respond well to the more bureaucratic approach favored by the professional educators. Parents praised teachers who ". . . don't wait for conferences to communicate" and those who are willing to call the parents at night to ". . . nip things in the bud."

Under the more specialized category of conferences, parents indicated their attitudes by giving only a 25% favorable response to this form of school-home communication, and 40% of the comments indicated that conferences were the most negative experiences parents remembered about school communication. Of particular interest to the committee was the finding that middle SES parents were about equally divided in ranking conferences as positive and negative, while not one lower SES parent listed the conference as a pleasant experience. Some of the reasons parents gave for their concerns about parent conferences were instructive. Lower SES parents commented on the style of language used and of feelings of being patronized by teachers. One mother mentioned a conference in which test scores about her child were being reported and remembered the teacher who, "seemed really hostile about the questions we were asking. I finally had to say 'calm down, we are all adults here.' It was like she felt we shouldn't ask questions." Another example of feeling patronized was given by a middle SES parent who reported, "When I saw the teacher I tried to explain that my daughter has a learning disability. The teacher acted as if I knew nothing about LD even though I have a Masters in Education."

Parents provided a litany of complaints about conferences ranging from the constraints of 10 minutes per conference in which the teacher was recalled as having done all the talking and none of the listening to the difficulty in getting teachers to agree to a conference or to return phone calls. The study concluded that differences in SES between teachers and lower income families puts additional strain on effective school communications and may add to the feelings of being demeaned in the conference setting.

The committee concluded the fourth session with a return to the two questions guiding their research. They felt they had learned a great deal of general information about types of parental involvement, and they felt they better understood why lower SES parents might be less responsive to the more formal bureaucratic procedures used at JMS. What was most lacking in their research review up to this point was some evidence regarding the important second question that asked about the effect of parental involvement on student achievement, particularly the achievement of predominately African-American students from lower income families.

A Study of Parental Involvement

Occasionally, serendipity provides needed assistance. In this case, Jolene received a handout in her Educational Administration class at the local university. The title, "Effects of Parental Involvement on Eighth Grade Achievement" (Ho & Willms, 1996), appeared to contain important information for both questions. This article is reproduced at the end of this chapter and we urge you to take the time now to read it carefully. Our discussion and critique of the study assumes you have done so.

We begin our discussion by examining the conceptual, operational, and empirical levels of the Ho and Willms article. We will explore all three of these, but we will pay particular attention to the operational level. There we will focus on the study's correlational design—the featured research component of this chapter.

Ho and Willms: The Conceptual Level

As stated in chapter 5, the conceptual level of a study explains the ideas that drive the research: the research *questions*, research *problem*, and the *rationale* of the study. We will describe these three aspects of the conceptual level and then examine the Ho and Willms study in relation to them.

Frequently, the title of a research article will provide the most succinct statement of the research question being addressed. Ho and Willms' title, "Effects of Parental Involvement on Eighth-Grade Achievement" leaves little doubt as to the central question being investigated in their study. The title could be recast as a question: "Does parental involvement increase achievement for eighth grade students?" While the title described the question in its general form, the authors made it clear rather early in the article that there were more specific questions that needed to be examined if they were to accomplish their research objective. They state "The purposes of the study reported in this article were fourfold" (p. 316). First, they attempted to clarify the construct of parental involvement both theoretically and empirically. Second, they sought to measure the degree of variation of each dimension both within and between schools. Third, they wanted to learn the relationship between parental involvement and family background variables. Finally, they wanted to examine the relationship between each type of parental involvement and student achievement.

The advantages of clearly stated questions (or clearly stated purposes, as Ho and Willms chose to describe them) should be apparent. By keeping our attention riveted to the questions, we can use them as guides through the remainder of the study. Often a study's methods become quite complex and even confusing. However, if we return to the basic questions that drove the research, and use them to judge the adequacy of the data to answer those questions, we can understand even very complex investigations.

Beyond the specific research questions of a study, we are also interested in examining the underlying problem to which these questions are addressed. If we ask why someone would be interested in these questions about parent involvement, we recognize that improving school achievement is the larger problem behind this study, a problem that is clearly of interest and importance to practitioners.

A third aspect of the conceptual level of a study is its rationale. A good rationale should provide an explanation of the linkages between and among the variables. We will review the four purposes listed by the authors to help us understand the study's structure and then evaluate their rationale for linking parental involvement and student achievement.

As we look at the four purposes of Ho and Willms, we can see the logic to their selection and sequencing in the study. First, it is easy to see that they were interested in a clear delineation of the construct of parental involvement. Their reading of the literature had persuaded them that it was important to have a better understanding of what different concepts may be embedded within that global term.

With a clearer understanding of parental involvement, it was important for Ho and Willms to examine how parental involvement was distributed among schools and parents, their second question. Recall our discussion in chapter 2 concerning achievement, where we pointed out that the total amount of achievement variation in a group of students can be broken into two components—a part that lies between schools and a part that lies among students within schools. Similarly, the total variation in each of the four types of parental involvement can also be broken into two components, enabling Ho and Willms to ask how much of each lies between and within schools.

Why is this question important? Their rationale for question two included a contrast of three explanations found in the literature for why parents might differ in their level of involvement. One explanation (the "institutional approach") was that school practices and policies and the behavior of school staffs were important contributing factors in determining the amount of parental involvement. If that were the case, there should be considerable variation among schools and proportionately less among parents within schools. Alternatively, the second and third theoretical explanations focus on attributes of the parents themselves. The second ("the culture of poverty approach") suggested that differences in parental involvement are a result of low SES parents placing less value on schooling than their higher SES counterparts. A third explanation ("the cultural capital approach") suggested that low SES parents lack the knowledge, skills, and contacts needed to successfully negotiate their way through educational institutions. If the second and third arguments have greater merit, proportionately more of the variation in parental involvement should be found among individuals rather than among schools. Thus, the institutional approach offers hope that schools might successfully increase parental involvement by deliberately changing their policies and practices. They are likely to be less effective in changing the values, attitudes, and skills of parents. Their second question is important, then, because it provides a clue about the likelihood that school administrators can successfully increase parent involvement.

The third purpose speaks to the linkage between types of parental involvement and family background variables. If the researchers were able to establish this link, it might help them explain the connection reported in the literature between family background variables and school achievement. While factors such as SES were empirically related to achievement, and while the literature had suggested that this may be due, in part, to a lack of strong parental involvement, there was little evidence supporting that claim.

The fourth and final question addressed by Ho and Willms asks about the relationship between each type of parental involvement and students' reading and math achievement. This question is reflected in the title of their article and is central to the study. Answering the three previous questions allowed the authors to address this central query. A rationale for this final question must explain how parental involvement could affect the reading and mathematics achievement of students.

The researchers provided partial answers to this question in their literature review as they examined the multidimensional aspects of the construct of parental involvement. They note that in some studies parental involvement had been found to be negatively correlated with school achievement. In these cases Ho and Willms reasoned that helping with homework or attending parent-teacher conferences may signal that a student is in academic or behavioral difficulty, thus explaining the seemingly anomalous findings that involvement has negative effects on achievement. In other studies, where measures of parental involvement included dimensions of high expectations and general monitoring of children's academic performance, involvement had positive effects on achievement. Thus, the authors reasoned that the various components of involvement would be differentially related to school success. Clearly Ho and Willms did not provide an explicit rationale explaining how each component of parent involvement would be related to reading and mathematics achievement. Nevertheless, by positing that differing forms of involvement would have differing effects, they did provide some conceptual help in understanding the relationships among the variables involved in their fourth question.

Ho and Willms: The Operational Level

The operational level addresses important issues of sampling, measurement, design, and data analysis. Because we focus our attention on correlational designs in this chapter we will pay particular attention to this component. We have previously stressed the value of clearly stated research questions and the importance of a logical rationale for a study, and these are vital, indeed. But good questions require good answers, and it is the operational level of a study that determines the quality of those answers. If any component in the research design process fails, the results can be felt throughout the study.

Sampling. In the Ho and Willms study, the researchers drew upon an existing data set (National Center for Education Statistics, 1989) and used a sample that had been drawn as a part of the National Education Longitudinal Study (NELS). The NELS sample was made up of 24,599 8th-grade students, the schools those students attended, and the parents of those students drawn from a probabilistic sample of 1,052 public and private schools in the United States. This was a large, randomly selected sample that should allow the researchers to generalize their results to all U.S. 8th-grade public and private school students and their parents, which represents a real strength of the study.

As a practitioner addressing concerns of application validity, several points may be noted. First, the size and representativeness of the sample should assure the reader that the results of the study are appropriate for a broad range of school settings. Second, the sample was limited to 8th-grade students, and in the opinion of our Jefferson Middle School committee, this focus was particularly appropriate. This study provides an excellent example of the distinction we have drawn between population validity and application validity. Clearly, the study has excellent population validity because the large, representative sample allows the researchers to generalize the results to the population of 8th graders. However, its application validity depends upon the particular characteristics of the practitioner's setting. In this case, the Jefferson Middle School committee can have high confidence that the results of the study can be considered appropriate for their 8th-grade students and parents, while a principal with grades 1–6 might judge the study's application validity for her or his school to be less appropriate.

Measurement. Measurement is the link between a construct and the empirical world. While at an abstract level it may be perfectly reasonable to expect a relationship between two variables, determining whether that relationship actually exists in the real world will require the translation of each of the variables into valid and reliable measures. In the case of Ho and Willms, it is important to examine how well parental involvement and student achievement were measured.

Parental involvement was measured by 12 items (See Table 1 in the Ho and Willms article, p. 320) that were selected from the NELS data set. While the use of an existing data set has obvious advantages for providing an inexpensive way to make use of a large, representative sample, it prevents the researcher from designing measures specifically for the research problem at hand. Ho and Willms were required to work with what was available in the existing file.

Recall that Ho and Willms were interested in defining and measuring different types of parental involvement. They did this by using an approach called *factor analysis* that examines the correlations among a set of items and produces clusters of items that correlate highly with each other. These clusters of items or factors are selected in a way that maximizes the correlation of the items within each factor while minimizing the correlation of that factor with other sets of items. These individual factors are then examined by the researchers and named based on the content of the items. This process needs to be stressed because naming the factors is clearly a subjective interpretation by the researcher and is not determined by the factor analytic procedures themselves. The computer provides a cluster of items that intercorrelate highly, but what the factor is called is based upon the researchers' interpretation of the items. You can examine the cluster of items for yourself by studying Table 2 in Ho and Willms (p. 321). The original 12 items were placed into 4 factors by the factor analytic procedures and then named by Ho and Willms. Home Discussion (4 items) was the first factor, followed by School Communication (2 items), Home Supervision (4 items) and School Participation (2 items). Do the names appear to capture the sense of the items contained in each factor? Would you have named any of them differently?

A second point needs to be stressed about the measurement of parental involvement. Ho and Willms reported that 4 factors or types of parental involvement were found in the study that had eigenvalues greater than 1. While an understanding of eigenvalues is not required for the practitioner, it is important to recognize that other types of parental involvement could have been extracted from these same data and that the ones that were found should not imply that these 4, and only these 4, types of parental involvement exist. The researchers reported that the 4 factors that emerged in this data set were the largest and most distinct clusters of items they found, and it is perfectly appropriate for them to draw this conclusion. Another study using another data set done by other researchers might have found a slightly different set of factors describing parental involvement. A clear knowledge of complex variables does not come easily or with complete certainty.

In addition to measuring parental involvement, another important variable in the study needed to be operationalized as well. Student achievement, as the major dependent variable, was of great importance to the researchers, and we need to know if it was measured validly and reliably. In contrast to the detailed description of procedures for measuring parental involvement, the amount of space devoted to telling us about the measures of academic achievement was very limited. On page 321 we are told they ". . . used standardized measures of academic achievement in reading and mathematics as the dependent variables." We are further informed in footnote 2 (p. 331) that they had initially analyzed measures of history and science achievement but that those were dropped because the results were virtually identical across all 4 dependent measures. While it is useful to know that they used standardized measures of achievement, we are left without any additional information about the particular battery of tests used and their reliability and validity. This may be a minor point in that nationally standardized tests can usually be assumed to have good validity and reliability, but it would be helpful to have more information than the researchers provided.

Design. Of particular interest for us in this chapter is the research design used by Ho and Willms as they examined parental involvement and student achievement. We stressed in chapter 4 that designs differ in their strengths and weaknesses, and it is important for us to recognize what each design can and cannot tell the practitioner.

While not readily apparent to the reader, Ho and Willms employed a correlational design in their study. How can you determine that this was a correlational design when the word "correlation" does not appear in the entire article? The practitioner must look beyond the highly technical language used in a study and ask rather basic questions about how the study was conducted. As discussed in chapter 4, each design has several characteristics that define it. Sometimes by a simple process of elimination it becomes apparent what design is being used, and once you know the design, it becomes apparent what the strengths and limitations of that particular study will be.

Both experimental and quasi-experimental designs require the manipulation of an independent variable, and both can be quickly ruled out as being the design for this study. Clearly, the researchers could not manipulate the type of parental involvement. All they could do was measure the type of involvement manifested by different parents. So, if it is not an experimental or quasi-experimental design, how can we determine what Ho and Willms actually used in their study?

The clues that the design used was correlational is taken from the frequent use of the word "relationship" to describe the outcomes of the study. Beginning with the second sentence in the abstract, attention is drawn to ". . . the relationship of each dimension with parental background and academic achievement" (p. 315). Throughout the article there are frequent references to relationships and associations of variables. These terms accurately describe a correlational design, and with that recognition we remember that caution must be taken in interpreting relationships of variables as being causal in nature. This caution is particularly appropriate because there are other terms used in the study that might inappropriately lead us to stronger inferences of causality than the design will allow us to draw. In the title itself we see the statement "Effects of Parental Involvement on Eighth-Grade Achievement." Elsewhere in the abstract there is a reference to "Parents' participation at school had a moderate effect on reading achievement." The word "effect" is frequently used to suggest a causal relationship in experimental research and may lead one to assume a similar causal connection in this study when it may not be warranted.

Let us examine the concept of correlation a bit more carefully and then explore why correlational designs impose limitations on our ability to infer causality. All correlational procedures provide the user with an estimate of how strongly two or more variables are related and state that estimate in values ranging from +1.0 to −1.0. The + sign indicates that the two variables are related in a *positive* fashion, which means that an increase in one variable is associated with an increase in the other variable. For example, a correlation of +.8 between height and weight would indicate, reasonably enough, that taller people tend to be heavier.

The − sign in the correlation indicates an *inverse* relationship between two or more variables. For example, a correlation of −.2 between class size and pupil achievement indicates that the larger the class size, the lower the achievement. Both negative and positive correlations can be equally meaningful; the sign simply indicates the direction of the relationship.

The *magnitude* of the correlation indicates the strength of the relationship. A correlation of −.2 between class size and achievement indicates that students in smaller classes tend to have higher achievement scores, but this relationship is much weaker than if the value were, say, –.8. A quick look at the magnitude of various correlations allows the reader to draw inferences about the strength of the relationships. Keeping the sign and the magnitude of a correlation in mind should allow you to draw meaningful inferences about comparing various relationships in the Ho and Willms and other research studies.

One final concept also discussed in chapter 4 will be useful in drawing inferences about correlations. Researchers talk frequently about ". . . the amount of variance accounted for." This concept is a logical extension of the magnitude of a correlation. When we ask how strongly two or more variables are related, we are really asking the question of how much difference a change in one variable might make in the other variable. Concretely, if the correlation is –.2 between class size and school achievement, how much of the difference in pupil achievement could be explained by class size? It makes sense that a correlation of –.2 will probably not be as powerful a predictor of pupil achievement than if the correlation were –.8. The task now becomes one of finding an easy way to estimate the amount of that difference, or, to use the terms with which we started this paragraph, ". . . the amount of variance accounted for."

Statisticians have provided us with an easy answer to this question. Simply squaring the correlation gives us the amount of variance accounted for by that particular variable. Thus, the –.2 correlation suggested previously indicates that only 4% of the variation in school achievement can be accounted for by class size. While clearly better than zero, this provides us with only a modest degree of accuracy in prediction. If the correlation between class size and achievement were, for example, –.8, then that would yield a value of 64% of the variance accounted for in school achievement on the basis of class size. It is useful to remember this, because it is easy to make a simple mistake when comparing correlations. To use a different example, if the typical correlation between a standardized ability test and high school grades is .6, and the typical correlation between SES and high school grades is .3, then many might conclude that the ability test is twice as powerful as SES in predicting grades. (.6 is twice as large as .3) In fact, the test is four times more powerful—it explains 36% of the variance in grades while SES explains only 9%.

The ultimate aim of most research is to provide us with information regarding cause-effect relationships among variables. We may engage in exploratory and descriptive research in the early pursuit of a topic, but we would like to reach the point where we can pinpoint possible causes for educational outcomes. In this vein, we need to remind ourselves that correlational designs are not strong designs to assess causality. Correlations do one thing very well and that is to provide us with rather precise estimates of the strength of relationships between and among variables. The question regarding the cause of those relationships is often more difficult to answer.

Consider the following example. If you were to correlate the number of substantive questions asked by middle school social studies teachers with pupil achievement in their classrooms, you would probably find a modest positive correlation between the two variables. Let us say the correlation is .3, which is statistically significant and accounts for 9% of the variance in achievement. Before you hasten to build a staff development program to increase the question-asking behavior of teachers, ask yourself what evidence you have that this relationship is a causal one.

Do students learn more when teachers ask substantive questions, or do classrooms filled with bright and motivated students allow teachers to ask more substantive questions, or could both suppositions have some validity? The existence of a correlation between two variables holds promise of what might be a causal link, but correlation is not direct evidence of it. Numerous examples can be found in everyday settings. Relationships between race and achievement, or gender and math ability are just two of the more obvious cases where correlations can be and frequently are interpreted as causal when, in fact, other variables such as SES, home environment, or societal expectations might be more likely explanations.

In summary, the results of the correlational study will be better understood if we keep several ideas in minds. First, the *sign* of a correlation indicates the direction of the relationship while the *magnitude* of the correlation indicates the strength of the relationship. Also, the existence of a correlation, even a large and consistent one, must be interpreted cautiously. Other evidence from other studies, preferably experimental designs, will need to be weighed before we can make definite statements about causality. We will return to this question of correlation and causality when we examine the results of the Ho and Willms study.

Data Analysis. This final component of the operational level is both extremely important and often quite confusing to practitioners. The data analysis section, usually found in the section labeled "Results," provides tables, reports of statistical analyses, discussion of relationships between and among variables, and statements about statistical significance of the findings. This section, often written in a manner that requires a high degree of statistical sophistication, is the part of the article that practitioners find most difficult to understand. While the highly technical procedures and concepts allow researchers to explain how they have analyzed their data, the nonstatistician is at a disadvantage.

There is an alternative to either becoming a statistician or becoming confused when approaching the data analysis section of a research report. The practitioner should return to the questions that have guided the research. What did the researcher claim to have found that responds to each research question set out in the beginning of the study? Has the researcher provided evidence that the results were not likely to be due to chance; that is, did the researcher provide evidence of statistical significance of the results for each question? Finally, has the researcher provided evidence of the practical significance of the results by discussing the size of the relationship in a correlational study or the size of the difference that a treatment made in an experimental study? Let us apply these three steps to the Ho and Willms study.

Recall that there were four questions involved in this study and that the first three allowed the researchers to reach the fourth one that was central to their interests. Their fourth research question examined the effects of parental involvement on 8th-grade achievement. In the interest of space, we will limit our application of data analysis concepts to this research question.

The researchers discuss their findings on p. 322 and focus the reader's attention on Table 6 (p. 327), which summarizes the results that bear on the relationship between parental involvement and student achievement. After providing a brief discussion of the relationship between SES, ethnicity, gender, and student achievement, the authors elaborate on the findings in Table 6. Take a look at the portion of the table entitled "Parent-involvement Factors." This small section gives you the information you need to determine the statistical significance of the relationship between each type of parental involvement and Mathematics and Reading. Notice the asterisks associated with 3 of the 4 parental involvement types. By glancing at the bottom of the table you will see that one asterisk (*) indicates statistical significance at $p < .05$ and 2 asterisks (**) indicate a level of statistical significance at $p < .01$. This quick check of statistical significance indicates that Home Discussion, School Communication, and School Participation had a relationship with both Mathematics and Reading that was not likely to be attributed to chance. Also, though there was no relationship with Mathematics, Home Supervision did have a statistically significant ($p < .01$) relationship with Reading. Thus, the researchers have provided you with the information you need to conclude that a relationship of this magnitude is likely to occur by chance less than 1 time in 100. By the same token, the lack of an asterisk indicates that the small relationship (.009) between Home Supervision and Mathematics might be the result of chance.

After examining one important facet of the data analysis process—statistical significance—we can now examine the question of the size or amount of the relationship between parental involvement and student achievement. Recall from our previous treatment of this concept that the practitioner needs to be concerned not only with the likelihood that a relationship could be the result of chance but also with the strength of that relationship. The data in a study may yield statistically significant relationships, but the practitioner requires some evidence of their importance. Let us return to the article for evidence regarding effect sizes.

On pages 326 and 327 the researchers provide a clear statement of the effect size of each type of parental involvement, basing their discussion on the same data found in the section of Table 6 that we have been examining. Ho and Willms indicate that the largest effect was found in the relationship of Home Discussion with Mathematics and Reading. While in an absolute sense 12% of a standard deviation might not seem large, we must place this in a context. While researchers generally consider effect sizes below .3 as small, we also need to consider the comparative cost of different attempts to raise achievement. If parental involvement could be increased at, for example, much less cost than lowering class size, then an effect size as modest as the .12 reported in this study might be considered cost-effective. We must always consider both the size of the effect and the amount of the financial, political, or psychological costs as we make determinations about whether an effect size is "large."

The remaining three types of parental involvement yielded even smaller effect sizes and will be mentioned only briefly here. First, notice that School Communication had a statistically significant ($p < .01$) relationship with student achievement but it was a *negative* relationship. As the authors point out, this means that children whose parents communicated more with the school had lower achievement scores. We will have more to say about this finding and its implication later in the chapter.

Second, the remaining two types of parental involvement had very negligible relationships with school achievement. School Participation, while statistically significant at $p < .01$, had an effect size of .03 of a standard deviation. This provides an excellent example of the difference for the practitioner between statistical and practical significance. While School Participation had a relationship that was very unlikely to be due to chance, the magnitude of the relationship was so small that it held little promise for the practitioner.

Finally, Home Supervision yielded a statistically significant relationship ($p < .01$) with Reading but was not related to Mathematics. In addition, the effect size of this variable also ranged from 1 to 3 percent of a standard deviation.

By examining the tables and following closely the text of the article, you can address the two essential issues of statistical and practical significance of the findings of any study. Notice that we did not consider the intricacies of the particular statistical procedure Ho and Willms used. It is not that we do not value the importance of sophisticated statistical techniques, nor that we think the article should not include that material. Rather, we believe that practitioners can understand even highly complex research articles by maintaining their focus on the question and by restricting their attention to the twin notions of statistical and practical significance. Regardless of the statistical procedure used, the researcher will often provide evidence on those two criteria.

Ho and Willms: The Empirical Level

Our final consideration of the Ho and Willms study involves its empirical level in which the researchers report the results of their efforts to provide answers to the questions that guided their study. We will explore these issues through the eyes of the Jefferson Middle School committee as we discuss the findings and their implications for the two questions that the committee framed as they began their assigned task.

We have stressed the need for caution when interpreting results from a correlational study. The relationships reported in this study could be interpreted in different ways. For example, while we might like to believe that the parents who were heavily engaged in Home Discussion were having a positive impact on their children's academic achievement, we must entertain the possibility that the reverse could be true. It is possible that high achieving students influenced their parents to increase discussion of school issues. It seems reasonable that the honor student who comes home requesting help with an English essay might elicit more interaction than her sister who brings back an unsatisfactory paper for the fourth time. We are not arguing that parental involvement did not impact student achievement in this study; we are simply reminding you that correlational data need to be interpreted cautiously.

Given that caveat, the committee looked at the major findings and conclusions as they were linked back to Ho and Willms' research questions. The first question dealt with the clarification of the construct of parental involvement, and, as we reported earlier, the authors had been successful in delineating four types of involvement through the use of factor analysis.

Their second question resulted in a less promising outcome for practitioners in general and for Jefferson Middle School in particular. The researchers wanted to know if schools varied widely in the amount of each type of parental involvement or if most of the variation lay within schools. The significance of this question can be understood a bit better as we near the end of this study. If schools do not vary in the amount of each type of parental involvement, then it would suggest that, in spite of administrators' claims, all the efforts in some schools to develop outstanding parent involvement programs have not made any difference. Even if there are significant effects of parental involvement on student achievement, this would be due to differences among the parents themselves and would not be due to efforts of teachers and administrators to effect school-wide differences.

An examination of Table 3 (p. 322) makes the point quite clearly. For 3 of the 4 types of parental involvement, over 90% of the variance was within schools. In fact, this is what Ho and Willms reported. They stated, ". . . it was impossible to identify reliably schools that were particularly effective or ineffective in inducing higher levels of parental involvement." (p. 328). Schools might differ in PTO attendance, but they did not differ in other forms of involvement. The authors were not making the strong claim that teachers and administrators could not develop effective programs of parental involvement that might make a substantive difference in student achievement: They were saying that they had not found schools to vary greatly on these dimensions.

Research question three concerned the relationship between parental involvement and Family Background, Student Background, and Ethnicity. Table 4 reports the results of those analyses. By reading across the rows under each type of parental involvement, you can determine both the statistical and practical significance of each of these variables. Further, since these coefficients are effect sizes,[1] they are directly comparable, so that you can judge the relative power of the various background and ethnicity factors. While the relationships are modest in size, SES was related ($p < .05$ or better) to all four of the parental

---

[1] We recognize that the fact that these are effect sizes may not be obvious to many readers. However, recall the suggestions we made in chapter 5 regarding tables. There we recommended that after reading a table's title, row, and column headings, the reader should understand what the numbers in the table's cells mean. It is usually unnecessary to know how those numbers were generated (in this case, what a hierarchical linear model is). Rather, it is only necessary to be able to interpret them. In order to do that, we suggested that you read the text that accompanies the table carefully. Often the author will explain how coefficients are to be interpreted. On page 324 Ho and Willms explicitly identify these coefficients as effect sizes.

involvement dimensions, with higher SES parents engaging in greater involvement than their lower SES counterparts. With the exception of its minuscule effect on Home Supervision (.024), SES had an approximately equal impact on Home Discussion, School Communication, and School Participation (.188, .175, and .161, respectively).

Regarding ethnic group differences in parental involvement, the text accompanying Table 4 reports these differences using Whites as the reference category. This means that all ethnic groups were compared to Whites; hence, a positive coefficient means the group scored higher than Whites on that form of involvement, and a negative coefficient means it scored lower. For example, Asian/Pacific Islanders reported lower levels of involvement than Whites ($p <$ .01) in Home Discussion ($ES = -.185$), School Communication ($ES = -.234$) and School Participation ($ES = -.188$), while exercising higher levels of Home Supervision (.183). Parental involvement for Blacks was reported as higher than Whites ($p < .01$) for Home Discussion, Home Supervision, and School Communication, and Blacks had exactly the same level in School Participation, but the effect sizes were small, ranging from .061 to .071.

This study provides a nice example of the importance of being able to read a table of results and not having to rely on the author's interpretation of that table. When the relationships in a study are relatively weak (as they were here) it leaves open greater possibilities for differing interpretations. If effect sizes in a study were reported to be .8 and .1 for two independent variables, it would be difficult to argue that the two were approximately equal in strength. However, the effect sizes contrasted in the Ho and Willms study are not so dramatically different, and alternative interpretations of the same coefficients are possible. For example, in their discussion they state, ". . . our findings provide little support for the conjecture that parents with high SES and parents in two-parent families are more involved in their children's education" (p. 328). Yet, the effect sizes of SES and two-parent families on most types of involvement were among the largest in their Table 4, and with one exception, all were in a positive direction. In the case of two-parent families, in particular, the effect sizes for Home Supervision (.291) and School Participation (.276) border the commonly accepted criterion for practical significance (.30), and in Table 4, which reports 40 separate coefficients, the effects of two-parent families are among the strongest presented.

As another example of the importance of interpretation, the effect size of SES on Home Discussion (.188) was termed "relatively small" (p. 324) while the effect size of being Black on the same variable (.064) was described in exactly the same words (p. 324). Yet it is also correct to say that SES was roughly three times more important than race in its effects on Home Discussion. Both interpretations are defensible. Practitioners need to remember that the researcher has an obligation to offer an interpretation consistent with the data, but practitioners have an obligation as well. They too need to examine the results of a study and draw warranted conclusions based on the data presented. A good study presents the results of its data analyses with sufficient clarity so that readers can draw warranted conclusions for themselves, rather than be required to accept the researcher's interpretations. Ho and Willms provided the results of their analyses in this way.

Ho and Willms' fourth research question dovetailed nicely with the second question of the committee. Jolene's committee had asked: *What evidence exists regarding the effect of parental involvement on student achievement, particularly in lower income African-American middle school settings?*

These results have been discussed previously and the findings appeared to be mixed. There was evidence of a statistically and practically significant relationship between Home Discussion and student achievement, but achievement's relationships with the other three types of parental involvement were much less clear. Mark characterized these findings to the committee as "Good News-Bad News" results. The good news was that parents' involvement with their children in the home was most strongly related to increased math and reading achievement. The bad news was that schools did not appear to influence this type of parental involvement. Conversely, it seemed to Mark that schools might influence PTO attendance and volunteering, but these activities were not associated with increased achievement. Stated most bluntly, those things that made a difference did not seem to be under the influence of the school, and the things that the school had worked hard to improve did not seem to make a difference.

Of course, Mark's comment was an overstatement of the findings, and Ho and Willms were not that pessimistic. Those parental behaviors that include, for example, working with their children in the home and providing both support and help with homework may not be impossible to impact, but they would not be as easy as encouraging a big turnout at the PTO meeting or making sure that parents came in for a parent-teacher conference. Ho and Willms phrased Mark's Good News-Bad News dilemma much more positively. They stated: ". . . there was little variation among schools in average levels of home discussion, which suggests that relatively few schools have strong influences on the learning climate in the home. We expect that big gains in achievement could be realized through programs that give parents concrete information about parenting styles, teaching methods, and school curricula" (p. 329). We hasten to add that Ho and Willms had no specifics on what such programs might look like, and they left to future research (or to Jolene and her committee) the task of developing such programs.

The Committee's Conclusions

After a very busy and extended committee session Jolene took an hour that evening and recorded the following notes in the journal that she had been keeping (see Figure 9.2 on the following page).

As the committee met for the final time they discussed what they had learned. First, the research literature had not yielded what had been sought, namely, an existing program that would be effective in their type of school. Sharlene commented on the innocence with which they had begun their efforts: "We were looking for a magic bullet to knock off Goliath and what we found were directions to put together a sling shot." They all agreed that a great deal of

JOURNAL NOTES

Recommendations on Ho and Willms
Jolene Watkins

It struck me that one way to bring our thinking together might be to see what we know about each question that guided our deliberations.

Question # 1: *What types of parental involvement are there and what is known about each type?*
    The four-fold classification of (1) Home Discussions, (2) Home Supervision, (3) School Communication, and (4) School Participation seems useful. Clearly, at Jefferson Middle School, we have been more preoccupied with School Communication and School Participation than with the other two types. Our parent-teacher conferences and concern about grade reports are examples of attempts at improving School Communication and our efforts to increase attendance at PTO meetings would be illustrative of working on increasing School Participation.

Question # 2: *What evidence exists regarding the effect of parental involvement on student achievement, particularly in lower income African-American middle school settings?*
    This question seems to be the more important one, and the answers appeared interesting if not particularly encouraging. The results seemed to indicate that increasing our efforts to improve School Communication and School Participation would not be a good use of our time. These types of parental involvement, while useful for other purposes, did not appear to have much impact on school achievement. What is needed is an effort to increase the type of parental involvement (Home Discussion) that did show greater promise in impacting school achievement. What we need is a plan that will help parents develop these skills.
    Several conclusions seem warranted from the Ho and Willms article. First, while a relationship was found between SES and Home Supervision, the strength of this relationship was less strong than commonly believed by many faculty members at JMS. Second, the research did not support the assumption that African-American parents were participating less than did white parents in their children's education. Both of these conclusions should give us pause, and they need to be shared and widely discussed with faculty colleagues.

Next steps: *I think we should draw up a brief plan for a report to Principal Davis. I believe we should keep it quite general. It appears that we must bring faculty, parents, and administrators along slowly to make sure everyone is committed to the overall goals of developing the types of parental involvement that appear to be linked to student achievement.*

F I G U R E   **9.2**   Journal Notes

learning had occurred; it just was not what they expected. Jolene reminded them of a line her research professor kept using in class: "Don't expect research to fix your problem."

They agreed that the research had given them a new way of thinking about their problem and that it was worth the effort. The Ho and Willms study had certainly challenged their initial assumptions. Clearly, finding more and better ways to get parents active at parent-teacher conferences and PTO meetings was not going to solve their problem, but it provided a way to begin. There were suggestions in the literature (e.g., Lindle, 1990; Hoover-Dempsey & Sandler, 1995) that outlined plans for developing a program of parental involvement. These two papers would help them as they and their colleagues sketched out parental involvement plans for JMS.

We close this chapter by sharing the action step taken by the committee. After a lengthy discussion and debate among the three members, they created a plan for action to share with the principal. As with most plans, its development and execution will depend on many factors. The committee felt that they had benefited from a review of the literature and had gained new insights into their problem.

Memorandum

TO: J. D. Davis

FR: Jolene Watkins

Mark Rigby

Sharlene Evers

RE: Parental Involvement Committee Plan

We would like to share our ideas for improving parental involvement at JMS. It is only in skeletal form, but we would like to discuss it with you at your convenience. Our plan calls for a three phase approach to the problem that will require the involvement of many teachers, parents and, of course, the principal.

The three phases are: (1) Redefinition of the Problem, (2) Strengthening Parental Involvement, and (3) Extending Parental Involvement.

Redefinition of the Problem

The first phase calls for time to be spent at several faculty meetings in which the committee will share the benefits of their search of the literature. In particular, we would like to carefully review one study that articulates four types of parental involvement and their relationships with school achievement. The committee feels strongly that unless the faculty engages some of the same material we have studied, it will be difficult to move to the next stage.

Continued

F I G U R E   *9.3*   Memorandum

Figure 9.3 continued

Strengthen Parental Involvement

Phase two will examine our current efforts in parent-teacher conferences and PTO but with a definite twist of emphasis. The current programs will be examined with an eye toward providing an entree into the type of parental involvement that has shown greatest promise for improving school achievement. Parent-teacher conferences might not be seen primarily as vehicles to convey information from the school to the parents about their children's academic program. A new emphasis might be developed that focuses on parents' involvement with their children in the home. This type of involvement was the one most strongly related to school *achievement in math and reading.*

Extending Parental Involvement

Phase three will require more time and effort and will include a sustained program of parental involvement that will coordinate all our efforts. Rather than separate efforts at PTO, parent-teachers conferences, and other voluntary efforts, the final stage will draw special attention to a new approach of home-school relations. Rather than present the details of such a program, we choose to paint it in broad strokes and develop the details at the next stage with input from both parents and faculty. Clearly, a committee that includes key faculty members, the principal, and several parents will be required if Jefferson Middle School is to take this important step in building a better learning environment for our pupils.

References

Comer, J. P. (1980). *School power.* New York: Free Press.

Comer, J. P. (1988). Is parenting essential to good teaching? *NEA Today, 6*(6), 34–40.

Goldring, E. B. (1986). The school community: Its effects on principals' perceptions of parents. *Educational Administration Quarterly, 22*(2), 115–132.

Goldring, E. B. (1991). Parental involvement and public choice in education. International *Journal of Educational Research. (15),* 229–352.

Ho Sui-Chu, E. & Willms, J. (1996). Effects of parental involvement on eighth-grade achievement. *Sociology of Education, 69,* 126–141.

Hoover-Dempsey, K. V., & Sandler, H. M. (1995). Parental involvement in children's education: Why does it make a difference? *Teachers College Record, 97*(2), 310–331.

Lightfoot, S. L. (1978). *Worlds apart: Relationships between families and schools.* New York: Basic Books, Inc.

Lindle, J. C. (1990). Five reasons to prepare your staff for parent involvement. *The School Administrator, 47*(6), 19–22.

Lindle, J., & Boyd, W. L. (1991). Parents, professionalism, and partnership in school-community relations. *International Journal of Educational Research. 15,* 323–337.

Litwak, E., & Meyer, H. J. (1974). *School, family and neighborhood: The theory and practice of school-community relations.* New York: Columbia University Press.

Mawdsley, R. D., & Drake, D. (1993). Involving parents in the public schools: Legal and policy issues. *West's Education Law Quarterly, 2*(1), 1–114.

Milne, A. M., Myers, D. E., Rosenthal, A. S., & Ginsburg, A. (1986). Single parents, working mothers, and the educational achievement of school children. *Sociology of Education 59,* 125–139.

National Center for Education Statistics. (1989). *National Education Longitudinal Study* (NCES Publication No. 90–482). Chicago: National Opinion Research Center.

A P P E N D I X

Effects of Parental Involvement on Eighth-Grade Achievement

Esther Ho Sui-Chu
J. Douglas Willms

The indicators of parental involvement in children's education vary considerably across studies, most of which treat parental involvement as a unidimensional construct. This study identified four dimensions of parental involvement and assessed the relationship of each dimension with parental background and academic achievement for a large representative sample of U.S. middle school students. The findings provide little support for the conjecture that parents with low socioeconomic status are less involved in their children's schooling than are parents with higher socioeconomic status. Furthermore, although schools varied somewhat in parental involvement associated with volunteering and attendance at meetings of parent-teacher organizations, they did not vary substantially in levels of involvement associated with home supervision, discussion of school-related activities, or parent-teacher communication. Yet the discussion of school-related activities at home had the strongest relationship with academic achievement. Parents' participation at school had a moderate effect on reading achievement, but a negligible effect on mathematics achievement.

Perhaps the most enduring finding in the sociology of education is that schooling outcomes are related to the socioeconomic status (SES) of children's parents (see, for example, White 1982). Much of the work in this field has been directed at determining the processes that contribute to this relationship, including structural processes at the level of the school, community, or larger society and microlevel processes associated with individual and group actions. Ethnographic research has bridged the gap between theories at both levels by introducing cultural elements that mediate processes at the macrolevel and by demonstrating how social and individual influences reinforce and interact with each other (Mehan 1992). Underlying the efforts to uncover the relationship between parents' SES and schooling outcomes is the belief that an understanding of the important processes will help schools and broader communities enhance children's education.

Background

A number of studies have suggested that parents of higher SES are more involved in their children's education than are parents of lower SES and that greater involvement fosters more positive attitudes toward school, improves homework habits, reduces absenteeism and dropping out, and enhances academic achievement (Astone and McLanahan 1991; Epstein 1987; Fehrmann, Keith, and Reimers 1987; Lareau 1987;

This article was originally published in *Sociology of Education*, April 1996, Vol. 69, pp. 126–141.

Muller 1993; Stevenson and Baker 1987). Thus, some of the association between students' outcomes and parents' background is probably attributable to different levels of parental involvement in school-related activities. If this is the case, then strategies that increase parental involvement may be an effective means of improving schooling outcomes and of reducing inequities in achievement among students with different social-class backgrounds.

Lareau (1987) described three conceptual approaches that researchers have used to explain the variation in parental involvement along social-class lines: the culture of poverty, the institutional approach, and the cultural-capital approach. According to the culture of poverty thesis, parental involvement varies because parents of different social classes have different values: Working-class parents place less emphasis on the importance of schooling and maintain a greater separation between their roles and those of school staff than do middle-class parents. In the institutional approach, institutions are the source of variation, either because school staff differ in their ability to involve working-class parents or because the subtle discriminatory practices that discourage these parents' participation (Becker and Epstein 1982; Lightfoot 1978).

The third approach—the one favored by Lareau (1987, 1989)—incorporates Bourdieu's (1977) concept of cultural capital. According to this thesis, schools are largely middle-class institutions with middle-class values, organizational patterns, and forms of communication. Children who are raised in middle-class environments have a form of cultural capital that enables them to adapt more readily to and to benefit from school life. Similarly, middle-class parents are more likely to feel comfortable relating to teachers and being involved in school activities. The cultural capital thesis is not inconsistent with the first two approaches and, in some respects, integrates them in that it emphasizes the roles of both schools and parents. However, in this approach working-class parents are not faulted for low aspirations, nor are teachers berated for discriminatory practices; rather, the approach emphasizes the class structures embedded in home and school life and the process by which parents with different dispositions (what Bourdieu called "habitus") realize success in the schooling system.

The purposes of the study reported in this article were fourfold. First, we attempted to clarify the construct, *parental involvement* by examining its dimensions, both theoretically and empirically. Some of the early studies (such as Morrison 1978) on the subject conceived it as involving parents in school activities; however, more recent studies (for example, Epstein 1986, 1987) have emphasized parents' actions at home, such as discussing their children's experiences at school and helping children with their schoolwork. In examining the effects of involvement on schooling outcomes, researchers have not adequately distinguished between these two general types of involvement. Our analysis identified two types of home involvement—one associated with discussing school activities and the other with monitoring a child's out-of-school activities—and two types of school involvement—one pertaining to contact between parents and school personnel and the other to volunteering in school and attending parent-teacher conferences and open-house meetings.

Second, we estimated the extent to which each dimension of parental involvement varies among students within and between schools. If variation in parental involvement stems largely from school practices and policies, one would expect to find considerable variation among schools in levels of parental involvement. According to the culture of poverty and the cultural capital theses, there would be large within-school variation in involvement that would be associated with the SES of the students' parents and the mean SES of the school.

Consequently, our third purpose was to understand the relationship between parental involvement and family background. We determined what proportion of the variation within and among schools in each dimension of involvement is attributable to parental background at the individual level and whether the variation among schools that remains after background is controlled is statistically significant. If significant variation among schools remains, the next issue is whether it is related to the mean SES of the school. We expected that there might be a contextual effect of the intake composition of the school on parental involvement, in that it may be easier to establish a climate of greater involvement if most parents are from middle-class backgrounds. Put another way, the question is: "Is a parent of average SES more likely to be involved in a high SES school or in a low SES school?" The same question can be asked with regard to a parent with above-average or below-average SES: Does the parent's involvement depend on the intake composition of the school? In exploring these relationships, we also included variables pertaining to ethnicity and family structure and examined whether some of the contact between home and school is attributable to students' learning or behavioral problems.

Finally, we examined whether variations in levels of school achievement are related to the four types of involvement. For our large, nationally representative sample of middle school students, we included measures of academic achievement in four subject areas and a more extensive list of background factors than those used in many previous studies. The analysis applied a multilevel statistical model to estimate school effects (Bryk and Raudenbush 1992; Raudenbush and Willms 1995). This approach provides an estimate of each school's effect on achievement, over and above the effects of parental background, and attempts to determine whether some of the effect is attributable to either individual-level contributions by parents or to the overall levels of parental involvement in the school.

Review of the Literature

The major large-scale studies of the determinants of educational achievement that have been conducted during the past two decades have incorporated a number of measures of parental practices at home or parental involvement in school. Studies with nationally representative samples have included the Sustaining Effects Study of Title 1 (Hoepfner, Wellisch, and Zagorski 1977), which covered students who were in grades 1–6 in 1976–77; the High School and Beyond (HS&B) study of the 1980 cohort of high school sophomores (National Opinion Research Center 1980), which followed a subsample of students to 1986; the Longitudinal Study of American Youth (LSAY) (Miller and Hoffer 1994), which followed a sample of 7th- and 10th-grade students in 1987 throughout their high school careers; and the National Education Longitudinal Study (NELS) (National Center for Education Statistics 1989), which sampled 8th-grade students in 1988 and followed them throughout high school. Research based on these data has been augmented with the Time Use Longitudinal Panel Study (Stevenson and Baker 1987), based on a nationally representative sample of American households, and a study of the practices of the parents of a large sample of elementary school children in Maryland (Epstein 1986, 1987).

The results of these studies are difficult to compare because the measures of parental involvement differ substantially. In their analysis based on data from the Sustaining Effects Study, Milne, Myers, Rosenthal, and Ginsburg (1986) used measures of whether parents helped with homework or attended parent-teacher conferences and three variables describing the time children spent doing homework, watching television, or reading; although the latter variables are affected by parental practices, we consider them indirect measures of parental involvement. Fehrmann et al. (1987) constructed a composite measure of parental involvement for the HS&B data that included measures of whether parents knew where their children were and what their children were doing, whether parents influenced their children's plans after high school, and whether parents closely monitored how well their children were doing in school. Astone and McLanahan's (1991) analysis of the same data included a measure of general supervision and measures of whether the parents had high aspirations for their children, monitored school progress, and talked regularly with their children.

In addition, Miller and Green's (1992) analysis of the LSAY data used a structural equation model, with parental involvement represented by measures of whether parents helped with homework, rewarded good grades, and communicated with teachers about school matters. Madigan's (1994) analysis of the LSAY data examined the effects of 10 indicators of parental involvement, associated mainly with whether parents encourage and reward work on mathematics at home. Muller's (1993) analysis of the NELS data also evaluated the separate effects of a number of parental practices.

Most of the analyses of the large data sets used some form of regression analysis, with one or two measures of SES (such as family income or parents' education) in the model. Some also included measures of family structure, ethnicity, and sex of the child. Thus, the estimated effects of parental involvement are adjusted effects; that is, they are the expected effects of involvement over and above the effects of family background. In attempting to account for the effects of family structure on reading and mathematics achievement, Milne et al. (1986) found *negative* effects of parents helping their White elementary school children with homework and suggested that this counterintuitive finding was attributable to the fact that parents helped more if their children were not doing well at school. Madigan (1994) also found negative effects for parents helping with homework, insisting that their children do their homework, or rewarding their children for good grades. Muller (1993), too, reported negative effects for parents monitoring their eighth graders' homework or providing more after-school supervision and significant negative effects for parents' frequent contacts with school or participation in parent-teacher conferences. Stevenson and Baker (1987) found positive effects for parents' attendance at meetings of parent-teacher organizations (PTOs) and parent-teacher conferences, but their data included only mother's education as a control for SES.

Both Milne et al. (1986) and Madigan (1994) found significant positive effects for parents' high expectations for their children, and Muller (1993) reported a significant positive effect for parents discussing school experiences with their children. Astone and McLanahan (1991) found large significant positive effects for parents' aspirations and general supervision on a range of educational outcomes and small positive effects for monitoring progress, but small negative effects for parents talking with their children. The parental-involvement construct used by Fehrmann et al. (1987), which consists of monitoring and supervision, was also positively related to children's academic achievement. In summary, these large-scale studies found that parents' high expectations for and general monitoring of their children's performance are positively related to children's academic achievement, whereas helping with homework and attending parent-teacher conferences do not have strong effects and may be negatively related to achievement.

The literature just described suggests that parental involvement is a multidimensional construct and should not be treated as a single construct. However, the inclusion of a large number of separate measures makes it more difficult to interpret the effects of any particular measure and can lead to multicollinearity. We attempted to overcome this problem by using 12 indicators of parental involvement, based on questions from both the student and teacher questionnaires of the NELS, and conducting a factor analysis to reduce them to four separate constructs.

The most serious limitation of analyses of data from large-scale surveys, and of most descriptive, qualitative studies, is that *causal* inferences are weak. However, causal inferences can be strengthened by better model specification. For example, the findings discussed earlier could suggest that helping with homework and attendance at parent-teacher conferences cause lower achievement; instead, they probably indicate that students with low academic achievement are more likely to receive extra help, and parents of children with a learning or behavioral problem are more likely to have contact with schools. By including measures of whether children had learning or behavioral problems, we could estimate the effects of parental involvement independent of the effects of learning or behavioral problems.

Some of the studies of parental involvement included measures of ethnicity but did not provide a clear picture of the extent to which it varies across ethnic groups. Coleman (1987) suggested that norms for academic success, and thus levels of parental involvement, may vary among ethnic groups. He noted the case of Asian parents in one school district who bought two copies of their children's textbooks: one for their children and one for them. But apart from norms for success, parents from some ethnic groups may not feel comfortable communicating with teachers or participating in school activities because of language barriers or differences in cultural values (see Delgado-Gaitan, 1991). Therefore, analyses should also include measures of ethnicity to understand the impact of ethnicity on parents' involvement and to assess the net impact of parents' involvement on students' achievement over and above the influence of ethnicity.

Data and Methods

Data for this study were taken from the NELS, which was based on a sample of 24,599 eighth-grade students and their parents and teachers, drawn from a national probability sample of 1,052 public and private schools in the United States. Compared with other nationally representative data sets, NELS is particularly strong in its coverage of items pertaining to parental involvement. Our analysis used data merged from the student and parent questionnaires.

The 12 items we selected to measure aspects of parental involvement are described in Table 1. A principal components analysis with varimax rotation identified four factors with eigenvalues greater than 1. These four factors accounted for 55 percent of the variance in the set of 12 variables (see Table 2 for the factor loadings). We labeled the four factors Home Discussion (with strong loadings on Talk with Mother, Talk with Father, Discuss School Program, and Discuss Activities), School Communication (Parent Contacts School and School Contacts Parent), Home Supervision (Limit TV Time, Limit Going Out, Monitor Homework, and Home After School), and School Participation (Volunteer at School and Attend PTO Meetings). For some purposes, it may be useful to disaggregate our measures further, for example, to include separate measures for volunteering and attendance at PTO meetings. However, we do not think that doing so would have changed our main results appreciably because the findings from the factor analysis suggested that

TABLE *1*

Selected Items for Parent-Involvement Variables

Talk with Mother (BYS50a)	How often have you talked to [your mother or female guardian] about planning your high school program? (0 = not at all, 1 = once or twice, 2 = three or more times)
Talk with Father (BYS50b)	How often have you talked to [your father or male guardian] about planning your high school program (0 = not at all, 1 = once or twice, 2 = three or more times)
Discuss School Program (BYS36a)	Since the beginning of the school year, how often have you discussed the following with either or both of your parents or guardians? . . . selecting courses or programs at school (0 = not at all, 1 = once or twice, 2 = three or more times)
Discuss Activities (BYS36b)	. . . school activities or events of particular interest to you (0 = not at all, 1 = once or twice, 2 = three or more times)
Monitor Homework (BYS38a)	How often do your parents or guardians . . . check on whether you have done your homework? (0 = never, 1 = rarely, 2 = sometimes, 3 = often)
Limit TV Time (BYS38c)	. . . limit the amount of time you can spend watching TV? (0 = never, 1 = rarely, 2 = sometimes, 3 = often)
Limit Going Out (BYS38d)	. . . limit the amount of time for going out with friends on school nights? (0 = never, 1 = rarely, 2 = sometimes, 3 = often)
Home after School (BYS40a-b)	[Is your mother or father]. . . at home when you return from school? (0 = never, 1 = rarely, 2 = sometimes, 3 = usually)
School Contacts Parents (BYP57a-e)	Since your eighth grader's school opened last fall, how many times *have you been contacted by the school* about . . . your eighth grader's (a) academic performance, (b) academic program for this year, (c) course selection for high school, (d) placement decisions . . ., and (e) behavior in school? (0 = none, 1 = once or twice, 2 = three or four times, 3 = more than four times)
Parents Contact School (BYP58a-c)	Since your eighth grader's school opened last fall, how many times *have you or your spouse or partner contacted* the school about . . . your eighth grader's (a) academic performance, (b) academic program for this year, and (c) course selection for high school? (0 = none, 1 = once or twice, 2 = three or four times, 3 = more than four times)
Volunteer at School (BYP59d)	Do you or your spouse or partner . . . act as a volunteer at the school? (0 = no, 1 = yes)
PTO (BYYP59a-c)	. . . (a) belong to PTO, (b) attend meetings of a PTO, and (c) take part in the activities of a PTO? (0 = no, 1 = yes)

T A B L E *2*

Factor Analysis of Parent-Involvement Variables

	Factor 1	Factor 2	Factor 3	Factor 4
Home Discussion				
Talk with Mother	.787	.019	.040	.022
Discuss School Program	.730	.012	.114	.004
Talk with Father	.706	.032	.061	.035
Discuss Activities	.605	−.029	.109	.105
School Communications				
School Contacts Parents	.032	.858	−.009	.092
Parents Contact School	−.013	.857	.032	.113
Home Supervision				
Limit TV Time	.080	.042	.711	.048
Limit Going Out	.060	−.007	.681	−.042
Monitor Homework	.173	.118	.607	−.056
Home after School	.006	−.170	.399	.194
School Participation				
Volunteer at School	.048	.040	.030	.846
Participates in PTO	.102	.175	.000	.790
Percentage of variance explained	20.1	14.3	10.8	9.6

parents who volunteered were also likely to attend PTO meetings. Unfortunately, the NELS data do not include detailed information on school and classroom policies and practices that may encourage parents to participate in school-related activities or dissuade them from doing so. This is a limitation of our study because if we knew that school policies on parental involvement varied, we could have accounted for that variation with direct measures describing school policy and practice.

A multilevel regression analysis fits a hierarchical linear model (HLM) to data that are organized hierarchically (Bryk and Raudenbush 1992)—in this case, students nested within schools. It enables the researcher to partition the variation in a variable into within- and among-group components and to examine the relationships among variables both within and among groups. Our first HLM analysis, which was a null model because it did not include any student background covariates, investigated the variation of each of the four dimensions of parental involvement within and among schools. We then extended the model to include measures of family SES,[1] family structure, whether students were considered by their parents to have learning or behavioral problems, and the students' sex and ethnicity. The analysis used dimensions of parental involvement as the dependent variables in separate regression equations. It showed not only the effects of different aspects of family background on each dimension of parental involvement, but the extent to which parental involvement varied among schools after student intake was controlled.

The second set of HLM analyses used standardized measures of academic achievement in reading and mathematics as the dependent variables.[2] The first analysis estimated the relationship between the achievement measures and the full set of student background variables, including both the individual-level and school mean

TABLE *3*

Percentage Variation of Parent-Involvement Factors Within and Between Schools

	Home Discussion	Home Supervision	School Communication	School Participation
Within schools	94.0	97.1	91.5	77.4
Between schools	6.0	2.9	8.5	22.6

SES. The mean SES of the school was included because a number of studies have indicated that the intake composition of a school can have a "contextual effect" on students' achievement, over and above the effects of individual-level characteristics (see Willms 1992 for a review). The second analysis added the four factors of parental involvement to discern whether they have an effect on achievement that is independent of family background. The model also included the mean level of participation for the school because we expected that a child's achievement might be affected more by the overall level of parental involvement in the school than by the involvement of the child's own parents.

The NELS data on the eighth-grade students do not include a measure of prior academic achievement, and thus the estimates of school effects derived from our hierarchical analysis may be biased (see Raudenbush and Willms 1995; Willms 1992). For example, if we had measures of children's cognitive skills on entry to kindergarten or Grade 1, it is likely that our estimates of the variation in school effects would have been smaller. This bias could lead to an overestimation of the effects of parental involvement, especially those pertaining to communication with and participation in school. This problem could have been acute if we were examining achievement in Grade 12 and trying to isolate the effects of schooling during students' high school careers. However, in this case, we expected this bias to be relatively small because we were interested in the cumulative impact of SES and involvement on achievement over the child's full elementary- and middle school careers.

Results

Table 3 represents the variation within and between schools for each of the parental-involvement constructs. It shows that over 90 percent of the variation in the first three types of involvement—Home Discussion, Home Supervision, and School Communication—was within schools and only about 3 to 9 percent of the variation was between schools. This finding means that the average level of involvement was relatively uniform across the 1,052 schools in the sample. However, 77.4 percent of the variation in levels of School Participation was within schools and 22.6 percent was between schools. Thus, schools differed considerably more in their average levels of School Participation (parents volunteering at school and attending PTO meetings) than in the other constructs. An important implication of these results for the study of school effects is that it is difficult to identify schools that have particularly high or low levels of parental involvement when the four types of involvement

T A B L E **4**

Hierarchical Linear Model Explaining Variation in the Four Parent-Involvement Factors

	Home Discussion		Home Supervision		School Communication		School Participation	
	Coefficient	SE	Coefficient	SE	Coefficient	SE	Coefficient	SE
Family Background								
Socioeconomic status	.188**	(.007)	.024*	(.007)	.175**	(.007)	.161**	(.008)
Number of siblings	−.041**	(.004)	.026**	(.004)	−.017**	(.004)	.007*	(.004)
Number of parents	.072**	(.015)	.291**	(.016)	−.079**	(.015)	.276**	(.014)
Student Background								
Female	.173**	(.012)	−.043**	(.013)	−.196**	(.012)	.004	(.011)
Learning problem	−.206**	(.026)	−.026	(.027)	.469**	(.025)	−.025	(.024)
Behavioral problem	−.191**	(.021)	−.116*	(.022)	.883**	(.020)	−.162**	(.020)
Ethnicity								
Asian/Pacific Islander	−.185**	(.027)	.183**	(.027)	−.234**	(.026)	−.188**	(.025)
Hispanic	.005	(.021)	.144**	(.021)	.014	(.021)	−.073**	(.020)
Black	.064**	(.022)	.071**	(.021)	.061**	(.021)	.000	(.021)
Native American	−.128*	(.057)	−.005	(.058)	−.142**	(.055)	−.071	(.053)
Residual Variance as a Percentage of the Total Variance								
Within schools	89.0		94.8		79.3		74.1	
Between schools	3.3		2.7		6.0		14.3	
Percentage of Variance Explained								
Within schools	5.3		2.4		13.3		4.3	
Between schools	44.9		6.6		29.4		36.8	

*$p < .05$.; **$p < .01$.

are considered together. Although a few schools may have had particularly effective strategies for fostering high levels of parental involvement at home or communicated more with parents, our results suggest that, on average, these dimensions of parental involvement did not vary markedly across schools. However, we found considerable variation among schools in parental volunteering and attendance at PTO meetings.

In the next analysis, we attempted to explain variation in the four factors of parental involvement with measures of family background and students' characteristics. Table 4 displays the estimates of the regression coefficients and their standard errors for models explaining each of the four constructs. An HLM analysis essentially estimates a separate regression model for each school. In these analyses, the outcome measures are factor scores, which have a mean of 0 and a standard deviation of 1.[3] The regression estimates shown are for the average within-school equation across the

1,052 schools (for example, the regression coefficient of SES, .188, is the weighted average of the 1,052 within-school coefficients of SES). The estimates represent the effects of a one-unit increase in the predictor variable, expressed as a fraction of a standard deviation (an effect size).

Consistent with previous research, SES had a statistically significant positive relationship with parental involvement. However, the effect sizes are relatively small. Except for Home Supervision, the coefficients ranged from .161 to .188, which indicates that the amount of involvement increased by about 16–20 percent of a standard deviation for each 1 standard deviation increase in SES. For Home Supervision, the effect was substantively insignificant—less than 3 percent of a standard deviation, indicating that parents with different levels of family background provided relatively similar levels of supervision.

The effect of the number of siblings was –.041 for Home Discussion, indicating that levels of discussion decrease by about 4 percent of a standard deviation for each additional sibling. The same is true for School Communication, but the effect size was less than 2 percent of a standard deviation. The effects of number of siblings on Home Supervision and School Participation were positive and relatively small. The third row of Table 4 displays the effects of number of parents (that is, of living in a single- versus a two-parent family) on parental involvement. The estimates indicate that levels of Home Supervision and School Participation were considerably higher in two-parent families (approximately 28 percent of a standard deviation higher) than in one-parent families. The effects on Home Discussion were also positive but much smaller, whereas single-parent families tended to have higher levels of School Communication. Note that these effects are net of the influence of family SES and other factors in the model.

Differences in the involvement of parents of male and female students were pronounced: Female students reported more discussion at home, while male students reported considerably more parental communication with the school. Levels of Home Supervision were slightly higher for males, but there was no difference between the sexes in levels of School Participation.

The coefficients for learning and behavioral problems indicate that children with these difficulties tended to have fewer discussions with and less supervision from their parents at home and that their parents participated less in school. However, levels of School Communication were considerably higher—the effects were 47 and 88 percent of a standard deviation for children with learning and behavioral problems, respectively.

The analyses also revealed some interesting differences among ethnic groups. In these analyses, White (other than Hispanic) was the reference category, and so the coefficients indicate differences between the designated group and Whites. Asian and Pacific Islanders had lower levels of Home Discussion, School Communication, and School Participation than did Whites but higher levels of Home Supervision; in each case, the effect was about 20 percent of a standard deviation. The differences between Hispanics and Whites were relatively small, except for Home Supervision, which was higher for Hispanics. The differences between Blacks and Whites were relatively small across all factors; overall, they suggest that parental involvement was slightly higher for Blacks, except for volunteering at school or attendance at PTO meetings. Finally, the results suggest slightly lower levels of Home Discussion and School Communication for Native Americans than for Whites, but these estimates are less accurate because of the relatively small number of Native Americans in the sample.

The bottom portion of Table 4 shows the percentage of within- and between-school variation explained by the set of background variables in the model. For example, the partitioning of the variance in Table 3 indicated that 6 percent of the variation in Home Discussion was between schools, and the background variables in Table 4 account for 44.9 percent of that between-school variation. Similarly, the background variables account for 5.3 percent of the 94 percent variation within schools.

At least two conclusions can be drawn from the analysis of explained variance. First, the background variables explained only a small proportion of the within-school variation. For Home Supervision, they accounted for only 2.4 percent of the variation, which suggests that there are a number of other unmeasured factors that determine the degree of parental supervision. The same is true for Home Discussion and School Participation, for which the background variables accounted for only 5.3 and 4.3 percent of the within-school variation, respectively. The model was somewhat better for School Communication, for which 13.3 percent of the within-school variation was explained. Second, there was very little variation among schools in Home Discussion, Home Supervision, or School Communication after parental background was taken into account. Only 6 percent of the variation in Home Discussion was between schools (Table 3), and the background variables in Table 4 accounted for 44.9 percent of it, which leaves a "residual variation" of 3.3 percent [(1−.449)*6.0%]. Similarly, the between-school variations in Home Supervision and School Communication that remained after parental background was controlled were only 2.7 percent and 6.0 percent, respectively. It was only in School Participation that schools differed substantially.

Since there was still considerable variation in School Participation among schools, we wished to determine whether the variation could be partially explained by the contextual factor, that is, the mean SES of the school. The results presented in Table 5 suggest that the socioeconomic context of the school did make a difference in the extent of participation in classroom volunteering and attendance at PTO meetings. The amount of School Participation increases by about 14 percent of a standard deviation for each 1 standard deviation increase in school mean SES. Thus, parents were more likely to volunteer or attend PTO meetings if their children attended high SES schools. The results also indicate that the outcome-SES slope is positively related to mean SES, although the effect is not large, which suggests that the increased likelihood of participation in higher SES schools is even greater for high SES parents than for low SES parents. The percentage of between-school variation in School Participation that was explained by the model increased by about 5 percent after the contextual effect of mean SES was taken into account.

In the final set of analyses, we examined the impact of parental-involvement factors on mathematics and reading achievement. In the first analysis, we estimated a null model for mathematics and reading, partitioning the variance into within- and between-school components. For mathematics, about 27 percent of the variation was between schools and 73 percent was within schools. For reading, approximately 20 percent of the variation was between schools and 80 percent was within schools.

The first and third columns of Table 6 display the results for models of the relationship between students' background and achievement and the SES of schools. The results indicate significant positive effects of SES on achievement and negative effects associated with learning and behavioral problems and with increases in the number of siblings. However, no significant differences were associated with single-versus two-parent families. One could conclude from these results that the lower

TABLE 5

Hierarchical Linear Model Explaining Variation in School Participation

Variable	Coefficient	SE
Adjusted School Mean		
Intercept	0.000	0.014
Mean SES	0.182**	0.021
Family Background		
Socioeconomic Status		
Average slope	0.138**	0.008
Mean SES	0.048**	0.011
Number of siblings	0.008**	0.004
Number of parents	0.277**	0.015
Student Background		
Female	0.003	0.012
Learning problem	−0.028	0.025
Behavioral problem	−0.162**	0.020
Ethnicity		
Asian/Pacific Islander	−0.189**	0.026
Hispanic	−0.062**	0.021
Black	0.015	0.022
Native/American	−0.059	0.055
Percentage of Variance Explained		
Within schools	4.3	
Between schools	42.1	

*$p < .05$.; **$p < .01$.

achievement scores often observed for children in single-parent families are associated with other factors, mainly SES. On the tests used in this study, the female students scored slightly lower in mathematics than did the male students, but nearly 20 percent of a standard deviation higher in reading. The differences among ethnic groups are similar to those reported in other studies of school achievement (see, for example, Rumberger and Willms 1992), with Hispanics scoring nearly 25 percent of a standard deviation lower and Blacks and Native Americans scoring about 40 percent of a standard deviation lower than Whites. Asians and Pacific Islanders scored about 20 percent of a standard deviation higher than Whites in mathematics and less than 10 percent of a standard deviation lower in reading. The model also includes the mean SES of the school, which is a proxy for the contextual effects of group composition (Willms 1986, 1992; Raudenbush and Willms 1995). The coefficients indicate positive contextual effects for both mathematics and reading, which suggests that students' achievement is higher in high SES schools, even after student background at the individual level is taken into account.

The model was extended to include the four parental-involvement factors, measured at the individual level, and the school-level mean of parental participation. The school-level means of the other three factors were not included because these factors

TABLE 6

Models Explaining Variation in Student Achievement

	Mathematics				Reading			
	Coefficient	SE	Coefficient	SE	Coefficient	SE	Coefficient	SE
Adjusted School Mean	−.005	(.010)	−.003	(.010)	.001	(.008)	.004	(.008)
Family and Student Background								
Socioeconomic status	.273**	(.007)	.255**	(.007)	.266**	(.007)	.250**	(.007)
Number of siblings	−.019**	(.003)	−.016**	(.003)	−.037**	(.004)	−.033**	(.004)
Number of parents	.019	(.013)	−.007	(.014)	.015	(.014)	−.020	(.014)
Female	−.055**	(.011)	−.087**	(.011)	.186**	(.011)	.156**	(.011)
Learning problem	−.704**	(.023)	−.653**	(.023)	−.708**	(.024)	−.652**	(.023)
Behavioral problem	−.260**	(.019)	−.185**	(.019)	−.219**	(.019)	−.137**	(.020)
Asian or Pacific Islander	.196**	(.023)	.210**	(.023)	−.082**	(.024)	−.067**	(.024)
Hispanic	−.223**	(.019)	−.222**	(.019)	−.215**	(.019)	−.213**	(.019)
Black	−.437**	(.020)	−.445**	(.020)	−.384**	(.020)	−.395**	(.020)
Native American	−.380**	(.050)	−.370**	(.050)	−.435**	(.052)	−.422**	(.051
Parent-involvement Factors								
Home Discussion			.124**	(.006)			.124**	(.006)
Home Supervision			.009	(.005)			.033**	(.006)
School Communication			−.051**	(.006)			−.056**	(.006)
School Participation			.030**	(.006)			.026**	(.006)
Effect of School-level Variables								
Mean School SES on adjusted school mean	.305**	(.015)	.294**	(.017)	.214**	(.014)	.191**	(.015)
Mean participation on adjusted school mean			.018	(.021)			.077**	(.018)
Mean participation on SES slope			−.018	(.012)			−.041**	(.011)
Percentage of Variance Explained								
Within schools	16.3		18.4		14.7		16.9	
Between schools	82.1		82.3		79.7		85.0	

*p < .05.; **p < .01.

did not vary significantly among schools. The results are shown in columns 2 and 4 of Table 6. They suggest that the most important parental-involvement factor at the individual level is Home Discussion. The estimated effect is approximately 12 percent of a standard deviation on both mathematics and reading achievement. This finding implies that an increase of 1 standard deviation in Home Discussion is associated with an increase in achievement of 0.12 of a standard deviation. School Communication has small negative effects—about 5 percent of a standard deviation—indicating that children whose parents communicated more with schools had lower achievement scores. As we discussed earlier, this effect probably stems from parents communicating with schools when their children were at risk academically.

The model also included indicators of whether a child had a learning or behavioral problem, and these variables mediated some of the observed negative effect of School Communication on achievement. However, more detailed measures of children's learning difficulties may account for all the observed negative effect. The other two individual-level measures of parental involvement, Home Supervision and School Participation, had very small effects, ranging from 1 to 3 percent of a standard deviation.

The school-level mean of School Participation had no effect on mathematics achievement but a positive effect on reading achievement. In schools where the average level of participation was 1 (student-level) standard deviation higher, the expected reading score was about 8 percent of a standard deviation higher. This finding suggests that a child's academic achievement did not depend so much on whether his or her own parents participated, but on the average level of participation of all parents at the school. Also notable is the decrease in the size of the contextual effect of school mean SES, which was about 11 percent smaller when the mean level of parental participation was added to the model. Thus, a moderate portion of the impact of school-level mean SES on reading achievement may be attributable to the effect of school participation. The relationship between reading achievement and SES was also related to the average level of school participation. The average reading-SES slope was 0.25, but in schools that had very high levels of participation, for example, schools where the parents were, on average, 1 standard deviation above the mean on the School Participation scale, the average reading-SES slope was less steep—on average only about 0.21 (0.25–0.04). Similarly, schools with lower levels of participation would have steeper reading-SES slopes. Thus, the effects of School Participation on reading scores were stronger for low SES students than for high SES students.

Discussion

Importance of Involvement at Home

The prevailing perception among educational researchers is that successful schools establish practices that foster greater communication with parents, encourage parents to assist children at home with their schoolwork and planning, and recruit parents to work as volunteers or participate in school governance. The argument is that these practices, in turn, lead to higher levels of schooling outcomes. This may be the case, but our findings suggest that such schools are uncommon. The findings indicated that levels of communication and levels of parental involvement in the home were about the same across all schools, so it was impossible to identify reliably schools that were particularly effective or ineffective in inducing higher levels of parental involvement. Schools did differ significantly in levels of involvement associated with participation as volunteers or attendance at PTO meetings, but this type of involvement had only a modest effect on reading achievement and a negligible effect on mathematics achievement. It was involvement at home, particularly in discussing school activities and helping children plan their programs, that had the strongest relationship to academic achievement.

Moreover, our findings provide little support for the conjecture that parents with high SES and parents in two-parent families are more involved in their children's education (Lareau 1987, 1989; McLanahan 1985; Milne et al. 1986). Although many of the relationships were statistically significant, the effects were not large, and their magnitude depended on the type of involvement that was considered. For example, family SES had virtually no relationship to the level of home supervision and was only moderately related to the other three dimensions of involvement. Parents in two-parent families were more likely to participate in the school and to provide higher levels of home supervision than were single parents, but the extent to which parents discussed school programs and activities or communicated with school staff was not related to family structure. Also, the results do not support the assumption that parents from ethnic-minority groups participate less than do White parents (Coleman 1987; Delgado-Gaitan 1991). For instance, we found that Hispanics had slightly higher levels of home supervision than did Whites, but were similar to Whites with respect to all other types of involvement. Blacks tended to have slightly higher levels of involvement than did Whites on all dimensions of involvement except school participation, for which their level of involvement was the same as that of Whites. Asian parents tended to provide more supervision at home than did White parents, but spent less time discussing school programs, communicating with school staff, and volunteering and attending PTO meetings. Overall, our measures of family background explained only about 10 percent of the variation in parental involvement across the four types of involvement. Consequently, we reject the culture of poverty thesis; the results do not support the notion that parents from working-class backgrounds place less emphasis on the importance of schooling or that they view education as the purview solely of the school.

Parental involvement was, however, associated with gender and whether a child had a learning or behavioral problem. On average, parents had more discussions about schooling with girls than with boys, whereas they tended to have more contact with school staff regarding boys' experiences at school. Parents of children with learning and behavioral problems tended to participate less in school and have fewer discussion about school activities with their children, but were more likely to have contact with school staff about their children's progress. These findings indicate that a considerable amount of the communication between schools and parents at this grade level pertains to problems that children are having in school.

Epstein (1995) presented a vision of what a successful partnership among schools, families, and communities might look like. Schools, families, and communities would jointly and separately conduct practices that influence children's learning and development. The partnerships would cause schools to be more like families, in that there would be a greater acceptance of all children and their families. They would also cause families to be more like schools: Families would emphasize the importance of schooling and provide regular assistance and learning experiences.

Our measure of home discussion captures, to some extent, the idea of "school-like families" that Epstein described, and we found that of the four types of involvement, home discussion was the most strongly related to academic achievement. However, there was little variation among schools in average levels of home discussion, which suggests that relatively few schools have strong influences on the learning climate in the home. We expect that big gains in achievement could be realized through programs that give parents concrete information about parenting styles, teaching methods, and school curricula. Our study lacked detailed data on the actual practices that schools had in place that could help families foster a stronger learning environment. Further research might examine the effects of particular policies and programs that support home learning.

SES and School Context

One aim of this study was to discern whether some of the advantage in academic achievement associated with high SES was attributable to different levels of parental involvement. Even though the relationship between levels of parental involvement and family SES was not strong, the extent to which parents were involved in their children's education did account for some of the advantages associated with SES. When our statistical models included measures of parental involvement, the effects of SES on academic achievement were reduced by about 7 percent. The inclusion of parental involvement also explained some of the negative effects associated with large families and of children having learning or behavioral problems. Perhaps what is more important, though, is that parental involvement made a significant *unique* contribution to explaining the variation in children's academic achievement, over and above the effects associated with parental background. Thus, parental involvement had an effect on achievement that was independent of children's family backgrounds.

Our analysis shows that children's academic achievement and the extent to which parents are involved in schools also depend on the intake characteristics of schools. Children scored considerably higher in both mathematics and reading if they attended a high SES school, irrespective of their own family backgrounds. In fact, our results suggest that the SES of a school had an effect on achievement that was comparable to the effects associated with the SES of a family. Similarly, irrespective of their own SES, parents were more likely to volunteer or attend PTO meetings if their children attended high SES schools than low SES schools. Although the benefits to children of having their own parents participate in this way were negligible the average level of participation in a school had a small but significant effect on reading achievement. This finding makes sense intuitively, since one would expect that when parents volunteer in school, they enrich the overall learning environment, strengthen social networks, and affect the norms and expectations for all children in the school (Brown, 1995; Lareau, 1989). The results also suggest that the effects of school participation were moderately related to the relationship between reading achievement and SES. Volunteering perhaps not only improves the quality of schooling, but also reduces inequality between social-class groups.

These findings are consistent with the theory that the contextual effect associated with attending a high SES school is attributable to a number of factors, including peer effects, teachers' expectations, the school disciplinary climate, parental involvement, and levels of material resources (see Willms 1986, 1992). They are also consistent with Coleman's (1987) thesis regarding social capital: The social networks and norms established by the school community complement the mission of the school. Coleman was drawing attention to differential dropout rates between public and Catholic schools; our findings suggest that some of the phenomena associated with social capital are apparent in the public sector as well. It is likely that when there is a strong concentration of high SES parents in a school community, an ethos of greater school participation is more easily established.

Notes

1. SES is a composite of five variables denoting family income and mother's and father's education and occupation. Data were taken from the parent questionnaire, but for students with missing data, we used data from the student questionnaire, if available. The composite was constructed by scaling the categorical variables on a logit distribution, following a procedure recommended by

Mosteller and Tukey (1977), and then averaging all nonmissing values for each student. The final scale was standardized to have a mean of 0 and a standard deviation of 1.

2. Our preliminary analyses also included measures of history and science achievement, but the findings are not reported here because the regression coefficients were virtually identical across the four achievement measures. The only exception was the coefficient estimating the differences between Asians-Pacific Islanders and Whites, which was less than 1 percent of a standard deviation and not statistically significant for both history and science.

3. The explanatory variables were centered on their grand means. Thus, the intercept for each within-school equation was the expected level of involvement for a student who had nationally average background characteristics. The average intercept across all schools was close to zero for each outcome measure, and thus these findings are not displayed.

References

Astone, Nan Marie and Sara S. McLanahan. 1991. "Family Structure, Parental Practices and High School Completion." *American Sociological Review* 56:309–20.

Becker, Henry J. and Joyce L. Epstein. 1982. "Parent Involvement: A Survey of Teacher Practices." *Elementary School Journal* 83: 85–102.

Bourdieu, Pierre. 1977. "Cultural Reproduction and Social Reproduction." Pp. 487–511 in *Power and Ideology in Education,* edited by Jerome Karabel and A. H. Halsey. New York: Oxford University Press.

Brown, Daniel J. 1995. "Schools with Heart: Volunteerism and Public Education." Unpublished manuscript.

Bryk, Anthony S. and Stephen W. Raudenbush. 1992. *Hierarchical Linear Models for Social and Behavioral Research: Applications and Data Analysis Methods.* Newbury Park, CA: Sage.

Coleman, James S. 1987. "Families and Schools." *Educational Researcher* 16:32–38.

Delgado-Gaitan, Concha. 1991. "Involving Parents in the Schools: A Process of Empowerment." *American Journal of Education* 100:20–46.

Epstein, Joyce L. 1986. "Parents' Reactions to Teacher Practices of Parent Involvement." *Elementary School Journal* 86:277–93.

———— 1987. "Parent Involvement: What Research Says to Administrators." *Education and Urban Society* 19:119–36.

———— 1995. "School/Family/Community Partnerships: Caring for the Children We Share." *Phi Delta Kappan* 76:701–12.

Fehrmann, Paul G., Timothy Z. Keith, and Thomas M. Reimers. 1987. "Home Influence on School Learning: Direct and Indirect Effects of Parental Involvement on High School Grades." *Journal of Educational Research* 806:330–37.

Hoepfner, Ralph, J. Wellisch, and H. Zagorski. 1977. *The Sample for the Sustaining Effects Study and Projections of Its Characteristics to the National Population.* Santa Monica, CA: System Development Corp.

Lareau, Annette. 1987. "Social Class Differences in Family–School Relationships: The Importance of Cultural Capital." *Sociology of Education* 60:73–85.

———— 1989. *Home Advantage: Social Class and Parental Intervention in Elementary Education.* Philadelphia: Falmer Press.

Lightfoot, Sarah Lawrence. 1978. *Worlds Apart.* New York: Basic Books.

Madigan, Timothy J. 1994, April. "Parent Involvement and School Achievement." Paper presented at the meeting of the American Educational Research Association, New Orleans.

McLanahan, Sara. 1985. "Family Structure and the Reproduction of Poverty." *American Journal of Sociology* 904:873–901.

Mehan, Hugh. 1992. "Understanding Inequality in Schools: The Contribution of Interpretive Studies." *Sociology of Education* 65:1–20.

Miller, Jon D. and Herman Green. 1992, February. "The Impact of Parental and Home Resources on Student Achievement and Career Choice." Paper presented at the meeting of the American Association for the Advancement of Science, Chicago.

Miller, Jon D. and Thomas B. Hoffer. 1994, April. "Longitudinal Study of American Youth: Overview of Study Design and Data Resources." Paper presented at the annual meeting of the American Educational Research Association, New Orleans.

Milne, Ann M., David E. Myers, Alvin S. Rosenthal, and Alan Ginsburg. 1986. "Single Parents, Working Mothers, and the Educational Achievement of School Children." *Sociology of Education* 59:125–39.

Morrison, George S. 1978. *Parent Involvement in the Home, School and Community.* Columbus, OH: Charles E. Merrill.

Mosteller, Frederick and John W. Tukey. 1977. *Data Analysis and Regression: A Second Course in Statistics.* Reading, MA: Addison–Wesley.

Muller, Chandra. 1993, February. "Parent Ties to the School and Community and Student Academic Performance." Paper presented at the conference on Sociology of Education, Asilomar, CA.

National Center for Education Statistics. 1989. *National Education Longitudinal Study* (NCES Publication No. 90–482). Chicago: National Opinion Research Center.

National Opinion Research Center. 1980. *High School and Beyond Information for Users, Base Year 1980 Data: Report to the National Center for Educational Statistics.* Chicago: Author.

Raudenbush, Stephen W. and J. Douglas Willms. 1995. "The Estimation of School Effects." *Journal of Educational and Behavioral Statistics* 20:307–55.

Rumberger, Russell W. and J. Douglas Willms. 1992. "The Impact of Racial and Ethnic Segregation on the Achievement Gap in California High Schools." *Educational Evaluation and Policy Analysis* 144:377–96.

Stevenson, David L. and David P. Baker. 1987. "The Family–School Relation and the Child's School Performance." *Child Development* 58:1348–57

White, Karl R. 1982. "The Relation between Socioeconomic Status and Academic Achievement." *Psychological Bulletin* 913: 461–81.

Willms, J. Douglas. 1986. "Social Class Segregation and Its Relationship to Pupils' Examination Results in Scotland." *American Sociological Review* 512:224–41.

—— 1992. *Monitoring School Performance: A Guide for Educators.* London: Falmer Press.

Esther Ho Sui-Chu, MA, is a Ph.D. candidate and research assistant, Department of Educational Studies, Faculty of Education, University of British Columbia, Vancouver. Her main fields of interest are sociology of education and research methods. She is currently completing her dissertation on the school climate of British Columbia elementary schools.

J. Douglas Willms, Ph.D., is a professor and UNB/CIAR Research Chair, Faculty of Education, University of New Brunswick, Fredericton. His main fields of interest are sociology of education and longitudinal research. He is presently working on a study of elementary school climate and a national longitudinal study of Canadian children.

This paper was prepared for the annual meeting of the American Educational Research Association, San Francisco, April 1995. The authors are grateful for the support they received from a grant from the Canadian Social Sciences and Humanities Research Council (Grant No. 410–92–1569) and for a grant from the American Educational Research Association, which receives funds for its AERA Grants Program from the National Science Foundation and the National Center for Education Statistics, U.S. Department of Education, under NSF Grant No. RED-92555347. Opinions expressed in this article are the authors' and do not necessarily reflect those of the granting agencies. The authors express their appreciation to Adrian Blunt, Frank Echols, and Sue-Ling Pong for their comments on an earlier draft of this article and to Anita van Weerden for assistance in preparing the manuscript. Address all correspondence to Dr. J. Douglas Willms, Faculty of Education, University of New Brunswick, P.O. Box 4400, Fredericton, N.B. Canada E3B 7A1.

10

School Climate and the Matter of Measurement

INTRODUCTION

Every practicing administrator knows that school improvement is a hugely expensive, high-stakes, and politically charged activity. Virtually every state has mounted extensive and costly programs intended to improve its schools, to make them accountable, and, in many cases, to attach substantial penalties for failure to meet state-imposed standards. Necessarily, such programs carry with them mandated assessment schemes. Obviously a state cannot decide that a school's or district's performance is unsatisfactory without setting standards, making those standards public, and establishing an assessment system to determine whether the standards have been met.

One of the many interesting aspects of these recent state-led school improvement efforts has been the extent of their reach. Only a decade or two ago, everyone knew which schools and districts were inadequate. They were the ones in which poor and minority children were taught by inexperienced or incompetent teachers, where expenditures per pupil were low, where facilities were in decay, and where even the mundane tools of teaching and learning, such as books and pencils, were in short supply. In brief, schools were judged by the quality and quantity of the resources they consumed. The new state assessment systems, however, have focused attention on school outcomes in addition to inputs, and thereby have made problematic what "everyone knew." If a school is rich in resources, it does not follow that it is superior. A focus on outcomes has made it possible for "good" schools, even those in wealthy, suburban communities, to be judged inadequate.

A second interesting aspect of these school improvement efforts is the strategy that some states have adopted to motivate local reform. Traditionally, state education departments have been responsible for school remediation. Education is, after all, a state responsibility. Goals were set, rules formulated, and the job of state education officials was to ensure local compliance. In effect, state bureaucracies wielded incentives, usually financial, to motivate local schools to improve. This was a classic, top-down approach to reform, and it ran head-on into Americans' strongly held value of local control and their suspicion of state bureaucrats. Savvy administrators and school boards could figure out ways to work around the regulations, secure the incentives, and continue business as usual.

More recently, however, some states have turned this classic approach on its head. In adroit moves they have made it possible for local citizens to seize the vanguard of reform in their own districts. They accomplished this by making available massive amounts of comparative data on the performance of all of the schools and districts within their borders. These data, available to anyone with access to the Internet, concern the resources schools consume, their organizational processes, and the performance of their students. As a consequence, it is now possible for ordinary parents and taxpayers to evaluate their own schools and to compare their performance with similar schools located elsewhere in the state. When they do this, they may not be pleased with their findings. The genius of this bottom-up approach to reform is obvious, though its effectiveness is still unclear (for evidence on this point see Haller, Nusser, & Monk, 1998). It is one thing for local administrators and school boards to get around obscure regulations promulgated by faceless bureaucrats in a distant state capital. It is quite another for them to get around indignant parents and taxpayers asking public, pointed, and informed questions about their own schools.

Our case involves just such a scenario, one that is likely to become much more common in the future. A wealthy suburban high school with excellent facilities, a well-trained staff, and supportive parents turns out to be less exemplary than everyone supposed. And this discovery is the result of a single parent's efforts to understand the "failure" of his son, leading him to dig beneath the conventional understanding that wealthy, suburban schools are necessarily good schools. In coming to grips with these events, the schools' principal learns a great deal about the quality of the education offered in her building, the nature of its educational climate, and the difficulties of measuring that abstract construct. In the process, she shapes a plan to improve the academic success of her school.

The Case: The Climate of Washington High School

Washington High is a moderately large high school located in a suburb of Springfield, a large southwestern city. The suburb, Alamo Gulch, is distinctly upper-middle class. Homes are large with spacious, well-tended lawns set on winding tree-shaded streets. BMWs or their equivalents are parked in the curving driveways. Most residents are business and professional people who work either in the high-tech firms located in Alamo Gulch or in the financial district in Springfield. The modal resident has a college diploma and a substantial proportion have graduate degrees. Census data show that Alamo Gulch has one of the highest per capita income levels in the state.

As might be imagined, residents are highly supportive of their schools. The community has never turned down a bond issue and, unless a proposed tax levy is extraordinarily high, there is seldom any serious protest over steadily rising school taxes. Indeed, the district's tax rate is one of the highest in the region. In return for this largesse, these supportive and well-educated parents expect that the Alamo Gulch Public Schools will provide a high quality education for their offspring. And by many measures the district meets this expectation. Every year almost 90% of the graduating seniors go on to some form of higher education, many to the state university, some to nearby four-year colleges, and some to the local community college. A few head east to ivy league institutions. Virtually no one drops out. Occasionally a student is named a national merit scholar. Scholastic Aptitude Test scores are always above average, and the district's pupils do equally well on the state's achievement tests, especially when compared with students attending school in the city of Springfield. Each year these data are faithfully reported in the Alamo Gulch Gazette; residents, professional educators, and the school board congratulate themselves on the quality of their schools; and things go on as before. Then, two years ago, Dr. McIver, a local physician, took an interest in the achievements of the graduates of the high school.

McIver's concern began as a personal matter. David, his son, who had nearly a straight A record at Washington High, was rejected by Harvard, Yale, and Princeton (though he had no problem getting into the state university). It seemed that David's scores on the SAT and on the state's achievement tests, while well above average, were also well short of the level demanded by the likes of Harvard. Further, the content of the essay he submitted along with his applications (which, unfortunately, neither of his parents had checked beforehand) was pedestrian at best and contained several egregious errors in grammar. Dr. McIver wondered how this could have happened. He thought of his son as a highly intelligent young man. This judgment was not just misplaced fatherly pride; David's percentile scores on a battery of intelligence tests were in the 90s, his grades were excellent, and many of his teachers had praised his native intellect and educational accomplishments. His English teachers had spoken highly of his writing skills.

In investigating the causes of his son's rejections, Dr. McIver learned about a web site prepared by the State Education Department (SED). Like an increasing number of states, the SED posted a plethora of school-level statistics for every school and district within its borders. For example, anyone interested could find the average achievement scores for any high school on the various state-administered tests as well as on the SAT. The percentage of each school's graduates that enrolled in postsecondary schools was given. Also available were data on every school's socioeconomic and demographic characteristics, its expenditures per pupil, the amounts spent on teachers' and administrators' salaries, dropout and attendance rates, and so on.[1] What caught Dr. McIver's eye was that while Washington High was certainly above average on the various measures of student achievement, it didn't seem to be very far above average. In particular, its students seemed to achieve at considerably lower levels than other schools serving equally affluent populations and spending less to educate their students.

His curiosity aroused, Dr. McIver took the trouble to check his subjective impressions. He dug up an old college statistics text to refresh his understanding, and then he discussed the matter with an epidemiologist he knew. They ran some simple multiple regression equations and computed adjusted achievement test scores for Washington High and for a random sample of high schools in the state. That is, they adjusted each school's scores to remove the effects of various factors believed to affect them, notably pupil socioeconomic status, race, ethnicity, and expenditures per pupil. What they discovered was that Washington High's students were actually performing below average, when these other factors were taken into account. Instead of being proud of their schools, their analysis suggested, Alamo Gulch residents might better feel a healthy dose of humility.

Dr. McIver first took the results of the analysis to Washington's principal, Raymond Welch, Ed.D. It was immediately apparent that Dr. Welch had no idea what multiple regression and adjusted scores were and had no interest in learning. "Washington is a good school," he retorted. "Everyone knows that. I don't know what your numbers mean, but they certainly can't mean that it's below average." The physician was peeved by trying to deal with a school administrator who had no understanding of an elementary statistical technique and no willingness to educate himself on the topic. McIver next took his results to the superintendent and the Alamo Gulch school board, where he met with much the same reaction. Now angry, he wrote a lengthy letter to the *Sun Times*, Springfield's daily paper, which served the entire metropolitan area. Not only did the *Sun* print his letter, it interviewed him and it did a series of feature articles on the story using the SED's web site to make its own direct comparisons of all of the schools and school districts in the region. On the *Sun*'s analysis, Dr. McIver was essentially correct: Alamo Gulch's schools were nothing special.

What followed next was predictable. It seemed that there were a substantial number of parents in Alamo Gulch who had similar experiences to Dr. McIver's—their sons and daughters had also been rejected from "good" universities, despite excellent grades from Washington High. Until McIver came forward, these parents had remained silent, assuming that they were alone and

---

[1] This practice is increasingly widespread. State education departments are posting "report cards" on the World Wide Web that contain extensive data on every school in that state. These data permit ordinary citizens to gain an extraordinary amount of information about the performance of individual schools and, if they wish, to carry out their own analyses of those data. Administrators need to be aware of this trend and be able to use and interpret these data to the public. For an example of these report cards and the kinds of data they contain, see the web site provided by New York: http://www.nysed.gov.

that their children were less capable then they had assumed. Also, most had been unwilling to publicly discuss their children's college rejections. Soon this group was joined by a larger set of concerned taxpayers who wondered why the schools weren't doing a better job, given the size of their tax bills.

Over the next two years Alamo Gulch's school board meetings came to be dominated by various facets of the controversy. A school budget was passed, but by the narrowest margin in the district's history. Numerous people objected to a sizable hike in teachers' salaries, and the proposed raise was scaled back considerably. Most notably, perhaps, Dr. Welch, Washington's principal, who was nearing retirement anyway, decided that it was a propitious time to resign and give more attention to improving his golf game. In his stead the board appointed Dr. Joanna Cambridge, with the mandate to fix whatever was wrong with Washington High School. Cambridge had recently received her doctorate in educational administration from the state university, she was steeped in the "effective schools" literature, and she was familiar with the recent research on improving academic performance. Unlike her predecessor, Cambridge also understood what regression equations and adjusted scores were.

Cambridge spent her first six months on the job carefully observing events in the school, without introducing any significant changes. She wanted, she said, "to fully understand Washington, its faculty, its students, and its educational processes, and to avoid precipitous changes." At the end of that time she had reached a diagnosis of Washington's problem. The trouble, she decided, lay with none of the usual things. Clearly students were bright, interested in school, and had high educational aspirations. They came from homes that were highly supportive of education. The teachers were, by and large, a dedicated, conscientious group, with high morale and well trained in their specialties. The problem, Cambridge decided, was that the climate of Washington High was simply not supportive of high quality academic work. Instead, it seemed to her that students held a tolerant, "laid back" approach to their education, an approach in which the dominant value was that everyone should be free to pursue his or her own individual goals. Those goals might concern cultivating an active social life (a particular favorite, she noted), excelling at sports, holding leadership roles in the varied and numerous extracurricular activities offered at Washington, success in various community projects quite unrelated to school, and, in a few cases, the pursuit of intellectual and academic excellence. It wasn't that students were opposed to scholarly achievement, they simply viewed it as one among many equally legitimate and praiseworthy goals. In brief, Washington High was characterized by a benevolent and free-wheeling individualism. If the school had a motto, Cambridge mused, it must surely be "Hey, whatever works."

Teachers abetted this student culture. The faculty was characterized by a fuzzy, warm-hearted view that the "whole child" was important, a view that had somehow become translated into a belief that all aspects of every student were equally deserving of school recognition and praise. High achievement in physics had no special claim for recognition over making the varsity tennis squad, becoming the prom queen, or editing the yearbook. Over the years the faculty had developed myriad elective courses, some of dubious academic value, which students freely substituted for the standard high school offerings. For example, many took "From Poe to Lovecraft: American Occult Literature," taught by a popular English teacher, instead of standard 10th grade English. Others met their science requirement with "Physics for Poets," which required no mathematics, and, if the truth be known, not much physics either. Because the students were bright, and because most were headed for college, academic distinctions were quietly suppressed. In particular, teachers seemed to feel that grading standards were not terribly important and, as a consequence, grade inflation was rampant. The modal grade at Washington High was an B+. Getting an A in calculus was no big deal. At the year-end awards ceremony, academic achievement was one among a multitude of achievements that were singled out for recognition, and it occupied no special place in the extensive list of student accomplishments. In short, Dr. Cambridge concluded that if student achievement was to be improved, the climate of Washington High needed to be changed: Scholarship and academic accomplishments needed to take a higher priority in the school's culture.

The problem was how to accomplish that. Cambridge quickly realized that her understanding of the nature of an organization's climate was severely limited. While the term climate was widely used (and she herself used it frequently), as soon as she began to think hard about the concept, she recognized that her understanding was quite shallow. Certainly she had no clear idea what the concept meant nor how to apply it in real life to her school. Given her relative ignorance, it followed that she could not be sure that her diagnosis of Washington's troubles was correct. She felt the need for a second opinion, perhaps one based on a different kind of evidence than a single person's judgment. And even if her assessment was corroborated, she needed advice about practical steps that she might take. These considerations led her to specify a number of questions that she would like to have answered. Eventually she narrowed these down to the following two:

1. What is "school climate"? That is, how has it been conceptualized? Do particular kinds of climates have especially positive effects on student achievement?
2. How is school climate assessed? Are there alternative, more objective, measures available that I might use to assess the climate of Washington High?

Armed with these questions, Dr. Cambridge set out to do some homework on her problem.

What Is School Climate? A Brief Introduction to the Research

The first thing that Joanna Cambridge learned about school climate was that there is no agreed upon definition of the concept. Hoy and his colleagues offer the following: "School climate is the relatively enduring quality of the school environment that is experienced by participants, affects their behavior, and is based on their collective perception of behavior in schools." It is those ". . .

internal characteristics that distinguishes one school from another and influences the behavior of its members" (Hoy, Tarter, & Kottkamp, 1991, p. 10). Precisely what "internal characteristics" are to be included is left unspecified. Other researchers, however, tend to equate school climate with the notion of "culture," the idea that groups that are in interaction over long periods of time develop a set of shared norms and beliefs that influence the views and behavior of group members (see, e.g., Coleman, 1961; Cookson & Persell, 1985; McDill & Rigsby, 1973). Other terms that are sometimes used in place of climate or culture include "ethos" (Lortie, 1975; Rutter, Maughan, Mortimore, & Ouston, 1979) or "ideology" (Willower, Eidell, & Hoy, 1967). What all definitions seem to have in common is the idea that schools and/or the groups that inhabit them possess a set of characteristics or beliefs that influence the behavior of individuals, over and above any influence of individuals' own characteristics. One implication of this conception is that the same student's behavior will vary in distinctive ways depending on the school that he or she attends.

In checking secondary sources, Cambridge was surprised to discover that the study of school climate had a relatively long history. Its empirical study goes back at least to the early 1960s, when Andrew Halpin and John Croft published *The Organizational Climate of Schools,* a work that surely has been one of the most influential studies in educational administration (Halpin & Croft, 1963). The instrument they developed, the *Organizational Climate Description Questionnaire* or OCDQ, has been used in well over 200 studies and in at least eight countries (Arter, 1987, p. 49). We shall spend a moment describing the OCDQ, because it is an important part of the history of educational administration, and its methodology is representative of many attempts to measure school climate.

Halpin and Croft conceptualized a school's climate as its "personality." They argued that schools differed from one another in their "feel" and that an observer moving among different schools could quickly spot these differences. While this feel was difficult to define, it was nonetheless apparent (Halpin & Croft, 1966). Indeed, the researchers were substantially influenced by Milton Rokeach's formulation of human personality types: Just as individuals may be characterized as having open and closed minds (Rokeach, 1960), schools may be characterized as having open and closed climates.

The OCDQ was an instrument initially designed to be administered to teachers and administrators of elementary schools. It consisted of 64 Likert items intended to measure four dimensions of teachers' interactions among themselves and four dimensions of principals' behavior. In regard to the former, the dimensions were disengagement (e.g., a sense of commitment to school goals), hindrance (e.g., a feeling of being unnecessarily burdened by prescribed procedures), esprit (e.g., the level of teacher morale), and intimacy (e.g., a sense of warm and friendly relations among teachers). The principal's behavior toward the staff was characterized by aloofness (e.g., maintaining social distance from the staff), production emphasis (e.g., exercising close supervision), thrust (e.g., setting an example for teachers as a means to achieving goals), and consideration (e.g., exhibiting warm and friendly behavior toward the staff). The questionnaire items resulted in eight subscales measuring these dimensions. In this regard the OCDQ is typical; most instruments offer measures of several "dimensions" of school climate, though the nature of those dimensions varies greatly. Items for each subscale were simple descriptive statements such as "The principal sets an example by working hard." These were responded to on a four-point scale measuring frequency of occurrence, from "very frequently occurs" to "rarely occurs." The responses of each school staff member to these eight subscales were then aggregated to the school level. By noting the pattern of subscale scores, schools could be characterized as having one of six different climates, and these were said to fall on a continuum from an open climate to a closed climate. An open school was characterized by being low on disengagement, hindrance, aloofness, and production emphasis, while they were high on esprit, thrust, and consideration. Schools with closed climates reversed this pattern. Clearly, Halpin and Croft believed that open schools were preferable to closed ones

Notice Halpin and Croft's research strategy, because it characterizes much (though not all) of the research on school climate. First, climate is presumed to be an attribute of a school, not of individuals. It is measured, however, by asking individuals to respond to a questionnaire and rate their school on a set of characteristics (e.g., the extent to which rules hinder the performance of their work or whether teachers have friendly relationships with each other). These ratings are then aggregated for all of the individuals in the school, usually by computing an average of individuals' ratings. These average scores, then, are taken as a measure of the extent that the school itself is rule bound, friendly, and so forth. In essence, respondents are used as observers of their school's climate. Second, climate is not taken to be a unitary concept: It has several dimensions and the instrument yields separate scores for each. Third, ideally individuals within a school will agree in their ratings—everyone perceives the school in the same way—while the aggregate ratings will differ sharply among schools—schools themselves will have quite different climates. (In fact, these two criteria are used to select items to include in the questionnaire.) Fourth, the theory behind the notion of school climate is important, for it drives the choice of dimensions to be measured. The Halpin and Croft measure was based (very loosely) on a psychological notion of personality—schools are like people; they have personalities. Hence, constructs like friendliness and commitment are candidates for measurement. A different theory, however, could lead to quite different dimensions. For example, considering a school as an organism that might be "healthy" or "unhealthy," one could ask about its ability to adapt to its environment, the clarity of its goals, or the adequacy of its internal communication (see Hoy et al., 1991; and Miles, 1965 for just such a view). Finally, the theory also drives the choice of respondents. There are at least four sets of observers that might reliably report on various aspects of a school's climate: administrators, teachers, students, and parents. Presumably some of these are better able to report on a particular climate dimension than are others.

Despite its popularity, the OCDQ came under a great deal of criticism. While schools might be shown to have open or closed climates, the existence of six intermediate and distinct climates was unsupported (Andrews, 1965). The metaphor of an organization having a personality, while intuitively appealing, is highly problematic. In psychology, personality is conceived as a relatively permanent aspect of an individual's nature that pervasively colors his or her interactions with other individuals. Personality is extremely difficult to change. Such a conception applied to school climate does not augur well for principals, such as Dr. Cambridge, who set out to change their school's climate. Further, the focus on school climate might be misplaced. Arguably what happens in the classroom has a more direct and powerful influence on students than does any school characteristic. It is notable that there are numerous studies of *classroom* climate that are founded on quite different theoretical premises (Fraser, 1986). Still further, the original OCDQ could only be used for elementary schools, though this defect (and others as well) was subsequently remedied with the development of substantially revised instruments for middle and high schools (Hoy et al., 1996b; Hoy et al., 1991). Finally, and most seriously in our view, the original OCDQ had no consistent empirical relationship to any student outcome, either affective or cognitive (Anderson, 1982; Arter, 1987). If, as we argued earlier, the fundamental responsibility of administrators is to ensure that their schools create prescribed changes in students, then an organizational attribute that has no effect on students loses significance. Aside from its historical importance, then, it is unclear that Cambridge would find the original OCDQ helpful in her quest to improve the performance of Washington's students.

Approaches to the Study of School Climate

The study of school climate burgeoned after the appearance of the Halpin-Croft work. Subsequent studies took a number of different approaches. Based on Tagiuri's scheme (Tagiuri, 1968), these have been categorized by Anderson (1982) as falling into four broad types, depending on the aspect of the school thought to be critical in setting its climate. Cambridge found Anderson's work particularly helpful. Not only did it provide a good overview of the voluminous research on climate, it also gave her a much-needed device for organizing her thoughts about it. An *ecological* approach focuses on the physical or material aspects of a school that are thought to influence student behavior or outcomes. Studies of the effect of school size on student relationships are one example of an ecological approach to climate (e.g., Barker & Gump, 1964; Goodlad, 1984; Haller, 1992). Under this view, Coleman's study, *Equality of Educational Opportunity*, EEO (Coleman et al., 1966), that we discussed in Chapter 2 is, in part, a study of school climate. Notice that physical attributes such as size don't directly shape student outcomes. Rather, they shape the nature and quality of the interactions that students have with each other and with the staff, and these interactions, in turn, affect student outcomes. Notice too that measuring ecological aspects of schools is reasonably straightforward—most people can agree on a way to measure the size of a school, for example.

A second approach to studying school climate is to examine what Tagiuri termed the school *milieu*. Milieu refers to the social composition of the school, typically meaning various sociodemographic characteristics of the student body. Investigators adopting this approach might compute the average socioeconomic status of students in each of a series of schools and then ask how these school averages affect achievement. For instance, do the educational aspirations of low SES students rise if they attend schools primarily serving middle class students? Studies of the effects of the racial composition of schools (e.g., Crain & Mahard, 1981) and of the effects of single-sex schools (e.g., Jimenez & Lockheed, 1989) on achievement are other examples of a milieu approach to climate. As in ecological approaches, milieu effects are presumably indirect. Attending an all-girls high school, for example, changes the nature of the interactions in the student body. It is said to free young women from the deleterious "rating and dating" environment found in ordinary high schools and thereby permits them to openly strive for academic success. Measurement issues in studies that approach school climate from a milieu perspective may be more problematic than in the case of ecological approaches (consider the common practice of computing the average socioeconomic level of a school based on the proportion of students receiving free lunches), but they generally present few technical difficulties.

A *social system* approach to the study of school climate is the third of Tagiuri's classifications. At this point concepts begin to become abstract and, because of differences in measurement, the results of studies are harder to compare. Social system refers to the patterned interactions among individuals and groups. In organizations, perhaps the most obvious of such patterns is the one we call "bureaucracy." A bureaucracy is characterized by hierarchical levels of authority, impersonal relations between bureaucrats and their clients, numerous rules and regulations, and a sharp division of labor, among other things (Weber, 1947). Thus, a bureaucratic organization creates a distinctive pattern of relationships among its members that distinguishes it from other kinds of organizations, such as social clubs. Organizations, including schools, vary in their degree of bureaucratization. Hence, researchers might ask whether that variation has any effect on student attitudes toward school (see, e.g., Anderson, 1973). Another social system view of schools might focus on the extent of parent involvement in decision making. Sharing decisions is another kind of patterned social relationship, and many believe it has an effect on student outcomes. Concepts such as bureaucracy and shared decision making are important: One can imagine them having direct effects on teacher and student behavior, in contrast to the indirect effects of school size and average pupil SES. But also notice the ambiguity inherent in any application to schools of such social systems constructs as bureaucracy and shared decision making. How should we measure a school's level of bureaucracy? On the one hand, we might take an objective approach and actually count the number of levels in its hierarchy, the number of rules in its student handbook, or the extensiveness of its job descriptions. On the other hand, we might argue that the important thing is how these are perceived by members of the organization, because it is their perceptions that determine their behavior. Thus, we might ask them, for example, to rate the importance of "following the chain of command in this school," or of "carefully following school policies." The issue is a fundamental one: Should we measure the world out there, or how people perceive that world?

Culture stands at the most abstract level of the approaches to school climate in Tagiuri's classification. Culture refers to peoples' belief systems, their values, and the meanings they attach to their experiences. When it is claimed that schools have cultures, it is meant that the individuals within each school share certain basic assumptions, values, and beliefs about students, teachers and the purposes of education, and further, that these assumptions, values, and beliefs are to a significant degree different from those shared by individuals in other schools. Further, the claim implies that these shared assumptions, values and beliefs are important because they affect the behavior of participants in each school. As a consequence of the variation in culture, behavior varies among schools. This view blurs the distinction between organizations and communities (or even societies). Indeed, its current popularity can be seen in the frequent descriptions of schools as communities. Notice that Cambridge has adopted a cultural understanding of her school's climate: Washington High's faculty and students, she believes, are characterized by a laissez-faire individualism, a set of values that places no particular merit on academic pursuits and achievements of the intellect. Because scholarly endeavors are not prized, student achievement is considerably lower than community support, parent values, and student ability suggest it should be.

A cultural approach to school climate requires that one examine the assumptions, beliefs, and values of the organization or of its members. Since the study of culture is the province of anthropologists, it would seem that examining school culture would require anthropological techniques—ethnography, for example. In fact, ethnographies of educational organizations are relatively rare, in part because they require sustained "living in" the culture. Good examples of educational ethnographies include Cusick (1973), Lightfoot (1983), Grant (1989), any of Peshkin's books (e.g., 1986) and Wolcott (1984). Instead, cultural approaches to school climate tend to adopt the kinds of techniques used by sociologists—interviews and questionnaires that ask organizational members to report on their own beliefs and values or on the beliefs and values that they think their school exemplifies. This strategy, however, raises the same kinds of aggregation problems noted earlier in connection with the social systems approach to school climate. Other problems occur as well, for example, respondents' willingness and ability to report their own or others' values accurately and the ability of brief items on questionnaires to capture important aspects of the amorphous concept of culture. Nevertheless, there are many examples of studies of school culture that have used this approach, for example, Bryk and Driscoll (1988), Phillips (1997), Willower, Eidell, and Hoy (1967), and Stern (1970).

What has Dr. Cambridge learned from a brief foray into the secondary literature regarding her first question: What is school climate? We would emphasize several ideas. First, the concept itself has no widely accepted definition. Nevertheless, it is generally agreed that schools possess climates, these climates vary, and these variations affect both students and educators in significant ways. Effects can be behavioral, cognitive, and affective. Second, the further we go up in these approaches, that is, from the ecological to the cultural, the more abstract and fuzzy are the definitions and the more difficult are the measurement issues presented. Third, however, the further we go the closer we seem to get to direct (and possibly more powerful) causes of achievement and behavioral differences among schools. Finally, the further we progress, the greater the potential effect of administrative interventions in a school's climate, and at the same time, the less obvious the means for exercising those interventions.

Measuring School Climate and Culture

Dr. Cambridge has tentatively diagnosed Washington's problems as cultural in nature, and she wants to check her diagnosis by finding another way to assess its organizational culture. Recall her second question: How is school climate assessed? Where might she go for help in finding high quality, objective measures to use in assessing Washington High's climate?

We will approach this question by first addressing its more general form: Where might administrators go to find expert guidance on the availability and quality of published tests and measurement instruments, regardless of their topic (e.g., tests of achievement or personality types)? School administrators should be aware that there are a vast number of available assessment devices for measuring individual, group, and organizational characteristics and performance. Further, careful descriptions and evaluations of many of these by experts in tests and measurements are available in a single source. Since the construction of valid and reliable questionnaires, tests, and surveys is a highly technical matter, it is almost never a good idea to construct a new instrument locally without first checking to see if a device of known quality already exists. For this purpose, *Tests in Print* (Murphy, Conoley, & Impara, 1994) and its companion volumes *The Mental Measurements Yearbooks* (the last volume of which is Plake & Impara, 1998) are excellent resources for the practitioner. When Cambridge checks these resources, she will find that there are several published measures of school climate available to her. For example, *The American Association of School Administrators* has published a set of instruments (*The Comprehensive Assessment of School Environments*) to assess school climate, among other secondary school characteristics.

Another good source of information regarding tests and measurements is available from the *ERIC Clearinghouse on Assessment in Education*. In addition to publishing numerous descriptions of available tests, the Clearinghouse maintains a web site (http://www.ericae.net/) that provides practitioners with brief coverage of a wide variety of measuring instruments.

Cambridge cannot rely on *Tests in Print* or the *Clearinghouse*, however, to find a suitable instrument to assess Washington High's climate. They list only commercially published devices that are in print and available for purchase. For many assessment topics this is sufficient. For others, such as school climate, most of the existing instruments are not commercially published; they are the products of researchers actively working in the area. These tests are described in reports of research and are often available only from the researchers themselves. Thus, Cambridge needs to search secondary, preliminary, and then the primary sources if she is to compile a reasonably comprehensive list of available instruments that might suit her purposes. Fortunately, the interest in school climate in the last few decades has led to the development of a substantial number of instruments. In addition, this popularity has resulted in several summary descriptions and critical discussions of available instruments that are specifically aimed at practitioners interested in assessing their own schools. Cambridge will find several of these in her search of the school climate literature. One of the more comprehensive was prepared by Gottfredson and her colleagues (Gottfredson, Hybl, Gottfredson, & Castaneda, 1986). However, other useful compilations and discussions of available instruments can be found in Arter (1987), Stockard (1985), and Witcher (1993). Depending on how one defines "climate," there are extant upwards of two dozen instruments for measuring it. (In the Gottfredson et al. survey, schools reported using 82 different measures!)

With a large number of instruments available, the practitioner faces the problem of deciding on the criteria for choosing among them. Wilson and McGrail (1987) offer several useful questions that administrators like Cambridge should consider. An appropriate choice depends on the answers given. They propose the following four queries: (1) For what purpose are climate data being collected? (2) Which climate variables should be assessed? (3) Whose opinion about climate should be sought? (4) How should data be gathered and reported? They note, for example, that if the administrator's purpose is to identify a school's strengths and weaknesses in order to plan improvements, the instrument chosen must measure that aspect of climate thought to be problematic. In the case of Washington High, an instrument that included a measure of a climate dimension such as "academic emphasis," "achievement press," or "high academic expectations" would be more appropriate than an instrument concerned with "order and discipline," "instructional leadership," or "sense of community" (all variables measured by some climate instruments and not others). Wilson and McGrail note that instruments' names are poor guides to the variables that they actually measure. For example, the "Effective School Battery," a popular measure of climate, does not assess some of the well-known effective schools components, such as having a clear school mission.

Interestingly, Wilson and McGrail do not suggest that practitioners inquire about an instrument's psychometric properties, specifically its reliability and validity. Clearly, however, a climate measure of weak or unknown validity (which, sadly, is all too common) is a poor choice under any circumstances. We should stress that psychometric considerations are not simply important when choosing a measure of climate—they are even more critical when considering measures of a school's effectiveness. There has been a tremendous emphasis over the last two decades in *school accountability*. In practice, a concern for school accountability has translated into a concern for achievement test scores. Thus, school administrators need to have a good working knowledge of the basic ideas of reliability and validity, since the quality of their schools (and hence their own performance as administrators) is being judged by measuring devices whose worth is substantially determined by the their reliability and validity. We will next discuss these topics in the context of a study of school climate, but their importance extends far beyond that subject.

Comparing Climate Measures: The Hoy, Tarter, and Bliss Study

In the course of her reading, Cambridge discovered a series of studies carried out at Rutgers and Ohio State University by Wayne Hoy and his colleagues. Beginning in the 1980s, the researchers set about constructing several measures of school climate and assessing their effects on various outcomes (Hoy et al., 1996a; Hoy et al., 1996b; Hoy & Hannum, 1997; Hoy & Sabo, 1998; Hoy, Tarter, & Bliss, 1990; Hoy et al., 1991). They substantially revised the original Halpin-Croft *OCDQ*, eliminating some of the methodological issues that had plagued it and developing alternative forms suitable for middle and high schools. Additionally, in response to the *OCDQ*'s lack of a theoretical base, they developed entirely new instruments grounded in the social systems theories of Talcott Parsons (Parsons, 1961; Parsons, 1967) and the organizational theories of Matthew Miles (Miles, 1969). The metaphor guiding the new instruments was that of organizational health: A school's climate could be healthy or unhealthy, and this could have profound effects on various outcomes. Finally, the researchers created distinct instruments for each school level. These instruments collectively are referred to as the *Organizational Health Inventory (OHI)*. In this chapter we will consider one of the studies growing out of the work at Rutgers, "Organizational Climate, School Health, and Effectiveness: A Comparative Analysis" (Hoy et al., 1990). In it Hoy, Tarter, and Bliss set out to compare directly the efficacy of two instruments, their revision of the *OCDQ*, which they named the Organizational Climate Description Questionnaire—Rutgers Secondary *(OCDQ-RS)* and the *OHI,* for explaining student achievement and teachers' commitment to their schools. We will examine this article in this chapter, paying particular attention to measurement issues. As in previous chapters, we will review its strengths and weaknesses at the conceptual, operational, and empirical levels. The article itself is reproduced in Appendix at the end of this chapter. (p. 368)

The Conceptual Level of the Hoy, Tarter, and Bliss Study

As usual, we suggest that you begin any critical reading of the conceptual level of a research report by identifying the question(s) that the study addresses. Hoy et al. couch the question they pose in slightly different ways in several places in their article (compare the stated purpose on page 369 with that on page 371). We prefer the latter for its greater clarity: "The purpose of the empirical phase of this investigation is to test the predictive utility of the two frameworks and their measures." Which is the better predictor?

Is this an important question for school administrators? On one hand, for someone like Joanna Cambridge it would seem so. Cambridge is concerned about her school's climate and she is seeking a good way to measure it. In particular, since she wants to improve student achievement at Washington High, she needs some assurance that the sort of climate being measured will have an impact on student learning. This study, then, might have a double advantage for her, since it provides a direct comparison of two different measures of school climate and their effects on two important school outcomes, one of which is student learning. On the other hand, however, the Hoy et al. study addresses a question that is perhaps primarily of interest to researchers working in the area of school climate. It is a study of the relative predictive power of two measuring instruments. It is unclear to us that many practitioners have a problem in their schools whose solution requires knowledge of the relative predictive power of the *OCDQ-RS* and the *OHI*. The point is that by phrasing good questions to guide the literature search process, useful and relevant studies may be found that were carried out by researchers for purposes seemingly irrelevant to the problems of practitioners.

Beyond the importance of an investigation's research question, we have stressed that practitioners should evaluate a study's rationale when judging its quality. Specifically, Cambridge needs to consider the quality of the Hoy et al. argument linking each measure of school climate with student achievement and teacher commitment. Why should we believe that school climate or health affects either reading and math achievement or teacher commitment? How sound is the study's theoretical reasoning?

Consider first the *OCDQ-RS*. Hoy et al. note the instrument's lack of a theoretical underpinning, at one place (page 372) referring to its predecessor as "starkly empirical" and admit that their revision suffers from the same defect. Whenever a measure lacks a rationale, there is little reason to expect it to predict any particular phenomenon, as Hoy et al. acknowledge when they hypothesize that "the closer a construct is to theory, the stronger its predictive power" (page 369). The only rationale offered for expecting that the *OCDQ-RS* will predict any school outcome is "because it has a long history of predictive use" (page 372). This, of course, is not a rationale at all, that is, an argument showing why organizational climate can be expected to affect either student achievement or faculty commitment. Indeed, Anderson's (1982) earlier review of the *OCDQ* (which Hoy et al. cite) is critical of the instrument precisely because it lacks predictive power.

What about the *OHI*? Do the authors offer a rationale for believing organizational health affects achievement or commitment? They stress that their measure is based on Parsons' theory of formal organizations (Parsons, 1961; Parsons, 1967). However, the question is not simply whether the instrument has a rationale that guided its construction (which is certainly a desirable feature of any measuring tool), but whether the researchers offer a cogent rationale, or theory, for expecting that organizational health affects student achievement and teacher commitment. The existence of a convincing argument linking independent with dependent variables is an important criterion for practitioners like Cambridge to consider in judging the quality of a study. In this case, Hoy et al. essentially argue (following Parsons) that healthy organizations will produce higher levels of instrumental and expressive outcomes. In schools these outcomes include measured achievement and teacher commitment; therefore, schools scoring high on the *OHI* will also score high on achievement and commitment. Cambridge may find this argument not entirely satisfactory. The problem is that it fails to link school health to the specific outcomes of achievement and teacher commitment. That is, schools produce a large number of instrumental and expressive outcomes (e.g., vocational training, athletic skills, school spirit, and community pride). The authors' rationale would have been strengthened had they made an argument linking school health to the specific outcomes they chose to measure.

The Operational Level of the Study

In this section we consider four aspects of the Hoy et al. methodology: sampling, measurement, design, and data analysis. We will give most attention to measurement and the questions raised by the issues of reliability and validity.

Sampling. There are two levels of sampling in this study (as there are in many climate studies): schools and teachers. In their discussion of their sampling procedures, Hoy and his colleagues note that they did not have a random sample of schools. Instead, they claim to have a diverse group of schools in a broad range of districts drawn from 17 of the 21 counties in New Jersey. Given the relatively large number of secondary schools involved (58), Cambridge can be somewhat assured that the sample is reasonably representative of the schools in New Jersey. However, she would be more assured if the researchers had provided some evidence of their sample's representativeness—of its population validity. They might have provided, for example, a table containing a few simple comparisons of readily available characteristics of their schools with those in the state, say, the percentage of pupils on free or reduced lunch, school size, and expenditures per pupil. Given Cambridge's concern about academics, information about the schools' level of achievement would have been useful. It would have been especially helpful to Cambridge (and possibly illuminating to Hoy and his readers) if the sample of schools had been divided into high and low SES groups and the analyses carried out separately for each. This would have given Cambridge a subsample of schools to examine that were like Washington High, increasing her ability to judge its application validity. It would also have opened the possibility of examining the personalogical validity of school climate. Perhaps organizational health has differential effects in high versus low wealth schools. We do not wish to make too much of this point regarding sampling. It is extraordinarily difficult to draw a large, truly random sample of schools. Further, journal editors may be unable to include nonessential tables in the articles they publish. Nevertheless, practitioners should take a skeptical view of studies based on convenience samples. Presumably all of the schools included in this study were volunteered by both their superintendents and their principals. It is possible that schools that are volunteered in this way differ in significant but unknown ways from other New Jersey schools.

The second level of sampling in this study concerned teachers. Here the researchers, quite properly, drew a random sample of teachers from within each school. This was critical. Were teachers to be volunteers, the study's results would be highly questionable because of the inevitable selection bias: People who volunteer tend to be those with strong opinions, either positive or negative, about the subject of the research. Further, the researchers drew separate random samples of teachers to respond to three different instruments: the *OCDQ-RS*, the *OHI*, and their measure of teacher commitment, the *Organizational Commitment Questionnaire (OCQ)*. That, too, was a good move; it ensured that the three measures were independent. In effect, one group of teachers within each school acted as observers of their school's organizational climate, a second group provided estimates of their school's organizational health, while the third group provided estimates of their colleagues' commitment.

One aspect of this within-school sampling strikes us as problematic. Notice that there were 872 teachers and 58 schools involved in the study. On average, then, there were 15 teachers drawn from each secondary school, and hence five who responded to any one of the three instruments. Since that is the average, in some schools even fewer teachers provided estimates of their school's standing on each instrument. Thus, whether a school scored as healthy or unhealthy, open or closed, or its staff as committed or uncommitted could depend on the judgments of a relatively few people in some of these schools. It would have been desirable if Hoy et al. had given us a few words about the within-school variation in their sample sizes.

Measurement. This is the concept that we wish to highlight in this chapter. Cambridge is seeking to identify an instrument to measure the climate of Washington High. She wants to corroborate her subjective judgment of its climate with a more objective assessment, a common situation for educational administrators. Often they need to objectively measure some aspect of their school or one of its programs. For example, in evaluating a new curriculum, an administrator may want to know whether students have learned more than they did under the previous version. Or a principal may wish to identify sources of student dissatisfaction with the school, and he or she will seek a questionnaire to assess students' opinions about various aspects of school life. These tasks require the selection of a measuring instrument. Two of the major criteria for evaluating the quality of a measuring device are its validity and reliability. We will examine these concepts as they apply to the measurement of organizational climate.

There were three measuring instruments used in the Hoy et al. study, besides the state achievement tests. We will confine our remarks to the *OHI*, though the considerations we raise, namely, validity and reliability, apply equally to the others. Further, since Cambridge is primarily concerned about Washington High's climate and its effects on students' academic success, we will focus on the authors' measure of achievement, not their measure of teacher commitment. We also need to stress an important limitation that practitioners need to be aware of when they try to assess the validity and reliability of an instrument used in a study. Often these instruments were developed by investigators other than the authors of the study under examination, or they were developed by the authors, but their development was fully described in a separate report. The latter is the case for both the *OCDQ-RS* and the *OHI*. This means that information needed to judge an instrument's psychometric quality may not be fully presented in a research report that used the instrument. In the case at hand, Cambridge would need to consult additional sources, in particular Hoy, Tarter, and Kottkamp (1991), where the creation of both instruments is more fully described.

One of the standard expressions of a test's validity is to say that it is valid if it measures what it purports to measure. The *Standards for Educational and Psychological Testing* define validity more precisely as the "appropriateness, meaningfulness, and usefulness of the specific inferences made from test scores" (American Educational Research Association, American Psychological Association, & National Council on Measurement in Education, 1985). It is the inferences that are valid or invalid, not the test itself. Gall, Borg, and Gall (1996) observe that it is helpful to think of these inferences as *claims*. In the case of an achievement test, for example, we infer that a student's score is a measure of how much the student knows about the subject matter being tested. What evidence has the test developer provided to support a claim that the score is a measure of the student's knowledge? In the case of the *OHI*, what evidence have the researchers provided that a school's score is a valid measure of its health? Cambridge needs to consider this matter and, more generally, any practitioner evaluating the worth of a study needs to consider the validity of its measurements.

While validity is a unitary concept, its assessment can be approached in at least four different but related ways. The first of these is usually referred to as *content validity*. A test has content validity if its scores adequately represent the conceptual domain being measured. For example, do the items on a history test fairly sample the content of the course that was taught? A test for a course that covered all of 20th century American history, but asked questions only about the Great Depression, has little content validity. Similarly, does an *OHI* score fairly represent the domain of organizational health? In "Organizational Climate, School Health, and Effectiveness: A Comparative Analysis" (briefly), and in *Open Schools/Healthy Schools* (more fully) the development of the *OHI* is described. It is clear from these descriptions that the *OHI* was constructed by deliberately creating test items that sampled each of the domains of the Parsonian theory of organizations. To the extent, then, that Parson's theory of organizations is a comprehensive description of the components of organizational health, it strikes us as reasonable to conclude that the items in the *OHI* are a comprehensive sample of that construct. That is, the instrument possesses good content validity.

Concurrent validity is a second approach to establishing the validity of an instrument. Evidence that a test has concurrent validity is provided when it is shown to correlate with other tests designed to measure the same construct. For example, when a newly created test of reading skills is shown to correlate strongly with the reading subtest of the well-established *Iowa Test of Basic Skills*, that is evidence of the new test's concurrent validity.

Hoy et al. provide little evidence regarding the *OHI*'s concurrent validity. On one hand this is understandable. If they used the total score from the instrument, that is, its measure of a school's overall health, they would need to find an existing measure of organizational health with which to correlate the *OHI*. Further, in Table 2 (see Appendix) they do provide the correlations between each of the subtests of the *OHI* and the subtests of the *OCDQ-RS*. With the exception of the moderate correlation (.64) between "Consideration" and "Supportive Behavior," most of the correlations are quite small. This tells us that most of the subscales of the *OHI* and the *OCDQ-RS* are measuring different constructs. But that is to be expected: The *OHI* was designed to measure something different than the *OCDQ-RS*.

There are available measures of other subscale constructs that Hoy et al. might have used to provide evidence of their instrument's concurrent validity. For example, their Academic Emphasis scale is conceptually quite similar to the Intellectual Climate subscale of Stern's *High School Characteristics Index* (Stern, 1970) and to the academic climate scales developed by McDill and Rigsby (1973). Similarly, there are a number of measures of teacher morale that have been in use for many years (e.g., Coughlan, 1970) that might have been correlated with the Morale scale of the *OHI*. Again, we should not expect such evidence in this article, which is not, after all, about scale development, but it would be appropriate to present it in technical reports or in the book that reports the entire series of studies that led to the *OHI*.

A third kind of evidence for the validity of inferences from a test is called *predictive validity*. In this case the test developer shows that the test successfully predicts the future behavior of individuals or groups. The most common example of predictive validity in education is the use of certain standardized tests to select individuals for college. The *SAT*, for example, was expressly designed to predict the college success of high school students. Hoy et al. offer no data on the predictive validity of the *OHI*, which is understandable. While they speak of "predicting" school achievement and teacher commitment, they are not using the term in the sense of predictive validity, that is, forecasting a future condition. Their primary measures taken on the schools in their sample were taken simultaneously.

The final kind of evidence usually presented to support inferences made from test scores is that of *construct validity*. A construct is a theoretical concept inferred from diverse phenomena and may be used to explain those phenomena (Gall et al., 1996). "Morale," for example is a construct. It is itself unobservable, but it represents a number of observable acts of a teaching staff: absenteeism, willingness to take on extra tasks, and turnover, for example. Further, the construct "morale" may be invoked to explain these acts: Teachers work hard in a school because they have high morale. The seven subscales of the *OHI* are intended to measure constructs (e.g., "Institutional Integrity") and the entire instrument is supposed to measure the overarching construct of "organizational health." We will devote most of our attention to this form of validity because it is particularly pertinent to Cambridge's concerns, and the study is rich in information relevant to it.

Construct validity is a more complex and comprehensive approach to establishing a test's validity than the other approaches we have described. It is not established in one specific way. Rather, multiple lines of evidence may need to accumulate before the construct validity of a test is established. Recall the example of a test of anxiety that we discussed in chapter 4. In order to establish the construct validity of such a test, its developer might hypothesize that anxiety scores will be high in people with heart disease, people in high stress occupations, and people clinically identified by psychotherapists as anxious. If the test distinguishes between people with and without these conditions, evidence of the test's construct validity is accumulated. The question, then, is what evidence has been provided that the *OHI* possesses acceptable construct validity?

There are basically two kinds of evidence of the *OHI*'s construct validity to be found in this article and in *Open Schools/Healthy Schools*. The first of these are the results of the authors' principal components factor analyses of their instrument. A principal components analysis is a statistical technique for identifying the underlying dimensions or factors in a data set. It is often used to reduce the number of variables in a study. In this case, Hoy et al. began with a 44 item questionnaire (i.e., 44 variables) and then showed that these 44 items really seem to be measuring just 7 factors, and that these factors correspond to the constructs they were trying to measure (i.e., Institutional Integrity, Initiating Structure, and so on). They show, for example, that the individual items created to measure Academic Emphasis do, in fact, hang together: They correlate substantially with the other items intended to measure Academic Emphasis and have much lower correlations with items intended to measure other constructs. Thus, if teachers judge that "[This] school sets high standards for academic performance," (one of the items intended to measure Academic Emphasis), those same teachers are likely to agree that "Students [in this school] seek extra work so that they can get good grades" (another item intended to measure the same construct). They also show, through their second order factor analysis, that all 7 of these factors are correlated moderately with each other, and offer this as evidence that a total score based on all 7 factors is a valid measure of organizational health, the overarching construct.

This procedure for establishing the construct validity of a measure is quite common and is especially so in the measurement of organizational climate. Practitioners like Cambridge should recognize it. It is one approach to construct validity, but it is not an especially compelling one. Notice the procedure: A group of experts in the field sit down and generate a series of questionnaire items that they believe will measure the constructs they are interested in, for example, "Institutional Integrity." They try to reach a consensus on which items seem valid. They then go over these items carefully to ensure that they meet certain criteria. Hoy and his colleagues specified those criteria as follows (Hoy et al., 1991, p. 65):

1. Each item reflected a property of the school.
2. The statement was clear and concise.
3. The statement had content validity.[2]
4. The statement has discriminatory potential (i.e., it will discriminate among schools).

Next, they administered the items meeting these criteria to a sample of respondents and factor analyzed the resulting data. They then selected those items that clustered together in the expected way, eliminated those that did not, and used those items as measures of the 7 constructs. Essentially, then, the factor analysis provided empirical evidence that the items clustered the way that the experts thought they would. This provides some evidence that the instrument has satisfactory construct validity, but it is not sufficient evidence.

Hoy et al. provide another kind of evidence of the construct validity of the OHI, but that evidence is not available in this article. Hoy and his colleagues have completed a number of studies using the instrument and have developed variations of it suitable to elementary and middle schools as well as high schools (Hoy et al., 1996a; Hoy et al., 1996b; Hoy & Hannum, 1997; Hoy & Sabo, 1998; Hoy et al., 1991). In these studies (as well as in the preliminary research involved in creating the instrument), the factor structure of the instrument in various levels of schooling and with different groups of teachers is quite similar. That is, the scales are relatively stable across situations. Arguably, this too counts as evidence for the construct validity of the *OHI*'s scales.

There is, however, another kind of evidence in the Hoy et al. article regarding the construct validity of their measure of organizational health. Recall that construct validity is usually established by showing that a measure discriminates between two or more groups that, on theoretical grounds, it ought to distinguish between. Hoy et al. argue on just such theoretical grounds that healthy schools should be more likely to meet their productive and expressive goals. In this case, students should evidence higher achievement and teachers should show greater commitment in healthy than unhealthy schools. Thus, rather than a study concerned with comparing the relative power of the *OHI* and the *OCDQ-RS*, their article can be read as a study of the *OHI*'s construct validity. Does the instrument sharply distinguish in the predicted way between schools with high versus low achievement and committed versus uncommitted teachers?

We suspect that Cambridge will conclude that it does not. Consider whether the *OHI* distinguishes high from low achieving schools. The evidence regarding this is found in Table 10.1, which we have reproduced below from Table 3 in the article. By itself the health instrument has a multiple correlation (the *R* in the top panel of the table) of .77 with average school achievement.[3] This is a respectable

---

[2] The correct term here is not "content validity" but "face validity." Face validity is much weaker evidence of a measure's validity. It involves only a subjective inspection of the possible items to judge whether their subjects seem reasonable examples of behavior representing the construct being measured (Gall et al., 1996, p. 250). As we discussed earlier, content validity is established by showing that a measure adequately samples the domain of possible behavior representing the construct.

[3] Think of a multiple correlation as analogous to an ordinary correlation between two variables. Instead of two variables, however, it represents the correlation between several variables combined together with one other variable. In this instance, the multiple correlation of .77 represents the relationship between a weighted combination of the 7 climate variables with average school achievement. Correlations involving two variables (sometimes called "zero-order correlations") are represented by the symbol *r*, multiple correlations by the symbol *R*.

T A B L E   *10.1*

Regression of Achievement and Commitment on Dimensions of School Health and SES

	Achievement		Commitment	
	r	beta	*r*	beta
Health variables only (n = 58)				
		Regression Number 1		
Institutional integrity	−.34**	−.44**	.32**	.16
Initiating structure	.10	−.17	.28*	−.15
Consideration	.11	−.02	.41**	.21
Principal influence	.18	.14	.41**	.21
Resource allocation	.33**	.04	.35**	.06
Academic emphasis	.63**	.62**	.41**	.25
Morale	.21	.13	.41**	.09
	*R = .77**		*R = .58**	
Health variables with SES				
		Regression Number 2		
SES	.82**	.57**	.26*	.15
Institutional integrity	−.34**	−.16	.32**	.24
Initiating structure	.10	−.07	.28*	−.14
Consideration	.11	−.03	.41**	.17
Principal influence	.18	.02	.41**	.20
Resource allocation	.33**	.07	.35**	.04
Academic emphasis	.63**	.31**	.41**	.23
Morale	.21	.07	.41**	.04
	*R = .87**		*R = .59**	

$*p < .05; **p < .01.$
Source: From Hoy, Tarter, & Bliss (1990, p. 272).

correlation. However, also notice that most of the strength of this relationship between school health and student achievement is due to the single variable of Academic Emphasis, which has a .63 correlation (*r*) with Achievement. Further, one school health variable, Institutional Integrity, is *negatively* associated with achievement, meaning that the healthier the school, the lower its students' achievement—opposite of what the theory suggests. Finally, 4 of the 7 climate variables are not significantly related to student achievement. These findings do not argue for the construct validity of the *OHI* as a measure of organizational health. Rather, they suggest that, at best, their construct of Academic Emphasis is able to distinguish between high and low achieving schools, but their construct organizational health cannot.

You can get further evidence on this matter by again examining Table 10.1 and recalling a few facts about correlations. (You will need to follow along in Table 10.1 as you read the next few paragraphs.) Recall that squaring a simple (zero-order) correlation (r) between two variables provides a measure of the power of one to affect the other. More precisely, squaring a correlation coefficient provides a measure of the amount of variation in one variable that can be predicted by variation in the other. Researchers usually say that a squared correlation measures how much of the variation in one variable can be "explained" by another. This explained variation is expressed as a percent. For example, in the bottom panel of Table 10.1 Hoy et al. give us the zero-order correlation (r) between school SES and school achievement. That correlation is .82. Squaring the .82 correlation between SES and achievement and multiplying the result by 100 tells us that the SES explains 67.24% of the variation in school achievement. In practical terms, this means that if we know the average SES of students in each of a set of schools, we can make reasonably accurate predictions of those schools' average achievement test scores.[4]

The same rule applies to a multiple correlation (R). Squaring a multiple correlation coefficient tells us the power of a group of measures, taken together, to explain the variation in a single variable. For example, look at the top panel of Table 10.1. The $R = .77$ tells us that all 7 subscales of the school health measure, taken together (ostensibly organizational health) have a substantial multiple correlation with Achievement and a more modest one with Commitment (.58). Squaring the former, we see that the *Organizational Health,* by itself, seems to explain 59.29% of the variation in schools' average achievement levels ($.77^2 \times 100 = 59.29$). That certainly seems to be a fairly large amount. Taken at its face, a school's climate explains over half of its average achievement. If we think now of construct validity, the *OHI* seems to nicely distinguish high from low achieving schools. This is evidence of good construct validity. However, the bottom panel of Table 10.1 tells a different story. There we see that both SES and the *OHI* scales together have a multiple correlation (R) with average school achievement of .87. Thus both SES and the 7 climate variables together explain 75.69% of the achievement variation ($.87^2 \times 100 = 75.69$).

Now consider: Table 10.1 tells us that by itself organizational health (i.e., all 7 of the climate variables) explains a substantial amount of achievement variation—59.29%. The table also tells us that by itself SES explains an even more substantial amount—67.24%. But both SES and health together explain only 75.69%. How can this be? The answer, of course, is that Organizational Health and SES are not independent; they are substantially related to each other, and much of this shared variation is also shared with student achievement. When this happens, it is not possible to judge the relative power of the two to affect achievement by simply examining the size of the correlations involved. More to

---

[4] A correlation between SES and achievement of .82 may seem extraordinarily high. Remember that Hoy and his colleagues are reporting a correlation between the *average* SES of all of the students in a set of schools and the *average* achievement levels in those schools. This is not at all the same thing as computing a correlation between SES and achievement among a group of individual students (which is usually about .3). It is a difference in the level of analysis—schools versus individuals. Correlations between what appear to be the same variables may differ very substantially at different levels of analysis.

the point, it is not possible to unambiguously judge the construct validity of the *OHI* by simply looking at its ability to distinguish between successful and unsuccessful schools, that is, by looking at its .77 correlation with achievement. Its apparent power to distinguish successful from unsuccessful schools may be due primarily to its relationship to SES.

All of this would have been more obvious (and Cambridge's life would have been easier), if Hoy et al. had developed a table that directly compared total health scores (not subscale scores) with SES. Using subscale scores certainly increased the multiple correlation of .77 by some unknown amount.[5] Doing that would have permitted a direct comparison of organizational health with SES. In any case, Cambridge would be justified in concluding that the *OHI*'s construct validity, at least in regard to achievement, is problematic. But since student achievement is arguably a very significant school outcome (and Hoy et al. make this claim on page 372 of their article), and it is certainly the most significant concern of Cambridge, a weak relationship between school health and student achievement is a serious matter.

In Chapter 9 we pointed out a case in which a researcher's interpretation of her data was not the only possible one. Here we see another example. Hoy and his colleagues have advanced an interpretation of the results of their analysis that is substantially at odds with another view. The point is not that anyone is necessarily wrong in these cases. Rather, the point is that data (like facts) never "speak for themselves." The same analysis can be (and often is) interpreted in quite different ways. This is why we have urged you to become reasonably comfortable with interpreting tables for yourselves. If you rely only on the text of articles to tell you what the researcher found, you are relying on the researcher's interpretation of his or her analysis. Simply by attending carefully to a table's title, its row and column headings and then trying to glean from the text what the numbers in cells mean, you will go a long way toward emancipating yourself from having to rely only on only one explanation for a study's findings. You do not necessarily need to understand the statistical techniques that generated those numbers. Simply by reading the numbers in Table 10.1 (e.g., noticing that several of the components of organizational health were uncorrelated or even negatively correlated with achievement), Cambridge recognized the problematic aspect of the *OHI*'s construct validity.

Reliability. Before a school administrator adopts an instrument for use in his or her school, it is important to assess its reliability as well as its validity. In this section we want to examine how Cambridge might assess the reliability of the *OHI*.

Every measuring device, no matter how well designed, is to some degree inaccurate. The most carefully constructed instruments—from ordinary rulers to

---

[5] This is because adding an independent variable to a multiple regression equation almost certainly will increase the multiple correlation, R. Adding an additional variable can never lower R. Thus, using the 7 subscale scores for each school produces a larger multiple correlation with achievement and commitment than would using a single total *OHI* score for the same schools.

atomic clocks—introduce some error into their measurements, and this is true for all educational measurements as well. In standard psychometric theory, a person's score on a test is thought of as being composed of two components, a true score (the actual amount of the attribute that is being measured) and an error component (some amount of error). Neither of these can be directly observed—they must be estimated. Reliability, then, is the amount of error in the scores generated by a test. A test's reliability is estimated by its *reliability coefficient,* a number that may vary between 0 and 1, where 0 indicates that scores contain only error and 1 indicates that scores contain no error. Since all measurement is to some degree inaccurate, no test will have a reliability coefficient of 1.

How much reliability should be demanded of a test? This depends on several factors, but perhaps the most important is the purpose of the test. In high stakes testing situations, where important decisions are to be made about individuals, very high reliability coefficients should be expected. For example, scores on a state test used to select students who will receive a high school diploma should have very little error in them, because denying someone a diploma is a very serious matter. A reliability coefficient over .90 seems reasonable.[6] On the other hand, when a test score is to be used to characterize groups in situations where nothing terribly significant rides on the score, lower reliabilities are acceptable. Cambridge's purpose of checking her subjective impression of Washington High's climate is an example of this situation. For her purpose, a reliability coefficient around .70 might be quite adequate.

How can a reliability coefficient be determined? *Parallel (or alternate) form reliability* is established by creating two equivalent forms of the same test and administering both to the same group. If the two tests have high reliabilities, the scores on the two should be strongly correlated. Because of the costs involved in creating two (or more) forms of the same test, this method is not often used. Understandably, Hoy et al. did not attempt to measure the reliability of the *OHI* in this way. (However, many of the publishers of the major standardized achievement tests offer alternative forms of their tests for use in the schools, and they do report their tests' reliabilities as alternate form correlations.)

Test-retest reliability is assessed by administering the same test to a group of people at two different times. Correlating the scores on the two tests provides an estimate of the test's reliability coefficient. Since a school's climate presumably changes rather slowly, particularly if there is no attempt to intervene and change it, Hoy et al. might have administered their instrument to teachers in the same school with several months between the two testings and then computed the

---

[6] Practitioners should not assume that all professionally developed high stakes tests have high reliabilities. As we write, a controversy over the Massachusetts Teacher Examination (MTE) is developing. A minimum score on that test is required before a person can be granted a license to teach in that state. A study evaluating the MTE purports to show that its test-retest reliability is very low, in some subtests approaching zero (Haney, Fowler, Wheelock, Bebell, & Malec, 1999). If that is correct, hundreds of persons who spent four or more years training to become teachers were unfairly denied a license. And perhaps even more alarming, hundreds who are actually incompetent are now teaching in Massachusetts schools.

correlation between the two sets of scores. This would have provided the test-retest reliability of the *OHI*. Alternatively, they might have selected two or more separate groups of teachers in each school to take the *OHI* at the same time. Since all groups would be observing the same phenomenon—their school's climate—the correlation of the sets of scores should be relatively high, if the instrument is reliable. (This is actually a measure of inter-rater reliability.)

A variation on this procedure was carried out by Nusser and Haller (1995). They administered an identical measure of a school's disciplinary climate to administrators, teachers, and students in a large sample of secondary schools. They found substantial discrepancies in the assessments of the three groups, and those discrepancies were patterned. Administrators consistently rated their school as having a better disciplinary climate than did that school's teachers, and teachers consistently rated the school as having a better climate than did students. This suggests, incidentally, that when measuring a school's climate, it makes a considerable difference who one asks to do the ratings. (More cynically, it also suggests that if an administrator wishes to show that a school has a good climate, he or she would do well to avoid asking students' opinions.)

A third type of reliability is often termed *internal consistency.* In this case, the individual items on an instrument that has been administered once to a group of persons are examined. Essentially, the method examines the correlations among all of the items measuring a construct: Each should be strongly and positively correlated with the others, if the test can be said to have high reliability. There are several ways of computing a test's internal consistency, and one of the most common is *Cronbach's alpha.* This is the method used by Hoy et al., who report alphas for each of the subscales of the *OHI* in the parentheses on the diagonal of Table 2 in the Appendix. As Cambridge reads the research literature on school climate, she will run into this measure of reliability frequently. Alpha can be interpreted as the correlation between the existing measuring scale and all other possible scales of the same length that might be constructed from the universe of items that measure the same construct. For example, Hoy et al. report that their Institutional Integrity subscale made up of 7 items (Hoy et al., 1991) has an alpha reliability of .91. One can imagine a hypothetical set of all items that measure institutional integrity and all possible 7-item scales made from those items. Theoretically, Hoy's measure of institutional integrity would correlate with these hypothetical scales at .91.

The alpha reliabilities shown in Table 2 for the *OHI*'s subscales range from .87 to .95. For measures of group characteristics that will not be used for consequential decisions, reliabilities over .7 are often considered adequate. Their subscales easily meet this standard.

What might Cambridge conclude about the validity and reliability of the *OHI*? On one hand, while subscale reliabilities are very high, she would be justified in having serious concerns about using the entire instrument, that is, all of its subscales, as a device to measure the climate of Washington High. The construct validity of the Organizational Health Inventory is clouded because of its weak relationship to school achievement. On the other hand, she might find the specific subscale Academic Emphasis to be useful. After all, her primary concern is the apparent lack of value placed on educational achievement at her school, and this subscale may possess adequate construct validity for measuring the stress put on academic work at Washington High.

We would also point out that in her review of the secondary literature on school climate, Cambridge will certainly have read various authors who have criticized the lack of reliability and validity of many climate scales and, in some cases, the lack of any data at all on these important considerations (Gottfredson et al., 1986; Morgenstern & Keeves, 1994; Stockard, 1985; Wilson & McGrail, 1987). Compared to many of the instruments in the extant literature, the *OHI* is of good quality.

Finally, we would be remiss if we did not mention that Hoy, Tarter, and Kottkamp (1991) provide a useful and specific set of directions to practitioners for administering, scoring, and interpreting the results of this instrument (and the *OCDQ-RS*). This is essential information for a practitioner interested in using any test, information lacking for most other measures of school climate.

Research Design and Data Analysis. We will close our examination of the Hoy et al. investigation with a brief discussion of the study's design and data analysis strategies. It is a correlational design, that is, its purpose was to ascertain how several measures of organizational health and climate were related to each other and how each was related to two outcome measures—student achievement and teacher commitment. Correlational studies are typically used for two purposes: to examine the relationships among variables or to predict a subject's future score on some measure. This study of school climate is an example of the former purpose.

We have discussed the strengths and weaknesses of correlational designs elsewhere in this book. We will not repeat that discussion here except to remind readers of the impossibility of proving causal relationships using correlational designs. Only true experiments approach that lofty criterion. Nevertheless, there can be no causal relationship between variables unless they are correlated, so that one can infer a causal relationship from a correlation. However, doing so is problematic because there are always alternative inferences to be made that may be equally or even more plausible. The strength of an inference regarding a causal relationship is dependent in large part on the power of a study's rationale or theory. When a study is grounded in a strong rationale that persuasively links independent and dependent variables, a researcher's inference of a causal relationship between those variables, after showing only that they are correlated, is considerably strengthened.

We alluded to this matter earlier in discussing the Hoy et al. rationale linking organizational health to student achievement. We suggested that their case would have been strengthened had they linked organizational health specifically to achievement, that is, by offering an explanation of exactly how a healthy school, as exemplified by high scores on Institutional Integrity and Initiating Structure, leads to higher mean scores on tests of reading, writing, and mathematics, and how healthy schools also create commitment in teachers. Refer again to their Table 10.1. In the lower panel we see that the only *OHI* variable that is significantly and independently related to achievement in the predicted direction is Academic Emphasis.[7] The inference, then, is that the latter causes higher achievement. That is not implausible: It seems reasonable that when teachers emphasize academic success, student achievement will be higher. But it is not the only plausible inference.

To see this Cambridge needs to know exactly what Academic Emphasis is. It will be necessary for her to refer to *Open Schools/Healthy Schools,* where the items that make up each of the *OHI*'s subscales are listed (Hoy et al., 1991, p. 188). Those items are simple descriptive statements scored on a four-point Likert scale from "rarely occurs" to "very frequently occurs."

1. Students in this school can achieve the goals that have been set for them.
2. The school sets high standards for academic performance.
3. Students respect others who get good grades.
4. Students seek extra work so they can get good grades.
5. Teachers in this school believe that their students have the ability to achieve academically.
6. Academic achievement is recognized and acknowledged by the school.
7. Students try hard to improve on previous work.
8. The learning environment is orderly and serious.

Cambridge should notice two things about these items. First, the name of the subscale suggests that it is a measure of the extent to which the school emphasizes academic achievement. However, four of the eight items (1, 3, 4, and 7) actually measure teachers' perceptions of student behavior, not their perceptions of the schools' emphasis on achievement. Compare items 2 and 3, for example. It is reasonable to suppose that in schools characterized by high achievement, teachers will be more likely to perceive that students seek extra work, that they try hard to improve, and so on. That is, Cambridge could reasonably conclude that the causal relationship is the opposite to the one hypothesized by Hoy et al. Achievement causes schools to have an academic emphasis, not the reverse. Second, the same argument can be made in regard to the remaining four items. In schools where students are achieving at a high level, teachers are likely to agree that students have the ability to achieve; those schools are likely to recognize and acknowledge academic achievement; and they are likely to set high standards for performance.

---

[7] We are referring to the beta values in the second column of Regression Number 2. In multiple regression analysis, beta weights can be interpreted as a measure of the effect of an independent variable on a dependent variable, when the effects of other independent variables are held constant. In this case, this means that Academic Emphasis and SES each had a statistically significant effect on mean school achievement, independent of any effects from institutional integrity, initiating structure, and so forth.

In part the criticism we are making is a matter of measurement; the one sub-scale that had a significant relationship to achievement is conceptually flawed. Such flaws may go undetected by statistical techniques (in this case, factor analysis), which simply show that the items in the scale are related to each other but cannot tell us why they are related.

But the criticism also highlights the danger of making possibly erroneous causal inferences in studies that use correlational designs. Researchers often slip into using causal language when describing the results of their correlational studies. It is natural for them to do so, since they are interested in establishing causality, yet they have no choice but to use correlational designs. Hoy et al., for example, wanted to know if healthy schools cause high achievement among students and strong commitment among teachers. But obviously they could not create an experiment in which they establish treatments producing different levels of organizational health and then assign schools randomly to those levels in order to observe the effects on achievement and commitment. Yet that is what is required before we can unambiguously say that organizational health causes achievement or commitment.

Researchers are not alone in slipping into unwarranted causal thinking. Practitioners are hardly free of this tendency. Cambridge, for example, seems to believe that there is something about the climate of her school that has caused achievement to decline. We suspect that most school administrators would subscribe to the notion that a school's climate is an important cause of student achievement, and perhaps it is. But we cannot know that based on the results of our research or our experience. For the moment then, sophisticated administrators should probably keep a simple rule in mind: *No statistical technique, no matter how sophisticated, is able to extract causal proofs from correlational data.* More fundamentally, however, we believe that these comments bear on the critical importance of a theoretical rationale in correlational studies that are meant to examine relationships among variables.

Practitioners interested in measuring some aspect of their school or its students must look beyond the names of potential instruments and their subscales. A test named "The XYZ Scale of Reading Comprehension" may or may not measure reading comprehension. Administrators who are interested in using some scale should examine the specific items that make it up. They need some assurance that each of the items plausibly tap the construct named by the scale's title. We have seen that the Academic Emphasis subscale of the *OHI* is problematic, despite its factor structure and high reliability. We can assure you that the *OHI* is far from being the only instrument with doubtfully titled scales.

Conclusions

What lessons might practitioners like Joanna Cambridge take from an excursion into the school climate literature and a search for a valid measure of that construct? We think there are several. Perhaps most importantly, the cognitive status of the concept of school climate has improved considerably since the original

OCDQ was developed by Halpin and Croft (1963). Nevertheless, much remains to be done. There is certainly no agreement on the nature of "the beast" as Anderson refers to it (1982), nor on ways to approach its measurement. In these regards, however, Hoy and his colleagues are to be strongly commended. While we have focused our attention on just one of their studies and have been critical of several of its aspects, the work carried out under their direction at Rutgers and Ohio State is one of the few sustained, theoretically unified, streams of research on school climate underway in this country. It is an excellent example of a process that is all too rare in educational administration—the slow, careful building of an empirical and theoretical foundation to an important idea. Practitioners interested in using the idea of school climate would do well to follow the future development of the *OHI*.

Beyond this, Arter (1987) provides some useful suggested steps for practitioners such as Cambridge, who want to assess the climate of their schools:

1. Decide why you want to gather information on educational climates. Climate information can be used for different purposes, for example, to improve achievement, to evaluate curriculum effects, or to compare one school to another. An instrument valid for one purpose may be invalid for another.

2. Decide what aspect of climate you want to look at. As was pointed out by Tagiuri 30 years ago (Tagiuri, 1968), organizational climate has several dimensions, and which dimension one chooses to emphasize is important. Of the seven dimensions of the *OHI*, for example, only one, academic emphasis, has consistently demonstrated substantial and meaningful relationships with student achievement. Given Cambridge's interest in student achievement, another instrument may be more useful. In this regard McDill, Myers, and Rigsby developed one that concentrates only on aspects of the achievement press of high schools and that provides a more nuanced set of measures than the *OHI* (McDill, Meyers, & Rigsby, 1967; McDill & Rigsby, 1973).

3. Decide how to best gather this information. Most climate assessments are carried out with paper and pencil instruments. However, other approaches may be better (e.g., naturalistic enquiry). Related to this is the question of from whom the information is to be collected: administrators, teachers, students, or parents. Different groups may come to quite different conclusions about a school's climate (Nusser & Haller, 1995).

Arter's final recommendation is that if you, as a practitioner, can find no instrument that meets your needs, you might develop one of your own. At this point we part company with her. Developing a valid and reliable instrument to measure a school's climate is an extraordinarily difficult undertaking, and is, in our view, well beyond the capabilities and time constraints of all but the most resource-rich school districts. The area of school climate may well be one where the prudent practitioner might better sit back and wait for the dust to settle before undertaking the task of creating an instrument to measure the hugely complex notion of school climate.

Joanna Cambridge's Notebook

Joanna Cambridge began her sojourn in the climate literature with two questions in mind:

1. What is "school climate"? That is, how has it been conceptualized? Do particular kinds of climates have especially positive aspects on student achievement?
2. How is school climate assessed? Are there alternative, more objective measures available that I might use to assess the climate of Washington High?

As she progressed through this literature, she kept a notebook and recorded her thoughts and findings about her discoveries, and how those discoveries might relate to her problem at Washington High. She did not order her notes in the sequence of her questions, though actually they responded to both. Rather, she jotted down thoughts as they occurred to her and as they were provoked by whatever she was reading. We have reproduced some of her notes in Figure 10.1, slightly edited to improve their readability. We also eliminated material that is largely irrelevant—primarily musings about the day's problems and many references to members of her staff and the community. All emphases are Cambridge's.

What is revealing about these notes is that they illustrate how Cambridge *used* the research literature to develop her own ideas regarding the climate at Washington High School. She did not simply seek the answers to her questions. Rather, her reading stimulated her own ideas and started her on the road to developing a plan to improve her school. She ended her reading with an entirely different purpose in mind than the one with which she started (measuring climate). Her actions epitomize our conception of a sophisticated, critical consumer of educational research. As we have said many times in this book, all that research can do is to help you think more intelligently about real problems.

Joanna Cambridge's Notes on the Climate Literature

- There is *much* more of this stuff than I expected. Stick with my questions or I'll spend all of my time in this library.
- Take a look at Halpin & Croft (OCDQ). Very early stuff—60s. Everyone refers to it, usually critically. If so many think it's worth criticizing, it's worth a few minutes of my time.
  - Re: H. & C. Climate as "personality" of a school. That metaphor seems a stretch—high schools aren't human beings. They classified schools as open-to-closed personality w/six dimensions. Didn't work empirically.
  - Re: OCDQ. It isn't useful to me. The focus is on principals and teachers and their interactions, it doesn't really concern kids & achievement. Also, OCDQ scores don't correlate w/achievement, which I need to attend to, or I'll have McIver *and* the school bd on my case. Forget the OCDQ. But it's interesting history.
- Anderson (RER, '82) is useful. Ditto Tagiuri (Tagiuri & Litwin '68). See also Hoy et al. '91. All give good discussions of the nature of organizational climate. Some generalizations:
  - It isn't one thing. There's no widely accepted definition. The underlying metaphor varies all over the place. Engineering (open systems), medicine (healthy or unhealthy orgs.), biology (adaptive orgs.), etc. There are at least 4 quite distinct approaches. More important, it turns out, given the different metaphors, there are several approaches to measurement. How am I going to measure it "objectively" at WHS?
  - There continues to be a problem with subscales, to say nothing of the overall measure of climate. Many don't correlate with student achievement. *Or anything else.* This also makes problematic my idea of objectively measuring WHS's climate.
  - There must be better measures available. Checked Mental Measurements Yearbooks and Tests in Print. One instrument developed by AASA (Comp. Assessment of Sch. Env., CASE) looks promising.
  - CASE has problems too. Maybe I should forget about measuring climate in WHS?
  - Bingo. Gottfredson et al. (1986), Wilson & McGrail (1987), and Stockard (1985) all provide useful secondary reviews of a number of climate instruments. Check these out; they'll save a lot of time.
- Looked at the empirical stuff by Hoy and others at Rutgers and OSU. They seem to be producing the bulk of the current studies involving the measurement of climate.
  - Again, subscale problems in Hoy, as above. But something called Academic Emphasis turns out to affect (maybe) achievement. It's one dimension of school climate that seems to make sense. Get earlier work by McDill and others and also Stern. They seem to have concentrated on academic press of school climate as well.
  - A measure of academic press, as in Hoy or McDill, etc. might serve my purposes. In the studies I've reviewed, these seem to have decent reliability.

Continued

F I G U R E   *10.1*   Joanna Cambridge's Notes on the Climate Literature

Validity seems to me to be dubious. If I can't get better evidence of validity, should I be using any of these instruments? *Can I claim, on the basis of any of them, that my school has an inadequate academic climate??*

- Suppose I use one of these (possibly invalid) measures and it tells me that the academic climate of WHS is just fine. Then what? If the instrument is wrong, not my diagnosis, I'll have wasted months and blown the chance to improve the climate of WHS.
- Q: How do I *know* that academic climate has an influence on achievement? A: I don't. All of these studies are correlational. But I think it does. Why else would WHS, which has everything going for it, have such a mediocre performance?

- I'm making a mistake. I really don't want to accurately measure the academic climate at WHS, I want to change it—make it more supportive of high achievement. Can I use these measures to help me change the climate at WHS? *Consider the following, Joanna*:

  - The measures are all suspect. Creating better ones is way beyond our means or expertise.
  - Suppose I took a selection of the items from the various academic emphasis scales and modified them slightly to make them fit our school, e.g., from Hoy's scale: "Washington High sets high standards for academic performance" or "Students at Washington respect others who get good grades." These are interesting topics to think and talk about.
  - I could organize small groups of administrators, teachers, students, and parents to take the test items and then simply sit around a table and talk about how they see WHS in regard to each. Basically, they'd ask: "What can these items tell us about our school?" Wouldn't that get people thinking about the academic climate of the school and how it might be improved?
  - We might spend six months, even a year, talking about this matter and focusing on the academic life of Washington. The goal would be to develop a school improvement plan, ways to make the school more conducive to and appreciative of academic work and the life of the mind. We just might be able to turn this situation around. After all, our students are bright, the staff is well trained, and parents are supportive. WHS should be one of the most academically successful schools in the state.
  - Make an appointment with the superintendent to discuss this. If he supports the plan, I might even contact Dr. McIver. It would be good to let him know that we're doing something about the problem at WHS.

References

American Educational Research Association, American Psychological Association, & National Council on Measurement in Education. (1985). *Standards for educational and psychological testing.* Washington, DC: American Psychological Association.

Anderson, B. D. (1973). School bureaucratization and alienation from high school. *Sociology of Education, 46*(3), 315–344.

Anderson, C. S. (1982). The search for school climate: A review of the research. *Review of Educational Research, 52*(3), 368–420.

Andrews, J. H. M. (1965). School organizational climate: Some validity studies. *Canadian*

Education and Research Digest, 5, 317–334.

Arter, J. A. (1987). *Assessing school and classroom climate. A consumer's guide.* Portland, OR: Northwest Regional Educational Laboratory. (ERIC Document Reproduction No. ED295301)

Barker, R. G., & Gump, P. V. (1964). *Big school, small school; high school size and student behavior.* Palo Alto, CA: Stanford University Press.

Bryk, A. S., & Driscoll, M. E. (1988). *The high school as community: Contextual influences and consequences for students and teachers.* Madison, WI: National Center on Effective Secondary Schools. (ERIC Document Reproduction No. ED302539)

Coleman, J. S. (1961). *The adolescent society: The social life of the teenager and its impact on education.* New York: Free Press of Glencoe.

Coleman, J. S., Campbell, E. Q., Hobson, C. J., McPartland, J., Mood, A. M., Weinfeld, F., & York, R. L. (1966). *Equality of educational opportunity.* Washington, DC: U.S. Government Printing Office.

Cookson, P., & Persell, C. (1985). *Preparing for power: America's elite boarding schools.* New York: Basic Books.

Coughlan, R. J. (1970). Dimensions of teacher morale. *American Educational Research Journal, 7*(2), 221–235.

Crain, R. L., & Mahard, R. E. (1981). Minority achievement: Policy implications of research. In W. D. Hawley (Ed.), *Effective school desegregation: Equity, quality and feasibility* (pp. 55–84). Beverly Hills, CA: Sage.

Cusick, P. A. (1973). *Inside high school: The student's world.* New York: Holt, Rinehart and Winston.

Fraser, B. J. (1986). *The study of learning environments.* Salem, OR: Assessment Research.

Gall, M. D., Borg, W. R., & Gall, J. P. (1996). *Educational research: An introduction.* (6th ed.). White Plains, NY: Longman.

Goodlad, J. I. (1984). *A place called school: Prospects for the future.* New York: McGraw-Hill.

Gottfredson, D. C., Hybl, L. G., Gottfredson, G. D., & Castaneda, R. P. (1986). *School climate assessment instruments: A review.* Baltimore, MD: Center for Social Organization of Schools, Johns Hopkins University. (ERIC Document Reproduction No. ED278702)

Grant, G. (1989). *The world we created at Hamilton High.* Cambridge, MA: Harvard University Press.

Haller, E. J. (1992). High school size and student indiscipline: Another aspect of the school consolidation issue? *Educational Evaluation and Policy Analysis, 14*(2), 145–156.

Haller, E. J., Nusser, J. L., & Monk, D. H. (1998). Assessing school district quality: Contrasting state and citizens' perspectives. In D. Chalker (Ed.), *Educational leadership in rural schools: Lessons for all educators.* Lancaster, PA: Technomics.

Halpin, A. W., & Croft, D. B. (1963). *The organizational climate of schools.* Chicago: Midwest Administrative Center, University of Chicago.

Halpin, A. W., & Croft, D. B. (1966). *Theory and research in administration.* New York: Macmillan.

Haney, W., Fowler, C., Wheelock, A., Bebell, D., & Malec, N. (1999). Less truth than error? An independent study of the Massachusetts Teacher Tests. *Educational Policy Analysis Archives, 7*(4) [On-line serial]. Available: http://epaa.asu.edu/epaa/v7n4/

Hoy, W. K., Barnes, K., and Sabo, D. (1996a). Organizational health and faculty trust: A view from the middle level. *Research in Middle Level Education Quarterly, 19*(3), 21–39.

Hoy, W. K., Hoffman, J., Sabo, D., & Bliss, J. (1996b). The organizational climate of middle schools. *Journal of Educational Administration, 34*(1), 41–59.

Hoy, W. K., & Hannum, J. W. (1997). Middle school climate: An empirical assessment of organizational health and student achievement. *Educational Administration Quarterly, 33*(3), 290–311.

Hoy, W. K., & Sabo, D. J. (1998). *Quality middle schools: Open and healthy.* Thousand Oaks, CA: Corwin Press.

Hoy, W. K., Tarter, C. J., & Bliss, J. R. (1990). Organizational climate, school health, and effectiveness: A comparative analysis. *Educational Administration Quarterly, 26*(3), 260–279.

Hoy, W. K., Tarter, C. J., & Kottkamp, R. B. (1991). *Open schools / healthy schools: Measuring organizational climate*. Newbury Park, CA: Sage Publications, Inc.

Jimenez, E., & Lockheed, M. E. (1989). Enhancing girls' learning through single-sex education: Evidence and a policy conundrum. *Educational Evaluation and Policy Analysis, 11*(2), 117–142.

Lightfoot, S. L. (1983). *The good high school: Portraits of character and culture*. New York: Basic Books.

Lortie, D. C. (1975). *Schoolteacher: A sociological study*. Chicago: University of Chicago Press.

McDill, E. L., Meyers, E. D., & Rigsby, L. C. (1967). Institutional effects on the academic behavior of high school students. *Sociology of Education, 40*(2), 181–199.

McDill, E. L., & Rigsby, L. C. (1973). *Structure and process in secondary schools: The academic impact of educational climates*. Baltimore, MD: Johns Hopkins University Press.

Miles, M. (1969). Planned change and organizational health: Figure and ground. In F. D. Carver & T. J. Sergiovanni (Eds.), *Organizations and human behavior* (pp. 375–391). New York: McGraw-Hill.

Miles, M. B. (1965). Education and innovation: The organization in context. In M. Abbott & J. Lovell (Eds.), *Changing perspectives in educational administration* (pp. 54–72). Auburn, AL: Auburn University.

Murphy, L. L., Conoley, J. C., & Impara, J. C. (Eds.). (1994). *Tests in Print IV*. Lincoln, NE: The Buros Institute of Mental Measurement, The University of Nebraska.

Nusser, J. L., & Haller, E. J. (1995, April 18–22). Alternative perceptions of a school's climate: Do principals, students and teachers agree? Paper presented at the Annual Meeting of the American Educational Research Association, San Francisco, CA.

Parsons, T. (1961). An outline of the social system. In T. Parsons, E. Shils, K. Naegle, & J. Pitts (Eds.), *Theories of society*. New York: Free Press.

Parsons, T. (1967). Some ingredients of a general theory of formal organization. In A. W. Halpin (Ed.), *Administrative theory in education* (pp. 40–72). New York: Macmillan.

Peshkin, A. (1986). *God's choice*. Chicago: University of Chicago Press.

Phillips, M. (1997). What makes schools effective? A comparison of the relationships of communitarian climate and academic climate to mathematics achievement and attendance during middle school. *American Educational Research Journal, 34*(4), 633–662.

Plake, B. S., & Impara, J. C. (1998). *The thirteenth mental measurements yearbook*. (Vol. 13). Lincoln, NE: The Buros Institute for Mental Measurements, University of Nebraska Press.

Rokeach, M. (1960). *The open and closed mind*. New York: Basic Books.

Rutter, M., Maughan, B., Mortimore, P., & Ouston, J. (1979). *Fifteen thousand hours: Secondary schools and their effects on children*. Cambridge, MA: Harvard University Press.

Stern, G. G. (1970). *People in context: Measuring person-environment congruence in education and industry*. New York: Wiley.

Stockard, J. (1985). *Measures of school climate: Needed improvements suggested by a review of the organizational literature*. Eugene, OR: Center for Educational Policy and Management, University of Oregon. (ERIC Document Reproduction No. ED267498)

Tagiuri, R. (1968). The concept of organizational climate. In R. Tagiuri & G. H. Litwin (Eds.), *Organizational climate: Exploration of a concept*. Boston: Harvard University, Division of Research, Graduate School of Business Administration.

Weber, M. (1947). *The theory of social and economic organization* (A. M. Henderson & T. Parsons, Trans.). New York: Free Press.

Willower, D. J., Eidell, T. L., & Hoy, W. K. (1967). *The school and pupil control ideology*. University Park, PA: Pennsylvania State University.

Wilson, B. L., & McGrail, J. (1987, April 20–24). *Measuring school climate: Questions and considerations*. Paper presented at the Annual Meeting of the American Educational Research Association, Washington, DC.

Witcher, A. E. (1993). Assessing school climate: An important step for enhancing school quality. *NASSP Bulletin, 77*(554), 1–5.

Wolcott, H. F. (1984). *The man in the principal's office: An ethnography*. Prospect Heights, IL: Waveland Press.

APPENDIX

Organizational Climate, School Health, and Effectiveness: A Comparative Analysis

Wayne K. Hoy
C. John Tarter
James R. Bliss

The theory-driven Organizational Health Inventory (OHI) was compared to the empirically derived Organizational Climate Description Questionnaire (OCDQ-RS) in predicting student achievement and teachers' commitment to the school. After controlling for the socioeconomic status of the 58 secondary schools in the sample, only academic emphasis, a subtest of the OHI, made a significant contribution to student achievement. While both instruments predicted commitment, the OHI explained more of the variance. The findings suggest that, at best, the influence of the principal is indirect on school achievement but direct on commitment. Further application of both the OHI and OCDQ-RS is recommended.

Despite decades of substantial empirical investigation, the meaning of organizational climate remains elusive (Anderson, 1982; Drexler, 1977; Halpin, 1966; James & Jones, 1974; Miskel & Ogawa, 1988; Moos, 1974; Stern, 1970; Tagiuri, 1968; Victor & Cullen, 1987). Nonetheless, the construct continues to attract organizational researchers. Climate may be a promising tool for the analysis of organizational behavior, especially because of the belief that a healthy climate can be achieved and that it promotes useful outcomes (Schneider, 1983; Victor & Cullen, 1988). Academics as well as practitioners are increasingly concerned abut understanding and managing the behavioral and normative systems of organizations (Howe, 1977; Hoy & Miskel, 1987; Schein, 1984, 1985, 1990; Schneider, 1975).

There is no standard definition of organizational climate; in fact, climate is conceptually complex and vague. Moreover, recent attention to culture has only added further confusion. Indeed, there is not general agreement concerning the difference between culture and climate. Ashforth (1985) suggests that culture consists of shared assumptions, values, or norms, whereas climate is defined by shared perceptions of behavior. Clearly, there is not a large conceptual leap from "shared assumptions or beliefs" (culture) to "shared perceptions of behavior" (climate), but the difference seems real enough. In this analysis, organizational climate is a broad term that refers to members' shared perceptions of the work environment of the organization (Hoy & Miskel, 1987). It is an enduring set of internal characteristics that distinguishes one organization from another and influences the behavior of its members (Tagiuri & Litwin, 1968).

This article was originally published in *Educational Administration Quarterly*, August 1990, vol. 26, No. 3, pp. 260–279.

The general purpose of this inquiry is to specify two competing frameworks and measures of organizational climate and to test the proposition that the closer a construct is to theory, the stronger its predictive power. In the case at hand, the Organizational Climate Description Questionnaire (OCDQ) (Halpin, 1966; Kottkamp, Mulhern, & Hoy, 1987) will be compared with the Organizational Health Inventory (OHI) (Hoy & Feldman, 1987) in predicting organizational effectiveness.

Organizational Climate: Open to Closed

Halpin (1966) was one of the first to conceptualize the domain of organizational climate. The inductive temper of his work is captured in his description of how schools vary in their atmosphere. "Anyone who visits more than a few schools notes quickly how schools differ from one another in their 'feel'" (p. 131). Halpin goes on to say that as one "moves to other schools, one finds that each appears to have a 'personality' of its own" (p. 131). It was that feeling of how schools differ that provided Halpin with a major impetus for the OCDQ research.

The original version of the OCDQ comprises eight dimensions: Four describe the characteristics of the faculty group, and four describe the components of teacher-principal interaction. Thus each school could be described in terms of a profile of the eight dimensions. Through factor analysis, six basic clusters of profiles, that is, six basic school climates, were arrayed along a rough continuum from open to closed. Open climates are those in which there is reality-centered leadership of the principal, a committed faculty, and no need for burdensome paperwork, close supervision, or a plethora of rules and regulations. Behavior of the principal and the faculty is authentic. The closed climate is the antithesis of the open.

The OCDQ has inspired hundreds of studies of the climate of schools (Anderson, 1982; Hoy & Miskel, 1987; Miskel & Ogawa, 1988; Silver, 1983; Sirotnik, 1980). Elements of the measure have predicted pupil control orientation (Appleberry & Hoy, 1969), alienation (Hoy, 1972), managerial systems (J. W. Hall, 1972), principal and school effectiveness (Anderson, 1964), school discipline (Nwankwo, 1979), and innovation (Brady, 1988). Although Halpin and Croft (1963) urged future researchers to revise, modify, and expand the OCDQ, until recently there has been remarkably little movement in that direction even as time, school conditions, and changes in society have eroded the utility of the instrument. Weaknesses in the instrument have been noted: Unionization and contractual requirements have rendered many of the items inappropriate; the validity of several dimensions is questionable; conceptual vagueness plagues the middle categories of the climate continuum; students are ignored in conceptualizing climate; its use is limited to elementary and nonurban schools.

In an attempt to meet these criticisms, two new versions of the OCDQ have been developed: one for elementary schools (Hoy & Clover, 1986) and one for secondary schools (Kottkamp, Mulhern, & Hoy, 1987). It is the secondary school version that is germane to this inquiry.

The revised version, Organizational Climate Description Questionnaire-Rutgers Secondary (OCDQ-RS), is based on the original Halpin and Croft measure and retains its inductive flavor. The revision uses five dimensions: Two dimensions describe principal behavior, and the other three describe teacher behavior. *Supportive* principal behavior is characterized by a genuine concern for the personal and professional welfare of teachers, whereas *directive* principal behavior is rigid, domineering management. *Engaged* teacher behavior reflects a faculty committed to their students and their school, whereas *frustrated* teacher behavior describes a general pattern of interference that distracts from the basic task of teaching. Finally, *intimate* behavior depicts a close network of social relations among the faculty.

A second-order factor analysis of the dimensions of the OCDQ-RS led to the identification of two factors, one of which was remarkably similar to Halpin and Croft's conception of openness; indeed, the factor was named *openness*. Openness if reflected in genuine relationships with teachers where the principal creates an atmosphere of concern and help (high supportiveness) and encourages teacher initiation of professional decision making (low directiveness). Open teacher behavior is characterized by sincere, positive, and supportive relationships with students, administrators, and colleagues (high engagement); teachers are committed to the school and the success of the students (high engagement); the work environment is facilitating, not frustrating (low frustration). In brief, openness in secondary schools refers to climates in which both teachers' and principals' behaviors are unprompted, energetic, goal directed, and supportive. Leadership acts emerge spontaneously from both teachers and administrators. Satisfaction is derived from both task accomplishment and need gratification. The second minor factor, intimacy, referred to strong and cohesive networks of social relations among the faculty; it stood alone as the second factor.

Organizational Health

Another approach in the description of organizational climate derives from literature on organizational health (Miles, 1969) and the school as a social system (Parsons, 1967; Parsons, Bales, & Shils, 1953; Parsons & Smelser, 1956). The notion of organizational health maintains that organizations not only survive in their environment but continue to cope adequately over the long haul and continuously develop and extend their surviving and coping capabilities (Miles, 1969). Such surviving and coping are the working out of Parson's imperative functions. Indeed, all social systems must solve four basic problems if they are to endure and prosper. These four needs are what Parsons (1961) calls adaptation, goal attainment, integration, and latency. In other words, organizations must solve the following: (a) the problem of acquiring sufficient resources and accommodating to their environment, (b) the problem of setting and implementing goals, (c) the problem of maintaining solidarity within the system, and (d) the problem of creating and preserving a distinctive value system. Etzioni (1975) has collapsed these four functions into two: (a) the instrumental needs of input and allocation, and (b) the expressive needs of social and normative integration.

Parsons (1967) also notes that schools have, as do all organizations, three levels of authority over these basic functions—technical, managerial, institutional. The technical level of the school is concerned with the teaching-learning process. The primary function of the school is to produce educated students. Furthermore, teachers and supervisors are the agents for solving the problems associated with effective teaching and learning.

The managerial level controls the internal administrative function of the organization. Principals are the administrative officers of the school. They allocate resources and coordinate the work. They try to develop teacher loyalty, trust, and commitment as well as motivate teachers and influence their own superiors. They mediate between all members of the organization.

TABLE *1*

Dimensions of School Health in Terms of Organizational Level and Function

Level	Function	Dimension
Institutional	Instrumental	Institutional integrity
Managerial	Instrumental	Initiating structure
	Instrumental	Resource allocation
	Instrumental	Principal influence
	Expressive	Consideration
Technical	Instrumental	Academic emphasis
	Expressive	Morale

The institutional level links the school with its environment. Schools need acceptance and legitimacy in the community. Both administrators and teachers need support if they are to perform their respective functions in a harmonious fashion without undue pressure from sources outside the school.

This broad Parsonian perspective provides the theoretical underpinning for school health. Specifically, a healthy school is one in which the technical, managerial, and institutional levels are in harmony; and the school meets its imperative needs as it successfully copes with disruptive external forces and directs its energy towards its mission.

The Organizational Health Inventory (OHI) is an example of theory directing the construction of a measure; the approach is deductive (Hoy & Feldman, 1987). The instrument consists of seven dimensions that capture the critical instrumental and expressive aspects of organizational function on three levels of responsibility and control. That is, each level (technical, managerial, and institutional) is tapped by measures that consider either instrumental or expressive activities or both (see Table 1).

The instrumental function of institutional integrity is the school's ability to cope with its environment in a way that maintains the educational integrity of its programs. Initiation of structure, resource allocation, and principal influence describe the respective managerial instrumental functions of task- and achievement-oriented leadership, the procurement of resources for instructional activities, and the ability of the principal to influence superiors on behalf of subordinates. Expressive managerial behavior is described by consideration, or the degree to which the administrator exhibits support and concern for the welfare of teachers. The technical instrumental function of academic emphasis is the extent to which the school is driven by a quest for academic excellence. Morale, the collective sense of affinity and pride, is the technical expressive dimensions of the school.

A second-order factor analysis of these school health dimensions yielded a single, strong factor called health. A healthy school is protected from unreasonable parental and community pressures. The board resists efforts of vested interest groups to influence policy (high institutional integrity). The principal is a dynamic leader, integrating both task- and relations-oriented leader behavior. Such behavior is supportive of teachers and yet emphasizes high performance standards (high initiating structure and consideration). Furthermore, the principal has influence with his or her superiors, which is demonstrated by the ability to get what is needed for the effective operation of the school (high principal influence). Teachers in a healthy school are committed to teaching and learning. They set high but achievable student goals, maintain high standards of performance, and promote a serious and orderly learning environment. Students work hard, are highly motivated, and respect their academically oriented classmates (high academic emphasis). Classroom supplies, instructional materials, and supplementary materials are readily available (high resource support). Finally, in healthy schools teachers like each other, are enthusiastic about teaching, and are proud of their school (high morale).

Research Question and Hypothesis

The purpose of the empirical phase of this investigation is to test the predictive utility of the two frameworks and their measures. The OCDQ-RS is a refinement of the OCDQ a starkly empirical measure developed through the factor analysis of teacher-teacher and teacher-principal interaction in schools. As we noted earlier, the OCDQ has been plagued by conceptual vagueness and psychometric problems. The OCDQ-RS addresses the psychometric issues, but the lack of a theoretical underpinning remains and may well limit its usefulness. In contrast, the OHI is an instrument built on the foundations of Parsonian social systems theory. Both of these climate instruments should predict organizational outcomes—the OCDQ-RS because it has a long history of predictive use (Anderson, 1982; Miskel & Ogawa, 1988), and the OHI because it is so closely tied to a theoretical framework that explains organizational behavior.

Both instruments in their own right identify important organizational attributes. Interestingly, however, neither of the instruments was designed to be a measure of effectiveness, the ultimate question of organizational analysis (R. H. Hall, 1972). Therefore, the focus of this inquiry is to do a comparative analysis of the power of these frameworks to predict important school effectiveness outcomes. Although the concept of organizational effectiveness is complex, most would agree that academic achievement of students is one of the criteria of school effectiveness. In Parsonian terms, achievement is one important instrumental outcome of the school; thus student achievement is a dependent variable of this study.

Inherent in the Parsonian emphasis on the integration of members into the organization is the idea that effective organizations will have members who share in the values of the organization, are willing to exert extra effort in their roles, and desire to continue their membership in the organization; commitment is central to organizational life (DeCotiis & Summers, 1987). In the absence of these characteristics, members will in all likelihood drift away from the organization. Therefore, teacher commitment to the school serves as an expressive outcome variable, and academic achievement is a student outcome variable. Nonetheless, both are important and serve as the criteria for testing the predictive utility of the competing climate frameworks.

The OHI, based on Parsonian social systems theory, is built on a stronger conceptual foundation than is the OCDQ-RS. Because the theoretical underpinnings of the OCDQ-RS are neither as clear nor as strong as the OHI, it is reasonable to hypothesize that the OHI will be a better predictor of the outcome variables than will the OCDQ-RS.

Method

Sample and Data

Data for the comparative analysis of the two frameworks were gathered using a sample of 872 teachers in 58 secondary schools in an Eastern industrial state. Although the school sample was not a random one, it was a diverse one representing a broad range of districts and spanning the range of socioeconomic status (SES). Participating schools came from 17 of the 21 counties of the state. If any group of schools was underrepresented, it was the large urban one.

Typically, data were collected by researchers at regular faculty meetings, but in a few schools, a faculty member collected the questionnaires. All respondents were anonymous. Because the unit of analysis was the school, separate random sets of faculty members were drawn from each school to respond to the Organizational Health Inventory (OHI), the Organizational Climate Description Questionnaire-Rutgers Secondary (OCDQ-RS), and the Organizational Commitment Questionnaire (OCQ); thus the measures were methodologically independent. Student academic achievement was measured by the High School Proficiency Test (HSPT), a statewide test of verbal and quantitative skills.

Measures

The Organizational Climate Descriptive Questionnaire-Rutgers Secondary (OCDQ-RS) is a 34-item instrument that measures aspects of school climate. All items are simple descriptive statements. Teachers indicate the extent to which each statement characterizes their school along a 4-point Likert-type scale from *rarely* to *very frequently occurs*. Four of the subscales of the OCDQ-RS cluster together to form a general measure of openness in school climate. The following items are samples for each scale: "The principal sets an example by working hard himself/herself" (supportive principal behavior); "The principal rules with an iron fist" (directive principal behavior); "Teachers help and support each other" (engaged teacher behavior); "The mannerisms of teachers in this school are annoying" (frustrated teacher behavior); "Teachers invite other faculty members to visit them at home" (intimate teacher behavior). In the current sample, all five scales have relatively high reliability coefficients, alphas ranging from .71 to .94. The stability of the factor structure of the OCDQ-RS supports the construct validity of the dimensions of the instrument (Kottkamp, Mulhern, & Hoy, 1987). A second-order factor analysis of all the subtests of the OCDQ-RS identified a strong openness factor consisting of the four subtests.

The Organizational Health Inventory (OHI) is a 44-item instrument that measures the seven elements of school health. Again, all items are simple descriptive statements. The following items are samples for each scale: "Teachers are protected from unreasonable community and parental demands" (institutional integrity); "The principal gets what he or she wants from superiors" (principal influence); "The principal puts suggestions made by the faculty into operation" (consideration); "The principal maintains definite standard of performance" (initiating structure); "Extra materials are available if requested" (resource support); "Teachers in this school like each other" (morale); "The school sets high standards for academic performance" (academic emphasis). Each scale has a relatively high reliability coefficient. Alpha coefficients range from .87 to .95. Construct validity was also supported by factor analysis (Hoy & Feldman, 1987). The results of a second-order factor analysis identify one strong general factor. This factor maps the schools that are strong on all seven of the elements of school health, and accordingly, it is called school health (Hoy & Feldman, 1987). A general index of the health of a school can be determined by simply adding the standard scores of the seven subtests; the higher the score, the healthier the school.

The Organizational Commitment Questionnaire (OCQ) is a Likert-type scale that measures the degree of involvement of participants in organizations. The measure is a revised form of the organizational commitment questionnaire developed by Porter, Steers, Mowday, and Boulian (1974). The OCQ measures three aspects of commitment to the organization: (a) acceptance of the goals and values of the organization, (b) willingness to exert extra effort on behalf of the organization, and (c) desire to remain in the organization. The original OCQ contained 15 Likert-type response items. Mowday, Steers, and Porter (1979) analyzed 2,563 employees in nine occupations and demonstrated the internal consistency, test-retest, and factorial reliability of the instrument as well as its predictive, convergent, and discriminate validity. The study at hand uses a 9-item version that Mowday and his colleagues used with four occupational groups. Alpha coefficients for the four groups range from .84 to .90. In the present sample the alpha was .91.

The High School Proficiency Test (HSPT) is a statewide examination to analyze academic performance in reading, writing, and mathematics. Our analysis used the reading and mathematics scores. Because these scores were correlated at .93, we used an average composite index of the two tests for the measure of academic achievement. The state has reported reliabilities of .94 for the reading measure and .95 for mathematics. The reading examination consisted of 87 items that tapped literal comprehension, inferential comprehension, critical comprehension, and study skills. The mathematics section consisted of 39 items that measured such standard arithmetic topics as fractions, decimals, percentages, algebra, and problem solving (New Jersey Department of Education, 1984).

Socioeconomic status for the school was measured by the use of state district factor groups (DFG). DFG is a composite index of SES based on a factor composed of the following eight variables: educational level of adults in the district, the occupations of adults in the district, the percentage of people who have lived in the district for the past 10 years, the number of people per housing unit, the percentage of urban population in the district, average family income, and the rates of unemployment and poverty. Districts are arrayed along a continuum from 1 to 10; the higher the number, the greater the SES.

Results

Descriptive statistics, alpha coefficients of reliabilities, and intercorrelations for all variables used in this study are reported in Table 2. As can be seen from the table, three of the health variables—institutional integrity ($r = -.34$, $p < .01$), resources allocation ($r = .33$, $p < .01$), and academic emphasis ($r = .63$, $p < .01$),—were correlated with academic achievement, but only one of the climate variables, teacher frustration ($r = .31$, $p < .01$), was related to academic achievement. All of the health variables were correlated with organizational commitment, and only teacher intimacy of the five climate variables failed to predict the teachers' commitment to the school; the remaining four variables were significantly associated with commitment. Not surprisingly, socioeconomic status was related to both academic achievement ($r = .82$,

T A B L E 2

Descriptive Statistics, Reliabilities, and Correlations Among Variables

Variables	N	X̄	SD	1	2	3	4	5	6	7	8	9	10	11	12	13	14
Health																	
1. Institutional integrity	58	18.6	2.7	(.91)													
2. Resource allocation	58	13.5	1.9	.19	(.95)												
3. Principal influence	58	12.9	1.8	.40**	.47**	(.87)											
4. Initiating structure	58	14.4	1.8	.33*	.23	.58**	(.89)										
5. Consideration	58	12.8	2.0	.35**	.25*	.30*	.39**	(.90)									
6. Academic emphasis	58	21.3	2.8	.11	.41**	.45**	.46**	.36**	(.93)								
7. Morale	58	25.0	2.6	.44**	.39**	.33**	.34**	.42**	.45**	(.92)							
Climate																	
8. Directive behavior	58	14.0	2.5	.01	-.02	.14	-.06	.38**	-.32**	-.03	(.86)						
9. Supportive behavior	58	18.2	2.7	-.29**	-.01	-.20*	.35**	.64**	.15	.16	-.09	(.94)					
10. Engagement	58	26.5	1.4	.29**	.30**	.39**	.16	.36**	.35**	.35**	-.21*	.39**	(.86)				
11. Frustration	58	12.3	2.0	-.26*	-.41**	-.38**	-.16	-.38**	-.39**	-.38**	.41**	-.31**	-.52**	(.85)			
12. Intimacy	58	8.8	.9	-.11	-.04	-.07	-.15	.02	-.04	.11	-.04	.05	.22*	.01	(.71)		
Effectiveness																	
13. Academic achievement	58	148.1	13.5	-.34**	.33**	.18	.10	.11	.63**	.21	-.11	.01	.21	-.31**	.02	(.92)	
14. Organizational commitment	58	29.6	3.6	.28**	.31**	.44**	.30**	.36**	.44**	.40**	-.22*	.29**	.45**	-.36**	.13	.02	(.91)
SES																	
District factor group	58	6.2	2.7	-.28**	.13	.15	-.04	.17	.53**	.13	-.20*	.03	.17	-.17	.03	.82**	.26*

*p < .05; ** p < .01.

$p < .01$) and organizational commitment ($r = .26$, $p < .01$), though much more strongly related to achievement than commitment.

The negative correlation between institutional integrity and academic achievement suggests that teachers perceive more pressure and intrusion from the community in schools where students achieve at higher levels. That is, the higher the academic achievement of the high school, the more likely teachers view the parents as a source of trouble. Parents in wealthier school districts may be more aggressive and, perhaps, more involved than are parents in districts of lesser means, an interpretation supported by the significant negative correlation between SES and institutional integrity. This explanation is further supported by the strong, positive correlation between academic emphasis and SES, as well as by the moderate, negative correlation between principal directiveness and SES.

All of the health variables and four of the five climate variables were significantly correlated with organizational commitment. Healthy schools have committed teachers. Open schools have committed teachers. But intimate schools, those with strong, cohesive social relations, do not necessarily generate teacher commitment. The relatively weak relationship of commitment to SES suggests that commitment is more a consequence of the inner workings of the school rather than of the community setting. Theoretically, SES should have a stronger relationship to achievement than to commitment because achievement is more a function of the school setting whereas commitment is a function of the social integration of school personnel (Parsons, 1961).

Although the zero-order correlations are instructive, they may be misleading. One of the problems facing educational researchers is determining the effect of one variable independently of others, a considerable problem in nonexperimental research. The relationship between variables such as academic emphasis and student achievement may well be the accidental consequence of their relationships with yet another variable, such as SES. Therefore, a series of multiple regression analyses was performed to examine the independent effects of health and climate on the effectiveness as well as to determine the net effect of all the independent variables on the dependent variables of effectiveness. Because there was no compelling theoretical basis for ordering the variables in the regressions, all the variables were entered as a block, that is, simultaneously.

We began our multiple regression analyses by examining the health variables in their explanation of the variance in each of the dependent variables. When academic achievement was regressed on the health variables, a multiple R of .77 ($p < .01$) explained approximately 59% of the variance. However, only institutional integrity (beta = $-.44$ $p < .01$) and academic emphasis (beta = .62, $p < .01$) had unique and independent effects on achievement of students. Because SES was strongly related to achievement, an important questions is, "Do these aspects of health make a unique contribution to achievement independently of SES?" To answer this question, SES was added to the health measures as a predictor variable. All of the independent variables then explained 75% ($R = .87$, $p < .01$) of the student achievement variance, but only SES (beta = .57, $p < .01$) and academic emphasis (beta = .31, $p < .01$) made separate and significant contributions to the explanation (see Table 3). When all of the independent variables (including SES) were used to predict organizational commitment, 35% of the variance was explained ($R = .59$, $p < .01$). None of the variables made a unique and significant contribution to commitment (see Table 3).

When academic achievement and commitment were regressed on the climate variables, the multiple R for achievement was not significant; however, the climate

TABLE *3*

Regression of Achievement and Commitment on Dimensions of School Health and SES

	Achievement		Commitment	
	r	beta	r	beta
Health variables only (n = 58)				
	Regression Number 1			
Institutional integrity	−.34**	−.44**	.32**	.16
Initiating structure	.10	−.17	.28*	−.15
Consideration	.11	−.02	.41**	.21
Principal influence	.18	.14	.41**	.21
Resource allocation	.33**	.04	.35**	.06
Academic emphasis	.63**	.62**	.41**	.25
Morale	.21	.13	.41**	.09
	R = .77**		R = .58**	
Health variables with SES				
	Regression Number 2			
SES	.82**	.57**	.26*	.15
Institutional integrity	−.34**	−.16	.32**	.24
Initiating structure	.10	−.07	.28*	−.14
Consideration	.11	−.03	.41**	.17
Principal influence	.18	.02	.41**	.20
Resource allocation	.33**	.07	.35**	.04
Academic emphasis	.63**	.31**	.41**	.23
Morale	.21	.07	.41**	.04
	R = .87**		R = .59**	

*$p < .05$; ** $p < .01$.

variables combined did explain 26% of the variance in commitment ($R = .51$, $p < .01$). Adding SES to the equations only confirmed the strong independent effect of SES on achievement but had little effect on teacher commitment (see Table 4).

Our final analysis considered the influence of all the independent variables, that is, SES, health, and climate properties, on the measures of effectiveness—student achievement and teacher commitment. In the explanation of student achievement, all of the variables combined to explain 75% of the variance ($R = .87$, $p < .01$). Of the teacher commitment variance, 42% was explained by the final regression equation ($R = .65$, $p < .05$). It is still the case that only SES and Academic Emphasis make significant and unique contributions to student achievement. None of the independent variables (including SES) made a significant and unique contribution to teacher commitment; the overall health and climate of a school determined the commitment teachers have to their school. These results are summarized in Table 5.

Regression of Achievement and Commitment on Dimensions of School Climate and SES

	Achievement		Commitment	
	r	beta	*r*	beta
Climate variables only (n = 58)				
		Regression Number 1		
Supportive behavior	.01	−.11	.35**	.19
Directive behavior	−.11	.04	−.21	−.06
Teacher engagement	.21	−.06	.45**	.28
Teacher frustration	−.31**	−.32	−.39**	−.14
Teacher intimacy	.02	.01	.05	−.02
	R = .32(ns)		*R* = .51**	
Climate variables SES				
		Regression Number 2		
SES	.82**	.80**	.26*	.17
Supportive behavior	.01	−.06	.35**	.16
Directive behavior	−.11	.02	−.21	−.05
Teacher engagement	.21	.02	.45**	.31
Teacher frustration	−.31**	−.14	−.39**	−.12
Teacher intimacy	.02	.07	.05	−.01
	R = .84**		*R* = .57**	

*$p < .05$; ** $p < .01$.

Discussion

Does the OHI provide a better instrument than the OCDQ-RS for the prediction of school effectiveness? The answer is a qualified yes. In predicting student achievement, we found that the dimensions of the OHI were strongly related to student achievement, and the climate measures were not. Even after controlling for SES, the acknowledged major predictor of student performance, the dimensions of health provided a substantial increase in the explanation of student achievement. In fact, the OCDQ-RS adds nothing to the explanation of student achievement that is not already explained by the SES and the OHI. In predicting teacher commitment, once again OHI was a slightly better predictor than the OCDQ-RS.

These comparative findings come as no surprise. As we explained earlier, the development of the OCDQ was not guided by a theoretical perspective, whereas the OHI was grounded in the theoretical work of Talcott Parsons. Recall that the dimensions of health were developed to measure aspects of Parsonian functional imperatives for the survival and growth of organizations. Healthy schools should have high scores on both instrumental and expressive activities. The combined influence of all the health variables in explaining student achievement was substantial; 59% of the

TABLE *5*

Regression of Achievement and Commitment on Dimensions of School Health, Climate and SES

	Achievement		Commitment	
	r	beta	*r*	beta
Health Variables (n = 58)				
SES	.82**	.57**	.26*	.15
Institutional integrity	−.34**	−.16	.32**	.21
Initiating structure	.10	−.06	.28*	.02
Consideration	.11	−.04	.41**	−.14
Principal influence	.18	.01	.41**	.18
Resource allocation	.33**	.06	.35**	.06
Academic emphasis	.63**	.29*	.41**	.20
Morale	.21	.06	.41**	.05
Supportive behavior	.01	.01	.35**	.21
Directive behavior	−.11	.01	−.21	−.25
Teacher engagement	.21	−.03	.45**	.16
Teacher frustration	−.31**	−.08	−.39**	.11
Teacher intimacy	.02	.04	.05	.06
	R = .87**		*R* = .65*	

$*p < .05; ** p < .01.$

variance was explained. In contrast, the climate variables explained an insignificant 10% of the variance.

It was also the case that SES was strongly related to both student achievement and organizational health. There is little doubt that wealthier school districts have higher levels of student achievement and healthier school environments. Our data reflect, however, that academic emphasis of the school makes a significant contribution to the explanation of school achievement that goes beyond the influence of SES. A careful examination of the construct of academic emphasis reveals that it embodies at least three of the six school effectiveness characteristics cited by Edmonds (1979). High student expectations, an orderly work environment, and a strong emphasis on academics are captured in this single health variable—academic emphasis. What is also clear from the analysis is that the value of positive or assertive leadership that Edmonds and others claim to be instrumental in effective student performance simply is not supported in the current sample. Not one of the six health and climate variables describing assertive leadership—initiating structure, consideration, influence, resource allocation, directiveness, supportiveness—made a unique and significant contribution to the explanation of student achievement.

These aspects of the leadership of the principal did not have a direct impact on student performance.

This research finding that the behavior of the principal is not directly related to instructional effectiveness has been anticipated by theoretical developments in the field. Bossert and his colleagues (1982) argued that the principal's role is one of affecting the climate and instructional organization available to the teaching staff. The links between administrative behavior and student achievement are complex. It may be that some principals can directly affect student learning by manipulating the instructional organization. Our findings, however, support the notion that the principal's influence is indirect, provided his or her actions lead to the development of a climate with a strong academic emphasis. Thus we hypothesize that one important way a principal influences student learning is by nurturing a climate of academic achievement, that is, developing a serious and orderly learning environment, strong academic press, and high student expectations. Our data support this hypothesis even controlling for SES.

Both the health and climate measures explained a significant amount of the variance in organizational commitment, but again the health measure proved a more robust measure than climate; that is, it explained more variance. It is theoretically provocative that in the regressions no single subtest of either health or climate makes a significant, independent contribution to teacher commitment Rather, it is the overall atmosphere or ethos (Good & Weinstein, 1986), whether measured as health or climate, that is associated with commitment. Therefore, we hypothesize that the patterns of principal and teacher behavior work together to ensure commitment. Perhaps leadership patterns of the principal need to complement the interaction patterns of teachers in order to produce strong teacher commitment.

We also hypothesize, based on the current results, that institutional integrity is an important component or side effect of SES. We recognize that this interpretation lends credence to the criticism that climate is a tautological duplication of context (James & Jones, 1974). We suspect that the negative relationship between institutional integrity and achievement identified in both the correlation and regression analysis may be a function of vigorous parental involvement that can affect the school's program by inducing high expectations. The term integrity has certain obvious connotations that may lead to confusion here. In Parsonian terms, institutional integrity is clearly a virtue. As suggested at the outset, however, different measures often get in the way of each other. The concept of institutional integrity is one that needs refinement both conceptually and operationally.

These preliminary findings suggest that, if practitioners or researchers are to use only one measure to map the domain of the climate of secondary schools, the OHI may be a more useful vehicle than the OCDQ-RS. But it seems premature to bury the OCDQ-RS. There are so few studies using either measure that important relationships might well be overlooked if one were to rely on one at the expense of the other. We suggest that health or climate measures be used where theoretically appropriate. For example, health is likely to be a better predictor of goal achievement, innovativeness, loyalty, and cohesiveness—variables directly linked to the functional necessities described by Parsons (1961). On the other hand, climate is likely to be a better predictor of openness in communication, authenticity, motivation, and participation variables associated with openness in interaction patterns as described by Halpin (1966).

Healthy schools and open climates may well be desirable ends in themselves. Even if unrelated to other outcome variables, these constructs are important in their own right. They signify organizational configurations that are good working environments, places where people feel comfortable with the purposes of the organization and their capacity to function as professionals. These are places that promote good mental health because of the cooperative and supportive relations, the low level of frustration, high levels of morale, and the expression of real engagement in the task at hand. Hence another important direction of research is to identify those personal and organizational variables that promote healthy schools and open climates.

Practical Implications

We have just suggested some research guidelines using the OHI and OCDQ-RS. A working school administrator also could use these instruments for formative evaluation of administrative practice, self-assessment of one's own practice, and as a guideline for organizational development and inservice.

The application of either the OHI or the OCDQ-RS for formative evaluation is not an unqualified recommendation. The essence of formative evaluation is that it is a continuous guide to the improvement of practice. For a principal, the subtests of the OHI and the OCDQ-RS seem to be more appropriate criteria for the evaluation of principal behavior than many of the current standards that masquerade as measures of administrative effectiveness. However, it is important that there exists a climate of collegiality and trust among teachers and administrators if the constructive use of these evaluative tools is to take place.

Principals may well find an application of these measures in self-assessment of their own administrative practice. Our experience demonstrates that a principal's perceptions of the health or climate of the school is frequently at variance with the perception of teachers. To discover such a discrepancy is not to uncover a problem but rather a symptom. The issue is not to determine in some objective sense whether the climate is open or closed, or healthy or unhealthy, but to find the root causes for discrepancy in perceptions. For example, the finding of high scores on teacher frustration would indicate that the teachers felt that current administrative practice was carried out with too heavy a hand. This is useful information, but it is more useful if the principal can determine why the feeling of frustration exists on the part of the teachers. In short, the measures provide a conceptual basis for the diagnosis and solution to some organizational problems.

Accurate descriptions of the organization are important, if one is to focus on organizational development. Development that is geared to addressing specific problems should be more effective than general injunctions to better teaching or improved performance. To extend the example in the preceding paragraph, the principal considering the problem of a heavy-handed administration might examine ways in which organizational objective can be met using the contributions of teachers in deciding methods of achievement instead of presenting the teachers with completed plans. There is no reason that teachers cannot work together as colleagues in both assessing the state of the organization and developing plans for improvement. If a secure atmosphere can be created in which teachers feel free to be candid in their appraisals of the work environment and their recommendations for change, then teacher programs for effective organizational development can become a reality. In the end, organizational development in the form of reflective teacher practice is critical to the professional development of the occupation.

References

Anderson, C. S. (1982). The search for school climate: A review of the research. *Review of Educational Research, 52,* 368–420.

Anderson, D. P. (1964). *Organizational climate of elementary schools.* Minneapolis: Educational Research and Development Council.

Appleberry, J., & Hoy, W. K. (1969). The pupil control ideology of professional personnel in "open" and "closed" elementary schools. *Educational Administration Quarterly, 5,* 74–85.

Ashforth, S. J. (1985). Climate formations: Issues and extensions. *Academy of Management Review, 25,* 837–847.

Bossert, S. T., Dwyer, D.C., Rowan B., & Lee, G. V. (1982). The instructional management role of the principal. *Educational Administration Quarterly, 18,* 34–64.

Brady, L. (1988). The principal as a climate factor in Australian schools: A review of studies. *Journal of Educational Administration, 26,* 73–81.

DeCotiis, T. A., & Summers, T. P. (1987). A path analysis of a model of the antecedents and conse-quences of organizational commitment. *"Human Relations, 40,* 445–470

Drexler, J. A. (1977). Organizational climate: Its homogeneity within organizations. *Journal of Applied Psychology, 62,* 38–42.

Edmonds, R. (1979). Effective schools for the urban poor. *Educational Leadership, 37,* 15–24.

Etzioni, A. (1975). *A comparative analysis of complex organizations.* New York: Free Press.

Good, T. L., & Weinstein, R. S. (1986). Schools make a difference: Evidence, criticisms, and new directions. *American Psychologist, 41,* 1090–1092.

Hall, J. W. (1972). A comparison of Halpin and Croft's organizational climates and Likert's orga-nizational system. *Administrative Science Quarterly, 17,* 586–590.

Hall, R. H. (1972). *Organizations: Structure and process.* Englewood Cliffs, NJ: Prentice–Hall.

Halpin, A. W. (1966). *Theory and research in administration.* New York: Macmillan.

Halpin, A. W., & Croft, D. B. (1963). *The organizational climate of schools.* Chicago: Midwest Administration Center of the University of Chicago.

Howe, J. G. (1977). Group climate: An exploratory analysis of construct validity. *Organizational Behavior and Human Performance, 19,* 106–125.

Hoy, W. K. (1972). Dimensions of student alienation and characteristics of public high schools. *Interchange, 3,* 36–52

Hoy, W. K., & Clover, S. I. R. (1986). Elementary school climate: A revision of the OCDQ. *Educational Administration Quarterly, 22,* 93–110.

Hoy, W. K., & Feldman, J. A. (1987). Organizational health: The concept and its measure. *Journal of Research and Development in Education, 20,* 30–38

Hoy, W. K., & Miskel, C. G. (1987). *Educational administration: Theory, research, and practice.* New York: Random House.

James, L. R., & Jones, A. P. (1974). Organizational climate: A review of the theory and research. *Psychological Bulletin, 81,* 1096–1112

Kottkamp, R. B., Mulhern, J. A., & Hoy, W. K. (1987). Secondary school climate: A revision of the OCDQ. *Educational Administration Quarterly, 23,* 31–48.

Miles, M. B. (1969). Planned change and organizational health: Figure and ground. In F. D. Carver & T. J. Sergiovanni (Eds.), *Organizations and human behavior* (pp. 375–391). New York: McGraw–Hill.

Miskel, C., & Ogawa, R. (1988). Work motivation, job satisfaction, and climate. In N. J. Boyan (Ed.), *Handbook of research on educational administration* (pp. 279–304). New York: Longman.

Moos, R. H. (1974). Systems for the assessment and classification of human environments: An overview. In R. H. Moos & P. M. Insel (Eds.), *Issues in social ecology,* Palo Alto, CA: National Press Books.

Mowday, R. T., Steers, R. M., & Porter, L. W. (1979). The measurement of organizational com-mitment. *Journal of Vocational Behavior, 14,* 224–247.

New Jersey Department of Education. (1984). *New Jersey statewide testing system high school proficiency test: 1983–1984 technical report.* Trenton: New Jersey State Department of Education.

Nwankwo, J. I. (1979). School climate as a factor in students' conflict in Nigeria. *Educational Studies, 10,* 267–279.

Parsons, T. (1961). An outline of the social system. In T. Parsons, E. Shils, K. Naegle, & J. Pitts (Eds.), *Theories of society.* New York: Free Press

Parsons, T. (1967). Some ingredients of a general theory of formal organization. In A. W. Halpin (Ed.), *Administrative theory in education* (pp. 40–72). New York: Macmillan.

Parsons, T., Bales, R. F., Shils, E. A. (1953). *Working papers in the theory of action.* Glencoe, IL: Free Press.

Parsons, T., & Smelser, N. (1956). *Economy and society.* Glencoe, IL: Free Press.

Porter, L. W., Steers, R. M., Mowday, R. T., & Boulian, P. V. (1974). Organizational commitment, job satisfaction, and turnover among psychiatric technicians. *Journal of Applied Psychology, 59,* 603–609.

Schein, E. H. (1984). Coming to a new awareness of organizational culture. *Sloan Management Review, 25,* 3–16.

Schein, E. H. (1985). *Organizational culture and leadership.* San Francisco: Jossey–Bass.

Schein, E. H. (1990). Organizational culture. *American Psychologist, 45,* 109–119.

Schneider, B. (1975). Organizational climate: An essay. *Personnel Psychology, 28,* 447–479.

Schneider, B. (1983). Work climates: An interactionist perspective. In N. W. Feimer & E. S. Geller (Eds.) *Environmental psychology: Directions and perspectives,* New York: Praeger.

Silver, P. (1983). *Educational administration: Theoretical perspectives on practice and research.* New York: Harper & Row.

Sirotnik, K. A. (1980). Psychometric implications of the unit-of-analysis problem (with examples from the measurement of school climate). *Journal of Educational Measurement, 17,* 245–282.

Stern, G. G. (1970). *People in context: Measuring person–environment in education and industry.* New York: Wiley.

Tagiuri, R. (1968). The concept of organizational climate. In R. Tagiuri & G. W. Litwin (Eds.), *Organizational climate: Explorations of a concept,* (pp. 1–32). Boston: Harvard University, Division of Research, Graduate School of Business Administration.

Tagiuri, R., & Litwin, G. W. (Eds.) (1968). Organizational climate: Explorations of a concept. Boston: Harvard University, Division of Research, Graduate School of Business Administration.

Victor, B., & Cullen, J. (1987). A theory and measure of ethical climate in organizations. In W. C. Frederick (Ed.), *Research in corporate social performance and policy.* (pp. 51–71). Greenwich, CT: JAI Press.

Victor, B., & Cullen, J. (1988). The organizational bases of ethical work climates. *Administrative Science Quarterly, 33,* 101–125.

CHAPTER 11

In Conclusion

INTRODUCTION

In the preface we shared our convictions regarding the development of sophisticated, critical consumers of educational research. In this closing chapter we leave you with a road map to continue your journey. Becoming knowledgeable and skilled practitioners is a task worthy of your best efforts, and we believe that the skills and understandings we have outlined in this book will contribute to that effort. We are also well aware that no book can complete this task for you, so we challenge you to continue that quest on your own. This chapter suggests some ways to do this.

Six Principles Revisited

In the preface we shared six principles that should guide administrators' use and understanding of educational research. Let us briefly revisit these and illustrate their significance and application to the cases and research studies that we have presented in previous chapters.

1. The problems studied by researchers are not the problems faced by practitioners.

While some might bemoan this state of affairs, we cannot wish the problem away. Nor would we if we could. Researchers serve their ends and those of practitioners best when they remain true to their goal of exploring educational phenomena to better understand them.

It remains the task of the thoughtful practitioner to understand that the researcher's pursuit of *understanding educational phenomena* is separate and apart from the administrator's need to *make an educationally defensible decision*. While it is inappropriate to expect the researcher's efforts to translate directly into practice, it is equally inappropriate to ignore the useful information that the researcher can add to the administrator's decision-making process. Understanding and appreciating the difference in focus of researchers and practitioners is an important first step in the journey toward wise and judicious use of educational research.

Certainly the distinction we are making can be overdrawn. Education is an applied field of research, just as is medicine, law, and engineering. The application of much educational research to practical administrative problems is reasonably obvious. Most of the studies that have been the focus of chapters 5–10 have been of this nature. Nevertheless, it is easy to misconstrue the problem posed in even a seemingly straightforward investigation. Consider, for example, the study by Finn and Achilles (1990) discussed in chapter 5. The question they address, "What is the effect of making a substantial reduction in class size on student achievement?" is immediately recognizable to every practitioner. However, the problem of their study is not class size. The problem is that many primary children are not learning to read and do arithmetic as well as they should. Reducing class sizes in the primary grades is a possible *solution* to that problem of low achievement. One of the most common mistakes made by practitioners is to confuse solutions with problems.

On the other hand, there are a number of investigations of educational phenomena whose practical application is murky at best. For example, applying the results of a study comparing the achievement attribution beliefs of students from six different Asian ethnic groups (Mizokawa & Ryckman, 1990) is less than transparent. Perhaps there are U.S. school districts that have a problem stemming from the fact that Asian students from different ethnic backgrounds achieve at different levels, but that problem is surely rare. Most educational research, of course, falls somewhere between the close-to-practice work of Finn and Achilles and the more distant-from-practice work of Mizokawa and Ryckman. The point, then, is that practicing administrators need to be clear about their own problem and be able to ferret out the problem lurking behind the questions posed by a researcher.

2. Research cannot be "applied" to practical problems in any straightforward manner.

This dictum may lie at the heart of many of the frustrations felt by educational administrators. Research texts may be unwitting accomplices in this confusion as they frequently stress the importance of "applying research findings to practice." An admonition to "apply research findings" suggests a simpler mechanism than we believe is possible, particularly in the social sciences. Beyond the complex issues of differences between the research context and the local setting of the school administrator (and these are legitimate concerns as well), research findings need to be tempered by a range of moral, ethical, and political considerations that cannot be avoided.

As an example, one of us had an opportunity to work with a district superintendent who had carefully examined the research literature on transitional classes and was convinced that such classes were ineffective at best and potentially harmful at worst. Intent upon applying research findings, this newly appointed superintendent enlisted this writer's help in implementing major changes in the primary curriculum of his district that would end a ten-year history of transitional classes.

After several days of meeting with teachers, building principals, and parents it became clear that transitional classrooms were held in high regard by nearly everyone. In fact, many of the best teachers had been placed in these classrooms, and teachers across the district opted to have their own children placed in these transitional classes because they were so convinced of their educational and social benefits.

The superintendent was wise enough to examine the local context before plunging ahead and applying the research findings. This was not a case of simple political expediency. In *this* context, at *this* time with *these* teachers, administrators, and parents, the evidence suggested that transitional classes were highly effective. To be sure, this evidence was not "scientific," but it was nonetheless evidence. To move precipitously to end a program based solely upon research would not only have threatened the brief tenure of the superintendent, it would also have been an over-reading of the research itself. In short, merely because the research indicated that these classes were ineffective, this did not, per se, make them a problem in this district. A careful assessment of all the factors impinging upon the administrator's decision led to a wiser course of action or, in this case, to a course of inaction.

3. Research problems have histories, and these histories are important for understanding and using research.

In an age of 30-second sound bites and an impatient public's demand for accountability, it is not surprising that educators are vulnerable to the press for instant change. Novel approaches that promise large gains are often undergirded with the beguiling appeal to "the latest research that shows. . . ." Somewhere between the wide-eyed novice who is tempted by the latest *Newsweek* claim for doubling reading achievement and the seasoned veteran who denounces all research evidence with a flippant "been there, done that" is our much beloved critical, sophisticated consumer of research.

A careful examination of the stream of research that has preceded the recent findings is vital to understand the complex theoretical and measurement issues surrounding every line of research. Consider the case of Joanna Cambridge and her problem at Washington High that we described in chapter 10. Had Cambridge not taken the time to peer into the history of the concept of school climate, she might have made a serious error. Recall that she initially set out to measure the climate of her school "more objectively," so she sought an existing instrument that she could use. Had she merely consulted some of the recent effective schools research, she might well have been unaware that, after 40 years of work, the very notion of school climate remains in serious conceptual disarray. When that is the case, valid measurement, no matter how objective, becomes problematic. Because she looked into the concept's research history, she radically revised her goal. Instead of trying to measure the climate of her school, she realized that she might better use items from available instruments as vehicles to provoke discussion and change of Washington's climate.

4. The research that bears importantly on any practical problem is usually too vast, amorphous, and inconsistent to be sensibly reviewed.

By the time an educational administrator needs to examine the research literature on a particular problem, this literature has usually accumulated in such massive quantities that one might risk injury attempting to lift it, let alone carefully read and synthesize it. In addition to its staggering size, the literature is often of uneven quality—conflicting in its findings and bearing little obvious relation to actual practice.

Consider, for example, the staggering amount of research on the teaching and learning of mathematics. This topic has been explored in great detail, and thousands of studies address many issues of marginal interest to the principal of a wealthy suburban, largely white junior high school seeking to improve 7th-grade math scores. If that principal enters the search term "math achievement" in an ERIC search, the computer will return over 8,000 entries. Modifying the search term to "junior high school or middle school and math achievement" will produce over 1,500 entries. Most of that material will be irrelevant. There will be, for example, hundreds of studies that explore gender, racial, and socioeconomic differences in math achievement, issues that may be of little interest to the principal.

Before being overwhelmed by the sheer bulk of the existing research, it is important that you pose a limited number of questions pertinent to your local problem. The answers to these questions are intended to help you make an educationally defensible decision. By limiting the questions, the task becomes manageable. Instead of the exhaustive (and exhausting) approach that asks, "What research exists on the teaching and learning of mathematics?" a more relevant question might be posed. Let us call it a guiding question: What math programs have been found to be successful in raising math computation and math reasoning scores of 7th and 8th grade children with characteristics similar to the ones in my school?

Notice how this question allows you to ignore large numbers of studies that may be interesting and well done but offer you little information regarding your more focused and practical problem. This guiding question has a chance of leading you to what is relevant and useful in the literature. To help ensure that this happens, you will need to ask and answer another question, one that should accompany each of your guiding questions: Why do I want to know that? That is, you should be able to offer a convincing reason for needing the answer to each of your guiding questions. Remember that finding the answer to a single guiding question may require hours of work searching a computerized database, sitting in the library, and reading what you have found. You will want a good reason for spending your time in these ways.

Recall the examples we provided in chapter 3 concerning the district with a dropout problem. Every guiding question that the administrators posed came with a good reason for its being asked. For example, they asked, "Are there identifiable characteristics of schools that promote high dropout rates?" They reasoned that it might be better to focus on school characteristics that cause dropping out, rather than on characteristics of students who drop out, since they were more likely to be able to do something about the former than the latter.

5. Much of the published research that bears on a practitioner's problem is not worth reading.

This principle guided us throughout the text as we stressed criteria for evaluating the merits of a piece of research. In this regard, however, note that much of what administrators often take as research is not research at all. That is, many of the articles that appear in magazines and journals aimed at practitioners are best described as editorials—opinions about some educational problem unbuttressed by any sort of evidence. Editorials are fine, of course, but responsible administrators would not base decisions that affect people's children on them.

One step above these editorials are the ubiquitous articles that *refer* to research, often with appropriate citations, while arguing for or against some solution to an educational problem. These articles are especially common in the journals aimed at practicing administrators. These essays can be helpful; they may stimulate your thinking, and they may prove useful secondary sources leading you to the primary research that bears on your problem. Nonetheless, you should be wary of relying on them when making important practical decisions, because the arguments they present are so often one-sided. That is, the author has a favored strategy for dealing with a problem, and he or she will carefully marshal the evidence that supports that strategy without examining with equal care the research that contraindicates it. As a professional person, you have an obligation to examine the research that supports *and* opposes a strategy for solving an educational problem. This especially is the case if you happen to favor the strategy yourself.

Finally, there is another kind of article that is common in the journals aimed at practicing administrators. These are typically written by practitioners themselves, and they describe a solution to a problem that the authors have implemented in their own schools or districts. We often refer to these as "how I did it in Peoria" articles. Again, there is nothing per se wrong with these if you treat them as essays, not research. They can be a source of ideas. What is striking about them, however, is that no matter what the problem, the solutions described almost always seem to work. If that were true, and given that tens of thousands of these essays have been written, we have to wonder that any serious educational problems are left to solve. The uniformly positive results reported in these articles should not surprise us. After all, savvy administrators will not rush to publicly describe—in print—a program that was an utter failure and for which they were responsible. It is not that authors deliberately misrepresent the programs they have implemented; rather, they describe them in the best possible light and, typically, offer no hard evidence of their effectiveness. In research design terms, these are one-shot case studies, without any sort of control group or statistical approximation of controls. These essays contain so many flaws that competent practitioners would not base important decisions on them. In brief, you need to distinguish editorials, one-sided essays, and glowing stories of success in Peoria from careful research.

If we seek verified and verifiable professional knowledge, we must necessarily lean heavily on empirical research—the sort of thing that fills the pages of mainline research journals. When we do that, however, we are confronted with their esoteric jargon and arcane statistics, and we need to make reasoned judgments about the quality of their findings. Can we trust their knowledge claims? Thus, in the end, research consumers cannot avoid technical criteria as they try to sift a few kernels of wheat from the considerable chaff in the available journals.

In this book we have offered a small set of criteria for assessing the quality of published studies. Certainly there are many others, but we have chosen those that permit practicing administrators to arrive at defensible judgments of quality without requiring them to earn a Ph.D. in educational research methodology. Undoubtedly you have noticed that we focused our attention on empirical research, and within that category, on quantitative empirical research. Our choice was deliberate. It is not that we believe that research must be empirical to be of value, or that quantitative studies are necessarily of greater worth than qualitative ones. Rather, we have found that practitioners have the greatest difficulty understanding, judging, and using the evidence adduced in quantitative empirical research.

We suggested that you be especially attentive to five major criteria when you judge whether a study provides you with credible evidence that is worth considering when you prepare to make a consequential administrative decision. These include the following.

The study's rationale. A clear rationale or theory provides the reader with an explanation of why certain variables will be related and why certain results should occur. If the expected results are found, our confidence in both the results and the underlying rationale are strengthened. Conversely, if the expected results do not appear, the researcher can use this information to refine the rationale or to construct a new one that accounts for the lack of results. Either way, our knowledge is advanced. When no clear rationale guides a study, or when no clear problem statement exists, the practitioner can learn little from it beyond a few isolated facts. The rationale is the glue that binds together the isolated facts and helps the researcher and the administrator make sense of them.

The validity and reliability of measurements. Obvious criteria for evaluating research include the validity and reliability of its measures. If you read a study purporting to show that a particular program has a strong positive effect on math problem solving, how do you know that the researcher has actually measured math problem solving rather than, say, math computation or even reading comprehension? If you need to improve math problem solving in your school, your goal will not be served by implementing a program that improves reading. There are several approaches that careful researchers might take to this matter of validity. Similarly, there are alternative ways to demonstrate the reliability of a researcher's measurements. The sophisticated consumer is aware of these alternatives and looks for them when reading quantitative, empirical studies. Absent explicit consideration of measurement validity and reliability, you are justified in substantially discounting a study's trustworthiness as a guide to action.

The nature of a study's research design. Causation is a central idea for many educational studies: Do smaller classes cause increased reading skills in primary children? Will greater parent involvement improve math achievement in 8th graders? Recall our discussion in chapter 1 of the practice of school administrators. School administrators, concerned as they are with implementing instructional programs that will result in better student outcomes, have a fundamental interest in the causes of those outcomes. Unfortunately, it can be impossible to convincingly show that a change in an educational program caused a change in student outcomes. There almost always is a possibility—sometimes a strong possibility—that a change in an outcome is not the result of the program but of another, extraneous variable. Research designs are essentially ways to try and rule out these other possible causes of change.

We described five research designs: descriptive, correlational, causal comparative, quasi-experimental and experimental. The first of these is not really concerned with issues of cause; rather, it seeks to describe a phenomenon. The remaining designs are often used in attempts to demonstrate causal relationships. However, only experiments are capable of this, and, unfortunately, it is difficult or impossible to apply them in education. (Recall chapter 10 and the difficulty Hoy and his colleagues had trying to show that a healthy climate causes student achievement.) If you must rely on nonexperimental research to help you decide whether to implement a program, you will need to be especially attentive to the rationales of studies you consult, to whether investigators attempted to control for reasonable alternative explanations for their results, and for the existence of other confirming *and* disconfirming studies.

Application validity. Because researchers are only rarely able to study the entire population that they are interested in, they must study a sample drawn from it. When they do this, and if they are careful, they will do their best to demonstrate their sample's external validity. Does it reasonably represent the target population? This question is addressed by considering the sample's population validity, its personalogical validity, and its ecological validity. As a practitioner, however, you will be less interested in these matters than in whether the study's findings can be applied to your school or district. We have called this *application validity*. This is simply a different perspective on external validity and utilizes the same information that the researcher considers. For example, using the descriptions provided of the investigator's sample, you can judge whether the study's participants (e.g., students, teachers, schools, districts, and so forth) resemble those in your situation. Similarly, you may be able to ascertain whether any treatment imposed in the study had differential effects on particular kinds of participants. Specifically, you should ask whether that treatment was particularly effective or ineffective with participants like those in your school or district. Finally, using whatever information is provided regarding ecological validity, you will need to decide whether the conditions that existed in the schools involved in the research reasonably resemble those in your location.

Statistical and practical significance. It is in the area of data analysis procedures that most practicing administrators find themselves at sea. Suppose a researcher uses logistic regression to determine whether an intervention reduces the likelihood that students will drop out of high school. Is that the right technique? Answering that question correctly requires a considerable amount of statistical knowledge and information about the researcher's data. Asking practitioners to master the knowledge required is tantamount to inviting them to ignore research.

We have approached this matter in two ways. First, in the beginning of this book we urged you to learn to recognize the major research journals in education and in your specific specialty within the profession. We did this, in part, to finesse the issue of data analysis. The major (read "good") research journals select the articles that they publish using a peer review system. Researchers who are experts on the topic under investigation carry out blind reviews of manuscripts. Their job is to advise the journal editors whether a study addresses an important question, whether it was competently conducted, and whether it should be published. In effect, experts have already decided that a published study's data analysis procedures were appropriate.[1]

Our second approach to the issue of data analysis has been to focus on the technical criteria of statistical and practical significance. These criteria are relatively easy to understand, and they enable practitioners to draw useful inferences about the meaningfulness of a study's results for their own situations. Statistical significance expressed in p values (e.g., $p < .05$) can help you decide whether an investigation's findings might simply be the result of chance. Beyond statistical significance, you will need to determine if findings are of sufficient magnitude to be of practical importance in your setting. An effect may reach statistical significance but be so small that, as a practical matter, it is not worth the resources required to gain it. Practical significance or effect size is expressed in fractions of a standard deviation (e.g., $ES = .5$) and gives the you a benchmark against which

---

[1] We are well aware of the problematic aspects of the peer review system. Nevertheless, it is the major institutionalized system of quality control in research, and it can provide the practitioner with some assurance that research techniques are appropriate. The issue is not whether the blind peer review system is perfect. It is not. Rather, the issue is whether it provides a practitioner a higher level of quality control than any of its alternatives. Clearly it does.

the magnitude of an effect can be assessed and compared with those from other studies. All other things equal, a method of teaching reading that yields an effect size of .4 is to be desired over a competitor's that yields an effect size of .2. Taken together, the criteria of statistical and practical significance can be of great help in judging the usefulness of research findings for your school.

6. When they are compiled and summarized, the results of trustworthy, relevant studies are an inadequate guide to practice.

We have stressed throughout the text that a simple summary of research findings can be a meaningless exercise and will not, in and of itself, help the practicing administrator find solutions to problems. The common recitations of "Smith says" or "Jones found" that are all too frequent in doctoral dissertations will not help an administrator make decisions until these findings are woven into a reasoned argument. This argument must fit the findings into a broader tapestry that includes values as well as political judgments, including the views of teachers, board members, parents, and fellow administrators.

Research findings may guide the administrator and may help inform a decision, but they cannot be considered apart from the practical context of the school setting. For example, research may conclusively show that distributing free condoms in schools results in reduced pregnancies and fewer instances of HIV transmission. In certain settings this research might lead an administrator to propose a free contraceptive program because it is effective in attaining these worthy objectives, and it is consistent with the values and goals of parents, teachers, and the larger community. It is certain, however, that other administrators in other settings would consider recommending the same program to be entirely inappropriate, given the values of their communities. Notice that the research findings did not change; a difference in value contexts led to opposite decisions.

The point, then, is that research findings cannot stand alone. Your school board will not—and certainly should not—care what "Smith says" and "Jones found." It is your responsibility to create an explicit argument that your school or district should (or should not) take some course of action concerning a problem. That means that you will have to construct a series of premises that lead logically to a recommendation regarding the problem that you face. Some of the premises in this argument will be normative—they will express your own, your board's, and your community's values and beliefs. Obviously these normative premises will not come from your reading of the research literature; they will come from your understanding of yourself, your profession, and your community. Other premises will be empirical. Some of these empirical premises will express relevant facts about your school, your students, and your town. These too will come from your knowledge of the local situation and, perhaps, from research that you conduct locally. Finally, some empirical premises will express relevant evidence that you have gathered from your reading of the research literature that bears on your problem. Your argument, then, is an amalgam drawn from these different sources. It is product of your own intellect. You will not find it in a library.

Educational Leadership, Research, and Change in a Democracy

In the first sentence of the introduction of this book we admitted that we have a point of view. That view, concerning the role of research in the practice of school administration, has been implicit and explicit throughout these pages. We also opened this book with a discussion of education's faddishness—the frequency with which American schools are swept by "solutions" to ill-defined or even nonexistent problems. Finally, in the introduction we suggested that school administrators have a substantial responsibility for the rise and spread of these fads. Now, at the close of this book, we want to return to these points.

Over the last few years we have asked practicing school administrators in our university courses if their school districts have a policy regarding retention in grade. Specifically, we ask if their districts set a minimum standard of performance for primary children and, if children fail to meet that standard, are they required to repeat a grade. Invariably, a significant number of administrators answer in the affirmative. We then ask these practitioners if they are aware of the large body of research suggesting that this practice is harmful, and that it does not have the effect it is presumed to have, that is, it does not improve achievement. Most practitioners have at least heard of this research (though few have actually read any of it). Finally, we ask these practitioners why, when they are aware of these findings, do they knowingly harm the children in their care?

Occasionally students will deny that the research is valid, or claim that it does not apply to their school. When pressed, however, these administrators cannot explain why it is invalid or inapplicable; they merely assert that it is. Most commonly, though, the practitioners' reaction is one of bemusement followed by the explanation that they are required by the public or the school board to implement these policies. It is difficult to keep the analogy to the "good soldier" from springing to mind.

Nevertheless, there is an important aspect of educational leadership hidden in these administrators' responses. Consider the following: In a republican form of democracy, schools, like every government institution, are supposed to serve the needs of the public, as those needs are expressed in the goals, policies, and regulations of their elected representatives (in this case, school boards). Boards, in turn, hire administrators to design and maintain systems to achieve their goals, carry out their policies, and implement their regulations. We all recognize this system, and we recognize that it makes school administrators employees of their boards. More specifically, it makes them public servants—an honorable title. It follows that if a community wants its children retained in grade, then that is what the community is entitled to get. In this normative view of educational governance, school administrators should not be free to ignore the wishes of school boards any more than administrators of a department of public works should be free to ignore the wishes of city councils. All of us would be irate, we suspect, if those who run the department of public works in our community were to decide, on their own, that garbage would be picked up biweekly rather than weekly, as the city council had decreed.

But school systems are not departments of public works, and educators are not garbage collectors. The difference is not that the work of the former is somehow more important than that of the latter. It would be difficult to make that case.[2] Rather, education is not a mechanical process and each educator must have some autonomy in how to best carry out his or her task. The goals of education cannot be achieved if schools are run like factories or departments of public works. Even more to the point, if educators are to function as professionals, they need to consider the needs of their clients, presumably their students, and how best to meet those needs. This requires that educators have a considerably greater level of discretion than garbage collectors. There is an inevitable tension, then, between public control of schools and the requirement for professional autonomy. This tension is often construed as one between bureaucracy and professionalism. But that is to misconstrue it. It is a tension between professional and democratic control of schools (Haller & Strike, 1997). On the one hand, the public has a legitimate right to control the education of its children. On the other hand, professional educators have a legitimate right to the autonomy required to properly educate those children.

Returning now to the matter of retention in grade, what should be the response of school administrators when their employers—school boards—require them to implement a retention policy? More broadly: *What should you do when you are required to serve the public, but the public wants the wrong thing?* And it is not just the public and its representatives who can want the wrong thing for children—teachers, teachers unions,[3] parents and—dare we say it—administrators and professors are all guilty of that on occasion. How should an administrator behave in these all-too-common situations?

It is in circumstances like these that we find many of the common understandings of administrative leadership to be shallow and inadequate. For example, we often hear administrators speak of themselves as "facilitators." But in this situation what is to be facilitated? If the school board wants to retain children in grade, should you facilitate its achieving this undesirable goal? Is that what leadership means? Similarly, we often read and hear discussions of "leadership styles," as if leadership were a kind of fashionable clothing that could be changed at will. Often these styles are described as "democratic" or "autocratic." If the faculty of your school unanimously demands that it wants you to get tough by suspending misbehaving students, what leadership style should you put on? Should you be democratic or autocratic in pursuit of this unwarranted goal? At the opposite extreme, we sometimes hear individuals described as born leaders, or as having charisma, indicating they possess character traits or personality attributes that enable them to lead regardless of the situation. These

---

[2] Consider the widespread devastation and epidemics that would occur if streets and stoplights were left in disrepair, garbage went uncollected, and sewers left to overflow.

[3] We are reminded of the comment by Albert Shanker, the former head of the American Federation of Teachers, that teachers unions would start looking out for the welfare of children when children start paying union dues (quoted in Gerson, 2000).

are not things that can be changed at will; they are either inborn qualities or they are gifts.[4] Suppose you want to increase the level of substantive parental involvement in your school because you are convinced that doing so will benefit your students. But also suppose that your teachers want parents to come to PTO meetings and conferences when they are called but to otherwise stay out of their hair. What should you do if you are a charismatic leader? And if you lack charisma—as virtually everyone does—what can you do? The problem with all of these views of leadership is that they are vacuous; they do not provide a practitioner with any concrete guidance when he or she is confronted with a specific, tough problem.

In contrast, our view is that educational leadership is substantially a cognitive matter. Good leaders are people who first and most importantly understand *where* to lead. They have a firm grasp of the values of their community and of their own profession. They are able to articulate these values to their school boards, their faculties, and their communities and to link these values to specific educational problems. Further, they are able to connect those values to relevant supporting empirical evidence. That is, they are able to make a cogent practical argument, one that weaves normative claims and verified evidence into a recommendation that one course of action is preferable over others. In brief, capable leaders are able to reason. Finally, they have the capacity to do all of this in a public context and in an articulate and persuasive manner.

In the case at hand then, this view requires that an educational leader be able to see that, while retaining children may conform to the board's values, doing so does not conform to other important public and professional values: For example, public schools should help not hinder learning, and they should not cause harm to children. Further, it requires that an educational leader know how to find and interpret the best available evidence that bears on the effects of retention in grade. Still further, it requires that the educational leader be able to construct a logically compelling argument based on these values and this evidence. He or she knows how to reason cogently. Finally, this view requires that the educational leader be skilled in rhetoric, that is, able to stand before his or her board and persuasively present the case against retention in terms that ordinary citizens can understand. In short, it requires that an educational leader be able to educate.

We are not so naive as to think that cogent arguments always carry the day. Clearly, they do not. But we believe that most school board members, teachers, parents, union members—and yes, even administrators and professors—are reasonably intelligent people of good will who want to do the right thing. We believe that they are likely to do just that when they understand the values and evidence bearing on a decision. As we said in the introduction, in a democratic society effective leadership should depend less on charisma, personality, and power than on reasoned persuasion, and that should especially be the case in

---

[4] The word "charisma" comes from the Greek and means "touched by God." Can we hope to stock our schools with principals who have been touched by God?

educational institutions, which, after all, are fundamentally committed to the development of the human capacity to reason.

The relevance of the sort of leadership we are describing is not confined to those occasions when groups are in conflict or when actions are proposed that conflict with important values, as our discussion above may seem to suggest. Leaders who recognize the importance of reason necessarily are also those who have a decent respect for the role of evidence in ordinary decision-making situations. It follows that they will *not* be frequent educational innovators in their schools. Before they implement new programs, they will demand some assurance that those programs work. Thus, they will approach every proposed innovation with a critically important demand: Show me the evidence. Where is the evidence that this innovation will do what its proponents claim? And they will be especially attentive to the quality of that evidence. Testimonials from other educators and unsubstantiated claims made by the inventors of new systems—like the sales pitches one hears at vending booths during the annual meetings of the American Association of School Administrators—will carry little weight. It follows, then, that the kind of leader we are envisioning will not be leading schools that experience frequent change. But then again, their schools will have missed the unwarranted turmoil created by Madeline Hunter, self-esteem programs, and the other fads and bandwagons that continue to characterize the American educational scene.

A Final Case

Let us leave you with a challenge as you continue grappling with the contribution of research to your decision-making process. Imagine the following situation.

As principal of an elementary school you have begun to hear comments from primary teachers about differences in the teaching of reading. A couple of your second grade teachers have been attending conferences and workshops on Whole Language Learning and are really excited about the use of this technique in their classes.

In contrast to the views of this group of teachers, several of your most respected teachers have been heard to grumble about the lack of phonics being stressed in first and second grade classrooms and their fears about the effect of this direction for reading achievement scores. Several articles have appeared on bulletin boards in the teachers' lounge about the negative impact of whole language learning on reading achievement. In response, an article appeared yesterday arguing strenuously for the positive effects of whole language learning on not only reading comprehension but reading motivation and on writing language skills.

While you are not thoroughly conversant with whole language methods, you know that it stresses the totality of the reading and writing process and, as the name suggests, approaches reading and writing from a more holistic perspective rather than building upon the traditional components of word sounds. Watson, Crenshaw, and King (1984) contrasted the approaches of "skills oriented" and "whole language" teachers in a manner that appeared descriptive of the two groups of teachers emerging in the faculty. Skills oriented teachers were described as focusing on small units of language, stressing the importance of mastering rules and phonics and drawing upon the use of workbooks, flash cards, and controlled vocabulary stories. In contrast, the whole-language teachers focused their attention on large units of language, permitted deviations from text in allowing miscues, and relied on library books, reference books, and child-authored stories rather than basal texts.

These differences, which began as slightly different emphases, were starting to take on the telltale signs of a border dispute. Implications were being felt for curriculum choices in the primary grades as teachers differed sharply on textbook selection. Smithey (1991) pointed to characteristics of whole language teachers that appeared to match what you are observing on your faculty when he wrote, ". . . whole language proponents viewed the development of reading and writing skills as occurring simultaneously, not in sequential order. Reading, writing, and oral language were not considered separate from other subjects but were utilized in every aspect of school including science, social studies, art, etc." (p. 12). As a final bit of pressure, the local university has been advocating whole language perspectives in their teacher education program, and several of the student teachers have introduced whole language learning in their classrooms with varying results, depending upon the orientation of the cooperating teacher. Truly, success seemed to be dependent upon the view of the beholder.

While healthy debate about effective ways to teach reading could be considered an ideal basis for improving instruction, you have reason to believe this issue might get out of control. Parents have become involved and letters to the editor in the local paper are beginning to appear, arguing on one side or the other of the issue.

What are you going to do? Several prominent faculty members in the local university are on record as favoring whole language learning. Involving them in a consulting capacity will be welcomed by one half of your staff and denounced by the other half as well as by many vocal parents.

You will need to consider your actions carefully. Perhaps a small committee comprising a couple of the more reasonable teachers from each of the two camps would be helpful. What if you chaired the committee of four teachers and gave them an initial charge to examine the research literature for help in addressing your problem?

On the other hand, is it a good idea to turn to the research literature at this time? Before you select and charge a committee, consider the following. Has the issue become so politicized in your school that the findings of the committee will be considered suspect by one side or the other? Will the selection of the committee members place them in an adversarial role that will preclude the possibility of careful consideration of the evidence? Will your position as principal place you in an arbiter role on the committee that could exacerbate the problem? Has the debate regarding the merits of phonics and whole language learning reached the stage where the window of opportunity has closed for the careful examination of research evidence? Are there other approaches that might allow for a compromise of these two positions that might reduce the strong emotions that have been raised? What does "compromise" even mean in these kinds of situations? How does one compromise two distinct philosophies and methods of teaching? By asking that teachers adopt a little of both? What possible sense can that make? In short, is this the time and is this the place to turn to the research literature for help in thinking more intelligently about your problem?

As if you needed more pressure in your job, we end this book by placing the task in your capable hands. What *are* you going to do next?

References

Finn, J. D., & Achilles, C. M. (1990). Answers and questions about class size: A statewide experiment. *American Educational Research Journal, 27*(3), 557–577.

Gerson, M. (2000, Spring). The right choice for schools. *The Public Interest, 139,* 121–126.

Haller, E. J., & Strike, K. A. (1997). *Introduction to educational administration: Social, legal and ethical perspectives.* Troy, NY: Educator's Press International.

Hoy, W. K., Tarter, C. J., & Bliss, J. R. (1990). Organizational climate, school health, and effectiveness: A comparative analysis. *Educational Administration Quarterly, 26*(3), 260–279.

Lortie, D. C. (1975). *Schoolteacher: A sociological study.* Chicago: University of Chicago Press.

Mizokawa, D. T., & Ryckman, D. B. (1990). Attributions of academic success and failure: A comparison of six Asian-American ethnic groups. *Journal of Cross Cultural Psychology, 21*(4), 434–451.

Smithey, G. F. (1991). *An investigation of the practice of whole language primary teachers in assessing and reporting students' reading progress* (Unpublished doctoral dissertation, University of Oklahoma.

Watson, D., Crenshaw, S., & King, D. (1984). *Two approaches to reading: Whole language and skills.* Paper presented at the annual meeting of the International Reading Association, Atlanta, GA. (ERIC Document Reproduction Service No. ED 247546)

Credits

Name Index

Abrami, P., 168, 179, 180, 181, 183
Achilles, C. M., 117, 119, 121, 124, 125, 126, 127, 128, 129, 130, 132, 134, 135, 136, 137, 138, 139, 140, 143, 146, 147, 385
Adams, D., 168
Advani, N., 263
Ageton, S. S., 260
Alexander, J. F., 288
Alexander, L., 122
Alkin, M. C., 69, 116
Allcorn, S., 222
Altheide, D. L., 94
Anderson, B. D., 342
Anderson, C. S., 341, 362, 364, 368, 369, 372
Anderson, D. P., 369
Andrews, J. H. M., 340
Appleberry, J., 369
Aronson, E., 170
Arter, J. A., 341, 345, 362
Ashforth, S. L., 368
Astone, N. M., 77–78, 80, 81, 315, 318
Atkeson, B. M., 263
Aussiker, A., 286
Averch, H. A., 41

Bacharach, S. B., 218, 235
Bachman, J. G., 259
Bader, B. D., 222, 223
Bailey, J. W., 263
Bain, H., 162
Bain, J., 121, 122
Baker, A., 244
Baker, D. P., 316, 317, 318
Bales, R. G., 370
Barker, R. G., 341, xx
Barnow, B. S., 38
Barth, R., 263, 288
Bartz, D., 245
Bear, G. G., 243
Bebell, D., 357
Becker,H. J., 316
Benson, C., 45
Berman, P. W., 287
Biddle, B. J., 221

Bliss, J. R., 346, 354, 368
Block, J., 261
Block, J. H., 261
Blunt, A., 332
Blyth, D. A., 247
Bock, R. D., 150
Bogotch, I. E., 16
Bolchoz, L., 288
Borg, W. R., 53, 67, 70, 96, 175, 350
Bossart, T. T., 41
Bossert, S., 168
Bossert, S. T., 379
Boulian, P. V., 374
Bourdieu, P., 316
Boyd, W. L., 297
Bracht, G. H., 104
Brady, L., 369
Brame, D., 288
Brantlinger, E., 245
Brent, B. O., xviii
Brewer, D. J., 77, 80
Brodie, F. M., 243
Brookover, W. B., 41
Brousseau, K. R., 219
Brown, B. L., 11
Brown, C. H., 261
Bryk, A. S., 43, 317, 320, 343
Buckley, N. K., 263
Bunch, K., 288
Bush, G., 122

Cahen, L. S., 161, 163
Cain, G. G., 38
Cambridge, J., 337, 338, 339, 341, 343, 344–345, 346–350, 351, 353, 356–357, 358–359, 360, 361, 362, 363, 364, 386–387
Campbell, D. T., 38, 134, 266
Canter, L., 285
Canter, M., 285
Carleton-Ford, S., 247
Carroll, S. J., 41
Castaneda, R. P., 345
Chamberlain, P., 288
Chambers, B., 168, 179, 180, 181, 183

Subject Index

Ablex Publishing Corporation, 70
Achievement. *See* Educational achievement
Adams Middle School case study, 239–242, 256
Administration, 8–9. *See also* School administration
Administrative practice
  effects of research on, 37–40
  role of research on, 17–19, 52
Administratively mutable, 11
Administrators
  issues facing new, 165–166
  knowledge of, 18–19
  nature of problems as addressed by, 54–60
  reviewing research from perspective of, 53–54
  role of, 9, 10, 84
African Americans
  educational achievement and, 27–28
  segregation and, 26–27
Alternate form reliability, 357
American Association of School Administrators, 344
American Educational Research Association (AERA)
  explanation of, 69
  journals published by, 69–70, 75
American Educational Research Journal (AERJ), 47, 75, 136, 147, 184
The American Journal of Education (AJE), 75
"Answers and Questions About Class Size: A Statewide Experiment" (Finn & Achilles), 146. *See also* Class size
  cross-sectional results, 151–156
  differential effects on whites and minorities, 154–156
  discussion, 161–162
  introduction, 147–148
  longitudinal results, 156–159
  procedures, 148–151
Application validity
  class size research and, 130–131
  as evaluation criteria, 390–391
  explanation of, 106–107
At-risk students, 177–179

Basic Skill First Test (BSF), 133
Behavior issues. *See* Discipline; "Managing Adolescent Behavior: A Multiyear, Multischool Study" (Gottfredson, Gottfredson, & Hybl)

Career ladders, 222–223, 226–231
Case studies
  class size, 114–117, 143, 144
  cooperative learning, 166–168, 190–192
  parental involvement, 294–296, 311–314
  school climate, 334–338, 360, 361–364
  school discipline, 239–242, 256–257
  teacher empowerment, 194–195, 212–216
Causal-comparative design, 96, 100
Causation, 98–99
Cause-and-effect, 98, 99, 305
Civil Rights Act of 1964, 22–23
Civil rights movement, 23
Class size. *See also* "Answers and Questions About Class Size: A Statewide Experiment" (Finn & Achilles)
  conceptual level and research on, 123–128
  early research on, 117–120
  economic issues and, 119
  educational achievement and, 118, 120, 127
  educators and, 118
  empirical level and, 135–140
  Finn and Achilles report and, 122–133, 135, 136, 143, 146–163
  Glass and Smith study and, 120–121
  Irontown case and, 115–117
  operational level and, 128–135
  Project Star and, 141–143
  pupil-teacher ratio vs., 119–120
  Tennessee studies and, 121–122
Clearinghouse on Rural Education and Small Schools, 70
Climate. *See* School climate
Coleman Report. *See Equality of Educational Opportunity (EEO)*
Comparative case study method, 208–209
The Comprehensive Assessment of School Environments, 344